SOCIAL WELFARE POLICY
From Theory to Practice

■

Bruce S. Jansson

University of
Southern California

WADSWORTH PUBLISHING COMPANY
Belmont, California
A Division of Wadsworth, Inc.

Social Welfare Editor: Peggy Adams
Editorial Assistant: Cathie Fields
Production: Sara Hunsaker, *Ex Libris*
Print Buyer: Martha Branch
Designer: Richard Kharibian; adapted by John Edeen
Copy Editor: Betty Duncan-Todd
Technical Illustrator: Lotus Art
Compositor: DEKR Corporation
Cover: Harry Voigt

Printed in the United States of America

2 3 4 5 6 7 8 9 10—94 93 92 91

Library of Congress Cataloging-in-Publication Data

Jansson, Bruce S.
    Social welfare policy : from theory to practice / Bruce S.
    Jansson.
        p. cm.
    Includes bibliographical references.
    ISBN 0-534-12600-6
    1. Social service—United States. I. Title.
HV40.J36 1990
361.973–dc20   89-16609
                                CIP

Preface

I first used the term *policy practice* in *The Theory and Practice of Social Welfare Policy* (Wadsworth Publishing Company, 1984) when searching for a term to describe an action or practice component of social welfare policy. In the ensuing years, I have become even more convinced that policy and funding realities of contemporary American society require social workers to become proactive participants in the shaping of policies—for ethical reasons (to try to redress inequalities and inequities), for professional reasons (to shape policies that serve the needs of clients and oppressed populations), and for pragmatic reasons (to protect the prerogatives and interests of the social work profession). A systems or ecological perspective, which distinguishes social work from other professions, demands that all social workers try to shape the rules that guide society, specific agencies, and specific programs.

It would be nice, in the crowded curriculum of professional education, to limit discussion of policy practice to several sessions or to simplify it to a few guiding questions or principles. In this text, however, we contend that social workers are unlikely to become effective participants in policy deliberations if they are not exposed to a range of concepts, skills, tasks, policy-making styles, and case examples. Nor do we have the luxury of limiting our policy-reform endeavors to those agencies where social workers are employed since many important policies that affect citizens, clients, and the profession are developed in the community and legislative bodies. If we believe the business of reforming policies to be a central part of professional work, we have to devote considerable attention to it.

Our discussion of policy practice needs to be attuned to the way policy is fashioned in the real world where a combination of skills is needed by people who wish to change existing policies. This text contends that social workers need to possess analytic, political, interactional, and value-clarification skills to be effective participants in policy deliberations. If we concentrate upon only one or two of these skills, we risk ignoring the importance of each of them to policy making.

In this new text, we use the term *policy practitioner* to describe the work of any social worker when he or she engages in policy-changing work. We build the first two-thirds of the text around the fundamental analytic, political, interactional, and value-clarification skills that social workers need to be effective policy practitioners.

Some people may fear that policy practice connotes a drastic departure from traditional methods of studying social welfare policy. This is not so; in fact, many topics that are covered in traditional analytic treatments of policy are included in this text, such as discussions of policy options that define strategies for financing social programs, allocating services and benefits, and structuring the human services system. A policy-practice perspective does not require us to dismiss concepts and issues that have been discussed in existing literature, but it does require us to ask how the concepts are relevant to those social workers who seek to change policies in specific settings.

This text is divided into five parts. In Part One we make the case that social welfare policy should contain a reform or change-oriented branch and that all social workers should participate in policy making in agency, community, and legislative settings. While cross-linkages exist, we contend that policy practice requires different skills and concepts than direct-service practice.

In Part Two we discuss analytic skills in considerable depth. We discuss techniques for analyzing and defining social problems in Chapter Two; we analyze an array of policy options that describe the structure of the human services delivery system, the ways services and benefits are financed, and strategies for shaping eligibility policies in Chapter Three; and we discuss methods of calculating trade-offs and developing policy proposals in Chapter Four.

If the discussion in Part Two emphasizes analytic techniques, Part Three discusses various "nonrational" factors that shape the selection of policies in specific settings such as political, interactional, and value-clarification factors. We define alternative kinds of power, sources of power, and assertiveness in Chapter Five. In Chapter Six we examine how policy practitioners assess patterns of support and opposition and develop political strategy.

Various interactional skills are discussed in Chapter Seven including techniques for persuading people to accept a policy position, methods of building personal credibility in specific settings, and techniques for working within task forces, committees, and coalitions.

Chapter Eight discusses numerous ethical or value issues that social workers confront in their policy practice. Alternative styles of ethical reasoning are discussed and linked to a set of questions that social workers should consider when they confront ethical issues pertaining to political tactics, content of proposals, the definition issues, and their policy objectives.

In Part Four we draw together our discussion of policy skills into a framework of policy practice that includes contextual factors, characteristics of the policy practitioner, policy tasks, and policy skills. In Chapter Nine we argue that policy practitioners, use the four policy skills to accomplish agenda-building, problem-defining, proposal-writing, policy-enacting, policy-implementing, and policy-assessing tasks. Instead of suggesting that a single approach should be used, we discuss how the values, setting, and stylistic preferences of policy practitioners shape their distinctive approaches.

We compare and contrast analytic, political, value-based, and consensus-building styles of policy practice and suggest that each style is useful in certain kinds of situations.

Like any other discipline with a practice component, people who engage in the practice of policy need to evaluate their work so that they can identify possible errors and improve their skills. We discuss specific methods of assessing the policy practice in Chapter Ten.

To review the concepts of preceding chapters, we devote Chapter Eleven to an extended and detailed policy-making case study, namely, the child development and daycare legislation from 1967 to 1989 in the U.S. Congress. This case illustrates the way people use analytic, political, interactional, and value-clarification skills to accomplish the various policy tasks.

In Part Five (Chapters Twelve and Thirteen), we discuss how social workers engage in the policy-implementing and policy-assessing tasks that occur after specific policies have been enacted. Chapter Twelve illustrates the many obstacles that often foil the implementation of policies. We discuss the flawed implementation of the Adoption Assistance and Child Welfare Act during the decade of the 1980s. We analyze alternative strategies for assessing policies in Chapter Thirteen.

In Part Six (Chapter Fourteen), we ask why social workers often do not engage in policy-changing work in agency, community, and legislative settings. We suggest that lack of comfort with power, assertiveness, and leadership have deterred many social workers from seeking to change their specific policies. But we also conclude that social workers can and should make a distinctive contribution to policy deliberations because of the greater emphasis that they place on social justice and beneficence than many other participants.

To facilitate discussion and additional reading, we have included considerable end-of-chapter materials. We have discovered that the use of a policy-practice perspective can revitalize the teaching of social welfare policy by concretizing policy in examples and cases and by linking policy to the ongoing professional work of social workers. A policy-practice perspective can be supplemented by various exercises and research projects supplied in Appendices A, B, and C.

To make this subject relevant to those social workers who would not normally engage in policy practice, we have minimized the use of jargon and have numerous concrete examples in each chapter. To be certain that policy practice is not limited to any specific setting, we have included examples from agency and from legislative settings.

This text is not, then, a revision of *The Theory and Practice of Social Welfare Policy* but is an entirely new book in its organization, approach, and style.

As social workers infuse their work with a social-reform dimension in agency, community, and legislative settings, they return to distant traditions of some of the founders of the profession who coupled their direct service, community, and administrative work with a broader vision. When surveying the policy landscape of the last decade of the twentieth century, few people would question the assertion that social problems and unmet needs abound in a society that is often indifferent to the needs of oppressed populations and poor people. While not a panacea, policy practice offers the promise of enhancing the relevance of social workers to broader issues in agency, community, and legislative settings.

ACKNOWLEDGMENTS

This project is the fruition of many years of thinking and writing about social welfare policy. Like any enterprise of this sort, I have accumulated many debts.

I received helpful comments on various drafts of this work from colleagues including Philip Engle, Wright State University; James Flanagan, Providence College; John D. Morrison, Aurora University; and Merlin Taber, University of Illinois, Urbana.

I am grateful for the help that I received from many people in constructing the extended policy case in Chapter Eleven, including the late Wilbur Cohen, Joseph Califano, Martha Phillips, and John Scales, as well as staff at the Lyndon Baines Johnson Presidential Library.

My collaborative research with June Simmons helped me to appreciate some of the subtler skills in policy practice, such as developing personal credibility in specific settings. My work as chair of the dissertations of Nora Gustavsson and Krishna Samantrai, who examined the implementation of the Adoption Assistance and Child Welfare Act of 1980, helped me fashion Chapter Twelve. Former students, including Andrea Karzen, Michele Wilson, Mary Hayes, and Stacy Stern, have contributed case material to this volume. My thanks for case material extend, as well, to the *California Journal* and to Marcia Mabee.

My long-standing social welfare policy colleagues—June Brown, Frances Feldman, Wilbur Finch, Maurice Hamovitch, Ramon Salcido, and Madeleine Stoner—at the School of Social Work, University of Southern California, have provided a stimulating environment as we have collaborated on curriculum. When he was Dean, Robert Roberts was unfailingly supportive of my writing. His successor, Rino Patti, generously allowed me to labor in peace during a sabbatical leave.

My ability to conceptualize and finish this project was helped by discussions, friendship, and friendly arguments with various colleagues in other schools of social work who have shown a particular interest in policy practice, particularly Ron Dear, Gerald Frey, Barbara Friesen, Aileen Hart, George Haskett, Marie Hoff, John Morrison, Mona Schatz, Elbert Segel, Will Richan, and Norm Wyers.

Sheryl Fullerton of Wadsworth Publishing Company patiently endured many drafts of the proposal that led to the final plan for this book. Peggy Adams, Wadsworth's social work editor, provided needed encouragement. Sara Hunsaker cheerfully guided this book through the production phase.

Of course, any errors of omission or commission in this work are wholly my own.

Many people have tolerated my work on this project, even when on vacation, including my parents, Betty McCorkel, and the members of the Tree Farm.

Betty Ann, Roger, and Stephanie provided a base of support that made this project feasible.

Contents

PART I

■

An Introduction to Social Welfare Policy and the Practice of Policy

We argue in Chapter One that social welfare policy is a multifaceted discipline that includes philosophical, analytic, and practice components. The philosophical component facilitates the making of critical and value-based assessments of the nature of the social response to social problems such as homelessness; we can ask, for example, whether Americans have been remiss in addressing this problem. The analytic component allows persons to identify and select policy remedies to social problems by using various techniques from the social sciences.

We argue in this introductory chapter, as well, that a compelling case can be made that social workers increasingly need to engage in the practice of policy, that is, in projects to reform policies in agency, community, and legislative settings. Policy practice requires, we will argue, the use of analytic, political, interactional, and value-clarification skills. We will argue that social workers should include policy practice in their professional work, whether they are direct-service, administrative, or community practitioners, if they wish to improve the human services system or address some of the social and economic causes of social problems.

Chapters Two through Thirteen of this text examine various policy skills and how they are used to accomplish specific tasks such as proposing, enacting, implementing, and assessing social welfare policies.

CHAPTER 1

■

Why Study Social Welfare Policy and the Practice of Policy, Anyway?

At first glance, social welfare policy seems to be a distracting diversion from counseling, administrative, and community work, which provide the focus of the work of most social workers. We will contend in this and remaining chapters, however, that social welfare policy should occupy a pivotal position in social work—to provide theory and perspectives about the human services and to equip social workers to assume leadership roles within the human services delivery system and in society.

We will attempt to answer two questions in this chapter. First, Why study social welfare policy? Second, Why study the practice of policy? As readers will soon discover, answers to these questions take us into a host of current realities in the human services system and into the theory of human behavior as well as direct-practice methodology.

THE MYTHOLOGIES OF AUTONOMOUS PRACTICE AND AUTONOMOUS CLIENTS IN THE SOCIAL SERVICES

If professionals and their clients are autonomous agents, whose work and lives are relatively insulated from their external environments, social welfare policy would occupy a tangential position in social work curriculum and professional practice. Some persons subscribe to a mythology of **autonomous practice,** which maintains that both professionals and their clientele are relatively insulated from external policies.[1] This notion of autonomous practice has had a curious and persistent strength in the social work profession, although, as we note subsequently, it has been challenged by many theorists and practitioners in recent decades.

The mythology of autonomous practice has been sustained by theories and practice strategies that have divorced direct-service practice from external policies. In classic Freudian theory, clinicians use a skillfully devised sequence of questions and comments to enhance their clients' cognitive understanding of the causes and nature of their problems, which are depicted as emanating from familial, childhood, and emotional causes. The helping relationship occurs in a sort of cocoon in which clinicians help clients resolve the riddles of the psyche.[2]

Classic organizational and administrative theory also gave scant importance to those external economic and social forces that influenced organizations. Managers were urged to emphasize "nuts-and-bolts" details of daily administration, such as budgeting, maintaining facilities, and hiring staff, which were widely assumed to constitute the core of administrative practice.[3] Community literature emphasized methods for establishing and organizing neighborhoods and community groups, usually by emphasizing community-development projects in which community workers sought to develop neighborhood councils or task forces. The policies of the external world that provided the context of particular communities were hardly mentioned in classic treatises by community-work theorists like Murray Ross.[4]

Of course, public policies and programs existed in the United States from the inception of the Republic and particularly in the aftermath of the Great Depression. But it was widely assumed in the 1950s and early 1960s that many social workers would work in nonprofit agencies such as child guidance or family counseling agencies, where their work would be insulated from the external world. Isolated from public officials and external policies in these nongovernment settings, social workers could, it was widely assumed, fashion their professional practice as they wished.[5]

The mythology of autonomous practice also obtained currency because of an understandable desire by some social workers to enhance their professional prestige. If physicians and attorneys engaged in private practice where their selection of clients, their fees, and their technical advice to their clients were dictated exclusively by themselves, why could not social workers also engage in autonomous practice? If professional status is partly determined by the autonomy of its practitioners, why not define social work practice to be described by carefully honed skills to help clients define, scrutinize, and remedy emotional conflicts? Although a private-practice movement did not gain strength until the 1970s and 1980s, many social workers envisioned their work in the 1950s and early 1960s as a kind of junior psychiatry where they could evolve autonomous practice even while salaried by nonprofit clinics.[6]

FORCES THAT DISRUPTED THE MYTHOLOGY OF AUTONOMOUS PRACTICE

The world of the human services changed dramatically in the decades following the early 1960s. The funding and structure of social agencies changed markedly; theorists increasingly recognized the impact of environmental factors on human behavior, communities, and organizations; and new paradigms of social work practice emerged. As various premises that undergirded autonomous practice were challenged by these various realities, the groundwork was laid for an enriched and more complicated set of direct-service, administrative, and community interventions—as well as for new conceptions of social policy.

Changes in the Funding and Structure of Social Agencies

Many social agencies in the 1950s could be neatly divided into public and nonprofit ones. A large group of nonprofit agencies received most of their funds from nonpublic fund appeals such as United Way or Red Feather agencies, sectarian fund-raising efforts like Federated Jewish Appeal, private donors, and fees.[7] These nonprofit agencies established their own fee structures, selected the kinds of client problems they wished to serve, decided which kinds of clients they wished to serve, and (in some cases) shunned certain kinds of populations, such as impoverished persons, whether by excluding them from service or by providing subtle clues to them in the early stages of their treatment that they should seek assistance elsewhere. Some family counseling agencies chose, for example, to disengage from serving poor persons on grounds they were insufficiently motivated to solve their personal problems or unable to participate in the kinds of talking therapies that the agencies emphasized.[8]

Even in public sector agencies such as mental institutions and welfare agencies where many social workers were employed, it was widely assumed that services could be rendered on terms dictated by professionals.[9] This belief was fostered by the common practice of establishing social service units within public agencies, where staff were given considerable latitude in determining which clients received services, as well as their duration and kind. For example, social workers in public welfare agencies, who often staffed the intake and eligibility services, gave intensive services to those clients who they believed needed and could benefit from them. Social workers seemed to have their private enclaves within the larger public bureaucracies—their own space—where they could work in largely autonomous fashion as they applied their knowledge of human behavior to fashion counseling strategies.[10] Because these child welfare units, social service units in public welfare agencies, and social work units in mental hospitals were often staffed by persons with master's degrees, they possessed considerable prestige within these bureaucracies that hosted them.

The relatively high esteem that social workers enjoyed in many public agencies was illustrated by the social service amendments to the Social Security Act in 1962 that provided federal incentives to local public welfare agencies to employ workers to provide services to welfare families. This policy obtained bipartisan support in the Congress and symbolized the esteem that social workers possessed in the public sector.[11] It was widely assumed in the wake of the passage of community mental health legislation of 1963 that professional social workers would assume major roles in providing services to deinstitutionalized patients in a range of community-based agencies.[12]

It was simplistic even in the early 1960s to maintain that social workers were autonomous agents, for their employing agencies often placed many restrictions on their practice—and, in turn, were themselves profoundly influenced by community and societal pressures. In his classic study of the YMCA, for example, Mayer Zald noted that the ethos or mission of the YMCA, as well as its need for revenues, dictated its emphasis on recreational programs, on services to middle-class (and fee-paying) consumers, and on suburban rather than inner-city services.[13] Some child guidance agencies socialized staff to prevailing psychiatric models and developed intake systems that selected certain kinds of clients while rejecting others. Some public agencies insisted that social workers implement relatively punitive policies, such as home visits, in welfare agencies to determine whether recipients were cheating or had live-in partners.[14] But the prevailing literature of the 1950s and the early 1960s discounted these kinds of intrusions on the work of professionals, who were perceived to be relatively autonomous in their work.[15]

A series of changes, however, shattered this idyllic world in both the public and nonpublic sectors. As illustrated by the mental health system, public services became more complex in the wake of policy changes in the 1960s, 1970s, and 1980s. Traditional nonprofit counseling agencies and public mental institutions were supplemented by an array of publicly funded community mental health centers, aftercare programs of mental hospitals, and profit-oriented psychiatric agencies and hospitals—specialized agencies that served such groups as substance abusers, halfway houses, board-and-care homes, and regional centers for specific groups such as developmentally disabled persons.[16] Such complexity in the sponsorship of services, as well as the diffusion of service roles to a host of specialized agencies, meant that social workers were increasingly influenced by interorganizational relationships in their work; they had to ask which clients "belonged" to whom, which ones should be retained or referred elsewhere, and whether collaborative services should be developed. Mental health agencies were sometimes integrated into larger human services agencies that placed an array of counseling, training, and welfare services under one roof.[17]

Organizational complexity was supplemented by increasingly complicated patterns of financing of services that in turn affected patterns of intake, the length of services, and the kinds of services that could be given to consumers. The funding of mental health services became shared by a variety of private insurances, public programs like Medicare and Medicaid, county and municipal authorities, the states, foundations, United Way and Jewish Federated Funders, and special federal and state programs for special populations such as disabled persons, substance abusers, and juvenile offenders.[18] Each funder placed specific restrictions on mental health services by prescribing their duration, the kinds of persons who could receive services, mechanisms for evaluating services, the training qualifications of staff, and the content of the services. Agency administrators became accountable to a dizzying array of funders and moreover had to consider how to increase their revenues from fee-paying clients to remain solvent.[19]

Decisions about the staffing of agencies became more complex in the wake of the development of new professions and new rules that often removed requirements that M.S.W.s receive job preference. The existence of social work in some agencies was endangered by these new rules; M.S.W.s were often supplanted by nonprofessionals, B.S.W.s, or members of other counseling professions in the late 1960s and the 1970s in many agencies such as public welfare and child welfare agencies.[20]

Additional restrictions were placed on agencies by the courts, which variously made rulings about the confidentiality of client-based information, about procedures for making involuntary commitments to mental institutions, about informed-consent procedures when medications or other treatments were used that had possible harmful side effects, about due-process requirements to be followed when removing children from their natural parents, and about minimum standards of service for the residents of institutions. Rulings from the various courts were so numerous and so pervasive that they constituted a sort of phantom welfare state that supplemented the programs and policies of legislators and government agencies.[21]

A veritable explosion of funding of social services by federal and local governments that occurred in the 1960s and 1970s fundamentally changed the nature of human services and reduced the role of private donors and federated fund-raising. Many nonprofit agencies received the bulk of their funds from public authorities.[22] Nor were public authorities chary about developing rules and regulations to govern how their funds were used by social agencies.

Moreover, an array of community groups, theorists, government authorities, and professional associations vied to shape these policies of legislatures, government agencies, insurance companies, and courts. Mental health services had become politicized in a manner that would have been unthinkable a decade earlier. In the case of procedures for involuntary commitments, for example, associations of patients often battled with chapters of the American Psychiatric Association; if the former wanted to tighten procedures to give patients more rights and to make commitments more difficult, the latter wanted to give professionals more discretion.[23] Groups representing specific groups, such as children, the elderly, and ethnic minorities, demanded more—or better—services for their groups, who they charged were excluded from services or given inappropriate ones.[24]

This politicization of services was fostered by the emergence of many philosophical and conceptual disputes. If some patient advocates suggested that many professionals wrongly labeled their clients by imposing diagnostic categories on them, some professionals retorted that these classifications were needed to promote scientific treatment.[25] If some persons wondered whether mental illnesses stemmed from poverty, unemployment, and environmental factors, other theorists continued to emphasize familial and emotional causes. Members of oppressed minorities, such as blacks, often contended that members of their groups were unfairly stereotyped or treated by social workers who, they charged, were more likely to declare them to have serious mental conditions even when they exhibited the same symptoms as other persons.[26] Child welfare workers were sometimes accused of imposing their cultural preferences on persons when they removed children from families because parents used physical punishment.[27] Theorists debated the relative importance of genetics, physiological imbalances, stress, poverty, unemployment, marital conflict, disability, role models, and other factors in causing mental disorders—and a remarkable array of treatment methods were developed that included psychodynamic, behavior modification, cognitive, transactional, gestalt, and existentialist schools.[28]

Professionals were increasingly circumscribed by pressures from the central administrations of their agencies, which increased in size and power to cope with the policy, funding, and political turbulence that they encountered. The central administrations of social agencies sought to navigate their organizations through the welter of external pressures that they increasingly encountered; they had to "market" their services to new clientele, keep abreast of current legal and policy developments, and meet the accountability requirements of funders.[29] Agencies often had to develop new services, discard ones that lost funds, and devise more efficient methods of delivering services to survive in the increasingly turbulent environment of the human services. The enhanced roles of the central administrations of agencies sometimes led to a variety of regulations and rules that reduced the autonomy of direct-service staff, who were asked to implement the rapidly changing services of their organizations.

Cognizant of these changes, organizational theorists increasingly argued that it was not possible to understand the internal dynamics of agencies without viewing them in their political and economic context. If traditional organizational theorists had emphasized the internal processes and structures of agencies, advocates of a political-economy perspective contended that these structures were profoundly shaped by the external policy, funding, and political environments of agencies.[30]

If the practice of social workers was influenced by policies that derived from sources within and external to their agencies, efforts to change or shape them necessarily became a part of their professional practice, if only for defensive reasons. A dramatic increase in the unionizing of social workers had begun by the late 1960s, for example, in the public sector and many nonprofit agencies.[31] Some social workers, as well as the National Association of Social Workers (NASW), increasingly attempted to influence those organizational and public policies that they believed to be inimical to the well-being of their clients or that jeopardized the rights of professional staff. NASW sought to become an advocate for those social workers who were fired because they objected to specific policies.

These combined shifts in the organization and funding of social services made it clear that social work practitioners were not autonomous agents. The work of direct-service staff, supervisors, administrators, and community organizers was profoundly shaped by the external policies of funders, courts, government agencies, and legislatures. These policies shaped both the terms and nature of social services as well as the working conditions of staff.

With the myth of autonomy shattered, it became even clearer that social workers, singly and as a profession, had to evolve strategies to influence these various policies, whether to improve their working conditions or to improve social programs so that they better address the needs of clients and the general population. We will note later that policy practice is used to correct deficiencies in a range of policies that influence the nature of the human services delivery system, as well as policies that determine the working conditions of staff within this system.

New Ways of Conceptualizing Human Behavior and Social Work Practice

We have noted that considerable social work–practice theory in the 1950s emphasized the role of familial and emotional factors in causing social problems. Although information about family members, employment, housing arrangements, and medical factors was often gathered and used to shape diagnostic assessments and treatment plans, these data often received secondary attention when contrasted with the resolution of the internal emotional conflicts of clients. As one example, many persons believed in the early 1960s that the poverty of women heads-of-household, whose numbers were swelling the rolls of the Aid to Families with Dependent Children (AFDC) program, could be redressed by providing social services to them— both to counsel them and to resolve marital problems so that their husbands did not desert them. Scant attention was given to the effects of social class, the absence of subsidized daycare, labor markets and training programs that discriminated against women, and racial discrimination.[32]

By the mid-1960s, however, a number of theorists began to place the external world in a more prominent position in human behavior. Some theorists, such as Abraham Maslow, emphasized the importance of meeting basic survival needs as a precursor to fulfilling higher-order creativity needs.[33] Robert White and other proponents of ego psychology suggested that humans possess a drive for competence; when they experience a chain of perceived failures, sometimes deriving from the deleterious effects of dis-crimination, people often become frozen, flee, or make ill-advised choices.[34]

Other researchers and theorists probed the effects of an array of peer and group influences on persons. Social psychologists observed the powerful role of group norms on their members, which sometimes influences them to take actions that are destructive to their well-being. The effects of roles in shaping behavior were widely discussed by sociologists and psychologists.[35] Many researchers examined the effects of situational stressors on human behavior, such as divorce and unemployment.[36]

Researchers probed the effects of social class on persons by examining the role of poverty, segregation, and poor housing on human behavior.[37] Debates raged about the precise effects of poverty on human behavior, but increasing numbers of theorists in the 1960s explored the way that oppressive social and economic conditions create and exacerbate social problems such as poor health, substance abuse, and truancy—and the way these problems perpetuate poverty.

Debates also emerged about the relationships between culture and pov-erty: Did poverty create certain cultural dispositions such as present-orientedness, or were these cultural characteristics artifacts of the imagination and faulty research instruments of middle-class researchers? To the extent they existed, were cultural characteristics such as present-orientedness ongo-ing and deeply rooted phenomena, or would they quickly disappear if per-sons were taken from oppressive environments and a condition of poverty? The existence of these debates illustrated the increasing awareness of rela-tionships among the social environment, social class, culture, and social problems of persons, even if considerable controversy existed about the nature of these relationships.[38] (In 1960, by contrast, a bibliography of academic writings on poverty consisted of less than a single page of citations.[39])

There was increasing recognition of the effects of culture upon social problems and the response of persons to existing services.[40] Although the United States had had waves of immigration to its shores and borders during its history, as well as an indigenous population of Native Americans, many academics and citizens had subscribed to the notion of a "melting pot" that eliminated cultural diversity as persons assimilated to the nation's dominant culture.[41] Feminists researched how women view the world differently than men and how their perspectives shape their interactions with men, other women, and external institutions.[42] As persons increasingly recognized that cultural diversity had not disappeared, they examined how culture shapes perceptions of social problems and the way they seek and respond to social services. Moreover, many persons noted that low-income persons were often averse to using the services of established social agencies, whether because they found their services to be irrelevant to their immediate needs, were fatalistic about improving their condition, or lacked the transportation or the time to use them.[43]

Systems of social support were implicated by many theorists in causing and sustaining social problems.[44] Research suggested that isolated persons who lacked familial, neighborhood, and workplace supports, such as friends and mentors, were more susceptible to illness and mental problems than were other persons.[45] Professionals increasingly referred clientele to support groups such as ones composed of victims of alcoholism and cancer, whose members sought not only to comfort victims but also to provide them with survival strategies and to help them negotiate bureaucratic systems.

Some research implicated the social service delivery system itself in causing or exacerbating social problems. When consumers must bear extensive transportation and financial costs to obtain medical services, for example, many delay seeking such services until their problems have become serious. Services that are excessively fragmented impede the development of effective and multifaceted interventions.[46]

Numerous theorists developed theoretical frameworks that included a range of environmental, policy, delivery-system, cultural, community, familial, and personal factors that shape human behavior. Thus, systems theorists placed human behavior and the problems of specific persons in a broad context that included societal, organizational, cultural, and familial factors. Carel Germaine and Carol Meyer, respectively, developed ecological frameworks of social work practice that required practitioners to obtain and use information about a range of environmental factors as they helped specific persons.[47]

As these various kinds of environmental influences on human behavior received increasing prominence in service and human behavior literature, the work of direct-service practitioners necessarily became more complex. A skillful social service professional had to ask whether the truancy of an adolescent, for example, derived from substance abuse, dyslexia, a perceived absence of economic opportunities, familial role models, culture, peer pressure such as from members of gangs, physical ailments, conflicts with school administrators or teachers, or conflicts with parents—or from some combination of these factors. Social workers could use counseling, advocacy, referrals to specialized reading clinics, support groups of other students, family therapy, a system of referrals to be coordinated by a case manager, or some combination of these interventions. Moreover, after examining the effects of diverse environmental factors on persons, social workers sometimes conclude that they should focus on providing consumers with assertiveness, survival, job-seeking, and legal skills so that they can cope with ongoing adversities and discrimination. This strategy, which has been called **empowerment,** extends to communities, whose members can learn political and organizing skills to obtain policy concessions from governments, funders, insurance companies, and others.[48] Because of the effects of the environment, culture, social class, and families on persons, services need to be tailored to the unique needs of specific populations. When programs provide only a single approach or remedy, their staff risk ignoring the diversity of human experience, which requires a range of service approaches.

As environmental factors were given more prominence in causing human problems, some theorists emphasized the role of advocacy by social work practitioners. To the extent problems of persons reflect oppression by landlords, welfare and other agencies, abusive spouses, and poor schools, should not social workers become advocates for individuals and classes of persons such as low-income tenants or welfare recipients?[49]

By the 1970s then, social workers were exposed to a more diverse set of practice materials than were their counterparts of the 1950s. The systems and ecological frameworks that were prominent in textbooks on human behavior and direct practice explicitly linked individuals to a range of community, institutional, and societal factors. If theorists of the 1950s had often assumed that human behavior among Caucasian and middle-class citizens extended to all persons, many theorists in the 1980s recognized that social class, gender, and ethnicity variables shaped the problems of persons, their perceptions of these problems, and their responses to specific kinds of interventions of the social service staff.

As social work practice increasingly emphasized environmental factors, partly in response to emerging research that implicated a range of factors in causing social problems of specific persons and populations, many theorists suggested that social workers needed to include advocacy in their work. **Case advocacy,** which seeks more equitable services for specific persons within existing laws, regulations, and entitlements, needed to be supplemented by **class advocacy,** which seeks to change defective laws and regulations and to develop new entitlements.[50] We will note later that class advocacy is an important part of policy practice.

NEW APPROACHES TO CONCEPTUALIZING SOCIAL WELFARE POLICY

Social welfare–policy literature had emphasized historical, philosophical, and policy-descriptive topics during the 1950s when its theorists were preoccupied with documenting the rise of social welfare institutions in a nation that had been relatively unresponsive to social problems like poverty and unemployment. Social welfare policy was widely perceived to be an orienting, rather than a practice, discipline that described and analyzed the context of social services. Policy theorists failed to develop an action or practice component for their discipline in the 1950s in part because of the strength of the myths of autonomous clients and autonomous social work practitioners. As a multitude of policies of legislatures, courts, funders, and agencies were perceived to impinge upon social workers and clients, social policy theorists were more likely to be aware of the need not only to describe and criticize policies but also to identify skills that social workers need to develop and enact policies. As we note in succeeding discussions, social welfare policy theorists gradually expanded the domain of their discipline to include a proactive and practice component. In the three decades after 1956 various social welfare theorists moved beyond historical, philosophical, and descriptive functions; they suggested that the discipline of social welfare policy could also include a range of interventions to allow social workers to conceptualize policy proposals, to secure their enactment, and to facilitate their implementation.

Developing Analytic Skills

In a seminal work in 1956, Eviline Burns analyzed strategies to help destitute, unemployed, and elderly persons.[51] Although her book contained historical materials, she analyzed a range of alternative approaches and strategies for addressing these economic social problems and, in the process, examined the comparative advantages of each. Burns suggested that an array of policy alternatives exist, that each has advantages and disadvantages, and that final choices require comparing their comparative strengths. She contrasted, for example, the comparative merits of various methods of financing and structuring welfare and Social Security programs. Neil Gilbert and Harry Specht, who portray themselves as disciples of Burns, continued this tradition by examining a variety of "dimensions of choice" that included a variety of policy alternatives with respect to service-delivery, financing, and allocation issues.[52] Like Burns, they examined the comparative advantages and disadvantages of various program and policy options such as alternative methods of designing the eligibility policies of programs. By identifying and comparing a range of policy options, Burns and her successors moved policy beyond the chronicling and describing of policy toward a process of selection and choice.

Alfred Kahn suggested that policy analysts should follow a series of conceptual steps when developing policy proposals; they should analyze the presenting social problem, develop policy alternatives, and devise policy proposals. He argued that policymakers should be rational and scientific in their approach.[53] Outside of social work, in fields like economics and public affairs, legions of theorists developed a host of analytic, research, and economic tools for facilitating the analysis of problems and the selection of policies.[54]

These kinds of analytic tools and approaches, which were developed within and outside of social work, advanced the notion that the discipline of social welfare policy should include a problem-solving and rational component rather than merely describing or chronicling the emergence of social welfare policies. Critics wondered, however, if policy-making can be as "rational" as these theorists suggested or implied because many policy analysts hardly mentioned politics, "old-boy" networks, and other realities that shape the selection of policies in specific settings.[55]

Value-Clarification Skills

In a widely used text, David Gil contended in 1970 that policymakers needed to use value considerations to make choices between contending policy alternatives; as a socialist, he strongly affirmed values of equality and redistribution to address a range of social and economic needs.[56] Gil's work was complemented by radical analyses of the controlling or regulating functions of some social welfare policies by Richard Cloward and Frances Piven, who contended that corporate and conservative interests often favored punitive programs, such as AFDC, that forced recipients into low-paying jobs by providing low benefits and by employing punitive devices to deter recipients from seeking welfare benefits.[57]

These radical perspectives provided a useful antidote to the analytic theorists, who often implied that values were incidental to the selection of policies. Moreover, they suggested that policy-making is not entirely a rational or scientific enterprise and that in many cases it is entirely or mostly irrational because political pressures often dictate choices. But some critics questioned these theorists as well; can policymakers maintain radical perspectives when they encounter pressures of interest groups and when policymakers need political skills to develop compromises?[58]

Politics, Implementation, and Policy-Making

Some theorists during the 1970s and 1980s began to analyze the intersection between politics and policy-making. Political skills were emphasized by a growing number of writers including Maryann Mahaffey, Andrea Dobblestein, Diane DiNitto, Thomas Dye, and Karen Haynes.[59] Ron Dear and Rino Patti collected empirical data to ask why some pieces of social legislation are enacted while others fail.[60] Mahaffey's edited volume discussed a range of testifying, lobbying, and coalition-building skills that are needed by policy advocates.[61]

In a seminal work in 1974, political scientists Jeffrey Pressman and Aaron Wildavsky contended that policy theorists had erroneously assumed that policy-making ceases once policies were enacted. They contended that in fact many policies are sabotaged or frustrated after their enactment by a range of organizational, political, turf-rivalry, and economic realities.[62] Many theorists explored various factors that determined the success of the implementation of specific policies in the decade following Pressman's book.[63]

Theorists who examined political and implementation realities usefully expanded the boundaries of policy beyond the relatively narrow scope that was established by policy analysts. Their work implied that the cerebral work

of policy analysis needs to be coupled with knowledge of political and organizational realities.

Developing a Range of Policy Skills

Curiously, few theorists in social welfare policy envisioned their discipline
to contain a practice or applied component even though the work of the
aforementioned theorists implied that a range of skills were needed to fashion, enact, and implement policies. This failure was probably caused by the
force of tradition, the mythologies of autonomous practice and autonomous
practitioners, and the assumption that other practice disciplines in social
work would assume policy-changing functions.

Social welfare policy had traditionally fallen into social reform, historical,
orienting, and descriptive categories. Even the analytic, political, and implementation literature, which supplemented policy literature in the 1970s and
1980s, usually failed to discuss how specific persons in specific settings might
actually try to shape policies. Because social welfare policy, like human
behavior on the direct-service side of the curriculum, had traditionally been
defined to be a theoretical discipline that provided background materials to
professionals, many theorists failed to perceive it as an applied discipline
as well.

When the Council on Social Work Education (CSWE) undertook a reap-
praisal of social work education in the late 1950s, many persons realized that
the profession needed to equip some graduates with the skills to manage
and plan the burgeoning social welfare programs of the nation, whether in
specific agencies or in the many sectarian or Red Feather fund-raising fed-
erations and planning councils.[64] The authors of CSWE's exhaustive report
equated *macro practice* with administrative, fund-raising, and planning functions and placed these practice tasks squarely under the macro-practice disciplines of community organization and administration.[65] Social welfare
policy, in short, retained its traditional position as a discipline that primarily
described the policies and programs of the American welfare state.[66]

Social welfare–policy educators and theorists might have developed an
interventive component of the discipline during the turbulence of the 1960s
when many educators sought to enhance the social reform capabilities of
social workers, but social reform was widely perceived to fall within the
domain of community organization where mobilizing techniques, such as
those of Saul Alinsky, were uneasily grafted onto the traditional materials of
that discipline.[67]

By the early 1980s, however, some theorists began to envision a practice
component to social welfare policy. In a work published in 1981, John Tropman contended that a range of *policy competencies* are needed by practitioners,
such as persuasive skills, political skills, and skills in using committee and
group processes to facilitate the development of policies.[68] Willard Richan

emphasized the importance of position-taking and debating skills when he argued that social workers, like lawyers, should be trained to develop and debate positions.[69]

Policy theorists had traditionally emphasized policy-making in legislative or government settings, but Tropman, Dean Pierce, and John Flynn suggested that policy skills are needed by executives and line staff within social agencies.[70] Indeed, Patti and Herman Resnick suggested that various staff including line workers could participate in developing innovations within agencies.[71]

In a work published in 1984, I coined the term *policy practice*, suggested that the discipline ought to articulate an interventive component, and contended that a range of social workers could engage in policy practice in agency, community, and legislative settings.[72] I suggested that a range of skills are needed by policy practitioners, including analytic or technical, political, interaction, and value-clarification skills. Drawing on the work of theorists in political and policy sciences, I suggested that policy practitioners should undertake a range of practice tasks such as developing, enacting, implementing, and assessing policies.[73]

WHAT'S WRONG WITH A CONTEXT-DESCRIBING OR ANALYTIC ROLE?

The central rationale for developing an interventive component for social welfare policy is simple: If many policies of the American welfare state are flawed—an inescapable conclusion with examining the extent of unmet suffering and inequality in the nation—how can we fail to discuss in social welfare–policy literature and curriculum specific skills and interventions that can be used by social workers to change them? Social workers need to assume policy-reform roles with respect to a host of festering social problems such as homelessness, child abuse, and AIDS. Nor should policy practice be restricted to society or community problems because social workers should seek to change those policies within specific organizations that are inimical to the interests of their clients. In the funding cutbacks of the 1980s, social work units in hospitals, schools, child welfare departments, and corporations have had to develop strategy to maintain their existence in bureaucracies that are often dominated by other professions.

Policy-practice skills could be delegated to other disciplines such as administration and community organization, but this decision would have unfortunate consequences. Those disciplines focus on other tasks and issues.[74] A discipline is needed that makes the development and changing of policies one of its central missions. Without a practice component, social welfare policy is an incomplete or partial discipline. Imagine the frustration of direct-service, administrative, or community-work staff if they could only analyze, describe, or assess their surroundings but lacked a practice component to correct or address the problems that they had discovered.

DEMYSTIFYING POLICY PRACTICE

Efforts to define and develop a policy practice are impeded, however, by various myths that are held by a range of social work practitioners and even some educators. The **great-person myth** maintains that policy practice is restricted to major policy breakthroughs such as initiatives like Medicare, Medicaid, and welfare reform. In fact, the work of direct-service staff and the well-being of clients and citizens are shaped by vast numbers of policies that extend from major ones, such as legislation that establishes major social programs, to a variety of policies in community and agency settings. The great-person myth allows most of us to abdicate our policy responsibilities in our daily work because it limits policy-making to high-level officials or to those reformers who champion ambitious pieces of legislation.

The **specialization or expert myth** suggests that policy-making rightfully belongs to policy specialists such as those with advanced analytic skills. Economists, program evaluators, and policy analysts have assumed increasingly prominent and important roles in policy discourse, but their role ought not be exaggerated. We have noted, for example, that political and implementation realities often intrude to circumvent even well-conceived policy proposals that derive from advanced and sophisticated policy analysis. Moreover, persons who actually implement policies and who see social problems firsthand should participate in the shaping of policies.

The **myth of powerlessness** suggests that professionals and ordinary citizens cannot contribute to policy-making because they lack the power resources of interest groups and politicians. As we discuss in Chapters Five and Six, policy-making often does not occur on a level playing field because some persons and interests possess more power than others. Many studies suggest, however, that a range of persons and groups can influence the course of specific policy reforms because policy innovations rarely stem from single crusaders but from the combined influence of a number of persons who often act in tandem through coalitions or professional associations where their power is enhanced by fusing it with other persons and groups.[75] Even direct-service professionals can sometimes develop and use power resources within their agencies and in their communities.[76]

By suggesting that *all* policy is public policy, the **legislative-policy myth** neglects a vast range of other kinds of policy including those agency-level, work-group, and community policies that influence the implementation of legislative policy. In the case of a community mental health center that receives most of its funds from state and federal sources, many policies are established *within* the agency because legislation often does not define many details of implementation.[77] Indeed, zones of discretion enable agencies to define many details of their programs within certain parameters established by high-level policy. Nonpublic agencies, even those that receive most of their funds from public sources, have considerable latitude in developing programs and policies, including the ability to decide which public funds they wish to seek.[78]

When demystifying policy, we do not want to run the danger of suggesting that policy practice can be easily pursued by anyone or that most people can obtain major successes on most occasions. Even experienced policy practitioners often do not succeed in obtaining the enactment of favored initiatives, as the failure of many policy initiatives suggests. If we become preoccupied with the problems and difficulties of practicing policy, however, we risk a sort of policy fatalism, which is itself a kind of myth.

WHO *ARE* POLICY PRACTITIONERS, ANYWAY?

While we have used the term *policy practitioner* with wild abandon, we have failed thus far to define who these persons are. We contend that many kinds of social workers are (or can become) policy practitioners. A small minority of them are persons who occupy specialized positions in the human services system or in the public bureaucracies of the nation; they are variously called *policy analysts, legislative assistants, lobbyists,* or *planners.* These persons are paid to engage in policy practice.

Most policy practitioners, however, couple this work with other work; indeed, the policy-practice component of their work is variable and shifting in nature and "piggybacks" their other professional work that absorbs most of their energies. Direct-service practitioners, supervisors, administrators, and community workers engage in policy practice *whenever* they develop and implement strategies to reduce the gap between preferred and actual policies—whether in their agencies, communities, or legislatures. During specific phases of their work, they may engage in no or little policy practice—only to become absorbed with it at another time. They sometimes engage in policy practice on the spur of the moment when, for example, they initiate a point in a meeting or in a discussion with a colleague or a superior. In other cases, they develop a long association with a specific project to change existing policies.

Is it wrong that policy practice is often performed by persons whose primary work involves direct-service, administrative, or community interventions? It cannot be denied that the effectiveness of some policy practitioners is diminished when they lack the time or resources to fully commit themselves to changing existing policies. Nor do many persons possess some of the skills or perspectives to make them effective participants in policy-making. Were we to reserve policy practice to specialists, however, we would run graver risks than we encounter by seeking to promote its use by a range of persons. A specialization strategy could render most of us unthinking defenders of the status quo and would deprive the human services system of the insights of a range of persons who directly encounter the defects in existing policies. High-level specialists have limited powers to obtain their policy preferences if external pressures do not exist from professionals, consumers, and interest groups to reform existing policies.

Although social work needs to develop and train policy specialists then, it also needs to equip a range of social workers with policy-practice skills and perspectives. Indeed, we will argue in Chapter Fourteen that policy practice serves to give social workers a leadership role that supplements their direct-service, administrative, and community functions.

DEFINING SOCIAL WELFARE POLICY

Definitions of social welfare policy abound. Some definitions emphasize the substance or content of social welfare policies; in this perspective, social welfare policies focus on the provision of resources and services to persons.[79] A course in social welfare policy that emphasizes this approach might devote itself to describing the myriad programs that exist in the American welfare state. Other persons emphasize the normative functions of social welfare policy, such as its traditional interest in redistributing resources and services to destitute or poor persons.[80] A course in social welfare policy that emphasizes this definition would stress the extent and nature of deprivation in society and the strategies that have been developed to address it. Other definitions emphasize the function that policies serve in defining the direction and use of social resources; a course that uses this approach would examine a range of policy options, choices, and dilemmas that confront policymakers.[81]

We cannot hope to resolve in this text the differences in nuance between various definitions of social welfare policy. But we wish to make a case that a definition that has a problem-solving orientation will promote an action or practice component of the discipline more effectively than will more abstract definitions. We define social welfare policy to be "collectively defined rules, regulations, procedures, and objectives to address social problems and those institutional problems that affect the implementation of specific policies." Our definition is similar to one developed by the late Richard Titmuss, the English social welfare-policy theorist.[82]

This goal-driven or problem-solving definition has several advantages. It emphasizes reasons why social welfare policies are constructed in the first place, namely, to address or alleviate social problems such as hunger, poverty, and mental illness. As can be seen from Table 1.1, social welfare policies address a broad range of social problems. Of course, no system of classifi-

TABLE 1.1   A Classification System of Social Problems

Material Resources Deprivation	Mental or Emotional Deprivation	Cognitive Deprivation	Interpersonal Deprivation	Deprivation of Opportunity	Deprivation of Personal Rights	Physical Deprivation
Inadequate income, housing, food	Various forms of mental illness	Developmental disability	Marital conflict Loneliness Destructive child–parent relations	Lack of education Lack of access to services or medical care Lack of fulfilling work	Lack of civil rights and liberties Victim of discrimination	Illnesses Disability

cation is perfect. Some problems cannot easily be classified: Is substance abuse a physical problem, a mental problem, or antisocial behavior? Our definition of social welfare policy suggests, as well, that social welfare policy often addresses institutional problems that affect the implementation of policies. As can be seen from Table 1.2, a range of institutional problems often block or impede the implementation of policies. Legislation that is enacted to provide prenatal services to those women in the inner city who are at risk of delivering unhealthy babies, for example, is likely to be ineffective if outreach services are not developed in the human services delivery system that is constructed to implement the legislative policy.

By stimulating us to ask whether specific policies *actually* address a social problem or whether other policies would be more effective than existing ones, a goal-driven definition stimulates efforts to change dysfunctional policies. It forces us to move from a policy-describing role to a role in critically examining and analyzing existing policies.

Moreover, a goal-driven definition places social welfare policy in step with other disciplines that possess practice components such as direct-service and adminstrative practice because all interventive disciplines seek to address presenting problems through various strategies or interventions. If a direct-service practitioner helps clients define their problems and mobilize themselves to redress them, administrators use an array of strategies to identify and redress various operating problems within specific organizations. In similar fashion, social welfare–policy practitioners address social problems such as poverty, mental illness, and substance abuse—not from the perspective of providing services to specific persons but to devise guiding principles to orchestrate an encompassing *strategy* that shapes the services or the distribution of resources that are ultimately provided and superintended by direct-service and administrative staff. (The terms *rules, regulations, procedures,* and *objectives* define this encompassing strategy.) When policy practitioners find that those programs that are established by policies do not effectively address specific social problems, they also seek to develop and enact policies to redress various institutional flaws or barriers. The literature on policy implementation suggests that policy practitioners do not cease their work once policies are officially enacted.[83]

This problem-solving definition of social welfare policy is sufficiently flexible to save us the problem of having to establish rigid boundaries between social welfare and other kinds of policies. Most commentators agree that public welfare, child welfare, medical, and job-training policies are social welfare policies, but less certainty exists about income tax, environmental, economic, transportation, and other policies.[84] Our definition suggests that specific policies *become* social welfare policies whenever they are germane to specific social problems or to institutional problems that impede the implementation of specific policies; thus, income tax proposals that increase (or decrease) resources that are available to poor persons *are* social welfare pol-

TABLE 1.2 Sources and Results of Problems Within the Service-Delivery System

Sources			Results
Mismanagement of Human Services Organizations	*Relationships Between Agencies and Programs*	*High-Level Policies*	*Direct Impact on Clients*
Lack of leadership	Lack of referral mechanisms	Vague policies	Discontinuity
Lack of monitoring and evaluation	Lack of joint programs	Insufficient resources to implement specific policies	Lack of referral mechanisms
Lack of innovation	Duplication		Excessive fees
Lack of planning	Turf rivalries		Cultural insensitivity
Internal conflicts between staff or units			Discrimination against certain clients
Wasted resources			Nonaccessibility
			Lack of case management
			Incompetent or poorly trained staff
			Poor matching of clients with needed services

icies when we consider their effects on social problems such as poverty and unemployment. (By the same token, some tax policies, such as policies that regulate how corporations depreciate their equipment, are not social welfare policies.)

Our definition does not limit us to legislative policies because many kinds of rules, regulations, and objectives exist in organizations and communities. We can illustrate the sheer variety of policies by examining some that are germane to the social problems of persons with serious mental problems who do not want to voluntarily enter mental hospitals. **High-level policies** are germane to this issue, including regulations established by state mental health officials, regulations of specific county mental health departments, various court rulings, and (possibly) regulations of federal authorities. Although these high-level policies influence their work, the mental health staff in the local units of a county mental health program—or the staff in different counties of a state who help this population—may implement high-level, formal, and official policies in strikingly different fashions. Staff in one county may commit a far larger number of persons, for example, than would staff in another county because they have developed different definitions of what constitutes an "imminent threat to themselves and to other persons." These **local and organizational policies** cannot be ignored when examining policies that are germane to mentally ill persons in this particular state.

We include **policy objectives** in our definition because they shape the actions and choices of officials, executives, and staff. When a state mental health agency declares it wants "to drastically reduce the populations of mental institutions," it commits its officials and staff to this objective and to programs that are consonant with it. (Imagine how the services of the staff might change if, instead, top officials declared their objective "to increase long-term institutional services for a range of mental conditions.") By the same token, we include **rules and regulations** in our definition because many social welfare policies establish parameters or constraints on the activities of officials, staff, and consumers. A rule that limits access to a program to persons who fall beneath specific income standards constrains both intake staff and consumers, whose decisions and access are shaped by it.

Everyone agrees that **formal,** or **written, policies** fall within the purview of social welfare policy, whether by legislation, court rulings, administrative guidelines, or budget documents. Less agreement exists about **informal,** or **nonwritten, policies,** but we often cannot understand how policies are implemented without examining them. When written policy contains relatively vague and ill-defined terms, officials and staff often must develop informal policies to "fill in the gaps." Some laws about involuntary commitment, for example, restrict it to persons who are an imminent danger to themselves or to others; staff who require a strict standard may resist committing someone who has not actually attempted suicide, for example, whereas other staff may believe threats of suicide fall within this definition. These standards *are* policies because, although not recorded in official policy, they have the same effect as written policy—that is, they are *collectively defined rules* that profoundly shape the actions of direct-service staff and their administrators.

Lest the reader believe that our definition of social welfare policy places no limits on policy, let us note various activities and subjects that fall outside its purview. It does not include the purely personal dispositions of specific staff or officials because policy is a phenomenon that collectively binds persons to specific rules and regulations. The personal positions of individuals do not become policy until they are concretized in the official or informal policies of legislatures, courts, or organizations.[85] The tasks of managing organizations do not fall within social welfare policy *unless* they are specifically germane to the implementation of specific policies. In similar fashion, the various planning and mobilizing functions of community organizers become relevant to social welfare policy *only* when they are used to develop, enact, or implement specific policies.

The controversial nature of social welfare policy stems from its collective or binding nature. Were no policies to exist, a state of anarchy would occur where staff members, consumers, agency directors, and public officials pursued whatever interests or tangents they espoused. Left to their own, for example, some staff might involuntarily commit most persons with mental conditions, even those with minor problems, to institutions, while other staff might commit none of them, even those with life-threatening conditions. Anarchy has its virtues, but these random and personal actions of staff would lead to confusion and, as we note later, unfortunate consequences for many consumers.

Anarchy would also frustrate the protection of the rights of vulnerable persons such as those with stigmatized social conditions or from oppressed groups such as racial minorities or poor persons.[86] By spelling out the nature of services and benefits that persons can receive, as well as rules about the determination of eligibility, policies establish entitlements that cannot be violated by those staff who dislike certain kinds of persons. Official policies also make clear to citizens what resources or services they can legitimately seek from social agencies.

Policy also provides a mechanism for the general public, their elected representatives, and the governing boards of organizations to articulate and enforce their preferences. In light of scarce resources, societies and organizations cannot undertake an unlimited number of projects and cannot serve all persons who seek or need assistance for any problem they possess. Policies provide a mechanism for establishing priorities.

If policies provide means for expressing the preferences of those persons who are vested with policy-making authority, they also provide a means of accountability and enforcement. Elected officials are ultimately accountable to their constituents, and their constituents decide whether to vote for them on the basis of the kinds of policies that the officials support and oppose.[87]

In turn, those agencies, programs, and staff that implement legislative policies are ultimately accountable to elected officials; if they flaunt legislative policies, they risk losing their funds and may be subject to prosecution. In similar fashion, the governing boards of agencies often enunciate policies that they expect the executive director and agency staff to implement.

DEFINING POLICY PRACTICE

We define **policy practice** as "the use of conceptual work, interventions, and value clarification to develop, enact, implement, and assess policies." *Conceptual work* includes the use of rational and analytic tools such as data gathering, research, identification of policy options, and the drafting of policy proposals. (We shall discuss conceptual work in Chapters Two, Three, and Four.) *Interventions* describe specific actions or verbal exchanges that policy practitioners make to increase the likelihood that specific problems will be deliberated, certain proposals will be developed, and specific policies will be enacted and implemented. These actions or verbal exchanges include discussions with other persons, presentations and other persuasive devices, debates and arguments, the use of specific power resources to modify the opinions or actions of other persons, and the use of group processes in coalitions, task forces, committees, and meetings. (We discuss political and interactional interventions in Chapters Five, Six, and Seven.)

Value clarification (or *ethical reasoning*) is needed at specific points during the policy-making process. Policymakers have to decide, for example, what objectives or goals they favor when analyzing problems and what criteria they wish to emphasize when comparing and selecting policy options. Do they seek, for example, drastic or major reforms or merely modest changes in existing policies? Do they want the least expensive policy, a policy that will provide the greatest benefit to consumers, a policy that reduces current inequities, or a policy that satisfies some combination of these (or other) criteria? The selection of objectives and criteria is necessarily shaped by the values of the policy practitioner.

Values intrude as well when persons decide why they engage in policy-making in the first instance. Do they identify with and seek to help certain powerless groups in the general population, the agency that employs them, or their particular work unit? Indeed, do they seek policy changes that will promote their personal advancement? Motives are often conflicted or numerous, and policy practitioners should analyze them to see if they conflict with specific ethical standards. Policy practitioners also have to decide what kinds of risks they are willing to take when they question existing policies—risks that can sometimes lead to loss of employment.

Policy practitioners need to wrestle with ethical issues that are germane to process or procedural matters. Under what circumstances are deceptive, dishonest, or manipulative behaviors ethical? When is it ethical to undermine the credibility of another person or faction? When seeking support for a policy, is it ethical (and when) to make exaggerated claims for it?

Ethical issues arise when considering the substantive content of policies. In the case of involuntary commitments of homeless persons with mental problems, for example, ethical principles conflict: Should laws facilitate commitments to protect the well-being of homeless persons, or should policies maximize their autonomy and self-determination? (We discuss value clarification in Chapter Eight.)

POLICY PRACTICE: SKILLS AND TASKS

The preceding discussion suggests that policy practitioners need at least four basic skills. **Analytic skills,** which are discussed in Chapters Two through Four, are used to identify policy alternatives, to compare their relative merits, and to develop recommendations. **Political skills,** which are discussed in Chapters Five and Six, are used to assess the feasibility of enacting specific policies, to identify power resources, and to develop and implement political strategy. **Interactional skills,** which are discussed in Chapter Seven, are used to develop contacts with influential persons, to develop supportive networks, to build personal relationships, to identify old-boy networks, and to use group process to facilitate one's policy objectives. **Value-clarification skills,** which are discussed in Chapter Eight, are used to identify moral considerations that are relevant not only to the shaping of policy proposals but also to political and interactional strategies that are used to obtain support for specific policies.

Other social work–practice disciplines also require the use of multiple skills. Direct-service practitioners analyze the problems of their clients, apply political skills when they engage in case advocacy, use interactional skills when fashioning helping relationships with clients, and recognize moral issues such as preserving the confidentiality of information obtained during the helping process. In similar fashion, administrators use analytic skills to diagnose problems and to select remedies, political skills to develop support for changes in agency programs, interactional skills to develop rapport with their staff and boards, and value-clarification skills to examine various program and strategy choices.

Policy practitioners use their policy skills to engage in six recurring policy tasks: agenda-setting, problem-defining, proposal-making, policy-enacting, policy-implementing, and policy-assessing tasks. When seeking to advance certain problems on the agendas of decision makers in agency, community, and legislative settings, they engage in **agenda-setting tasks.** John Kingdon's pathbreaking research on the formation of agendas in the federal arena identifies a variety of conceptual and political tools that are used by policy practitioners to place specific issues, problems, or policies in a preferential position on the agendas of policymakers.[88] Policy practitioners analyze presenting issues or problems when they engage in **problem-defining tasks.** In the case of social problems such as homelessness, for example, policy practitioners develop taxonomies of homeless persons, gauge its prevalence in specific communities, and analyze its causes.

When engaging in **proposal-making tasks,** policy practitioners identify policy options, compare and contrast their comparative merits, and meld or combine them into an embracing proposal. Proposals can be relatively simple, such as a proposal to change the intake policies of an agency, or complex and multifaceted, such as legislation that establishes a major social program. Policy practitioners engage in **policy-enacting tasks** when they develop and implement strategy to obtain the passage or approval of a policy proposal in a specific setting. In the case of protracted and conflictual political processes, strategy may encompass an extended period of time, require the expenditure of major amounts of time and resources, and demand frequent revisions. On other occasions, strategy may be limited to a single presentation at a critical meeting or personal discussions with a few highly placed decision makers.

The policy-implementing and policy-assessing tasks of policy practitioners intersect with disciplines of administration and program evaluation. When policy practitioners engage in **policy-implementing tasks,** they identify various reasons why a specific policy is not adequately implemented and develop corrective strategies and policies. As the expansive literature on policy implementation suggests, policy practitioners must often seek changes in official policy during the implementing process to correct those facets of existing policy that contribute to poor implementation of policy. In many cases, they find that official policies cannot be implemented because of insufficient resources. These policy tasks are supplemented by a range of administrative ones such as hiring competent staff.

When engaging in **policy-assessing tasks,** policy practitioners decide what criteria will be used to evaluate a policy or program and what kinds of changes need to be made in the wake of negative evaluations. This policy work intersects with evaluative research because evaluations require a range of research decisions and tasks. (We discuss the six policy tasks in Chapters Ten through Thirteen and note that analytic, political, interactional, and value-clarification skills are needed to accomplish each of them.)

IS POLICY PRACTICE "RETOOLED" DIRECT-SERVICE PRACTICE?

Surface similarities between the skills employed by direct-service staff and policy practitioners ought not suggest that someone can become adept at policy practice merely by adapting direct-service skills to policy practice.

Policy practice and direct-service practice, while often linked, are markedly different.[89]

The work of direct-service practitioners centers on the problems of specific clients and their families. Practitioners possess considerable autonomy in these therapeutic interventions as they diagnose problems, develop and sustain helping interventions, assess the progress of their clients, and terminate the intervention. Although referrals, case management, advocacy, and multidisciplinary approaches require them to interact with other professionals and institutions, their interactions with clients provide the *primary* focus of their work. Policy practitioners must frequently interact with other persons in the external world during the course of their work because policies are social and collective phenomena. Few persons have the luxury of brainstorming or conceptualizing a new policy and enacting it without considering the responses of others, encountering opposition from one or more sources, building a base of support, and superintending its progress through a decision-making process because *each* task requires interactions with other persons.

Policy practitioners and direct-service practitioners possess markedly different goals. Direct-service staff usually want to change some attributes of their clients, whether their manner of functioning, the way they think about specific personal or familial problems, patterns of relationship, their self-esteem, or specific kinds of competencies such as their ability to find and retain employment. Policy practitioners rarely seek *therapeutic* changes, although they often try to change the opinions or actions of specific persons. In many cases, they develop knowledge of the attributes of persons in order to "work around them" and to develop estimates of the feasibility of securing policy objectives; when a policy practitioner knows, for example, that an executive director of a specific agency abhors a specific policy and possesses the power to prevent its enactment, he or she will likely think twice before proceeding to propose it unless some strategy can be devised to modify the executive's position or to develop a method of decreasing the executive's power to sabotage the measure.

Direct-service staff often enounter issues of power and influence in their interactions with clients and when they seek to help persons cope with institutions and programs. When working with involuntary clients in probation, child welfare, and institutional settings, for example, social workers often have to use professional and court-sanctioned power resources to compel clients not to withdraw from services—yet they must also skillfully build their clients' trust by not making excessive use of their power. When seeking to be advocates for clients, they use their power resources to induce or compel other agencies and persons to provide specific kinds of assistance to their clients. And, when trying to empower their clients, they often teach them how to be assertive and how to develop and use power.

Power is even more endemic to policy practice, however, because many persons possess a personal stake in policy deliberations. When a state mental health agency advocates changes in procedures for involuntary commitments to mental hospitals, for example, it is likely to become embroiled in controversy because different groups, professionals, and officials possess different conceptions of whether, when, and how persons should be involuntarily committed to institutions. The American Civil Liberties Union (ACLU) and patient-rights advocates fear the arbitrary or excessive use of authority by professionals and courts, whereas some professional associations and local officials want to make involuntary commitments less difficult. Some budget and public officials may oppose expanding the commitment powers of professionals because they fear it could lead to escalating costs that would occur if markedly more persons were institutionalized.

Direct-service staff are trained to assume a sort of benevolent neutrality; they want their clients to decide, after weighing options, feelings, and realities, what course of action they wish to take. While direct-service staff often give suggestions or shape the decisions of clients in subtle ways—perhaps more profoundly than they sometimes realize—they nonetheless subscribe to the tenet of self-determination except in those situations where clients violate laws or norms of decency, as in the instance of child abuse.[90] While policy practitioners sometimes assume a relatively background role where they try to help other persons shape their positions, much as a therapist to client, they often take sides in controversies. As interested and involved parties to a dispute, they openly solicit support from other persons, even when their positions offend others. If direct-service staff are sometimes afraid to exert power over clients for fear of sabotaging self-determination, policy practitioners seek and use power to further their cause. Indeed, as we will argue in Chapter Five, direct-service practitioners often need assistance in developing assertiveness skills so that they do not carry into their policy practice some of the reservations about the use of power that exist in direct-service practice.

Policy practitioners have different "clients" than do direct-service practitioners. Specific persons, families, or groups constitute the clients of direct-service practitioners, whose primary objective is to help improve their well-being by working with them. They obtain their clients in several ways: They (or their agencies) may be directly approached by persons who voluntarily seek assistance, or they may be assigned involuntary (or semivoluntary) clients in protective services, probation, or institutional settings.

But policy practitioners are not *assigned* policy issues by their superiors unless they are a legislative aide or full-time policy analyst in government or private organizations. Rather, they initiate or join a faction that seeks to change policy, or, in rarer instances, they try to change policies by themselves. As they engage in policy practice, they have to decide who their "client" is by determining their primary point of reference. Do they ultimately seek policy changes to help certain kinds of persons or communities in the external world, to advance the interests of their organizations or work units, or to further their own policy preferences or interests? In many cases, policy practitioners possess multiple points of reference; someone may support the initiation of a new social program to help certain consumers *and* to obtain new resources for their agency *and* to obtain a promotion to an administrative post in the new program. When they possess multiple allegiances, policy practitioners must decide how to resolve tensions that sometimes arise when practitioners try to juggle competing demands and interests imposed on them—a fact often illustrated in the work of legislators who often try to appease competing interests when they shape specific pieces of legislation.[91]

SIMILARITIES BETWEEN POLICY PRACTICE AND DIRECT-SERVICE PRACTICE

Were policy practice and direct-service practice wholly antithetical, it would be difficult, perhaps impossible, to shift from one to the other. Although they are substantially different, sufficient similarities exist that persons often couple both direct-service practice and policy practice in their professional work. In a sense, each discipline needs the other one. The work of direct-service staff is often frustrated by policies that make their work difficult, as reflected by onerous caseloads, unnecessary red tape, and misdirected regulations. Policy practitioners need direct-service practitioners because their policies must ultimately be implemented and they stand to gain from the insights of direct-service staff about issues, problems, and dilemmas in addressing various kinds of social problems.

Direct-service staff possess skills and perspectives that can contribute to their effectiveness in policy deliberations.[92] Listening skills allow them to detect hidden meaning, hidden agendas, conflicted feelings, anger, resentment, and inclinations to compromise or to "hold out." These kinds of feelings, emotions, and attachments are critical to policy practice because they shape the actions of persons and allow policy practitioners to guess what kinds of actions or positions specific persons are likely to take during policy deliberations.

Direct-service staff also possess sophisticated skills in working with these kinds of feelings, emotions, and attachments. Direct-service practitioners who engage in policy practice may decide, for example, to help someone articulate their conflicted feelings about the advisability of changing a specific policy, particularly if they believe this activity will promote support for a specific policy. Process skills are needed by policy practitioners when they participate in committees, meetings, and task forces.

Both policy practitioners and direct-service practitioners have to persevere in the face of uncertainty and a lack of tangible and immediate results. When working with difficult problems, direct-service staff often realize that they do not have the luxury of extended interventions and that they often cannot influence a range of factors, such as environmental stressors, that cause or exacerbate the problems of their clients. They often do not know whether their work will lead to lasting improvements in the lives of their clients or whether short-term gains will be erased in the course of time. In similar fashion, policy practitioners often feel that they lack the time and resources to modify existing policies, particularly when powerful, well-funded, and opposing interests exist or when their cause lacks popularity or salience to decision makers. In both policy-practice and direct service–practice arenas, social workers need to struggle to maintain idealism and hope in the face of uncertainty and when their work is not immediately rewarded with tangible successes.

POLICY-SENSITIVE PRACTICE, POLICY-RELATED PRACTICE, AND POLICY PRACTICE

Similarities and differences between direct-service practice and policy practice can be summarized by exploring distinctions among policy-sensitive practice, policy-related practice, and policy practice itself. Much direct-service practice, such as interviewing skills, has little or nothing to do with the development and enactment of policies. Policies are clearly relevant to direct-service practice, however, because the lives of clients and the work of social workers are influenced by an array of agency, community, and societal policies. Social workers use **policy-sensitive practice** when they incorporate policy realities into their work with clients by using an ecological or systems framework to shape their direct-service practice. A social worker who helps a battered woman and who uses an ecological framework is likely to view her problems as emanating, at least in part, from the sexism of the broader society and from sexual oppression within her marriage. Moreover, the social worker is likely to view the task to be to empower the woman not only to cope with the abusive spouse but also to negotiate other harsh realities, such as gender-segregated and low-paid work, as she seeks emancipation from her spouse. To the extent the woman has internalized sexism that is widespread in the broader society and believes her spouse has the right to batter her, the social worker may help her realize this fact. But such counseling, while cognizant of policy matters, is not policy practice because it does not focus on developing, enacting, implementing, and assessing policies in the external world.

In other cases, direct-service practitioners engage in **policy-related practice** when they use skills, such as the use of power and negotiation, to assist specific clients.[93] Such case advocacy is also informed by knowledge of existing policies because the case advocate wants to be certain that specific persons "receive their due" under existing policies. Because the case advocate seeks fair treatment of specific persons under existing policies, however, he or she does not engage in **policy practice,** which seeks the development and enactment of policies in specific settings. In a sense, the case advocate seeks the fair implementation of existing policies for specific persons.

Policy practice occurs when direct-service practitioners (or anyone else) engage in class advocacy, that is, seek policy reforms that benefit a range of persons. Of course, policy-sensitive and policy-related practice often develop into class advocacy as social workers discover that the social problems of specific persons require the development of new or revised policies. Indeed, it was precisely to develop this progression that the NASW established its National Center on Practice and Policy in 1986.

Distinctions among policy-sensitive practice, policy-related practice, and policy practice also apply to administrators and community organizers. We noted that traditional administrative materials emphasize internal "nuts and bolts" tasks of administrators, such as managing their personnel and developing budgets. Even when engaging in these traditional functions, however, policy-sensitive administrators are aware of external policy realities as they develop the internal activities and programs of their agencies. They develop programs and hire staff, for example, that will position their agency to receive resources from external funders. As they actively seek resources from external funders, advocate for specific clients, and coordinate with other agencies, they engage in policy-related administrative practice; as with the case advocacy of direct-service practitioners, these activities require them to use power and negotiation. When administrators seek to change external social policies or to develop agency-based policies such as mission statements, they engage in policy practice.

Policy-sensitive community organizers are aware of the policies of city, county, state, and federal authorities that impinge upon those communities and groups that they seek to organize and mobilize. Indeed, these community organizers seek to alert community and other groups to opportunities, as well as constraints, of existing policies. When helping communities or groups to negotiate for resources from high-level authorities under existing policies and programs, community organizers engage in policy-related practice. When they help communities and groups mobilize to change existing policies, community organizers engage in policy practice.

As we noted earlier, a relatively small group of social workers are employed as policy specialists, whether as policy analysts, policy evaluators, lobbyists, or aides to legislators. Unlike most direct-service, administrative, and community-organizing staff, these specialists engage in policy practice on a full-time basis. While they specialize in policy practice, they use the same combination of analytic, political, interactional, and value-clarification skills that other social workers employ to accomplish agenda-setting, proposal-writing, policy-enacting, policy-implementing, and policy-assessing tasks.

Policy-sensitive practice, policy-related practice, and policy practice are depicted in Figure 1.1. To the extent that direct-service staff, administrators, and community organizers participate, policy practice engages the entire profession of social work in activities that supersede their ordinary or usual work. While it is often difficult and promises no certain successes, policy practice returns the profession of social work to the vision of some of its founders, such as Jane Addams, who worked tirelessly to improve the social conditions of powerless and oppressed populations such as children, immigrants, and workers.

FROM STATIC TO DYNAMIC DESCRIPTIONS: DESCRIBING THE WORK OF POLICY PRACTITIONERS

Policy practice does not, of course, occur in a vacuum. The context provides both constraints and opportunities. Many economic, organizational, political, and interpersonal factors, as well as existing policies, provide the context for

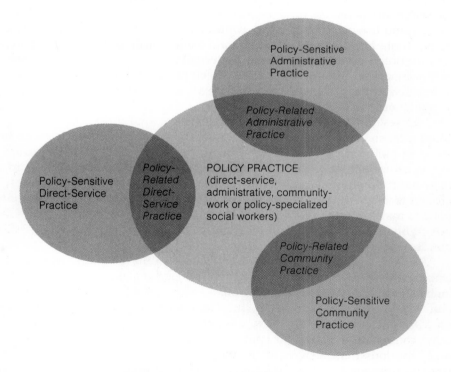

Figure 1.1   Policy-Sensitive Practice, Policy-Related Practice, and Policy Practice

a specific episode of policy practice. Nor can historical factors be ignored; an issue or problem that has been associated with considerable conflict on a prior occasion, for example, is more likely than issues with different traditions to be associated with it on future occasions. Nor can we understand the policy practice of specific persons without understanding their objectives in specific situations, as well as many influences on them, such as peer pressure, motivations, and prior experiences.

To obtain a dynamic, rather than a static, conception of policy practice then, policy skills, policy tasks, policy context, and the objectives and dispositions of specific policy practitioners need to be viewed in tandem. Some readers may at this point throw up their hands and declare, "But this is too complicated to comprehend, much less to learn!" Several gentle reminders, however, may make policy practice appear less forbidding. First, *all* practice disciplines occur within a context, demand the use of multiple skills, require the addressing of specific tasks, and involve the personal objectives and disposition of practitioners. Indeed, a dynamic concepton of practice is described in extensive practice literature in direct-service, administration, and community organization.[94] When faced with conflict between warring units in their organizations, for example, administrators engage in conflict-reduction or mediation tasks, develop specific objectives that define how rapidly and to what extent they wish to resolve the conflict, and use a range of political, analytic, interactional, and value-clarification skills. We have already noted that direct-service practitioners use a range of skills, develop professional objectives when helping specific persons, and engage in specific tasks such as developing a helping contract with specific clients.

Relatively few theorists have developed dynamic models of policy practice, however. Existing texts often describe policy-making as involving a single skill such as analysis. Or they describe policy-making to be a series of steps or guiding questions—an approach that minimizes the uncertainties and evolving nature of policy practice, not to mention its political and interpersonal components. Many case studies, as well as the practical experiences of policymakers in many kinds of settings, suggest that policy practitioners, no less than other practitioners, need to evolve strategy by selecting those interventions and conceptual tools that are most likely to obtain their policy preferences in particular situations.[95]

We seek to develop a dynamic model of policy-making in social welfare by discussing policy-making as *deliberations* in specific agency, community, and legislative settings in which participants use various skills to advance their policy preferences. Contextual factors, such as cultural, political, legal, and economic factors, and historical precedents shape the course of the deliberations profoundly. They sometimes provide *constraints* by limiting the policy options that participants can or do consider. If specific policy practitioners are aware that widespread opposition exists to a specific policy option, for example, they often discard or modify it to make it more acceptable. In other cases, contextual factors provide *opportunities* as persons perceive political support, research, precedents, and legal rulings or as resources support or suggest the need for specific policies (see Figure 1.2).

Of course, the policy context does not remain constant or fixed during policy deliberations; indeed, as we will note in many later chapters, policy practitioners often want to modify the context to make it more conducive to the enactment of specific policies. As policy practitioners change the opinions of specific persons, for example, they modify political and technical components of the context, just as they influence interpersonal components when they become acquainted with other persons.

Policy deliberations describe the interactions of persons who participate in policy-making (see the central portion of Figure 1.1). One or more **policy initiators** begin work to change existing policy, whether by overturning an existing policy, by recommending modifications of existing policy, or by proposing new policies. Policy initiators may enter policy deliberations at many points; they may seek, for example, to promote an issue on the agendas of decision makers, may participate in the processing of the issue, may seek enactment of a proposal, or may concentrate on the implementation or assessment of an existing policy.

It would greatly simplify matters if we could assume that policy initiators perform their work in isolation, as some theorists who provide step-by-step analytic frameworks seem to suggest. But policy initiators usually do not

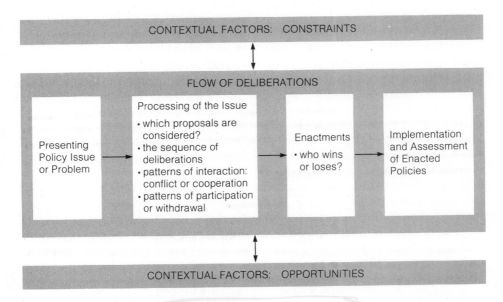

Figure 1.2   Policy-Making: An Overview

have the field to themselves because other persons participate in policy deliberations. Some may join the ranks of policy **initiators.** Others are **bystanders** who take no part in policy deliberations. Still others are **policy responders** who seek to modify or change the policy proposals of the initiators. A final group, the **opposers,** decides to block or modify the proposals of the initiators. These various groups often do not remain stable through time because persons may shift from one to another group as policy deliberations proceed. Indeed, initiators often want to expand their ranks by adding persons from other groups—although they sometimes find opposers equally determined to convert persons to their positions. Nor do all groups emerge in policy deliberations; thus, an opposing group may not form when a consensus develops behind a proposal.

Different levels of conflict are associated with specific issues during policy deliberations. Some issues excite high conflict throughout policy deliberations or during specific portions of those deliberations, whereas other issues are resolved with minimal or no conflict. We can determine the level of conflict by examining the actions and rhetoric of participants. In the case of high conflict, persons use emotion-laden language, make vigorous efforts to out-maneuver other participants, use extraordinary tactics such as filibusters, publicize the issue by appealing to the mass media, and try to enlist persons to support their positions. Polarization between factions and groups often occurs, such as conflict between political parties or conservatives and liberals in legislative settings, between population groups and neighborhoods in community settings, and between management and line staff in organizational settings. The absence of these kinds of actions and alignments usually suggests relatively low-conflict or consensual deliberations.

Policy deliberations often extend over a period of time in specific settings. A piece of legislation, for example, is considered in a variety of subcommittees, committees, and floor debates before it is forwarded to elected officials, such as the president or governor, for approval or veto. Proposals in agencies often proceed through sequences of deliberation that similarly involve a variety of meetings, committees, and officials. Other issues, however, are decided rapidly, such as decisions that are made in the staff meetings of an agency to modify internal policies.

At some point, proposals are enacted, whether in their original or amended form, or rejected. When analyzing these outcomes, we often ask, Who won and who lost? In many cases, patterns of amendments and changes in enacted proposals lead us to conclude that various participants obtained a portion of their policy wishes. In some cases, we decide that apparent victors were in fact losers because their proposals are so diluted as to be meaningless, as Peter Bachrach and Morton Baratz note when they discuss decisionless decisions.[96] Ultimately, of course, we also ask which segments of the population benefited or were harmed in the wake of the enactment or defeat of a policy proposal, a question that forces us to assess or evaluate policies. If persons obtain the enactment of a new social program whose benefits are distributed exclusively to affluent persons, for example, we might declare poor persons to be losers.

Once a policy has been enacted, policy deliberations focus on its implementation and assessment (see Figure 1.1). The purpose and the provisions of many enacted policies are only partially realized during their implementation. As we discuss in Chapter Twelve, policy practitioners often seek to make reforms both in enacted policies and in the bureaucratic systems that are devised to implement them.

Policy practitioners frequently assess the programs or activities that are established in the wake of the enactment of policies to see if they fulfill certain objectives or criteria. As one example, many researchers have analyzed the Food Stamp Program to see if its benefits have decreased malnutrition among specific segments of the population. As we will discuss in Chapter Thirteen, the assessment of policies is a complex undertaking.

SUMMARY

Social welfare policy has traditionally emphasized historical, philosophical, and program-descriptive content, but a new dimension of the discipline, which we have termed *policy practice*, is gaining prominence in policy literature. Policy practice describes and analyzes the skills and strategies of persons who seek to modify existing policies to make social welfare institutions more responsive to the needs of consumers.

Policy practice shares some similarities with other disciplines, such as direct-service, administrative, and community practice, but it is significantly different from them in its focus and in the skills that its practitioners use. We contend that policy-practice skills and concepts should be an important part of the practice competencies of all social workers, no matter what their specialization. A compelling rationale can be made to place policy practice within the broader discipline of social welfare policy.

A variety of social workers can and should engage in policy practice, but a series of myths and a misguided notion of autonomous practice have impeded the emergence of policy practice. Moreover, policy theorists have been remiss until recently in developing the concepts, frameworks, and skills needed to facilitate policy practice.

A framework describing the playing field of policy practice is needed to identify both contextual realities and the course of deliberations. A range of political, economic, ideological, technical, and interpersonal factors shape the course of policy deliberations, as well as the positions and beliefs of participants in them. A presenting issue, problem, or policy provides the focal point of policy deliberations. Deliberations are described by the length, patterns of participation, and the amount or level of conflict that occurs within them. In the wake of policy enactments, attention turns to processes of implementation and assessment.

To receive the attention it deserves, policy practice needs to be supplemented by direct-service methodologies that emphasize environmental and policy factors such as policy-sensitive practice, which includes direct services that attend to environmental realities, and policy-related practice, which includes case-advocacy and empowerment services.

Political, value-clarification, interactional, and analytic skills are needed in policy practice, as we discuss in more detail in the succeeding seven chapters. Various theorists have emphasized one or several of them, but all are needed by skillful practitioners.

QUESTIONS FOR DISCUSSION

1. In a social agency with which you are familiar, define (a) a specific social problem that is addressed by its staff and (b) collective strategy, as influenced by specific rules, regulations, procedures, and objectives, that shapes the activities of staff with respect to that problem.

2. In an agency with which you are familiar, identify some informal policies that shape the actions of staff in addressing a social problem.

3. In an agency with which you are familiar, identify policies that have different points of origin, i.e., stem from sources external to an agency, from high-level sources within an agency, and from specific units within the agency.

4. Discuss how the collective or binding nature of policy often contributes to controversy and conflict when people try to change existing policies or to initiate new policies.

5. The rights of minorities and stigmatized persons would be trammeled in a world without policies. Discuss.

6. Take a clinical case with which you are familiar. Discuss and distinguish between policy-sensitive direct-service practice, policy-related direct-service practice, and policy practice as they might stem from or be associated with this case. How do the three kinds of practice differ from one another? (Perform the same exercise with respect to administrative or community practice in a specific agency or community.)

7. Discuss various mythologies that have made social workers disinclined to engage in the practice of policy. How are these mythologies transmitted and sustained?

8. Discuss the following statement: "It is not feasible or practical for most social workers, whose primary responsibilities lie elsewhere, to engage in

the practice of policy. Therefore, this kind of practice should be reserved for persons who specialize in it."

9. Why are direct-service social workers ill equipped to engage in the practice of policy? What sensitivities and skills facilitate their participation in policy practice?

SUGGESTED READINGS

Definitions of Policy and Social Welfare Policy

Brian Hogwood and Lewis Gunn, *Policy Analysis for the Real World* (London: Oxford University Press, 1984), pp. 12–31.

Martin Rein, *Social Policy: Issues of Choice and Change* (New York: Random House, 1970), pp. 5–8.

Richard Titmuss, *Commitment to Welfare* (New York: Pantheon, 1968), p. 156.

Materials That Link Policy to Direct-Service Practice

Chauncey Alexander, "Professional Social Workers and Political Responsibility" in Maryann Mahaffey and John Hanks, eds., *Practical Politics: Social Work and Political Response* (Washington, D.C.: National Association of Social Workers, 1982), pp. 22–25.

Robert Goodin, *Reasons for Welfare: The Political Theory of the Welfare State* (Princeton, N.J.: Princeton University Press, 1988), pp. 123–228.

Seymour Halleck, *Politics of Therapy* (New York: Science House, 1971), pp. 11–38.

Yeheskel Hasenfeld, "Power in Social Work Practice," *Social Service Review*, 61 (September 1987).

Michael Sosin and Sharon Caulum, "Advocacy: A Conceptualization for Social Work Practice," *Social Work*, 28 (January-February 1983): 12–17.

Harold Weissman and Andrea Savage, *Agency-Based Social Work: Neglected Aspects of Clinical Practice* (Philadelphia: Temple University Press, 1983).

Overviews of Policy Deliberations

James Anderson, *Public Policy-Making* (New York: Praeger, 1975).

Bruce Jansson, *Theory and Practice of Social Welfare Policy: Analysis, Processes, and Current Issues* (Belmont, Ca.: Wadsworth Publishing Co., 1984), pp. 49–55.

Policy Practice

Bruce Jansson, *Theory and Practice of Social Welfare Policy*, pp. 24–28, 53–60.

John Tropman, "Policy Analysis," in *Encyclopedia of Social Work*, vol. 2 (Washington, D.C.: National Association of Social Workers, 1987), pp. 268–283.

Policy Practice in Specific Settings

Ron Dear and Rino Patti, "Legislative Advocacy," in *Encyclopedia of Social Work*, 18th ed., vol. 2 (Washington, D.C.: National Association of Social Workers, 1987).

Maryann Mahaffey and John Hanks, eds., *Practical Politics: Social Work and Political Response* (Silver Springs, Md.: National Association of Social Workers, 1982).

Herman Resnick and Rino Patti, *Change from Within: Humanizing Social Welfare Organizations* (Philadelphia: Temple University Press, 1980).

NOTES

1. See, for example, Carol Meyer, "The Search for Coherence," in Carol Meyer, ed., *Clinical Social Work in the Eco-System Perspective* (New York: Columbia University Press, 1983), p. 17. Also see Carol Meyer, "Direct Practice and Social Work: Overview," in *Encyclopedia of Social Work*, 18th ed., vol. 1 (Silver Springs, Md.: National Association of Social Workers, 1987), pp. 412–413.

2. Meyer, "Direct Practice," p. 412.

3. Yeheskel Hasenfeld, *Human Service Organizations* (Englewood Cliffs, N.J.: Prentice-Hall, 1983), pp. 12–33.

4. Murray Ross, *Community Organizing* (New York: Harper and Row, 1955).

5. The "private agency casework ideal" is discussed by Stanley Wenocur and Michael Reisch in *From Charity to Enterprise: The Development of American Social Work in a Market Economy* (Urbana, Ill.: University of Illinois Press, 1989), p. 260.

6. See Harry Lurie, "The Development of Social Work Programs," in *Yearbook* (New York: National Association of Social Workers, 1960), p. 47, and Werner Boehm, "The Contributions of Psychoanalysis to Social Work Education," *Social Casework*, 39 (November 1958): 487–493.

7. Elmer Tropman and John Tropman, *Encyclopedia of Social Work*, vol. 2, pp. 827–828.

8. Richard Cloward and Irwin Epstein, "Private Agencies, Disengagement from the Poor: The Case of Family Adjustment Agencies." In George Brager and Francis Purcell, eds., *Community Action Against Poverty* (New Haven, Conn.: College and University Press, 1967), pp. 40–63.

9. The common tendency to deny that social workers are influenced by the agency context or that they, in turn, control or influence clients, was discussed by Robert Taylor, "The Social Control Function of Casework," *Social Casework*, 39 (January 1958): 17–21.

10. Wenocur and Reisch discuss the "private agency ideal in the public sector" in *From Charity to Enterprise*, p. 260.

11. Gilbert Steiner, *Social Insecurity: The Politics of Welfare* (Chicago: Rand McNally, 1966), pp. 176–204.

12. U.S., Joint Commission on Mental Illness and Public Health, *Action for Mental Health* (New York: Science Editions, 1961), pp. 150–151.

13. Mayer Zald, *Organizational Change: The Political Economy of the YMCA* (Chicago: University of Chicago, 1970). Also see Robert Scott, "The Selection of Clients by Social Welfare Agencies: The Case of the Blind," in Yeheskel Hasenfeld and Richard English, eds., *Human Service Organizations* (Ann Arbor, Mich.: University of Michigan Press, 1974), pp. 485–499.

14. Joel Handler, *Reforming the Poor: Welfare, Policy, Federalism, and Morality* (New York: Basic Books, 1972), pp. 25–46.

15. Taylor, "The Social Control Function of Casework."

16. Ted Watkins, "Services to Individuals," in James Callicutt and Pedro Lecca, eds., *Social Work and Mental Health* (New York: Free Press, 1983), pp. 45–68.

17. Laurence Lynn, *The State and Human Services: Organizational Change in a Political Context* (Cambridge, Mass.: MIT Press, 1980).

18. U.S., President's Commission on Mental Health, *Report to the President*, vol. II (Washington, D.C.: Government Printing Office, 1978), pp. 497–537.

19. Stephen Webster and Mary Wylie, "Strategic Planning in a Competitive Environment," *Administration in Mental Health*, 15 (Fall 1988): 25–44.

20. David Hardcastle, "The Profession: Professional Organizations, Licensing, and Private Practice," in Neil Gilbert and Harry Specht, eds., *Handbook of the Social Services* (Englewood Cliffs, N.J.: Prentice-Hall, 1981), p. 675.

21. Donald Brieland and John Lemmon, *Social Work and the Law* (St. Paul, Minn.: West Publishing Co., 1985), and Lester Schroeder, *The Legal Environment of Social Work* (Englewood Cliffs, N.J.: Prentice-Hall, 1982).

22. Lester Salamon and Alan Abramson, *The Nonprofit Sector and the New Federal Budget* (Washington, D.C.: Urban Institute Press, 1986).

23. U.S., President's Commission on Mental Health, *Report to the President*, vol. IV, pp. 1362–1516.

24. Brenda McGowan, "Advocacy," *Encyclopedia of Social Work*, vol. 1, pp. 89–95.

25. An attack on labels is made by Thomas Szasz, *Insanity: The Idea and Its Consequences* (New York: John Wiley, 1987). A defense of diagnostic categories is made by Robert Spitzer, Janet Williams, and Andrew Skodol, "DSM-III: The Major Achievements and an Overview," *American Journal of Psychiatry*, 137 (February 1980): 151–154.

26. Victor Adebimpe, "Overview: White Norms and Psychiatric Diagnoses of Black Patients," *American Journal of Psychiatry*, 138 (March 1981): 279–285.

27. Andrew Billingsley and Jeanne Giovannoni, *Children of the Storm* (New York: Harcourt, Brace, Jovanovich, 1972), pp. 218–239.

28. David Mechanic, *Mental Health and Social Policy*, 3rd ed. (Englewood Cliffs, N.J.: Prentice-Hall, 1989), pp. 37–40.

29. Noel Mazade, "Mental Health in Transition," *Administration in Mental Health*, 14 (Spring-Summer 1987): 232–240.

30. Yeheskel Hansenfeld, "Power in Social Work Practice," *Social Service Review*, 61 (September 1987): 475–476.

31. Dennis Chamot, "Professional Employees Turn to Unions," *Harvard Business Review*, 54 (May 1976): 119–127.

32. Gilbert Steiner, *State of Welfare* (Washington, D.C.: Brookings Institution, 1971), pp. 35–40.

33. Abraham Maslow, *The Farther Reaches of Human Nature* (New York: Viking Press, 1971).

34. Robert White, *Ego and Reality in Psychoanalytic Theory* (New York: International Universities Press, 1963).

35. See, for example, Peter Berger, *Invitation to Sociology: A Humanistic Perspective* (Garden City, N.Y.: Anchor Books, 1963), pp. 93–121.

36. Thomas Keefe, "The Stresses of Unemployment," *Social Work*, 29 (May-June 1984): 264–268.

37. For discussion of theorists in the 1960s who probed the effects of these factors on human behavior, see William Wilson, "Cycles of Deprivation and the Underclass Debate, *Social Service Review*, 59 (December 1985): 544–551.

38. See Barbara Solomon, "Is It Sex, Race, or Class?" *Social Work*, 21 (November 1976): 420–421.

39. Henry Aaron, *Politics and the Professors* (Washington, D.C.: Brookings Institution, 1981), p. 17.

40. Wynetta Devore and Elfriede Schlesinger, *Ethnic-Sensitive Social Work Practice* (St. Louis: C.V. Mosby, 1981).

41. Nathan Glazer and Daniel Moynihan, *Beyond the Melting Pot* (Cambridge, Mass.: MIT Press, 1963), pp. 288–291.

42. Nancy Russo, "Women in the Mental Health Delivery System: Implications for Research and Public Policy," in Lenore Walker, ed., *Women and Mental Health Policy* (Beverly Hills, Ca.: Sage, 1984).

43. The classic discussion is found in August Hollingshead and Shirley Redlich, *Social Class and Mental Illness* (New York: John Wiley, 1958), pp. 253–303.

44. Gerald Caplan, *Support System and Community Mental Health* (New York: Behavioral Publications, 1974).

45. Benjamin Gottlieb, *Social Support Strategies: Guidelines for Mental Health Practice* (Beverly Hills, Ca.: Sage, 1983), pp. 31–64.

46. Neil Gilbert, "Assessing Service-Delivery Methods: Some Unsettled Questions," *Welfare in Review*, 10 (May 1972): 25–33.

47. Carel Germain and Alex Gitterman, *The Life Model of Social Work Practice* (New York: Columbia University Press, 1980) and Carol Meyer, *Social Work Practice: A Response to the Urban Crisis* (New York: Free Press, 1970).

48. Solomon, *Black Empowerment;* and Hasenfeld, "Power in Social Work Practice."

49. McGowan, "Advocacy," pp. 90–91.

50. Ibid., p. 91. Also Michael Sosin and Sharon Caulum, "Advocacy: A Conceptualization for Social Work Practice," *Social Work*, 28 (January-February 1983): 12–17.

51. Eviline Burns, *Social Security and Public Policy* (New York: McGraw-Hill, 1956).

52. Neil Gilbert and Harry Specht, *Dimensions of Social Welfare Policy* (Englewood Cliffs, N.J.: Prentice-Hall, 1974).

53. Alfred Kahn, *Theory and Practice of Social Planning* (New York: Russell Sage, 1969).

54. Yeheskel Dror, *Venture in Policy Sciences* (New York: Elsevier North Holland, 1971), and Edward Quade, *Analysis for Public Decisions*, 2nd ed. (New York: Elsevier North Holland, 1982).

55. See Edward Banfield, "The Public Interest," in Neil Gilbert and Harry Specht, eds., *Planning for Social Welfare* (Englewood Cliffs, N.J.: Prentice-Hall, 1977), pp. 44–49.

56. David Gil, *Unravelling Social Policy* (Cambridge, Mass.: Schenkman, 1976).

57. Richard Cloward and Frances Piven, *Regulating the Poor: The Functions of Public Welfare* (New York: Pantheon, 1971).

58. The need for compromises in political arenas is discussed by Ron Dear and Rino Patti, "Legislative Advocacy," in *Encyclopedia of Social Work*, vol. 2, p. 37.

59. Maryann Mahaffey and John Hanks, eds., *Practical Politics: Social Work and Political Response* (Silver Springs, Md.: National Association of Social Workers, 1982); Diane DiNitto and Thomas Dye, *Social Welfare: Politics and Public Policy* (Englewood Cliffs, N.J.: Prentice-Hall; 1983); Andrew Doblestein, *Politics, Economics, and Public Welfare* (Englewood Cliffs, N.J.: Prentice-Hall, 1980); Karen Haynes and James Mikelson, *Affecting Change: Social Workers in the Political Arena* (New York: Longman, 1986).

60. Ron Dear and Rino Patti, "Legislative Advocacy: Seven Effective Tactics," *Social Work*, 26 (July 1981): 289–297.

61. Mahaffey and Hanks, *Practical Politics*.

62. Jeffrey Pressman and Aaron Wildavsky, *Implementation* (Berkeley, Ca.: University of California Press, 1974).

63. For example, see Erwin Hargrove, *The Missing Link* (Washington, D.C.: Urban Institute, 1981); Eugene Bardach, *The Implementation Game* (Cambridge, Mass.: MIT Press, 1977); and Walter Williams, *The Implementation Perspective* (Berkeley, Ca.: University of California Press, 1980).

64. See Werner Boehm, *Objectives of the Social Work Curriculum of the Future*, vol. 1 (New York: Council on Social Work Education, 1959).

65. *Ibid.*, pp. 144–145.

66. See Irving Weissman, *Social Welfare Policy and Services in Social Work Education*, vol. XII (New York: Council on Social Work Education, 1959).

67. Saul Alinsky, *Reveille for Radicals* (New York: Vintage Books, 1969).

68. John Tropman, et al., *New Strategic Perspectives on Social Policy* (New York: Pergamon, 1981), pp. 181–247.

69. Willard Richan, "A Common Language for Social Work," *Social Work*, 17 (November 1972): 14–22.

70. John Flynn, *Social Agency Policy: Analysis and Presentation for Community Practice* (Chicago: Nelson-Hall, 1985); Dean Pierce, *Policy for the Social Work Practitioner*

(New York: Longman, 1984); John Tropman, *Policy Management in the Human Services* (New York: Columbia University Press, 1984).

71. Herman Resnick and Rino Patti, eds., *Change from Within: Humanizing Social Welfare Organizations* (Philadelphia: Temple University Press, 1980).

72. Bruce Jansson, *Theory and Practice of Social Welfare Policy: Analysis, Processes, and Current Issues* (Belmont, Ca.: Wadsworth Publishing Co., 1984), pp. 24–28.

73. *Ibid.*, pp. 24–28.

74. See, for example, the range of nonpolicy subjects in anthologies in community work and administration as illustrated by Fred Cox, et al., *Strategies of Community Organization* (Itasca, Ill.: F.E. Peacock, 1983), and Simon Slavin, ed., *An Introduction to Human Service Management* (New York: Hayworth, 1986).

75. See Robert Dahl, *Pluralist Democracy in the United States* (Chicago: Rand McNally, 1967).

76. Rino Patti and Herman Resnick, "Changing the Agency from Within," *Social Work*, 17 (July 1972): 48–77. Also see Chauncey Alexander, "Professional Social Workers and Political Responsibility," in Mahaffey and Hanks, eds., *Practical Politics*, pp. 26–27.

77. Variations between policies of community mental health centers are discussed by Franklin Chu and Sharland Trotter, *The Madness Establishment* (New York: Grossman, 1974).

78. Bruce Jansson, "Public Monitoring of Contracts with Nonprofit Organizations: Organizational Mission in Two Sectors," *Journal of Sociology and Social Welfare*, 6 (May 1979): 362–374.

79. Martin Rein, *Social Policy: Issues of Choice and Change* (New York: Random House, 1970), p. 5.

80. *Ibid.*, p. 5.

81. *Ibid.*, p. 5.

82. Richard Titmuss, *Commitment to Welfare* (New York: Pantheon, 1968), p. 156.

83. Pressman and Wildavsky, *Implementation.*

84. Rein, *Social Policy*, pp. 6–9.

85. The same point is made by Mackie with respect to "moral rules" when he argues that "privately imagined rules or principles of action are worthless . . . we need expectations and claims (to have) moral rules." J.L. Mackie, *Ethics: Inventing Right and Wrong* (London: Penguin Books, 1977), pp. 146–148.

86. Robert Goodin, *Reasons for Welfare: The Political Theory of the Welfare State* (Princeton, N.J.: Princeton University Press, 1988), pp. 123–228.

87. See Lewis Froman, "Interparty Constituency Differences and Congressional Voting Behavior," *American Political Science Review*, 57 (March 1963): 57–61.

88. John Kingdon, *Agendas, Alternatives, and Public Policies* (Boston: Little, Brown, and Co., 1984).

89. Haynes and Mikelson, *Affecting Change*, pp. 15–22.

90. Taylor, "The Social Control Function," and Hasenfeld, "Power in Social Work Practice."

91. Carol Weiss, "Ideology, Interests, and Information," in Daniel Callahan and Bruce Jennings, eds., *Ethics, the Social Sciences and Policy Analysis* (New York: Plenum Press, 1983), pp. 213–248.

92. Chauncey Alexander, "Professional Social Workers and Political Responsibility," in Mahaffey and Hanks, eds., *Practical Politics*, pp. 22–25.

93. See Harold Weissman and Andrea Savage, *Agency-Based Social Work: Neglected Aspects of Clinical Practice* (Philadephia: Temple University Press, 1983).

94. Charles Garvin and Brett Seabury, *Interpersonal Practice in Social Work: Processes and Procedures* (Englewood Cliffs, N.J.: Prentice-Hall, 1984); George Brager, Harry Specht, and James Torczyner, *Community Organizing*, 2nd ed. (New York: Columbia University Press, 1987); and Rino Patti, *Social Welfare Administration: Managing Social Programs in a Developmental Context* (Englewood Cliffs, N.J.: Prentice-Hall, 1983).

95. Read any extended case study of policy-making as it actually occurs in agency, legislative, and community arenas. See the mixture of political, analytic, and interactional skills that are used by Eric Redman, for example, when he seeks passage of a piece of legislation in *Dance of Legislation* (New York: Simon and Schuster, 1973). Also read the cases in Edward Banfield, *Political Influence* (New York: Free Press, 1961). Many biographies of policymakers discuss the combination of skills that are used by them; see, for example, Doris Kearns, *Lyndon Johnson and the American Dream* (New York: Harper and Row, 1976).

96. Peter Bachrach and Morton Baratz, *Power and Poverty* (New York: Oxford University Press, 1970), pp. 17–38.

PART II

■

Analytic Skills in Policy Practice

Policy theorists use the term *policy analysis* to describe various techniques for dissecting and measuring problems, comparing and assessing policy alternatives, and selecting those alternatives that receive relatively positive assessments. At the outset of Chapter Two, we provide an overview of the analytic style of policy practice. We discuss methods of analyzing social problems in Chapter Two to illustrate our discussion by analysis of the social problem of substance abuse. To sensitize readers to the kinds of policy options that often arise in social welfare, we discuss a variety of financing, organization, and service-delivery options in Chapter Three. These recurring policy options are frequently encountered by policy practitioners, no matter what their setting. To illustrate our discussion, we examine the way a proposal might be developed to provide federal funding for shelters that help battered women. Policy practitioners often examine the comparative merits of specific policy options when they develop policy proposals. We call this activity *analytic reasoning,* which we discuss in Chapter Four. We also discuss how policy practitioners meld or combine specific options into an embracing proposal in Chapter Four.

Policy-practice cases are included at the beginnings of Chapters Two through Four to introduce readers to concepts that are discussed in these chapters.

CHAPTER 2

■

Analytic Skills in Policy Practice: Defining, Measuring, and Conceptualizing Social Problems

American society, like all industrialized societies, is beset by social problems like homelessness, family abuse, substance abuse, mental illness, and physical illness. These problems have defied resolution despite the determined efforts of legions of reformers. Policy analysts seek to bring to these problems a modicum of rationality; they implore policy practitioners to carefully analyze social problems, to identify a range of relevant policy options, to evaluate the merits of specific policy options, and to select those options that meet stringent standards of merit. In this chapter, we examine how policy analysts approach social problems such as substance abuse.

A POLICY-PRACTICE CASE FROM THE HUMAN SERVICES SYSTEM

A social worker who wishes to develop a new program to address unmet needs of consumers has to define specific social problems, collect data about their prevalence, propose specific interventions, and convince decision makers that new policies are needed to address the problem. In Policy-Practice Case 2, a social worker tries to develop a preventive program in a mental health agency.

The social worker devotes considerable time to analyzing the social problems that would be addressed by the LEAPS project, that is, the Learning Everything About Parenting Service. She ponders developing a research survey to ascertain what kinds of problems the project might address among families with latency and adolescent children. Would it address a variety of social problems, such as suicides and substance abuse, or focus on a specific one such as substance abuse? To what populations might LEAPS be targeted?

What kinds of outreach or publicity would most effectively make the program relevant to specific kinds of parents?

As she ponders these questions, the social worker engages in policy analysis that focuses on defining, measuring, and conceptualizing specific social problems. Because social welfare policy seeks to ameliorate social problems, as we discussed in Chapter One, this portion of policy practice is vitally important to social workers, who are well positioned to be aware of unmet needs in the communities where they work.

THE DESIRE TO ENHANCE THE QUALITY OF POLICY CHOICES BY USING POLICY ANALYSIS

It is small wonder that many people want to improve the quality of policy choices because various welfare, crime, substance-abuse, public-housing, urban-development, and economic-development policies have failed to accomplish their objectives. Many factors conspire to make existing policies ineffective. Persons, groups, and institutions with a preponderance of power often select those policies that are congruent with their interests, as is illustrated by agencies, professions, corporations, government agencies, and officials who often support policies that will increase their revenues, their prestige, their monopolies of specific kinds of services or tasks, and their power—sometimes with scant regard to the needs of those citizens who need their assistance. Tradition often assumes a major role in shaping policies even when considerable evidence suggests existing policies are outmoded and ineffective. Professional wisdom, which often fosters effective services, can sometimes lead practitioners to support dysfunctional policies such as the excessive reliance of many surgeons on radical mastectomies, hysterectomies, and heart bypass operations. Nor are policymakers immune from societal prejudices and misconceptions, as well as fads and presumed panaceas.

Why not, some theorists wonder, subject policy choices to careful deliberations to minimize the effects of power, tradition, fuzzy intentions, and intuition? Why not establish decision-making rules in advance so that only those policy options that obtain positive evaluations are chosen? Why not make extensive use of research so that objective information guides policy choices?[1]

As *Webster's* definition of the term *analysis* suggests, the analytic approach emphasizes "breaking up of a whole into its parts to find out their nature."[2] Most analytic frameworks or approaches suggest a careful and step-by-step process of defining policy problems, collecting information, and reaching policy solutions after an extended and deliberative process.[3] As can be seen in Table 2.1, analysis of presenting policy problems (Step 1) is followed by efforts to select policy remedies by comparing the strengths and weaknesses

POLICY-PRACTICE CASE 2

EXPANDING A PREVENTIVE PROGRAM IN A MENTAL HEALTH AGENCY

I work for a community mental health center (the Hobart CMHC) attached to a local hospital that provides it with some of its funds. The Hobart CMHC is currently in a state of fiscal crisis because the local hospital is experiencing marked budgetary deficits; indeed, there have been layoffs of clerical and administrative staff.

Thus, Hobart CMHC as a community mental health center has become like Cinderella, a participant in a hospital family that views her as an unwanted stepchild. Like Cinderella, Hobart is becoming aware of its need to look to external sources for deliverance.

It would be too presumptuous of me to consider the program proposal I will set forth in this paper to be Hobart's fairy godmother. However, perhaps it could be like the glass slipper, an instrument for creating inroads into the process of orienting Hobart to the concept of community mental health and a means for educating the local hospital to the validity of that concept.

Proposal

In 1970 the family–child division of Hobart CMHC began a program called the Preschool and Infant Parenting Service (PIPS). The aim of this program was to reach parents of young children (birth through five years) who had concerns about their children's development and behavior. A "warm line" free telephone service was established. Parents could call into the clinic and within twenty-four hours receive direct assistance from either staff clinical social workers, child development specialists, or volunteer paraprofessionals specifically trained for this program. Medical questions were not in the realm of service; rather, the objective was to provide suggestions, alternatives, information, referrals, and/or reassurance to callers. The name "warm line" denoted the kind of response and the fact that this was not to be correlated with crisis or "hot line" kinds of programs. Calls averaged about forty-five minutes in length, and, generally, families who called received follow-up calls (callers may choose to remain anonymous, however).

Besides the warm line, the PIPS program offered a variety of brief services usually about six weeks in length. Mothers and fathers with "normal" concerns about raising their children could rap with other parents in various group settings led by a staff member. A twenty-five-dollar fee per family was charged for the six-week groups. The PIPS program was considered an early (secondary) prevention program whose objective was to enlarge the population using Hobart CMHC while increasing the comfort experienced by "normal" families in using this kind of clinic. Every family participating is interviewed and evaluated separately, and families with serious problems are referred to other programs at the local hospital. PIPS was initially funded by a small federal grant, which has expired; it is now funded by the local hospital. It is a small operation that has never been evaluated for its impact and is currently in jeopardy of being eliminated.

To provide more comprehensive mental health services and thereby increase community support and participation, I am seeking an expansion of the present PIPS program through increased publicity and staffing and through the addition of a second level that would initiate a similar service for families with children of latency and adolescent ages. With tongue in cheek, I must admit that I have already accomplished the first task of program development, that of devising an appropriate acronym. The new program is to be called LEAPS (Learning Everything About Parenting Service). Allowing myself the freedom to fantasize, I could envision a LEAPS program with its "warm line" and group technology serving families at all levels of the life cycle, including three-generational problems. (Hobart's catchment area has a large senior citizen population, yet program development for that group has been minimal.)

The idea for a LEAPS program evolved from observations of the warm line. Each time that PIPS advertised its warm line service through the communications media, warm line would receive calls from families with children over the age of five. Staff time and availability to respond to these families are limited, so these calls could not be adequately serviced. Professionally, I feel that expansion to a LEAPS program could lead to better services for a larger population.

Four sequential steps are needed before LEAPS can be implemented. One step is to make a comprehensive documentation of the LEAPS program, which would include a definition of the LEAPS mission as it correlates with stated and implied goals for Hobart CMHC and its family–child unit. LEAPS would have to be described as a program able to provide broader services to people needing help with emotional problems and to provide mandated consultation and prevention objectives through an innovative approach to treatment in the family and child mental health field.

Documentation needs to include a description of program operation and specific populations served. It should also anticipate statistics such as estimates of the numbers who would utilize this service, operational costs, probable space needs, staffing needs and costs, and equipment needs and costs, including telephone and audiovisual materials. Some of these estimates could be based on studies of similar programs, including the PIPS project, suicide prevention, and other hot line services.

A preliminary market research survey could add additional credence to the documenter's sense of "felt need." It would also alert the public to the potential service and provide an avenue for community input in the planning stage. Market research is important because it puts the consumer in the position of contributing to decision making.

The description of staff could strategically emphasize in-house control through appointment of a staff member as clinical administrator. To satisfy attending staff, a psychiatrist could be designated to act as program consultant. This might also serve to reinforce public legitimation of the project.

Continued

POLICY-PRACTICE CASE 2
(continued)

Because of the present dearth of funds, use of existing staff would be prudent. To mitigate conflicts with PIPS personnel, the PIPS staff should be LEAPS core personnel. The validity for hiring a community worker who had additional communications and public relations expertise could be justified in terms of economics, that is, saving staff time. I feel that infusion of new blood schooled in community work could be an important asset to the LEAPS program. Most of the present staff needs to be educated to the nuances of consultation and community outreach because few have participated in community projects.

Also, methods for record-keeping and evaluation need to be improved. One important statistic that PIPS is not gathering is the number of referrals it makes to the family–child unit or other programs at Hobart CMHC. There has been much speculation that PIPS is a viable "feeder" for Hobart CMHC, and information to that effect would point to an additional success of the program. Built-in methods of evaluation and research seem to be needed also as justification for continued funding.

A second step is to obtain approval from internal sources, that is, people within the agency structure. My first targets would be those whom I perceive to be key personnel. The originator of the PIPS program is the wife of Dr. Jones, an influential physician. He is a pivotal person in terms of his influence as administrator at Hobart CMHC and as an envoy for the local hospital to key persons in positions of power. My observation of a parenting project now in existence at Hobart CMHC bears witness to the necessity for seeking support from Dr. Jones for any new proposal. The parenting project, a longitudinal study of children and their families, was funded and staffed independently and was approved by officials at the local hospital without seeking aid from Dr. Jones, the Hobart CMHC chief. Consequently, the project staff is faced with obstacles such as lack of space and is subject to the criticism of Dr. Jones's chief, who publicly questions the validity of the study.

A third step involves community support for the project. I know several influential persons on the advisory council of PIPS who want an enlarged project that serves a larger section of the population. External support may also be obtained from the county child welfare agency, which is understaffed but working to develop a preventive strategy.

A crucial fourth step is to obtain funding from external sources. Informal contacts with officials from several local foundations suggest the possibility of funding for a larger program, especially if part of the funds can be assumed by Hobart CMHC and the county child welfare department. Hobart CMHC has several ongoing private fund-raising groups, and perhaps one of these groups could be persuaded to dedicate fund-raising for a new program. Present financial difficulties preclude asking for a portion of existing funds. This program might need to be presented as a one-year "demonstration" project when funding sources are initially approached.

SOURCE: This case is adapted from one by Andrea Karzen, M.S.W. Names and locations have been altered.

TABLE 2.1   The Analytic Style of Policy Practice: Recurring Questions

Step 1   Analyzing the Presenting Problem

- How do we define it so that it can be distinguished from other related problems?
- Can we establish a typology that defines subvarieties of the problem?
- How do we measure the prevalence of the problem?
- How do we locate persons or institutions that possess a specific problem or, in the case of prevention, could develop it?
- How do we assess the relative importance of the problem to society, to some group in the population, or to specific institutions?
- What factors cause the problem?

Step 2   Finding a Policy Remedy That Will Effectively Address the Problem

- What policy remedy will most effectively prevent or redress the problem?
- Besides effectiveness in preventing or addressing the problem, what other criteria should be considered when locating a policy remedy?
- What array of policy options should be considered?
- What data exist to suggest how options "score" on various of the selected criteria?
- What policy option is preferable?

Step 3   Convincing Other Persons to Accept the Recommendations

- Disseminating technical data
- Disseminating policy recommendations

of specific options (Step 2). Finally, analysts disseminate their recommendations to convince decision makers to adopt their findings (Step 3).

PROBLEMS AS HUMAN INVENTIONS: SOME CONCEPTUAL ISSUES IN DEFINING AND MEASURING THEM

As they wrestle with defining, measuring, and analyzing problems, whether population-based ones or ones within the human services system, policy analysts frequently confront the fact that problems are not "real" or "objective" entities but constructs of the human mind.[4] Take the examples of poverty, child abuse, and indebtedness. Persons have argued in prior eras and in the contemporary period about the definition of poverty: Does it exist when persons suffer life-threatening conditions such as hunger? Is it best measured by an inability to purchase some "acceptable" amount of goods and services (and what level or amount is sufficient to place someone at, below, or above poverty?)? Or is it measured by comparing the economic condition of certain persons, such as low-wage workers, with other persons, high-wage workers, or "rich" persons?[5] Moreover, is poverty best defined as the ability or inability to purchase certain amounts of services and goods, or must one *also* be involuntarily subjected to economic deprivation? Indeed, must one *also* possess negative mind sets like hopelessness and alienation? (These stipulations would cast Mother Teresa outside the pale of poverty and would require us to examine not only the resources that persons possess but also their routes into poverty and their attitudes about it.) One could also examine the length or chronicity of economic deprivation; someone who is temporarily deprived of resources in the wake of loss of a job or a bad day at the track might not be defined as poor in contrast to persons who experience poverty for extended periods.

Other conditions in the external world are also subject to widely varying interpretations by experts and citizens. Some experts tell us that 40 percent of us (or more) suffer from "serious mental illness," whereas others place the numbers at 10 percent.[6] Estimates of the numbers of alcoholics, child abusers, and children who are neglected also vary wildly.[7] While the variations in estimates are partly a function of problems in obtaining information from persons who do not want to disclose stigmatized conditions to researchers, they also underscore the role of judgments, values, and culture in shaping definitions of social problems.[8] A mild bout of depression is, for some experts, "mental illness" but merely a "normal response to a life event" for other experts. Routine drinking of several martinis after work represents alcoholism to some persons but is merely social drinking to other analysts.

We have discussed social problems to this point, but our comments apply equally to problems in the human delivery system. Persons variously discuss fraudulent use of services, bureaucratic waste, unresponsiveness of services to consumers, red tape, duplication of services, and discrimination. Were we confronted with extreme examples of these problems, we could agree that they exist, as illustrated by an executive who pockets agency funds, a consumer who must negotiate fifty forms to obtain eligibility to a program, or flagrant denial of services to consumers based on their race or gender.

Values, culture, and traditions shape our perceptions of these conditions. Conservatives suggest, for example, that most federal programs are unresponsive to consumers, inefficient, or associated with red tape or fraud.[9] Some fraud exists in many programs, for example, because it is impossible for intake staff to personally verify every piece of information given by every applicant. But what rates and kinds of fraud are needed to make it a serious problem? As in the case of poverty, decisions about thresholds and definitions influence how persons evaluate the external world. To some persons, *any* incorrect information by an applicant—or any "bending of the rules" by intake workers—constitutes fraud, whereas others impose a less stringent standard. Some persons are not concerned about fraud unless it exceeds a threshold of 10 percent of applicants who receive benefits or services to which they are not entitled, whereas others view it as a problem if it exceeds 5 percent.[10] Persons sometimes make a determination by comparing different programs; liberal defenders of programs like AFDC and Medicaid note, for example, that lower rates of fraud exist in these programs than in the tax collections of the Internal Revenue Service.[11]

As our examples of poverty and fraud suggest, policy problems are slippery concepts. We can disagree about their seriousness, their causes, the relationships of specific problems to other problems, their implications for society, the definition of specific problems—and, not surprisingly, about strategy to address or to prevent them.

THE ANALYTIC CHALLENGE IN CLASSIFYING PROBLEMS

Policy analysts are undeterred by this conceptual thicket and seek to use systematic and deliberate approaches to bring rationality to our discussion of policy problems. They want to define problems with considerable precision, develop typologies to identify subvarieties, measure the prevalence of specific problems, assess the importance of problems so that major ones can be distinguished from trivial ones, and examine the causes of problems.

Definitional and classification issues are immediately encountered by policy analysts. Analysts seek more specific terms to supplement broad ones like mental illness, alcoholism, and substance abuse because broad terms usually embrace a variety of subproblems that differ significantly from one another.[12]

To illustrate our discussion, let's examine the attempt by Mark Moore to define specific kinds of heroin users (see Figure 2.1). First, he identifies heroin users at various *stages of development*, as can be seen by analyzing the model from the left (a "susceptible" but nonaddicted population) to the center (various kinds of "unsupervised users") to the right (users who are receiving services or who reside in jails). Moreover, he tries to analyze patterns of movement between these various stages (see the various arrows in the model).

Moore distinguishes between various kinds of unsupervised users in the left-center part of the model when he uses descriptions like "joy popper," "drug dabbler," "addict," "hustler," "drug-dependent," "conformist, "maturing-out user," and "burned-out user." To develop this typology of unsupervised users, he used a set of distinguishing characteristics to sort specific users into various categories. Moore's distinguishing characteristics include manifestations, phase of problem development, causation, and threshold. **Manifestations** are specific outward actions or behaviors that allow policy analysts to distinguish between different kinds of persons. Some substance

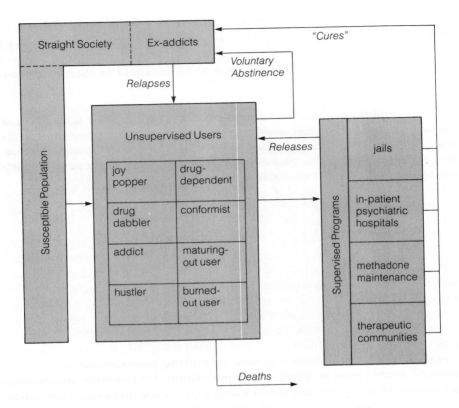

Figure 2.1   Dynamic Model of the Heroin-Using Population

SOURCE: © 1976 by the Regents of The University of California. Reprinted from *Policy Analysis* (vol. 2, no. 3, p. 256) by permission.

abusers, for example, do not appear to be mentally impaired or mentally disoriented, whereas the behaviors of others suggest that their addiction has damaged their mental functioning and capacities. Counseling staff would probably need to obtain medical tests of the latter kind of abusers in contrast to persons who appear to be mentally unimpaired. When analyzing the **phase of problem development,** the analyst distinguishes between persons who are at risk but have not yet developed a problem, persons who are in the early stages of a problem, persons who have serious problems, and persons who are in the latter phases of a problem; in Moore's scheme, chronicity and duration are suggested by descriptions like "susceptible population," "joy popper," "addict," "maturing-out user," and "burned-out user." When examining **causation** of a problem, the analyst identifies specific kinds of persons who developed the problem in a similar fashion. In Moore's scheme, for example, "conformist" suggests that some persons take drugs because of their susceptibility to peer pressure, whereas "drug-dependent" suggests psychological or physiological factors that contribute to usage.

Analysts must also wrestle with issues of **threshold** in their definitions of problems. How much heroin use is required, for example, to make one fit one of the subgroups under "unsupervised users"? If persons imbibe heroin several times a year at social events, do they exceed a threshold that allows them to be classified as a "joy popper" or as a "drug dabbler"? In the case of alcoholism, at what threshold of consumption do we classify persons as "social drinkers" or as "alcoholics"? What level of anxiety or depression must be exceeded to call persons "anxious" or "depressive"? Of course, these judgments are often influenced by cultural factors. Cocaine use, for example, was relatively widespread in all social classes in the United States in the early part of the twentieth century; thus, many persons possessed a far looser definition of addiction than do many contemporary Americans, who sometimes equate addiction even with the occasional use of drugs such as cocaine.

Analysts often encounter the difficult problem of determining the standard to be used in deciding the level or threshold. If they use a **relative standard,** they establish thresholds by comparing the actions, behaviors, or resources of one group with those of the rest of the population. If the national norm for drinking were two drinks a day, an alcoholic by a relative standard might be someone who consumed, say, five or more drinks a day. Of course, a relative standard suggests a flexible or moving threshold; as the average usage of alcohol rises and falls in the population, for example, so also does the threshold of usage that citizens and experts use to define alcoholism. Alternatively, we can use an **absolute standard** in which we establish a threshold on the basis of expert opinion. Perhaps physicians contend that persons who imbibe more than two drinks a day, or who use alcohol in the morning, are alcoholic because this threshold appears to suggest compulsive patterns of use or to cause physical damage. Unlike relative standards, such absolute standards do not rise and fall with patterns of popular usage; if *everyone* in the United States consumed more than two drinks a day, for example, the expert who used the two-drink threshold would declare the entire adult population to be alcoholic.

By using concepts such as stages of development, manifestations, causation, thresholds, relative standards, and absolute standards, policy analysts develop **typologies.** Difficult as typologies such as Moore's are to develop, they increase our precision when discussing specific kinds of social problems. If we make *no* effort to develop classification schemes, we encounter serious problems. First, we cannot develop policies and programs that *specifically* address the idiosyncratic needs of special groups of consumers.[13] Moore's scheme suggests, for example, that we should develop programs for at-risk populations that are different from programs that we develop to assist current addicts. Perhaps, as well, we need different programs for users whose addiction is caused or exacerbated by social factors, such as "conforming users," than for users whose usage is linked to physiological or psychological dependence. Second, if we have no classification system, it is difficult to evaluate the effectiveness of specific strategies. As we couple classification systems with service strategies, we can evaluate whether certain kinds of counseling (or other remedies) are most effective with specific kinds of drug users. Third, a classification system allows us to establish priorities. If research suggests that certain kinds of users are most likely to become long-term users, for example, federal or state authorities might prioritize those programs that target those kinds of users with preventive, counseling, or other services.

Our discussion of classification systems with respect to heroin use applies with equal measure to other social problems such as mental illness, poverty, child abuse, and marital discord. Many analysts and professionals have developed typologies of mental illness, for example, such as the *DSM–III* manual of the American Psychiatric Association.[14] When testifying before Congress in 1988 about welfare reform, some experts distinguished different kinds of impoverished persons such as unwed teenage mothers, recently divorced older women, and victims of structural unemployment.[15] Because research suggested that unwed teenage mothers were most likely to be on welfare rolls for ten or more years, the welfare reform legislation of 1988 required local authorities to give priority to this group in its training, counseling, and educational programs.

To be candid, analysts encounter formidable technical obstacles when trying to construct classification systems like Moore's. Critics can ask, for example, whether his subtypes of heroin users are mutually exclusive; can "addicts" be neatly distinguished, for example, from "drug-dependent persons" and from "conformists"? Classification systems sometimes create categories that lead policy-makers and direct-service staff to stereotype specific kinds of persons.[16] Thus, specific persons who appear to belong to specific groups may be erroneously categorized or labeled. Some black psychiatrists allege, for example, that mental health workers wrongly classify many blacks to be schizophrenic because of a combination of racism as well as a propensity to mistake for pathology some behaviors that derive from their social class or from black culture.[17]

Persons who construct classification systems often enounter a dilemma regarding the breadth of their categories. If relatively few categories are used, such as dividing the heroin population into preaddict, addict, and recovered-addict categories, it is difficult to develop specialized programs to assist those persons whose needs are inadequately defined by these simple categories. If *many* categories are developed, the analyst risks making artificial distinctions between persons who in fact share many commonalities.[18] We have already asked, for example, whether the various categories in Moore's scheme are mutually exclusive; is it possible in fact to distinguish between "joy poppers" and "drug dabblers"?

USING ANALYTIC SKILLS TO MEASURE THE PREVALENCE OF POLICY PROBLEMS

Policy practitioners often have to demonstrate or prove to skeptics that specific problems are sufficiently important that they merit attention by agency staff, funders such as foundations and United Way, government officials, and legislators. Moreover, they have to discuss the nature and causes of specific problems in sufficiently convincing terms that persons believe that interventions can be devised to address them. Much as the fabled blind man who gradually develops a composite concept of an elephant, various technical approaches exist to facilitate measurement of the prevalence of social problems.

Legislators, funders, and executives are more likely to invest scarce resources in programs if they believe that those programs address widespread problems. Concepts such as rates, prevalence, and incidence are commonly used as measures of the relative magnitude of social problems.[19] These measures allow the analysis of the distribution of problems at a given time. **Rates,** for example, measure the ratio of persons, such as white males between ages eighteen and twenty-five who are arrested for drunk driving in a specific year, to a larger reference group, such as the total number of white males in the population in that year. (The number is expressed as a percentage.) **Incidence** measures the ratio of *new* cases, such as the number of new arrestees in the white male population in the age bracket eighteen to twenty-five during 1990, to a larger reference group, such as the total number of white males in the population in that year. (The number is expressed as a percentage.) **Prevalence** measures the number of persons who are in a specific population *at a specific time;* thus, a policy analyst might want to know the ratio of the number of persons currently under prosecution for drunk driving to the total number of drivers on a specific day of a particular year. Each measure provides a somewhat different estimate of the seriousness of a particular problem. These kinds of data are often available from city, county, state, or federal government agencies or from research literature from the social and health sciences.

When data are not available from government agencies or research literature, policy practitioners develop other measures of the distribution of specific social problems. Jonathan Bradshaw contrasts felt-need, expressed-need, expert-need, and comparative-need measures.[20] **Felt need** measures the importance of social problems by examining the extent persons *believe* they experience certain kinds of problems. An agency might interview a sample of working mothers with preschool children, for example, to assess the extent they believe they cannot afford existing day-care centers or whether they have so-called latchkey children. Of course, persons sometimes exaggerate their actual needs—or, in the case of stigmatized conditions such as substance abuse, underreport them.

Expressed need measures the importance of social problems by examining the extent persons *actually seek* specific kinds of services. A policy practitioner might examine the length of waiting lists at drug-treatment centers, for example, or the number of calls that a hot line receives about substance abuse. Although service-related behaviors of clients are useful, they may not accurately reflect actual needs of consumers. Some persons do not seek or inquire about existing services, for example, because they believe they cannot afford them, do not like existing agencies, are not aware of existing services, fear they will receive punitive or ineffective services, or fear that they may be prosecuted. (Persons who are addicted to illegal substances such as cocaine may fear that drug-treatment staff will reveal their names to the police.)

Policy practitioners sometimes use the **expert-need** approach by consulting experts, such as social scientists, social work practitioners, local executives, or government officials, to obtain their estimates of the importance of specific problems. Experts can provide convincing evidence about specific problems, such as the extent of alcoholism among women, which is drawn from current research. Of course, the biases or values of experts can importantly influence their positions and their credibility; someone who believes, for example, that alcoholism only occurs if persons imbibe many drinks each day will provide a lower estimate of the seriousness of alcoholism than will someone who uses a less rigorous standard.

In a **comparative-need** approach, the existence of unmet needs is also inferred indirectly by comparing the distribution of services in different communities. Assume, for example, that certain neighborhoods possess relatively many drug-treatment programs, while others, with similar demographic characteristics, have relatively few. We can infer with considerable confidence that there is more unmet need for drug-treatment services in the neighborhoods with fewer treatment programs.

Our case that a specific social problem needs remedial action is strengthened, of course, when we use several or all of these approaches to gauge the importance of specific social problems or needs. If we were trying to obtain support for drug-treatment programs in a specific neighborhood, for example, we might obtain information about the numbers of persons on the waiting lists of existing centers (expressed need), obtain data from high school students about the perceived seriousness of substance abuse among adolescents (felt need), provide data that demonstrated that a neighborhood was underserved when contrasted with similar neighborhoods (comparative need), and obtain information from selected experts (expert need).

Data about social problems are more dramatic when they include trend data suggesting that a specific problem is becoming more serious, data that can include felt-need, expressed-need, comparative-need, or expert-need sources.[21] Someone may be able to show that substance-abuse problems have dramatically increased in a specific jurisdiction during the past several decades by noting rising levels of deaths from overdoses and longer waiting lists for drug-treatment programs.

LOCATING WHERE PROBLEMS EXIST WITHIN SOCIETY: FINDING THE "NEEDLE IN A HAYSTACK"

It does us little good to determine that a problem is relatively widespread if we cannot locate and reach its victims or, in the case of preventive programs, its potential victims. To find the current victims of a problem, various social science tools can be used. Census data, which are collected in a major national survey every ten years, do not collect data about problems such as substance abuse or mental illness—nor do they yield information about specific persons because the data report information in aggregate terms for specific geographic regions.[22] Its data are nonetheless important to social service personnel because social scientists have discovered associations between specific demographic or economic factors and specific social problems. Poor persons are more likely than affluent persons, for example, to experience specific medical problems, to be unemployed, to have poor housing, and to be subjected to pressure from drug dealers to use substances such as heroin. Persons with specific racial characteristics are more likely than other persons to possess specific conditions such as sickle-cell anemia and Tay–Sachs disease. By using economic, housing, demographic, and ethnic data, policy analysts can *infer* high rates of certain kinds of social problems in specific neighborhoods and in specific subareas within them.

Nor do policy analysts need to confine themselves to census material. Local public health offices, various state agencies, municipal and county authorities, and some federal agencies such as the National Institute of Mental Health collect or compile various kinds of population-based data.[23]

Census and other public data can also be used to shape marketing, outreach, and advertising strategies. An agency could decide to concentrate an outreach or advertising strategy toward certain sections of neighborhoods, for example, because of a high concentration in them of specific kinds of persons such as working women (day care), adolescents (substance abuse), or elderly persons (home health-care services).[24]

DISTINGUISHING IMPORTANT FROM TRIVIAL PROBLEMS

Because finite resources exist for human services, policy analysts often have to decide which of them should receive priority. Data about the prevalence of a problem are useful, but they can be misleading because some widespread problems are relatively trivial in nature. While an oral surgeon estimates that

25 percent of the population have cosmetic defects of their teeth or jaws, a critic might respond that these cosmetic problems are not as important as social problems such as poverty. In similar fashion, some experts have argued that marijuana use, while widespread, represents a relatively trivial problem when compared to heroin or cocaine use.[25]

How do we determine which specific problem deserves priority? Analysts often try to examine the impact of problems on their victims, their families and friends, and society. Considerable research suggests, for example, that alcoholism is a serious social problem because it often has disastrous consequences for its victims by causing a range of health problems, absenteeism, and loss of employment. These direct effects are supplemented by a tragic toll on families, including abusive behaviors and divorce. By providing a role model of excessive drinking to their children, alcoholic parents increase the likelihood that their children will become alcoholics when they become adults. Numerous researchers have probed the economic effects of alcoholism on society, including the taxes that are lost when alcoholics are unable to work, the economic effects of decreased productivity on corporations, the considerable medical costs that are borne by society to help alcoholics, and the economic and human costs of deaths and injuries that are caused by drunk drivers.[26]

The documentation of the costs to victims, families, and society of a specific social problem is often accompanied by evidence that specific programs can reduce these costs. In some studies of the effectiveness of programs that treat alcoholism, for example, policy analysts contend that specific investments of resources in preventive or ameliorative programs will save society some of the current costs of alcoholism by decreasing destructive behaviors such as absenteeism and drunk driving, by decreasing alcohol-related illnesses such as hepatitis, by decreasing wife battering and child abuse, and by increasing the tax revenues that society receives as absenteeism and disability rates decrease.[27] In programs with a high benefit–cost ratio, every dollar of expenditure in a social program, such as alcohol-treatment centers, leads to the reduction of many dollars of the current costs to society of specific social problems and to the increased tax revenues, which would otherwise be reduced by the social problems, that accrue from employed persons.

ANALYZING THE CAUSES OF SOCIAL PROBLEMS

Many interventions in the human services are developed in a trial-and-error manner. Medical advances have occurred, for example, when physicians have accidentally found that certain medications or certain diets solve or redress specific illnesses, even though they do not understand why they are effective. Some policy proposals do not purport to address the basic causes of social problems, but, instead, to diminish deleterious effects of them, such as the suffering or harm that is experienced by some of their victims.[28]

Alternatively, we can try to develop theories about the causes of problems to help us develop interventions that address specific causes of a problem—a difficult task because many social problems, such as substance abuse, are caused by myriad psychological, familial, physiological, peer, economic, and community factors. To provide a method of simplifying complex realities, theorists often use theories and research drawn from the social sciences, economics, and biology.

Paradigms

Policy analysts often bring to their work conceptual lenses that powerfully shape or guide their work. Indeed, most theorists emphasize certain kinds of causal factors when they analyze problems. In **public health** or **ecological perspectives,** social problems are perceived to be caused by environmental factors such as occupational, economic, familial, peer, neighborhood, or advertising ones.[29] Many environmental factors have been implicated as causes of alcoholism. Members of certain occupations, such as reporters who are subject to deadline and competitive pressures, have high rates of alcoholism. The targeting of youth by the liquor industry has increased alcohol use by adolescents and college students. Peer pressure contributes to alcoholism among businesspeople, who often drink heavily during their many social and business interactions with peers and with clients. Persons who use a public health perspective often emphasize community, occupational, and societal interventions to arrest alcoholism, such as placing limits on the advertising of the liquor industry, reducing the stress in certain occupations, and developing preventive services for persons who are subject to high-level stress.

Persons with **radical perspectives** implicate economic and social inequalities, as well as the thwarted economic opportunities of certain populations, as causes of specific social problems.[30] Some radicals argue, for example, that the alienation and desperation of low-income persons contribute to relatively high rates of certain kinds of substance abuse in inner-city neighborhoods. The economic desperation of many persons in low-income communities stimulates some of them to become drug dealers within their communities. Radicals are likely to indict persons and interests who have an economic stake in perpetuating social problems like alcoholism, such as the mass media, liquor interests, and international drug dealers. Because they implicate economic and political factors, radicals are often skeptical about the effectiveness of counseling remedies.

Analysts who use **medical** or **disease models** explore physiological factors that are associated with substance abuse.[31] Considerable research suggests that genetic factors assume a major role in alcoholism, as well as cocaine, heroin, and other drug use. Research suggests that various physiological factors sustain an addiction, so that some persons find it nearly impossible to arrest addictions. These kinds of analysts often seek physiological remedies such as medicines that can counter the addictive effects of a drug, substitute drugs such as methadone (in the case of heroin), detoxification, and early warning systems for children who possess a genetic predisposition.

Persons who emphasize **intrapsychic factors** explore personal and familial causes of substance abuse. Perhaps, some contend, alcoholics drink to escape personal and familial dilemmas, to rebel against controlling parents, or (in the case of males) to escape dependence on their mothers. Analysts who emphasize intrapsychic factors often seek various kinds of counseling remedies.[32]

In a departure from traditional counseling, some persons adhere to **behavioral frameworks.** Some social problems can be redressed in this perspective by providing some mixture of rewards and disincentives to the victims of specific social problems such as smoking. Peer pressures serve both to reward persons when they withdraw from addictive behaviors and to punish persons who continue addictive behaviors.[33]

Some persons, such as those who believe that certain social behaviors are criminal, emphasize **deterrent strategies.** Many persons want to criminalize the use or sale of many addictive substances, including marijuana, cocaine, and heroin, just as temperance crusaders sought to criminalize the use and sale of alcohol in prior eras. Some analysts believe that social problems can be redressed by raising the financial costs to those consumers who use them; why not, they ask, dramatically raise the cost of cigarettes and alcoholic beverages or make the users of addictive substances pay higher premiums for their health insurance?[34]

A vigorous debate often occurs among theorists, analysts, and researchers who adhere to various of the preceding paradigms. Opponents of criminalizing drugs contend, for example, that it invites some persons, such as rebellious adolescents, to become addicts. Persons who implicate economic and environmental factors often contend that counseling represents an ineffective strategy. Research evidence is often selectively cited by contending groups to support their specific remedies and to attack proposals of persons who use different paradigms.

These various frameworks and causal factors are not mutually exclusive; indeed, some experts argue convincingly that complementary strategies are often needed.[35] Some persons respond favorably to one approach, such as a specific kind of counseling, whereas others respond to behavior modification or to membership in support groups like Alcoholics Anonymous. Deterrent measures, such as increasing the cost of alcohol or cigarettes, appear to deter usage by some persons, but they may be even more effective when supplemented by counseling programs and by reductions in the advertising of the manufacturers of alcohol and cigarettes in the mass media.

Social Science Research

Policy analysts who use research to examine the causes of specific problems encounter formidable obstacles. Unlike laboratory research where environmental, dietary, and physiological factors can be controlled and where animals can be followed for extended periods, policy analysts cannot usually create controlled environments to probe the causes of specific social problems. They must usually examine factors that are associated with specific problems *after* those problems have arisen; thus, they can explore genetic, demographic, economic, advertising, and community factors that appear to be associated with drug use and alcoholism. Alcoholics are more likely than nonalcoholics, for example, to come from families with one or more alcoholic parents—a finding that implicates genetic factors or that suggests that exposure to role models can shape behavior.[36]

Some research seeks not to contrast victims with nonvictims but to explore the lives and environments of victims to develop theories about how and why they developed specific problems. One researcher initiated a study of 2000 "drinking groups" in the bars of a major city, for example, to examine the effects of cultural, peer, and personal factors that contribute to alcoholism.[37] Considerable research examines case records of victims, as well as their self-reports, to develop theories about the emergence of specific problems in specific kinds of persons.

If some social science research probes the causes of social problems by examining their development and causation, other research expands our understanding of social problems by analyzing the effectiveness of existing programs. A positive evaluation of a social program can provide clues about the causes of social problems. Take the case, for example, of an evaluation of a program that provided prisoners with a financial subsidy when they were released from prison. Researchers wanted to know if this subsidy would reduce the rate of recidivism of those ex-offenders who received the subsidy; so they compared their rates of recidivism with other prisoners who did not receive financial subsidy when they were released. When the evaluation showed that fewer of the subsidized ex-offenders committed new offenses, the researchers concluded that financial hardship was an important cause of crime.[38]

Biological Science

Biologists and medical researchers have begun to expand our knowledge of some social problems by comparing the genes of victims of some social problems with the genes of other persons—or by examining the rates of specific social problems like alcoholism in twins who have been placed with different adoptive families at birth. Because those twins who are children of alcoholic parents are far more likely to be alcoholics than are other children even when they are placed in adoptive families where no substance abuse exists, the researchers surmise that genetic predisposition is an important causal factor. These kinds of studies have implicated genetic factors in a growing number of social problems such as schizophrenia, depression, and alcoholism.[39] Moreover, some researchers believe that genetic factors may predispose some persons to multiple addictions; many alcoholics, for example, also have been or are simultaneously addicted to substances such as cocaine.[40]

Economics

Economic perspectives and research have enriched our understanding of the causes of specific problems, patterns of utilization of existing services, and the comparative merits of alternative policies.[41] Economic research provides useful information about the response of employers to addictive behaviors of employees, the impact of advertising of alcohol on consumer behavior, the effects of fees in deterring or promoting the use of drug-treatment programs, and the cost–benefit ratios of alternative policies that seek to redress alcoholism.

Much research in economics focuses on the effects of economic motivations on the actions and behaviors of persons. Economists can explore, for example, why some persons become drug pushers by examining the financial rewards that are associated with it. Or they ask, What economic factors, such as fear of loss of employment or the costs of treatment-related fees, shape the decisions of some persons to seek, or not to seek, help for their problems?

In turn, economists also examine how the financial motivations of institutions and corporations shape their actions and, at least in some cases, contribute to the development of some social problems. Take the example of cigarette companies where financial motivations of the tobacco growers in various states, coupled with the profit motives of large corporations, contribute to the problems in eradicating the tobacco industry. Indeed, political pressures from growers and corporations make it difficult to eliminate the massive subsidies of the federal government to tobacco growers.

In the case of advertising, economists explore the effects of external stimuli on the behaviors of specific kinds of consumers. An economist might ask, for example, Does advertising of wine coolers that is targeted to teenagers actually affect their purchases of this product?

If economists often examine the effects of financial considerations on the actions of persons and institutions, they also examine larger questions such as the way the policies of governments influence economic activity in the private sector. Economists variously explore the way taxes on products, such as cigarettes, would influence the purchases of cigarettes by consumers and the extent such taxes would be borne disproportionately by specific groups in the population, such as blue-collar families where rates of smoking are relatively high.

Economists also examine the effects of specific government policies on the general employment and economic growth of the nation. Because unemployment and poverty are social problems in their own right, as well as problems that cause or exacerbate other problems, this kind of research is important to persons in social welfare policy. Of course, as debates between schools of economic theory suggest, considerable controversy exists about the effects of specific economic policies on the general economy: *supply-side economists* emphasize the need to develop tax policies that provide large-scale investors, such as corporations and affluent persons, with relatively abundant capital; *monetarists* emphasize the need to maintain a delicate balance of the money supply to avoid the twin perils of inflation and recession; and *Keynesian* or *demand-side economists* emphasize the need to provide consumers with adequate purchasing power to keep consumer demand at adequate levels to stimulate the production of goods and services. Many hybrid models of economic theories exist.[42]

Even this cursory discussion suggests that macro or societal economics is concerned with examining relationships between the supply of money, the purchasing power of consumers, and the investment of capital—and the effects of these factors, singly and in tandem, in producing specific economic effects such as unemployment, inflation, and economic growth. Disagreements among economists stem from the sheer complexity of these relationships, as well as the fact that many additional factors, such as the economic policies of other nations, intrude. To return to our example of substance abuse, for example, the internal policies of the nation to control drug trafficking are often confounded by the policies of Latin American, Asian, and Middle Eastern nations, as any examination of drug trafficking suggests.

VARIATIONS IN PROBLEMS AND THEIR CAUSES

Specific social problems vary in both their causes and their manifestations in different sections of the population. Alcoholism appears, for example, to have different causes and to take different forms among male and female victims.[43] Unlike men, whose alcoholism often stems from occupational stress and peer pressure, alcoholism of many women begins during points of family crisis such as in the wake of divorce or marital discord or after the death of a child. Unlike the drinking of men, which tends to occur in bars or with friends, many women sustain relatively secretive styles of drinking. These differences in both the causes and manifestations of alcoholism suggest that different kinds of treatment, as well as different kinds of preventive services, may be needed by men and women. Moreover, members of different groups often respond in different fashion to services. Spanish-speaking families, for example, often defer to male heads-of-household before seeking assistance for specific problems, unlike many Caucasian families where women often take the initiative in seeking services for specific problems.[44]

Variations in the causes and manifestations of problems pose major challenges for policy analysts because they suggest that generalizations about the causes and nature of specific social problems are hazardous, as well as the kinds of services that are likely to be effective. We have already noted that many experts contend, for example, that a veritable smorgasbord of services for alcoholics may be needed to address the different needs of specific persons and specific populations.

LINKING ANALYTIC SKILLS TO OTHER POLICY SKILLS

When we return to Policy-Practice Case 2 at the start of this chapter, it is clear that analytic skills often have to be supplemented by political, interactional, and value-clarification skills if policy practitioners wish to be effective in securing support for new policies and programs to address unmet needs. Analytic skills are important because they allow us to marshal technical evidence to show that a specific social problem is important; thus, the social worker in Policy-Practice Case 2 contemplates the use of a survey to ascertain what kinds of problems families with latency and teenage children might wish the LEAPS program to address.

As the case suggests, however, the social worker encountered some political obstacles. She notes, for example, that her proposed LEAPS program might be viewed with some animosity by the current staff, as well as the originator of the PIPS program (the Preschool and Infant Parenting Service), which *already* had a telephone warm line. Its staff might fear that LEAPS would compete with it for scarce funds or that the new program might diminish some of their prestige. (She contemplates securing support from Dr. Jones, an influential physician whose wife had initiated PIPS.)

She also realizes that she needs interactional skills. If a task force is established to develop the proposal, the social worker can assist it in its deliberations by using a variety of group skills. Moreover, she will need to engage in numerous personal discussions with persons such as Dr. Jones to persuade them that a new program is needed.

Value-clarification skills are needed to decide (among other things) whether the new program will address sufficiently important social needs that it merits the expenditure of scarce agency funds. Might other social needs be more important? Are preventive programs, which address the needs of consumers before problems become serious, as necessary as curative programs, which address the needs of teenagers, for example, who already possess serious problems of substance abuse? She will need value-clarification skills as she decides what kinds of political tactics to employ; is it ethical, for example, to use deception to outflank possible opponents to the LEAPS program?

Even this brief discussion of Policy-Practice Case 2 suggests that analytic skills, which we have discussed in this chapter, need to be coupled with the other kinds of policy skills that we discuss in succeeding chapters.

SUMMARY

Concepts in this chapter, such as the causes of social problems, prevalence, systems of classifying social problems, and variations in social problems, figure prominently in the work of policy analysts, who hope to develop disciplined and scientific approaches to social problems. Skillful policy practitioners use these concepts both to develop policy proposals and to secure support for them from legislators, executives, and other decision makers. They also draw on supportive research and theories from the social sciences, biology, and economics.

We ought not minimize, of course, the controversy that often exists with respect to attempts to define, measure, or conceptualize specific social problems. Ideology often influences what kinds of data and perspectives specific policy practitioners favor or question. Competing camps of experts often take divergent positions in disputes about the causes and nature of specific problems. Moreover, as any perusal of legislative hearings suggests, many decision makers devote little time to examining relevant research or concepts but rather proceed directly with the devising of policy remedies.

Even with these provisos, however, thoughtful policy practitioners use analytic techniques to inform their proposals and to buttress their arguments. Nor should the political uses of policy analysis be ignored; as policy practitioners appear informed of current streams of research, they enhance their credibility among those decision makers who value expertise.

QUESTIONS FOR DISCUSSION

1. It is sometimes argued that "the way in which persons define a problem influences how they proceed to solve or address it." Discuss this statement as it applies to alcoholism or substance abuse.

2. Using a social agency with which you are familiar, discuss the influence conceptual frameworks have on how staff perceive and address specific social problems. Discuss conceptual frameworks that are absent in this setting, and speculate why they are absent.

3. Take any major social problem and try to develop a definition of it. Try using both relative and absolute approaches. How is your definition influenced by your values or your cultural predispositions?

4. Take any major social problem and try to develop a speculative typology that identifies a variety of persons who possess it. What problems do you encounter as you undertake this task?

5. Discuss the statement, "social workers place insufficient emphasis on public health or radical paradigms when analyzing specific social problems."

6. Discuss the strengths and weaknesses of several alternative ways of measuring the prevalence of a specific social problem in a specific community. Is it possible to use several kinds of information in tandem?

7. Discuss how a specific social problem takes different forms (or manifestations) and has different causes in specific subsections of the population. Discuss some implications of these variations for the human services delivery system.

SUGGESTED READINGS

Developing Typologies

David Ellwood, *Poor Support: Poverty in the American Family* (New York: Basic Books, 1988).

Policy Agendas

John Kingdon, *Agendas, Alternatives, and Public Policies* (Boston: Little, Brown, 1984).

Louis Keonig, *An Introduction to Public Policy* (Englewood Cliffs, N.J.: Prentice-Hall, 1986), chapter 4.

Julie Kosterlitz, "Not Just Kid Stuff," *National Journal*, 20 (November 19, 1988): 2934–2939.

Controversies in Defining and Conceptualizing Social Problems

Herbert Fingarette, "Alcoholism: The Mythical Disease," *Public Interest*, 91 (Spring 1988): 3–22.

John Kaplan, "Taking Drugs Seriously," *Public Interest*, 92 (Summer 1988): 32–50.

Ethan Nadelman, "The Case for Legalization," *Public Interest*, 92 (Summer 1988): 3–31.

William Wilson, "Cycles of Deprivation and the Underclass Debate," *Social Service Review*, 59 (December 1985): 541–559.

Steven Wineman, *The Politics of Human Services: A Radical Alternative to the Welfare State* (Boston: South End Press, 1984).

How Culture and Values Influence Definitions of Social Problems

Arnold Green, *Social Problems: Arena of Conflict* (New York: McGraw-Hill, 1975).

Barbara Solomon, *Black Empowerment* (New York: Columbia University Press, 1976), pp. 299–313.

Technical Approaches to Analyzing and Measuring Social Problems

Jonathan Bradshaw, "The Concept of Social Need," in Neil Gilbert and Harry Specht, eds., *Planning for Social Welfare* (Englewood Cliffs, N.J.: Prentice-Hall, 1977), pp. 290–297.

U.S., National Institute of Mental Health, *A Working Manual of Simple Evaluation Techniques for Community Mental Health Centers* (Washington, D.C.: Government Printing Office, 1976), pp. 99–146.

NOTES

1. See Alfred Kahn, *Theory and Practice of Social Planning* (New York: Russell Sage, 1969); Robert Mayer and Ernest Greenwood, *The Design of Social Policy Research* (Englewood Cliffs, N.J.: Prentice-Hall, 1980); Yeheskel Dror, *Venture in Policy Sciences* (New York: Elsevier North Holland, 1971); and Edward Quade, *Analysis for Public Decisions*, 2nd ed. (New York: Elsevier North Holland, 1982).

2. *Webster's New World Dictionary* (New York: Simon and Schuster, 1982), p. 16.

3. Mayer and Greenwood, *The Design of Social Policy Research*, pp. 67–76.

4. Arnold Green, *Social Problems: Arena of Conflict* (New York: McGraw Hill, 1975), pp. 67–115.

5. Victor Fuchs, "Redefining Poverty," *Public Interest*, 8 (Summer 1967): 88–96.

6. For example, problems in measuring rates of mental illness among children are discussed by Jeanne Giovannoni, "Children," *Encyclopedia of Social Work*, 18th ed., vol. 1 (Silver Springs, Md: National Association of Social Workers, 1987), p. 251.

7. See Jon Conte, "Child Sexual Abuse," *Encyclopedia of Social Work*, vol. 1, pp. 255–256.

8. Green, *Social Problems*, pp. 67–115.

9. Martin Anderson, *Welfare* (Stanford, Ca.: Hoover Institution Press, 1978), pp. 160–161.

10. Frank Thompson, *Health Policy and the Bureaucracy: Politics and Implementation* (Cambridge, Mass.: MIT Press, 1981), pp. 134–147, 176–178.

11. Liberal defenders of social programs often cite their low rates of fraud. See Winifred Bell, *Contemporary Social Welfare* (New York: Macmillan, 1983), p. 24, and Sar Levitan, *Programs in Aid of the Poor*, 5th ed. (Baltimore: Johns Hopkins Press, 1985), p. 79.

12. See J.K. Wing, *Reasoning About Mental Illness* (London: Oxford University Press, 1978), chapter 2.

13. Ibid., chapter 2.

14. Robert Spitzer, Janet Williams, and Andrew Skodol, "DSM-III: The Major Achievements and an Overview," *American Journal of Psychiatry*, 137 (February 1980): 151–154.

15. See testimony of David Ellwood in U.S., Senate, *Hearings*, Subcommittee on Social Security and Family Policy of Committee on Finance (March 2, 1987), pp. 105–111.

16. See Thomas Szasz, *Insanity: The Idea and its Consequences* (New York: John Wiley, 1987).

17. Victor Adebimpe, "Overview: White Norms and Psychiatric Diagnoses of Black Patients," *American Journal of Psychiatry*, 138 (March 1981): 279–285.

18. See David Mechanic, *Mental Health and Social Policy*, 3rd ed. (Englewood Cliffs, N.J.: Prentice-Hall, 1989), pp. 16–44.

19. Martin Bloom, *Primary Prevention: The Possible Science* (Englewood Cliffs, N.J.: Prentice-Hall, 1981), pp. 173–174.

20. Jonathan Bradshaw, "The Concept of Social Need," *New Society*, 30 (March 1972): 640–643.

21. John Kingdon, *Agendas, Alternatives, and Public Policies* (Boston: Little, Brown, 1984), pp. 95–99.

22. See U.S., National Institute of Mental Health, *A Working Manual of Simple Program Evaluation Techniques* (Washington, D.C.: Government Printing Office, 1976), pp. 99–146.

23. Ibid., pp. 99–146.

24. Phillip Kotler, *Principles of Marketing*, 4th ed. (Englewood Cliffs, N.J.: Prentice-Hall, 1989), pp. 42–46.

25. Steven Mirin, et al., "Casual versus Heavy Use of Marijuana, A Redefinition of the Marijuana Problem," *American Journal of Psychiatry*, 127 (March 1971): 1134–1140.

26. U.S., Department of Health and Human Services, Public Health Service, *Alcohol and Health: Report to U.S. Congress on Alcohol and Health* (Washington, D.C.: Government Printing Office, 1987), pp. 1–27.

27. Shelley Wood, "Alcoholism," *California Journal*, 5 (June 1974): 199–201.

28. Herbert Simons, *Persuasion: Understanding, Practice, and Analysis*. 2nd ed. (New York: Random House, 1986), pp. 165–167.

29. U.S., *Alcohol and Health*, pp. 97–119.

30. Steven Wineman, *The Politics of Human Services: A Radical Alternative to the Welfare State* (Boston: South End Press, 1984).

31. For a critique of the medical model in substance abuse, see Dorothy Nelkin, *Methadone Maintenance: A Technological Fix* (New York: George Braziller, 1973).

32. Judith Lewis, *Substance Abuse Counseling* (Pacific Grove, Ca.: Brooks/Cole, 1988).

33. Norman Krasnegor, ed., *Behavioral Analysis and Treatment of Substance Abuse* (Washington, D.C.: Government Printing Office, 1979).

34. Esa Osterberg, "Alcohol and Economics," in E. Mansell Pattison and Edward Kaufman, eds., *Encyclopedic Handbook of Alcoholism* (New York: Gardner Press, 1982), pp. 418–420.

35. William Miller and Hester Reid, "Matching Problem Drinkers with Optimal Treatments," in William Miller and Nick Heather, eds., *Treating Addictive Behaviors: Processes of Change* (New York: Plenum Press, 1986), pp. 175–204.

36. Robin Murray and James Stabenau, "Genetic Factors in Alcoholism Predisposition," in Pattison and Kaufman, eds., *Encyclopedic Handbook of Alcoholism*, pp. 3–30.

37. Thomas Maugh, "The Slower the Music, the Faster the Drinking," *Los Angeles Times* (November 28, 1988), pp. 1 and 3.

38. Richard Berk, et al., "Social Policy Experimentation: A Position Paper," *Evaluation Review*, 9 (August 1965): 387–431.

39. See, for example, Murray and Stabenau, "Genetic Factors in Alcoholism Predisposition."

40. Mirin, "Casual versus Heavy Use of Marijuana," p. 1137.

41. For an overview of research in economics, see Joseph Stiglitz, *Economics of the Public Sector*, 2nd ed. (New York: W. W. Norton, 1988).

42. John Kenneth Galbraith, *Economics in Perspective: A Critical History* (Boston: Houghton Mifflin, 1987).

43. Vasanti Burtle, ed., *Women Who Drink: Experience and Psychotherapy* (Springfield, Ill.: Charles C Thomas, 1979).

44. Vicente Abad, "Mental Health Delivery Systems for Hispanics in the United States: Issues and Dilemmas," in Moises Gaviria and Jose Arana, eds., *Health and Behavior: Research Agenda for Hispanics* (Chicago: Simon Bolivar Hispanic American Psychiatric Research and Training Program, 1987).

CHAPTER 3

■

Policy Analysis:
Recurring Policy Options in the
Human Services

We discussed in Chapter Two some methods of defining, measuring, and conceptualizing social problems. Our focus shifts in this and the next chapter to analytic techniques that are used to develop policy proposals to address these kinds of policy problems. We examine in this chapter a wide range of policies that shape the structure, content, and nature of the human services. We do not pretend to cover all policies but merely a variety of important ones that frequently recur in the human services delivery system.

To illustrate our discussion, we examine some analytic challenges that would confront a policy practitioner who wished to develop a proposal to provide federal funding of shelters for battered women. Indeed, after discussing many policy options during the chapter, we emerge with the outline of a proposed piece of legislation.

A POLICY-PRACTICE CASE FROM THE HUMAN SERVICES

When social workers develop new programs within the human services system, or restructure existing ones, they have to identify a range of policy options and make difficult choices between them. In Policy-Practice Case 3, for example, a social worker seeks to develop an innovative Community Emergency Service Program (CES) for families that need immediate assistance.

The social worker had to develop the broad outlines or structure of the program by defining the nature of its intake policies, the content of its services, and its relationships with other agencies. By discussing options with many persons, as well as reviewing a model program that had been developed in Nashville, Tennessee, she selected six components that are discussed in Policy-Practice Case 3. To select these six components, however, she had to use analytic skills because the six components were developed only after reviewing a range of policy options, comparing and contrasting their relative merits, and (finally) selecting specific options to provide the structure of the completed proposal.

At a more modest level, social workers often scrutinize specific policies within the human services system such as the nature of the intake system, specific protocols or procedures for certain kinds of clients, the nature and extent of outreach services, and the mix of preventive and curative services. In each case, they often identify and compare a range of policy options before proposing specific changes in existing policy. We examine a range of policy options that often recur in the human services delivery system in this chapter.

RECURRING ISSUES WHEN DESIGNING POLICY INNOVATIONS

When devising policies in social welfare, practitioners have to address or resolve a number of issues (see Table 3.1). To resolve each of these issues, policy practitioners have to make informed choices between policy alternatives—choices that can sometimes be difficult, particularly when a variety of criteria, such as efficiency, effectiveness, equity, and feasibility, are considered.

To illustrate our discussion, let's place ourselves in the vantage point of a hypothetical policy practitioner in the nation's capitol who wants to develop a federally funded program for the victims of spousal abuse.[1] She works for a shelter in Baltimore but is connected with a coalition of service providers, feminists, victims of spousal abuse, and professionals who want the federal government to take a more active role in addressing this problem. (Their group is called the Stop Wife-Battering Coalition.) The policy practitioner knows that a variety of local programs have been initiated for this population,

TABLE 3.1   Recurring Issues When Designing Policy Proposals

1. Establishing a mission or set of objectives

2. Designing the structure of service or program delivery

3. Planning the infusion and circulation of resources

4. Devising the content and form of services or benefits

5. Rationing scarce resources

6. Addressing community and regional factors

7. Orchestrating policy oversight

POLICY-PRACTICE CASE 3

A SOCIAL WORKER DEVELOPS POLICIES FOR
A NEW PROGRAM

I was one of several coordinators assigned to develop an innovative program to provide community emergency services (CES) to families in a large metropolitan area. (The word *we* is used subsequently to describe the coordinators.)

This model for a service system is taken from the program developed in Nashville, Tennessee. Nashville had one large children's institution that housed the majority of the children coming into placement. Public welfare staff members became aware of a lack of any real preventive system or alternatives to placement and developed a program model that incorporated six components (described later in this case) that could help a family in crisis.

In 1977 an unincorporated area was chosen by Region 2 HEW (now the Department of Health and Human Services) as a possible site for the implementation of CES. It was felt that this community had a problem, recognized by many people in the community, in delivering services to certain kinds of families. An initial exploration suggested that the community would be receptive to the program; thus, it was decided by an administrator in the public welfare agency that we should be assigned to the CES program to work with the community on devising policies.

Our initial focus as staff coordinators hired by the public welfare agency was to do a needs assessment in the community, identifying the problem areas, diagnosing causes, and formulating solutions. The next step was to develop a constituency and devise strategies to effect necessary action. The regional administrator of the public welfare agency was helpful in providing two resources at this point. First, we were given a list of various agencies and personnel in the community involved in providing services to families. Key persons were identified who could give information on the community's problems and on existing programs. We used this list and expanded it by contacting people informally to sound out problems experienced by the community. Second, we were given access to records of emergency family situations dealt with by the public welfare agency during the past two years. These records covered both day and evening situations and revealed that major defects existed in the community that could be addressed by the CES program.

During the day, emergencies of families were handled by the public welfare office and various other community agencies in the area. But the various services sometimes overlapped and were not very well coordinated. The most severe problems, however, arose during the evening when no viable services for families existed. Children from families in crisis were picked up by the sheriff and placed in foster homes in surrounding communities or at Duncan Hall (a county detention facility) because no emergency foster homes were available in the community.

These children, many of whom spoke only Spanish, were traumatized by the experience of placement outside their homes in a strange community where no one understood or could even communicate with them. Often children of a parent hospitalized on an emergency basis went to Duncan Hall because no foster homes were available in the community at night for such families. Adolescents who were having family problems came into the court system because they were found on the streets at night. Some children came into placement because adequate housing was not available for the entire family. Finally, records revealed that service programs among various agencies in the community were not coordinated. In some instances, we found that various agencies were providing the same services to some families and none to others or were competing with one another for clients. And some families fell through the cracks of intake criteria in agencies and were denied services in a crisis.

In the CES program, six components were developed:

1. Twenty-four-hour emergency intake
2. Emergency homemaker caretaker
3. Emergency foster-family homes
4. Emergency shelter for adolescents
5. Emergency shelter for families
6. Outreach and follow-up

Our next step was to develop a constituency and devise strategies to effect action. This task was accomplished in several ways. First, we went into the community to meet with various persons and agencies about the problem they had identified and about what could be done from the community perspective. Next, we attended meetings of established groups in the community to learn more about community leaders and agencies, including the Interagency Coordinating Council, a group of ninety agencies that meet on a monthly basis and share resources and new program information. We went to these meetings to begin to establish linkages with already existing agencies.

However, we began to face political problems. People in the community had strong feelings about the public welfare agency, some of which were negative. They asked whether the coordinators were really going to implement the services. In one instance, an agency executive in a small, private, community-based agency accused our agency of always talking but never producing results. We restated our commitment to the program and asked for community participation in the planning committees in order to make it both a public welfare and community system. Community people responded to our enthusiasm.

After a month and a half of reconnaissance work in the community, a large general meeting was held at a neighborhood center to bring together various community and agency personnel. The general meeting accomplished its goals of imparting information, getting support, gaining legitimacy for the program, and establishing community linkages.

Six planning committees were formed focusing on the six components. People were given sign-up sheets at the general meeting and signed up for

Continued

POLICY-PRACTICE CASE 3
(continued)

whichever component was most closely related to their interests or agency services. Meetings were held on a weekly basis, and we acted as facilitators. In December, two months later, another general meeting was held to inform people of the accomplishments of the various committees with the hope of setting a time for implementation of the program.

After the first CES general meeting, a meeting was set up with administration of the public welfare agency to discuss what resources they would offer. It soon became obvious that, for a number of reasons, the key division chief did not fully support or understand the new CES project, which he described as an extension of an already existing twenty-four-hour hot line program in the public welfare agency. We were not part of the ongoing administrative staff and therefore lacked credibility with this executive and had not developed linkages within the department. Further, the executive had the approval of his superior to explore the program, not to approve it. (We were asking him to approve the plan to implement CES.) We realized we had made a tactical error and resolved to develop intradepartmental support for the CES program.

We spoke at meetings within the agency, informed line-staff supervisors and middle-management staff about CES, and asked for suggestions. We informally contacted staff in various offices of the public welfare agency to discuss the program and get support. These strategies were so successful that, when we requested a budget for CES, we were told that approval was likely by early January and that CES would begin on a trial basis by March. Resources offered by other community agencies helped keep projected costs relatively low.

It was the planning committee, however, that really influenced the public agency to sponsor the program. The twenty-four-hour intake committee found a twenty-four-hour phone line that CES could use. They set up intake guidelines for families coming into the program, and they established written agreements with agencies in the program regarding what services they would provide and who the contact person for each agency would be after regular working hours. Further, the public welfare agency agreed that six children's services workers would be assigned to make home calls for the CES program at night.

For each of the committees, plans were submitted that recommended various resources. The emergency shelter committee was instrumental in getting support from the county board of supervisors. Further, a powerful supervisor helped facilitate working relationships with other county agencies by putting the CES coordinators in touch with key persons in these agencies, that is, the county medical center, mental health, and the probation department.

By the first week in January, the public welfare agency had assigned eight homemakers to the program, two of whom were available immediately to CES. Emergency foster homes that were bilingual and bicultural were developed in the Hispanic area especially for the CES program. Arrangements were made with already existing adolescent group homes in the community to set aside beds for the CES program. The emergency shelter for families committee, in working with the Chicana center, had found an old church building that they were working to have ready in one month. On the outreach component, various private and public agencies made written commitments to supply services once the program became operational.

In planning the project, responsibility for providing services was divided up among the public welfare agency and the various community agencies. As the project moved closer to implementation, the promise of delivery of services became a basis for attaining legitimacy with community agencies, which maintained or developed closer ties with CES. We built linkages both externally (outside DPSS) and internally (inside DPSS) because we knew that the program could not function in their absence. Service responsibilities among agencies were clearly defined, and community agencies gained prestige through association with the project.

SOURCE: This case is adapted from one developed by Mary Hayes, M.S.W. Names and locations have been altered.

mostly by underfunded nonprofit agencies that have sought assistance from a variety of foundations, private benefactors, and public sources such as the Department of Housing and Urban Development. Despite the determined efforts of their founders, these centers have proved to be woefully inadequate in helping the rising numbers of women who seek relief from spousal abuse. The coalition tentatively titles their proposed program the Federal Shelter Program.

Establishing a Mission or Set of Objectives

While developing this program, the policy practitioner has to develop some objectives or a mission for the Federal Shelter Program. We noted in Chapter One that policies usually contain explicit or implicit objectives that provide an overarching rationale or direction for them. The preambles of legislation often provide this rationale.

When discussing the issue of shelters with the aides of various legislators, she finds no consensus on the mission or objectives concerning the federal role pertaining to spousal abuse. Some legislators are uninterested in the issue, which they believe has been grossly exaggerated in its importance and magnitude; indeed, one aide contends it is a "figment of the imagination of do-gooder social workers, who want to create more jobs for themselves." Other legislators favor a "get-tough" strategy that would provide federal funds and policy requirements to local units of government to find, prosecute, and imprison offenders, but they demur from direct federal assistance to shelters, which they believe should be funded by local jurisdictions. Still other legislators want to provide federal assistance to the national network of shelters that protect and offer shelter to battered women and their children.

While believing that better law enforcement is needed, our policy practitioner, as well as other participants in the Stop Wife-Battering Coalition, decides to emphasize federal assistance to shelters because she believes that abused women need the immediate protection that is afforded by residence in shelters. (They realize that many women lack the resources to find alternative sources of safe shelter.) They want a service component included within the shelter program as well, to help women cope with their predicament and to link them to legal, welfare, job-placement, and other services.

Their mission or objectives then emphasize federal financial assistance to shelters to facilitate their construction, rehabilitation, and maintenance and to provide services to women who reside in them. This mission has important consequences for the kinds of policies that they will develop; had they adopted a different mission, such as one that emphasized an enhanced federal role in aiding in the prosecution of spouse abusers, their subsequent proposal would have taken an entirely different form.

Designing the Structure of Service or Program Delivery

With a general direction established, this policy practitioner and her allies encounter some practice issues: Where should they affix ultimate responsibility for overseeing the new program, and what kinds of agencies should receive funds for the program?

Affixing Ultimate Responsibility   Programs and agencies are typically classified in policy sectors such as mental health, health, child welfare, public welfare, and gerontology. Large bureaucracies and programs have been established that administer programs and policies within these sectors, and the staff and officials who work within them typically identify themselves with them.

The assignment of specific programs to a sector is often a relatively arbitrary choice and sometimes occasions turf battles between rival claimants. In the case of the Head Start Program, for example, the federal Office of Education and the federal Office of Economic Opportunity (OEO) vied for it. In truth, it could have been placed in either of them because it possessed educational components as well as the parent and community participation that was emphasized by OEO.[2]

To return to our example, the policy practitioner has to decide who should receive the ultimate responsibility for the program. Were the Federal Shelter Program assigned to the National Institute of Mental Health, for example, its major focus could become the provision of counseling services (with less emphasis on the provision of shelter services), whereas social services might be deleted were it assigned to the Department of Housing and Urban Development. Of course, the policy practitioner could decide to make it an independent agency that reported directly to the president—possibly linking it to other programs that assist victims of violence, including children.

She needs to decide not only which department of government should receive ultimate jurisdiction but also to develop policies germane to myriad operational details. Should state officials—perhaps a state agency designated by the governor to be the state agency to oversee the operations of this program—choose the specific agencies that would receive the federal funds? Or should that decision be made by federal authorities who would themselves receive applications for funds from specific agencies at the local level?

Who should collect statistics about the shelters that are established so that legislators can be informed about the use of federal funds? Who should attend to program problems such as the possible misuse of funds by some shelters or their failure to comply with local building codes? Who should determine the eligibility policies of shelters within a specific state? Should these policies be contained within the federal legislation, be left to federal officials to define after the legislation had been enacted, or be left to the discretion of state officials?

In the halcyon days of the 1960s, legislators often made federal officials responsible for many funding and operational decisions. Indeed, in many federally funded programs in the War on Poverty, local agencies applied directly to federal authorities for funds, and federal officials inspected and audited local projects. In subsequent decades, authority has increasingly been vested in state, regional, or county officials, who ultimately report some details of local programs, such as program statistics, to federal funders. (In the Reagan administration, even this reporting was minimized because he wanted to divest federal roles in favor of state and local ones.)

As in the choice of the appropriate sector, the policy practitioner has to wrestle with the comparative advantages of using the various levels of government.[3] If she believes that many local units would be particularly unreceptive to the needs of battered women, she could opt to vest responsibility with the federal government, but she would realize, as well, that it is difficult for federal officials to superintend the operational details of thousands of shelters. Alternatively, she could choose a middle course by directing the federal funds to state authorities while requiring them to follow specific standards and to report specific kinds of information to federal authorities.

Kinds of Agencies Receiving Funds   The policy practitioner has to decide which kinds of agencies can receive federal funds. Should nonprofit, public, or profit-oriented agencies or some combination of these receive funds?[4] Nonprofit agencies have boards of directors, but their members are not allowed to have a financial stake in the agency nor do the boards have shareholders or other investors who receive dividends. (Their surpluses must be reinvested in the agency, whose staff receive fixed salaries.) Nonprofit agencies are exempt from state and federal taxes, and donations of contributors can usually be deducted from their income under tax codes, provided the agencies have received a tax-exempt status with the Internal Revenue Service and with state authorities who oversee nonprofit agencies. Profit-oriented agencies are owned by private investors, whether private owners or owners of stock, who expect a financial return on their investment. (Owners may assume a major role in overseeing their agencies or may cede management to outside managers who work under their general direction.) Public agencies are usually funded exclusively by public authorities and from those fees that they collect from consumers. In actual practice, complex hybrids exist. Many nonprofit agencies, as well as some profit-oriented agencies, receive contracts from public authorities or provide services to consumers whose bills are partially reimbursed by federal, state, or local authorities. Some nonprofits even possess profit-oriented subsidiaries.

The policy practitioner has to weigh the real (and imagined) strengths and weaknesses of these kinds of agencies when deciding whether to include them. Because public agencies lack a profit motive, they have no economic incentive to deceive or shortchange consumers. Indeed, theorists, such as the late social welfare theorist Richard Titmuss, contend that public agencies reinforce altruism by strengthening the notion that society should both fund and implement social programs.[5] Many critics have assailed public agencies, however. They often are bedeviled by red tape and by civil service and unionized employees who cannot easily be removed when they are ineffective. Although ultimately accountable to elected officials, many public agencies do not make extensive use of community resources such as volunteers and support groups. Because public agencies have often emphasized services to poor persons, they are often shunned by working and middle-class citizens, who may also believe them to be excessively bureaucratic in their operations.[6]

Nonprofit agencies are often believed to be more innovative than public agencies because they are often less constrained by regulations that define the programs and by procedures of public agencies.[7] Because they tend to be smaller than public agencies and have boards that are composed of residents, some of them are probably more responsive to the needs of specific communities. Some critics nonetheless question whether nonprofit agencies are more innovative than public agencies and note that their boards are often dominated by community elites, with scant participation by ordinary citizens.[8] Some of them engage so aggressively in marketing and fund-raising activities that they are indistinguishable from profit-oriented agencies.

In similar fashion, profit-oriented agencies have their defenders and detractors. Many advocates of privatizing the human services—that is, giving profit-oriented organizations expanded roles in delivering services—contend that private markets enhance the efficiency of the human services while

promoting the responsiveness of services to the needs of consumers. They suggest that inefficient agencies or ones that were not responsive to consumers lose their clientele to more responsive competitors.[9] This optimistic portrayal of for-profit agencies is vigorously challenged by many critics who point to the current practices of many profit-oriented nursing homes and day-care centers, which sometimes use deceptive advertising to entice consumers to use them, cut the quality of their services to increase their profits, and refrain from serving those persons who cannot pay their fees.[10]

Planning the Infusion and Circulation of Resources

The policy practitioner realizes that fiscal resources are the lifeblood of the human services system and that many shelters desperately need funds to survive. Besides the funding choices, she has to examine alternative sources of funds for social programs, mechanisms for shaping the level of funding of specific programs, and funding channels.

Sources of Funds for Social Programs   Policy analysts must choose among a variety of funding sources.[11] The extensive **general revenues** of local, county, state, and federal governments are used to fund many programs. The federal government has emerged since the 1930s as the major funder of social welfare programs because it possesses greater tax-raising capabilities than do state or local governments. Most federal revenues derive from the federal income tax, which produces far more revenue than the limited income taxes of many states, as well as their property, sales, excise, and license taxes.

General revenues provide a useful source of funds for social programs because they constitute large amounts of unrestricted funds. By the same token, however, many claimants exist for general-revenue funds, such as the thousands of existing social programs and the Defense Department. Moreover, when taxpayer revolts cut tax rates, as happened in both federal and state governments in the 1980s, access to general revenues became even more problematic.

Payroll taxes are a useful source of revenue that is used to fund the nation's Social Security and Medicare Programs. These taxes take a certain percentage of the payrolls of employees or of employers—or tax the payrolls of both employees and employers simultaneously. While payroll taxes are a predictable and stable source of revenues, it is virtually impossible to develop new payroll taxes because Social Security and Medicare already preempt considerable shares of the payrolls of employers and employees.

Consumer payments fund a significant share of the nation's social programs—whether fees that are imposed by agencies or by private practitioners such as counselors and physicians. Consumer payments deter the frivolous or unnecessary use of social and medical services and sometimes (in the case of sliding fees) provide a means of requiring relatively affluent persons to shoulder part of the operating costs of programs. They often deter poor persons from seeking needed services, however.

Special taxes, such as taxes on marriage licenses, alcoholic beverages, and auto licenses, are often earmarked for specific programs. As one example, special taxes on marriage licenses are used by many states to fund shelters for battered women. Like payroll taxes, special taxes provide a stable source of revenues for specific programs, but they are often opposed by political interests, such as liquor companies, that fear the taxes will erode their markets by raising the costs of their products.

Private philanthropy, which includes federated community fund-raising drives like United Way and appeals for Jewish and Catholic agencies, corporations, foundations, and individual donors, has long been eclipsed by government as the major source of funding for social programs.[12] Private philanthropy provides many agencies with funds that are often less restricted than government monies because they are not usually earmarked for specific programs. As with the general revenues of government, however, many claimants exist for scarce philanthropic funds. Established agencies or ones that emphasize popular causes, such as hospitals, attract a disproportionate share of these funds.

Determining Levels of Funds Euphoric in the wake of the enactment of legislation, reformers often discover that the program subsequently receives inadequate funding. The funding of public programs usually follows a two-step procedure.[13] First, legislatures **authorize** funds by stipulating in the mandating legislation how much money (an upper limit) can be allocated for a specific program in a given year. Second, the legislature **appropriates**— that is, actually commits—a specific amount of money to the program in a specific year. But programs often receive far less funds than were authorized for them because available funds are outstripped by the demands on them during the annual appropriations process. Intensely political from start to finish, the appropriations process leads to winners (programs that receive their authorized levels) and losers (programs that receive far less than their authorized levels).

Legislatures sometimes provide **open-ended funding** for some programs, where they agree to fund whatever costs those programs incur in a specific year. Medicare and the Social Security Programs illustrate such open-ended funding, which can be contrasted with the more usual pattern of establishing an upper ceiling on the funds that can be appropriated for a program in a specific year.

Funding Channels Once funds exist for a social program and some combination of public, nonprofit, and profit-oriented agencies have been chosen, funding channels need to be devised to distribute resources from funders. We can visualize the flow of funds from the federal government to agencies to occur through channels, or routes (see Figure 3.1).

Government funders often provide funds directly to the agencies that deliver social programs (Route 1). These agencies can be given project grants where the federal government provides funds to a shelter to provide services to battered women. The government could establish specific regulations to specify the content or nature of services or could give local agencies relatively wide latitude. Alternatively, funders can **contract** for specific services by asking local agencies to participate in a competitive bidding process for contracts that specify the kinds of services the government wishes to provide.[14] If a project grant provides funds for the general purpose of providing assistance to battered women, a contract details in specific terms what the government seeks to purchase, such as "5000 days of residential services to battered women who live in Fargo, North Dakota."

Alternatively, some persons argue that federal funders should provide resources directly to consumers (Route 5). For example, some persons favor the use of **vouchers,** that is, funds that consumers use to purchase specific services, such as day care. Government can place parameters on the kinds of services or commodities that can be purchased and can require agencies or providers to meet certain licensing standards. Alternatively, government funds can make so-called **vendor payments** to reimburse providers for specific services they provide to specific consumers.[15] As an example, the Medicaid Program reimburses hospitals and physicians for the medical services they provide to particular patients.

In the federal-state channel (Route 2), funds are distributed by the federal government to the states, which then distribute the funds to specific agencies. Advocates of state government support this policy because it gives states enhanced roles in the human services system. Indeed, advocates of **block grants,** which are sums of relatively unrestricted funds that the federal government gives to states or to local units of government, argue that they give state and local governments the flexibility to use the funds as they wish and to adapt their programs to local needs.[16] Opponents of block grants often contend that they provide local jurisdictions with a *carte blanche* that invites the use of federal funds for trivial or misdirected programs or that allows them not to serve powerless or stigmatized groups such as racial minorities. These persons often favor federal funding of specific programs that require agencies or local governments to use them for specific social problems or populations and moreover to adhere to numerous regulations that are established by federal authorities. (These programs, such as the Head Start Program, are often called **categorical programs.**) In the Reagan administration, a number of large block-grant programs were established that included a maternal and child health block grant and a social services block grant. While some restrictions were placed on the use of these funds by the states, their funds were relatively unrestricted compared with those of the fifty-seven

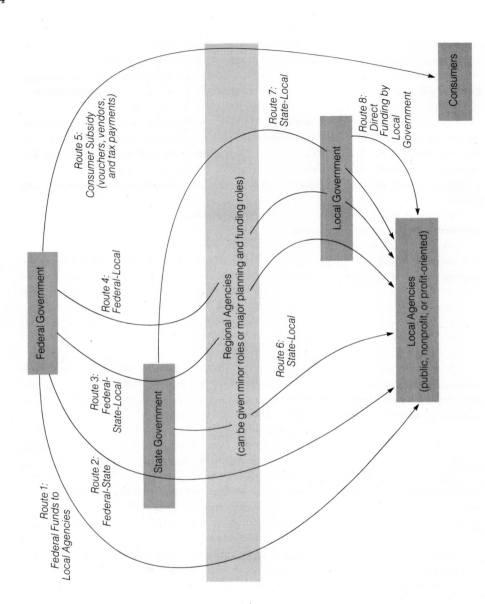

Figure 3.1   Selected Funding and Decision Channels, or Routes

categorical programs that they replaced. Alternatively, the federal government can fund local governments directly (Route 4)—a tactic that would be favored by some mayors and county supervisors who chafe at the extraordinary power of government. In this case, local governments would fund local shelters for battered women within their jurisdictions.

In similar fashion, states use myriad channels when they distribute their funds to local programs. They can distribute the funds directly to agencies (Route 6) or can use local governments as the conduit for distributing the funds to agencies (Route 7).

Like other policy options, each funding channel has its defenders and its detractors. Persons who favor the use of vouchers contend that it promotes healthy competition among agencies for clientele and decreases the need for government bureaucracy. Critics, however, point to many defects in market schemes. Although armed with vouchers, many low-income consumers cannot find quality providers because relatively few of them locate their agencies or practices in low-income areas.[17] Persons who want to maximize the role of the federal government want to have it directly fund agencies or consumers, whereas persons who want to increase the role of the states, such as many conservative politicians, want federal authorities to distribute funds to the states in the form of unrestricted block grants.

Indirect Financing   The preceding discussion has focused on direct methods of financing social welfare programs by federal and state governments. The purchase of social welfare services can also be financed indirectly through the tax system.[18] As reflected in policies that allow persons to deduct interest payments on their mortgages or to deduct health expenditures, consumers are sometimes given **tax deductions** that allow them to deduct specific social welfare and housing expenditures. **Tax credits** allow taxpayers to subtract monies that they used for specific programs from their tax payments to the government; thus, many working women fund a portion of their daycare expenditures by subtracting a child-care credit from the taxes. **Tax exemptions** allow the taxpayer not to have to pay taxes on specific income. Someone who is allowed to exempt from taxable income a specified sum for each dependent, for example, subtracts that amount from total income and then calculates tax payments due the government.

In these various indirect methods of financing social welfare then, monies are provided to citizens not by direct appropriations from government but by the less obvious route of tax concessions. The advantage of using the tax system is that it does not require appropriations and thus avoids political uncertainties. Because many Americans are not even aware of the magnitude of tax concessions, however, they sometimes escape legislative scrutiny. Tax concessions often benefit relatively wealthy persons disproportionately as illustrated by the tax deductions for mortgage interest payments for persons with expensive homes that vastly exceed deductions for home-owners with modest homes. (Tenants receive no assistance from the tax codes.) The government gives persons who use tax-subsidized benefits a free hand in choosing their services; persons who receive daycare credits are not required, for example, to use high-quality or licensed daycare in order to receive their tax credits.[19]

Some Funding Choices of the Policy Practitioner   With the preceding discussion as background, the policy practitioner has to decide how large to make the authorizations of the legislation, to what extent states should match federal funds, whether funds should be given to the states with relatively few restrictions, and whether taxes on marriage licenses could be used in some states to fund shelters.

When examining funding channels, she has to review her predilections about the various levels of government. If she decides to emphasize the role of states in superintending the program, she could decide to place the program within an existing block-grant program, although she might require state authorities to earmark certain funds from the block grants for the shelters. If, by contrast, she wants to emphasize the role of the federal government, she may decide to have federal authorities directly fund local agency applicants, or she may develop a categorical program that provides funds to those states that followed specific guidelines in using the funds.

She decides to ask for an authorization level of $450 million in the first year with authorizations to rise to $600 million within three years. Although she wants more funds than this for the program, she realizes that conservatives, as well as some moderates and liberals, will object to a larger program during a period of federal budgetary deficits. She selects Route 2 from the funding channels, that is, the provision of federal funds to states that in turn fund local shelters. She would have preferred direct federal funding of shelters, but she doubts that this policy is politically feasible in an era when many politicians favor increasing the power of the states.

Devising the Content and Form of Services or Benefits

As she develops an initial outline of the Federal Shelter Program, the policy practitioner has to establish an orienting framework to provide direction for the service component of the shelters, and she has to decide what kinds of staff should deliver these services.

Establishing an Orienting Framework   We can return now to our discussion of conceptual frameworks in Chapter Two, where we contrasted public health, intrapsychic, deterrent, and other paradigms that are frequently used in social welfare policy. As she wrestles with services, the policy practitioner has to articulate an orienting framework on which to base her selection of a services strategy.

The policy practitioner realizes that women who have been subjected to abusive behavior often experience multiple problems such as legal, psychological, familial, medical, and economic ones. Many of them contend with issues of divorce and police protection, suffer from anxiety and depression, have children with them who were traumatized by family violence and disruption, possess serious physical problems that stem from the violence, and contend with a loss of income in the wake of separation from their spouses. These considerations prompt the policy practitioner to favor the provision of multifaceted services that are integrated with residential services. As she struggles with defining the services, she decides she wants some combination of advocacy, crisis intervention, and referral services that are integrated through a case-management system.

She is also aware, however, that many paradigms exist in the human services, including ones that stress intrapsychic factors. She is certain that some shelters will not provide *any* social services because they lack funds or are preoccupied with residential services. Thus, she decides to specify in the legislation those services that will be required by shelters that receive federal subsidies, including crisis intervention, referral services, and case-management services, to attend to the multiple needs of battered women.

Of course, she realizes that formal requirements often do not shape the *style* of services. She does not want the shelters to become institutions like hospitals or nursing homes that are merely places of residence for battered women; indeed, she wants them to be linked to their surrounding communities and to feminist organizations. Moreover, she wants them to be advocates not only for individuals but also for battered women generally, by supporting policies to increase prosecutions of spousal abusers and to include battered women in existing state programs that provide financial reimbursement to the victims of other violent crimes. How can she promote these intangible attributes in her legislative proposal? Besides case-management and other services, she decides to require advocacy for battered women, the use of volunteers, and, as we will discuss later, participation by victims of battering on the governing or advisory boards of shelters. Even with these kinds of stipulations, she realizes that many shelters might in fact resemble those nursing homes that provide primarily custodial services because it is far simpler to define the formal attributes of facilities than to shape their informal qualities such as their sensitivity, advocacy, or responsiveness to community needs.

Staff and Licensing Issues   The policy practitioner realizes that the provisions that mandate specific kinds of services will come to naught if the shelters do not employ competent staff. She also knows, however, that considerable competition can develop between rival professions when members of certain professions seek to give priority to their members.

Before we can understand her predicament, we need to briefly discuss the way professions, including social work, develop their power and credibility. Professions are developed for reasons of both altruism and self-interest.[20] Members of specific professions want to protect consumers from incompetent persons (altruism), but they also want to reserve the use of their title and access to certain jobs, as well as private practices, to those persons who meet certain basic requirements (self-interest). Both altruism and self-interest lead professionals to want professional monopolies where they exclude those "outsiders" who have not received certain kinds of training. Professions have to establish certain minimal educational and training requirements, both to be certain that their members possess certain competencies and to distinguish these members from the general public and from other professions. (If no minimum requirements exist, *anyone* can use the title of the profession and can pose as a member of the profession—with disastrous consequences for the credibility of the profession because consumers and employers are likely to believe that "the title means nothing.") To protect their members, then, professions specify minimum training and education provisions and develop methods for monitoring them; thus, graduate schools of social work, whose graduates use the degree M.S.W., cannot be accredited by the Council on Social Work Education (CSWE), the national accrediting body, unless they provide minimal classroom and field-work requirements.[21] Similarly, persons who claim they have the B.S.W. degree must complete specified undergraduate education and field-work requirements that are specified by CSWE. Programs that are not accredited by CSWE can graduate students, but their graduates would likely experience problems in obtaining employment and they would have difficulty in recruiting faculty.

But professions are rarely content, again for reasons of altruism and self-interest, to rely exclusively on accreditation of professional schools to enhance their status. They also want government to use its **licensing powers** to restrict to members of their professions the use of certain titles, the performing of certain tasks, and the holding of certain positions.[22] **Licensing of titles** occurs, for example, when state laws stipulate that titles like "licensed clinical social worker," "physician," or "attorney-at-law" are restricted to persons who have met certain training or educational requirements, including graduation from programs that have been accredited by their professions and certain kinds of postgraduate professional and training requirements. For example, licensing requirements for persons who use the title Licensed Clinical Social Worker (LCSW) in some states require a certain number of hours of professional employment that is supervised by a licensed clinical social worker (LCSW). **Licensing of tasks or functions** precludes persons who have not met certain training requirements from performing specified tasks, such as surgery or the prescription of drugs in the case of physicians. This latter kind of licensing represents an even more potent form of protection for a profession because, unlike the licensing of titles that apply merely to the terms that persons use to describe themselves, it reserves certain tasks to members of a specific profession.[23] Imagine the power that would suddenly accrue to licensed clinical social workers, in those states that license this title, if *all* counseling was reserved to them in the manner that surgery is reserved to physicians!

Professions often try to reserve to themselves certain positions in government agencies by having them classified. When government authorities require certain credentials for a civil service position, such as stipulating that only social workers with master's degrees can fill supervisory positions in some child welfare agencies, they disallow members of other professions from competing for that position. It is small wonder that professional social workers have been perturbed by the phenomenon of declassification, which removes the requirement that persons must possess a social work degree to hold many positions in child welfare agencies, in welfare programs, or in other programs.[24] Political controversies are often associated with issues of licensing and classification because rival professions often contend with one another to reserve certain tasks or positions for themselves or to prevent other professions from monopolizing them.[25]

School guidance counselors ✓ School Social Workers.

Our policy practitioner has to decide whether to require the shelters that receive federal funds to hire certain kinds of professionals for specific jobs. The legislation could stipulate, for example, that each shelter must have a director of social services who has an M.S.W. degree and that specific kinds of case-management and counseling services must be provided by the members of specific professions who have had (at least) a supervised practicum in clinical work. Such requirements might enhance the quality of social services that are given by the shelters and might also facilitate efforts by shelters to augment their fees by receiving payments from health insurance in those states where insurance companies reimburse the services of counseling professions. But the policy practitioner realizes that these kinds of staffing requirements would carry some disadvantages. They will substantially increase the cost of maintaining the shelters because shelters will have to pay the relatively higher salaries that professionals command. Those professions that are excluded by the legislation from directing the shelters, such as marriage and family counselors and psychologists, could oppose the legislation. Some feminists may even argue that "professionalizing the shelters" will detract from their use of volunteer and community supports. The policy practitioner decides to require the shelter directors to possess an M.S.W. degree and to require the direct-service staff to have had a supervised practicum, but she decides not to specify their professional affiliation.

Preventive Versus Curative Services   Critics argue that preventive programs can lead to significant savings by decreasing the costs of welfare, mental health, health, and other existing programs by providing primary prevention (preventing problems prior to their emergence) or secondary prevention (detecting and addressing social problems soon after their emergence).[26] But only a fraction of existing social welfare expenditures are directed to programs that provide consumer education or early detection efforts (secondary prevention) or to projects to address basic causes of problems like spousal abuse, such as substance abuse and poverty in those populations that are at high risk of engaging in family violence (primary prevention).

When contemplating whether to provide a major preventive component, the policy practitioner confronts difficult dilemmas. The number of women on the waiting lists of existing shelters makes it difficult to justify an expenditure of large sums on prevention. It is difficult to know how to prevent abusive behavior in light of the complexity of the problem and the absence of definitive research because abusive behaviors are probably caused by some combination of personal exposure to abuse as a child, marital discord, substance abuse, cultural factors, sexism, situational stressors such as unemployment and poverty, the ownership of guns by many Americans, national culture that promotes violence, and (possibly) a genetic predisposition toward violence of some persons.[27] While large-scale reforms and national reforms could redress some of these causes, the policy practitioner could not easily address them in her legislative proposal. If primary prevention is difficult to accomplish, she nonetheless wonders if her legislation could facilitate the early detection of abusive behaviors (secondary prevention). As members of her coalition brainstorm the issue, they decide that local hot lines can, if properly advertised, encourage women to seek early assistance; thus, she decides to include in the bill a section that enables some shelters to qualify for funds to establish and maintain a hot line in their geographic region.

Rationing Scarce Resources

The term *rationing* may seem like an anomaly in the human services because it sounds like something that is reserved to the economies of wartime, Third World, or Eastern Bloc nations. Rationing is necessary, in light of insufficient resources, to assist all (or even most) consumers who use social programs, however; every social agency and social program must engage in some form of rationing.[28] Our policy practitioner must grapple with this issue as she plans the legislation because the resources that Congress might approve for her legislation will not be sufficient to address the magnitude of demand for services by battered women, who have formed long waiting lists for existing shelters. Moreover, were the Federal Shelter Program enacted, it is likely that many women who do not currently use services would seek them as they learned that they were available.

Formal or Direct Methods of Rationing   Perhaps the most common method of restricting access is by income, such as by limiting access to persons who fall beneath the official poverty line. The use of income mea-sures poses some problems, however.[29] An income limitation would deny access to shelters to those women whose incomes are above the requisite income unless there is a sliding-fee scale to allow shelters to charge fees that are calibrated to the amount of income of abused women. An income limi-tation will require shelter staff to engage in the time-consuming work of checking the financial records of applicants. Imagine, as well, the financial problems encountered by many abused women whose finances are in a state of chaos when they have left their spouses; can shelter staff accurately identify actual available income, as opposed to total family income, in these circumstances? Income-based eligibility, however, has some advantages. It allows social agencies to focus scarce resources on those persons who are least able to purchase alternative services.

Alternatively or in conjunction with income-based eligibility, the policy practitioner can place diagnostic eligibility criteria in the legislation, such as the extent of danger to women, the chronicity or severity of the abusive behavior that they have experienced, or the extent of personal trauma of applicants. As in the instance of mental health institutions, which often limit access (or at least involuntary commitments) to persons who are a danger to themselves or to others, the policy practitioner can limit use of shelters to women who have been actually abused rather than subjected only to verbal threats. Diagnostic criteria have the advantage of allowing intake staff to limit the use of programs to persons who appear to have the most serious problems—not an unimportant consideration when dealing with battered women whose lives are sometimes in danger—but they place applicants at the mercy of the diagnostic skills of intake staff, who may misread the seriousness of a situation or who may allow their own preferences to shape their judgments.[30] Indeed, the subtle (and overt) biases of intake staff may make them respond more sympathetically to certain persons, such as mem-bers of their own racial or ethnic group or women with certain kinds of problems.

When analyzing her options, the policy practitioner needs to decide whether to use a number of eligibility criteria in tandem. She can, for exam-ple, limit free services to persons earning less than a certain amount *and* require shelter staff to give priority to women "in serious danger of serious injury." Of course, she cannot resolve rationing issues without returning to certain value premises or to her purpose-defining or mission policies. If she wants a national network of federally subsidized shelters that provide a resource to most battered women, she may seek eligibility policies that are relatively nonexclusionary. Carried to its fullest, she can even declare shelters to be an entitlement with open-ended funding, much like Medicare or Social Security that receives automatic and open-ended funding of whatever ser-vices are provided by shelters to abused women during a given year.

We should note that buck passing is common with respect to eligibility.

In order not to make difficult and sometimes controversial choices, federal or state legislators often yield eligibility decisions to states or agencies. Such ceding of eligibility standards in programs like AFDC has some merit because standards of living and demand for services vary in different parts of the nation, but critics contend that more conservative and poorer states restrict eligibility excessively when given this power.[31]

Indirect Methods of Restricting Access   Social agencies and programs devise policies that indirectly influence patterns of access. One method of rationing is to place upper limits on the intensity or duration of services. To allow more persons to receive assistance, a program administrator can decide, for example, to limit residence in a shelter to a certain number of months. When placing limits on services, policy practitioners must ask, How do we balance effectiveness with equity? If the intensity, duration, or amount of services or benefits is markedly reduced, many consumers receive program benefits (equity is increased), but services may be distributed so thinly that persons receive little, hence ineffective or inadequate, assistance.[32] Policy practitioners must make difficult choices then when considering the relative intensity or amount of program benefits.

Another common method of rationing program resources in social agencies and programs is to adopt a first-come, first-served policy in which consumers are given services in order of application. This approach appears at first glance to be equitable because no favoritism is possible. But this policy also has drawbacks, particularly when certain kinds of persons are excluded from services by it. Some persons, such as low-income persons or geographically isolated populations, may not know about specific services, may use them at later times than other persons (when their problems have become particularly serious), or may be most likely to drop off of waiting lists.

Some critics argue that social agencies should earmark or reserve resources for underserved populations, much as affirmative action or quotas are used to reserve employment slots for women and racial minorities. They should also, according to this argument, develop outreach services to these populations and examine service-utilization patterns to provide outreach to consumers who prematurely terminate.

Some social agencies ration services by *discouraging* specific populations from utilizing them. Overt discrimination is probably less serious than subtler forms.[33] In some cases, specific service approaches, such as extended "talking therapies," are not likely to be used by low-income populations who want tangible assistance with their economic and social problems. In similar fashion, the lack of bilingual and ethnic minority staff can deter use of services by ethnic minority consumers.

Rationing can be affected indirectly in many other ways, including the placement of facilities, the use of specific program titles, and the selective use of outreach. When facilities are placed in low-income areas, they promote their use by poor persons, just as facilities in many suburban areas favor affluent populations. The importance of titles becomes obvious when one examines the implications of calling an agency "free clinic" instead of "women's free clinic." Patterns of outreach and advertising also influence access; if staff advertise their program to relatively affluent populations, for example, they shape and bias access toward these persons and away from other populations.

6. Use of fees constitutes another method of restricting access. As fees increase, low-income consumers are less likely to seek services or more likely to terminate at the earliest possible point. Some policies, such as the restriction of services to the usual hours of employment of consumers, impose a hidden but substantial burden on working persons and poor persons who must in effect pay a fee by taking time from their employment.

Our policy practitioner reluctantly decides that she has to impose some kind of rationing on shelters financed by the Federal Shelter Program because of the enormity of unmet needs. She decides to restrict access to three months of residence in shelters "unless the woman remains in imminent danger of physical abuse." She requires the shelters to disseminate information about their shelters to a broad range of community groups. She establishes a sliding-fee schedule for applicants, but allows it to be waived when family finances are disrupted by dislocation.

Addressing Community and Regional Factors

We noted earlier that the policy practitioner wants the shelters to be embedded in the community fabric to endow them with special qualities such as sensitivity, friendliness, and informality. Of course, no legislative strategy can ensure that these kinds of qualities are possessed by staff, particularly when the latter do not value them or when high-level officials do not monitor services. She decides she can indirectly promote these qualities through policies germane to the governance and the use of community-support systems by the centers.

Whether in pieces of legislation, court rulings, or high-level administrative regulations, official policies are often riddled with loopholes or ambiguities—because insistence on defining all the fine points would jeopardize their passage or because high-level officials do not foresee specific problems that will occur when the policies are enacted. If the policy practitioner inserted in the Federal Shelter Program a requirement that local agencies must provide "advocacy" for battered women and must "conduct outreach to segments of the population who are not aware of social services for battered women," she would prescribe relatively vague objectives that would be interpreted and implemented in different fashions by various shelters. *All* shelters possess limited resources; thus, some might decide to devote relatively little effort toward these objectives. Moreover, some staff would not prioritize these objectives because they do not value them when compared to other objectives such as providing residential services or clinical services to battered women. Undeterred, the policy practitioner nonetheless wants to develop linkages with community-support systems to include self-help groups, professionals in the community who have extensive contact with women (such as beauticians and hair stylists), female community leaders, and agencies that link women to schools, job-placement, medical, and other agencies, as well as to free clinics.

Because decisions about the priorities and objectives are resolved both by the staff of particular shelters and by their boards, the policy practitioner, herself a feminist, decides to require that the boards appoint 51 percent of their membership from current or prior victims of wife battering, female leaders in the community, and professionals from the community who work in self-help and other agencies. She hopes that this policy requirement will advance the implementation of many of her policy objectives by including persons on boards who are more likely to be sympathetic to them than the business and professional persons who usually dominate the boards of agencies. Because boards often assume the role of merely assenting to those policies that are favored by the executive director, the policy practitioner also decides to include in the legislation a requirement that the boards will review programs and budgets to ascertain that the shelters provide the full range of services that are included in the legislation, including advocacy, the use of community-support systems, and outreach.[34]

Policy practitioners sometimes favor the development of regional entities that are also accorded major roles in funding local agencies and in shaping and planning policy choices.[35] Thus, Area Agencies for the Aging (AAAs) and regional boards for various programs funded by block grants of the states assume these roles. These regional entities, some persons argue, are able to coordinate services of agencies in a relatively broad geographic area, to identify underserved jurisdictions, and to monitor the services of agencies in their areas. The policy practitioner could advocate, for example, regional boards be established and given substantial roles in funding and overseeing the programs of local shelters. She ultimately decides not to include regional entities in her legislation because some members of the coalition fear that many conservatives, who tend to oppose the creation of "additional levels of bureaucracy," would oppose the legislation if they were added.

Orchestrating Policy Oversight

If the boards and staff of local agencies have a major role in shaping the content and direction of services, officials in local, regional, state, and federal bureaucracies often assume a considerable role in monitoring and assessing the implemented programs, as well as in issuing administrative regulations about how various high-level policies will be operationalized. We call these monitoring, assessing, and regulations-issuing functions *policy oversight*. **Monitoring** examines the extent local agencies actually implement official policies; **assessment** or **evaluation** evaluates the implemented policies (e.g., by measuring the extent the services help the recipients); and **regulations** provide steps, procedures, and reporting mechanisms implementing agencies must use.[36]

We have already noted that the policy practitioner fears that local agencies, if left to their own, will neglect some important policies. She realizes, however, that it is unlikely that federal officials will be able to oversee the programs of far-flung shelters under the Federal Shelter Program. She decides to support a division of labor by requiring federal officials to provide administrative regulations but to require the states to use a certain percentage of the funds of the Federal Shelter Program, say, 3 percent, for the monitoring of local programs by the lead agency of each state that distributes the federal funds to local agencies. Moreover, she decides to require each state to establish a Licensing Advisory Board, which is composed of state fire, social service, and health officials to develop minimum standards that must be met by each shelter.

FROM ANALYSIS TO POLITICS

As we will note in the next chapter, it is relatively simple to list available policy options and to make preliminary choices, as reflected by the policy proposal of the policy practitioner. After identifying a range of policy options, she made some tentative policy choices, as seen in Table 3.2. But she and other members of her coalition, who are relatively liberal feminists, have not yet encountered the hardships of the political process—much less some agonizing choices that will need to be made when she encounters persons who are not favorably disposed to her proposal.

LINKING ANALYTIC SKILLS TO OTHER POLICY SKILLS

When we refer back to Policy-Practice Case 3 at the start of this chapter, we discover that analytic skills in identifying, comparing, and selecting policy options must often be teamed with other policy-practice skills if policy practitioners wish to be effective. Recall that the social worker wants to obtain the approval of a Community Emergency Services Program (CES) for families that need immediate assistance. (Such emergency services are needed for families where wife battering, child abuse, child neglect, severe marital conflict, illness, homelessness, and other conditions exist.) Although the social worker is confident that she has developed an analytically sound proposal that includes six components, she has to convince public authorities and

TABLE 3.2   Tentative Policy Options for the Federal Shelter Program

1. Establishing a mission or set of objectives:
   - Establishes a program to combine assistance with construction and rehabilitation of centers with funds to promote a range of social services to the victims of spousal abuse.

2. Designing the structure of service of program delivery:
   - Places the Federal Shelter Program in the Department of Health and Human Services.
   - Uses only nonprofit agencies.
   - Devises some standards at the federal level but requires each state to establish a lead agency to actually administer the funds to local nonprofit agencies.

3. Planning the infusion and circulation of resources:
   - Establishes an authorization level of $450 million to rise to $600 million within three years.
   - Uses Route 2 (see Figure 3.1).

4. Devising the content and form of services or benefits:
   - Uses an ecological paradigm.
   - Requires a broad range of services to include referral, crisis, case-management, advocacy, legal, and outreach services.
   - Funds a regional hot line in designated regional areas.
   - Requires the shelter directors to possess an M.S.W. degree and requires direct-service staff to have had a supervised practicum.

5. Rationing scarce resources:
   - Establishes a sliding fee but allows it to be waived when family finances are disrupted by dislocation.
   - Establishes an upper limit of three-months' residence to be waived when resident remains in imminent danger of physical abuse.
   - Gives priority to women in imminent danger of physical abuse.

6. Addressing community and regional factors:
   - Requires outreach to underserved segments of the population.
   - Requires linkages with community-support systems.
   - Requires advocacy.
   - Requires 51 percent of the board composition to consist of women who are current or former victims of spousal abuse, who are staff in agencies or support groups that serve this population, or who are community leaders.

7. Orchestrating policy oversight:
   - Earmarks 3 percent of funds for monitoring activities of the lead state agencies.

decision makers that the proposal should be funded—a not easy political task in an era of scarce public resources. Indeed, she teams political and interactional skills together; by engaging in many community meetings, as well as personal discussions with highly placed officials (interactional skills), she *also* constructs a constituency for the proposal (political skills). Indeed, the social worker finds that she has to use interactional and political skills to develop support for CES within the department where it would be housed. She needs value-clarification skills as she decides whether and how to develop community pressures on the officials who are her employers and as she decides whether to accede to various attempts by department officials to diminish the scope and size of the proposed program. (Political, interactional, and value-clarification skills are discussed in succeeding chapters.)

SUMMARY

We have discussed in this chapter an array of policy options that analysts often encounter when constructing social welfare proposals. When making policy choices, policy practitioners must often grapple with the dilemma that each policy option, such as a specific method of determining eligibility, has merits and weaknesses. Because some choices that appear meritorious on certain grounds may carry other disadvantages, policy practitioners must frequently examine trade-offs to determine, on balance, which options appear preferable. In the case of complex and multifaceted proposals such as the Federal Shelter Program, choices need to be made with respect to (at least) seven issues that include establishing a mission, devising a structure of services, infusing programs with resources, devising the content and form of services or benefits, rationing scarce resources, addressing community and regional factors, and orchestrating policy oversight.

The policy practitioner in this case had not yet encountered the kinds of political opposition she will confront if the Federal Shelter proposal advances into the legislative process. She was able to anticipate some kinds of opposition, such as conservative dislike of regional agencies, but she knows that unexpected sources of opposition will arise. She anticipates that these initial choices will have to be changed in the push-and-pull of the political process.

QUESTIONS FOR DISCUSSION

1. The focus or mission of a program is often profoundly shaped by where it is placed within a bureaucracy or agency. Discuss.
2. The increasing use of profit-oriented agencies to deliver social services poses a threat to the quality of services in the welfare state. Discuss.

3. How does the tax system currently fund a variety of social programs and activities? Discuss some advantages and disadvantages in using the tax system to fund social welfare programs.

4. Take two alternative routes or channels for funding social programs and discuss their comparative strengths and weaknesses (see Figure 3.1).

5. The founders of social programs are often disappointed to find that their programs receive considerably fewer resources in succeeding years than they had hoped. Discuss in the context of the appropriations and authorizations process.

6. Licensing, accreditation, and classification policies have emerged from a combination of self-interest and altruism. Discuss this statement as it applies to the social work profession.

7. The advocates of preventive services often encounter a difficult problem in securing funds for them. Discuss why this is so.

8. Social agencies accomplish rationing by a variety of explicit and official policies and by some informal and less obvious policies. Discuss in general terms or with respect to a specific agency.

9. In Policy-Practice Case 3, discuss how the social worker needed a variety of policy-practice skills to design and secure acceptance of the CES program.

SUGGESTED READINGS

Federal, State, and Local Relationships

Paul Gorman, "Block Grants: Theoretical and Practical Issues in Federal/State/Local Revenue Sharing," *New England Journal of Human Services*, 4 (Spring 1984): 19–23.

Richard Nathan and Fred Doolittle, "Federal Grants: Giving and Taking Away," *Political Science Quarterly*, 100 (Spring 1985): 53–74.

Profit-Oriented, Nonprofit, and Public Agency Relationships

Harry Carroll, Ralph Conant, and Thomas Easton, eds., *Private Means—Public Ends: Private Business and Social Service Delivery* (New York: Praeger, 1987).

Harold Demone and Margaret Gibelman, *Services for Sale* (New Brunswick, N.J.: Rutgers University Press, 1989).

Alfred Kahn, "Public Social Services, the Next Phase," *Public Welfare*, 30 (Winter 1972): 15–25.

Lester Salamon and Alan Abramson, *The Nonprofit Sector and the New Federal Budget* (Washington, D.C.: Urban Institute Press, 1986).

Stan Smith and Deborah Stone, "The Unexpected Consequences of Privatization," in Michael Brown, ed., *Remaking the Welfare State* (Philadelphia: Temple University Press, 1988), pp. 232–252.

Organizational Issues in the American Welfare State

Michael Murphy, "Organizational Approaches for Human Services Programs," in Wayne Anderson et al., eds., *Managing Human Services* (Washington, D.C.: International City Management Association, 1977), pp. 193–229.

Fiscal Issues

Harold Demone and Margaret Gibelman, eds., *Services for Sale* (New Brunswick, N.J.: Rutgers University Press, 1989).

Herman Leonard, *Checks Unbalanced: The Quiet Side of Public Spending* (New York: Basic Books, 1986).

Paul Terrel, "Financing Social Welfare Services," in Neil Gilbert and Harry Specht, eds., *Handbook of the Social Services* (Englewood Cliffs, N.J.: Prentice-Hall, 1981), pp. 380–410.

Professional and Staffing Issues

Bruce Fretz and David Mills, *Licensing and Certification of Psychologists and Counselors* (San Francisco: Jossey-Bass, 1980), pp. 9–29.

David Hardcastle, "The Profession: Professional Organizations, Licensing, and Private Practice," in Gilbert and Specht, eds., *Handbook of the Social Services*, pp. 666–688.

Allocation Issues

Richard Frank, "Rationing of Mental Health Services: Simple Observations on the Current Approach and Future Prospects," *Administration in Mental Health*, 13 (Fall 1985): 22–29.

Neil Gilbert and Harry Specht, *Dimensions of Social Welfare Policy* (Englewood Cliffs, N.J.: Prentice-Hall, 1986), pp. 66–91.

Richard Titmuss, "Laissez-Faire and Stigma," in Brian Abel-Smith and Kay Titmuss, eds., *Social Policy: An Introduction* (London: Allen and Unwin, 1974), pp. 33–46.

Prevention

Martin Bloom, *Primary Prevention: The Possible Science* (Englewood Cliffs, N.J.: Prentice-Hall, 1981).

Neil Gilbert, "Policy Issues in Primary Prevention," *Social Work*, 27 (May 1982): 293–297.

Staff Discretion

Robert Goodin, *Reasons for Welfare* (Princeton, N.J.: Princeton University Press, 1988), pp. 184–228.

NOTES

1. For an overview of one effort to secure federal legislation to fund shelters for abused women, see the *Congressional Quarterly Almanac*, 35 (Washington, D.C.: Congressional Quarterly, Inc., 1979), pp. 508–509. Also see Liane Davis and Jan Hagen, "Services for Battered Women: The Public Policy Response," *Social Service Review*, 62 (December 1988): 649–667.

2. Bruce Jansson, "The History and Politics of Selected Children's Programs and Related Legislation," Doctoral Dissertation, University of Chicago, 1975, pp. 66–67, 76–77.

3. See Paul Gorman, "Block Grants: Theoretical and Practical Issues in Federal/State/Local Revenue Sharing," *New England Journal of Human Services*, 4 (Spring 1984): 19–23; Robert Fulton and Ray Scott, "What Happened to the Federal/State Partnerships?" *New England Journal of Human Services*, 4 (Fall 1984): 38–39; and Allen Imersheim, "The Influence of Reagan's New Federalism on Human Services in Florida," *New England Journal of Human Services*, 5 (Spring 1985): 17–24.

4. Some overview literature on auspices includes Ralph Kramer, *Voluntary Agencies in the Welfare State* (Berkeley, Ca.: University of California Press, 1981); Bruce Jansson, "Public Monitoring of Contracts with Nonprofit Organizations," *Journal of Sociology and Social Welfare*, 6 (May 1979): 362–374.

5. A defense of public agencies is made by Richard Titmuss, *The Gift Relationship* (New York: Pantheon, 1971) and Alfred Kahn, "Public Social Services: The Next Phase," *Public Welfare*, 30 (Winter 1972): 15–25.

6. For an overview of some criticisms of public agencies, see Ralph Kramer, "From Voluntarism to Vendorism: An Organizational Perspective on Contracting," in Harold Demone and Margaret Gibelman, eds., *Services for Sale* (New Brunswick, N.J.: Rutgers University Press, 1989), pp. 101–102.

7. For a critical overview of the emergence and roles of nonprofit agencies in the federally funded welfare state, see Eleanor Brilliant, "Private or Public: A Model of Ambiguities," *Social Service Review*, 47 (September 1973): 384–396.

8. For criticisms of voluntary agencies, see Kramer, "From Voluntarism to Vendorism," pp. 102–103.

9. For a defense of profit-oriented agencies, see Emanuel Savas, *Privatizing the Public Sector: How to Shrink Government* (Chatham, N.J.: Chatham House Publishers, 1982).

10. For criticism of profit-oriented agencies, see Harold Demone and Margaret Gibelman, "Privatizing the Acute Care General Hospital," in Harry Carroll, Ralph Conant, and Thomas Easton, eds., *Private Means—Public Ends: Private Business and Social Service Delivery* (New York: Praeger, 1987), pp. 50–75.

11. For an overview of funding options, see Paul Terrell, "Financing Social Welfare Services," in Neil Gilbert and Harry Specht, eds., *Handbook of the Social Services* (Englewood Cliffs, N.J.: Prentice-Hall, 1981), pp. 392–394.

12. *Ibid.*, pp. 398–399.

13. Classic accounts of the authorizations and appropriations processes are found in Richard Fenno, *The Power of the Purse* (Boston: Little, Brown, 1966) and Aaron Wildavsky, *Politics of the Budgetary Process* (Boston: Little, Brown, 1964).

14. See Demone and Gibelman, *Services for Sale.*

15. A defense of voucher and vendor payments is made by John Coons and Stephen Sugarman, *Education by Choice: The Case for Family Control* (Berkeley, Ca.: University of California Press, 1978). A criticism of them is made by Frederick Thayer, "Privatization: Carnage, Chaos, and Corruption," in Carroll, Conant, and Easton, eds., *Private Means—Public Ends,* pp. 146–170.

16. Various points of view on block grants can be found in Richard Nathan and Fred Doolittle, "Federal Grants: Giving and Taking Away," *Political Science Quarterly,* 100 (Spring 1985): 53–74 and Richard Williamson, "The 1982 New Federalism Negotiations," *Publius,* 13 (Spring 1983): 11–33.

17. Thayer, "Privatization."

18. See Herman Leonard, *Checks Unbalanced: The Quiet Side of Public Spending* (New York: Basic Books, 1986).

19. *Ibid.,* pp. 251–265, for criticism of the use of the tax system.

20. Bruce Fretz and David Mills, *Licensing and Certification of Psychologists and Counselors* (San Francisco: Jossey-Bass, 1980).

21. David Hardcastle, "The Profession: Professional Organizations, Licensing, and Private Practice," in Gilbert and Specht, eds., *Handbook of the Social Services,* p. 677.

22. *Ibid.,* pp. 679–683.

23. *Ibid.,* pp. 666–687.

24. Robert Teare, *Classification Validation Processes for Social Services Positions* (Silver Springs, Md.: National Association of Social Workers, 1984).

25. S. Khinduka, "Social Work and the Human Services," *Encyclopedia of Social Work,* 18th edition, vol. 2 (Washington, D.C.: National Association of Social Workers, 1987), p. 691.

26. A defense of preventive services is made by Martin Bloom, *Primary Prevention: The Possible Science* (Englewood Cliffs, N.J.: Prentice-Hall, 1981).

27. Cautionary comments on prevention are made by Neil Gilbert, "Policy Issues in Primary Prevention," *Social Work,* 27 (May 1982): 293–297.

28. For a discussion of rationing, see Richard Frank, "Rationing of Mental Health Services: Simple Observations on the Current Approach and Future Prospects," *Administration in Mental Health,* 13 (Fall 1985): 22–29.

29. A general discussion of means tests is found in Neil Gilbert and Harry Specht, *Dimensions of Social Welfare Policy* (Englewood Cliffs, N.J.: Prentice-Hall, 1986), pp. 82–84.

30. For a discussion of staff discretion, see Robert Goodin, *Reasons for Welfare* (Princeton, N.J.: Princeton University Press, 1988), pp. 184–228.

31. For differences in eligibility standards for AFDC when states establish their own eligibility standards, see Joseph Heffernan, "New Directions in Welfare Reform

Debate: The Problems of Federalism," *Journal of Sociology and Social Welfare,* 15 (December 1988): 3–27.

32. See Noel Tichy, *Organization Design for Primary Health Care* (New York: Praeger, 1977), p. 100.

33. For subtle forms of discrimination and rationing, see Sharon Sepulveda-Hassell, *An Assessment of the Mental Health Treatment Process: Eliminating Service Barriers to Mexican Americans* (San Antonio, Texas: Intercultural Development Research Association, 1980) and David Ramirez, *A Review of Literature on Underutilization of Mental Health Services by Mexican Americans: Implications for Future Research and Service Delivery* (San Antonio, Texas: Intercultural Development Research Association, 1980).

34. A similar tactic was used in the Head Start Program; see Jansson, "The History and Politics of Selected Children's Programs," p. 131.

35. For discussion of regional agencies, see Eli Ginzburg, ed., *Regionalization and Health Policy* (Washington, D.C.: Government Printing Office, 1977).

36. For a discussion of monitoring, see Bruce Jansson, "The Political Economy of Monitoring: A Contingency Perspective," in Demone and Gibelman, eds., *Services for Sale,* pp. 343–359 and Kenneth Wedel and Nancy Chess, "Monitoring Strategies in Purchase of Service Contracting," in Demone and Gibelman, eds., *Services for Sale,* pp. 360–370.

CHAPTER 4

■

Thinking Analytically:
From Trade-Offs to
Policy Proposals

In Chapter Three we discussed how policy practitioners identify an array of policy options that they wish to consider when developing policy proposals. Policy practitioners sometimes wish to engage in systematic comparisons of competing policy options where they follow a careful, step-by-step process that draws upon available research and knowledge and that allows them to develop quantitative rankings of competing options. We will discuss this process of comparing and evaluating competing policy options in the first portion of this chapter.

Policy practitioners must often incorporate specific policy options in a broader proposal that also addresses administrative and logistical issues and provides a rationale for the proposal. Moreover, they need to fashion their proposal to make it appealing to specific decision makers or funders. We discuss the challenges of constructing policy proposals in the latter portion of this chapter.

A POLICY-PRACTICE CASE FROM THE HUMAN SERVICES SYSTEM

In Policy-Practice Case 4, we examine a policy memorandum prepared by a social worker for the Commissioner of the Department of Mental Health (DMH). The author examines various policy options with respect to services for developmentally disabled and mentally ill persons in her state; she thinks that there should be total deinstitutionalization, liquidation of existing state schools, or implementation of a purchase-of-service (POS) system of community care where public authorities reimburse nongovernmental agencies for providing specific kinds of community-based services.

To compare and contrast these issues, she prepares a memorandum for

POLICY-PRACTICE CASE 4

MEMORANDUM FOR THE COMMISSIONER:
Deinstitutionalization: Recommendation
for Planning

I. POLICY ISSUE

In the context of the development of the next series of five-year plans, what should be the role of state hospitals for the mentally ill and state schools for the mentally retarded in comprehensive community care? Specifically, should DMH care for its remaining institutionalized clients totally within existing institutions, totally in the community through the mechanism of purchase of services (POS), or somewhere in between? How can the department shape its personnel policy accordingly?

Recommendations: DMH's goal for its mentally retarded clients should be total deinstitutionalization, liquidation of existing state schools, and implementation of a total POS system of community care. The goal for mentally ill clients should be liquidation of existing state hospitals, leaving a residual role for small institutions, one in each of the seven regions to serve violent patients. The proposed facilities would be operated by private auspices under state contract. Community-care services should be totally POS. DMH's personnel policy should be, implicitly, a policy of attrition. Explicitly, DMH should work closely with unions to arrange for three options: (1) early retirement, (2) training and transfer to other state positions, (3) training and transfer to a limited number of community-service settings under public auspices to preserve vesting but without civil service protections, for example, municipal hospitals, state university–sponsored settings, and so forth.

II. SUMMARY AND ANALYSIS OF ISSUES

The impetus for deinstitutionalization is founded on a belief, buttressed by research findings, that large institutions inhibit and discourage potential for independent functioning for mentally ill and mentally retarded individuals. This belief, particularly prevalent for the past twenty years, underlies passage of the Community Mental Health Centers Act of 1963 and various subsequent presidential directives to reduce the rolls of public institutions for the mentally retarded. Legal developments, especially several Supreme Court decisions, have hastened deinstitutionalization by prohibiting involuntary commitment without provision of treatment. Social programs such as Medicaid, Medicare, Title XX, and SSI have provided heretofore absent funding sources for community services. The result of these developments has been a nationwide census reduction of 370,000 in a twenty-year period (1955–1975) in public mental hospitals and 24,000 in an eight-year period (1967–1975) in public "schools" for the retarded. In Massachusetts corresponding reductions have been 7000 in the state hospitals, 1971–1978, and 1100 in the state schools for the retarded, 1971–1977.

Current situation—What has happened to deinstitutionalized clients? It is a well-known fact that many "deinstitutionalized" individuals have been "reinstitutionalized" in nursing homes without resources, and frequently inclination, to meet the needs of mentally disabled residents. Many other individuals reside in substandard boarding houses, do not receive rehabilitation or treatment services, frequently decompensate, and are readmitted to state hospitals. Still other individuals are simply "lost to follow-up."

This situation is the result of three factors: (1) gaps in services in the community for a deinstitutionalized population; (2) presence of funding sources for services not tailored to the needs of the mentally disabled individual but offering a protective environment; (3) pressure from mounting costs and a desire to avoid legal suits to deinstitutionalize quickly, thus precluding planning to fill service gaps and foster receptive community attitudes.

What should the optimal community care system look like? What is needed? The literature abounds with descriptions of successful and unsuccessful community-care programs for the deinstitutionalized mentally disabled. The same essential program elements emerge again and again as keys to success or failure. They are (1) targeting of chronic patients: a priority commitment; (2) linkage with other resources, for example, vocational rehabilitation, and so on; (3) functional integrity: provision in the community of the full range of functions that are associated with institutional care; (4) individually tailored treatment; (5) cultural relevance and specificity: programs tailored to the realities of local communities; (6) specially trained staff attuned to the unique survival problems of mentally disabled clients living in noninstitutionalized settings; (7) hospital liaison: public or private beds; (8) internal evaluation.

The problem at hand is how to move states like Massachusetts from their current situation of half-filled institutions and inappropriately and underserved community-based clients to a fully community-based model incorporating the eight key program elements.

III. AVAILABLE OPTIONS

Option 1: Don't try. Discontinue deinstitutionalization—devote scarce resources to upgrading institutions.

■ *Pro:* This option has appeal for those who doubt the potential for growth of mentally disabled individuals and who, due to concern or contempt, want them off community streets. It is administratively simpler, leaving the state in complete control. However, it is likely to be more costly because community-based programs can utilize federal funding sources such as SSI and Medicaid.

■ *Con:* Research offers strong support that large institutions reduce individualization, thereby decreasing opportunity for ego development necessary for the establishment of independent functioning. Current concern for civil liberties will not tolerate this option, particularly in regard to the mentally ill.

Continued

POLICY-PRACTICE CASE 4
(continued)

Option 2: Develop a total community-care system incorporating the eight key program elements using POS.

- *Pro:* A major criticism of POS has been that the state loses control and is dominated by providers. However, this has largely been due to a lack of state planning, an abundance of direct-service oriented and trained personnel versus management-trained personnel, and a state "inferiority complex." These deficiencies can be altered. State legislatures must be persuaded to continue to provide funds to support institutional care as well as new funds for the development of community services. Once community settings are in place, institutional expenditures can be converted to community expenditures, and further new funds can be discontinued. This interim support of two systems provides the hiatus needed for important planning efforts. Administrative personnel can be retrained and direct-service personnel phased out. Liquidating property assets, converting direct-service expenditures into POS monies, provides the state with buying power it need not be afraid to exercise; community mental health centers and other financially distressed community-service settings will welcome state funding.

- *Con:* Community programs, exemplified by community mental health centers, reject the chronically mentally disabled as "unrewarding." Community residents reject the mentally disabled out of fear and disgust and concerns about property devaluation. Although some programs may welcome state funding, delayed payment creates prohibitive cash-flow problems.

Option 3: Develop a community-care system incorporating the eight key elements using POS but reserve a residual role for small, regionally located, state institutions for the treatment of violent mentally ill individuals. The proposed facilities would be privately managed and staffed. Develop a limited number of direct-service community programs under other public auspices such as municipal hospitals and state university–sponsored settings. Staff them with transferred institutional personnel.

- *Pro:* This option is particularly suited to the mentally ill. Violent patients frequently cannot safely be treated in community-hospital settings. Presence of small, secure institutions in each region will provide more humane, cost-effective care than will preserving and maintaining large institutions for this purpose. The rationale for private administration, as for POS versus direct services, rests on the assumption that personnel currently serving in the state institutions are so imbued with the institutional practices that suppress client development that they would simply recreate those negative practices in the proposed institutions. Literature describing successful retraining of institutional personnel into community settings refers to early deinstitutionalization efforts. Most of the best personnel have now left the state systems. Private community programs are fiercely resisting incorporating the remaining state personnel, even the professionals. However, because unions are strong and have influence with state legislators, and out of a sense of fairness, employee concerns about jobs and retirement benefits must be attended to. Three options may meet the needs of state personnel while preserving the state's policy of attrition: (1) early retirement benefits, (2) training and transfer to other state positions, (3) training and transfer to community settings under other public auspices. The latter option is designed for those who are vested and lack mobility. It is hoped exposure to more privatelike administration without civil service protection will encourage either positive change or resignation.

■ *Con:* Any residual institutional role is dangerous because it will be overutilized. The incentives needed to attract private management and professional staff for the proposed secure facilities would outweigh any cost effectiveness smaller facilities would provide. The assumption that all state personnel are recalcitrant and "untherapeutic" is unfair and untrue.

Recommendation: Choose Option 2 for the mentally retarded and Option 3 for the mentally ill.

Rationale: Although deinstitutionalization is a goal for both the mentally retarded and the mentally ill, differences in the nature of their disabilities and in existing funding sources call for differences in policy.

Mental retardation, by and large, is a stable condition. Research has shown that individualized educative efforts can significantly improve the functioning of many retarded children and adults. To encourage individualized growth, in 1972 the federal government authorized Title XIX reimbursement for small, fifteen-bed facilities that supply occupational, socialization, and physical therapy, as well as psychological, social work, medical, and dental services. The funding provision for these facilities under Title XIX in conjunction with the relatively stable condition of mental retardation permits planning for a totally contracted community-care system. The ICF/MRs are frequently the first step for many retarded individuals to less restrictive settings such as group homes and supervised apartments. Much of the success of currently functioning ICF/MRs and group homes is due to the intense vigilance and advocacy of the parents of retarded individuals.

The mentally ill, by contrast, have few if any advocates (families are often nonexistent for one reason or another), lack federal support for settings comparable to the ICF/MRs (in fact, if more than 50 percent of a nursing home's residents are found to be mentally disabled, federal support ceases), and suffer from a frequently fluctuating disease process requiring a range of different treatment methods. As a result, standby inpatient beds, as noted in the eight key program elements, must be available, and some of these beds must be in a secure setting to protect others from violent patients and suicidal patients from themselves.

Continued

POLICY-PRACTICE CASE 4
(continued)

The personnel issue is the same in both cases, and the recommendation described applies to both.

IV. IMPLEMENTATION FACTORS

How can legislators be persuaded to continue to support both an institutional system and development of community-based services? They must be impressed with the horrors of a poorly planned deinstitutionalization process. Plenty of examples exist, probably even locally. Use them to gain crucial planning time.

How can unions be persuaded to comply with an implicit policy of attrition that will no doubt be perfectly explicit to them? The state administration must impress on local legislators—that is, those whose areas are most affected by deinstitutionalization—that institutions are inhumane, anachronistic relics that must be abolished (I understand a Senator Backman has been vocal in this regard; this can be pointed out) but that the state wishes to be fair to employees caught in the middle.

DMH management should be sure to broaden the base when dealing with unions. Don't meet just with union leaders; involve rank and file and respected professionals. DMH should be sensitive to employee anxieties and committed to retraining and relocation efforts. New York State has been successful in this area and offers a good model.

What about the future? Should the state's goal be permanent dismantling of all direct-care services? No. Once the current system has been dismantled and POS has been in operation for a while, DMH should evaluate the cost effectiveness of providing direct-care services versus POS, especially for outpatient services. Prof. Barry Friedman of the Heller School at Brandeis offers an excellent analytic model to this end. It is the stigma and ingrained practices of the current state system that must be destroyed. There is no reason why DMH, instituting the proper incentives, could not rebuild a direct-care system under a new philosophy of care.

SOURCE: This case was prepared by Dr. Marcia Mabee.

the commissioner in which she provides some contextual or background material and then discusses a range of available policy options including Option 1 (discontinue deinstitutionalization), Option 2 (develop a total community-care system using POS), and Option 3 (Option 2 but with a residual role for small, regionally located, state institutions).

The policy practitioner identifies the pros and cons of these three options as a prelude to recommending that the commissioner accept Option 2 for developmentally disabled clients and Option 3 for mentally ill clients. By systematically and carefully comparing these options, she hopes to provide a technically convincing rationale to the commissioner for her recommendations.

As we discuss in this chapter, social workers need to develop skills in making these kinds of analytic comparisons of policy options because decision makers often insist on this kind of analytic reasoning before they make changes in existing policies.

TRADE-OFFS: MAKING SYSTEMATIC COMPARISONS OF THE RELATIVE MERITS OF SPECIFIC POLICY OPTIONS

To make systematic comparison of policy options, policy practitioners often proceed in a deliberate process; they identify options, select and weight criteria, and rank options and develop a decision-making matrix.[1] To further expose this analytic style of reasoning, we have selected a simple example to illustrate and demystify it. In our example, officials of an overcrowded school district weight the merits of alternative policies before selecting a preferred course of action.

Identifying Options

Policy analysts rarely feel comfortable with a single policy option because they want to compare and contrast the merits of alternative policies as a prelude to making a final selection. Someone seeking to end malnutrition in certain segments of the population might examine, for example, the merits of direct food distribution to certain persons, changes in the existing food-coupon or Food Stamps Program, and changes in the benefits of existing welfare programs to give low-income persons more funds to purchase food. These three policy options might in turn be contrasted with the effects on food consumption of an expansion of income tax credits to poor persons. By identifying these four options and perhaps others as well, the policy analyst hopes to avoid premature commitment to a specific policy before it has been contrasted with alternative ones.

The options that policy analysts sometimes examine are not alternative policies but yes-and-no options. Take the case of a state-funded social program that has never been formally evaluated. Deciding that they can no longer take its effectiveness for granted, state officials decide to subject it to a rigorous program evaluation that will determine whether the program provides sufficient benefits to merit its continuation. In this case, the options are "continue the program" and "terminate the program"—a choice that many policy analysts would hope would be made on the merits of the issue rather than because one or another political faction has the power to obtain its preferences.

Selecting and Weighting Criteria

Although policy analysts want to select a preferred or optimal policy, they cannot do so unless they identify those criteria that will be used as a basis of comparison. In simple cases, a single criterion is used; given three policy options, for example, and the single criterion of cost, the cheapest policy option would be selected. In most cases, however, analysts identify an array of criteria because several (or more) criteria must be considered in most situations. Policy analysts must often consider, for example, the criteria of administrative feasibility *and* the costs of specific policy options when addressing a specific policy problem. When more than one criterion is selected, policy analysts need to weight their relative importance.

To illustrate the selection and use of multiple criteria, let's take the example of a school district that has overcrowded schools and that has to decide whether to build more schools (Option 1) or to keep the facilities in year-round use by giving each student and each teacher three six-week breaks that are staggered during the academic year rather than the traditional eighteen-week vacation in the summer (Option 2). (By staggering the breaks, the school would be filled during each month of the year.) As they discuss this issue in a public meeting, a variety of criteria emerge. One school official believes that "cost is the most important criterion" because, he argues, "our district is strapped for funds." A leader of the teachers' union contends that the morale of many teachers will be "devastated if many teachers have to take three six-week vacations during the year rather than the traditional eighteen-week vacation in the summer"; she insists that "teacher morale" be an important criterion. Some working women with several children in schools wonder if their day-care problems will be exacerbated by the year-round option because "it will be difficult to find day-care programs that will care for our children for short six-week blocks of time at scattered points during the year." Moreover, these parents insist that "day-care considerations" be included as an important criterion.

Even this brief example suggests the sheer number of criteria that can be considered by policy analysts. When multiple criteria exist, someone has to decide which of them are most important, which are relatively trivial, and which should not be considered at all. As should be clear from this example, both the selection of criteria and their weighting are strongly influenced by value and political considerations. If the teachers' union has considerable power, for example, it is more likely than otherwise to persuade the school board to seriously consider the impact of a year-round schedule on morale of teachers. By contrast, unrepresented or powerless groups, who might be harmed in important ways by a scheduling change, may find their concerns relegated to a secondary status in policy deliberations. Let's assume, for example, that many low-income students need income that they obtain from summer jobs and that they are unlikely to be able to obtain this income if they receive six-week vacations that are scattered throughout the year. Unless someone articulated this problem who was moreover taken seriously by school board members, this economic issue might not be considered at all.

Varieties of Criteria

Some value-based criteria are illustrated by listing terms like *equality, equity, social justice,* and various freedoms such as the right to free speech and the right to privacy, the right to receive accurate and honest information, and the right to self-determination.[2] (Moral philosophers, religious leaders, the due-process clause of the Fourteenth Amendment to the Constitution, and the Bill of Rights variously discuss these value-based criteria, which we discuss in more detail in Chapter Eight.) Other consumer-outcome criteria define the effectiveness of specific policies in redressing specific social problems. In the social services, for example, persons often scrutinize the implications of various policy options for the well-being of consumers. To return to our example of the schools, one could ask, Do students learn more effectively when given a single three-month summer vacation or three six-week vacations scattered throughout the year? Of course, the extent of effective learning constitutes only a single measure of student well-being; others, such as their social and developmental well-being, could be considered as well. Still other economic criteria are reflected by terms like *efficiency* and *cost.* School board officials want to know the relative costs of the option of constructing new school buildings and the option of mandatory year-round attendance because they have scarce resources. Of course, it is relatively complicated in some analytic problems to compute the costs of various policy options. The old adage "penny-wise and pound-foolish" illustrates the reality that the selection of options that save funds in the short term is sometimes more costly than other options in the long term. In this case, a decision *not* to build more schools would bring immediate and short-term savings, but the board might find it encountered long-term costs if it had to eventually build new buildings, say, in fifteen years, when the costs of land and construction have risen dramatically. Indeed, the short-term savings of delaying construction could eventually be more than offset by the costs of the deferred construction. Costs can be difficult to assess as well because specific policy choices are often associated with relatively hidden costs. Were the school board to decide *not* to construct new buildings, it might find that teachers would demand higher salaries to compensate them for "the inconvenience of teaching on a year-round schedule."

Feasibility criteria pertain to the specific policy options, for example, their political and administrative practicality. An option might appear attractive on numerous grounds but be rejected because it could not be implemented or was not politically feasible. As one example, some persons believe that it would be wise to decriminalize certain drugs, such as cocaine, by selling them at relatively cheap prices in state-regulated stores. Many practical details could confound the administration of the new policy. If cocaine were legalized, what about countless substances such as PCP ("angel dust") and others not even yet invented? If they were legalized as well, the state-regulated stores might possess a wide assortment of mood-altering substances on its shelves. Who would fund the cost of growing or manufacturing the currently illegal drugs? Should poor persons be allowed to use their food stamps to purchase them? Could federal authorities easily override the laws in the various states that declare various mood-altering substances to be illegal? Would limits have to be established to provide ceilings on the amount of drugs that someone could purchase, or could persons obtain unlimited quantities? Could drugs in such an open market be kept from adolescents or schoolchildren—or would older friends, siblings, or even some parents supply them? Some politicians would likely decry "a policy that will corrode the morals of our youth by making drugs too accessible."

A final group are **externalities criteria,** which assess the extent a policy option has favorable or unfavorable impact on institutions or persons who appear at first glance to be unrelated to a policy. If drugs were decriminalized, including hallucinatory ones, policy analysts would have to ask whether driving accidents would markedly increase as drug use was made legal. This externality could not be dismissed as trivial because as many as 50,000 Americans die each year from the effects of driving while under the influence of alcohol—a decriminalized and accessible drug. This negative externality might be offset, however, by some positive ones. The reduced price of drugs and the increased availability in state-regulated stores would drive criminal elements, gangs, and foreign profiteers from drug dealing and would make it unnecessary for addicts to steal to support their habits.

Some analysts suggest that we combine several criteria into single measures as reflected by terms like *cost effectiveness.*[3] In cost-effectiveness studies, for example, analysts want to know which policy will yield the most benefits to consumers at the lowest cost or, to use the vernacular, provide "the most bang for the buck." One policy option may yield considerable benefit to consumers but at a prohibitive cost; another option may yield few benefits but at a low cost; and a third option may provide considerable benefits at a relatively modest cost. A policy analyst who wants a cost-effective policy would probably select the third option because it balances the twin objectives of cost and effectiveness.

Ranking Options and Developing a Decision-Making Matrix

To facilitate the selection of policies, policy analysts often construct a decision-making matrix that allows them to portray graphically the options and the criteria.[4] In our case of the school board, they want to display the two policy options (year-round attendance versus major construction of new buildings with traditional summer vacations) and four criteria (cost, teacher morale, parental day-care considerations, and students' educational achievements).

As can be seen in Table 4.1, a decision-making matrix places the options and criteria in the form of a table.

Because the school board wants to select a preferred policy, its members must rank the relative merits of two options by placing numbers in the various cells of the decision-making matrix to allow the selection of the policy option with the best score. To place scores in the various cells, however, the school board must first rank the relative importance of the four criteria across the top of the matrix. As with any rating system, some rules have to be established.[5] While they could easily have selected another scoring mechanism, they decide to rank each criterion from .001 to .999, based on their estimate of its importance to them. Moreover, they decide that the four scores, or rankings, of the criteria must add up to 1.0 to force them to decide the comparative or relative value of the various criteria. The board decides to rank cost as .50, teacher morale as .15, day-care needs of parents as .10, and student learning as .25.

By ranking the criteria in this manner, the board has decided that cost "counts" the most, that day-care needs of parents and teacher morale count the least, and that the educational needs of students receive middle-range importance. (These rankings of the criteria are placed directly beneath each of them in parentheses at the top of Table 4.2.)

The board must next rank the relative merits of each of the two policy options with respect to each of the four criteria by using some combination of research data, the opinions of experts, and their "best guesses." As in the case of the criteria, the board must develop some ranking system; it decides to rank the options from 1 (poor) to 10 (outstanding) and places these rankings in circles next to each policy option (see Table 4.2). The board rates the full-year option as 8 with respect to cost because it will be less costly than a major construction program, and it ranks the new-construction option as 3 because of the high cost of construction. By contrast, the board gives a higher

TABLE 4.1   A Decision-Making Matrix

	Criteria			
Policy Options	Cost	Teacher Morale	Day-Care Needs of Parents	Student Learning
Schedule year-round attendance with staggered vacations				
Initiate a major construction program				

TABLE 4.2. Rankings of Policy Options by Criteria

Policy Options	Cost (.50)	Teacher Morale (.15)	Day-Care Needs of Parents (.10)	Student Learning (.25)	Total
			Criteria		
Schedule year-round attendance with staggered vacations	⑧ 4	④ .6	③ .3	⑩ 2.5	7.4
Initiate a major construction program	③ 1.5	⑦ 1.05	⑧ .8	⑩ 2.5	5.85

(handwritten annotations: "ranking of criteria"; "summary score")

ranking (7) to the new-construction program than to the year-round option (4) with respect to teacher morale because most teachers want to continue to have summer vacations rather than staggered vacations. In similar fashion, the board decides that the new-construction program ranks relatively high with respect to the day-care needs of children (8) because working parents have persuaded them that it *would* be difficult to arrange day-care for children if their vacations are staggered; the year-round option receives a ranking of only 3 on this criterion. Both policy options receive the same score of 10 with respect to student learning because the board is not persuaded that either option will jeopardize that.

The board must now develop scores for each option that reflect *both* its ranking of the options with respect to the criteria (the circled scores) and the relative importance of the various criteria (the numbers in the parentheses after each criterion).[6] It adopts the simple rule of multiplying the circled score in each cell by the weight given to that criterion to reach a summary, or final score, in each cell. (The summary scores are underlined in Table 4.2.) The year-round option thus obtains a score of 4 with respect to cost (.50 × 8 = 4), while the major construction program obtains a score of 1.5 with respect to cost (.50 × 3 = 1.5). It can be seen that the year-round option obtains a higher summary score than does the construction program with respect to cost, the same score with respect to student learning, and lower scores with respect to teacher morale and to day-care needs of parents.

Which option should be selected? When the board adds the underlined scores in the various cells next to each option, it finds that the year-round option achieves a somewhat higher score (4 + .6 + .3 + 2.5 = 7.4) than does the construction option (1.5 + 1.05 + .8 + 2.5 = 5.85). The biggest difference between the two options occurred with respect to cost, partly because the board gave such importance to this criterion in its deliberations.

Of course, had the board not been quantitatively inclined, it could have made *qualitative* estimates of the rankings of the two policy options with respect to the four criteria. However, it would still have had to take into account the relative importance of the four criteria, rank the policy options with respect to the criteria, and reach a judgment about the relative merits of the two policy options.

The term *trade-offs* is frequently used to connote the process of assessing the comparative advantages of two or more policy options. In the case of the school board, the two competing options can be visualized as occupying the ends of an old-fashioned balance scale; the analyst seeks to discover which option has the most *weight*, that is, has the greatest net score on those criteria that the policy analyst has identified and weighted.[7] In the case of the board, it selects the first policy option even though it realizes that the second option is superior to the first on the criteria of the teachers' morale and the day-care needs of parents.

When reviewing this example of a decision-making matrix, it is important to dwell not on the details of the scoring rules that the school board adopted but rather on its *style* of analytic reasoning because other numeric rules could easily have been used to rank the criteria, to rank the various options, and to develop summary scores. When using an analytic style of reasoning, the policy analyst breaks the selection process into a series of sequential steps that eventually lead to an overall score of specific options. As we will discuss in more detail in Chapter Eight, the use of policy matrices or tables, such as Table 4.2, does not necessarily eliminate controversy or conflict because persons can disagree about the criteria, their relative importance or weights, and the scores of specific options on those criteria. Had they been part of the deliberations, for example, some parents might vigorously contest the board's assertion that the new-construction option was superior to the year-round option with respect to day care because the board could incorporate into the new buildings some child-care facilities. Or some teachers might have objected to the assertion that year-round schools are more harmful to teacher morale than schools with traditional summer vacations. Considerable guesswork and intuition often enter into the rankings even if some policy analysts believe that they are scientific in their approach.

When policy analysis occurs *before* a policy is enacted, as in the case of the aforementioned local school district, analysts encounter the challenge of predicting the outcomes, costs, and consequences of policies prior to their enactment; in many cases, these kinds of estimates turn out to be inaccurate. The school board could discover, to their subsequent chagrin, that they grossly underestimated the costs of a policy option or its effectiveness in redressing a social problem.

Even when data exist, they can often be disputed. Perhaps researchers had found another school district that had already adopted a year-round schedule and concluded that its teachers had decided, on balance, that they liked it. A skeptic might ask if this research was flawed; perhaps an inadequate sample of teachers was surveyed, the data-gathering instruments were inadequate, or the teachers in the other district possessed different preferences than did those in the school board's district.

DEVELOPING BROADER POLICY PROPOSALS

To this point, we have discussed techniques that policy analysts use to select specific options, but many policy proposals consist of a number of options that are bundled together into a larger proposal. We noted in Chapter Three, for example, that the woman who developed the Federal Shelter Program included in her proposal a number of policy options that included various service, funding, and licensing options. When developing these proposals, policy analysts often undertake integrating, scenario-building, support-demonstrating, and revising tasks.

A high-level official in the Kennedy and Johnson administrations once told me that persons who "take a stab" at drafting a proposal often obtain considerable power precisely because their version, although the initial one, establishes certain ideas and options that often are retained in subsequent versions. When initially configuring a proposal, a policy practitioner does not usually want to become excessively absorbed with details; the initial version should contain essential points and an overarching rationale. In the case of legislation, an initial version might contain a title, a brief preamble containing the purpose of the legislation, a discussion of various policy options that describe the content and structure of the program, and some practical administrative and budgeting details. Many policy proposals are supplemented by appendix materials that contain some fiscal and implementation details such as an estimate of the likely costs of the proposal.

Establishing a Rationale

Few proposals will succeed if decision makers do not believe an important reason exists for considering and enacting them because proposals that are perceived to be trivial are usually discarded in the push-and-pull of crowded schedules of decision makers. Either as part of a proposal or in a brief and attached statement, policy practitioners have to establish a convincing rationale at the outset of their proposal.[8] In the case of proposals that describe new policies and programs, the rationale might emphasize deficiencies of existing policies that the new policy is intended to address, such as unmet consumer needs, gaps or omissions in existing services, or the ineffectiveness of existing services in addressing an important social need. When new service approaches are proposed, framers of proposals often specify the innovative or creative nature of their proposal.[9] Perhaps it uses an innovative-service approach to addressing the needs of certain clients by transferring techniques that are currently used with other populations or problems. (Someone in a mental health clinic could propose to use biofeedback technology, which has traditionally been used in medical settings, in stress-reduction programs.) Perhaps an innovative technique is used to provide outreach services to a population that currently does not seek or use a specific service. Perhaps an innovative method of linking together the services of different agencies is identified, such as linking schools, hospitals, and mental health clinics in a specific region to address the substance-abuse problems of adolescents. Perhaps new kinds of staff will be used in a program.

Some innovative policies and programs rest on the kinds of research and conceptual work that we discussed in Chapter Two. Someone may propose targeting services on some specific population that is particularly at risk of developing specific problems, such as children whose parents have severe substance-abuse problems. Perhaps an innovative program draws on research showing that persons who lack supportive ties to family and community resources are most likely to develop specific kinds of problems; in such cases, innovative services to link persons to support systems might be developed.

Or perhaps research on cultural and ethnic factors suggests that innovative kinds of services are needed for specific subgroups in the population, such as a different approach to help Spanish-speaking women address substance-abuse problems or to help black youth in inner-city schools to learn safe-sex practices to slow the spread of AIDS.

Linking the Proposal to a Theory of Causation

We can return full circle to our discussion of social problems in Chapter Two. Because most policy proposals purport to address specific problems, they should not only refer to these problems but demonstrate that the policy remedies are relevant to the causes of the presenting policy problem. Take the case of the school board; its proposed policy—the year-round option—makes little sense if it is not linked to some analysis of the problem of "school overcrowding." Is this a truly serious problem? Do trend data suggest that it is getting more serious? Do past and projected demographic data about birth rates and population movement in and out of the area suggest that it will become more serious? Or take the issue of battered women that we discussed in Chapter Three. A proposal to develop federal subsidies for shelters would obtain more support if its framers analyzed the problem of wife battering in the context of its incidence and causes. Were the proposal to purport to provide *preventive* services to decrease current rates of spousal abuse, its framers would have to link their proposed remedies to prevailing research and theory about the causes of the problem.

Integrating Tasks

We discussed some specific policy options earlier in this chapter, but policy practitioners often do not confine themselves to merely listing a single option that they have selected from a number of them. Many proposals contain *clusters* of options that, when taken together, describe a new social program, an innovation, or a change in existing policy. As we noted in Chapter Three, for example, a policy practitioner who developed legislation for federal funding of shelters for battered women would have to define a range of policy options in the proposal from the list of seven policy issues that were described in Table 3.1.

One method of integrating proposals is to identify with clarity the administrative and decision-making mechanisms to be used to allow them to be implemented in expeditious fashion.[10] Take the example of a grant proposal, which an agency executive produces, that describes a new program that the agency wants funded by a foundation. The foundation will want to know who is charged with the ultimate responsibility of administering the project, what goals or objectives provide a direction for the various activities within the project, and what central priorities exist in the project that provide it with some internal focus. Moreover, it would expect some logical linking of the rationale or purpose of the proposal and the policies, procedures, and budgets that were outlined in it. If a proposal was written to establish outreach services to a neglected and foreign-speaking population, for example, but no mention was made of the need to hire bilingual staff, the foundation staff might wonder if the goals could be achieved.

Proposals must also be integrated or meshed with existing institutions, laws, and programs. New programs or procedures do not exist in a vacuum but must coexist with existing programs, procedures, institutions, and laws. When writing proposals, practitioners should ask whether coordinating mechanisms are needed, whether existing agencies and programs are likely to cooperate with new ones, and whether certain goals of a new program will be frustrated by certain policies or procedures of existing programs. Will those persons who must approve the policy proposal fear that it intrudes on similar services and programs that are already provided by other agencies and programs?

Many policy proposals then contain a variety of materials and content. They contain some policies that define the objectives, goals, or purpose of a proposal; instrumental policies that define how those objectives, goals, or purposes will be implemented; and policies that define budgetary, decision-making, and implementing details. Some proposals discuss certain theoretical and research materials about the nature of the social or institutional problems that are addressed by the proposal, as well as a proposed strategy to evaluate the policy after it has been implemented.

Scenario-Building Tasks

Often as an appendix or accompanying document, proposal writers often have to convince readers that their proposal is not only conceptually sound and important but also that it will *actually* achieve the major objectives that its framers identified.[11] Many readers of proposals are justifiably cynical because they have seen so many impressive proposals that failed during their implemention.

We should note that most policy proposals contain or are supplemented by materials that discuss the details of their implementation. A proposal to begin a new pilot or demonstration program in an agency, for example, may contain details about timetables or schedules to be followed when beginning it; methods to be used to evaluate it; budgetary details about supplies, salaries, and facilities; and methods to be used to publicize it.

Writers can convince readers that their proposals will be effective by developing plausible scenarios in which these implementation strategies assume a prominent part. They can develop time lines or schedules that show, for example, what the project will look like three, six, nine, and twelve months after its enactment in terms of cost, services rendered, staff hired, and other program details. They can provide flowcharts to show how clients will move through a new program from intake to the completion of services. They can illustrate referral patterns from external sources to the program and from the program to outside agencies.[12]

Scenario building can help the framers of proposals identify possible errors in them at the outset. It is common, for example, to believe that a project can achieve greater results than its staff and resources can deliver— something that funders, such as foundations, are adept at spotting. The framer of a proposal may underestimate the time it takes to get a project into operation, to publicize the program, or to make linkages with other agencies whose programs intersect with it.

Of course, operating programs often work differently than their framers intended, as unexpected problems and obstacles emerge. The framers of proposals can identify error-detection devices that they will use during their implementation, such as evaluations, monitoring, outside reviews, and oversight by specific bodies such as advisory groups or boards. Indeed, many foundations and government funders require that proposals contain a plan for evaluating new programs after they have been implemented—a topic we discuss in more detail in Chapter Thirteen.[13]

Seeking and Establishing Support for the Proposal

Policy practitioners have to decide where to route their proposals in the first instance. In the case of legislative policies, the answers are often obvious because legislative aides, as well as government officials, often provide advice about those legislators and legislative committees who are interested in specific kinds of policies. Within relatively small agencies, proposals reach the desk of the executive director, and the director often participates in developing them. In larger bureaucracies with multiple divisions, units, and layers, proposals can take various routes. An initial sponsor is needed who can guide it to those persons who can promote it initially and during its ascent to higher authorities.

When proposals are directed to external funders, policy practitioners have to draw on the extensive literature on grant writing that provides detailed information on government, foundation, and corporate sources of fundings, which is beyond the scope of this text. Suffice it to say that many funding alternatives exist for most proposals. Some research is needed to determine which sources are appropriate for specific proposals. Once potential sources such as particular foundations or particular government agencies are identified, policy practitioners have to craft their proposal to address the issues, the information, and the requirements that particular funders desire.

Decision makers often want evidence that a proposal has widespread support, to provide further evidence of its technical merit and to demonstrate that it will not be sabotaged after its enactment.[14] Evidence of support for legislative proposals is marshaled by finding legislators who will formally sponsor them; their names are placed at the top of drafts of the proposals that are considered by legislative committees. Drafters of legislation often try to assemble a broad list of sponsors that includes persons from both parties from various regions of the state or nation and (where possible) with different perspectives and ideologies. Evidence of support for a proposal is also obtained during public testimony before legislative committees when a range of groups and persons, as well as well-known figures, support it. When submitting nonlegislative proposals, such as a proposal for an innovative program, to funding sources, such as foundations, drafters of proposals often attach letters of support or endorsement from executives in other agencies, experts, and community leaders to attest to the importance of the proposal and to the ability of the proposal writer to implement it.

Revising Tasks

Proposals rarely emerge full-blown from first drafts but are successively revised. In the legislative process, amendments are made to bills as they are "marked up" in successive committee deliberations. Indeed, legislative committees often publish copies of marked-up bills that show precisely how they altered a prior version; lines are drawn through excised words and new provisions are italicized so that persons can see precisely how a committee altered the original version. Grant proposals, which are policy and program statements to foundations, government authorities, and other funding bodies, are often revised successively as they emerge from "think pieces" to final versions. In some cases, for example, the framer will write a one-page version and circulate it to other persons including a staff person in a foundation or government agency. Another and succeeding version—say, four or five pages in length—will be circulated for comments to various persons as a prelude to developing a finished and more lengthy version.

Considerable skill is needed to translate complex ideas into readable prose. Excessive jargon and verboseness, complex sentences, and poor syntax needlessly diminish interest in a specific proposal.[15] Many decision makers, such as legislators, lack a technical understanding of specific programs and issues and are disinclined to read complex and lengthy materials. Policy practitioners can sometimes err, of course, in the opposite direction; if their proposal is too brief and fails to address important issues, their work may be discarded as superficial. Drafters of policy proposals have to skillfully use analytic, political, and value-clarification skills in tandem, as they develop policy proposals. Perhaps political considerations dictate leaving certain topics out, using certain words rather than others, and developing a title for the proposal that makes it more appealing to certain persons.

POLICY ANALYSIS: PUTTING IT ALL TOGETHER

Policy analysts usually aim to construct proposals to articulate their ideas about changing existing policies. We can visually conceptualize the proposal-building process as the melding or combining of concepts and subjects that we have discussed in the last three chapters (see Figure 4.1). We identify four overlapping zones. Zone 1 emphasizes the theoretical and conceptual tasks that we discussed in Chapter Two. By drawing on relevant research in the social sciences, for example, the policy practitioner hopes to ground a policy proposal in existing knowledge of specific social problems, interventions, and populations. In Zone 2, the policy practitioner identifies a range of policies, as we discussed in Chapter Three and this chapter, and then proceeds to compare and contrast policy options as a prelude to selecting some of them for the final proposal. Policy practitioners have to construct a completed proposal and present it to decision makers, whether legislators, government officials, or agency executives. Such proposals often emerge only after an extensive process of consultation and revision (Zone 3). Finally, as we discussed in this chapter, the policy practitioner has to develop a proposal that includes some logistical and practical details such as its administrative structure and implementation strategies (Zone 4).

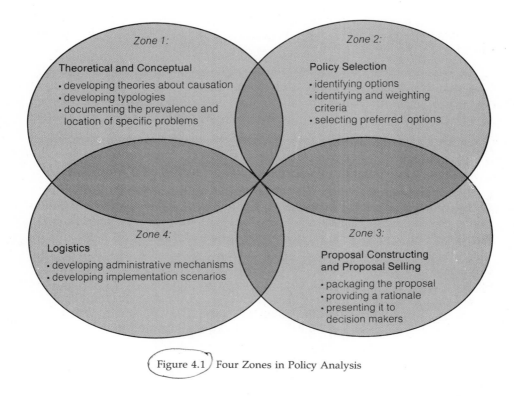

Zone 1:

Theoretical and Conceptual

- developing theories about causation
- developing typologies
- documenting the prevalence and location of specific problems

Zone 2:

Policy Selection

- identifying options
- identifying and weighting criteria
- selecting preferred options

Zone 4:

Logistics

- developing administrative mechanisms
- developing implementation scenarios

Zone 3:

Proposal Constructing and Proposal Selling

- packaging the proposal
- providing a rationale
- presenting it to decision makers

Figure 4.1 / Four Zones in Policy Analysis

LINKING ANALYTIC SKILLS TO OTHER POLICY SKILLS

As we noted when discussing the policy-practice cases at the beginnings of the preceding two chapters, policy practitioners often have to couple analytic skills with political, interactional, and value-clarification ones. Recall that Policy-Practice Case 4 provides a memorandum that a social worker had prepared for the Commissioner of the Department of Mental Health with respect to policies to guide the deinstitutionalization of developmentally disabled and mentally ill clients in her state.

She notes, for example, political skills are needed to deal with opposition that will stem from unions who oppose dismantling of institutions because many of their members, who currently work in them, could lose their jobs. She does not discuss interactional skills, but one can imagine how the commissioner would need them in the extended negotiations, committee deliberations, and personal discussions with legislators, the governor, and many government officials. Value-clarification skills are needed as well. What ethical dangers lurk behind the use of purchase of service, that is, extensive use of private and profit-oriented providers who would seek to provide community-based services of various kinds? Might some of them place profits ahead of the provision of quality services?

Clearly then, analytic skills need to be teamed with other skills when developing and seeking support for specific policy proposals. We will argue in Chapter Ten that some policy practitioners make the false assumption that they can rely exclusively on a single skill, such as analytic skill, in their practice of policy.

SUMMARY

Policy analysts possess a noble objective: They want the emerging techniques of the social sciences and economics, as well as disciplined and careful analysis, to provide rational solutions to various policy problems. Nor should their quest be dismissed because politicians, decision makers, and professionals have often proceeded with scant attention to existing research or to systematic analysis of problems and their causes.

In the succeeding four chapters, however, we will discuss various, "nonrational" components of policy-making, such as political, interactional, and value-based ones. Like it or not, policy-making in the real world is often not dominated by technical or policy-analysis experts because realities like power, old-boy networks, vested interests, and ideology often shape policy choices.

QUESTIONS FOR DISCUSSION

1. The solution to a policy problem is profoundly shaped by the selection and weighting of criteria. Discuss referring to the example of the school board in this chapter or referring to Policy-Practice Case 4 at the start of this chapter.

2. Discuss some kinds of criteria that often recur in policy analysis.

3. In many cases, the criteria that are used by policy practitioners conflict with one another, i.e., an option that ranks high with respect to one criterion can rank low with respect to another criterion. Take the examples of cost and quality of services and discuss how these criteria often conflict in the human services system.

4. Develop your own decision-making matrix with respect to a policy issue or problem in a social agency with which you are familiar. Try to score the options using the technique discussed in this chapter. What predicaments and uncertainties did you encounter?

5. Policy analysts often encounter the challenge of predicting how specific policy options will fare before they are enacted and implemented. Discuss

this statement with reference to either the case of the school board (see Table 4.1) or Policy-Practice Case 4.

6. Play devil's advocate with respect to either the case of the school board (see Table 4.1) or Policy-Practice Case 4. Develop a rationale for an entirely different conclusion or recommendation in these cases, whether by selecting different criteria or options or by scoring the options in different fashion. What does this exercise tell us about the limitations of policy analysis?

7. Discuss some major challenges that policy practitioners confront when developing broader policy proposals that they wish to present to decision makers of funders.

SUGGESTED READINGS

Overviews of Analytic Approaches to Policy Making

Brian Hogwood and Lewis Gunn, *Policy Analysis for the Real World* (London: Oxford University Press, 1984).

Carl Patton and David Sawicki, *Basic Methods of Policy Analysis and Planning* (Englewood Cliffs, N.J.: Prentice-Hall, 1986).

Applications to Social Welfare

Kent Portney, *Approaching Public Policy Analysis: An Introduction to Policy and Program Research* (Englewood Cliffs, N.J.: Prentice-Hall, 1986), pp. 111–112.

Critical Discussions

John Dryzek and Brian Ripley, "The Ambitions of Policy Science," *Policy Studies Review*, 7 (Summer 1988): 705–719.

William Dunn, "Methods of the Second Type: Coping with the Wilderness of Conventional Policy Analysis," *Policy Studies Review*, 7 (Summer 1988): 720–727.

Martin Rein, "Value-Critical Policy Analysis," in Daniel Callahan and Bruce Jennings, eds., *Ethics, the Social Sciences, and Policy Analysis* (New York: Plenum Press, 1983), pp. 96–100.

Charles Wolf, "Ethics and Policy Analysis," in Joel Fleishman, Lance Liebman, and Mark Moore, eds., *Public Duties: The Moral Obligations of Government* (Cambridge, Mass.: Harvard University Press, 1981), pp. 131–141.

Developing Broader Proposals

Mary Hall, *Getting Funded: A Complete Guide to Proposal Writing*, 3rd ed. (Portland, Ore.: Continuing Education Publications of Portland State University, 1988).

Armand Lauffer, *Grantsmanship and Fund Raising* (Beverly Hills, Ca.: Sage Publications, 1983).

Craig Smith and Eric Skjei, *Getting Grants* (New York: Harper and Row, 1980).

NOTES

1. The analytical process of identifying and selecting options is discussed by Edward Quade, *Analysis for Public Decisions*, 2nd ed. (New York: Elsevier North Holland, 1982); Alfred Kahn, *Theory and Practice of Social Planning* (New York: Russell Sage, 1969); Yeheskel Dror, *Venture in Policy Sciences* (New York: Elsevier North Holland, 1971); Robert Mayer and Ernest Greenwood, *The Design of Social Policy Research* (Englewood Cliffs, N.J.: Prentice-Hall, 1980); and Brian Hogwood and Lewis Gunn, *Policy Analysis for the Real World* (London: Oxford University Press, 1984).

2. Bruce Jansson, *Theory and Practice of Social Welfare Policy* (Belmont, Ca.: Wadsworth Publishing Co., 1984), pp. 51–52.

3. See Tony Tripodi, Phillip Fellin, and Irwin Epstein, *Differential Social Program Evaluation* (Itasca, Ill.: Peacock, 1978), pp. 101–104.

4. See, for example, the "decision matrix technique" of Robert Francoeur in *Biomedical Ethics: A Guide to Decision Making* (New York: John Wiley, 1983), pp. 127–137.

5. Ibid., pp. 127–137.

6. Ibid., pp. 127–137.

7. Tichy portrays competing policy options on the ends of a balance throughout *Organization for Primary Health Care* (New York: Praeger, 1977).

8. Craig Smith and Eric Skjei, *Getting Grants* (New York: Harper and Row, 1980), pp. 173–181.

9. Ibid., pp. 173–181.

10. Armand Lauffer, *Grantsmanship and Fund Raising* (Beverly Hills, Ca.: Sage Publications, 1983), pp. 238–246.

11. Ibid., pp. 80–84.

12. Ibid., pp. 236–246.

13. Mary Hall, *Getting Funded: A Complete Guide to Proposal Writing*, 3rd ed. (Portland, Ore.: Continuing Education Publications of Portland State University, 1988), pp. 127–144.

14. Smith and Skjei, *Getting Grants*, p. 152.

15. Marya Holcombe, *Writing for Decision Makers* (Belmont, Ca.: Lifetime Learning Publications, 1981).

PART III

■

Nonrational Components of Policy Practice: Political, Interactional, and Value-Clarification Skills

If discussion in the preceding three chapters emphasized some analytic techniques and approaches to developing social welfare policies, the four chapters in Part III discuss some nonrational components of social welfare policy. In Chapters Five and Six, we discuss concepts like power, assertiveness, force-field analysis, salience, stakes, strategy, and campaigns. Because policy is a binding and collective phenomenon, people often have to overcome formidable opposition to specific proposals from others who do not want to be "bound" in specific ways, whether because their interests will be adversely affected, they oppose a new policy on value-based or ideological grounds, or they believe them to be defective on technical grounds. The development and use of power often enable people to obtain their policy preferences in specific settings.

Policy practitioners often have to use persuasive techniques to entice other persons to accept specific policies. We discuss argumentation and debates in Chapter Seven as strategies for securing support for specific policies. We also note that policy practitioners sometimes seek to obtain support for a policy by drawing other people into a consensual and participatory process where group process itself becomes a tool for developing and rallying support behind policies. We discuss some credibility-building strategies, as well, in Chapter Seven.

We discuss value-clarification and ethical-reasoning skills in Chapter Eight. Policy practice is "shot through" with value considerations at virtually every turn in the road. People have to identify those values that are germane to the selection of policy options, such as social justice, equity, and preservation of the freedom or self-determination of others. When engaging in politics, people have to wrestle with ethical issues such as whether it is correct to lie, to tell partial truths, and to exaggerate the merits of a specific policy. As we discuss in Chapter Eight, resolution of these kinds of ethical issues requires us to engage in ethical reasoning.

CHAPTER 5

■

Political Skills in Policy Practice: Power and Assertiveness

Policy analysts often contend that "might does not make right," but their vision of a rational decision-making process, one largely purged of political and value considerations, has often been ignored in legislative, government, community, or agency settings. In the next two chapters, we examine the role of politics in policy-making. If power realities often shape decisions, effective policy practitioners cannot pretend they do not exist; indeed, they need to develop skills in the give-and-take of the political process, no matter the setting. In this chapter, we discuss the nature and varieties of power and the issue of assertiveness, as a prelude to discussing methods of developing political strategy in the next chapter.

A POLICY-PRACTICE CASE FROM THE HUMAN SERVICES SYSTEM

The need for political skills in policy practice is illustrated in Policy-Practice Case 5, where a social work intern tries to develop an innovative program in a mental health agency. She notes that the agency, which considers itself to be an advocate for the mental health needs of children, lacks a program to help children whose parents have been institutionalized because of psychiatric problems. She hopes to obtain approval for an eight-week crisis model of services to these children but soon realizes that she encounters numerous political barriers. Would private-practice psychiatrists and staff in area hospitals, who admit patients to mental hospitals, cooperate with the new program by making referrals to it? Would officials within the agency support a preventive program when they believe existing funds should be devoted to programs to address the existing mental problems of children and adults? Would the executive director, who wishes to use existing resources to eliminate a waiting list, oppose the innovation on grounds that it diverts funds from this priority?

As she ponders these kinds of questions, the social work intern examines her own power resources such as her ties to her preceptor, Mr. Jones. She thinks about how she can best present the proposal to him to increase the likelihood that he will support it. She subsequently discusses with him a two-phase political strategy to obtain support for the proposal to lead (she hopes) to eventual approval of the project by the executive director and the board of the agency.

This policy-practice case, which emphasizes political barriers to the acceptance of a new policy, is not unusual because opposition often exists to new policies in agency, community, and legislative settings. Had the intern been unable to think and act in political terms, she would most certainly have failed to obtain approval for this proposal.

A POLITICAL PARADIGM

We enumerated the kinds of questions that policy analysts often ask at the outset of Chapter Two. In similar fashion, we present a political paradigm, which identifies the kinds of questions that people with political perspectives often pose when they confront specific policy problems (Table 5.1, p. 135).

Unlike policy analysts, who select options that are preferable on technical grounds, people who use a political paradigm usually do not want to waste their scarce political resources and time on losing issues when instead they might invest them in winning ones.

Because of their preoccupation with power, people who ascribe to the political paradigm devote considerable time to calculations of political feasibility; they examine patterns of support and opposition that are associated with specific issues, options, and proposals not only before they begin but also during the course of deliberations. By making these calculations, they hope not only to assess whether a proposal can be enacted but also to develop political strategy to enable them to outmaneuver likely opponents.

A political paradigm differs markedly from the analytic approaches that were discussed in the preceding four chapters. If the analyst wants to discover technically superior solutions to problems by using quantitative and analytic techniques, the adherent of the political approach wants to understand existing political realities as a basis for selecting feasible options and developing effective political strategy. If the analyst assumes that "the truth will win out," the politician assumes that "might will prevail." If analysts devote most of their time to technical tasks, political practitioners devote considerable time gauging political realities, developing power, and implementing political strategy.

POLICY-PRACTICE CASE 5

A SOCIAL WORK INTERN TRIES TO DEVELOP A PREVENTIVE PROGRAM IN A MENTAL HEALTH AGENCY

It is curious that the Mountain View Child Guidance Clinic considers itself an advocate for the mental health needs of children when it neglects the children of the psychiatrically hospitalized parent. Such children are in crisis and experiencing extreme family disequilibrium at the time of the parent's hospitalization. They need immediate assistance in understanding and dealing constructively with feelings and thoughts associated with this experience. It is preferable that this intervention occur at or near the time of the crisis, when defenses are most fluid and before maladaptive patterns of functioning have been solidified. To meet this need, I am trying to develop, as an addition to the existing structure of brief services offered by the clinic, a crisis group for children of psychiatrically hospitalized parents.

I am hoping that the program can proceed on the eight-week crisis model currently adhered to by the clinic; however, several alternatives in programming are possible. A fixed membership group composed of children experiencing the recent hospitalization of a parent could be used, with the number of children in the group to be based on demand with an upper limit of ten. Referrals and screening for the group could be accepted up to one day prior to first meeting, but, once the group has started, no new members would be added. Such groups would be offered at overlapping intervals of four weeks. Alternatively, an ongoing open-ended group with children rotating through an eight-week membership could be used so children could be accepted into a group as soon as they were referred, a strategy that would avoid any delays and limits on membership.

Implementation of this program would be based on referrals from local psychiatric hospitals. The coordination and cooperation necessary for such a program would be a landmark in the clinic's history. Although cooperative interrelations with other mental health agencies in the area is a stated goal, the clinic is openly competitive in its relationships with other child-related services. Providing this new service would add to the clinic's prestige in the community. Its success would depend on the referrals of psychiatrists who assist patients admitted to various public and private psychiatric hospitals in the area. Should the clinic bypass the authority of the physician and accept referrals directly from the social service departments, it would alienate some physicians.

Announcements could be sent to the hospitals, their social service departments, and specific physicians. The service must be offered as a support service for both the physician and the hospital.

The politics of this agency dictate, alas, that the new program not be called preventive lest funders and policymakers not favor it. Because they believe that no room exists in the budget for prevention, this program will be called crisis intervention.

Four local hospitals could be approached with announcements of the new clinic program. A follow-up phone call would add a personal touch and hopefully clinch the process. As a staff member, I would personally persuade physician–friends of its merit while soliciting membership and support.

A number of barriers frustrate change in this agency. The clinic focuses its energy on the quantity rather than the quality of services. Of primary importance to the executive director is avoidance of a waiting list. To this end, he mobilizes all forces, and any program change that would deter this aim is automatically shelved. Further, staff are usually inundated with work and so have little time to create innovative services. Similarly, the agency values efficiency in programming and expenditures. Clinic executives believe that they cannot afford to risk any revenue by applying funds to areas other than those directly funded and approved. Another barrier to innovation is disinclination of the agency staff to participate in program development, which deprives the agency of new program ideas. Staff members come to work to glean what fulfillment is available through the clients themselves but leave the business of the clinic to the bureaucracy.

I am only a student intern in this agency, but I want to get this innovation off the ground prior to the end of my field experience. Considering the nature of the agency, it is essential to introduce the change in an administratively sanctioned way through approved channels. Therefore, I initially broached the idea of the innovation to the director of outpatient services, Mr. Jones, who is my preceptor for short-term and intake cases. On first mentioning the plan, I was careful to make it appear as an idea that I had developed in the course of discussions with him. I interpreted it as consistent with comprehensive mental health care for children, an ideal he had often espoused. Underscoring the validity of the time-limited approach, which he likes, and stressing its efficiency in terms of the waiting list, I ventured to actually propose a pilot plan. He groaned and suggested that I "write it up," with no explanation as to what that meant. Rather than irritate him further, I did not mention the project for several weeks. I then told my regular field instructor that I was discussing with Mr. Jones a new program for children of hospitalized patients, and I received her approval to use this as a learning experience in program design.

Several weeks later, I found that Mr. Jones had totally forgotten my plan. But, in further discussion, he expressed strong interest and even brainstormed an initial strategy with me that would allow the innovation to gradually gain support in Mountain View Child Guidance. He argued that we should develop a two-phase strategy. In Phase 1, I would develop a pilot project as a student intern that would not need formal clearance from high-level executives or the agency board. (He would notify the executive that a student intern was establishing a pilot group-treatment program for children of institutionalized parents.) He urged a "low profile" during this initial period. Subsequent to initiation of the project, he would develop a strategy for formal program proposal that would go to the executive director and (hopefully) eventually to the board, a strategy that would require formal

Continued

POLICY-PRACTICE CASE 5
(continued)

earmarking of agency funds for the program. He hoped that my experience in devising a pilot project would provide useful information that could be used when writing the formal proposal and making a case for it in oral presentations to the executive and the board. He concluded with the statement, "You know that you will have to do the entire program in the pilot phase. All the screening and everything." He seemed tantalized by the idea of obtaining increased service with no additional expenditure of staff time.

To date, I have succeeded in involving Mr. Jones in planning sufficiently to encourage his sense of investment in the program. I have abided by the rules of the game in recognizing his authority and decision-making powers and deemphasizing my own initiative. My short-term strategy, then, is to begin the program myself. But a number of obstacles could still interfere with program acceptance by key decision makers even during the pilot phase.

One obstacle is the issue of community coordination. Currently, the clinic engages in superficial coordination with local mental health agencies, only exchanging cases sporadically on a case-by-case basis. No clear plan exists for coordination of services. This program will necessitate an intermediate type of coordination: a case-planning coordination organized into a whole-family approach. The current fragmentation in treatment of families with a disturbed member would be a danger in this program because it would undermine the purpose of comprehensive care. What are the factors involved in this coordination process?

First is the issue of goal conflict. On the surface, there appears to be little; both the psychiatric hospitals and the clinic serve and are concerned with the mental health needs of families. But is that really the case? In fact, the hospitals view treatment of the parent–patient from a pathology model rather than a family systems perspective. In that case, they may choose to refer the child not for group but for individual treatment as an "impaired" family member. It will be important to impress on these staff members that the crisis groups that I form help the child in crisis rather than providing long-term therapy. With regard to the power relationships between agencies, the major snare seems to be the physicians' autonomy. The administrators of area psychiatric hospitals may also perceive the group for children as highlighting their own program deficiencies and choose instead to provide a similar service themselves.

At present, the agencies do not consider themselves to be interdependent. Instead, they coexist in separate realms of the psychiatric community and rarely communicate. More positively, though, they may cooperate with this project not only because of the obvious needs of the children but also because child and adult agencies are in fact complementary services in the community that do not usually compete for the same clientele.

To alleviate some of the tension between agencies and to facilitate the common goal of improved community mental health, I will plan individual visits to each hospital's social services department. Possibly I will be invited to present this program to the monthly medical staff meeting, a direct encounter with most of the staff physicians. In addition, I will invite representatives of each hospital to the clinic for an orientation and open house, which should improve relationships between clinic and hospital and emphasize the community nature of the project.

Within the clinic itself, a political process will ensue in the initiation of this program. When Mr. Jones seeks its official approval, he must submit to the medical director for confirmation; he in turns takes it to the executive committee for approval, and they then present it to the board of directors for final approval. However, because Mr. Jones is the most powerful person in the agency, his approval should lead to its acceptance. A complicating factor is the director of training, Ida Brown. To be candid, she does not particularly like Mr. Jones and often opposes any proposals initiated by him.

She may interfere in the decision-making process by pushing for a nondecision; that is, she may suggest the plan be initiated only after lengthy study or pending location of special sources of external funding. Further, many in the agency focus on the child as patient, a focus that clashes with the program's preventive mission.

I also see several other groupings developing. One is composed of the senior administrator and the chief of program development (also the director of support services). These two men are allied in their unstated mission of increasing clinic prestige and influence in the community. They will probably support the program from their positions of stated commitment to enriching the quality of service available to the community. This would appear reasonable and underscore the senior administrator's interest in the efficient business operation of the clinic.

The executive director himself will probably support the program in deference to Mr. Jones, to whom he defers on all issues pertaining to the outpatient part of the agency. The outpatient service functions virtually independently from the day treatment and other components of the agency.

The medical director is also a figurehead, whose medical degree is valued by the agency. He will most assuredly remain neutral lest he find himself in the middle of a political battle. He appears to have little power in the agency.

The board of directors also has little power in this agency. They are most concerned with what mural is painted on which wall and how chairs are grouped in the waiting room. Program development is not their expertise, and they usually abide agreeably with decisions made by the executive director.

In implementing this program, Mr. Jones will want a strong evaluation component. A before-and-after study can easily be incorporated into the proposal. The instrument used requires ratings of the child by parent and by therapist. Further, evaluation of parents is possible. Consider a parent whose spouse has just been hospitalized and is left to care for the children alone. Such a parent would almost certainly benefit from receiving some group services.

Continued

POLICY-PRACTICE CASE 5
(continued)

In the future, I see this program as an integral part of the clinic's services, if it can survive pilot and approval stages. The children served during their first experience with a parent's hospitalization may choose to return themselves for assistance at the time of a rehospitalization. And children who have experienced numerous parental hospitalizations will be able to compare previous episodes with the one eased by clinic services. We may then see self-referrals by children and families, reducing the need for referrals by physicians.

Another possibility is the development of similar programs within the area hospitals themselves as part of their social services to families. In this case, the clinic could serve those children whose parents have been recently discharged from the hospital, that is, after the hospitals have discontinued services. An enlargement of the program is therefore possible to assist the returning parent to readjust to his or her family.

Mr. Jones wants me to assist him in writing the formal proposal after my pilot project has been in operation for five months. The project has made me realize that good clinical skills need to be supplemented by program design and legitimation skills. How else can social workers develop and institutionalize innovative services?

SOURCE: This case is adapted from one developed by Stacy Stern, M.S.W. Names and locations have been altered.

IN DEFENSE OF POLITICS

Policy analysts often declare that persons who are preoccupied with political realities are opportunistic, power-hungry, or wedded to special interests. Some truth often exists in various of these assertions, but they obscure some of the important functions of politics in policy-making. Before we discuss some of these functions, let's define the word *politics* with more precision. Some people equate it with government policy-making; indeed, one part of Webster's definition declares it to be "the policies and aims of a government [and] the conduct and contests of political parties."[1] Certainly, these government and political party functions belong within a definition of politics, but what about "wheeling and dealing" in other settings such as social agencies, professional associations, and communities? Webster comes to our assistance by also including in his definition "the political connections or beliefs of a person [and] the plotting or scheming of those seeking personal power, glory, position, or the like."[2] Although Webster's use of words like *plotting* and *scheming* suggests a certain disdain for such activity, he usefully notes that politics includes power-related struggles in *any* setting.

At the risk of rewriting the dictionary, let us hazard our own definition;

TABLE 5.1   A Political Paradigm

Deciphering the Distribution of Power with Respect to an Issue

- What persons, interests, and factions are likely to participate in deliberations associated with a specific option or proposal, and what are their respective power resources?
- What are their likely positions on a specific policy proposal, and how strongly do they hold them?

Identifying Personal Political Stakes in an Issue

- What are the political benefits and risks that I will encounter if I participate in the deliberations that are associated with a specific issue, option, or proposal?
- Should I be a leader, a follower, or a bystander?

Deciphering the Political Feasibility of Specific Policy Options

- What patterns of opposition and support are likely to be associated with specific policy options?
- Which of them, on balance, should be supported?

Developing Political Strategy

- What power resources do I (or my allies) currently possess that are relevant to the deliberations of this option or proposal?
- What power resources might I (or my allies) develop that will be relevant to the deliberations of this option or proposal?
- What strategies will we use in a specific and upcoming time frame?

Revising Strategy

- What changes in strategy are suggested by the evolving political realities, including the likely "moves" of opponents?
- What changes in my role are suggested by the evolving political realities?

politics represents "efforts by persons in a range of government and non-government settings to secure their policy wishes by developing and using power resources." When defined in this manner, politics becomes relevant not only to highly placed officials but also to *anyone* who tries to influence the selection of policies in a specific setting.

It is difficult to imagine a world where politics does not exist because political processes are endemic to social discourse. Were such a world to exist, people who lacked the formal authority to develop policy positions would have no recourse but to obey existing policies or to seek remedies through other means such as force. In dictatorships, of course, opposing parties and politicians face these grim prospects, but democratic regimes allow interests, factions, and individuals to occupy legitimate roles in policy deliberations even if some of them possess greater power resources than others.

The political process provides a method of addressing the many value-laden issues in policy-making that defy resolution by using analytic and technical methodology. When people possess different values or reach different conclusions, they can resolve their differences by seeking to shape policy choices in the give-and-take of policy deliberations. Some policy analysts claim to be purely objective or scientific in their approach, but even a casual examination of their methodology reveals many value-laden choices.[3] To illustrate some of the nonrational components of policy analysis, we can return to our discussion of criteria, options, results, and decision-making rules. Recall from Chapter Four that these criteria are those objectives, such as efficiency, effectiveness, and equality, that are used, singly and in tandem, to evaluate policies. Because criteria are those objectives that specific persons value, they are not selected in the first instance by rational or scientific techniques.[4] Officials who emphasize the cost or efficiency of policies, for example, are less likely to emphasize their effectiveness or adequacy—or their effects in redistributing resources to poor people from affluent people. Conservatives, liberals, and radicals often disagree about the selection of criteria; when assessing specific welfare-reform proposals, for example, radicals are less likely to be concerned about the cost of the proposal than are conservatives and are more likely to favor policy options that redistribute resources to poor people. Of course, as noted earlier in the last chapter, policy analysts can use multiple criteria, but they still have to weight their relative importance in either quantitative or qualitative terms; such weighting, like the choice of criteria in the first instance, is strongly influenced by values.

The selection of options is similarly shaped by the values and interests of policy analysts. When complex issues arise, such as the feminization of poverty, many policy strategies can be identified and analyzed—including various revisions of the AFDC Program, revisions of the tax code, children's allowances, job-creation programs, and policies to increase and enforce support payments of absentee fathers. In turn, an infinite number of permutations within these broad strategies can be identified; for example, the AFDC Program can be revised in hundreds of ways that variously describe different levels of payment, different amounts of day-care subsidies, and different kinds of job training. Because it is impossible to examine all possible policy options, people can only choose some of them for intensive analysis, but this selection process is profoundly shaped by values. Conservatives, for example, would probably not even choose to examine policy options to radically increase the level of payment to AFDC women, to guarantee them extended and free day care, or to provide them with long-term training. Indeed, it is interesting when examining the selection of a policy to identify policies that were not even or seriously considered by policy analysts.

Even when people agree on the options, as well as criteria, they may reach dramatically different conclusions about which policy option to select. Because policies are often selected *before* strong evidence exists, considerable guesswork is needed to predict their likely cost or effectiveness. People who are predisposed against an option are less likely to give it the benefit of the doubt, in contrast to its defenders who often discount negative possibilities.

Even this brief discussion suggests that policy analysis, far from reducing policy selection to a value-free exercise, is riddled with value-laden choices. Moreover, the tangible interests of specific persons and groups often shape their positions independently of their values or analytic judgments. The political process provides one mechanism for resolving these kinds of choices in the give-and-take of deliberations; because some people possess different values than others, they can use the political process to inject their perspectives about criteria, options, and preferred policies—an option that would not necessarily be present if we ceded policy choices to a group of cloistered experts.

THE NATURE OF POWER

If politics is both inevitable and, at least in some cases, beneficial, policy practitioners have to understand concepts like power and develop skills in using it. We can begin by discussing the elusive concept of power, which lies at the heart of politics. Power is difficult to define or to observe, as is illustrated by a simple example. After John is implored by his wife to make pancakes one morning, he makes a batch of them. When John makes these pancakes, does he take this action because Mary wanted him to do so or for some other reason, such as his own predilection for them? What "power resources" specifically did Mary possess, such as persuasiveness, that led him to make pancakes? Did he make pancakes because another member of the family wanted him to do so or because Mary wanted them? If even this situation defies analysis, imagine how more difficult the analysis of power becomes in complex situations where many participants vie with one another over extended periods of time about complex policy issues.

Let's begin our discussion of power with a simple two-person situation where X is labeled the "sender" of power and Y the "receiver" and where X wants Y to take an action that Y would not normally have taken. We can argue that X succeeds in exercising power when Y takes an action that he would not otherwise have taken. To return to Mary and John, Mary exercises power only when she influences John to make pancakes when he would not otherwise have made this decision.[5] (Mary did not exercise power if John would have made pancakes anyway or if he made them due to the intervention of another family member.)

How does X influence Y to take an action he might otherwise not have taken? If X uses force—that is, physical coercion—Y has no (or virtually no) choice, as is illustrated by a criminal suspect who is forced to enter a police car at gun point. Were Mary to make John cook pancakes by holding a gun to his head, she would have forced him to make them. Like Peter Bachrach and Morton Baratz, we contend that "force" is not "power" because little or no choice is given to the person against whom it is used.[6]

When power *is* used, it involves transactional rather than unilateral relationships and choices.[7] The receiver in a power transaction (Y) has a choice whether to accede to suggestions of the sender (X). If John would have decided *not* to make pancakes despite Mary's entreaties but decides to make them because of her request, he is involved in a power transaction that differs from interactions that involve the unilateral use of force. When we declare the exercise of power to be transactional then, we argue that it is not possible to understand it by examining only one of the partners in the transactional relationship. Both X (and X's actions or verbal expressions) and Y (and Y's responses to X's entreaties) are integral to power-wielding transactions.

In most power transactions, the receiver (Y) has some or considerable latitude; he can decide whether to accede to the actions or expressions of X. In some situations, of course, it is difficult to determine where voluntarism begins and coercion ends; people who are in desperate economic straits may believe they have little choice but to accede to specific requests if they fear they will lose their jobs, pay increases, or promotions. Even in such cases, however, receivers have some latitude because some people *do* leave jobs to follow the dictates of their conscience.[8]

The effective or successful use of power confirms the old adage that "it takes two (at least) to tango." We can portray power relationships graphically by placing arrows between X and Y (Figure 5.1).

This transactional nature of power exercising has important consequences for political strategy. Even in this simple two-person example, success in using power hinges on a number of considerations. Mary has to decide in the first instance to exercise power, that is, must decide that a particular issue warrants the expenditure of her power. She has to select a kind of power resource that she believes will be effective in influencing John's behavior, and she has to use the power resource sufficiently skillfully that John accedes to her wishes. Were she *too* insistent, for example, John might decide not to make pancakes.

Figure 5.1   The Transactional Nature of Power

Power is often wielded in transactions that involve more than two persons. If Mary believed that John was unlikely to accept her request for pancakes, for example, she might ask someone else, like a daughter or son, to make the request.[9] In this case, two sets of transactional relationships would exist; Mary (X) would have to use power resources to entice her child (Z) to make entreaties to John (Y), and the child would then need to persuade the father to make the pancakes. (See Figure 5.2, where the dashed line between X and Y signifies the fact that X exerts power over Y by indirect means.) Such indirection commonly occurs in power transactions not only in families but also in legislatures and agencies.

KINDS OF POWER RESOURCES

What kinds of power resources do people use to persuade others to take actions or positions that they would not otherwise take or assume? Policy practitioners can employ many kinds of power resources during policy deliberations, including person-to-person, substantive, procedural, and process ones. In each case, a sender (or the sender's emissary) seeks to change the actions or opinions of one or more receivers by using a specific kind of power resource.

Person-to-Person Power

Policy practitioners sometimes exert power in personal discussions with other individuals—a kind of power that we term **person-to-person power.** In their classic article, John French and Bertram Craven discuss the uses of expertise, coercion, reward, charisma, and authority as power resources.[10] When using *expertise,* senders display their personal credentials and (presumed) knowledge to convince others that they should adopt certain positions. For such entreaties to be effective, of course, receivers have to believe that specific senders *are* experts. They use or threaten sanctions or penalties when using

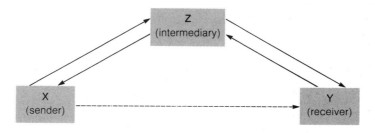

Figure 5.2   The Exerting of Power by Indirection

coercive power; someone might suggest that someone else will lose a job, a promotion, or a desirable position if they do not accede to a specific policy. This power resource is effective only if the receivers believe the sender (or the sender's allies) can implement the threat and if they truly fear the threat; if they are not sufficiently offended by the threat, they may refuse to accede to it. (Considerable bluffing occurs in the politics of all settings.)

When using *reward power,* policy practitioners promise inducements to other persons, such as promotions, pay increases, financial or other support in upcoming campaigns, and bribes—or they promise a reciprocal, or quid pro quo, arrangement where they indicate they will support a policy request of someone else on a future occasion if that person accedes to a specific request. Lyndon Johnson skillfully used reward power not by providing rewards each time a legislator supported one of his policies—an approach that would have made politicians expect rewards on frequent occasions—but for an extended pattern of supportive votes.[11] Like the use of coercive power, the use of reward power can backfire if it is used in a manner that offends the ethical sensibilities of persons who believe that they are unfairly pressured to adopt positions.

Charismatic power exists when people use personal attributes of leadership, moral authority, and personal persuasiveness to stimulate followers or disciples to follow their wishes. In similar fashion, people who possess *authority* over others, such as executives, are often able to persuade others to follow their wishes because many people stand in awe of those who occupy high-level positions. (They may also hope that they will receive rewards and avoid sanctions by following the suggestions of their superiors.)

We have discussed person-to-person power as it is used in dyads, but it can also be used when a sender gives presentations to larger groups. An executive might say to her staff, for example, "support this policy or our agency will suffer severe financial repercussions" (coercive power); or a politician might say to a neighborhood group "get out the vote for my candidacy if you want this neighborhood improvement" (reward power). Indeed, political campaigns involve efforts by candidates to influence the opinions of the general public through the use of political advertisements and debates with opponents.

Person-to-person power can also be exercised indirectly through the use of third parties. Someone may ask someone else to intervene with a person, as illustrated when a politician asks an ally to persuade a fellow legislator to support a specific piece of legislation. In other cases, someone may suggest that another person or institution, such as a funder, will harm or reward them if they fail to adopt certain policies. In still other cases, someone may invoke someone else's expertise when seeking support for a specific policy; an executive may invoke research findings of a respected academician, for example, to support a specific policy. Indirection exists, as well, when a person asks a third party to directly intervene with someone else, such as direct-service staff asking their supervisors to talk directly to the executive of an agency about a policy proposal.

The exercise of these various kinds of person-to-person power is most effective when the sender, or user, selects the kind of person-to-person power that a particular person, or receiver, is likely to honor. Someone may be receptive to the use of expertise, for example, but unreceptive to the use of coercion. Effective users of power often possess considerable knowledge of the needs and predispositions of those persons whom they seek to influence.

We have already noted that effective users of power not only select those power resources carefully that they wish to use in specific situations but also apply them in skillful fashion. Policy practitioners who use expertise as a power resource, for example, are certain to have marshaled evidence and arguments that are persuasive to those persons whom they wish to influence.[12]

Power resources can be used singly or in tandem. Someone may use a combination of a "carrot" (reward power) and a "stick" (coercive power) to persuade someone to support a specific policy. Or someone may try using differing power resources over a period of time; finding that the use of rewards fails, someone may then use coercive- or expertise-power resources.

Substantive Power

People often support or oppose a policy not because they have been subjected to specific entreaties to support or oppose it but because they like or dislike its substantive content. Policy practitioners exercise **substantive power** when they shape the content of policies to elicit support from specific persons. Assume, for example, that two persons favor providing low-income housing subsidies in a government program, but one wants the subsidies to be given primarily to people falling beneath poverty standards while the other wants the subsidies to go, as well, to people with moderate incomes. The initiator of a housing-subsidy proposal might decide not to define the precise income levels within the legislation in hopes that *both* persons would vote for it. Indeed, *vagueness* is often an effective substantive-power tactic, particularly when persons disagree about specific details of a proposal.[13] Vagueness can, of course, be counterproductive in certain situations because an "excessively vague" proposal can attract the opposition of those persons who strongly favor including specific measures in it. Some Democrats, who feared that a vague national day-care proposal would be implemented in punitive fashion by the Reagan administration, insisted that it include specific federal standards such as specified minimum child-to-staff ratios, even though some politicians objected to this provision.[14]

Policy practitioners exercise substantive power when they make additions to or deletions from a policy proposal to enhance support for it from specific decision makers. In the aforementioned day-care proposal, child-care advocates inserted many provisions that were designed to allay opposition from conservatives, such as a relatively modest ceiling on the costs of the program and the inclusion of many provisions that gave the states significant roles in shaping the details of programs within their boundaries. These additions and deletions can occur at the outset—when legislation or proposals are initially drafted—during the give-and-take of deliberations, or on the floor of Congress. Substantive power often involves mutual compromises and agreements where someone agrees to modify or delete a provision in exchange for a reciprocal concession from another faction, with respect to another provision.

Policy practitioners encounter difficult dilemmas when using substantive power. They may make a certain change in a policy proposal to obtain the support of a specific person only to find that they have alienated someone else. When they make numerous concessions to obtain the support of opponents, policy practitioners sometimes find their proposals to be so diluted that they become, in the words of Bachrach and Baratz, "decisionless decisions," that is, merely symbolic measures.[15] As one example, Senator Hubert Humphrey and Representative Augustus Hawkins initiated a legislative proposal in the 1970s to require the federal government to create jobs whenever the national unemployment rate exceeded 3 percent. By the time the legislation was enacted, it included only a vague statement that the federal government would seek full employment, but it possessed no requirement that specific actions be taken by the government, such as developing public works when considerable unemployment existed.[16] To avoid excessive compromises, skillful policy practitioners often refrain from offering changes in a proposal until they are certain that compromises are needed for its passage.

Substantive power is also illustrated by the coupling of a relatively unpopular proposal with more popular ones. In so-called Christmas-tree legislation in Congress, politicians place various unenacted proposals in a single and larger piece of legislation just before the session ends at the end of December; politicians who oppose certain of the measures in this multifaceted legislation nonetheless vote for it because it contains some of their own measures.[17] Or a controversial proposal may be attached to a popular proposal in hopes that it will be swept to victory by the support for the popular one, as foes of abortion discovered when they attached a proposal that prohibited the use of Medicaid funds for abortions to appropriations bills for the Department of Health and Human Services.[18]

Proponents of a proposal often shape it so that it is nonthreatening to potential opponents. A proposed program may be deliberately designed and portrayed as a "pilot project" or as a "demonstration project" to defuse opposition to it.[19] The proponents of a measure may place a proposed program under the jurisdiction of a specific unit of government to make it more appealing to potential opponents. Proponents of the Supplementary Security Income (SSI) Program, a federal program to provide income to destitute elderly and disabled persons, enhanced support for it by proposing that it be placed under the jurisdiction of the Social Security Administration, a unit of government that is more acceptable to conservatives than those units of governments that administer welfare programs such as AFDC.[20] The names or titles of proposals are often selected to make them more acceptable to conservative politicians; thus, Senator Moynihan emphasized "family-support payments" rather than "welfare payments" when discussing a welfare-reform initiative in 1988—a tactic that made it more acceptable to conservatives.[21]

Christopher Matthews contends that many successful politicians eschew discussions of basic principles when discussing legislation.[22] They realize that the "real battle" in the legislative process often involves the precise details of legislation—that discussion of fundamental principles can often alienate valuable allies who possess different perspectives from their own. They often remain silent or noncommittal about basic principles in order to concentrate upon the details of legislation. Of course, this substantive-power tactic can be used to excess: policy practitioners often need to enunciate basic principles to rally support for a measure and to assert important values.

Procedural Power

Policy is often fashioned by **procedural power** in the course of a complex chain of deliberations and decisions. In legislatures, for example, numerous people, committees, and bodies must sequentially assent to a policy before it can be finally enacted. A bill that is introduced in the House of Representatives must normally proceed through deliberations in a subcommittee, a committee, and the full House before repeating a similar sequence in the Senate (Figure 5.3).

A conference committee of congressional members tries to resolve differences in the House and Senate versions of a piece of legislation, which is then sent back to both chambers for their final approval. (If it cannot resolve the differences, the legislation often dies.) The legislation then proceeds to the president, who either signs it or vetoes it; two-thirds vote of both the House and Senate is required to override a presidential veto. Similar parliamentary procedures exist in state legislatures as well as in some municipal governments.[23]

Many parliamentary techniques and strategies exist for circumventing specific steps in this process. Clever strategists often try to bypass those persons, committees, and meetings that they believe are unfavorable to their proposal, while routing the proposal to more favorable settings. In some cases, for example, a specific legislative proposal can be considered by various committees but is steered by party officials to the committee that is most favorably disposed to it. They sometimes shorten the normal procedures by "leap-frogging" a meeting or procedure when they think this will favor their proposal. They use person-to-person–power resources with those individuals who are strategically located in the decision-making process, such as chairs

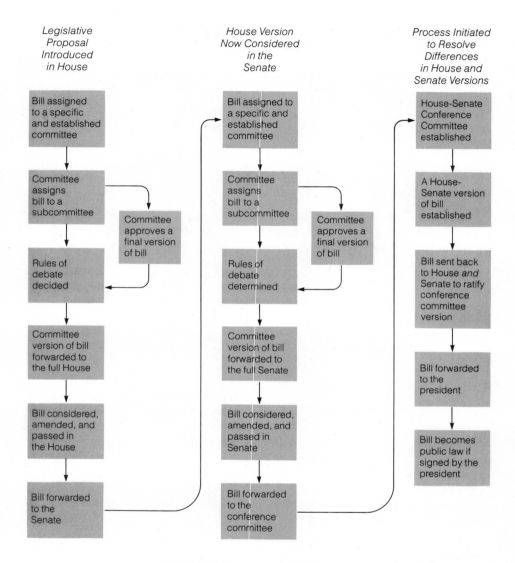

Figure 5.3   Route Followed by One Bill in the Federal Congress

of important committees, not only to obtain their support for a specific measure but also to secure their assistance with logistic details. The chair of a committee can place a proposal in a preferred position on the agendas of specific meetings, can insist that certain policies should be returned for further subcommittee deliberations, and can abbreviate lengthy deliberations to facilitate or to impede the enactment of a specific measure. Clever strategists are well versed in parliamentary procedures; they know how to outmaneuver legislative foes by using those amending, blocking, and sidetracking tactics on the floor of Congress that are allowed by parliamentary rules of a specific chamber.[24]

The use of specific procedural tactics can sometimes be counterproductive, however. Someone can be accused of unfairly seeking to stifle dissent by rushing a proposal through Congress, by "stacking the cards" in favor of (or against) a proposal, or by bypassing normal channels. Also in Chapter Eight we will note that ethical objections can be raised when persons exclude others from policy deliberations.

When proposals are initiated, it is necessary to ask which persons control the decision-making apparatus at specific points, whether they favor a proposal, and whether proponents can overcome opposition. In the case of the Senate during the early years of the Reagan administration, Republicans held the power of the various Senate committees because their party possessed a majority of Senate seats. These Republican chairs worked in liaison with White House staff members, who assisted them in mobilizing party support for those bills that were favored by Republicans. Disgruntled Democrats discovered that many of their legislative initiatives never made it beyond these committee gatekeepers, even when they had considerable support in the House, whose committees were chaired by Democrats. When the Democrats regained control of the Senate in the 1986 elections, they regained control of the chairs of the Senate committees, which they in turn used to scuttle many of the legislative proposals of the Reagan administration.[25]

Complex and simple procedures for decision making exist, as well, in agencies. In the former case, a staff member, staff committee, or executive may initiate a proposal to develop a new agency program. The proposal may be developed by a staff committee, come to the full staff for consideration, and be taken to the board of directors by the executive. The board may then refer it to a board committee as a prelude to taking a final vote. (In some cases, funders may also be included, particularly when the board wants their participation to ensure funding for the program.) Although many major revisions in agency policy are considered through complex decision procedures, simpler options sometimes also exist. A hospital social services director who wants to develop social work services on the neurology ward, for example, may merely obtain the concurrence of the medical director of neurology. Only after the staff member has been on the service for some time may he even seek formal approval from a higher official in the hospital— perhaps when he decides he needs additional funding for the position from the hospital's budget.

Process Power

Policies are shaped in the give-and-take of policy deliberations, which are described by their tenor, tempo, and scope of conflict. *Tenor* describes their level of conflict; *tempo* describes their timing, pace, and duration; and *scope of conflict* describes the numbers and kinds of persons who participate in them.

Policy practitioners use **process power** when they take actions or make statements to shape the tenor, tempo, or scope of conflict of these processes in a manner that they believe will help them secure their policy preferences. Let's begin with the crude analogy of a schoolyard dispute to illustrate process power. The two parties to this conflict not only have to develop their positions in the dispute but also have to decide *how* to resolve their dispute. For example, each has to shape the tenor of deliberations; do they use brute strength (a fight), an amicable discussion, or some middle course in which they do not fight but shout at each other? Each has to decide, as well, what tempo of deliberations will help their cause; do they seek a speedy settlement or protracted deliberations? They decide who they want to participate in the conflict; if they want a narrow scope of conflict, they try to exclude most other persons from their interaction while they invite others to join the fray if they believe a broad scope of conflict will help their cause.[26]

A bully who possesses physical superiority might decide to initiate a fight, whereas the proverbial "ninety-pound weakling" might want to expand the scope of conflict to include other (and more powerful) allies. Some protagonists believe that a speedy resolution of an issue will benefit their cause by not allowing opponents to mobilize opposition to their positions. In some cases, people decide that their cause will be aided by relatively low conflict where resolutions are obtained in behind-the-scenes deliberations. As one example, some presidents decide that controversial issues are best resolved by blue-ribbon and bipartisan committees to avert the controversy that is often associated with partisan politics.[27]

The preceding discussion suggests then that individuals can sometimes shape or influence the political process by their actions or their statements. Someone who wishes to intensify conflict, for example, uses emotion-laden words, makes references to fundamental values that are at stake, enlarges the scope of conflict by publicizing the issue or entreating friends to join the deliberation, or uses unusual tactics like the filibuster in legislative settings.[28] These people can also state political intentions that make it clear that they do not want amicable resolution, such as "we plan to fight to the finish" or "we will accept no significant changes in our proposal." People who believe that conflict will be detrimental to their cause take actions or make statements that diminish conflict, such as emphasizing the technical features of a proposal, identifying common interests that all parties to the conflict share, and discouraging those persons from participating who will raise the level of conflict. Policy practitioners influence the pace of policy deliberations by encouraging or discouraging amendments to a policy or by shortening or lengthening the time that is allocated to its discussion.

The *timing* of the initiation of a policy proposal, like the level of conflict, often favors a specific side in a policy dispute. If someone introduces a proposal at an inopportune moment, its chances may be imperiled no matter how skillful its defenders or how great its merits. Whether in agency or legislative settings, such background factors as budgetary deficits, an agenda that is crowded with other proposals, or an unsympathetic executive can provide a harsh environment for a policy proposal. When a favorable context exists, a proposal that was defeated at a prior time may suddenly "sail through" the political process.[29]

It must be remembered that policy practitioners often possess limited power to influence the nature of political interaction. Someone who wants to limit conflict, for example, may find her goal sabotaged by opponents who succeed in escalating conflict. Someone who wants to restrict the scope of conflict may be unable to stop someone else from publicizing it in the mass media, as the frequency of leaks to the press in government settings suggests. Even skillful policy practitioners sometimes miscalculate. Someone who introduces a proposal at a supposedly opportune moment may soon discover that various background factors emerge that scuttle it. Moreover, policy processes often develop a momentum that defies attempts to change them; when conflict becomes heated, for example, it is often difficult for persons to diminish it even when they wish to reduce it.[30] Traditions also frustrate the work of policy practitioners because issues that have been associated with high conflict on prior occasions, such as national health insurance, are often associated with it on successive occasions.[31] Morton Deutsch reminds us, as well, that the nature of an issue powerfully shapes the course of conflict; policies that propose truly massive changes in the status quo, such as major and costly pieces of social legislation, are more likely to be associated with polarization between liberals and conservatives than are more modest proposals.[32]

The Power of Autonomy

We have argued in the preceding discussion that power is effectively exercised when someone influences the actions or opinions of someone else. In some cases, however, people possess power when they can free themselves from the attempts of others to control *their* actions and opinions. This kind of power—or should we call it negative or defensive power?—allows people to "call their own shots," a not insignificant kind of power in situations where people might otherwise be circumscribed by myriad policies that they found objectionable.[33]

People with **autonomy** possess, in effect, the ability to develop with their colleagues some of their own policies, sometimes in defiance of existing ones, as an example from medicine illustrates. Responding to changes in the reimbursement rules of Medicare authorities, many hospitals enacted stringent rules that required the discharge of elderly persons soon after the completion of surgeries. Because some social workers believed this early-discharge policy was detrimental to the physical and mental well-being of some elderly patients, they discovered various ways of circumventing the policy, such as arguing that no suitable convalescent-home vacancies existed. Because hospital administrators could not easily check the veracity of this claim in each case, social workers were able to use their autonomy to modify the existing policy even, in some cases, when vacancies *did* exist. We discuss the ethical merits of this practice in Chapter Eight, but it illustrates how autonomy allows some people to shape the implementation of policy, some-times in defiance of official or high-level policy.

VANTAGE POINT: EXTERNAL VERSUS INTERNAL PRESSURE

We have discussed to this point various kinds of power that policy practi-tioners use. In some cases, they try to influence policymakers from an exter-nal vantage point, whether from community groups, external agencies, coalitions, interest groups, or professional associations. In other cases, they use these kinds of power from the vantage point of positions that are located within specific bureaucracies, legislatures, or agencies.

Exerting Pressure from External Sources

Legislators' positions on specific issues are often shaped by external pressures that are exerted on them by lobbyists, interest groups, experts, officials within the government, and constituents. These pressures may be exerted during personal interactions in legislators' offices, at social occasions, during legis-lative hearings, or by correspondence. In some cases, the pressure is exerted directly on legislators, while lobbyists and constituents try on other occasions to persuade their aides.[34]

Strategists often try to mobilize pressure from a number of these sources to build sufficient support to convince legislators that they will suffer severe repercussions if they oppose a measure. But pressure must be carefully timed, focused, and planned so that it constructively contributes to support for a specific proposal.[35] "Pell-mell," or unfocused, pressure can sometimes be counterproductive, as illustrated by letter-writing campaigns that use form letters (politicians like individualized expressions of support) or by conflicting testimony at legislative hearings by members of a coalition that supports a specific policy. Pressure is sometimes particularly effective when it is carefully timed to precede important votes.

Supporters of a proposal often form coalitions of diverse groups and institutions to exert pressure on politicians.[36] Coalitions serve many pur-poses. By including many kinds of members and organizations, they mobilize pressure on politicians from diverse constituencies. Members of coalitions can diminish contradictory messages that legislators receive during the legislative process when they reach common agreements about the kind of policy they favor and the kinds of arguments that they wish to use to support it. Moreover, coalitions that draw on diverse interests are often more successful than are single organizations in obtaining coverage from the media, whose cooperation is often needed to promote interest in the issue by the general public. Members of coalitions often pool their resources to further enhance their power; they can arrange a coordinated letter-writing campaign that draws on funds, combine their mailing lists, coordinate their separate lobbying resources, and pool their funds to hire a lobbyist or staff person.

Coalitions are useful, but they can be difficult to organize and maintain.[37] Someone has to be willing to invest considerable time and energy in forming and sustaining them because meetings, negotiations, mailings, and telephone conversations are often needed. When coalition members cannot agree on the details of a policy, their united front is imperiled. Members may find it difficult to agree on the central leadership and the staffing of their coalition because they fear that some people will seek leadership to obtain publicity or credit for themselves or will commit them to policies and actions that they have not fully discussed. Coalition members may fear that their leadership is not responsive to their suggestions.

These kinds of costs, or problems, that are associated with coalitions sometimes lead policy practitioners to decide to "go it alone" when mobilizing pressure for a specific measure. In some cases, the costs of coalitions exceed their benefits, particularly when considerable conflict, vying for leadership, and absence of common interests exist. In many cases, however, the absence of a coalition dooms a measure to defeat. Far more measures cross the desks of legislators than they can possibly enact; if a threshold of support for a measure is not achieved—particularly ones associated with controversy and with strong or potential opponents—legislators may choose to oppose or avoid it.

When they form coalitions, policy practitioners have to decide what structure, or form, they should take. It is easier to form coalitions of like-minded persons and groups because less effort is needed to fashion agreements on policy or strategy matters; however, coalitions that represent a broad range of perspectives and groups can sometimes exert more effective pressure on legislators.[38] Recent efforts to obtain increases in the funding for federal food programs and federal housing programs contained diverse groups such as civil rights groups, agribusiness, advocates of low-income housing, and advocates of moderate-income housing.[39]

External pressure can be placed not only on legislatures and government agencies but also on social agencies. As Yeheskel Hasenfeld and other organizational theorists who subscribe to a political-economy perspective note, policies within organizations are shaped by many forces that exist externally to them.[40] Funders, courts, community groups, and community leaders shape the internal policies of organizations in many ways and in varying degrees. People who are concerned with policies of specific organizations can in some cases seek to change them by directly approaching people and institutions in their external environment. Thus, a feminist organization that believes an agency that provides job-placement services is failing to help women could approach its funders, such as the local Job-Training Placement Agency (JTPA), or it could develop a delegation of community leaders to approach its administrators.

Exerting Pressure from Internal Sources

Decision makers often respond to pressure that is placed directly on them by "insiders," whether fellow legislators or, in the case of agencies, by staff within their agencies. Policy practitioners who are not themselves legislators or aides to legislators often seek to promote interactions among legislators and their aides to build support for a specific piece of legislation. They can elicit from a supportive legislator or aide the names of other legislators and aides who can facilitate the enactment of a specific measure. They can ask a legislator or aide to discuss a proposal with another legislator or aide or to route to them, over their signature, a proposal. Policy advocates often seek the sponsorship of a specific proposal by a range of legislators, including some who are particularly influential, such as the chair of a committee or a party leader.[41]

Advocates of a change in policy within an organization often cultivate alliances with other staff and executives within the organization.[42] Informal and preexisting alliances or factions often provide a useful source of support for a policy change—alliances that often exist because of shared interests or perspectives. Or a new coalition can be formed to specifically develop and support a specific proposal.[43] Union leaders have become increasingly powerful participants in the policy-making of agencies and government bureaucracies; although they often emphasize "bread-and-butter" issues, such as those that shape the working conditions and wages of their members, they sometimes take positions on policy issues.[44]

BUILDING CREDIBILITY AS A MEANS OF ENHANCING POWER RESOURCES

Because people who use power resources are only effective if others respond favorably to their requests, suggestions, or demands, it is logical to ask, What attributes of people increase the likelihood that others will respond affirmatively to them? (We discuss tactics to increase personal credibility only briefly in this chapter, since a section of Chapter Seven is devoted to this topic.) Proponents of power-dependence theories suggest that many people who obtain power make others dependent on them and are more likely to be effective users of power than others.[45] The concept of power dependence is particularly useful to social work units in larger organizations, whether in hospitals, schools, corporations, or courts. When their staff are perceived to fulfill a number of functions within them, they are more likely to obtain the credibility that makes other staff respond favorably to their policy sugges- tions. Contrast, for example, a social work unit in a hospital that contents itself only with facilitating the release of elderly patients from the hospital with one that provides a variety of counseling, financial advising, and com- munity services in various units or services of the institution. The staff and leaders of the latter unit are more likely to be asked to contribute to the development of policy than are the staff and leaders of the former unit—and to be heeded when they make program and policy suggestions.

People enhance their power by increasing their connections with others, and particularly strategically situated individuals such as aides to legislators and administrators, high officials, and people with special expertise. These kinds of connections serve many purposes. They allow people to obtain "insider information" about possible or impending developments *before* they occur. They obtain tips or suggestions about strategy from these connections, such as how to approach certain people, whether a specific proposal is politically feasible, and *when* to initiate a proposal. These connections some- times agree to serve as emissaries to other highly placed officials. Personal links to a range of people in a bureaucracy or agency increase the likelihood that someone will be asked to comment on proposed policies *before* they are officially introduced by other persons.

Many personal characteristics, such as honesty, diligence, empathy, and willingness to "put in the extra mile," increase the power resources of some people. When lobbyists are asked to list the attributes that enhance their effectiveness, they often place honesty at the top of the list because "straight shooters" obtain a positive reputation with legislators who depend on accu- rate information in fashioning proposals.

POWER DIFFERENTIALS IN POLICY-MAKING: HOW IMPORTANT ARE THEY?

Our discussion to this point may convey the misleading impression that power wielding occurs on a level playing field—that is, that each of us, if we put our minds to the task, can be as successful as others in obtaining the enactment of policy proposals. This optimistic conclusion ignores harsh real- ities such as power differentials that give some people a significant advantage in power transactions.

Executives, legislators, and highly placed government officials possess **formal authority,** for example, by virtue of their positions that give them powers to approve or disapprove certain policy initiatives, to initiate pro- posals, and to obtain access to program, budget, and technical information.

Their positions give them access to other highly placed people who yield information and assistance that are not available to others. They are often more likely than others to command obedience from other people when they issue directives or make recommendations. In some cases, as considerable research suggests, authority figures can sometimes obtain the obedience of subordinates or other people, even when their suggestions are ethically flawed.[46]

Leaders, staff, and lobbyists of certain interest groups, institutions, and professional associations possess extraordinary power that derives not only from their technical expertise but also from their access to constituencies that can exert external influence on those decision makers who do not heed their policy suggestions. In turn, their expertise and clout make it simpler for them to cultivate personal relationships with decision makers, which further enhances their power. Some interest groups increase their power, as well, by making large contributions to the campaigns of those politicians who support their positions. In a compelling account of the role of the mass media and large interest groups such as the American Association of Retired Persons (AARP) and political action committees (PACs) in influencing policies, Hedrick Smith contends that power is increasingly wielded in legislative settings by those groups and lobbyists that possess well-organized, grassroots constituencies, extraordinary resources, and access to the mass media.[47]

Individuals who possess power over the shaping and enactment of budgets, such as those legislators who sit on appropriations committees and those officials who develop budgets in bureaucracies, often possess extraordinary power because "those who pay the piper dictate the tune." A professor of mine once lamented the common tendency of social workers to seek jobs in the personnel sections of many organizations because the staff in the budget and fiscal departments usually possess more power to shape the policies and programs of bureaucracies. Officials in the federal Office of Management and Budget (OMB) are powerful players in the establishment of domestic policy in the executive branch of the federal government because they superintend the shaping of the president's budgetary recommendations.

Nor should we overlook the role of cultural symbols in giving certain persons and groups more power than others. Officials who are affiliated with programs that benefit socially acceptable groups or programs, such as children, health, and education, are often more able to influence the decisions of funders and legislators than are people who are associated with socially stigmatized groups such as mentally ill people, welfare recipients, or ex-offenders.[48]

Discrimination patterns in the broader society influence power transactions. Rosabeth Kanter's extended discussion of problems that women encounter in large organizations suggests that they are often excluded from decision making because of gender-based prejudice and because they lack access to old-boy networks.[49] Members of various minority groups often encounter similar problems.

Although few people would disagree that power differentials exist, some theorists, such as C. Wright Mills, suggest that a "power elite," such as leaders of well-financed interest groups, exists in many situations; this elite monopolizes power and consigns other people and interests to marginal roles.[50] Indeed, tightly organized factions or interests—or even a single person—often possess such extraordinary power that they control the course of policy deliberations. Were we to accept this thesis in every situation, however, we could easily succumb to resignation, fatalism, and cynicism. Other theorists like Robert Dahl, who are called "pluralists," suggest that a myriad of interests and people shape policy choices in most situations.[51] They point to multiple interest groups that participate in the shaping of specific policies in municipal, county, state, and federal jurisdictions to support their contention. Who is right? The answer may well be, Each side is correct in certain situations. In some situations, specific people and interests possess such power that they are able to powerfully shape the course of deliberations. Other policy choices are associated, however, with a political process where just about anybody can successfully join the fray. In yet other situations, certain people and interests may possess a preponderance of power in setting agendas and shaping choices, but determined and well-organized groups may be able to force them to make important concessions. As we discuss in the next chapter, policy practitioners need to realistically assess the actual distribution of power in specific settings.

CAN DIRECT-SERVICE STAFF BE "PLAYERS"?

Our discussion of power differentials may lead some people to the pessimistic conclusion that policy-making is an elitist enterprise that is dominated by high-level officials and powerful interests. Many theorists contend, however, that even people "at the bottom of the heap," such as direct-service staff, possess considerable power resources.[52] Direct-service staff certainly possess considerable person-to-person–power resources such as expertise that stems from their personal knowledge of problems of an agency's clientele. Many supervisors and executives value suggestions from direct-service staff about a range of agency matters. Because direct-service staff are perceived to be indispensable to other staff or officials in their organizations, they are more likely to be effective players in policy-making.

Direct-service staff also possess considerable reward and coercive power. As they do their work well, they enhance the reputations and credibility of their superiors, who often recognize that attentiveness to the program and policy concerns of direct-service staff further enhances the quality and productivity of their work. When unions exist, direct-service staff possess coercive power that derives from the implied or stated threat to disrupt their work if certain demands are not granted; these demands primarily involve salary and work-load issues, but unions sometimes seek changes in policy that are directly relevant to the needs of consumers. Even when unions do not exist, direct-service staff can vigorously protest some policies by directly making their case to high-level staff.

Direct-service staff often possess access to certain points in the decision-making processes of agencies, such as staff meetings, retreats, meetings of specific units, and meetings with supervisors. They sometimes participate on task forces or committees, which are established by boards of directors, where they can use these forums to promote support for specific proposals.

Direct-service staff often possess power that derives from their autonomy.[53] Many regulations shape the interventions of direct-service staff in specific settings that govern the length and intensity of services, recommended procedures or services, and priorities, but regulations are difficult to enforce because the work of direct-service staff is relatively shielded from high-level scrutiny. Moreover, it is often possible to *bend* some rules without technically violating them. Carried to an extreme, autonomy can bring anarchy when staff systematically disobey existing policy, but it nonetheless represents an important kind of power that can be used by direct-service staff.

Direct-service staff do not, of course, possess many of the power resources of executives, funders, or legislators, so they need to imaginatively enhance their power resources and selectively choose issues and situations where they can influence policy deliberations.

THE PROBLEM OF ASSERTIVENESS

People sometimes fail to seize strategic opportunities to shape policies because they fatalistically assume that they cannot win. In some cases, as our discussion of power differentials suggests, the deck *is* stacked against them; but in many other cases, individuals undermine their effectiveness by becoming excessively fatalistic.

The effective use of power requires people to decide in the first instance that they possess power resources, that they can use them effectively, and that they want to use them. The word *assertiveness* describes this proclivity to test the waters rather than to be excessively fatalistic.

Assertiveness is undermined, however, by two dispositions that lead some people to chronically underestimate their true power resources. First, some people have a victim mentality, which disposes them to believe that other people usually or always conspire to defeat or to frustrate their preferences.[54] A director of a social work department in a hospital might believe, for example, that nurses and physicians will systematically oppose *any* proposals of social workers. Second, some people are fatalistic about the use of power in a more general sense; they believe that successful power wielders are necessarily high-level persons or officials—or powerful interests. Such fatalism suggests that people who fall outside these exalted categories cannot effectively participate in policy deliberations.

Both the victim mentality and fatalism create self-fulfilling prophecies. If people believe that others conspire against them and that power can be effectively used only by a restricted group, they do not seek to develop or use personal power resources. If they are perceived in turn to be disinclined to participate in policy deliberations, other people are more likely to run roughshod over them, to ignore their occasional suggestions, and to exclude them from policy deliberations. These negative experiences operate in turn to further reinforce the victim mentality and fatalism as the vicious circle continues and speeds its course.[55]

The preceding discussion suggests that people with a victim mentality and fatalism ignore the diverse and numerous kinds of power resources that most of us possess or can develop that allow us to participate in the shaping of events in many situations. Fatalists falsely assume that each of us possesses a fixed supply of power resources that cannot be increased as we enhance our credibility, expertise, connections, and other sources of power. Even when people *are* relatively powerless, they can take steps to change this situation by finding allies, establishing relationships, developing expertise, and obtaining information.

What can individuals do to avoid the trap of nonassertiveness?[56] They can try to realistically assess both the risks and the possible benefits that are likely to accrue from responsible efforts to change defective policies. They can use forthright and honest communication in many situations rather than evading difficult issues prematurely. In some cases, they can test the waters by asking other people how they perceive an existing policy or issue. They can consult with trusted colleagues about troublesome policies or about the efforts of specific persons to run roughshod over themselves. When they fear reprisals for whistle-blowing, they can ask themselves and others whether they will likely encounter real risks or whether they have developed unrealistic fears.

A case example illustrates an assertive orientation to power. The director of a department of social work in a hospital observed that unsuccessful requests for increased budgetary resources for her department often were followed by more successful requests because the unsuccessful entreaties had educated top officials to programs of the social work department. Indeed, she surmised that some officials actually developed some guilt about denials of well-presented and well-justified requests. So she decided not to be intimidated but to make successive requests for funds for her department. She discovered that the skillful and relatively frequent requests for funds led to successive increases in the budget of her unit. Unlike departments with more timid executives, her department gained size and stature as she assertively sought resources for her department on successive occasions.[57]

SUMMARY

We have discussed the nature and varieties of power because power is critical to policy practice in legislative, government, community, and agency settings. Power is a transactional phenomenon that can be understood only by examining perceptions, actions, and responses of the participants in a power transaction. Our discussion suggests that many kinds of power resources exist and that skillful policy practitioners are adept at using a variety of them in specific situations.

Policy-making does not occur on a level playing field because some persons and interests possess more power resources than others. Formal authority or position in bureaucratic and policy-making hierarchies, access to resources and powerful constituencies, and policy-making skills give some participants an advantage. Considerable theory and evidence nonetheless suggest that many individuals and groups can shape policy outcomes in many situations, including direct-service staff who can sometimes use power resources such as expertise, autonomy, indispensability, reward, and coercion to advance their policy preferences.

People who possess a victim mentality or who believe that the use of power is unethical or unprofessional often create a self-fulfilling prophecy that impedes their ability to participate in policy deliberations. Such policy passivity makes them unlikely to influence the selection of policies—a failure that often strengthens their fatalism and their sense of victimization.

If power lies at the heart of politics, its effective use requires the development of strategy, which we discuss in the next chapter.

QUESTIONS FOR DISCUSSION

1. Review Policy-Practice Case 5. Identify various kinds of power resources (including person-to-person, substantive, process, and procedural ones) that the social worker plans to use to secure the adoption of the service innovation.

2. What does Policy-Practice Case 5 tell us about the power of low-level persons within agencies—in this case, the student intern who wants the agency to adopt a specific innovation? What constraints, as well as opportunities, stemmed from the low position that the intern occupied in the agency?

3. Referring to Policy-Practice Case 5, discuss the exercising of power by indirection, for example, by using third parties.

4. Discuss the assertion that people with an analytic or technical style of policy-making have falsely given politics a "bad rep." What are some

positive or necessary functions of politics within agencies, communities, and societies?

5. Discuss the statement "Social workers are often uncomfortable with power and often think that its acquisition and use are extraneous to professional practice."

6. Discuss the assertion that the victim mentality and fatalism create self-fulfilling prophecies.

7. By using a situation with which you are familiar where you (or someone else) were (or are) subjected to arbitrary and ongoing control, discuss assertiveness options that could have been (or could be) considered.

SUGGESTED READINGS

The Nature of Power

Peter Bachrach and Morton Baratz, *Power and Poverty* (New York: Oxford University Press, 1970).

Varieties of Power

John French and Bertram Raven, "The Bases of Social Power," in Dorwin Cartwright and Alvin Zander, eds., *Group Dynamics: Research and Theory* (New York: Harper and Row, 1968), pp. 259–269.

Lewis Froman, *The Congressional Process: Strategies, Rules, and Procedures* (Boston: Little, Brown, 1967).

Christopher Matthews, *Hardball: How Politics Is Played* (New York: Summit Books, 1988).

Hedrick Smith, *The Power Game: How Washington Works* (New York: Random House, 1988).

A Defense of Politics

Eric Schattschneider, *The Semisovereign People* (New York: Holt, Rinehart, and Winston, 1960).

The Uses of Power from Internal Vantagepoints

Bruce Jansson and June Simmons, "The Survival of Social Work Units in Host Organizations," *Social Work*, 31 (September 1986): 339–344.

Herman Resnick, "Tasks in Changing the Organization from Within," in Herman Resnick and Rino Patti, eds., *Change from Within: Humanizing Social Welfare Organizations* (Philadelphia: Temple University Press, 1980), pp. 200–212.

The Uses of Power from External Vantagepoints

Karen Haynes and James Mikelson, *Affecting Change: Social Workers in the Political Arena* (New York: Longman, 1986).

Nancy Humphreys, "Competing for Revenue-Sharing Funds: A Coalition Approach," *Social Work,* 24 (January 1979): 14–20.

William Whitaker, "Organizing Social Action Coalitions: WIC Comes to Wyoming," in Maryann Mahaffey and John Hanks, eds., *Practical Politics: Social Work and Political Response* (Washington, D.C.: National Association of Social Workers, 1982), pp. 136–158.

Power Resources of Direct-Service Staff

Michael Lipsky, *Street-Level Bureaucrats: Dilemmas of the Individual and Public Service* (New York: Russell Sage, 1980).

David Mechanic, "Sources of Power of Lower Participants in Complex Organizations," *Administrative Science Quarterly,* 7 (December 1962): 349–364.

The Problem of Assertiveness

Rosabeth Kanter, *Men and Women of the Corporation* (New York: Basic Books, 1977), pp. 158–197.

Linda MacNeilage and Kathleen Adams, *Assertiveness at Work* (Englewood Cliffs, N.J.: Prentice-Hall, 1982).

Stanley Milgram, *Obedience to Authority* (New York: Harper and Row, 1975).

NOTES

1. *Living Webster Encyclopedic Dictionary of the English Language* (Chicago: English Language Institute of America, 1977), p. 737.
2. Ibid., p. 737.
3. Martin Rein, "Value-Critical Policy Analysis," in Daniel Callahan and Bruce Jennings, eds., *Ethics, the Social Sciences, and Policy Analysis* (New York: Plenum Press, 1983), pp. 96–100.
4. Bruce Jansson, *Theory and Practice of Social Welfare Policy* (Belmont, Ca.: Wadsworth Publishing Co., 1984), p. 51.
5. Peter Bachrach and Morton Baratz, *Power and Poverty* (New York: Oxford University Press, 1970), pp. 17–38.
6. Ibid.
7. Ibid.
8. For discussion of dilemmas of the receivers of power resources, see Stanley Milgram, *Obedience to Authority* (New York: Harper and Row, 1975).
9. Edward Banfield, *Political Influence* (New York: Free Press, 1961), pp. 307–314.

10. John French and Bertram Raven, "The Bases of Social Power," in Dorwin Cartwright and Alvin Zander, eds., *Group Dynamics: Research and Theory* (New York: Harper and Row, 1968), pp. 259–269.

11. Doris Kearns, *Lyndon Johnson and the American Dream* (New York: Harper and Row, 1976), pp. 190, 224–227.

12. See Christopher Matthews, *Hardball: How Politics Is Played* (New York: Summit Books, 1988), pp. 21–43.

13. Jansson, *Theory and Practice*, p. 184.

14. Julie Rowner, "Daycare Package Clears First Hurdle in House," *Congressional Quarterly Weekly Report*, 46 (July 2, 1988): 1833–1836.

15. See Bachrach and Baratz, *Power and Poverty*, pp. 17–38.

16. *Congressional Quarterly Almanac*, 34 (Washington, D.C.: Congressional Quarterly Service, Inc., 1978), pp. 272–279.

17. Jansson, *Theory and Practice*, p. 184.

18. Joseph Califano, *Governing America* (New York: Simon and Schuster, 1971), p. 67.

19. Gerald Zaltman and Robert Duncan, *Strategies for Planned Change* (New York: Wiley-Interscience, 1977), p. 100.

20. Vincent Burke and Vee Burke, *Nixon's Good Deed: Welfare Reform* (New York: Columbia University Press, 1974), pp. 195–204.

21. U.S., Congress, Senate, Committee on Finance, *Hearings Before the Subcommittee on Social Security and Family Policy*, pp. 2–14 (January 23, 1987).

22. Matthews, *Hardball*, pp. 144–154.

23. Lewis Froman, *The Congressional Process: Strategies, Rules, and Procedures* (Boston: Little, Brown, 1967).

24. Eugene Bardach, *The Skill Factor in Politics* (Berkeley, Ca.: University of California Press, 1972), pp. 234–240.

25. Bruce Jansson, *Reluctant Welfare State: A History of American Social Welfare Policies* (Belmont, Ca.: Wadsworth Publishing Co., 1984), pp. 212–214, 222.

26. Eric Schattschneider, *The Semisovereign People* (New York: Holt, Rinehart, and Winston, 1980), pp. 20–46.

27. Jansson, *Reluctant Welfare State*, p. 217.

28. Morton Deutsch, *The Resolution of Conflict: Constructive and Destructive Processes* (New York: Yale University Press, 1973), pp. 124–152.

29. John Kingdon, *Agendas, Alternatives, and Public Policies* (Boston: Little, Brown, 1984), pp. 1–22.

30. Deutsch, *The Resolution of Conflict*, pp. 124–152.

31. Ibid., p. 368.

32. See Theodore Lowi's discussion of the politics of redistributive measures in "American Business, Public Policy, Case Studies, and Political Theory," *World Politics*, 16 (July 1964): 677–715.

33. Michael Lipsky, *Street-Level Bureaucrats: Dilemmas of the Individual and Public Service* (New York: Russell Sage, 1980).

34. George Sharwell, "How to Testify Before a Legislative Committee," in Maryann Mahaffey and John Hanks, eds., *Practical Politics: Social Work and Political Response* (Washington, D.C.: National Association of Social Workers, 1982), pp. 85–98.

35. Ibid., pp. 81–84.

36. For a theoretical discussion of coalitions, see Samuel Bacharach and Edward Lawler, *Power and Politics in Organizations* (San Francisco: Jossey-Bass, 1980), pp. 48–69. Also see George Brager, Harry Specht, and James Torczyner, *Community Organizing*, 2nd ed. (New York: Columbia University Press, 1987), pp. 193–200; and Bardach, *The Skill Factor in Politics*, pp. 215–230.

37. For a discussion of the "costs" of coalitions, see Charles Adrian and Charles Press, "Decision Costs in Coalition Formation," *American Political Science Review*, 62 (June 1968): 556–564.

38. Nancy Amidei, "How to Be an Advocate in Bad Times," *Public Welfare*, 40 (Summer 1982): 41.

39. Ibid., p. 42.

40. Yeheskel Hasenfeld, *Human Service Organizations* (Englewood Cliffs, N.J.: Prentice-Hall, 1983).

41. Ron Dear and Rino Patti, "Legislative Advocacy: Seven Effective Tactics," *Social Work*, 26 (July 1981): 290–291.

42. Herman Resnick, "Tasks in Changing the Organization from Within," in Herman Resnick and Rino Patti, eds., *Change from Within: Humanizing Social Welfare Organizations* (Philadelphia: Temple University Press, 1980), pp. 210–212.

43. Ibid., pp. 210–212.

44. Denis Chamot, "Professional Employees Turn to Unions," *Harvard Business Review*, 54 (May 1976): 119–127.

45. Richard Emerson, "Power-Dependence Relations," *American Sociological Review*, 27 (February 1962): 31–40. Also see D.J. Hickson et al., "A Strategic Contingencies Theory of Organizational Power," *Administrative Science Quarterly*, 16 (June 1971): 216–229.

46. Milgram, *Obedience to Authority*.

47. Hedrick Smith, *The Power Game: How Washington Works* (New York: Random House, 1988).

48. Richard Fenno, *The Power of the Purse* (Boston: Little, Brown, 1966), pp. 366–390.

49. Rosabeth Kanter, *Men and Women of the Corporation* (New York: Basic Books, 1977), pp. 129–163.

50. C. Wright Mills, *The Power Elite* (New York: Oxford University Press, 1956).

51. Robert Dahl, *Pluralist Democracy in the United States* (Chicago: Rand McNally, 1967).

52. David Mechanic, "Sources of Power of Lower Participants in Complex Organizations," *Administrative Science Quarterly*, 7 (December 1962): 349–364.

53. Lipsky, *Street-Level Bureaucrats.*

54. Kanter, *Men and Women of the Corporation,* pp. 158–160, 196–197.

55. Ibid., pp. 196–197.

56. Various strategies are discussed by Linda MacNeilage and Kathleen Adams, *Assertiveness at Work* (Englewood Cliffs, N.J.: Prentice-Hall, 1982).

57. Bruce Jansson and June Simmons, "The Survival of Social Work Units in Host Organizations," *Social Work,* 31 (September 1986): 339–340.

CHAPTER 6

■

Developing Political Strategy

We have emphasized the nature and varieties of power, but we have not yet discussed how policy practitioners use their power resources to develop and implement political strategy in agency, community, or legislative settings. The word *strategy* describes "a planned sequence of actions and verbal exchanges in a specific time frame to increase the likelihood that a proposal will be enacted."

Four challenges confront policy practitioners when they devise political strategy. First, they have to establish some political objectives that define what they want to achieve during a specific period of time. Second, they have to understand those existing political realities that provide the context or starting point for developing strategy. Third, they have to develop and implement strategy that identifies actions and discussions that will enable them to obtain their policy objectives. Finally, they need to revise their strategy should they find it to be ineffective, whether because they made some miscalculations at the outset or because changing events have rendered their original strategy obsolete. In the hurly-burly of unfolding events, of course, policy practitioners do not follow these steps in a neat progression.

A POLICY-PRACTICE CASE FROM THE HUMAN SERVICES

Recall that Policy-Practice Case 5 (pp. 130–134) discussed the efforts of a social work intern to obtain a preventive program in a mental health agency. (The program would provide eight-week crisis services to the children of parents who were institutionalized because of their mental problems.) Although it was important for her to identify her sources of power, such as her connections with a preceptor (Mr. Jones), she had to incorporate, some-how, these kinds of power into a coherent political strategy.

Before she could develop a political strategy, however, she had to take a reading of those political realities that were germane to the case. She quickly decided that many political barriers existed, such as the dislike of many top officials of preventive programs, the scarce resources of the agency, and patterns of competition among the agency, area hospitals, and psychiatrists. However, she also identified various individuals and forces that were or could become supportive of her innovation, such as Mr. Jones and the desire by some officials to develop innovative projects that would enhance the prestige of the agency.

After considering these realities, she and Mr. Jones developed a two-phase strategy that would begin with a low-key approach (the developing of a pilot project by the intern with no consultation or approval from highly placed officials) and would lead to a formal presentation to the executive director after the project had already demonstrated its success.

This kind of strategizing in the context of political realities of the situation is discussed in this chapter. Social workers need these kinds of political skills because, as Policy-Practice Case 5 suggests, even relatively small and inexpensive proposals often encounter opposition from multiple sources. Ill-considered strategy often leads to failure; had this intern immediately sought approval from the executive director for the project, for example, she would probably have failed. Although intelligent and skillfully implemented strategy does not guarantee success, it often increases the likelihood that policy practitioners will obtain their policy preferences.

ESTABLISHING SOME ORIENTING OBJECTIVES

To develop intelligent strategy, policy practitioners have to first answer the question, Why am I participating in the political process? They have to decide what side they are taking as well as how much and what kind of policy changes they seek.

To Affirm, to Amend, to Oppose, or to Be Bystanders?

First, strategists have to decide whether to:

1. Initiate their own proposal (an affirmative position).
2. Change their or others' proposals (an amending position).
3. Oppose the initiatives of others (an opposing position).
4. Assume no role (a bystander position).

These choices are important because they commit the strategist to certain obligations and risks. People who develop a proposal have to invest considerable time in research, discussions, meetings, and negotiations and may expose themselves to criticism from those who question it. Advantages accrue to the initiators of proposals, however. By seizing the initiative, they make it more likely that their ideas will figure prominently in ensuing policy deliberations.

In contrast to strategists who initiate proposals, some people decide to amend them. Assume, for example, that someone is generally in accord with another person's position but does not wish to invest time in developing a proposal. By amending the proposal during policy deliberations, this person can advance his or her preferences for specific changes.

People sometimes assume a blocking or negative role to stop the enactment of an objectionable proposal. It is easier in some respects to block proposals than to develop them because opposers need only pinpoint their flaws or errors—a simpler task than developing them in the first instance. Blockers encounter risks of their own, however. They can be perceived to be "nay sayers" who lack constructive alternatives and may be accused of opposing changes because they benefit from existing policies.

Strategists sometimes adopt bystander roles, that is, they remain aloof from the deliberations that are associated with an issue. Perhaps they believe that they lack power to influence outcomes, want to save their scarce political resources for a future issue, believe that involvement in deliberations will require them to antagonize one or both sides in a controversy, or want to stay on the sidelines until they can assume a mediating role.

Roles of strategists are often shaped, of course, by their analysis of the distribution of sentiment, salience, and power with respect to a particular issue or proposal. If the prognosis for passage of a proposal is extremely bleak, for example, some practitioners are reluctant to develop proposals— just as they might not obstruct a proposal that had attracted widespread support. As we will note in Chapter Eight when we discuss advocacy, policy practitioners sometimes oppose objectionable policies or develop proposals in the face of overwhelming odds, whether because they believe fundamental principles are at stake or because they want to convince some segment of their constituency that they will champion their interests.

What Policy Changes Are Sought?

Policy practitioners often encounter the perennial question, Do we want relatively major or incremental changes? This choice, like other policy choices, is often difficult to make. A policy practitioner may believe that major changes are needed to provide assistance to a particular group of consumers or to revitalize an existing program. But fundamental changes are often not politically feasible and moreover require relatively large investments of time and energy.[1] Political realities importantly shape this choice; if a considerable number of people oppose a specific initiative, for example, policy practitioners may have to settle for relatively modest changes in existing policy. In some cases, policy practitioners have the modest objective of sensitizing or educating people about a particular policy problem or issue because it is impossible to develop and enact policies if people do not first believe that a problem exists.

Selecting a Time Frame

Policy practitioners often ask, Do we want specific changes to be enacted in the short term, such as during a specific and upcoming meeting, during the present year, or during the present session of a legislature—or are we willing to accept a longer time frame?[2] People with a long-term perspective do not need to develop strategy that will bring instant results, although they encounter the formidable challenge of maintaining interest in an issue when tangible results are not forthcoming. The selection of a time frame is linked both to the distribution of power and to the policy objectives of a practitioner; when the distribution of power is unfavorable with respect to an issue or proposal, for example, it is difficult to obtain its immediate enactment no matter how skillful its proponents.

GROUNDING STRATEGY IN CURRENT REALITIES

As with any community-work, administrative, or direct-service intervention, political strategy has to be firmly linked to existing realities including the distribution of power, various contextual factors, situational realities, impending developments, and the nature of the setting.

Analyzing the Distribution of Sentiment, Salience, and Power That Are Associated with Specific Issues

Kurt Lewin, the noted social psychologist, pioneered the concept of force-field analysis to facilitate the analysis of the distribution of power in specific situations.[3] To obtain a rough estimate of the support for a proposal, Lewin suggests that we enumerate persons (by name) and indicate the strength of their support or opposition in numeric terms, say, from 1 (relatively weak support or opposition) to 10 (relatively powerful support or opposition). Their names and the degree of their support or opposition can be illustrated in graphic form (Figure 6.1) by placing the opponents on the underside of a line and the proponents on its topside. (The line lengths correspond to the strength of their opposition to or support of the policy.) The preponderance of sentiment in opposition to the policy in Figure 6.1 is discerned by comparing the number and length of lines beneath the horizontal line to the lines above it.

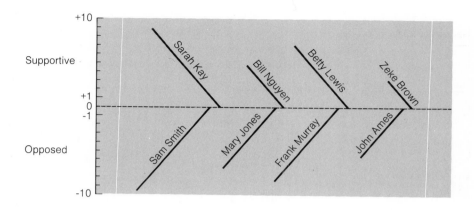

To gather a more complete depiction of the strength of support of and opposition to a specific policy proposal, we would need to obtain additional information. First, we need to know the relative ability or power of someone to shape policy on a specific issue because people with such power could be particularly critical to our strategy development. The chair of a committee that considers an issue, for example, often has more power than someone who does not occupy this strategic position. Second, we need to estimate the relative salience or importance that specific individuals attach to an issue. Someone might have strong convictions on an issue and be well positioned to affect policy, for example, but not be interested in the issue, whether because he believed it fell within someone else's purview or because he was more interested in other issues.

Michael O'Leary and William Coplin have developed a simple scoring system to assess the distribution of power and sentiment with respect to an issue.[4] Take the example of a family of four persons who must consider two issues: (1) whether to have Grandma move into the house in the wake of a recent bout of illness and (2) whether to allow an eighteen-year-old son to own his own car. The two parents (Mary and Frank) and the two children (Sam and Diane) have decided to reach these decisions democratically, but, as we noted in the preceding chapter, policy-making does not usually occur on a level playing field. Assume that we know the family well enough to construct the data in Table 6.1, where the positions, salience, and power of the family members are scored. (The initials M, F, S, and D stand, respectively, for the four family members—mother [Mary], father [Frank], son [Sam], and daughter [Diane].)

First, we give a score to each person with respect to their formal positions on our issues (extending from −10, very negative, to +10, very favorable).

TABLE 6.1 A Scoring Chart for Estimating the Distribution of Sentiment, Salience, and Power

	Issue 1: Grandmother				Issue 2: Car			
	M	F	S	D	M	F	S	D
Positions on the issues (−10 to +10)	10	−5	2	4	4	2	10	8
Salience (1 to 10)	8	8	3	4	7	7	7	7
Power to influence the outcome of this issue (1 to 4)	3	3	1	1	3	3	2	1
Totals for each participant (multiply the numbers down each column)	240	−120	6	16	84	42	140	56
Grand total for each issue (add together the totals for each person)		142				322		

The higher the to total score, the more likely the proposal will succeed. Sam's getting a car is more likely than Grandma's moving in.

Table 6.1 shows that Mary strongly favors allowing her mother to reside in their home (she receives a score of 10), whereas Frank opposes the move (he receives a score of −5). (The children are mildly supportive and receive scores of 2 and 4.) It can be seen that *all* family members support allowing Sam to have a car (Issue 2) because they, respectively, receive scores of 4, 2, 10, and 8, although, predictably, the two children support this policy more strongly than either of their parents.

Second, we score each person with respect to the salience, or importance, that they attach to each issue on a scale extending from 1 (low salience) to 10 (high salience). Both parents attach considerable importance to each of the issues, as can be seen by their scores of 8 on the issue of Grandma and 7 on the issue of Sam's car. The children attach much more importance to the issue of the car (they both are scored as 7 on Issue 2), while attaching less importance to Grandma's residence in their home (their scores are 3 and 4 on salience).

Third, we estimate the relative power of persons to influence the choices with respect to each issue on a scale extending from 1 (low power) to 4 (high power). The parents possess far more power than do the children, as is reflected by their scores of 3 on each of the issues when compared to the scores of 1 or 2 of the children on each of the two issues.

To obtain an overall reading of the distribution of sentiment, salience, and position on each of the two issues, we multiply the scores of each person on each issue. Mary receives a score of 240 ($10 \times 8 \times 3$) on Issue 1 and 84 ($4 \times 7 \times 3$) on Issue 2, whereas Frank receives scores of -120 on the issue of Grandma ($-5 \times 8 \times 3$) and 42 ($2 \times 7 \times 3$) on the issue of Sam's car. The two children receive considerably higher—that is, more favorable—scores on the issue of the car (they receive, respectively, scores of 140 and 56) than on the issue of Grandma, where they receive scores of 6 and 16.

After finding the total score of each person on each issue, we simply add the scores of the various participants on each issue to obtain a score for all participants with respect to a specific issue. Because a higher score indicates a more favorable prognosis for a proposal, it appears that Sam is more likely to have a car ($84 + 42 + 140 + 56 = 322$) than is Grandma to obtain residence in the family home ($240 + -120 + 6 + 16 = 142$). Table 6.1 clearly shows that a single *negative* score by a powerful participant can markedly decrease the likelihood that a specific issue will be enacted (see Frank's negative score with respect to Grandma's move to his home).

A numbers approach to force-field analysis may seem farfetched, but the skeptical reader should realize that this kind of analysis, crude and imperfect as it may be, is sometimes used by politicians in legislative bodies who keep numeric tallies to determine the prognosis for specific pieces of legislation.[5] If a proposal is associated with an extremely low or unfavorable score, policy practitioners may decide the situation is hopeless, *unless* they can develop strategy that enables them to change the positions, to alter the salience, or to modify the power of persons who support their position.

Moreover, the exercise of identifying important participants, as well as their positions, salience, and power, helps policy practitioners develop strategy.[6] The data in Table 6.1 suggest a variety of strategy options. Assume that Mary wants Grandma, that is, *her* mother, to move to her home. She could try to change Frank's position on the issue at least toward a neutral position, *or* she could hope to reduce the salience he attached to the issue (perhaps by contending it would be a brief stay), *or* she could try to isolate him from the decision-making process, thus reducing his power to influence the outcome of the issue. She could seek to alter the positions, salience, and power of the children with respect to the issue—perhaps by promising them support for the car in return for their support on the grandmother issue! Coalitional power is not discussed in Table 6.1, but Mary could try to increase her power by "ganging up on" Frank by forming a coalition with her children. Or she could try to add *new* participants to the struggle.[7] Perhaps she could persuade Grandma to make an impassioned plea to Frank or secure the support of the family physician who might say that residence in the family's home would be more beneficial to Grandma than entering a nursing home. Or perhaps she could enlist support from other relatives who might even offer to visit Grandma after her move to the family home.

We should note certain dangers in force-field analysis. If people wrongly estimate the positions of certain persons, they may falsely decide that the prognosis for a position is more favorable or less favorable than it really is. This misreading of evidence may lead them to commit two kinds of errors: they may falsely refrain from pursuing an issue or proposal that could be enacted, or they may promote an issue or proposal that cannot be enacted.

These errors in calculating positions, salience, and power at a specific time can be compounded by another kind of error. When we estimate at Point 1 that a proposal is or is not politically feasible, we sometimes assume that the current distribution of sentiment, salience, and power will remain constant at Points 2, 3, and so on. In fact, positions, salience, and power often change during the course of deliberations. Indeed, effective reformers are skillful at transforming bleak and seemingly hopeless situations into more positive ones by developing and implementing strategy. Indeed, our discussion of some of Mary's strategy options suggests how strategists can seek to modify existing realities.

These cautionary notes about force-field analysis do not render it useless. If we make no effort to gauge the nature and extent of support and opposition to specific measures, we can often proceed blindly to commit ourselves to issues that are not politically feasible. As important, if we make no estimate of the degree of difficulty in enacting or obtaining approval for a policy, we cannot make an estimate of the amounts of time and political resources that we need to commit to it. Better to go into battle, some would say, with our eyes open to the realities that we confront.

Identifying Contextual Realities That Shape Deliberations with Respect to an Issue or Policy

Although it is useful to tally the relative support of and opposition to a policy, these calculations need to be supplemented by broader considerations that tell us *why* certain persons take specific positions or how they are likely to act when an issue or policy is injected into policy deliberations. Analysis of prior traditions of deliberation, vested interests, and the underlying values of participants provides a more complete understanding of the positions— and likely actions—of people than does merely estimating their current positions.

Prior Traditions   Some issues or policies are considered de novo, but many have been considered on prior occasions. The responses of decision makers to specific issues or policies, as well as interest groups and the general public, are often shaped by their recollections of these prior deliberations or by reports or accounts of the prior deliberations.[8] Deliberations are more likely to be conflictual, for example, when an issue has been associated with ideologic polarization on prior occasions, as illustrated by controversy that arises whenever Congress considers national health insurance, gun control, or federal prohibitions on abortion. Indeed, many politicians avoid these kinds of issues because they do not want to become embroiled in controversial issues that pit various groups within their constituencies against one another—or that commit them to an extended legislative battle with uncertain outcomes. In organizations, too, participants sometimes refrain from reintroducing issues or policies that have been associated with controversy on prior occasions.

Policy practitioners can sometimes erroneously conclude, however, that the traditions that have been associated with an issue or policy will continue. After a veto by President Nixon of legislation that would have funded a national day-care program (among other things), children's advocates found it difficult to persuade many legislators to reintroduce or support similar legislation. But a determined coalition nearly obtained the enactment of major day-care legislation in 1988 when a combination of factors, including pressure from corporations and from an expanded pool of female workers, created a more favorable environment. Indeed, skillful strategists try to offset the negative effects of traditions by emphasizing those developments that have made an issue or position more feasible than on a prior occasion. Supporters of the day-care proposal in 1988, for example, noted that many more women were in the workforce than in the early 1970s and that many corporations had become convinced that subsidized daycare was needed for them to attract and retain female employees.[9]

Vested Interests   The positions of persons on specific issues or policies are often powerfully shaped by their perceptions of their interests. In some cases, they fear issues or policies will harm their interests.[10] Politicians may fear, for example, that a certain policy will antagonize some of their constituents, enable the other party to expand its constituency, or allow an opposing politician to obtain an electoral advantage. An executive of a social agency or government bureaucracy may fear that a proposal will shift resources or program responsibilities to rival agencies, impose controls or regulations on their activities, or diminish their revenues. Alternatively, people support specific issues or policies because they believe that the policies will enhance, for example, their power, prestige, or resources.

It is sometimes difficult to predict how people will calculate the impact of a policy or issue on their interests. In the case of specific politicians, for example, they may not know how their constituents will respond to a proposal, may mistakenly assume that they will obtain support (or opposition) from specific constituents, or may not realize that some "losses," such as antagonism from one interest group, will be offset by gains from other groups. Skillful strategists often try to identify some positive implications of a position on the interests of those people whose support they hope to garner. For example, supporters of the day-care proposal in 1988 told many politicians that they risked losing a large share of the female vote if they opposed the proposal.[11]

(3) *Degree of Cohesion of Likely Opponents and Proponents*   Although we can sometimes calculate with considerable precision the positions of specific individuals on an issue or policy, our analysis is incomplete if we fail to examine the relationships among them. Assume, for example, that we discover that the support of and opposition to a proposed policy are evenly balanced—a discovery that makes us predict a stalemate because neither side will prevail. To our astonishment, the proponents subsequently win a one-sided victory because, unlike their opponents, they possess close working relationships that allow them to evolve strategy to facilitate their cause and to work together to implement it. (Opponents are, by contrast, disunited.) Moreover, the nature of the leadership that is associated with specific issues is often vitally important. If leaders with knowledge, commitment, political expertise, and considerable power support a specific issue, it is more likely to be successful. Moreover, successful leaders are adept at assembling and maintaining supportive coalitions.

Situational Realities

Situational realities often shape the course of policy deliberations. In legislative settings, for example, the fate of specific policies is often influenced by the proximity of elections, the balance of power between contending parties, institutional rivalries among powerful legislators in various legislative committees, rivalries among members of different legislative chambers, the budgetary situation, changes in leadership, the extent of competition with other proposals for attention, and the remaining time in a legislative session.[12]

These kinds of background factors variously influence the extent of interest in specific issues and the extent of conflict that is associated with them. When national elections are imminent, for example, politicians of both parties begin to jockey for position; they want to take "out-front" positions that will appeal to major segments of their existing constituencies *or* draw some of the constituents of opponents to their side. These positions may be affirmative or negative; liberal Democrats from northern cities, for example, may champion the enactment of certain social programs and publicly oppose conservative initiatives such as efforts to rescind regulations that promote affirmative action. Conservatives not only promote issues that will solidify support among their traditional constituencies but also advance social measures that will attract some Democrats to their cause; thus, George Bush developed a tax-credit scheme to fund daycare for middle-class women in the summer of 1988 to counter a more liberal proposal from Michael Dukakis.[13] By the same token, however, impending elections may make members of both parties inclined to avoid those issues where they can achieve no partisan advantage or where significant political risks exist. Some liberal Democrats who normally champion policies to allow federal financing of abortions may try to avoid this divisive issue in the year preceding an election.

Personal and institutional rivalries often exacerbate conflict as well as efforts to initiate proposals. Legislative committees may jealously attempt to preserve their jurisdiction over certain kinds of issues; when their leaders hear rumors, for example, that another committee will soon develop a proposal, some of the members may rush to develop their own proposal to preempt the issue. This kind of rivalry can exist between committees within a legislative chamber—or between rival committees in different chambers, as is illustrated by rivalry between leaders in the House Committee on Education and Labor and leaders in the Senate Committee on Labor and Public Welfare. In the early phases of the development of child development legislation in 1971, for example, these two committees developed proposals in the context of considerable rivalry.[14]

Situational factors also influence the political process in organizations. Neither elections nor party rivalries exist in organizations, but the succession of leaders, internal institutional and personal rivalries, tensions between the boards and staff of agencies, budget realities, and developments among external funders can significantly influence the politics of specific proposals.[15] In the wake of the advent of a new executive, for example, a relatively fluid political situation exists; both the executive and various individuals and factions within the organization position themselves by developing positions on those issues and proposals that are on the policy agenda and by seeking support for them. Indeed, many theorists contend that many of the major changes in the policies of organizations occur in the aftermath of new leadership.[16]

Institutional and personal rivalries exist within most organizations as different factions and units vie for scarce resources, possess somewhat different views of "where the organization should be heading," and seek credit and recognition for their respective programs. As in legislative settings, these rivalries sometimes influence the positions of competing persons and factions on specific proposals or issues; thus, someone may oppose the initiative of rivals *because* it was initiated by them or initiate a proposal in order to "beat them to the punch." The structure of many organizations invites institutional rivalry because they are often divided into specific sections or units that have overlapping jurisdictions and that seek funds from the limited budget of the organization.[17] Considerable competition often exists, for example, between nursing, psychology, and social work units within hospitals as each seeks enlarged functions and budgets.

Predicting Future Developments

We have noted that computations about the relative support for a policy can falsely imply that political interaction is static in nature and can be analyzed by merely estimating the prognosis of a measure at a single point. In fact, the politics of specific measures *evolve* as supporters, opponents, and bystanders interact and as events unfold. Assume, for example, that a person who is relatively neutral with respect to a policy proposal at Point 1 observes at Point 2 a "nasty and unethical effort by someone to steamroll his perspective." She may become sufficiently incensed by this power maneuver that she joins the fray by opposing the proposal. As this example illustrates, it is sometimes difficult to develop strategy because people's positions on specific issues change during the give-and-take of the political process.

The give-and-take of the political process also shapes the kinds of political strategies that people use. If supporters of a particular measure decide that they need only to quietly spirit a measure through a legislative committee and subsequently on the floor of Congress to secure its enactment, they may quickly develop more militant strategies if they learn that opponents plan to attack the measure in emotional terms and to publicize it in the mass media. Indeed, a large group of theorists have developed a body of knowledge, which is called *game theory*, that examines how persons and factions respond to the tactical maneuvers of opponents.[18]

Because people change their positions and their strategies in the course of deliberations and in response to the actions of opponents, effective practitioners have to revise their strategy at successive points and in response to anticipated events as well as the tactical moves of others.

Adapting Strategy to the Setting

Strategy needs to be tailored to the setting, that is, to the specific agency, community, or legislature where an issue is deliberated. Strategy that is effective in legislative settings, for example, can be counterproductive in agency settings as the following discussion suggests.

Conflict is endemic to legislatures because it allows legislators to publicize their policy preferences to their constituents.[19] If liberals cultivate the support of their constituents by advocating social reform measures, conservatives increase their constituency support by opposing them and by introducing relatively conservative measures like proposals to reduce taxes. The electoral process, which rewards politicians who enhance their base of support and punishes those who antagonize constituents, promotes open conflict.

In agency settings, however, executives, members of boards, and staff are not elected by the general public but are appointed or hired by executives, by the boards of agencies, or (in the case of top officials in government agencies) by mayors, governors, or presidents. Public, regular, and sustained conflict is not common in organizations for several reasons.[20] Staff have to work together on a daily basis, so continuing and open conflict could disrupt agency programs. People in subordinate positions who engage in open and frequent conflict are often viewed to breech the "chain of command" that exists in all organizations. Staff and board members often believe that controversy about their agency can diminish public support and funding for it, particularly when it reaches the general public or the mass media. Although publicized conflict is correspondingly less common in organizations than in legislatures, the executives of large government agencies, as well as some smaller ones, are adept at using the press to publicize the achievements of their organizations to obtain a public relations advantage.[21]

Other differences between legislatures and agencies exist. A hierarchy exists in both settings, extending from party leaders and chairs of committees to recently elected legislators or executives and board members to staff. Recently elected legislators, who exist at the bottom of the legislative hierarchy, can nonetheless support initiatives that run counter to their party or their party leaders because they possess an independent source of power that derives from their constituents.[22] Because subordinates in organizations lack this independent base of power, however, they can be fired, demoted, denied pay increases, denied promotion, or given distasteful jobs. Although unions, civil service regulations, and professional ethics diminish these kinds of reprisals, they do not eliminate them.

These comparisons between agencies and legislatures illustrate how settings influence the selection of strategy. A staff member in an organization who sought to publicize dispute within the agency to the community—a tactic commonly used in legislative settings—could experience negative repercussions because the tactic violates the norms of most organizations. (He might nonetheless assume this risk if he felt the issue to be so important that he was willing to incur possible risks.) Policymakers also have to adapt their strategies to the idiosyncratic norms and traditions of specific organizations and legislative committees. The staff in some organizations are used to relatively conflictual tactics, whereas the staff in other organizations spurn them. If some legislative committees, such as the House Committee on Labor and Education, are used to relatively wide-open conflict between liberals and conservatives, the appropriations committees of both Houses of Congress pride themselves on quiet and private deliberations where they seek behind-the-scenes solutions to budgetary issues.[23]

BUILDING SCENARIOS TO CONSTRUCT POLITICAL STRATEGY

Our discussion thus far has emphasized a *future-looking activity* (the setting of objectives) and a *present-oriented activity* (examining current realities such as the distribution of power and sentiment that are germane to deliberations about a specific issue or policy). Political strategy allows us to conceptually link the present with the future by identifying likely actions and verbal exchanges that allow policy practitioners to obtain their policy preferences.

Developing Alternative Scenarios
That Are Linked to Strategy Options

Policy practitioners begin a process of sorting through a series of political options, much like a quarterback who surveys possible plays that can be used when confronted with a specific situation on the football field. Indeed, creative strategists run through successive what-if scenarios in which they try to predict whether various combinations of actions or statements could increase their likelihood of obtaining their policy preferences.[24]

To graphically portray these what-if scenarios, imagine three possibilities. In Scenario 1, the policy practitioner asks, What would happen if I (or my allies) made a *single* presentation at an appropriate meeting or with a decision maker to suggest a specific policy or course of action? This presentation might involve (1) a request that a specific policy problem be taken sufficiently seriously to be placed on the agenda of a committee or (2) a policy option that should be seriously considered. In some cases, of course, this single presentation, which represents a minimal or modest strategy, will suffice, particularly if the practitioner's assessment of current realities suggests that a propitious and supportive environment exists.

When policy practitioners decide, however, that such a modest strategy will probably be unsuccessful, they necessarily turn to other, more ambitious strategies. Practitioners sometimes develop at least two additional scenarios. In Scenario 2, they develop a somewhat more ambitious strategy; perhaps, for example, the single presentation is coupled with various discussions with key decision makers before and after a pivotal presentation in order to make them more sympathetic to a specific policy. Scenario 3 is even more ambitious and could involve developing a coalition, cultivating a constituency, coupling presentations with many personal discussions, allocating specific roles and tasks to a range of people, and mixing internal pressure with external pressure. As an example of ambitious strategy, for example, a coalition of organizations, which included the Children's Defense Fund as a central participant, developed a legislative proposal for federal day-care subsidies in 1988. Its members not only had personal liaisons with a range of legislators and government officials but also exerted extensive external pressures on congressional members through letter writing and articles in the mass media.

Let's contrast the three preceding strategies with an ad lib, or improvisational, one. In some cases, policy practitioners decide *not* to develop a strategy but to make comments or to seize opportunities as they arise in specific situations.[25] Perhaps, at an opportune moment, they inject an idea or issue into the discussions of a committee, staff meeting, or with an official in their organization. Improvisational strategies are sometimes useful because policy practitioners lack the time or do not know "the lay of the land" sufficiently to allow the development of more refined strategies. However, unlike the three preceding strategies, improvisational strategies may not enable the policy practitioner to mobilize and use power resources in a systematic fashion.

Policy practitioners do not have to invest major resources in this preliminary development of three or four strategies because they are interested only in developing the *broad outlines* of strategy at this point. In effect, they ask, Does this issue or policy require a major investment of resources and time on my (and my allies') part, or should we address this issue with a modest *or* improvisational strategy?

Selecting One of the Strategies

Pragmatic considerations and stylistic preferences shape the selection of strategy. Policy practitioners obviously want to select a strategy that will increase the chances for obtaining their policy preferences, so they review strategy options in light of the various kinds of current realities that were discussed in the preceding section of this chapter. If their force-field analysis suggests that extraordinary opposition exists to their proposal, for example, they may select a relatively ambitious strategy that is relatively complex and that requires a significant investment of time and energy. Policy practitioners want a strategy that is sufficiently robust to offset the kinds of opposition that their proposal will likely encounter.

They have to consider their own resources and time. Accordingly, they often want to develop a strategy that allows their measures to follow a "path of least resistance."[26] If a proposal can be enacted by using a relatively simple strategy that does not require many resources and much time, most policy practitioners will select it. In some cases, even when they fear a more ambitious one is needed, they proceed with a relatively modest strategy because they lack time to devote to an issue—or place higher priority on another.

The strategy choices of practitioners are also influenced by their stylistic preferences. Individuals often have distinctive styles when participating in the political process, whether in legislative, community, or agency contexts. Consider the case of political candidates for the presidency in 1988.[27] Paul Simon, the Democratic senator from Illinois, was an "old-fashioned Populist" who championed social programs to help minorities and poor people at numerous points during his career. He was often less interested in securing the passage of specific bills than in championing social and moral causes. Like Jesse Jackson, the candidate whose career had begun in the ministry and the civil rights movement, Simon hoped to educate the public to the merits of an expansive welfare state. Richard Gephardt and Robert Dole,

Democratic congressman from Missouri and Republican senator from Kansas, respectively, had long assumed functions in Congress as mediators or facilitators where they performed vote-counting, parliamentary, and measure-shaping functions to expedite the enactment of specific pieces of legislation. (Their positions as leaders in Congress and their parties required them to assume these mediating tasks on frequent occasions.) Both were accustomed to frequently changing their personal positions to fashion compromises that would allow specific measures to be enacted. Senator Albert Gore, Democratic senator from Tennessee, preferred to select certain high-visibility issues that were associated with a broad consensus, such as the development of federal laws to establish a National Organ Donation Service and to outlaw the commercial sale of organs. (He carefully avoided the kinds of controversial issues that Jackson and Simon preferred to address.) George Bush, the Republican vice president, had contented himself with a variety of background positions in the executive branch where he filled a variety of implementation, ceremonial, and mediation roles and where he avoided stating his own positions on many issues. Indeed, many people were unable to pinpoint his personal positions on a range of issues.

This discussion of political styles suggests that each of us possesses distinctive approaches to politics. Some of us are "out front and direct" in stating our positions, whereas others prefer discussing them in private deliberations. Some people like to precipitate conflict by advancing controversial positions, whereas others like to serve as mediators. Some people prefer initiating and enacting policies, whereas others prefer implementing roles.

Each of these styles of politics has advantages and disadvantages. Mediators usefully facilitate compromises but sometimes are accused of failing to develop their own perspectives. (Dole and Gephardt encountered the charge that they often shifted positions.) Champions of ideologic positions initiate bold changes but sometimes lack the skills of compromise that are needed to get them enacted. (Many persons perceived Simon and Jackson to be ideologues.) Persons who only select "sure winners" or who avoid controversial issues are seen to lack courage or leadership, charges that were levied against Gore and Bush.

The personal styles of policy practitioners often extend to the kind of political interaction that they favor. Let's distinguish between high-conflict and polarized politics, high-conflict but consensual politics, low-conflict and technical politics, and moderate conflict but compromise-oriented politics.[28] People who use a **high-conflict and polarized style,** such as those who introduce national health insurance legislation into Congress, deliberately introduce controversial policy measures that they know will polarize others into supportive and opposing camps. Not wary of conflict, such people are not afraid to use conflict-inducing tactics; thus, an initiator of national health insurance would criticize the "self-serving tendencies" of the American Medical Association, the greed of health-care providers and insurance companies, and the inequalities of the current health-care system. This style of politics is useful in a number of situations. It can be used to educate citizens and to build reform-oriented constituencies even in those cases where little chance of passage is likely. People can also use this style when they believe their side possesses a numeric majority in Congress or in a deliberative body—or could obtain a majority if the general public were to become sufficiently aroused by the proposal to pressure their legislative representatives. When the Democrats obtained sweeping majorities of both houses of Congress in the New Deal and the Great Society, Presidents Franklin Roosevelt and Lyndon Johnson, respectively, were able to obtain sweeping legislative reforms by using a conflictual style of politics.[29]

A **high-conflict and consensual style** occurs when policy makers want to obtain credit for a highly popular measure, such as increased funding for a specific program. In such cases, both sides in a political conflict advance proposals that they claim will "do the most" for the program and contend that the proposal of their opponents is insufficient. Because the measure is extremely popular, however, both sides seek an eventual solution in order not to be tagged as obstructionists, so they are willing in the final analysis to compromise with their opponents. In this style of politics conflict is combined with a willingness to compromise, unlike the high-conflict and polarized style where both sides seek to defeat their opponents during a protracted period of conflict.

A **low-conflict and technical style** of politics is most suited to issues that could potentially become controversial if they were perceived to involve major reforms. Seeking to obtain passage, strategists portray the issue as "merely technical or small scale" in nature. They shun publicity for the measure, provide a technical rationale for its passage, and make extensive use of parliamentary maneuvers such as attaching the measure to another, more popular measure to usher it quietly and quickly through the legislative process.

Strategists seek a **moderate-conflict but compromise-oriented style** of politics when they want to foster a give-and-take process of deliberations.[30] The measure lacks widespread public support, cannot be presented as "merely technical" in nature, and is somewhat controversial. Its advocates want to encourage a give-and-take process of deliberations that leads to the adoption of an eventual compromise that is acceptable to all parties. Unlike conflictual politics, however, and like the politics of technical issues, much of the compromising and amending process occurs in the proverbial "smoke-filled rooms" of committees and party caucuses.

Of course, strategists often cannot succeed in stimulating the style of politics that will lead to enactment of their measure. Someone who favors the technical style may find that it quickly becomes associated with polarized conflict. Conversely, someone who wants moderate conflict and consensus building may discover the issue is so widely dismissed as "merely technical" in nature that its politics conform to the low-conflict and technical style of politics.

These styles, which have been discussed regarding legislative settings, also exist in organizations. On rare occasions, people in organizations try to stimulate polarized politics that divide their staff and officials into contending factions. On other occasions, people seek support for issues by portraying them as technical or minor ones. For example, people sometimes propose a time-limited pilot or demonstration project to decrease opposition by others who would object to a major innovation.[31] Skillful strategists can use a variety of styles and can select a style that will help them achieve their policy objectives in a specific situation.

Revising the Strategy in Light of Emerging Realities

The preceding discussion fails to capture, however, the evolving or fluid nature of strategy-making. We have already noted that it is often difficult to predict who is likely to support or oppose a specific policy. People cannot engage in strategy-making without considering the current and expected actions of possible opponents of the policy. How cohesive and organized are they? For example, do they possess coalitions, leadership, and strategies, or are they merely scattered individuals? If they possess strategy, what is it likely to be, how are they likely to attack the substantive content of the proposal, which persons are they likely to try to convince, and what procedural powers might they use? Of course, strategists may have little or no idea about the strategies of opponents, but they need, at least, to consider them.

To the extent that they can guess likely strategies of opponents, strategists need to decide whether and how they can be countered. Assume, for example, that opponents argue that a specific policy will be excessively costly. Proponents might try to show that it will allow the reduction of some costs, might alter the content of the proposal to make it less costly, or might contend that the additional costs are offset by benefits to clients. Anticipation of the strategy of opponents allows proponents to more effectively counter it.

Of course, interventions that are devised at Point 1 need to be revised at subsequent points as policies evolve, as events unfold, as new configurations of support and opposition to a policy develop, and as strategies of opponents change. At each successive point, strategists encounter the same challenge as confronted them initially, namely, how to capitalize on and strengthen the sources of support for their policy and how to offset or neutralize opposition.

In this evolving process, the policy itself may change markedly. In legislative settings, for example, modifications occur in the provisions of the legislation in the give-and-take of committee deliberations, in floor debates, and during negotiations between proponents of the bill and various legislators and their aides.[32] At certain points, proponents concede to certain changes in the legislation to decrease opposition to it, whereas in other cases, the changes are imposed on them by people or factions that possess the power to secure specific changes.

FLESHING OUT THE DETAILS: DEVELOPING STRATEGY

Policy practitioners have to identify specific power resources that can enable them to achieve their policy preferences in a specific situation. It is rarely sufficient to identify those power resources that, at a single and climactic moment, can bring the enactment of a policy. Instead, a sequence of power transactions, often extending over a period of months or years, provide the groundwork that allows a proposal to be developed, to obtain some initial clearances, and to reach a culminating vote or process of ratification. A number of people may collaborate in the devising and implementing of these power transactions. Strategy usually requires, then, the successive and repeated uses of power, often by many people and in many situations, over an extended period of time.

Moreover, some overall style or approach is needed when devising strategy. Is a low-conflict or high-conflict approach to be used? Will strategists seek to mobilize a relatively large constituency or group to work together to pressure decision makers, or will they rely on behind-the-scenes discussions? Will they seek a sweeping or major reform or settle for a relatively modest one?

A detailed strategy identifies specific actions and verbal exchanges that one or more persons will take or make during a specific time frame to achieve those policy objectives. Many kinds of strategies exist. Some are relatively ambitious and involve many people; others are relatively simple and involve planned actions or verbal exchanges of one person. Some strategies, such as ones to secure the enactment of a major piece of legislation, cover an extended time frame, whereas others are devised for a single event such as an important meeting. Although diversity is important, effective strategy addresses certain issues that can usefully be placed in six categories (Table 6.2).

Establishing a Time Frame and Policy Goals   The enactment of a proposal usually occurs in the course of a series of maneuvers, meetings, discussions, presentations, and other interactions. People who seek enactment of their proposals often develop objectives within specific time frames that contain one, several, or more episodes or events.[33] Someone may wish during specific time frames, for example, to obtain an affirmative vote during an

TABLE 6.2   Six Issues Often Addressed by Strategy

Establishing a Time Frame and Policy Goals
- What do proponents wish to achieve within a specific time frame?

Specifying the Content of a Policy Proposal
- What minimal features or content should the policy proposal contain?
- What points are negotiable or compromisable?

Finding and Organizing the Proponents of a Proposal
- Who will provide leadership?
- Who will perform what tasks?

Establishing the Style or Approach to Be Used
- What decision routes will be sought?
- What kind of process or interaction is sought in terms of the level of conflict and the scope of conflict?

Matching Specific Power Resources with Specific Persons and Situations
- What kinds of person-to-person, substantive, process, and agenda-setting power resources will be used?
- Who will use these power resources and in what situations?

Revising the Strategy
- How should the game plan be revised in light of the strategies of opponents?
- What changing events or background factors suggest a change in strategy?

important meeting, to establish a supportive coalition, or to get an item placed on the agenda of a meeting. By defining goals and time frames as events unfold, policy practitioners can focus their work and provide discipline to it.

Specifying the Content of a Policy Proposal   The ultimate objective of policy practitioners is to secure the enactment of a proposal, but they must often ask, Precisely what proposal? They have to decide what points or contents of a proposal are sufficiently important to them, thus resisting efforts to change or delete them. Policy practitioners encounter difficult dilemmas: if they are willing to compromise excessively, they run the risk of "ending up with nothing"; but if they are excessively rigid or dogmatic, they may be unable to obtain the enactment of any proposal.

Finding and Organizing the Proponents of a Proposal   The proponents of specific measures often want to pool their resources, ideas, and power resources, but they cannot accomplish this objective if they are not organized in some fashion. In the case of relatively small and homogeneous groups, such as colleagues in a social agency, coordinating mechanisms are relatively simple to form and may build on the leadership and communication patterns that already exist.[34] Coordination is more difficult when relatively heterogeneous groups or interests are represented and when many of them are involved. Patterns of mistrust sometimes exist, as well as fundamental differences about the nature of the policy or proposal.

As we discuss in more detail in the next chapter, proponents need to address issues of coordination, leadership, the building of constituencies, the resolution of conflict, division of labor, and communication. Moreover, they must attend to these issues not only at the outset but also as events unfold. Perhaps some people lose interest or become disenchanted with the cause, disagreements develop about strategy, some people fear others unduly seek credit for a proposal, or others become restive in the wake of apparent setbacks.

Even before these coordinating mechanisms can be established, a pool of proponents needs to be developed. Strategists have to avoid extremes of fatalism and naïveté when searching for potential allies. Fatalists wrongly assume that specific persons will oppose a certain initiative; thus, liberals sometimes assume that moderates and conservatives will necessarily oppose social reforms without fully considering constituency, value, and other factors that *might* impel them to support a specific proposal.[35] Naïve strategists wrongly assume that an initiative will attract support from an array of persons and interests, even when evidence suggests that it will be controversial. Unaware of political realities, these strategists fail to take actions or engage in discussions to avert or offset opposition.

When deciding whether certain people, groups, or interests will support a proposal, strategists examine *motivating* factors. Do their traditional or past positions on a similar issue suggest a sympathetic orientation? Are they likely to believe that their vested or tangible interests, such as constituency support, resources, or prestige, could be protected or advanced by a proposal? Will an existing or potential ally command sufficient respect from certain people to sway them to support an issue? Will certain others perceive a proposal to support the central mission of an organization? These kinds of motivating factors are difficult to identify and analyze, but they provide important clues. In many cases, of course, people have mixed motivations; values may dispose some to support a policy, for example, but their vested interests may suggest opposition.[36]

Establishing the Style or Approach to Be Used　We noted in the preceding discussion that an overarching style, or approach, is needed. Practitioners need to decide what kind of political interaction and what kind of procedural or parliamentary approaches will be most advantageous to their proposal.

Will behind-the-scenes and nonconflictual deliberations suffice, or is more conflictual and publicized interaction advisable? To the extent a choice exists, which committee will provide a specific proposal with a relatively favorable treatment? Should the introduction of an initiative be delayed until background conditions are more favorable?

These kinds of choices may be vigorously contested, of course, by others, such as the opponents of a specific measure. By defining the style, or approach, that is beneficial to their measure, however, proponents hope to shape events rather than merely responding to the initiatives of other people.

Matching Specific Power Resources with Specific Persons and Situations To realize their strategy, the proponents of a policy must use their power resources in specific situations. They use the various kinds of power resources that we discussed in Chapter 5, but their challenge is to decide *who* uses *what power resources* in *what situations.* If a number of people are involved in a project, they can divide responsibilities for talking with specific people, making presentations, doing research, developing lists of supporters, and other functions. As an example, people who seek policy changes in an agency may decide that "Joe will propose a place on the agenda at an upcoming staff meeting to discuss a modification of the intake procedure, Mary will comment on inadequacies in the existing procedure at the staff meeting, Tom will make some supportive comments, and Elise will suggest the need to form a task force to devise a new policy." Moreover, this group might decide to approach certain people before the staff meeting to obtain support for the change in agency policy. In similar fashion, a coalition of groups seeking a change in federal day-care policy might decide to obtain the sponsorship of an important legislator for a specific policy and might allocate certain lobbying tasks to various persons.

Revising the Strategy Proponents who hold rigidly to a specific strategy often imperil their success. Perhaps they made miscalculations when they established their strategy, such as underestimating the strength of the opposition. Or perhaps specific opponents devised a counterstrategy to circumvent them, much as a chess player outwits an opponent. Or perhaps background and unanticipated events powerfully shaped deliberations. The proponents of a measure need then to modify their strategy and to respond improvisationally to unanticipated events.

DEVELOPING STRATEGY: A SIMPLE ILLUSTRATION

How do strategists put together a strategy from all the elements that we have discussed? Much like chefs who visualize different combinations of ingredients before trying them, strategists brainstorm several alternative strategies and then speculate how events might unfold if each of them were used. Let's consider two examples, a relatively simple one and a more complex one, to discuss the way strategists think about strategy.

We return to the case of the family that was attempting to decide whether Grandma should move into their home or Sam should have a car (see Table 6.1). Recall that the family consisted of two parents (Frank and Mary) and two children (teenager Sam and his younger sister, Diane). Sam wanted a car but encountered a relatively bleak situation. The two persons with the greatest power to influence deliberations on this issue (his parents, Mary and Frank, who each received a high score of 3 on a 4-point scale that measured "power to influence outcomes") were only mildly disposed to let him have a car (Mary and Frank, respectively, scored 4 and 2 on the 10-point scale that measured their positions). Moreover, both his mother and father attached considerable importance, or salience, to the issue—a fact that suggested that they would work hard to obtain their policy preferences. While his younger sister was decidedly supportive (she received a score of 8 on the 10-point scale that measured their positions), Sam knew that she possessed relatively little power to shape the outcome (she received a ranking of only 1 on the 4-point scale).

Sam concluded that nothing would happen if he took no action. Nor was he confident that events would change if he took minimal action, such as asking several times if he could have a car. Asking the question, What would happen if I took no or minimal action? confirmed the essential accuracy of the data in Table 6.1 and made clear to him that he *had* to develop strategy if he wanted to increase the chances of obtaining his policy preferences. He decided, first, to try to change his father's position on the issue by diminishing some of Frank's fears about Sam's use of a car. He offered to pay all gasoline costs and to contribute one-half of its insurance costs from the earnings of a summer job. Moreover, Sam conceded that other members of the family could use the car on those occasions when either parent needed it. He hoped, as well, to heighten his sister's interest in the car by promising to share it with her when she reached the driving age in two years.

DEVISING STRATEGY: A MORE COMPLEX ILLUSTRATION

An example of alternative scenarios is provided in the case study of a young legislative aide (Eric Redman) who wanted to devise a proposal to develop a National Health Service Corps to provide federal funds for salaries of young physicians who agreed to work for two years in clinics that serve low-income citizens in rural and urban areas.[37] He initially wanted to develop a relatively modest strategy to extend the existing public health program that allows some physicians to perform certain public health duties in lieu of serving in the armed forces. (At the time of the case study, physicians were required to serve in the armed forces.) To accomplish this goal, he (and his allies) would merely need to convince public health officials in the Public Health Service (PHS) to modestly expand their existing program to also fund a public health service corps that provided medical services to poor people. Indeed, Redman was not certain that legislative approval was even needed for his modest proposal; perhaps the PHS could implement it by merely expanding their current practice of exempting some physicians from military service— but some of them would now provide medical services to poor people instead of providing traditional public health services.

At the other extreme, however, Redman could imagine developing and seeking enactment of a relatively ambitious piece of legislation. This ambitious proposal might have the advantage of allowing a larger program than one that was merely "tacked on" the existing public health program, but it would also present major political problems. Might some politicians believe that the National Health Service Corps would be a kind of national health insurance, which has traditionally evoked extraordinary political controversy and conflicts between liberals and conservatives? Moreover, would not the relatively conservative and Republican president veto the legislation even if it were enacted because of the power of the conservative wing of the Republican party? And would not the American Medical Association use its remarkable lobbying resources to defeat a bill that placed large numbers of physicians in public and salaried positions? (The PHS had escaped this controversy because its physicians were allowed only to "prevent" illnesses through inoculation and educational programs rather than to provide medical services to patients.)

As he compared the more modest proposal with the more ambitious proposal, Redman did a force-field analysis and concluded that he had to select the modest proposal if he hoped to be successful. But he soon had to revise his strategy when he discovered that the existing public health legislation forbade PHS physicians from actually treating ill patients. Moreover, officials in the federal bureaucracy, whose cooperation was needed to expand the PHS to include treating low-income patients, refused to cooperate with him, whether because they did not want to work with the legislative aide of a prominent Democratic senator or because some high-level officials did not favor the proposed program.

Correspondingly, Redman enlisted the assistance of some legislative aides to draft a piece of legislation that described and authorized funds for a National Health Service Corps. His earliest and relatively modest strategy thus had to be revised in light of changing events and new information. He proceeded to assemble a group of legislative sponsors that included prominent politicians from both political parties.

This example describes Redman's successful and evolving strategy to enact his policy proposal.[38] He consistently used a low-profile and nonconflictual political style to obtain broad bipartisan support for his measure and to avoid opposition from conservatives that would have doomed his legislation to certain defeat. He developed a low-conflict style of politics by shunning publicity in the mass media, emphasizing the small size of the intended program, and skillfully using rivalries between various politicians in Congress to entice them to develop competing versions of the legislation. His low-profile strategy was successful, although he had to mobilize external pressures on specific legislators at specific points—and on the president just before he finally signed the legislation. He skillfully built support for the legislation among rural legislators from both parties—who traditionally oppose social reforms—by emphasizing the relevance of the program to rural populations that are chronically unable to obtain sufficient medical personnel.

SUMMARY

Political strategy provides a method of actualizing power resources by combining and sequencing them into a pattern of actions and verbal exchanges. Skillful strategists can sometimes convert a seemingly hopeless situation into a more promising one by carefully analyzing the existing distribution of power and sentiment, by developing what-if scenarios, by selecting a well-considered strategy, and by revising strategy as circumstances change.

Considerable guesswork is needed when devising strategy because of the sheer number of imponderables. It is often difficult to gauge where specific persons or interests stand with respect to a specific issue or proposal—or to predict how they will respond to specific arguments or presentations. A strategy that seems meritorious at one time may be rendered useless by unexpected tactical maneuvers of opponents.

Undeterred by these practical problems, skillful policy practitioners view power and political strategy as indispensable tools and resources for increasing the likelihood that they will achieve their policy objectives.

QUESTIONS FOR DISCUSSION

1. Review Policy-Practice Case 5 at the start of Chapter 5. Conduct a force-field analysis of the situation that the social work intern confronted as she contemplated securing support for her innovation. Who did she guess would support or oppose the innovation and with what intensity? Were background factors generally supportive of the reform? From her description of the situation, would you rate the prognosis as unfavorable, mixed, or favorable? What problems or difficulties did you experience when attempting a force-field analysis—and what did they tell you about the limitations of this process?

2. By reviewing Policy-Practice Case 5, discuss the following dilemmas, tasks, and realities that policy practitioners encounter when they develop political strategy:
   a) Since it is often difficult to predict whether a specific project is feasible in the early stages, people often under- or overestimate the opposition to it.
   b) It is often necessary to dilute, modify, or rename a policy proposal to increase support for it.
   c) Coalitions are often difficult to form and maintain but are often critical to the success of an initiative.

3. In addition to the role of initiating a proposal, discuss other roles that policy practitioners can assume in the political process, such as bystanding, opposing, and amending roles.

4. Compare and contrast the politics of agencies and legislatures with respect to levels of conflict and strategy. Do your comparisons suggest the need for different kinds of strategy in the two settings?

5. Discuss the assertion that skillful strategists often develop several alternative strategies before selecting one of them for implementation.

6. Compare and contrast different styles or models of politics.

7. Referring to Policy-Practice Case 5, use the six issues in Table 6.2 to define the "game plan" that the social work intern developed.

SUGGESTED READINGS

Gauging Political Feasibility

George Brager and Stephen Holloway, *Changing Human Service Organizations* (New York: Free Press, 1978), pp. 57–92.

William Coplin and Michael O'Leary, *Everyman's Prince* (North Scituate, Mass.: Duxbury, 1976).

Kurt Lewin, *Field Theory in Social Science* (New York: Harper and Row, 1951).

Shaping Policy Agendas

John Kingdon, *Agendas, Alternatives, and Public Choices* (Boston: Little, Brown, 1984).

Understanding and Predicting the Likelihood of Conflict

Morton Deutsch, *The Resolution of Conflict: Constructive and Destructive Processes* (New Haven, Conn.: Yale University Press, 1973), pp. 124–152.

Developing and Implementing Political Strategy

Eugene Bardach, *The Skill Factor in Politics* (Berkeley, Ca.: University of California Press, 1972), pp. 183–240.

Ron Dear and Rino Patti, "Legislative Advocacy: Seven Effective Tactics," *Social Work*, 26 (July 1981): 289–297.

Eric Redman, *Dance of Legislation* (New York: Simon and Schuster, 1973).

Building and Using Coalitions

George Brager, Harry Specht, and James Torczyner, *Community Organizing*, 2nd ed. (New York: Columbia University Press, 1987), pp. 193–200.

NOTES

1. The need for compromises in policy making is discussed by Ron Dear and Rino Patti, "Legislative Advocacy," *Encyclopedia of Social Work*, 18th ed., vol. 2 (Washington, D.C.: National Association of Social Workers, 1987), p. 37.

2. George Brager and Stephen Holloway, *Changing Human Service Organizations* (New York: Free Press, 1978), pp. 107–128.

3. Kurt Lewin, *Field Theory in Social Science* (New York: Harper and Row, 1951).

4. William Coplin and Michael O'Leary, *Everyman's Prince* (North Scituate, Mass.: Duxbury, 1976), pp. 7–25.

5. Stephen Frantzich, *Computers in Congress* (Beverly Hills, Ca.: Sage, 1982), pp. 248–250.

6. Coplin and O'Leary, *Everyman's Prince*, pp. 20–25, 170–175.

7. Eric Schattschneider, *The Semisovereign People* (New York: Holt, Rinehart and Winston, 1960), pp. 1–19.

8. See the discussion of the traditions, objectives, and ideology of organizations in Brager and Holloway, *Changing Human Service Organizations*, pp. 57–66.

9. See Julie Kosterlitz, "Not Just Kid Stuff," *National Journal*, 20 (November 19, 1988): 2934–2939.

10. The role of tangible interests of persons in shaping their position is discussed by Brager and Holloway, *Changing Human Service Organizations*, pp. 85–92.

11. Feminist pressure is discussed by Kosterlitz, "Not Just Kid Stuff," pp. 2934–2939.

12. See John Kingdon, *Agendas, Alternatives, and Public Choices* (Boston: Little, Brown, 1984), pp. 152–170.

13. Warren Miller and Donald Stokes, "Constituency Influence in Congress," *American Political Science Review*, 57 (March 1963): 45–56.

14. Bruce Jansson, *History and Politics of Selected Children's Programs*, Dissertation (University of Chicago, 1975), pp. 248–274.

15. The political economy framework identifies these kinds of factors; see Yeheskel Hasenfeld, *Human Service Organizations* (Englewood Cliffs, N.J.: Prentice-Hall, 1983), pp. 43–49.

16. See Perry Smith, *Taking Charge* (Washington, D.C.: National Defense University Press, 1986), pp. 17–26.

17. Samuel Bacharach and Edward Lawler, *Power and Politics in Organizations* (San Francisco: Jossey-Bass, 1980).

18. See Thomas Schelling, *The Strategy of Conflict* (Cambridge, Mass.: Harvard University Press, 1960).

19. Schattschneider, *Semisovereign People*, pp. 1–19.

20. Sissela Bok, "Blowing the Whistle," in Joel Fleishman, Lance Liebman, and Mark Moore, eds., *Public Duties: The Moral Obligations of Government Officials* (Cambridge, Mass.: Harvard University Press, 1981), pp. 204–209.

21. Laurence Lynn, *Managing the Public's Business* (New York: Basic Books, 1981), pp. 128–130.

22. The decline in party discipline, as well as the increased importance of television, has given many legislators more leeway in shaping their own positions. See, for example, Nelson Polsby, "Goodbye to the Senate's Inner Club," in Norman Ornstein, ed., *Congress in Change: Evolution and Reform* (New York: Praeger, 1975), pp. 205–208.

23. Richard Fenno, *Power of the Purse* (Boston: Little, Brown, 1960), pp. 193–195.

24. Game theorists are particularly inclined to simulate scenarios, albeit from a relatively limited perspective. See Schelling, *Strategy of Conflict*.

25. See Eugene Bardach, *The Skill Factor in Politics* (Berkeley, Ca.: University of California Press, 1972), pp. 188–189.

26. Brager and Holloway, *Changing Human Service Organizations*, pp. 140–141.

27. The characterizations of these candidates stem from a variety of journalistic commentaries in the *New York Times* and the *Los Angeles Times*.

28. Also see comparisons of consensus, collaborative, and contest styles of strategies in Rino Patti and Herman Resnick, "Changing the Agency from Within," *Social Work*, 17 (July 1972): 48–57.

29. Both of them were able, as well, to appeal to important conservatives. See Bruce Jansson, *Reluctant Welfare State: A History of American Social Welfare Policies* (Belmont, Ca.: Wadsworth Publishing Co., 1984), pp. 134–145, 164–166.

30. See Lowi's model of "distributive" politics in "American Business, Public Policy, Case Studies, and Political Theory," *World Politics*, 16 (July 1964): 677–715.

31. Brager and Holloway, *Changing Human Service Organizations*, pp. 194–195.

32. Bardach, *Skill Factor in Politics*, pp. 183–194.

33. Ibid., pp. 235–236.

34. Herman Resnick, "Tasks in Changing the Organization from Within," in Herman Resnick and Rino Patti, eds., *Change from Within: Humanizing Social Welfare Organizations* (Philadelphia: Temple University Press, 1980), pp. 210–212.

35. Nancy Amidei, "How to Be an Advocate in Bad Times," *Public Welfare*, 40 (Summer 1982): 41.

36. Carol Weiss, "Ideology, Interests, and Information," in Daniel Callahan and Bruce Jennings, eds., *Ethics, the Social Sciences, and Policy Analysis* (New York: Plenum Press, 1983), pp. 213–248.

37. Eric Redman, *Dance of Legislation* (New York: Simon and Schuster, 1973).

38. Ibid.

CHAPTER 7

■

Interactional Skills
in Social Welfare Policy

Were we to terminate our discussion of policy practice with analytic and political skills, we would not identify an array of skills that policy practitioners need, whether they practice in agency, community, or legislative settings. Let's call interactional skills "the X factor" in policy practice, that is, a set of skills not commonly covered in existing literature that case studies, biographies of policymakers, and accounts of policy-making suggest are critical to the success of policy practitioners.

Although not claiming that other skills are not also needed, we discuss four kinds of interactional skills. First, policy practitioners need skill in building their personal credibility because other people are more likely to respond favorably to the suggestions of someone they believe to be credible. Second, policy practitioners needs skills in networking where they develop supportive links with an array of people who can help them with specific initiatives. Third, policy practitioners need skills in policy persuasion so that they can effectively persuade others to support specific positions. Fourth, they need skills in group process because most policies are developed by committees, task forces, and boards—and pressure is exerted on decision makers by interest and advocacy groups, coalitions, and social movements.

A POLICY-PRACTICE CASE FROM THE HUMAN SERVICES

As Policy-Practice Case 7 suggests, people who seek to influence policy—in this case, two "low-budget lobbyists" who, respectively, seek reforms for children and AIDS patients—encounter a range of challenges that extend beyond yet intersect with the analytic and political ones that we have discussed in preceding chapters.

Their first challenge is to obtain personal credibility with legislators so

POLICY-PRACTICE CASE 7

LOW-BUDGET LOBBYISTS

The phone rang a dozen times before a harried Rand Martin could grab it, and then he disconnected the caller when he tried to put the line on hold while he finished another call. Such is life when you're between secretaries and cursed with a cheap, quirk-filled phone system.

He probably would get little sympathy from Sherry Skelly, who lacks not only a secretary but, until recently, a desk, typewriter, and an office as well. Until she managed to scrape up the money, she had been using a donated hallway as her headquarters. She still makes do with a single phone line and an answering machine, however.

Martin and Skelly are lobbyists, Martin for the AIDS-oriented Lobby for Individual Freedom and Equality, and Skelly for the California Children's Lobby. You can tell they are lobbyists because they work bills, meet with legislators and consultants, and testify at hearings. And their pictures are in the secretary of state's *Directory of Lobbyists*.

But if you look for the other signs that so clearly signify "lobbyist" to most of the public, you won't find them. The organizations they represent never show up on the lists of heavy campaign contributors. They keep their fingers crossed when they send their cards in to legislators on the floor seeking a few words, for, unlike their heavyweight counterparts, Martin and Skelly are unable to command an audience. They don't have legions of staff to keep them posted on the dozens of bills they must track. And if they hit the Sacramento hot spots at night, it is to relax and enjoy themselves. Their budgets and salaries don't provide for the few rounds of drinks or dinner that might further connections with lawmakers and legislative staff.

In short, what these two lack is money.

Of course, they are not alone. The Fair Political Practices Commission lists 762 registered lobbyists. Ranking lobbyists by affluence, there are only eleven big operators at the top. Those receive in excess of $500,000 in client fees and spread around comparable hundreds of thousands of dollars in campaign contributions.

Much lower in rankings are the lobbyists for public interest groups— California Common Cause, Consumers Union, American Civil Liberties Union—along with lobbyists for state agencies, departments, and commissions. Although they have no money to grease the wheels of power, they usually have enough resources to track bills, produce position papers, and rally the public.

Scraping dead bottom are a subgroup of public interest entities, like LIFE and California Children's Lobby, that are typified by annual budgets that detail how many stamps may be used and how many photocopies may be made in one month. Martin runs his operation on a budget of $80,000, including office rent, his salary and a secretary. Skelly gets by on $63,000.

Clearly neither of them is in it for the money. And if it were true that money turns the wheels inside the Capitol, then one would expect the work that Martin and Skelly do to be mostly futile. So who are these penny-pinching lobbyists, how do they get by, and what can they possibly accomplish?

"A lobbyist is a be-all," says the twenty-seven-year-old Skelly. "I feel like I'm a mediator and a resource who can provide expertise on an issue. If you have no money, you end up working closely with consultants, and consultants are very detail-oriented."

Expertise, a flair for detail, credibility—these are the tools an empty-pocket lobbyist brings to work every day. Some of the weight such a lobbyist carries is personal, earned over years of giving consistently good advice and testimony; some of it comes part and parcel with the organization he or she represents.

The Children's Lobby, for instance, is an umbrella group for child-care providers, child-care educators, and parent groups around the state. Skelly says the Lobby has a twenty-year track record of grass-roots activism that makes it an effective advocate on children's issues.

"It's a very sophisticated network," she says. "With the phone tree we have, we can get forty calls into a member's office on a particular bill within an hour. These people know the [legislative] members in their areas; they write letters, make phone calls, and involve the parent groups. This committed network has been developing for the past ten or twenty years, and now it's primed and ready to go."

Skelly, who has been with California Children's Lobby for almost a year, says she is the only full-time lobbyist for children's issues in Sacramento. Although that has the drawback of spreading one person too thinly over hundreds of bills, it does mean that Skelly has become a focal point for children's issues, and she has become a natural funnel for information, studies, and trends.

But beyond the clout of her organization, Skelly works on developing her own ties and credibility. She knows about one-quarter of the members of both houses.

"When I meet a member, I don't just talk about my bills," she says. "Education bills, minimum wage—if I know a certain member's interested in something this year, then I talk about that. Then they know I'm interested in their concerns and views and not just pushing my agenda."

Just as important are her consultant contacts. "Consultants tap into us [lobbyists] as a resource. You have to prepare good amendments for bills, make good suggestions well in advance of hearings, if you are going to have an influence on the outcome."

The thirty-four-year-old Martin, who has been a lobbyist on health issues for three years, says he is always working on recognition and credibility with both legislators and consultants. Unlike Skelly's organization, Martin's group is still learning to flex its political muscles.

And while children's issues may be simmering on a front burner this year, Martin's issue has been boiling over at high speed for a couple of years.

Martin was instrumental in forming the Lobby for Individual Freedom

Continued

POLICY-PRACTICE CASE 7
(continued)

and Equality, an umbrella organization for forty-two organizations around the state concerned about AIDS, and he has been its sole lobbyist since its beginnings on June 1, 1986.

The first full year of operation, he felt swamped, working out of his living room to track 65 bills. Confronted with 142 bills this year, last year is beginning to look calm in retrospect.

"The number of bills, so many legislators and staff to get to know, plus keeping a fledgling organization afloat—it's been difficult," Martin says.

And the difficulties aren't just in the part of the job that deals with bills. He has learned quickly that a discount lobbyist not only needs to keep an eye on developments in the Capitol but also is needed to educate, guide, and cajole the groups he represents. One of his biggest tasks is forming his backers into a cohesive, effective voice.

"Gays and lesbians have always been very adept at turning people out on a single issue, but they've been unable to do it on a consistent basis," Martin says. "LIFE has been working to build that kind of network. LIFE is an example of a newfound political maturity that acknowledges the need to have a continuous visibility in politics."

But networking and consensus building are slow processes, and the AIDS issue is moving very quickly. "Building a network is a longer road than the one to gaining personal access to an individual legislator, but it's every bit as important," Martin says.

Important, yes; comfortable, no. Martin is often caught between a legislative agenda that threatens to move ahead without LIFE and purists on his board who believe compromise is synonymous with evil. "It puts us in a tough position, because we have liberal legislators who want to side with us telling us we have to give on some things," Martin says. "But then we have those who believe LIFE needs to maintain a pure image in the gay–lesbian community. And there's a need for those kinds of people: they create such a pure position, we look like moderates in comparison."

So Martin frequently finds himself in the role of an educator, not just to consultants and legislators, but to his own people who need to understand how the process works and what is probable, feasible, and impossible.

Skelly agrees with the vision of a lobbyist as an educator. She conducts seminars and attends the monthly meetings of a half-dozen child-oriented organizations. It's important for the folks back home to understand how Sacramento works and how they can affect what comes out of the Capitol.

"The Children's Lobby network can produce a teen parent, her mate, and a baby to give testimony at a hearing," Skelly says. "We can call on experts in the field and find out anything a legislator might want to know. These people are on the scene where state programs are actually working, so they are in a good position to know what's wrong and what needs to be done. They need to be able to convey that information to the legislature."

Skelly says such personal testimony at hearings can have a "significance beyond dollars."

But dollars do count, no matter how optimistic or well-armed with statistics a lobbyist may be.

"A lobbyist without money just doesn't have the access," Martin says. "It's most visible in committee when lobbyists are giving testimony. The committee members sit up and listen when it's someone with clout or money; they pay attention."

Martin says matter-of-factly, with little bitterness to his voice, there is just a regretful acceptance of reality: Lobbyists without the big-buck bang have to be more diligent in preparing arguments, supplying statistics, and proposing improvements—and sometimes to no avail.

"You take a lot of frustration home. But then there have been people we've turned around on a particular issue," Martin says. "I think we've had a lot of impact on Dr. Filante [Assemblyman William Filante] and helped build his leadership on the AIDS issue among Republicans."

Skelly says her biggest victory came last year when she helped place $500,000 in the 1987–88 state budget for California State University campus child care. The governor had already vetoed a $1.2 million expenditure, so getting the partial funding past his blue pencil was a plus. "These campus centers had been struggling along for twenty years without any state funding, and many of them were on the verge of closing," she says. "So this was the first time general-fund money was ever committed to campus child care, and I was very excited about it."

The upbeat Skelly can't remember a defeat that left her depressed in the past, but even an optimistic nature won't block reality this year. The Children's Lobby's top priority is a statutory cost-of-living adjustment for child care, and the governor has already vetoed similar legislation in the past. And the governor placed an equitable cost-of-living adjustment in his budget proposal this year, cutting the ground out from under Skelly's arguments by removing the need for immediate action. "I have to admit I'm beginning to anticipate a problem," she says.

Martin's victories and defeats have come, as they so often do in politics, in contrary fashion. His biggest victories have been killing two of GOP state Senator John Doolittle's ten-bill AIDS package, and his worst defeat was the passage of a bill to test prostitutes for AIDS.

Victories that come by defeating bills are often fleeting. One of Doolittle's bills would have substantially relaxed AIDS test confidentiality laws, including turning results over to public health officials, and the other would have allowed widespread testing in psychiatric institutions. Those two are dead, but other measures this year are likely to accomplish at least some of Doolittle's goals.

The prostitute bill's passage was the type of convoluted fluke that leaves lobbyists with nightmares. The bill swept out of the Assembly, not as a well-reasoned policy decision, but on a Gang-of-Five tidal wave, while Martin

Continued

POLICY-PRACTICE CASE 7
(continued)

watched helplessly. "It happened so fast, and most of it was behind closed doors," Martin says, "so we really couldn't do much about it."

Had the Gang of Five, a group of dissident Democrats, not been trying to find common ground with Republicans so they could successfully challenge Speaker Willie Brown, the prostitute bill would have stayed buried in committee or at least could have been modified to be less objectionable to LIFE, Martin says. But it is just one of several bills that Martin expects to mark on the loss side, a factor that leaves him feeling stressed and makes his shoestring-budget operation all the more depressing.

"Burnout is common with public interest lobbyists," Martin says. "The ones you see around the building who have been here for twenty or thirty years are the ones who work for industries, big-buck clients."

So if the offer came from a big-time lobbying firm, would he switch?

"I couldn't leave LIFE dangling in midsession," says Martin, who is gay and deeply committed to the fight against AIDS. "But in the longer term, yes, I'd probably move on. You can have a deep personal commitment to an issue, but it only lasts until burnout hits."

Martin, whose father is a Washington, D.C., lobbyist, is already well sidetracked from the career in theater he had hoped for. He keeps his hand in by acting and directing with a Davis community theater group, but his future is in the Capitol. "It's in my blood," he says simply. "The more and more I've been involved in government activities, the more I've been fascinated with what is going on in Sacramento."

The fascination is still there for Skelly, as well. "I really enjoy lobbying. It's exciting and stimulating."

Skelly didn't start out to be a lobbyist. An active role in trying to start a child-care program at UC Santa Barbara put her in the limelight when the university's student association needed a lobbyist. Two years there and another year with the Children's Lobby have satisfied her itch to do something professionally that focuses on children.

"I have a bottom-line commitment to education and children's issues. I might move on to something else in the future. But I'm pretty dedicated to children's issues and, right now, I couldn't imagine doing anything else."

SOURCE: Adapted from Kathy Beasley, *California Journal,* 1988.

that their proposals and suggestions will not be ignored or not taken seriously. Lacking the resources and vast constituencies of some lobbyists, they begin their work at a decided disadvantage, but both of these lobbyists have managed to obtain significant successes by persistence, hard work, and research. Both lobbyists seek access to networks of persons within the legislative and bureaucratic systems of their state's capital because they realize that many decisions are shaped during discussions and social encounters of informal old-boy networks. They must not only seek access to existing networks, such as old-boy networks, but also establish new networks that consist of existing or potential allies of reforms for children or AIDS victims. Indeed, both lobbyists cultivate a statewide constituency of these allies, whether the "telephone tree" of the children's advocate or the advisory board of the advocate for people with AIDS.

Both lobbyists must frequently persuade people to support specific policies, to join certain causes, to donate funds to support their work, or to take certain actions such as withholding support from a punitive policy with respect to AIDS victims.

Both lobbyists have had to develop and use skills in organizing, facilitating, and mobilizing groups. Both must relate to and organize social movements, that is, grass-root groups that seek to modify existing policies in specific communities and in their state. To overcome their disadvantages when compared to better funded lobbyists with massive constituencies, such as lobbyists representing specific business interests, they need to develop and use coalitions of reform-minded groups that can pool their scarce resources at strategic times. Their group skills are useful when analyzing the workings of specific legislative committees; they must predict, for example, when the internal dynamics of a committee suggest that it will support or oppose a policy and whether specific interventions, such as discussions with specific legislators (or their aides), may "turn the balance."

INTERACTIONAL SKILLS AS EXTENSIONS OF ANALYTIC AND POLITICAL SKILLS

To illustrate the importance of interactional skills, let's imagine the work of a person with advanced analytic or political skills who lacks interactional skills. In the case of a policy analyst, someone might fashion a technically superior report that brilliantly identifies policy options and develops a policy proposal but cannot convince others that the proposal ought to be adopted. Or a political strategist might skillfully decipher political realities and fashion a compelling political strategy but fail to convince others to join in or to implement the strategy. Indeed, when called on to use person-to-person–power resources, such as those discussed in Chapter Five, this strategist might fail to convince others to accede to her wishes because of the awkward, heavy-handed, or poorly timed nature of the intervention.

In one sense then, **interactional skills** are the "action" or "doing" components or extensions of analytic and political skills. Ideas and proposals must be presented in skillful fashion to individuals and groups if they are to be accepted; people have to organize and sustain problem-solving and action-oriented groups if ideas are to be developed and if pressure is to be placed on decision makers; and power resources have to be skillfully used in interpersonal dealings. Lacking these kinds of interactional skills, policy practitioners could not influence the course of policy deliberations.

BUILDING PERSONAL CREDIBILITY

Whether they are attorneys, physicians, or social workers, professionals require a certain level of personal credibility if they are to be effective with their clients. Without this credibility, they would soon find their practices to be jeopardized because clients would not seek or heed their services. In similar fashion, the personal credibility of people who seek to influence the course of policy deliberations influences the degree to which others are unlikely to heed their suggestions, proposals, criticisms, arguments, and power resources. **Credibility** then can be defined as personal characteristics that other people value and that influence their responsiveness to the initiatives of specific policy practitioners.[1]

Because a number of personal characteristics often enhance the credibility of specific individuals, many tactics can be used, singly and in tandem, to increase it. Policy practitioners can try to appear reasonable and pragmatic, to appear as team players, to increase integrity, to increase authoritativeness, to develop a positive track record, and to possess positive associations. We will note, as well, that some Machiavellian tactics are often used to enhance personal credibility, although not without ethical and practical risks.

Appearing Reasonable and Pragmatic

Policy practitioners can sometimes increase their credibility with decision makers who possess different values or priorities by *not* emphasizing the underlying principles or values of a proposal and, instead, by focusing on its substantive details or provisions.[2] Assume, for example, that a policy advocate wants to redistribute resources to poor people by substantially increasing the benefits of the Food Stamps Program and that this person possesses a radical perspective. When dealing with the aide of a conservative legislator, such as Senator Robert Dole of Kansas, the policy practitioner might decide to downplay his radical ideology in order to emphasize both the details of the reform and the objective of "increasing revenues of distressed farmers on the Great Plains." By downplaying his ideology, which is dissonant with the ideology of conservative politicians, the policy practitioner will seem more credible to the aide than would an openly radical person.[3]

This strategy can be carried to extreme if policy practitioners sacrifice their preferences excessively in their zeal to appear reasonable and pragmatic. Indeed, it can be counterproductive if other people perceive the policy practitioner to be disingenuous.

Appearing as Team Players

As we discussed in Chapter Six, adherents of power-dependence theory suggest that our credibility increases as we become indispensable to others, who view us as credible because they are dependent upon us.[4] To illustrate this theory, contrast two social work units in two hospitals. The unit in Hospital 1 contents itself with providing crisis-intervention services to patients in several of the services of the hospital, whereas the unit in Hospital 2 fills a large number of functions besides the traditional counseling ones. The staff assume highly visible roles in facilitating the expeditious discharge of elderly patients, do financial counseling to patients, help provide social services to victims of rape, serve as intermediaries between the hospital and the Department of Children's Services with respect to suspected cases of child abuse and neglect, operate a substance-abuse clinic for patients with alcohol- and substance-abuse problems, and administer a program that provides home-based services to frail elderly persons. Top decision makers in Hospital 2 depend on the staff for a range of services—indeed, they can hardly imagine how their hospital could function without this social work department. By contrast, top decision makers in Hospital 1 hardly know that the social work unit exists—much less that it is necessary to the functioning of the hospital. According to power-dependence theory, they are more likely to heed suggestions of the director (or other staff) of the expansive social work unit (Hospital 2) rather than the other unit (Hospital 1).[5]

Power-dependence theory suggests then that policy practitioners can increase their stature by assuming a range of functions within their organizations that supplement the relatively narrow or traditional functions of their job descriptions. As one director of a social work unit once said to me, "I might even consider washing windows!" These expansive functions serve several purposes; they make high-level administrators feel beholden to units and individuals who perform a variety of positive tasks for the agency—and they make these units and individuals appear to be team players who have the broader interests of the institution in mind.

Besides assuming a range of functions, policy practitioners can enhance their credibility by assuming initiatives within *specific* change-oriented projects. Assume, for example, that a social worker has a casual conversation with an administrator about some problem in a hospital, such as "the remarkable turnover of nursing and social work staff in the pediatrics unit during the past five years, which has severely jeopardized the quality of services and the morale of staff." If the social worker seized the initiative by offering to conduct a survey of the staff as a prelude to a meeting to discuss possible causes of the turnover, she makes the administrator dependent on her by performing some necessary work—and her willingness to volunteer these services makes her appear to be a team player. If she continues to assume additional roles on this project, such as chairing or staffing a committee, she continues the proactive and positive role that she assumed at the inception. We can imagine that her credibility with respect to this issue would be enhanced by these assertive actions.

People can also increase the likelihood that they are perceived as team players by shaping policy proposals germane to the mission (or set of shared purposes) of specific organizations.[6] The mission of an organization consists of those objectives or goals, or methods of operations, that officials and staff of an institution emphasize or prefer. Let's assume, for example, that top officials in a mental health clinic wish to increase services to adolescent and elderly populations, to develop some satellite programs to help chronically ill people in outlying areas, to increase revenues from foundations and corporations, and to increase revenues from fee-paying clientele. These various goals define some of the priorities of officials of this organization, although it is possible that unanimity does not exist. A policy practitioner would enhance his credibility by developing and supporting policy proposals that are consonant with one or several of these objectives.

Of course, ethics place limits on the use of this tactic because we should not develop or support proposals that are consonant with values or priorities that are morally objectionable. If a hospital wished not to serve *any* poor patients who lacked requisite insurance, even ones with emergency conditions, a social work unit ought not seek funds for additional staff to help "screen out and transfer" all such people—even if this proposal were consonant with the objectives of top officials of the institution.[7]

Increasing Personal Integrity

Some people may rightly wonder whether some of the preceding tactics for increasing personal credibility might not imperil the integrity of policy practitioners; if we must constantly appear to be reasonable and to be team players, what room is left for outspoken advocacy for specific causes or for *not* being team players when we think "the team" needs fundamental reforms?

Policy practitioners can take heart, perhaps, in the effectiveness of a number of legislators who combined more moderate approaches with principled and outspoken positions on certain issues. Hubert Humphrey, Phillip Hart, and Claude Pepper often championed social causes before they became popular or fashionable, with some risk to their political well-being. Yet these politicians were highly successful legislators who were overwhelmingly reelected on numerous occasions and who enjoyed immense popularity among their legislative peers. Perhaps one reason for their credibility was that many people and legislators perceived them to be persons of integrity, that is, persons who were able to "draw the line" when their most fundamental beliefs were challenged.[8] In these cases, such as civil rights legislation in the case of Humphrey and attacks on Social Security in the case of Pepper, they became determined advocates. Even when they disagree with them, people often admire others who possess certain values that they will take risks to defend. And they often do not respect people who, like willows, bend with every passing breeze. Of course, even the aforementioned politicians had to determine when to invest their energies and to take risks; on many issues, they were more willing to adopt accommodationist strategies.

Increasing Personal Authoritativeness

When we want to change a specific policy in an agency, community, or legislative setting, we often encounter opposition that stems from a suspicion that change is not warranted. Perhaps some faction (or person) wants merely to increase its own interests. Perhaps the existing policy is meritorious. The policy practitioner can often diminish such inertia by conveying a sense of authoritativeness about the subject, whether by citing important research, documenting similar change projects in other (and similar) settings, and citing reputable experts.[9] Or the policy practitioner may develop some evidence that buttresses the case for changes in existing policy. In the aforementioned case of the turnover of staff in the pediatrics service of a hospital, the social worker might obtain evidence to document the extraordinary rate of turnover as well as evidence of low staff morale by using a standardized instrument that measures staff morale. As individuals appear to be authoritative with a specific issue, they probably increase the likelihood that they will be perceived as authoritative with respect to other issues on future occasions.

Developing a Track Record

The preceding discussion suggests that credibility cannot easily be obtained by the mere use of rhetoric; people have to observe firsthand, or hear secondhand from others, that someone is competent, trustworthy, or authoritative—or that their unit or department performs services or functions that are indispensable to themselves or to their organizations.

The value of secondhand reports to the establishing of credibility should not be ignored. As people make sensible suggestions or initiate useful policies and as they engage in responsible efforts to change existing policies, they obtain reputational advantages from others whom they have directly encountered and from those who have heard positive feedback about them from other people.

Possessing Positive Associations

Credibility can be viewed both as the property of individuals *and* as a phenomenon that stems from their associations and affiliations. To illustrate this point, assume that a hospital administrator receives requests for additional funding successively from the directors of two units within the hospital. The first request comes from a director whose unit has been marked by chronic and repeated turmoil and that is not perceived by the administrator to provide quality services. The second request comes from the director of a unit that is widely viewed as outstanding; unlike with the first unit, the hospital administrator has received many positive reports about its services and its staff. Although both directors may possess similar personal characteristics, we can guess that the hospital administrator will be more likely to heed the request from the second unit.

The lesson for social workers who work in bureaucracies is a simple one. Personal credibility stems in part from association with well-regarded and effective units that in turn stem in part from the quality of their work and the reputations of the staff who compose them.[10] Credibility must often be enhanced by indirection, that is, by enhancing the services of those units that employ social workers in the first instance.

Increasing Credibility: Machiavellian Tactics

Some individuals try to enhance their credibility by using negative tactics such as harming the reputations of others, buckpassing, sandbagging, turf or empire building, and impugning the personal motives of other. Those who use Machiavellian tactics often begin with the premise that a win-lose situation exists where they can obtain reputational gains only if they harm the reputations of others. (In the case of political campaigns, where candidates are pitted against one another and where only one person can be elected, win-lose situations often exist, but some persons extend this logic to many situations.) In the case of buckpassing, people blame others for specific failures or problems in hopes that they can escape personal complicity.[11] In sandbagging tactics, people seek to diminish the legitimate successes of others by contending that other factors or people, perhaps even themselves, were "really responsible" for these successes.[12] As any participant in bureaucratic politics can attest, many people excel in turf or empire building where they seek not only to accumulate power and responsibility but also to obtain these commodities by wresting them from others.[13] When impugning the motives of others, people diminish the initiatives of other people by suggesting that they reflect ulterior and evil motivations such as greed and a desire for power.[14]

These negative tactics are sometimes effective, as many defeated candidates for political office can attest; indeed, some politicians, such as Richard Nixon, obtained remarkable power by making considerable use of them. In some cases, individuals *do* develop policy initiatives primarily to advance their own power or prestige, and they sometimes should be attacked for their ulterior motives. But these negative tactics can often erode the credibility of those who use them because others may believe that these people who resort excessively to negative tactics lack moral qualities that they value. As we note in the next chapter, these tactics can also violate ethical norms.

NETWORKING

Networking refers to the nature, number, and range of supportive relationships that people possess.[15] These relationships are important to policy practitioners in a number of ways. Individuals who possess broad networks develop "early-information systems" that provide them with information about issues, problems, and trends that are relevant to their work as policy practitioners. Perhaps the priorities and objectives of top decision makers in an agency will be decisively changed in coming months in ways that will affect their units and the services of the agency. Policy practitioners who possess broad networks can call on other individuals for advice and assistance as they develop policies and strategies; when seeking to remedy a specific problem in the agency, someone may ask a trusted colleague, for example, Where should I start?

Many kinds of networks exist. *Lateral networks* consist of peer or colleagial relationships, whereas *vertical* and *subordinate* *networks* consist, respectively, of persons who are superior to and beneath the position of a person in an organizational chart. People have relatively *heterogeneous networks* when they have supportive relationships with others in a range of positions both within and outside their work. A social worker in a hospital possesses a heterogeneous network, for example, when it includes members of different professions and members of different units or departments of the institution. Some relationships in networks are short term, perhaps fashioned in response to a specific issue or problem, while others are long-standing ones.

Many strategies can be used to expand personal networks. They include enhancing one's visibility, seeking inclusion in decision-making and planning bodies, cultivating mentors, obtaining access to informal groups such as old-boy networks, and developing links with social movements.

ENHANCING PERSONAL VISIBILITY

Some people develop networks by increasing their visibility in specific bureaucratic, community, and legislative settings. Indeed, one school of management, which is called "Management by Walking Around," exhorts managers to broaden their personal networks. Some individuals resort to visiting "watering holes" or places where persons socialize to expand their circle of acquaintances.[16]

Of course, the nature of relationships during these personal contacts becomes important to the policy practitioner. Christopher Matthews tells the story of the young Lyndon Johnson, who lived in a boardinghouse in Washington, D.C., when he first arrived as an aide to a legislator. To meet other aides of legislators who lived in the same boardinghouse, he brushed his teeth three or four times each morning and took several showers to meet them. In these encounters, he asked them about their jobs and their interests—a tactic that convinced each aide that he cared about him.[17]

Indeed, practicing politicians often employ a tactic that can be used by other persons. Although purely exchanging information and socializing are important, both as ends and as methods of establishing relationships, they need to be supplemented by actively seeking advice, support, or suggestions from others. As Matthews notes, people usually like to be asked for advice and assistance because it makes them feel important and wanted.[18] Of course, too much can be made of a good thing when individuals make excessive requests.

Obtaining Inclusion in Formal or Ad Hoc Decision-Making Bodies

Most agencies establish ad hoc, or ongoing, committees or task forces from time to time to examine specific problems or issues. Besides formal, or official, committees and task forces, less formal and ad hoc groups are sometimes convened where people meet to discuss specific issues and problems.

Membership on some of these committees or task forces is sometimes limited to those who are invited to participate by top officials in an organization, but individuals can seek membership by displaying an interest in a specific issue. Or individuals can initiate groups by suggesting that a committee be established to examine a specific problem. The deliberations of committees and groups offer an excellent opportunity to obtain an inside position on important issues, to improve one's personal credibility, and to extend one's personal network.

Seeking Mentors and Inclusion in Old-Boy Networks

When researching why women have difficulty obtaining promotions in corporations, Rosabeth Kanter implicates their exclusion from mentoring relationships and informal associations of influential and up-and-rising men in old-boy networks.[19] Males, she observes, are informally assigned to or develop relationships with high-level (and male) officials. These officials develop a mentoring relationship with these men where they receive advice and information about the internal workings of the corporation, its politics, taboo subjects, informal factions, upcoming policy issues, and possibilities and strategies for obtaining promotion. Mentors introduce these neophytes to a range of acquaintances, including important officers of the corporation, both in formal decision-making arenas and in informal or socializing situations. On occasion, mentors "go to bat" for neophytes when they need high-level assistance from other officers.

Mentors introduce neophytes to informal cliques and relationships. As J. McIver Weatherford notes with respect to legislatures, old-boy networks span the legislative, bureaucratic, and lobbying spheres of government as people move between them in their employment.[20] In both state and federal capitals, for example, powerful legislators possess an intricate network of acquaintances—many of them former aides—in lobbying and bureaucratic capacities. They "tap into" these rich networks at many points in their work; a legislator might contact acquaintances within government agencies when contemplating whether to introduce legislation, when seeking to help a constituent who has a specific problem, and when scanning the horizon for issues that he might use to enhance his reputation as an initiator of new legislation.

These old-boy networks contain in effect a wide-ranging set of contacts that provide assistance, information, business contacts, and job possibilities to persons who belong to them and who cultivate them. Many high-level decisions are made in the social and informal relationships between those who are in these networks; people not included in them are not only not consulted about these decisions but also fail to obtain the advantage that derives from obtaining advance notification of upcoming shifts in policy.[21]

The workings of the mentor system and the old-boy networks are manifestly unfair, at least from the perspective of those who are not included within them. Lacking allies within them, many women and racial minorities are excluded from them, as well as "loners," that is, those who are disinclined to invest the time and energy to maintain a network of relationships.[22] Declarations about their evil nature, however, will not cause them not to exist—nor are the moral victories of people who disdain them likely to erase the decided disadvantages that they encounter from avoiding them.

Developing Links with Social Movements and Other Pressure Groups

Some people develop linkages with specific groups that possess an interest in specific issues such as AIDS, reforms for children, disabled persons, and mentally ill persons. These groups, which often possess minimal resources, have members who are highly knowledgeable about specific issues and who are deeply committed to them.

As volunteers or members of social movements, individuals can supplement their professional work with an action or policy dimension that extends beyond the boundaries of their agency.[23] In some cases, they can bring pending issues and policies to the attention of staff in their agencies. Or they may inform some clients of specific social movements or specific actions, such as protests, that they are organizing, though they need to be certain that their clients do not believe that receiving services is conditioned upon their participating in these activities.[24]

POLICY PERSUASION

A considerable part of the work of policy practitioners involves the use of language to influence the attitudes, preferences, and actions of other people.[25] We may try to influence someone in an interpersonal discussion, through speeches to larger audiences, through memoranda, through formal reports, in debates or arguments, or through messages, such as guest editorials, in the mass media. In each case, we initiate these various kinds of communications to change the actions or beliefs of others.

It is difficult to understate the importance of **policy persuasion** to policy practice. If the ultimate goal of policy practice is to secure the enactment (or the defeat) of specific policies, skilled policy practitioners need to convince other people to support specific policies; however, they often face significant challenges when other people are deeply opposed to their position, are apathetic, or encounter peer or group pressure to oppose it.

In short, persuaders need to develop persuading strategy to overcome obstacles to their positions. People who are highly skilled in the art of persuasion tailor their messages to specific audiences and situations to increase the likelihood that they will influence them in an intended direction.

As in the case of using power resources, persuasive encounters are transactional in nature—that is, persuaders hope to change the beliefs or actions of their audience (which may extend from individuals to large groups to the general public in mass-media communications)—but their endeavor requires activity *both* by them (the sending of a message) and the audience, whose members decide either to heed (and be changed by) the message or to ignore (or not to be changed by) it[26] (see Figure 7.1). No matter how loudly persuaders shout at someone or how articulately they make their case, their efforts come to naught unless the audience decides the message is meritorious and that its prescriptions should be heeded.

The social context can often be important. A specific persuader might have convinced some people to accept certain beliefs or take certain actions if she had had the luxury of interacting with them in relative isolation, but she may find her work to be frustrated on a specific occasion by "external noise," such as peer pressure or competition from messages of other senders, not to mention inertia that stems from traditional habits or beliefs of her audience.[27] Such external noise is illustrated by the problems of political campaigners who seldom have the luxury of extended personal discussions with voters; faced with the competing messages of opposing candidates, pressure from members of their families and friends, and encumbered by

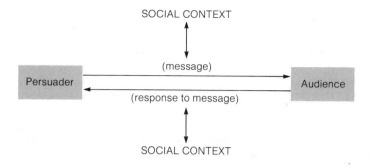

Figure 7.1   Persuaders, Audiences, and the Social Context in Persuasive Encounters

traditional political loyalties, politicians often fail to secure the votes of some people who might otherwise be sympathetic to their candidacy.[28]

The major difference between the use of political resources and persuasive encounters involves the vehicle that modifies beliefs and actions. When people use the kinds of political resources that were discussed in Chapter Five, such as various kinds of person-to-person power, they do not usually develop a complex message such as a speech. Indeed, power can be exerted by brief sentences such as "vote for me if you want more money for your cause," "attend this meeting and register your opposition to XYZ policy," or "if you support me on this issue, I'll support you on that issue." Moreover, as we noted in Chapter Five, power is often exerted in nonverbal ways. If someone routes a policy to one committee rather than to another one because the members of the first committee are more favorably disposed to it, she uses power indirectly and without having to construct *any* verbal or written message.

Messages, whether verbal or written, are the vehicle of persuasive encounters. Although they may contain implied threats or rewards—that is, the use of power resources—they often contain internal logic, assertions, arguments, and a "call for action." Even in relatively brief messages, persuaders rely primarily on the content of the message to convince the audience to change their beliefs or actions. As we will discuss later, persuaders possess many options when constructing messages in specific situations.

ESTABLISHING PERSUADING OBJECTIVES WITH SPECIFIC AUDIENCES

Before persuaders can decide how to fashion a message, they have to establish **persuading objectives.** Do they want major or minor changes in the beliefs or actions of the audience? Are they content merely with maintaining the existing beliefs or habits of an audience, or do they want to change them markedly?

Varieties of Objectives

Objectives can be ranked on a continuum extending from ambitious to modest.[29] Persuaders with ambitious objectives hope to make dramatic changes in the beliefs or actions of the audience. At the most ambitious level, persuaders hope to markedly modify the beliefs of an audience *and* to convince them to take specific actions such as enlisting in a project to change a policy, engaging in specific tasks, or pressuring decision makers to support a proposed policy. At a somewhat more modest but still ambitious level, a persuader may be content, at least in the short term, merely to try to modify the beliefs of an audience, perhaps as a precursor to eventually causing them to take certain actions such as supporting a specific policy. (As we will discuss later, changes in people's beliefs do not necessarily cause them to change their actions.)

Persuaders with relatively modest objectives may wish merely to educate or sensitize an audience without (at least for the moment) inducing them to change their beliefs or to take specific actions. Perhaps hoping to convince an executive in an agency to eventually support a new policy or program, a staff member might route to him an informational memorandum that discusses a specific unmet need in the community or a promising pilot project of another agency.

Efforts to maintain certain beliefs and the customary actions of an audience fall between the ambitious and modest ends of the continuum. Assume, for the moment, that persuaders in a specific agency fear that someone else will soon attack or question a favored program and that they want to "head off" this possibility by maintaining, or even strengthening, the support of an agency director of the existing program. Assume, as well, that the executive has provided relatively generous funding of it. These persuaders need to develop messages that confirm or buttress existing support of the program so that the director will not be unduly influenced by the impending attack on the program.[30] While this endeavor sounds relatively modest in nature, it is more ambitious than persuasive projects that merely educate or sensitize because the persuaders wish to influence beliefs *and* actions.

To make matters somewhat more complex, we also need to distinguish between the short- and long-term objectives of a persuader. When planning a specific message on a specific occasion, a persuader may have a relatively modest objective such as sensitizing or educating an audience about a specific issue or policy. But the persuader may anticipate a *campaign* or sequence of messages to an audience that have the ultimate—and ambitious—effect of changing their beliefs *and* rallying them to support a new policy. Indeed, intelligent policy practitioners often hope to persuade people "bit-by-bit." A campaign might consist of some interpersonal discussions, a memorandum, and a formal presentation, each planned to educate an audience and to move them toward support of a policy.

It is more difficult to develop a campaign of presentations, of course, than to convince an audience in a single presentation to support a policy or to change their beliefs. Numerous discussions, memos or reports, and presentations may be required. The policy practitioner not only must manage the campaign but also must decide during it when to proceed beyond a goal of educating the audience to a more ambitious goal of seeking their support for new policies and beliefs. Much as someone who seeks funds from a donor, the policy practitioner may proceed too cautiously or too rapidly from modest to ambitious objectives.

Varieties of Audiences and Social Contexts

Policy practitioners often try to "diagnose" audiences, even if they do not use the therapeutic classifications of direct-service practitioners. They often want to know the beliefs of an audience, their degree of motivation or ego involvement in an issue, their fears and hopes, and the extent to which they are subject to situational or historical factors that might influence their response to a message.[31]

When examining beliefs of audiences, policy practitioners gauge the degree of opposition or hostility to their messages. Audiences are most hostile to a message when they oppose its value premises *and* its fundamental logic, or argument.[32] When liberal policy practitioners seek expansion of the nation's welfare programs and wish to address a conservative audience, they are likely to find the audience disagrees with (1) their value premises that society is obliged to help impoverished people and that government should expand its social welfare roles and (2) their assertion that unemployment and low-paying jobs rather than the size of existing welfare grants have caused welfare rolls to expand. Many conservatives adhere to the value premise that government is not obligated to help most poor people and that the existing welfare system exacerbates the welfare problems by encouraging dependency.

Audiences are less hostile when the value premises and logic of the message are relatively close to their own beliefs or when they possess relatively flexible or undefined positions. When an audience has a fairly broad zone of tolerance, it is relatively tolerant of ideas, values, or perspectives that differ from its existing orientations. Persuaders encounter a difficult challenge when the zone of tolerance is relatively narrow and the persuaders seek to make major changes in the attitudes or beliefs of the audience.[33]

Audiences also differ in their levels of motivation or involvement in specific topics. All of us have experienced or been part of apathetic or indifferent audiences that could not care less about a specific message. Perhaps we have been inundated with messages about a specific subject, do not perceive its relevance to us, or have been subjected to particularly boring messages on the same subject on prior occasions.[34]

To the extent an audience is hostile to a position or policy, persuaders have to try to diagnose why its members are opposed to it. Indeed, the functional school of theorists suggests that audiences are most receptive to messages that are relevant to the fears and hopes of its members.[35] When a new policy or program is proposed in an agency, for example, some staff may fear it will jeopardize certain of their current reponsibilities or powers, will divert funds from existing projects that they favor, or will lead to new and difficult burdens that they do not wish to shoulder, such as learning new skills or working longer hours. Skillful persuaders carefully allay these kinds of fears in their messages.

In similar fashion, persuaders often identify positive factors that could motivate some members of an audience to support a policy. A new policy in the aforementioned agency, for example, might allow staff to develop new roles and skills, might enhance the job security of staff by adding an important source of new revenues, and might enhance the prestige of the agency and some of its staff. Moreover, many professionals respond favorably to policy and program initiatives that address important or unmet needs of clients.[36]

The social context may contribute to the audience's response to a particular measure. If a social agency is in a cut-back mode, for example, its staff are unlikely to be responsive to a message that supports the development of a costly program initiative. Audiences are often influenced by historical factors. Assume, for example, that a specific issue or policy has been discussed on prior occasions when some members of the audience were present. Their recollections of these discussions, which are often transmitted to others who were not present, can powerfully shape the responses of people. If an issue was a divisive one, for example, it may be associated with extensive conflict when it is reintroduced. By contrast, policy issues that are associated with positive traditions often have a better chance of acceptance by an audience.[37]

To this point, we have assumed that audiences are relatively homogeneous in nature, that is, that all their members possess specific orientations toward a subject or a message. In fact, audiences often contain a range of perspectives; one faction may be highly disposed to support a new policy, for example, while another faction may be opposed. In the case of these mixed audiences, persuaders encounter the challenge of segmenting the audience by identifying various factions or subgroups within it.[38] They have to decide how to address the different needs of the various subgroups in their messages—a formidable challenge if these factions possess divergent perspectives. Perhaps one section of a message can contain elements that appeal to one segment of the audience ("some of you fear that . . ."), while another section can address another segment ("others of you believe that

. . ."). Even in the case of audiences with divergent perspectives, persuaders can identify and appeal to common values, hopes, or aspirations; they can note, for example, that "despite the differences among us on this issue, we all agree that this agency needs to diversify its services."

Meshing Objectives and Audience Realities

Persuaders often encounter the difficult dilemma of establishing objectives that are too modest or too ambitious. In the former case, persuaders may falsely believe that an audience is so hostile to their messages that they can only hope to achieve minor changes in their positions or actions. This mistaken judgment predisposes them to be too timid. In the latter case, persuaders establish unrealistic expectations because they falsely believe that their audiences are (or soon can be) similar to themselves. Persuaders with liberal perspectives may, for example, possess unrealistic expectations that they can convert an extremely conservative audience to accept a policy that stems from liberal premises, only to find that the message merely reconfirms the preexisting beliefs of an audience that unites against "these knee-jerk liberals."

SELECTING A PERSUADING STRATEGY

With objectives, audience, and situation in mind, policy practitioners develop a persuading strategy by drawing upon a variety of options that include selecting a medium; choosing an audience; developing a basic format, or outline; picking a presentation style; and deciding the order of persuasive interventions. After discussing these various options, we will illustrate persuading strategy with some practice examples.

Selecting a Medium

Persuaders rely on symbols, such as words and visual aids, to influence the ideas and actions of audiences, but they can deliver or present these symbols in many ways, such as through the use of speech, written documents, graphic aids, or some combination of these methods. Because these modes of communication are so familiar, we often do not consider their relative merits.

Spoken communication allows presenters to interact with the audience. As they perceive fears and hopes that impede or facilitate a positive response, presenters can address them; indeed, they can elicit these perceptions and emotions during the course of their presentation. Spoken communications allow a persuader to be flexible; if they are skilled at "thinking on their feet," persuaders can change their message in midstream to respond to unforeseen developments. When persuaders want an audience to become emotionally involved in an issue, they often use arguments that culminate in a "call to action," where members agree to actively work to support or promote a specific cause.[39]

Written communications, such a memoranda, letters, and reports, have the virtue of allowing precise communication, unlike spoken communication where definitions and details are often relatively vague. When presenters seek commitments of an audience to a course of action, they can seek relatively precise and binding agreements; a memo may seek a straw poll, for example, by asking people to check specific categories at the end of the memo, such as "agree or support," "disagree," or "undecided." Written communications are useful for relatively technical subjects, such as the details of the implementation of a specific policy or a summary of existing research, because it is difficult to convey technical subjects in relatively brief addresses.[40]

Graphic communications, such as the use of graphs and slides, provide a means of simplifying complex and technical materials. Graphic materials are often useful for capturing the attention of a hostile or indifferent audience; someone who seeks support for vulnerable populations, for example, can use pictures or slides to promote sympathy or interest. If used to excess, however, graphic materials can be counterproductive.[41]

Choosing the Audience

When we think of presentations, we customarily conceive them as one-shot episodes, where people seek to influence an audience through a single encounter such as a formal presentation. Viewed in this manner, persuaders have one (and only one) chance to convince an audience to take a specific position on an issue. In fact, skilled persuaders rarely approach their work in this manner because they realize that they are more likely to be effective if they develop a strategy that uses a sequence of persuasive encounters. Even when a formal presentation culminates the sequence, it may be preceded by a variety of written, interpersonal, and other communications. A persuader might decide, for example, to use some informal and one-on-one encounters as information-gathering tools to discover where people stand on specific issues and what kinds of fears or objections they possess. This persuader may use these informal encounters to reduce the uncertainties that may be associated with subsequent verbal or written presentations that prepare the way for a culminating presentation, such as a speech or a report.[42]

Developing a Basic Format, or Outline

Persuaders often develop a basic format, or outline, for specific communications. These formats are critically important because they establish an integrating logic for a presentation. As with other strategy choices, persuaders have to decide which kind of format to use with specific audiences because each has strengths and weaknesses.

Persuaders sometimes use a relatively simple, **opinion-eliciting format.**[43] Assume that you do not know the positions of a specific audience; rather than developing a formal presentation, you might wish merely to develop a series of leading questions to probe the opinions and knowledge of specific persons. (This kind of format is similar to nondirective questions in some clinical encounters.)

Rational formats are presentations that use scientific or formal logic, as is illustrated by classic debate strategy.[44] (This format is similar to the analytic approach that we discussed in Chapters Two, Three, and Four.) Someone may begin a presentation, for example, with a discussion of an existing social or institutional problem, where she presents evidence to document its importance. She may proceed to a discussion of its causes or its distribution in the population as a prelude to examining alternative policy and program options. After weighing the comparative merits of these options, the presentation may conclude with a proposal. Rational presentations then use evidence and reasoning to progress from a statement of the presenting problem to discussion of its causes to examination of one or more solutions to a concluding position. Persuaders who use this kind of presentation aspire to impress an audience with their logic, evidence, and force of reasoning so that the audience decides that they have been led to the most reasonable conclusion that is possible in the circumstances.

Many variations are possible when using a rational format. Presenters can tell the audience in the introduction that they will recommend a specific option or proposal. Or they can merely tell the audience that they will present them with a conclusion at the end of the presentation after discussing the presenting problem and various possible solutions. (With relatively hostile audiences, it is often wise not to divulge the ultimate policy that the presenter favors, but presenters hope that the process of reasoning will diminish audience hostility so that they are more ready to respond favorably when the proposal is presented.[45]) In some cases, presenters do not have to begin their presentation with an analysis of a major social or institutional problem but can begin with a discussion of some problem or deficiency in existing policies, such as their cost. They can then introduce an alternative policy, perhaps a minor revision that is superior in some respects to the existing policies. This kind of rational argument is somewhat less demanding than presentations that purport to develop entirely new policies to address major social or institutional policies.

Persuaders must meet certain obligations when making rational presentations.[46] They have to show that their proposed policy or program will be superior to existing ones. They have to show that their proposed policy will remedy the defects of existing policies more effectively than any other remedy. They have to show that their policy remedy is feasible in its polit-ical, administrative, and cost dimensions. They have to use evidence or data convincingly. They have to convince an audience that they have made proper use of relevant theory from the social sciences, economics, or other disciplines.

As a review of the rhetoric of social movement leaders suggests, some presenters use **emotional, or value-dominated, presentations.**[47] Rather than initiating a presentation with an analysis of a problem, these presenters begin with an assertion of moral outrage or indignation. Basic value premises are asserted, such as "how can Americans allow economic inequalities of this dimension to continue?" or "how can Americans resort to the taking of life (the death penalty) to curb crime?" Once the value premise is stated, both the proposed policy and the rejected policy are judged primarily as they reflect or repudiate the value premise.

Like rational presentations, emotional presentations may include refer-ences to statistics, research, and theory. An opponent of the death penalty may contend, for example, that research suggests that the death penalty does not deter homicides. But value premises are nonetheless dominant in emo-tional presentations. Emotional presentations often conclude with a "call to action" where the audience is asked to join a cause, to vote for a candidate, or to pressure officials to adopt a specific policy.[48]

Emotional presentations are most useful with audiences that share spe-cific values with the persuader. The leader of a social movement who is speaking to its members—people who already possess a sense of moral outrage at an existing policy—stresses their shared values both to maintain their level of motivation and to urge them on to greater activity. Emotional presentations can be used with some indifferent, or apathetic, audiences, but indifference can turn to antagonism if the presenter fails to motivate the audience by appealing to a common, or shared, value.[49]

Directive communications are used to mobilize people behind a specific course of action. The persuader wants to quickly convince people to take an action such as attending a meeting or writing a legislator. He emphasizes the urgency of the situation, the fact that "time has run out" and no alternatives exist, and the support of the action by other influential or credible persons. In directive communications, emphasis is placed not on an extended process of reasoning to convince people to change their beliefs but on the immediate task of convincing them to take a specific action.

Picking a Presentation Style

Policy practitioners sometimes encounter hostile audiences who possess val-ues or beliefs that predispose them to oppose a specific message. In other cases, they encounter apathetic audiences who are uninterested in specific issues, problems, or policies.

Various techniques can decrease hostility. The persuader can identify common values, perspectives, and practical concerns that link the persuader to the audience.[50] Perhaps the persuader shares certain memberships, educational affiliations, demographic traits, or other characteristics with some members of the audience. Persuaders can sometimes appeal to higher values that can be used to bind themselves to the audience.[51] Some policy advocates seek support from conservatives for social programs by appealing, for example, to their patriotism; if Americans want the nation to remain competitive in international markets, these advocates could argue, they need to develop programs to redress the high dropout rate in schools.

Persuaders need to establish their credibility with hostile audiences. They may cite authorities or experts whom the audiences are likely to respect. They can discuss their own credentials or experiences that make them credible to the audience. To connote an aura of reasonableness, presenters can present "both sides" of complex issues and freely admit that alternative viewpoints are inevitable when addressing complex issues. In some cases, they can reach their eventual proposal or position only after rejecting or refuting alternative positions.[52]

Humor can often calm tense situations. Perhaps persuaders can make fun of themselves so that the audience perceives them as unceremonious and unpretentious.[53] If told with skill, anecdotes at the start of presentations can ease audiences into subjects that they find difficult or stressful.

Apathetic audiences present similar challenges to persuaders. It is important with apathetic audiences not to overwhelm them with complex arguments or data, which can serve to intensify their apathy. Nor is it wise to tell the audience that they *should* care about the issue or policy because this intrusive technique is likely to make them retreat even further into apathy. The skillful persuader needs to make the presentation interesting and lively, to stress relatively few themes or arguments, to present a relatively simple argument, and to offer interesting and unusual evidence or data that the audience has not heard on prior occasions.[54]

Deciding the Order of Persuasive Interventions

Besides deciding which of the preceding formats or outlines to use with specific audiences, persuaders have to make some other strategy choices such as deciding the order, or sequence, of points within their presentations and the nature of their introductions and conclusions. Moreover, they have to decide to what extent they should alert an audience to some of the counterarguments that can be made against their positions or whether instead to concentrate on the strengths of their positions.

Single-Sided or Two-Sided Arguments? Should persuaders present the strongest possible argument for a specific policy where they emphasize arguments that affirm it (a single-sided argument), or should they instead present both sides of an issue (a two-sided argument)? Persuaders might contend, for example, that a new policy is needed, acknowledge that it has some liabilities (such as its cost), but then contend that it is desirable "on balance" after considering both positive arguments and some negative considerations. Conversely, they might decide to emphasize the strengths of their proposal and hope that possible opponents do not emerge who find its weaknesses.

Findings of some social psychologists suggest that two-sided arguments are particularly useful for critical or hostile audiences; by admitting some negative considerations, the persuader anticipates and defuses some criticisms of the audience and, in the process, appears to be a reasonable and open-minded person. If presenters emphasize the weaknesses of their position excessively, however, they risk providing ammunition to opponents.[55]

(2)   *How Much Dissonance to Seek?*   All persuaders want to change their audiences, whether by changing their beliefs, their actions, or a combination thereof. But they have to decide how much dissonance to introduce, that is, discrepancy between the beliefs of the audience and the proposal of the presenter. If they ask for massive changes, they risk alienating their audiences. If they ask for minor changes, they risk undermining support for those policies that they favor.

When persuaders anticipate a hostile audience, they should probably refrain from suggesting massive changes from the outset. Perhaps several presentations should be sought and planned, with the first of them seeking to educate and sensitize the audience rather than securing commitments to major changes. When encountering sympathetic audiences, persuaders can overstate their case and secure public commitments to relatively major changes.[56]

(3)   *Climax or Anticlimax?*   Social psychologists have researched the merits of making the strongest points, or arguments, at the end or at the beginning of a presentation. Their findings, however, are contradictory, but some evidence exists that audiences pay the most attention to the introductory and concluding portions of communications. The weakest points then should usually be inserted in the middle sections of communications.[57]

(4)   *Who Should Present?*   When a choice exists, persuaders need to carefully ponder who should take the lead in presenting information to specific audiences. With hostile or apathetic audiences, presenters should be selected who are relatively credible with them or who possess styles of communication that are suited to overcoming hostility and apathy. Multiple presenters— several persons take responsibility for specific portions of a presentation— are sometimes useful.[58]

(5) *Creating the Setting for Persuasion*   Skillful persuaders sometimes find or create settings where their messages are most likely to be heeded by specific audiences. Perhaps relatively intimate or friendly settings can be substituted for formal settings to increase the rapport between presenters and specific audiences. Perhaps seating arrangements can be devised to facilitate exchanges between the presenter and the audience. Perhaps graphic aids, such as slides, can be used to overcome the apathy of an audience. In some cases, the audience can be broken into smaller groups that reconvene at a later point to share their solutions to specific problems.[59]

(6) *Honoring Protocols and Expectations*   Audiences often possess specific expectations about presentations. In the case of testimony to legislative committees, for example, legislators expect presentations to be relatively brief, that is, to not exceed ten or fifteen minutes.[60] (Detailed materials and the text of the presenter's comments are submitted separately.) Audiences may also possess expectations regarding the formality, tenor, and style of a presentation. An audience composed of persons who perceive themselves to be experts on a specific subject expect the presenter, for example, to offer alternative viewpoints, whereas an audience of activists often expect a "call to action." To understand these kinds of expectations, presenters need to talk with members of the audience before their presentations or with people who are familiar with the audience.

PUTTING IT ALL TOGETHER: SHAPING PERSUADING STRATEGY

The preceding discussion suggests that persuaders have a variety of options when developing a persuading strategy. Choices have to be made in the context of the audience, the social context, and the objectives of the persuader. To explore the development of strategy, let's discuss a variety of audiences that the lobbyist in Policy-Practice Case 7 might consider when trying to make specific presentations to various kinds of audiences. Recall that Rand Martin, who established the Lobby for Individual Freedom and Equality (LIFE), seeks legislative reforms for AIDS victims. These hypothetical vignettes illustrate the nature of reasoning that persuaders use as they develop strategy for specific audiences.

The Hostile Audience

Assume that Martin wants to convince some conservative Republicans— people most likely to be critical of the gay community and to believe that AIDS victims "brought it on themselves"—to support a major legislative initiative to expand the state's funding of home health–care programs to serve AIDS patients. These services would cover an array of homemaker, visiting-nurse, and physical-therapy services and would be provided not only to Medicaid recipients but also to persons who are considerably above the poverty line. (The state's home-health services are currently funded mostly by counties and only for individuals who meet restrictive income standards.) Admittedly, the new program will be expensive because many AIDS victims who are not eligible for existing county programs will need extended home-health services.

With this skeptical and hostile audience, Martin decides to seek two presentations: the first to capture their interest and to cut through their stereotypes and the second to obtain their suggestions for legislative strategy.

Even before the first presentation, he obtains the assistance of several sympathetic Republican legislators, who agree to moderate the sessions and to expedite discussion. He wants to fashion an introduction that will lead some of the conservatives to perceive the problem in human and personal rather than abstract and ideological terms. He decides to present several case histories of HIV-positive people who have encountered many personal dilemmas when seeking access to home-based services. (To decrease the chances that they perceive the problem as belonging only to "gay radicals," he concentrates on several cases of conservative Republicans who have contracted the disease.) He also wants to make analogies to elderly persons and to disabled persons to ensure that the legislators understand that home-health needs and problems of the AIDS population are similar to those encountered by other, more acceptable populations. He concludes the first presentation with a question-and-answer format regarding the dimensions of the problem.

During the second presentation, he uses a rational format with a two-sided argument. After quickly summarizing some factual information from the first session regarding the dimensions of the problem, he quickly moves to some alternative remedies including the cost implications of establishing different levels of eligibility for home-health services, the merits of working through local nonprofit agencies when compared to using home-health programs of the counties, and the merits of focusing the services on specific subgroups of AIDS patients. (Some legislators wonder if the program should emphasize home-health services for AIDS victims who can still work but who have bouts of disability because they are least covered by the county home-health programs.) After discussing the merits of these various options, he provides them with a tentative draft of a legislative proposal that a bipartisan group has drafted but not yet introduced into the legislative process.

The Sympathetic Audience with Some Hostile Members

Assume that the legislative proposal is introduced into a legislative committee, that most of its members are sympathetic, but that a minority of its

members are hostile. Martin, who hopes to intensify support for the proposal, encounters a dilemma that is experienced by persons who encounter
"mixed audiences." Should he "write off" the minority and direct his comments to the sympathetic members, or should he target his comments to the
hostile minority because he expects the majority to support the proposal?

Martin decides to focus his comments on the majority but to include
points in his presentation that can attract some "swing votes" from the
minority. For the sympathetic majority, who do not need an extended argument but want a brief and dramatic message to energize them to support
the proposal, he uses a relatively emotional format rather than a rational
one. Indeed, he focuses his presentation about a particularly poignant case.
To appeal to the hostile minority, however, he selects a case that illustrates
how the provision of a homemaker and other services can allow some people
with AIDS to remain productive members of the labor force (and hence
taxpayers) for a longer period than if these services were unavailable.

The Expert Audience

Assume that the lobbyist seeks support for the proposal from an audience
of hospital administrators, whose professional association is a powerful lobby
within the state. Unlike most legislators, who possess scant knowledge of
the intricacies of health-care programs, hospital administrators are familiar
with existing programs. With this audience, Martin decides to emphasize
practical cost and administrative issues such as how the proposal would be
implemented, how the state would monitor it, and how it would affect the
lengths of stay of AIDS patients who are admitted to hospitals.

To enhance his rapport with this audience, Martin cites evidence and
arguments that he had obtained from a hospital administrator as well as
some hospital social workers who specialize in discharge planning. Because
the proposal's funds would be funneled through nonprofit agencies, he
discusses how these agencies would coordinate their services with hospitals.

Some Interpersonal Discussions

During the progression of this legislation from initial proposal to drafted
legislation to (hopefully) enacted legislation, the lobbyist would have innumerable interpersonal discussions with legislative foes and friends of the
legislation, officials in the state's government bureaucracies, local officials,
and community activists. These interpersonal discussions would take many
forms. Some of them would be information-soliciting contacts to discern the
positions, biases, and perspectives of people. In these nondirective contacts,
Martin would maintain a background and fact-finding posture. Of course,
his patience would be tested in those contacts where individuals assume a
hostile stance toward people with AIDS, such as a legislator who maintains

that "the approach to the AIDS problem is to require all testing centers to turn over the names of all persons who test positive for the AIDS virus to public health officials." As Lewis Dexter suggests, the lobbyist should remain "benevolently neutral" in some of these hostile discussions. While he need not capitulate to these legislators by disingenuously agreeing with them, he does not need to attack them, either.[61] Indeed, he might indicate that "we share in common a desire to bring this epidemic under control, but what ideas do you have about how to help some AIDS victims remain productive members of society in the interim?"

In some of these interpersonal discussions, Martin uses a directive-communication format where he seeks to mobilize support for a position or proposal. He might wish to secure a commitment from a leader of an action-oriented group to mobilize support for the legislation by obtaining letters and phone calls from the constituents of key legislators. He might use a combination of flattery and emotional language such as indicating "we've turned to you many times in the past and you have never let us down . . . how do you think we can place pressure on these five legislators who are 'swing votes.'?"

Still other interpersonal discussions might follow a rational format, such as ones with health experts. In these conversations, the lobbyist might seek assistance in defining the magnitude of the home-health needs of AIDS patients, cost implications of specific provisions in the legislation, and administrative considerations.

COMBATIVE PERSUASION

We have emphasized "friendly persuasion" in the preceding discussion by presenting a variety of techniques that persuaders use to change the beliefs and actions of an audience. Rather than confront or attack the audience, persuaders try to use written and verbal language that engages the audience in a cooperative and transactional enterprise. When used skillfully, audiences are hardly aware that their perspectives have changed or that the persuader has spent considerable time in developing a persuading strategy.

When using **combative persuasion,** persuaders use confrontive strategies to modify the opinions and actions of other people, who are typically viewed as adversaries.[62] Two kinds of combative situations exist. In some cases, persuaders engage in one-on-one confrontations to change an adversary's position by using coercive persuasion. In a confrontational meeting, for example, the leader of a social movement might demand that the executive of an agency modify its services to become more responsive to the needs of a specific population. In other cases, persuaders engage in debates or arguments with an adversary hoping to convince *observers* to accept their points of view rather than those of the adversary (who is also seeking to influence the positions of the observers). In a staff meeting, for example, someone might engage in a debate with one person trying to convince other members of the staff to accept her position. We can illustrate the use of combative persuasion by discussing adversarial debates, coercive or "hard-line" messages, and negotiations.

Adversarial Debates

Three parties exist in adversarial debates: the persuader, the adversary, and an audience of observers. Formal debates that follow a structured format rarely exist in the real world, aside from debating teams, but argumentative situations often exist.[63] Perhaps someone presents a proposal in a staff meeting, which is criticized by one or more persons and then defended by its initiator. Perhaps someone testifies against a legislative proposal to a legislative committee, as in the case of the AIDS lobbyist who opposes mandatory testing of prostitutes for the human immunodeficiency virus (HIV) that causes AIDS. Perhaps someone engages in an argument with an individual in the presence of another person. Persuaders sometimes hope to change the minds of both their immediate adversary and an audience that hears their argument.

Many tactics can be used to criticize someone's position or proposal.[64] Let's assume that a legislator wishes to introduce a bill to require all testing services, both public and private, to give to state public health officials the names of *all* persons who test positive for HIV. Assume, as well, that the lobbyist in Policy-Practice Case 7 wants to defeat this measure and that he is invited to a public forum to engage in discussion with the legislator who initiated the measure.

Martin can use many kinds of arguments to cast doubt on the merits of the proposal. He can attack the *values* of the legislator because the proposal possesses implicit or explicit value premises. *Any* value premise can be contrasted with a competing or alternative value premise. While the legislator values "control" to protect the public's health, Martin favors protecting the privacy and freedom of people who test positive for HIV. (Such privacy, he contends, conforms with traditions that are embedded in the Bill of Rights and are particularly needed by persons who could be subjected to discrimination, such as those who are HIV-positive but may remain symptom-free for many years before they are diagnosed with AIDS.) He can attack the *workability* of the proposal. In theory, public health departments would interview HIV-positive individuals to obtain lists of persons with whom they have had sexual relations and in turn alert each of them to their possible infection with HIV. However, it is an extremely time-consuming process to develop these lists and to contact the persons on them—particularly in light of the lack of sufficient staff to implement this policy. "If public health officials lack the staff to adequately accomplish their existing functions, how can we expect them to assume these added functions?" Martin might ask. He might attack the *motives* of the legislator by suggesting that "he is more interested in finding the names of HIV-positive persons than in providing them with humanistic services." He might attack some *unanticipated* or *adverse consequences* of the proposal; might not many people who fear that they have been infected with the virus decide not to seek *any* testing if they feared that the results would not be kept confidential? (Aware of the considerable job-related and social discrimination that gay people, as well as AIDS victims, have encountered, many people would likely forgo testing because they feared their identities would be revealed to employers, landlords, and others.)

He might attack *the use of specific analogies* by the legislator. Assume that the legislator contends that the divulging of the names of persons who are infected with syphilis and gonorrhea has long been required by public health departments and that this information has led to successful efforts to alert sexual partners to their possible infection. To attack the use of this analogy to other sexually transmitted diseases, Martin might attack the effectiveness of this approach in stemming the spread of syphilis and gonorrhea by noting that they are currently epidemics *despite* these practices. Moreover, the dangers of discrimination against victims of these treatable diseases are not nearly as marked, he might argue, as with persons who are HIV-positive. Unlike syphilis and gonorrhea, the initial infection with HIV is often followed by a lengthy period—sometimes as much as ten years—when the person has no serious symptoms, much less the disease of AIDS. "If we breech the confidentiality of persons with a disease of such duration," Martin might argue, "we risk extended damage to their careers and reputations that does not occur with treatable diseases like syphilis."

The lobbyist could question the *uses of data* as well as the *analytic assumptions* of the legislator. Assume, for the moment, that the legislator contended that the proposal had already been used in Colorado and that it had been "successful." Martin could question the veracity of this claim by criticizing the merits of specific quantitative studies that the legislator used to buttress this claim. Martin could variously criticize the methods that were used to collect data, the applicability of the Colorado data to his state, and the way the legislator interpreted the data. (We discuss methods of criticizing quantitative studies in more detail in Chapter Thirteen.)

He could attack *implicit models of human motivation* in the legislator's rationale for the proposal. The imposition of mandatory reporting of the names of HIV-positive persons by testing centers to the public health department implies that most HIV-positive persons will not *voluntarily* cooperate with public health officials—an assumption that in turn suggests that most HIV-positive persons lack a strong sense of social responsibility. Martin might assert that many HIV-positive individuals are (or can become) concerned about former and current sexual partners *if* given access to high-quality counseling that does not infringe on their confidentiality. At the point that they receive their test results, for example, they could be told about the availability of voluntary counseling as well as the need to inform current and prior sexual partners of the risks they encounter. Martin could reframe the issue from "how do we *force* HIV-positive persons to assume social responsibility?" to "how do we provide educational and counseling assistance to HIV-positive persons to show them how to channel their inherent altruism?" (The remarkable generosity of gay people toward AIDS victims, as reflected by a proliferation of support networks, provides support for this contention.)

Martin could attack the legislator's conception of the *chain of events* that would follow the enactment of his proposal. The legislator assumes that (1) testing centers will provide the names of HIV-positive people to the state's public health department, (2) this department will contact HIV-positive people, (3) HIV-positive people will agree to provide the names of their previous and current sexual partners (or persons with whom they have shared needles when using drugs), (4) public officials will contact many or most of these sexual partners, and (5) the sexual partners will agree to be tested for HIV, will practice "safe sex," and will provide public officials (if they test HIV-positive) with names of their sexual partners. Martin could contend that this chain of events would often be broken at one, two, or more points in the real world. We have noted that public health departments often lack the staff to make these contacts. When forced (more or less) to divulge names, some HIV-positive persons might decline to be cooperative because of the violation of their privacy *and* the imposition of mandatory procedures. In the case of anonymous or casual sexual encounters or the sharing of needles, HIV-positive persons might be unable to supply the names of partners. Because of the mobility of the population, it would be difficult to locate some of the sexual partners even if authorities possessed their names.

The lobbyist might also identify *points of vagueness* in the legislator's proposal that might make it seem less attractive to other people. Perhaps his proposal fails to describe how the testing services, some of them private ones, will be linked to the state's public health department. Perhaps the proposal fails to discuss how the mandatory-reporting policy will be evaluated to assess its effectiveness in slowing the spread of HIV.

Martin could point to *unacceptable trade-offs* in the legislator's proposal. He might commend the legislator, for example, for wanting to stem the spread of HIV (a desirable objective) but argue that this objective, noble as it may be, should not be achieved at the cost of the privacy of tens of thousands of individuals (a violated objective) or at an exorbitant cost. When making this kind of argument, the lobbyist is saying in effect that we need to find methods of stemming the spread of HIV that do not violate personal privacy and that are not so costly.

In some cases, people contend that an adversary's proposal will be *rendered moot or ineffective* by future events that they have not foreseen. Assume, for example, that impending technology allows individuals to test themselves for HIV in the privacy of their homes; such technology would render moot the mandatory-reporting law because many people would bypass public or private testing centers. Or assume that legal rulings might render the mandatory-reporting law unconstitutional or delay its implementation.

The lobbyist need not only criticize the legislator's proposal but could also argue that *an alternative proposal is more meritorious* in what debaters call a comparative advantages approach. Because the tracking of sexual partners is an expensive proposition, Martin could argue that scarce public resources ought instead be invested in public education projects such as efforts to promote safe sex by the use of condoms. Perhaps scarce resources should be invested in teaching addicts and prostitutes how not to become infected and how not to spread the disease to other people. The lobbyist might conclude that "the state will get a far better return on funds invested in an educational program than in a mandatory-reporting program."

People who use combative debating techniques often try to catch their adversaries off guard by asking questions that they did not anticipate. Perhaps they have found a recent piece of research that their adversaries have not read and that makes their proposal seem less desirable than they assert. Perhaps they introduce a development that will render the innovation ineffective or moot that the adversary has not considered. By surprising their opponents with points they had not considered, the policy practitioner hopes to make them appear to be ill prepared.

Coercive, or Hard-Line, Messages

Policy practitioners sometimes use coercive, or hard-line, messages with decision makers who, they believe, would otherwise be opposed to their positions.[65] Perhaps someone works for, volunteers with, or is a member of a social movement such as one that helps disabled persons, AIDS victims, minority groups, or a specific community. Or someone is placed in a position as a negotiator for a specific group whose task is to exact the best possible bargain for a specific faction.

People who use coercive messages usually begin with the assumption—often a correct one—that cooperative or conciliatory messages will not work because political and ideological factors, discriminatory attitudes, or the force of tradition makes decision makers unwilling to accept their policy proposals. Or perhaps they feel that existing resources are already so committed to other programs or causes that policymakers are unwilling to fund those programs that they seek.

With this assumption in mind, people develop messages that are framed to make decision makers perceive the demands as important. The message often contains several elements.[66] A formal request is made for a specific policy or program or for a process that obtains commitments to include the leaders or members of a specific group in the decision-making process. Moral, or value, elements are introduced, sometimes with the use of specific (and flagrant) examples. Threats are sometimes included in the message, whether explicit or veiled; persuaders may imply or say that they will take further steps such as litigation, protests, or the sending of delegations to even higher authorities, if decision makers do not comply with the request. (Of course, threats also contain implied incentives or rewards such as the promise *not* to use coercive measures if the request is granted.) In many cases, an implied threat to publicize the issue through the mass media is made if the media have not already been apprised of the issue.

People who use coercive messages often try to influence the social context of the persuading encounter. They may insist that the decision maker listen to a delegation rather than one or several persons. They may try to physically surround the decision maker with members of their group. In some cases, persuaders inform the mass media of the encounter before it has occurred in order to place even more pressure on decision makers.

Coercive messages can be effective in some situations, particularly when no recourse exists and when decision makers believe themselves to be vulnerable to adverse publicity or to other coercive measures if they do not heed the requests of the persuaders. But coercive messages also carry certain dangers with them. If decision makers believe that they are not vulnerable to coercion, they are unlikely to comply with the requests and may in fact harden their positions *and* take retaliatory measures.[67] Assume, for example, that some staff in an agency used coercive messages with their executive director with respect to a specific issue; were the director to not sympathize with them and to believe they lacked the power resources that they claimed, she might fire, demote, or otherwise retaliate against the leaders of the delegation. Moreover, once coercive messages have been initiated by one side in a dispute, a vicious circle of escalating intransigency and reprisal often begins that makes it increasingly difficult for opposing sides to cooperate.[68] Both sides more likely will view the conflict as win-lose rather than win-win conflict, so each side believes that *any* concession to the other side is a defeat for themselves.

Negotiations

Negotiations occur when two or more parties to a conflict, who possess different positions, meet to develop a final position.[69] Skillful negotiators want to emerge from the negotiations with their positions intact, but they realize that they can seldom achieve this goal. To increase this possibility, negotiators sometimes rank the importance of specific provisions within a proposal to decide which are nonnegotiable, which are relatively unimportant, and which might be changed in return for concessions from the other side. They also try to analyze the positions, motivations, and power resources of their opponents to decide if they will be relatively tough negotiators, whether they possess power resources that will allow them to use coercive measures if concessions are not granted to them, and which provisions are relatively important to them. Negotiators also decide whether they can afford an impasse, where no solution is found, or whether they need a compromise solution.

Of course, these choices and preferences, made before negotiations begin, may change during the course of negotiations. Skillful negotiators do not prematurely grant concessions to their adversaries because they want to see if they can induce them to make most of the concessions. Moreover, they concede only those points (if possible) that are relatively unimportant to their side. To avoid antagonizing their followers, negotiators often consult extensively with their backers before making specific concessions. If both sides believe it is necessary to resolve the conflict, concessions emerge in the course of deliberations where each side, much like a poker player, gradually reveals where it is willing to make concessions. (Delays, using veiled or open threats, and offering inducements are often used to persuade the other side to make greater concessions than it wants to make.)

In some cases, policy practitioners are cast into the role of serving as mediators in disputes. Mediators often use a variety of techniques to decrease conflict, such as meeting separately with the parties in a conflict to reduce open confrontations, lowering the level of rhetoric, and identifying common values and interests that the parties share.[70] For mediation to be successful, each party to a conflict has to believe that the mediator does not manipulate the situation to the advantage of either side.

SKILLS IN USING GROUP PROCESS

When discussing policy practice, it is sometimes tempting to portray it as an individualistic enterprise, but in fact policies are usually fashioned collectively by groups, whether small groups such as boards of directors or large groups such as legislatures. It is difficult to overstate the importance of groups within this collective process such as committees, task forces, and informal groups in agencies, communities, and legislatures.[71] Moreover, an array of groups, such as interest groups, social movements, and coalitions, exert pressure on decision makers from external vantage points.

Many kinds of groups exist, but policy practitioners are particularly concerned with task, or work, groups, that is, groups that "focus on producing or influencing something external to the group itself."[72] (By contrast, treatment, therapy, and educational groups emphasize the personal growth or learning of members of the group.) Policy practitioners participate in task groups for two central reasons. First, they want these groups to develop policies to address an array of social and institutional problems. Second, they want groups to take actions, such as exerting pressure on decision makers, to expedite the passage (or the defeat) of specific policies.

Why Use Task Groups?

Task groups are integral to the policy-making process because they serve representational, political, and cognitive functions. In dictatorial governments (or even in organizations with autocratic leaders), policies are fashioned by individuals or by closely knit factions that stand apart from the citizenry, residents, or staff. Democratic institutions, by contrast, are based on the assumption that policies should be fashioned by a decision-making process that accords significant decision-making roles to collective bodies that include members who "represent" specific interests.[73] Elections and the appointive powers of executives and political leaders are commonly used to select the members of decision-making bodies whether within organizations, communities, or legislatures. (Of course, these elective and appointive processes often lead to the exclusion of important interests, so a considerable part of the political process is devoted to securing greater representation for specific interests.)

Although individuals often possess considerable power, they often turn to groups to magnify their power by commingling it with others'.[74] As Policy-Practice Case 7 suggests, lobbyists derive their power in considerable measure from their association with constituencies that are organized into coherent groups that can raise funds, establish telephone trees, oversee letter-writing campaigns, and develop positions on policy issues. Informal factions, unions, professional groups, and specific work units mobilize pressure on executives within organizations at strategic points when their interests are threatened or when they wish to initiate policies.

People also turn to groups for cognitive reasons.[75] When confronting a serious problem, individuals often find it useful to pool their ideas to reach a joint solution that is superior to the choices of individuals. Of course, using groups to make decisions is not a panacea because groups sometimes make flawed choices.

Varieties of Policy-Related Groups

A remarkable range of policy-related groups exist.[76] Some groups concentrate on making *and* enacting policies, whether the boards of agencies, legislative committees, or legislatures themselves.[77] These groups often rely, however, on policy recommendations that stem from "feeder groups" such as deliberative committees, subcommittees, task forces, study groups, or commissions; these various groups emphasize the development of recommendations that they forward to decision-making entities.[78] Some of these groups are ongoing entities such as a program committee of an agency or the Select

Subcommittee on Children and Youth in Congress. Other recommending groups are established by executives or political leaders to study specific problems and to make recommendations and are terminated when they have issued their recommendations.

Other task groups specialize in implementing policies.[79] Assume, for example, that a county mental health and substance-abuse agency has developed a new and coordinated program to offer services to students in the school district. To oversee the operations of the new program, the agency could establish an ongoing overseeing committee, which might decide to suggest changes in specific policies if they believed the new program was not realizing its objectives. A multitude of ongoing coordinating committees exist, as well, to promote communication and policy development between various agencies.

An additional assortment of groups has developed to advocate the policy preferences of specific factions or interests. Unions have become a potent power source in the human services system by mobilizing vast numbers of employees in public and nonprofit agencies.[80] Community organizations, such as those modeled on the theories of Saul Alinsky, represent specific neighborhoods.[81] A remarkable array of groups serve as advocates for specific groups and institutions that command varying degrees of power and resources. Social movements describe an assortment of groups and an overarching purpose that seek to advance the needs or perspectives of a specific segment of the population such as the civil rights or welfare rights movements of the 1960s or, more recently, the movement to help homeless people.[82] Various coalitions merge the resources and power of discrete groups.[83]

Different Roles of Policy Practitioners in Task Groups

Policy practitioners can assume the roles of leaders, staff, or members within task groups; indeed, the nature of their work within these groups is powerfully shaped by the specific role that they assume. *Leaders* can be compared to the conductor of an orchestra or the quarterback of a football team. They facilitate the work of the group by helping it develop a mission or set of objectives and acquire resources (such as funds and staff). They expedite its ongoing work by developing agendas and presiding at meetings. They help shape its structure and membership by developing subcommittees and a nominating process. They intervene at specific points to promote participation (e.g., by members) and decision making. As troubleshooters, they avoid or diminish excessive internal conflict or dysfunctional processes such as the scapegoating of specific members. If the president or chair of a group is its most important leader, various officers also exist, such as treasurers and secretaries, who assume important logistic tasks.[84]

Staff are expediters and facilitators for the leaders of groups and their members. As expediters, they collect information, assemble materials, perform secretarial functions, and attend to logistic details to allow the leaders and members of specific groups to concentrate on developing ideas and taking specific actions. As facilitators, they attend the meetings and functions of groups and take specific actions to promote group processes to allow the group to achieve its goals. They often work with leaders of groups between meetings to help them plan upcoming sessions and accomplish specific tasks.

The staff's role places certain limits, however, on their interventions within groups. Their role requires considerable circumvention and restraint because they are background facilitators and expediters rather than members or leaders. They may disagree with the decisions of leaders and members, but they usually refrain from confrontive statements of their own perspectives, although this rule can be broken under certain circumstances.[85]

Members of task groups are more than foot soldiers; they provide ideas, participate in specific tasks, provide the group with power by linking it to specific interests, lead specific subgroups within the task group, provide resources, and (in the case of some members) assume the leadership of the group after a period of apprenticeship. While leadership is crucial, few task groups are successful without motivated and active members.[86]

WHAT TASK GROUPS NEED
TO ACCOMPLISH THEIR WORK

Many task groups are highly successful ones that establish and realize their objectives in the course of their deliberations and their activities. Other groups flounder, are split asunder, procrastinate, or dwindle to nothingness, however, as many of us have experienced in our professional and personal lives.

Theorists and researchers have implicated an array of factors that lead some task groups to be relatively successful and to cause other groups to be failures. These factors include the group's mission, leadership, developmental needs, procedures, structure, deliberative and interactional processes, staff and resources, and relationships with the external environment. Indeed, many theorists and researchers suggest that we need to examine the structure and processes of groups, as well as the actions of specific persons in them, to understand why some of them succeed while others fail.

Mission

Successful groups have to develop a mission that defines the objectives or goals of the group. Although the mission often changes during the course of deliberations and events, members should decide what they want to accomplish during the early stages of the formation of a group. Several dangers exist. A group may establish unrealistic expectations such as securing the enactment of a major piece of legislation in a brief period; when it cannot accomplish its objectives, the morale of its members and the reputation of its leaders may be harmed. It may fail to develop a consensus about its objectives, so that different factions and members possess different expectations. In some cases, overt or manifest expectations may clash with hidden ones as when leaders possess personal agendas that they do not share with members.

Its mission also includes agreements about procedural matters such as the frequency of meetings, the way leaders are selected, its size, and its relationship to external bodies. Without agreements about these matters, as well as about their major goals, groups can be bedeviled by a succession of controversies and misunderstandings.

 Leadership

Successful groups possess skillful leaders who have an array of qualities that facilitate their work. Skilled leaders walk a tightrope between alternative vices: they want to be directive and assertive, yet not dominate; to encourage dissenting perspectives, yet not allow the group to become encumbered with excessive or destructive conflict; to assume a range of tasks, yet encourage group members to engage in many tasks; to represent the group to the external world, yet not become excessively absorbed with seeking personal credit; and to emphasize the accomplishment of the objectives of the group, yet not to the extent that the social and emotional needs of group members are neglected. Unskilled leaders are characterized by adjectives that describe one or another of these alternative vices, such as domineering, passive, confrontive, agitative, dictatorial, and creditmongering.

Skilled leaders are cognizant of specific developmental, structural, and process needs of groups at specific points in their existence and develop strategies to address them. A leader might discern, for example, that "this group needs to engage in relatively unstructured brainstorming" at this point in its existence or that "we need to reach closure on this topic" at another point.

The preceding discussion suggests the need for certain value orientations by leaders. Effective leaders are committed, for example, to democratic values—that is, they want to give group members a considerable role in shaping their decisions, although leaders realize that discussion can be carried to excess. They do not want the group to engage in actions that are destructive to certain participants, such as the scapegoating of members with legitimate and dissenting perspectives.

Developmental Needs

Groups develop, or evolve, through time as they strengthen their missions, engage in deliberations, and accomplish tasks. In early phases, for example, they have to develop initial agreements about their mission, leadership, and procedures, as well as realistic expectations. During middle phases, they need to develop and routinize procedures, experience successes that instill and maintain a sense of momentum, and develop a division of labor that allows (and requires) a range of people to participate in the activities of the group. They should also modify and update their mission. In later phases, some groups should terminate themselves when they no longer are needed, whereas others need to regenerate by developing a new or revised mission and new members.

Some groups do not progress between these stages of development. Having not established their mission, some groups keep returning to the question, Why do we exist? Other groups fail to change their mission as events unfold. With their original mission accomplished or rendered obsolete, some groups continue to exist when they should be terminated.

Procedures

Some people falsely equate leadership and group effectiveness with minutes, agendas, and bylaws, which are procedures. Procedures, however, serve a useful purpose.[87] They allow thoughtful people to review the accomplishments of the group and, in the case of agendas, to anticipate and plan forthcoming events. They provide a history of the group that can be periodically reviewed to ascertain how the group has evolved and to analyze what new tasks it might undertake. Bylaws provide mechanisms for selecting leaders, replenishing membership, dividing tasks among officers and subcommittees, and handling funds.

Structure ⑤

All groups have to organize themselves internally to facilitate a division of labor by establishing subcommittees or ad hoc groups. They have to decide how large they wish to be to accomplish their mission and, in the case of groups that pressure decision makers, to obtain political clout. They have to examine their relations with external bodies; do they wish to merge with other groups, to participate in coalitions with other groups, or to maintain an independent existence?

These kinds of structural issues pose significant challenges to specific groups. A group that becomes excessively decentralized with numerous committees, for example, may lack central direction, but a group that is too centralized may fail to delegate responsibilities to its members. A group may lose its identity if it merges with other groups or becomes excessively active in coalitions, but it may lack clout if it remains isolated from other groups.[88]

Deliberative and Interactional Processes

To be productive, groups need to develop modes of deliberation and interaction that allow their members to examine an array of options, to assess their strengths and weaknesses, to make informed choices, and to develop strategies to implement their choices. Positive modes of deliberation include an open atmosphere where members feel free to contribute ideas, where dissent is permissible, where persons believe their ideas will be taken seriously, and where brainstorming precedes the selection of ideas.[89] Moreover, group members need to sufficiently respect each other, as well as the deliberative process, and honor those decisions that the group makes.

The decision-making process can be stifled or abbreviated, however, if leadership and group processes do not favor dissent, a period of brainstorming, and a democratic process. The social psychologist Irving Janis suggests that some groups succumb to "group-think," where they move too rapidly to unanimous positions, scapegoat dissenters, and fail to consider fully the strengths and weaknesses of their positions.[90] Intolerant leaders, membership that fails to represent a variety of perspectives, and truncated deliberations contribute to this phenomenon.

Janis, Robert Bales, and other researchers suggest that groups should progress through a series of stages when considering specific issues. They should engage in a process of brainstorming where their members identify an array of options in a risk-taking and tolerant atmosphere.[91] With care and considerable effort, they should gradually reduce these options so that a group of final candidates emerges. Only after an extended process of considering the strengths and weaknesses of these options should the group develop its final position. But this progressive movement from large numbers of options to final choices can only occur if group members feel free to risk themselves and if the group tolerates internal dissent.

Staff and Resources

Groups that engage in relatively complex work need staff and resources to help them accomplish logistic tasks, to provide them with technical assistance, and to facilitate the work of leaders and members. Staff can be provided by institutions such as agencies, or they can be volunteers. Resources can come from institutions, from memberships, from special events, from private donors, or from corporate or foundation donors.

Resource- or staff-poor groups operate at a marked disadvantage when compared to other groups. As Policy-Practice Case 7 illustrates, "low-budget lobbyists," while successful in achieving some goals, are disadvantaged when compared to lobbyists who are affiliated with staff-intensive and resource-rich groups. Of course, resources and staff do not guarantee success because staff, much like leaders, need to possess various group-process skills to be effective.

Relations with the Environment

Groups exist in a social and organizational context that can facilitate or impede their work. They are often established by highly placed decision makers who develop remedies to problems, oversee the implementation of policies, or provide them with advice. Although these mandates are often accompanied by donations of staff and resources, groups receive varying degrees of autonomy; if some of them are given considerable independence, others become political appendages of those officials who establish them. (These officials may not allow them to examine a full range of options and may seek to control them by appointing members to them who are beholden to themselves.) Effective groups need to negotiate or obtain some independence if they wish to develop their own identities, while still maintaining linkages to officials in their environment.[92]

INTERVENTIONS TO ADDRESS DYSFUNCTIONAL PROCESSES

We have discussed some attributes of effective groups and some factors that impede their performance. Because policy practitioners often work with and through groups, they need skills in developing interventions that offset or prevent these kinds of factors.

These interventions are in turn conditioned by their roles; leaders, members, and staff assume somewhat different roles in groups. If staff usually assume a relatively background and facilitating role, leaders and members can more assertively participate in the give-and-take of a group's deliberations. If leaders directly shape agendas and procedures, staff usually offer behind-the-scenes suggestions about them to leaders. If leaders often summarize and clarify the statements and positions of members and ascertain if agreement exists, members are often more free than leaders to state their opinions in a forthright way.

Subject to the constraints and opportunities that are provided by these different roles, all participants can use certain kinds of interventions to improve the functioning of specific groups. They must first, however, diagnose or anticipate specific problems such as the process, structural, and other problems that we noted previously. Interventions include behind-the-scenes discussions, comments made during group deliberations to develop ideas, the assumption of some leadership functions, using power, mediation, the direct assumption of specific tasks, using humor, and discussions with persons and institutions that are external to the group.

No matter what their position within a group, persons can discuss strategy with other group members outside the formal sessions.[93] In the case of the scapegoating of a member who makes important but dissenting contributions, for example, a member can discuss strategy with another member or with the leader to avert or decrease this activity. As with all interventions, some dangers exist. When persons discuss strategy extensively behind the backs of others, they risk bypassing the normal deliberative processes of a group.

Participants in groups can make many kinds of comments during meetings to facilitate the development of ideas and proposals, such as "don't we need to spend more time discussing this idea?" "isn't it time to reach closure?" "can we couple this idea with one that was made earlier?" and "is there a different way to look at this problem?" They can suggest using certain procedures to foster consideration of ideas, such as "shouldn't we break up into smaller groups to seek solutions to this problem?"[94]

Even when they are not themselves leaders, participants in groups can assume some of the functions of leaders on specific occasions. Assume, for example, that a leader appears to move a group prematurely toward closure on a specific issue; a member or a staff member can say, "I would like to hear more about another option that was briefly raised a few minutes ago." Persons who are adept at the use of parliamentary tactics can sometimes use them to inject new perspectives and to delay decisions. Or members can directly contact leaders between meetings to add additional issues to agendas or to register their opinions on procedural, process, or structural matters. Of course, members and staff can risk alienating leaders or can erroneously usurp their functions if they do not use discretion.[95]

Like any collectivity, participants in groups bring with them or develop power resources. It might be nice if the deliberations and processes of groups were purely reflective and scholarly in nature, but political realities often intrude. Disagreements often develop about specific issues or even the leadership, processes, or structure of groups. Participants in groups often use their power resources to shape decisions, whether by invoking their expertise, asserting their authority, or suggesting parliamentary procedures that will (they think) give them an advantage over someone else.[96] Members sometimes try to influence the positions of other members by interceding with them between meetings. Factions often develop within groups that adhere to specific positions.

Persons need to use power resources in groups with discretion and in a manner that does not excessively override the normal deliberative processes of a group. Excessive use of power resources by the group members can render them into miniature legislative bodies whose members substitute threats, coercion, and parliamentary maneuvers for normal deliberative processes. At the same time, however, power resources sometimes need to be used to overcome stalemates, to stop destructive activities like scapegoating, to bring decisions that are acceptable to "important players" in the environment of a group, or to make groups more responsive to the needs of specific groups or to needs that they have neglected.

We have discussed the use of mediation in the preceding discussion of combative persuading strategies. All groups need persons who are willing to assume the role of mediator at specific points in their deliberations, particularly when groups become polarized into competing factions.[97] Mediators can help group members to identify their common values and how each of them will benefit from the development of compromises. They can suggest specific structural or process strategies that can diminish conflict, such as bringing to the group an outside facilitator who possesses a neutral perspective. They can identify specific compromises that may allow each side to a conflict to believe that its central concerns have nonetheless been addressed.

Participants in groups can sometimes "take the bull by the horns" by volunteering to undertake difficult or conflict-producing tasks that other members shun. When a subcommittee of a group completes a task or develops a position on a difficult issue, for example, it gives to all group members a sense of accomplishment and momentum.

We have noted that humor is often used by persuaders to defuse conflict. Effective participants in groups inject humor into their deliberations at key points to ease tension, to place members at ease, and to encourage persons not to take their positions (at least on some occasions) too seriously.[98] Humor can sometimes be used to discuss specific problems of the group, as in the case of a leader who says, "if we don't watch out, our propensity for small talk will mean we do not reach a decision on this matter until it is too late."

SUMMARY

We have covered many topics that have not received extensive attention because they do not neatly fit into the analytic and political frameworks that have dominated most policy literature. We have argued that various interactional skills, such as the building of personal credibility, networking, persuading, and group process, are needed by policy practitioners at many points in their work.

Because their effectiveness hinges in part on the perceptions of other persons of their personal characteristics, policy practitioners need skills in building their personal credibility. Credible practitioners are often perceived to be team players, reasonable, trustworthy, and authoritative. Networking skills are needed to develop and use contacts with a range of people in specific agency, community, and legislative settings. These contacts provide inside information, facilitate the development of strategy, and enhance one's personal credibility. Persuading skills are needed during the process of developing policies when designing and presenting messages, whether in interpersonal discussions, formal presentations, or written reports. Policy practitioners sometimes use combative strategies that include argumentation and the coupling of messages with use of power resources to entice recalcitrant decision makers to make specific decisions. Because policies are usually fashioned by collectivities such as groups, policy practitioners need to be adept at participating in them, facilitating their work, and engaging in troubleshooting interventions to offset or avert factors that impede their functioning.

At various points in this and in preceding chapters, we have alluded to ethical or moral problems that policy practitioners confront in their work. We argue in the next chapter that policy practitioners frequently need value-clarification and moral-reasoning skills to address a variety of issues in their work.

QUESTIONS FOR DISCUSSION

1. Review Policy-Practice Case 7 from the vantagepoint of Sherry Skelly.
   a) Discuss in general terms why political and analytic skills need to be supplemented by interactional skills for her to be effective in her work.
   b) Identify an array of interactional skills that she needs in her work.
   c) Discuss various strategies she and Rand Martin use
      ■ to build personal credibility with legislators
      ■ to build networks of various kinds (discuss lateral, vertical, and subordinate ones)
      ■ to enhance their persuasiveness with legislators.

2. Discuss the assertion that the power and persuasiveness of a policy practitioner are closely linked to perceptions that others possess of his or her personal credibility.

3. Discuss the implications of power-dependence theory for staff and leaders of social work units in larger bureaucracies (such as hospitals) that wish to increase their credibility with other officials and staff.

4. Discuss some Machiavellian tactics that people use to enhance their credibility. Under what circumstances (if any) might these kinds of tactics be appropriate?

5. Identify various strategies that a social worker in a social agency might use to create and expand personal networks that might be useful at some point during his or her policy practice within that agency.

6. Discuss the assertion that "the workings of the mentor system and old-boy networks are manifestly unfair, at least from the perspective of those

persons who are often not included within them." What are some implications for women and racial minorities, who are often excluded from networks?

7. Discuss the statement "There are many similarities between the use of power and efforts to persuade an audience to change its positions." (Compare and contrast Figures 5.1 and 7.1.)

8. Select a policy position or topic and design a presentation strategy for
   a) a hostile audience
   b) an audience with mixed orientations toward your topic
   c) an apathetic or disinterested audience.

9. Discuss an array of criticisms a debater can make of someone else's proposal if he or she wishes to engage in adversarial or combative persuasion.

10. Discuss the assertion that social workers are often inclined to make premature and unnecessary concessions or compromises during negotiations.

11. With respect to a task group with which you are familiar, discuss various factors that promote:
    a) the success of the group
    b) failure to accomplish objectives
    c) possible interventions to facilitate more effective decision making by the group.

12. Compare and contrast the roles of leaders, members, and staff of task groups.

13. Assume that you staff a committee whose members refuse to examine a range of alternatives and prematurely select one position. Discuss some options you might consider to help the group to enlarge its conceptual horizons.

SUGGESTED READINGS

Building Personal Credibility

Richard Emerson, "Power-Dependence Relations," *American Sociological Review*, 27 (February 1972): 31–40.

Bruce Jansson and June Simmons, "Building Department or Unit Power Within Human Service Organizations: Empirical Findings and Theory Building," *Administration in Social Work*, 8 (Fall 1984): 41–50.

Bruce Jansson and June Simmons, "The Ecology of Social Work Departments: Empirical Findings and Strategy Implications," *Social Work in Health Care*, 11 (Winter 1985): 1–16.

Christopher Matthews, *Hardball: How Politics Is Played* (New York: Summit Books, 1988), pp. 21–33, 59–73, 144–154, 194–211.

Networking

Rosabeth Kanter, *Men and Women of the Corporation* (New York: Basic Books, 1977), pp. 129–163, 181–197.

Noel Tichy, *Strategic Change: Technology, Politics, and Culture* (New York: John Wiley, 1983), pp. 69–94.

J. McIver Weatherford, *Tribes on the Hill* (New York: Rawson, Wade, 1981), pp. 87–111, 250–253.

Policy Persuading

Milan Dluhy, "Policy Advice-Givers: Advocates? Technicians? or Pragmatists?" in John Tropman, et al., eds., *New Strategic Perspectives* (New York: Pergamon, 1981), pp. 202–217.

Austin Freeley, *Argumentation and Debate*, 6th ed. (Belmont, Ca.: Wadsworth Publishing Co., 1986).

Marya Holcombe and Judith Stein, *Presentations for Decision Makers* (New York: Van Nostrand Reinhold, 1983).

Michael Pfau, "A Systematic Approach to Opposing Policy Change," in David Thomas and Jack Hart, eds., *Advanced Debate: Readings in Theory, Practice, and Teaching* (Lincolnwood, Ill.: National Textbook Co., 1987), pp. 39–45.

Willard Richan, "A Common Language for Social Work," *Social Work,* 17 (November 1972): 14–22.

George Sharwell, "How to Testify Before a Legislative Committee," in Maryann Mahaffey and John Hanks, eds., *Practice Politics: Social Work and Political Response* (Washington, D.C.: National Association of Social Workers, 1982), pp. 85–98.

Herbert Simons, *Persuasion,* 2nd ed. (New York: Random House, 1986).

Negotiating and Mediating

Jay Folberg and Alison Taylor, *Mediation* (San Francisco: Jossey-Bass, 1984).

Margaret Gibelman and Harold Demone, "Negotiating a Contract: Practical Considerations," in Harold Demone and Margaret Gibelman, eds., *Services for Sale* (New Brunswick, N.J.: Rutgers University Press, 1989), pp. 131–148.

Working with Task Groups

Paul Ephross and Thomas Vassil, *Groups That Work* (New York: Columbia University Press, 1988).

Irving Janis, *Victims of Groupthink* (Boston: Houghton Mifflin, 1972).

John Tropman, Harold Johnson, and Elmer Tropman, *The Essentials of Committee Management* (Chicago: Nelson-Hall, 1979).

NOTES

1. See Herbert Simons, *Persuasion,* 2nd ed. (New York: Random House, 1986), p. 130. Also see discussion of credibility by George Brager, Harry Specht, and James Torczyner, *Community Organizing,* 2nd ed. (New York: Columbia University Press, 1987), pp. 342–347.

2. Christopher Matthews, *Hardball: How Politics Is Played* (New York: Summit Books, 1988), pp. 144–154.

3. Rochelle Stanford, "Beleaguered Lobbyists for the Poor—Taking Allies Where They Can Find Them," *National Journal,* 12 (September 20, 1980): 1556–1560.

4. Richard Emerson, "Power-Dependence Relations," *American Sociological Review,* 27 (February 1962): 31–40 and D.J. Hickson et al., "A Strategic Contingencies Theory of Organizational Power," *Administrative Science Quarterly,* 16 (June 1971): 216–229.

5. For research findings on power-dependence theory in hospital settings with social work departments, see Bruce Jansson and June Simmons, "Building Department or Unit Power Within Human Service Organizations: Empirical Findings and Theory Building," *Administration in Social Work,* 8 (Fall 1984): 41–44, 49–50.

6. See Bruce Jansson and June Simmons, "The Ecology of Social Work Departments: Empirical Findings and Strategy Implications," *Social Work in Health Care,* 11 (Winter 1985): 1–16.

7. Bruce Jansson and June Simmons, "The Survival of Social Work Units in Host Organizations," *Social Work,* 31 (September 1986): 342.

8. Joel Fleishman, "Self-Interest and Political Integrity," in Joel Fleishman, Lance Liebman, and Mark Moore, eds., *Public Duties: The Moral Obligations of Government Officials* (Cambridge, Mass.: Harvard University Press, 1981), pp. 67–77.

9. Eugene Bardach, *The Skill Factor in Politics* (Berkeley, Ca.: University of California Press, 1972), pp. 204–206, 216–220.

10. Jansson and Simmons, "Survival of Social Work Units," p. 341.

11. Matthews, *Hardball,* pp. 207–209.

12. Ibid., pp. 203–204.

13. J. McIver Weatherford, *Tribes on the Hill* (New York: Rawson, Wade, 1981), pp. 87–111.

14. Matthews, *Hardball,* pp. 194–211.

15. Noel Tichy, *Strategic Change: Technology, Politics, and Culture* (New York: John Wiley, 1983), pp. 69–94.

16. Weatherford, *Tribes on the Hill,* pp. 20–24. Also see Tom Peters and Nancy Austin, "MBWA (Managing by Walking Around)," *California Management Review,* 28 (Fall 1985): 9–34.

17. Matthews, *Hardball,* pp. 21–33.

18. Ibid., pp. 59–73.

19. Rosabeth Kanter, *Men and Women of the Corporation* (New York: Basic Books, 1977), pp. 181–184.

20. Weatherford, *Tribes on the Hill*, pp. 87–111.

21. Ibid., pp. 87–111.

22. Ibid., pp. 250–253.

23. See how a social movement led to legislative reform in Wyoming in William Whitaker, "Organizing Social Action Coalitions: WIC Comes to Wyoming," in Maryann Mahaffey and John Hanks, eds., *Practical Politics: Social Work and Political Response* (Washington, D.C.: National Association of Social Workers, 1982), pp. 136–158.

24. See Frances Piven and Richard Cloward, "New Prospects for Voter Registration Reform," *Social Policy*, 18 (Winter 1988): 2–15.

25. Willard Richan, "A Common Language for Social Work," *Social Work*, 17 (November 1972): 14–22.

26. Simons, *Persuasion*, pp. 18–21.

27. Donald Cegala, *Persuasive Communication: Theory and Practice*, 3rd ed. (Edina, Mn.: Bellwether Press, 1987), pp. 13–15.

28. Simons, *Persuasion*, pp. 227–251.

29. Cegala, *Persuasive Communication*, pp. 70–75, 97–98.

30. Simons, *Persuasion*, pp. 23–24, 141–142.

31. Karlyn Campbell, *The Rhetorical Act* (Belmont, Ca.: Wadsworth Publishing Co., 1982), pp. 69–118.

32. Ibid., pp. 101–116.

33. Simons, *Persuasion*, p. 25.

34. Campbell, *The Rhetorical Act*, pp. 69–118.

35. Cegala, *Persuasive Communication*, pp. 152–155.

36. Stan Paine, G. Thomas Bellamy, and Barbara Wilcox, *Human Services That Work* (Baltimore: Paul Brooks, 1984), pp. 42–44.

37. Morton Deutsch, *The Resolution of Conflict: Constructive and Destructive Processes* (New Haven, Conn.: Yale University Press, 1973), pp. 124–152.

38. Segmentation is discussed extensively in marketing literature: see Phillip Kotler, *Principles of Marketing* (Englewood Cliffs, N.J.: Prentice-Hall, 1989), pp. 42–46. Also see Simons, *Persuasion*, pp. 143–146.

39. George Brager and Stephen Holloway, *Changing Human Service Organizations* (New York: Free Press, 1978), pp. 199–203.

40. Ibid., pp. 199–203.

41. See Marya Holcombe and Judith Stein, *Presentations for Decision Makers* (New York: Van Nostrand Reinhold, 1983). Bardach notes that graphics that depict quantitative facts need to be kept simple; see *Skill Factor in Politics*, pp. 200–201.

42. Holcombe and Stein, *Presentations for Decision Makers*.

43. Cegala, *Persuasive Communication*, pp. 101–106.

44. For an excellent discussion of rational arguments, see Austin Freeley, *Argumentation and Debate,* 6th ed. (Belmont, Ca.: Wadsworth Publishing Co., 1986).

45. Simons, *Persuasion,* pp. 148–150.

46. Michael Pfau, "A Systematic Approach to Opposing Policy Change," in David Thomas and Jack Hart, eds., *Advanced Debate: Readings in Theory, Practice, and Teaching* (Lincolnwood, Ill.: National Textbook Co., 1987), pp. 39–45. Also see Allan Lichtman, Daniel Rohrer, and Joseph Misner, "The Role of Empirical Evidence in Debate: A System Approach," in Thomas and Hart, eds., *Advanced Debate,* pp. 298–309.

47. Milan Dluhy, "Policy Advice-Givers: Advocates? Technicians? or Pragmatists? in John Tropman et al., eds., *New Strategic Perspectives* (New York: Pergamon, 1981), pp. 202–217.

48. Ibid., pp. 202–217.

49. Cegala, *Persuasive Communication,* pp. 189–199.

50. Simons, *Persuasion,* pp. 153–154.

51. Ibid., pp. 124–129.

52. Ibid., pp. 148–154.

53. Ibid., pp. 210, 213.

54. Ibid., pp. 153–154.

55. Cegala, *Persuasive Communication,* p. 136.

56. Simons, *Persuasion,* p. 153.

57. Cegala, *Persuasive Communication,* p. 134.

58. Brager, Specht, and Torczyner, *Community Organizing,* pp. 342–343.

59. Paul Ephross and Thomas Vassil, *Groups That Work* (New York: Columbia University Press, 1988), p. 157.

60. George Sharwell, "How to Testify Before a Legislative Committee," in Mahaffey and Hanks, eds., *Practical Politics,* pp. 85–98.

61. Lewis Dexter, "Role Relationships and Conception of Neutrality in Interviewing," *American Journal of Sociology,* 62 (September 1956): 153–157.

62. Simons, *Persuasion,* pp. 253–254.

63. Ibid., pp. 190–192.

64. Pfau, "A Systematic Approach to Opposing Policy Change."

65. See Brager, Specht, and Torczyner, *Community Organizing,* pp. 355–357.

66. Simons, *Persuasion,* pp. 253–256.

67. Ibid., pp. 259–261.

68. Ibid.

69. For an overview of negotiating strategy, see Margaret Gibelman and Harold Demone, "Negotiating a Contract: Practical Considerations," in Harold Demone and Margaret Gibelman, eds., *Services for Sale* (New Brunswick, N.J.: Rutgers University Press, 1989), pp. 131–148. Also see Brager, Specht, and Torczyner, *Community Organizing,* pp. 366–381.

70. See Jay Folberg and Alison Taylor, *Mediation* (San Francisco: Jossey-Bass, 1984) and Joseph Palenski and Harold Launer, *Mediation, Contexts and Challenges* (Springfield, Ill.: Charles C Thomas, 1986).

71. John Tropman, Harold Johnson, and Elmer Tropman, *The Essentials of Committee Management* (Chicago: Nelson-Hall, 1979), pp. ix-xiii.

72. Ephross and Vassil, *Groups That Work*, p. 1.

73. Tropman, Johnson, and Tropman, *Essentials of Committee Management*, pp. xiii-xiv.

74. See Samuel Bacharach and Edward Lawler, *Power and Politics in Organizations* (San Francisco: Jossey-Bass, 1980), pp. 48–69; Brager, Specht, and Torczyner, *Community Organizing*, pp. 193–200; and Bardach, *The Skill Factor in Politics*, pp. 215–230.

75. Robert Bales and Fred Strodtbeck, "Phases in Group Problem Solving," in Dorwin Cartwright and Alvin Zander, eds., *Group Dynamics: Research and Theory* (New York: Harper and Row, 1968), pp. 380–398. Also see David Sink, "Success and Failure in Voluntary Community Networks," *New England Journal of Human Services*, 7 (1987): 25–30.

76. Tropman, Johnson, and Tropman, *Essentials of Committee Management*, pp. 141–203 and Ephross and Vassil, *Groups That Work*, pp. 16–27.

77. Tropman, Johnson, and Tropman, *Essentials of Committee Management*, pp. 179–186.

78. Ephross and Vassil, *Groups That Work*, pp. 16–18, 22–24.

79. Tropman, Johnson, and Tropman, *Essentials of Committee Management*, pp. 196–203.

80. Denis Chamot, "Professional Employees Turn to Unions," *Harvard Business Review*, 54 (May 1976): 119–127.

81. Saul Alinsky, *Reveille for Radicals* (New York: Vintage Books, 1969).

82. Simons, *Persuasion*, pp. 253–261.

83. Bacharach and Lawler, *Power and Politics in Organizations*, pp. 48–69; and Brager, Specht, and Torczyner, *Community Organizing*, pp. 193–200.

84. Tropman, Johnson, and Tropman, *Essentials of Committee Management*, pp. 5–23. For a compilation of literature on leadership, see Ralph Stogdill, ed., *Handbook of Leadership: A Survey of Theory and Research* (New York: Free Press, 1974).

85. Tropman, Johnson, and Tropman, *Essentials of Committee Management*, pp. 38–48.

86. Ibid., pp. 24–37.

87. Ibid., pp. 63–139.

88. Ephross and Vassil, *Groups That Work*, pp. 84–87, 166–183.

89. Irving Janis, *Victims of Groupthink* (Boston: Houghton Mifflin, 1972).

90. Ibid.

91. Bales and Strodtbeck, "Phases in Group Problem Solving."

92. Ephross and Vassil, *Groups That Work*, pp. 84–87, 166–183.

93. Tropman, Johnson, and Tropman, *Essentials of Committee Management*, pp. 39–42, 44–46.

94. Ephross and Vassil, *Groups That Work*, p. 164.

95. Tropman, Johnson, and Tropman, *Essentials of Committee Management*, p. 45.

96. There is surprisingly little discussion of the positive and needed uses of power in committees and task groups; power is usually viewed to be destructive of group processes.

97. Folberg and Taylor, *Mediation*.

98. Ephross and Vassil, *Groups That Work*, pp. 158–159.

CHAPTER 8

■

Value Clarification and
Moral Reasoning

We have discussed analytic, political, and interactional components of social welfare policy in preceding chapters. Useful as these skills are to policy practice, however, they fail to provide guidance to policy practitioners who confront moral issues and dilemmas. Should a social worker who dislikes a policy lie or deceive opponents to obtain a political advantage? In light of scarce resources and long waiting lists, should a social agency give priority to certain kinds of clients or consumers, such as low-income people? Should policy practitioners seek policies to radically redistribute social resources to low-income people or be relatively content with the existing distribution of resources? Should social policies allow mental health practitioners to involuntarily commit disturbed mental patients whenever they fear they could harm other persons—or should commitments be allowed only when persons have actually attempted to harm themselves or others?

Even this brief listing of ethical questions and moral issues suggests their pervasiveness in policy practice. These kinds of questions and issues are moral ones because they involve identifying and weighting of personal values, using value-laden words such as *ought, should, responsibility,* and *duty.* As we discuss later, no one can escape moral dilemmas and judgments in policy practice, even those policy analysts who pride themselves on their use of scientific and data-gathering methodology.

In this chapter then we discuss the nature of ethical reasoning, a moral-reasoning framework, and a variety of ethical issues that are confronted by policy practitioners.

A POLICY-PRACTICE CASE FROM THE HUMAN SERVICES

Policy-Practice Case 8 discusses a seemingly mundane matter: Should patients in a mental agency have access to their charts and under what circumstances? The charts had been kept in a highly public place where patients could see their name printed in bold letters on their charts.

For many years, the question of client access to charts was not raised and was not perceived by staff to be an ethical issue. In similar fashion, relatively few social workers, physicians, or nurses in medical settings believed patients should have access to their charts.

Yet this issue *is* an ethical issue because it involves the rights of patients and the duties of professionals. If we assume that self-determination is a basic right, then can we exercise it if we lack full knowledge of our diagnosis and prognosis? And does that require that we have full access to the repository of such information, our charts in both medical and mental health settings?[1]

That persons have not exercised their rights, as in the case of asking to see charts, does not mean that those rights do not exist. Nor is it sufficient to dismiss the issue by arguing that access to charts is inconveniencing to staff (who must supply them) because the conveniences of staff should not override their duties to fundamental principles.

At the same time, some arguments *can* be raised about the right of patients to see their charts. Might access in some cases exacerbate mental distress, whether by a mental patient with a serious condition or a medical patient with a terminal illness? What if a patient does not *want* to know her condition?

This example illustrates then the need to become conversant with ethical or moral reasoning, which is a process of thinking to reach ethical conclusions to moral issues such as the one presented in Policy-Practice Case 8. As this case suggests, social workers encounter ethical issues even in the seemingly mundane details of their professional work.

The case also illustrates the way ethical issues intertwine with politics. The social workers in this case found that many obstacles existed to changing the existing policy of the agency with respect to access to records.

ETHICAL AND NONETHICAL ISSUES: HOW DO THEY DIFFER?

Lest we imply that policy practitioners are confronted at every point by ethical issues, it is useful to note that "ethical issues" are specific kinds of issues. Issues are ethical or moral *when they cannot be resolved without considerable recourse to personal values that define some "right" or "good" objective or criterion.*[2] When persons make statements such as "don't lie," "allow terminally ill persons to decide when they wish to forgo extraordinary medical measures," or "redistribute resources to poor people," they imply that certain kinds of actions or policies represent better or superior values than do alternative actions or policies; not lying is better than lying, allowing terminally

POLICY-PRACTICE CASE 8

ACCESS BY PATIENTS TO THEIR CHARTS: AN AGENCY ISSUE

As a staff member in a mental health agency, I believe that patients should have access to written case records. In absence of knowledge about their diagnosis and problems, how can they fully participate in making a treatment plan? Far from causing them to become upset, reading and discussion of case materials is likely to promote thoughtful participation in contract making between social worker and consumer. But I now work in an agency where few patients see their records. This case provides a good example of the preliminary phase of the policy-making process. I assumed a survey role as I examined prevailing policies and identified a policy issue that, I believe, merits further attention in this agency.

The Agency

The agency (henceforth anonymously referred to as "Center B") is located on the grounds of a state hospital and was itself once a ward and part of that hospital. In 1969 Center B negotiated a contract with the county of Los Angeles under the terms of the Short–Doyle Act. This new contract meant that Center B, which had been a ward of the state hospital, was now to be separated from the hospital but still partially under its control. Center B was also to maintain its location on the grounds of the state hospital.

Center B's formal mandate comes from both the county and the state. Funding, for example, is shared by both the county (10 percent) and the state (90 percent), and the approval of the agency's policies and constitution is also a shared responsibility. Although the mandate is passed down and approved by two sources, the state actually has more direct control over Center B. Center B, for example, although no longer part of the state hospital, must abide by the hospital's administrative manual and policies.

Center B is a community mental health and day-treatment facility where patients receive psychiatric treatment only during daytime hours, returning to their own homes in the evening. Center B provides a variety of services: group therapy, individual counseling, occupational therapy, recreational therapy, chemotherapy, and vocational rehabilitation. These services are used by individuals with some mental disorder or life crisis who are able to function on at least a minimal level.

Specifically, Center B's patient population consists of individuals who have been hospitalized and do not need full-time care but are not quite ready to adjust to life outside a hospital setting, as well as persons who will always need some kind of supportive and therapeutic influence. Such patients would otherwise be hospitalized but can function when provided partial services.

Most of the patients served are in the lower-income bracket, and many must depend on some kind of government assistance—supplemental Social Security income, general assistance, or AFDC. Most patients have had very little formal education and are between twenty-five and forty-five years of age.

Charts are maintained for each person served by the agency and contain information regarding personal history, a psychiatric evaluation conducted at the initial intake interview, any correspondence that relates to the person, and daily notations charting progress at the center.

The staff is run on an "equalized interdisciplinary" principle, that is, each staff member functions as both a group and an individual therapist. All staff members perform basically the same functions in their involvement and treatment of patients.

The staff consists of three social workers, two nurses, four psychiatric technicians, one marriage counselor, one psychologist, and one psychiatrist who functions as the agency's executive director. The entire staff meets formally once a week for an hour and a half. The director has an agenda, and each staff member adds to the agenda before the meeting. The agenda is kept on the secretary's desk, where each staff member has access to it.

The Issue

At Center B all patients are on some kind of chemotherapy schedule and must walk through Center B's main office to collect their medications. When passing through the main office, each patient comes in visual contact with the medical charts, which are located in a three-sided cabinet. Each chart has a patient's name printed in bold letters and is held in a slot that enables easy visual access to the name.

In December of 1974, several staff members at Center B became quite concerned about patients loitering in the main office and about some asking to see their charts. This problem was put on the director's agenda and brought up at a Thursday staff meeting. After much discussion, the entire staff agreed on a proposal to keep patients out of the main office as much as possible. Technicians and nurses were to hand the patients their medication, and the patient was then to be instructed to leave the office area immediately. Patients were to remain in the office area only if they had some financial business with the billing clerk. Furthermore, patients who wanted to see their charts were to be referred to their personal staff therapist, who would decide whether to show it to them.

My research was directed toward interviewing a staff member from each of the disciplines represented at the agency to obtain an overall picture of staff attitudes regarding this issue. Of the six staff members I interviewed, all had at one time during the year been asked by a patient to see his or her chart.

All therapists felt that patients had the right to see their charts, yet they also felt that granting them this right was dependent on patients' ability to accept, understand, and fully interpret the material they read. Controversy centered on the issue of patients' rights versus therapists' discretion.

One of the most frequently used reasons for not allowing patients to see their charts was that it might jeopardize the patient–therapist relationship. Each therapist I interviewed was very much concerned that the patient might become angry, hostile, or intimidated by the therapist's written

Continued

POLICY-PRACTICE CASE 8
(continued)

remarks, and that the therapist would have to start building the relationship all over again or that the patient might not even be willing to continue.

The design of Center B ensures that all patients come into contact with a number of different therapists each day, although they may also have an individual therapist. Patients are considered almost a "community project," meaning that each therapist at the agency can feel free to talk to or help any patient. Because of this unique "community project" design, comments are made in each patient's chart by many members of the staff. Thus, therapists feared that patients might not trust any of them if the patients knew that the therapists shared information with one another. Many therapists also feared that they (the therapists) would not feel free to chart as they wished. Essentially, they were concerned about losing privacy and freedom in the types of notations they would be able to chart.

During my interview with the director, he suggested that patients might be able to file slander suits against either an individual or the entire agency if they felt a comment to be malicious or harmful toward them. Although he felt that this situation was unlikely to occur, his comment suggested yet another rationale for opposing policy change. Some staff also feared a sort of domino effect: as one patient obtained access, others would also seek it.

It was also important to consider the attitudes of the staff toward mentally ill patients. Four out of the six staff members I interviewed felt that patients' requests for their charts were probably a symptom of their illnesses. Several staff members explained that requests to see a chart might be a sign of paranoia or of feelings of insecurity or distrust toward the therapist or staff. Patients were also not felt to be equipped to read, accept, and understand chart material.

Three of the therapists stated that, when confronted by a patient, they would flatly state that it was agency policy not to show patients their charts.

In fact, patients have exerted little pressure for a change in the access-to-records policy. I think it is important to analyze this situation in a historical context. To begin with, the majority of Center B's patients have been discharged from the state hospital but still need some kind of therapeutic influence and support. At the hospital, patients were expected to follow hospital rules and schedules and were not allowed to disrupt hospital procedures. There was little room for individual freedom.

This approach actually reinforces the concept of mental illness. A patient is seen—not only by the layperson but by professionals as well—as sick, out of control, and dependent. Therefore, patients coming from the hospital are put in a passive role and are seen by hospital personnel as dependent on them for help and treatment. Patients do not create demands to be met by the staff; rather, the staff is seen as setting the rules that the patient must follow. Essentially, patients are the recipients of an agency service over which they have no control.

Staff members as a whole were unwilling to let patients read their charts. As a result, a number of tactics were used to put an end to the issue once it was raised by a patient. The most widely used tactic was to tell patients that agency policy did not allow them to see their charts.

Another tactic was to actually sit down with patients and explain why they could not see their charts.

Another method of dealing with the issue was to allow patients to read only specific excerpts from their chart. Some therapists, for example, would not let patients read the diagnosis, the correspondence, or the notations of other therapists but would allow patients to read their own notations. Still another method was to explain to patients that the therapist wanted to think about letting patients see their chart. In this way, the therapist would put the issue off for an indefinite period of time, even though the issue eventually required a solution.

None of the therapists I interviewed had, at any time during their employment at Center B, allowed patients to see their entire chart, nor had any of the other therapists, as far as they knew.

An interesting aspect of the issue was the legal ambiguity regarding the patients' rights to see their charts. According to the agency's administrative manual (which is the state hospital's manual as well), Center B staff did not have to provide access because the section discussing confidentiality of information does not discuss the issue. A comprehensive list is presented of persons other than the patient who may or may not have access to the chart, but nothing about patient rights is mentioned. The administrative manual interprets its policies from the Welfare and Institutions Code, which also noticeably omits any mention of patients' rights to see their charts.

During my research of the issue, I found a lack of information for dealing with the issue not only in the hospital's and Center B's procedures but also in the Welfare and Institutions Code. I did manage to find one source published by the American Medical Association that made some attempt to explicitly state a patient's rights. This source maintained: "In the absence of any statutory or court precedent that gives the patient the right of personal access to the medical record, hospital policy must be followed."

Because neither state statute nor hospital administrative policy makes any provisions, the issue of patients' rights to see their charts is open to agency interpretation. Historical precedent set down by the state hospital has been to not allow patients to see their charts. Within this framework, Center B's director did indeed initiate an innovative policy when he allowed staff members to decide individually whether to provide access, yet they have chosen to adhere to traditional practice.

My personal experience with allowing consumers access to records suggests that they benefit from it, that is, are more likely to become collaborative participants in decision making during their treatment. Further, I believe that these consumers have certain rights that cannot be arbitrarily ignored. At this point, some sentiment exists that prevailing policy is defective. But, if I pursue this issue, I will need to think carefully about how to proceed because there is relatively little interest in policy change and even considerable sentiment that patients should not obtain access.

SOURCE: This case is adapted from one developed by Michele H. Wilson, M.S.W. Names and locations have been altered.

ill persons to control their medical fate is better than making their medical decisions for them, and equalizing economic resources is better than allowing marked inequality to exist.

An **ethical dilemma** exists when policy practitioners encounter two (or more) choices or actions that *each* reflect or represent one or more of their values. In most situations when we interact with other people, we do not lie because (1) we value honesty, (2) the choice of not lying reflects this value, and (3) the alternative course of action (i.e., lying) repudiates honesty. In such situations, we do not experience an ethical dilemma; indeed, it would rarely even occur to us to resort to lying. In other situations, however, we might decide that lying, although still unattractive, allows us to achieve a valued objective. Persons might lie to a terrorist who was holding many people hostage, for example, if they believed that this deceit would save the lives of innocent victims. When the value of honesty competes with the value of saving the lives of people, persons experience an ethical dilemma because two courses of action exist that *each* reflect important values.[3]

We face many dilemmas, of course, but they only become ethical dilemmas when alternative choices or actions each reflect important values and when the resolution of the dilemma is not immediately apparent. I do not experience an ethical dilemma when I have to decide, for example, whether to take a coffee break now or twenty minutes from now. Nor do ethical dilemmas exist when matters can be resolved purely by recourse to factual or empirical information, as when we wish to compare the cost of two alternative policies and make a final choice based entirely on economic considerations.[4]

Of course, we sometimes decide that other persons wrongly believe that they do not encounter an ethical dilemma when, in fact, they do. Physicians who have routinely prolonged the lives of terminally ill patients without consulting them may falsely believe that only one course of action (the prolongation of life) possesses normative merit. Indeed, as we note later, policy practitioners sometimes need to convince other people that they do in fact confront an ethical dilemma in a specific situation.[5]

Ethical issues and ethical dilemmas often exist when value-laden words like *duty* and *responsibility* exist. Someone might say to the aforementioned physicians, for example, that they have a *duty* to consult terminally ill patients before seeking to prolong their lives. Or someone might say to someone who considered lying to someone else that he had a *responsibility* to tell the truth in this situation. By contrast, it is not likely that someone might tell me that I had a duty to take a coffee break at a specific time or that I have a responsibility to choose a particular movie rather than another on a particular Friday evening.

THE FUNCTIONS OF ETHICS:
ESTABLISHING BOUNDARIES, RECOGNIZING
DILEMMAS, AND FACILITATING CHOICES

Ethical reasoning both simplifies and complicates choices of policy practitioners. It simplifies choices by declaring certain options unacceptable, at least in most situations. We have noted, for example, that few persons frequently resort to lying even if they lie (or partially lie) on a few occasions. In similar fashion, most of us do not routinely betray confidences, do not routinely support policies that discriminate against certain kinds of persons, and do not routinely defy those existing policies that we are charged with implementing. Ethics then establishes certain boundaries or limits for most of our choices in most situations.[6]

Because we take those kinds of boundaries or limits for granted, we often fail to recognize their importance. Imagine a world in which you dealt with people who routinely lied to you, who routinely resorted to devious Machiavellian strategies, or who frequently chose to develop policies that discriminated against certain kinds of persons. With no boundaries to acceptable choices and actions, life would become an unpredictable, tumultuous, and dangerous enterprise where powerful persons might routinely use their power to ruthlessly oppress others, as well as those kinds of clients or consumers that they happened to dislike. Certain widely accepted ethical rules or duties, such as honesty and fairness, establish boundaries that preclude consideration of specific kinds of options.

The preceding discussion emphasizes the choice between "all-good" and "all-bad" options; when deciding whether to lie, for example, ethics facilitates selection of the all-good option (do not lie) and rejection of the all-bad option (lie). In many situations, however, choices are far more complicated than this; people may encounter two "partly good" options, two "partly good" and "partly bad" options, and two "all-good" options.[7] In these situations when both competing options reflect positive values of the decision maker, awareness of ethics facilitates the recognition of a dilemma. Take the example of racial discrimination and assume that we are troubled by the fact that disproportionate numbers of racial minorities are underrepresented in professions when contrasted with Caucasians. While we do not normally agree to discriminate against persons by virtue of their race, we could decide to waive certain admissions standards to a school of social work to allow more members of a racial minority to obtain admittance. This *is* a form of discrimination because its practical effect is to give some minority-group applicants an advantage in the admissions procedure, but it is a different kind of discrimination than conventional racial discrimination because (1) it is used to help a group increase its representation in a profession rather than to exclude a group, (2) it is limited in its effects to a specific number (and a relatively small number) of slots, and (3) it seeks to rectify the effects of past injustice that led specific groups to be grossly underrepresented.[8] Even with these provisos, however, an ethical dilemma exists because competing values are reflected in alternative admissions procedures. Although the application of identical admissions requirements for all applicants would advance the value of fairness, it could jeopardize the objective of increasing the proportion of minority students, that is, the value of equality. No easy answers exist to dilemmas like this one, but ethics helps us recognize and grapple with them.

Ethical reasoning provides a means or methodology for resolving dilemmas like this one, but, as we note later, it does not necessarily lead to a consensus about specific issues.

A BRAMBLED THICKET: VARIETIES OF ETHICAL REASONING

When seeking information on some subjects, such as the flora of the Outer Hebrides, curious readers can obtain an authoritative source and emerge with the notion that they have obtained an objective and irrefutable rendering of the truth. In the case of moral philosophy or ethical reasoning, however, numerous approaches have been defined that are strikingly different from one another, such as utilitarian, intuitive, egoistic, deontologic, and mixed (or hybrid approaches). Moreover, theorists from these various schools also suggest that situational factors—such as the motives of persons, responsibilities to an organization or profession, and political realities—shape ethical choices. We have to grapple with alternative approaches to ethical reasoning to merge them with our own style.

Despite their differing approaches, moral philosophers or ethicists want to develop (at least) three kinds of concepts; they want to define the good, the right, and methods of reasoning to facilitate choices in specific situations.[9] The **good** describes end-states, that is, the nature of the "good society." When discussing the good society, ethicists describe how an ideal society should be constructed or even, as in the case of socialists, how social resources might be distributed within it. When discussing the **right,** ethicists develop general rules or duties that describe a right-functioning society, such as a rule of honesty or a rule of freedom. When discussing **methods of reasoning,** ethicists identify the way persons make moral choices when they confront ethical issues or dilemmas.

These methods of reasoning often tell us how to derive definitions of the good and the right. Nor should we underestimate the importance of defining the good, the right, and methods of ethical reasoning. If we lacked *any* guidance, we would find it difficult to decide whether to lie in a specific situation, whether to consult a terminal patient about withdrawing or continuing specific medical treatments, and whether to favor policies like affirmative action.

Utilitarians

Utilitarians have dominated ethical philosophy during the last century and have been the most influential shapers of moral reasoning in public-policy literature.[10] The utilitarian approach to moral philosophy, which found its guiding tenets shaped by philosophers like Jeremy Bentham in the nineteenth century, can best be described by the phrase "maximizing the total happiness of society."[11]

Although nuances exist within the ranks of utilitarians, their basic logic can be described in relatively simple terms. Society is composed of a large number of individuals who want and deserve to be happy, but their happiness is often jeopardized by ill-conceived policies of society that are established by nonthinking rulers who in turn are often motivated by their own ambitions, traditions, or pleas of special interest groups such as lobbyists. Policymakers are needed who empathize with the needs of the entire population and who try to discern what would make them happy. Thus, disinterested and wholly rational, rulers select that policy option that would maximize the total happiness of society. We can see then that utilitarians describe the good as maximizing happiness, the right as those specific policies that maximize happiness, and the ethical reasoning process as an investigative or research process to decipher what policy options will most advance societal happiness.[12]

We can understand how this approach works in practice by briefly describing the work of a health-care provider and a public-policy analyst.[13] A health-care provider, who has to operationalize the word *happiness* because it is an abstract concept, decides that it consists of (1) the wants or desires of the patient; (2) the wants or desires of family members, particularly the spouse of the dying patient; and (3) the costs to the patient and society. The provider then lists two or more options and develops a score for each of them by using quantitative or qualitative measures (see Table 8.1).

In the case of Table 8.1, then, a utilitarian would identify the likely positive and negative consequences of the two options with respect to a specific patient and select the option that was associated with the greatest (net) positive consequences. Assume that a dying patient wants termination of heroic measures to extend his life, that his family members strongly support his request, and that this policy will save considerable money for both the patient and society. From a utilitarian perspective, then, Option 2 in Table 8.1 is preferable to Option 1 because it is associated with a preponderance of positive consequences.

Of course, utilitarians, or consequentialists, encounter formidable scoring challenges because they must somehow aggregate the various consequences

TABLE 8.1   Consequences Associated with Specific Service Options

Option 1: Use All Medical Means to Prolong Life

- Wishes–wants of patient
- Wishes–wants of various family members
- Costs to patient
- Costs to society
- Other consequences

Option 2: Use No Medical Means to Prolong Life

- Wishes–wants of patient
- Wishes–wants of various family members
- Costs to patient
- Costs to society
- Other consequences

into a single score that allows them to decide, on balance, which option is preferable. In some cases, a specific option may contain both negative and positive consequences so that it is difficult to know, on balance, whether it is associated with net positive consequences. Assume, for example, that a comatose person made it known when he was still conscious that he did not want life prolongation but that his surviving relatives adamantly want him to remain on a life-preserving respirator, when consulted by the health-care provider. A decision not to prolong life would presumably satisfy the needs or desires of the dying man but not those of his relatives. Moreover, how would the subject of cost figure into the calculations? Life prolongation would be more costly to the family, but should this consideration outweigh the desires of the family members?[14] Messy as the calculations may be, utilitarians adamantly insist that the exercise is worth the effort because it forces us to ignore our "gut" or subjective impulses and to make choices based on objective data that reflect specific and aggregate negative and positive consequences.

In similar fashion, policy-making analysts try to gauge the consequences of policy options. Assume, for example, that you were charged with writing legislation in a state that determined whether terminally ill patients could demand that health-care providers not prolong their lives. As a utilitarian, you would identify an array of possible options such as allowing terminally ill and "competent" patients—that is, persons still capable of making rational choices—(1) to insist that life-prolonging procedures such as the use of a respirator not be used or (2) to demand that providers actually terminate their lives by administering life-ending substances or by withholding water or food. (The first option is called passive euthanasia because providers allow life to end by *not* taking certain actions, whereas the second option is called active euthanasia because the provider actually shortens life by administering lethal substances or by withholding food or water.)

You would need to identify various consequences of these two options when drafting your legislative proposal. You might decide, for example, that both forms of euthanasia were meritorious when compared to existing policies because many comatose patients currently are subjected to respirators and other life-prolonging techniques despite their expressed wishes when they were conscious and despite the wishes of relatives who do not want life to be extended. (Many physicians and hospitals currently fear malpractice suits from a dissenting relative if they do not use all possible measures to prolong life, even if the patient and the patient's relatives favor not prolonging life.) Euthanasia appears more responsive to the wants or desires of some patients and their relatives and would moreover drastically reduce the health-care costs of patients and their families, as well as those of society.

Some utilitarians would probably agree that passive euthanasia should be legitimated by law but only with specific safeguards such as the concurrence of several physicians that the patient *is* terminal (e.g., unlikely to live more than six months) and that the patient (or the patient's relatives in the case of a comatose person) has made the choice in a rational and deliberate fashion. Under these circumstances, passive euthanasia would enhance the wants or needs of the patient (or the patient's relatives) and would moreover save the patient and society the costs of additional medical procedures during the prolonged life of the patient. However, some utilitarians would oppose passive euthanasia even under these circumstances, whether because they feared it could jeopardize reverence for life (a widely held value) or because they feared that some patients might be pressured to accede to euthanasia to save funds, whether by relatives or government officials. (In this latter case, the policy would undermine the wants or desires of patients.)

If they prioritize meeting the needs or wants of patients (or their relatives) and the saving of funds for patients and for society, some utilitarians would favor a policy that supports active euthanasia, subject to the same kinds of restrictions that we noted with respect to passive euthanasia. Because they base their ethics *entirely* on calculations about the tangible consequences of policies, utilitarians can only oppose policies that can demonstrate negative consequences for society. In this case, then, utilitarian reasoning could lead to acceptance of the administration of lethal substances to comatose patients or to the withholding of food and water from them to hasten death.

In many cases, utilitarians use cost–benefit analysis to determine whether a particular policy is meritorious.[15] To simplify their work, they usually reduce the expected costs and benefits of a policy to monetary terms. On the cost side of the ledger, they calculate the costs of implementing a policy. On the benefit side of the ledger, they identify (1) costs that society currently expends that might be saved if the policy were enacted and (2) the monetary value of positive and new contributions that would accrue to society if the policy were enacted. In the case of social services to frail, elderly persons, utilitarians would calculate the cost of providing homemaker, counseling, nutritional, recreational, and other services. In similar fashion, they would calculate the current costs of placing many frail, elderly persons in nursing homes and hospitals, as well as the financial and other burdens of persons who currently care for them. Then they would ascertain how many of their current costs would be saved if services were provided to these patients that allowed them to escape institutionalization and that allowed some of their relatives, currently burdened by caring for them, to become more productive (and tax-paying) members of society.[16] Much like a banker who looks for a good investment, they might find a policy, such as providing services to preschool children, that "realized" an even greater return on invested public funds.

Deontologists

Vigorous criticisms of utilitarianism have been voiced by a range of moral philosophers over the past century. We have already noted some practical problems in calculating whether a policy advances the public good, such as the problem of identifying and weighting consequences, as well as scoring specific options with respect to them.[17] Many people contend moreover that it is impossible to dispassionately identify and select those measures that enhance the general happiness because most of us, by virtue of our interests and affiliations, identify with and seek measures to assist specific segments of society, whether our professions, our religions, our social classes, or specific problems or issues that we seek to resolve because of our personal interest in them.[18]

Moreover, the logic of utilitarianism can lead its proponents down some strange and unethical paths. If utilitarians believe that a policy will enhance the overall happiness of society, they should logically support it even if it harms specific individuals or groups. Someone could support active euthanasia for old people, for example, on grounds that the policy, while killing some older people, would divert social resources from an unproductive and elderly population to other, more productive segments of the population, such as children.[19] Indeed, if cost–benefit analyses found that children's programs were associated with a more favorable benefit-to-cost ratio than were programs for older citizens, some utilitarians might conclude that we should drastically decrease the funding of programs for senior citizens and divert the monies to children's programs.[20] Such pitting of groups against one another, in a grim and competitive game, would have dire consequences for society, however, because certain groups such as elderly persons could find themselves abandoned by a society that sought to invest its resources in other citizens.

A group of moral philosophers, known as deontologists, have often made these kinds of criticisms of utilitarians. Should not society, they contend, develop certain first-order or basic moral rules that provide guiding principles for society—ones that cannot be overridden by the calculations of some utilitarians?

But how do deontologists derive these kinds of principles? Some of them consult precepts of major religions or religious writings such as the Koran or Bible. Others cite the work of philosophers such as Immanuel Kant, who identified a number of first-order principles.[21] Still others, such as contemporary philosopher John Rawls, obtain first principles by a process of reasoning.[22] Rawls asks, What moral principles would rational persons establish if they could devise the ideal society at its inception? Such rationality would be jeopardized, he argues, if persons knew their wealth or other characteristics because they would construct moral rules (in the case of the wealthy) to protect their personal interests. To be certain that people will be rational, Rawls insists that they operate behind a "veil of ignorance" when they construct their rules, that is, that they not know their own social class, skills, level of education, or any other personal attribute and that they not know the characteristics of their society such as its level of wealth or size.[23] Rawls concludes that rational persons would establish two basic moral principles: (1) the rule of liberty or freedom and (2) the principle of social justice. His reasoning about the principle of social justice is particularly interesting. Not knowing their likely wealth and fearing that they might not inherit or possess great wealth, rational people would decide to put strong limits on inequalities in wealth; indeed, they would choose to create a society where inequalities in wealth and opportunities could exist *only* if the inequalities could be demonstrated to help less advantaged people. Thus, high salaries of certain occupations could be justified only if it could be shown that they were needed to attract talented persons to them who would in turn provide needed services to less advantaged people.[24] Rawls includes elements of utilitarianism in his theory since he insists that social justice would bring practical benefits such as increases in the morale—hence the productivity—of many citizens who are currently poor.

Deontologists then seek to establish moral principles that take precedence over calculations of the consequences of specific choices. While differences exist among them, deontologists have variously derived a range of first-order ethical principles that include "honesty," "freedom," "self-determination," "confidence-keeping," "not-killing," "due process," "beneficence," "equality," and "social justice." In addition, some ethicists contend that society and subparts of it, such as organizations, possess certain rights such as the right to public order. (See Table 8.2; these terms are placed in quotations because considerable controversy about how to define them exists within philosophical literature.)

By establishing first-order principles, deontologists avoid some of the

TABLE 8.2   Various First-Order Ethical Principles

- "Autonomy": The right to make critical decisions about one's own destiny
- "Freedom": The right to hold and express personal opinions and take personal actions
- "Preservation of life": The right to continued existence
- "Honesty": The right to correct and accurate information
- "Confidentiality": The right to privacy
- "Equality": The right of individuals to receive the same services, resources, opportunities, or rights as other persons
- "Social justice": The right of equal access to social resources
- "Due process": The right to procedural safeguards when accused of crimes or when benefits or rights are withdrawn
- "Beneficence": The right to receive those treatments, services, or benefits that allow one to establish or maintain a decent standard of well-being
- "Societal or collective rights": The right of society to maintain and improve itself by safeguarding the public health and welfare, avoiding unreasonable or unnecessary expenditures, and preserving public order

peculiar choices that utilitarians are forced to consider. Take the example of active euthanasia, where physicians can administer lethal substances. A medical deontologist, such as Robert Veatch, can oppose it on grounds that it violates the first-order principle of "not taking life," whereas some utilitarians *might* support active euthanasia if their calculations indicated that it enhanced the overall happiness of society.[25] Indeed, to make this point even more tellingly, some deontologists note that utilitarians could support medical experimentation on involuntary human subjects because the research findings, such as a cure for cancer, might outweigh the harm to the subjects. (A deontologist who adhered to the first-order principles of self-determination and beneficence, which would be violated by such medical experimentation, would necessarily oppose such experimentation.[26])

Intuitionists, or Subjectivists

Both deontologists and utilitarians are attacked by intuitionists, that is, moral philosophers who maintain that we should make ethical choices by recourse to our "everyday and personal ethics." These philosophers make the same criticisms of utilitarians as do the deontologists, but they also attack deontologists on several grounds. People in the real world do not make ethical choices by identifying first-order principles that they rigidly apply to all situations.[27] Let's take the example of lying. A deontologist, who would often subscribe to the first-order principle of honesty, would usually condemn lying. In practice, however, we often engage in outright lying or in "partial lying" as several examples suggest. Assume, for example, that you are engaged in a political struggle with another faction, that you are convinced that your side in the dispute is correct, and that you believe that a victory by your side is vitally important. An opponent corners you in the hallway and asks, "Is it true that you are going to use XYZ tactic?" Also assume that you believe that honest divulging of the tactic would jeopardize the victory of your faction. It is conceivable that you would lie in this situation by not divulging the tactic because you believe adverse consequences would flow from honesty. Unlike utilitarians, however, you would probably make this choice not from some elaborate calculation, but "intuitively," that is, by consulting your sense of right and wrong in this specific situation.[28]

Some intuitionists also note that both utilitarians and deontologists fail to recognize the pluralism of society by embracing moral choices that extend to all people in society, whether the maximizing of societal happiness (for utilitarians) or first-order principles (for deontologists). In fact, moral rules and choices often vary between locations and between issues in a pluralistic society, as is illustrated by variations in the laws of the legislatures of different states on a range of moral issues including euthanasia.[29] Moreover, both utilitarians and deontologists suggest that moral choices are essentially rational or objective undertakings when in fact they are often made in the push-and-pull of the legislative process. On issues such as abortion and euthanasia, choices are not made by moral philosophers who make scientific estimations of likely consequences of specific choices or by deontologists who objectively identify and apply first-order principles but by legislators who respond to the temper of the times and the desires of various groups.[30]

Egoists

Some theorists appear to equate moral actions with the self-interested actions of individuals—a finding that conflicts with utilitarianism, deontologism, and intuitionism. Adam Smith, the eighteenth-century philosopher, assumed, for example, that the self-interested actions of individuals would lead to economic growth and prosperity.[31] In similar fashion, many contemporary political scientists subscribe to the notion that the self-interested actions of different interests lead to the development of sound policies.[32] Even though Smith and pluralists see the need for laws, we use the word *egoists* to describe them because they imply that moral rules and laws should emanate from self-interested actions of individuals and groups. This conception of morality is strikingly different from those of utilitarians and deontologists, who seek moral rules through a process of calculations and reasoning where they try to identify the common good *or* moral rules that transcend the wishes of specific factions or persons within society.

Nor should the role of personal interests be discounted in moral reasoning because we often support moral rules that advance our own interests, even when we claim to be wholly objective.[33] Some people engage in charity work, for example, because they find it meets some of their personal needs.

We sometimes support policies because we have been sensitized to specific needs through personal experiences such as the mental illness of a relative. Some politicians are elected because they espouse the needs of specific groups in the population. Indeed, it is often difficult to decide what our "true" motivation is; do we seek specific moral rules or policies to advance our personal interests or needs or from "genuine altruism"? By suggesting that rule making is objective and disinterested, deontologists and utilitarians overlook the reality that our needs often shape our choices.

Egoists encounter problems of their own, however. When carried to an extreme, egoism could lead to anarchy and the exploitation of powerless populations.[34] *Some* factions and individuals possess more power than others and have no compunction about seeking moral rules and policies that advance their interests. Unrestrained by the moral rules of deontologists or by the need to make calculations of the consequences of utilitarian policy, powerful interests can use their power to exploit powerless populations, as was illustrated in the South before the civil rights movement when the dominant white population developed laws to enhance and retain its power over a subjugated black population.

Situational Factors and Affiliations

Many moral philosophers concede that situational factors and affiliations shape the moral decisions of specific individuals—independently of their style of ethical reasoning. The role of situational factors is illustrated by the case of a professor of social work who took a sabbatical in Taiwan. When he saw a man beating his son in the street, he immediately went to the defense of the child, only to discover that a large (and unfriendly) crowd soon assembled. In Taiwanese culture, parents are widely perceived to have total responsibility for their children, even to the point of using physical force that would be viewed as child abuse in the United States. Of course, one could hold that he should have been undeterred by local customs, but the case raises the possibility that our moral choices are sometimes shaped by situational factors such as culture. In parallel fashion, some people contend that the U.S. government should not intervene when foreign nations select kinds of governments, such as dictators on the left or the right, whose political philosophy is unacceptable in the United States but acceptable in these nations. An anthropologic perspective suggests that persons in specific cultures develop certain rules to facilitate social harmony, that is, establish rules that govern our actions so that we know what to expect from friends and strangers. But the content of these moral rules is not constant because their nature changes as societies evolve and as new developments occur, such as technological advances. "Do not drink alcohol," was, for example, a moral maxim that led to the enactment of temperance laws in many states and in the nation during the nineteenth century and the early part of the twentieth century, but relatively few people have supported temperance in the middle and latter portions of the twentieth century.[35]

Affiliations shape our moral choices, as well. Employees in specific organizations, for example, are responsible to help them survive and to effectively meet their missions or objectives. Individuals who maliciously undermine an organization (e.g., by absconding with its funds, by inciting internal conflict, or by undermining its leaders) are widely viewed as violating ethical duties that are associated with the role of employee. Indeed, organizations and superiors also possess ethical responsibilities toward their employees and subordinates.[36]

In similar fashion, members of professions possess certain obligations toward their profession. Because members benefit from the use of a professional title and because professions serve social objectives, they are morally obliged not to unnecessarily harm their profession by engaging in activities that discredit it, such as engaging in sexual relations with clients or seeking to discredit professional colleagues for malicious reasons. Indeed, members possess a duty to participate in their professions to enhance the development and use of knowledge, to participate in the shaping of their internal policies, and to urge them to take moral positions in social problems.[37]

EMERGING FROM THE BRAMBLED ETHICAL THICKET

Many readers may wonder how it is possible to emerge from the brambled thicket of moral philosophy with its diverse approaches to moral reasoning. No single philosopher and no single approach to ethical reasoning have dominated moral discourse; indeed, academic literature is filled with numerous attacks and counterattacks as one or another theorist finds points of vulnerability in the work of other theorists.

This diversity of perspectives extends not only to the method of moral reasoning but also to substantive moral conclusions to specific ethical problems—sometimes even by persons who use the same mode of reasoning! To return to the issue of active euthanasia, for example, a variety of ethical opinions exist among people who are recognized experts; if some ethicists contend that individuals should be able to obtain the assistance of medical personnel in terminating their lives (subject, of course, to certain procedural safeguards such as an extended decision-making process), other experts are adamantly opposed to active euthanasia.[38]

The diversity of perspectives leaves us in a quandary when we confront specific ethical problems. If so many approaches exist, how can we develop convincing and credible solutions to ethical dilemmas? If ethical experts cannot agree, how can those of us who are not deeply versed in the intricacies of moral philosophy decide?

We could, of course, simply adopt one of the schools of moral philosophy as our own. Or we could select the tenets of a specific philosopher as our own and apply her style of reasoning to specific problems. This approach would suggest, however, that someone *had* achieved an approach to moral reasoning that was clearly superior to other approaches. Moreover, this approach would make it difficult to communicate with the proponents of other approaches to moral reasoning.

The decision to adopt someone's work as definitive might engender moreover the illusion that an objective approach to moral reasoning exists. We have noted that ethical dilemmas exist when different choices or actions are associated with specific (and often competing) values. Because individual values are not objective but reflect culture, upbringing, religious orientations, political ideology, and even vested interests, it should not be surprising that people often reach different ethical conclusions, even when they use the same kind, or style, of ethical reasoning. Unlike scientific inquiry where experimental data can be obtained in successive experiments, moral inquiry is profoundly influenced by the values of the ethicist. A Marxist philosopher and Ronald Reagan could discuss the nature of social justice for years, for example, and would unlikely reach a consensus either about the preferred distribution of property in society or the correct style of moral reasoning.

We need not be deterred by the brambled thicket of moral philosophy, however, if we realize that no one has a monopoly of moral truth and indeed that each style, or approach, has some merit. This simple truth is often overlooked in the zeal to develop or to find a single style of ethical reasoning.

"TAKING PAUSE" AS THE ULTIMATE PURPOSE OF ETHICAL REASONING

Our ascent from the brambled thicket is facilitated by recognizing that the ultimate purpose of ethical reasoning is not to obtain a single or objective truth but to force ourselves to "take pause"[39] when considering alternative courses of action or alternative choices. With some kinds of decisions, we have little need to take pause, such as trivial ones or ones that can readily be made by analyzing factual information. If we must choose between two rival policies when the only criterion is "administrative feasibility" and if it is readily apparent that only one policy is administratively feasible, a choice can be made quickly and with considerable confidence. In similar fashion, we do not need to take pause when making minor decisions about our personal schedules.

Issues that are associated with two or more alternative resolutions that *each* reflect important values and consequences should not be hurriedly or impulsively resolved. We should feel "tugged" in different directions, and we should feel that each alternative option is serious and cannot easily be dismissed.[40] Were we to hurriedly or impulsively resolve such issues, we might later decide that we had compromised important values and overlooked important consequences.

To illustrate the nature of these special kinds of issues, let's contrast some issues that do and do not require taking pause. We do not ordinarily have to ponder whether to lie, for example, because the choice of not-lying is clearly superior on both value and consequential criteria. If we routinely lie, we not only repudiate honesty (a value) but also jeopardize our reputations (a consequence). But people sometimes have to ponder the option of lying when both it and the alternative of not-lying *are* associated with important values and consequences. Health-care providers often encounter ethical dilemmas, for example, when deciding whether to disclose to patients their true medical conditions, particularly when they encounter life-threatening conditions like cancer. On one hand, the option of full disclosure is appealing because it advances the value of honesty and the ethical principle of self-determination because patients often need facts about their medical condition to participate in medical decisions. Patients who do not know that they are terminally ill, for example, are unlikely to participate intelligently in decisions about further surgeries. On the other hand, the option of not-disclosing the true condition of patients is appealing when patients request that health-care providers not tell them if they are terminally ill or even if they have a disease like cancer. Moreover, it is possible that some patients could experience serious mental problems if providers told them the true extent of their illness.

Health-care providers have to decide not only whether to tell "the complete truth" or to actually lie (e.g., to tell people they have a good prognosis when in fact they are terminal) but also whether to take various intermediate positions. Perhaps a provider should in some cases be noncommittal, except when specifically pressured by patients to tell them additional facts—a course of action that is a form of lying but that is not as blatant as providing them with false information.

In the preceding example then, an important ethical dilemma exists because alternative courses of action exist that are associated with important values and consequences. If people do not take pause when confronted with this kind of ethical dilemma, they might take actions that are inferior to other possible actions, on both value-based and consequential criteria. But events often conspire to hide ethical dilemmas from people; indeed, ethical reasoning is needed not only to facilitate choices but also to recognize ethical dilemmas in the first instance. In the case of lying in medical settings, the increasing tendency of health-care providers to disclose information is relatively recent. In the case of terminal illness, many health-care providers have not told patients about their medical prognosis because (1) medical staff believed it to be less traumatic for themselves (who wants to tell someone that she has a terminal illness?), (2) medical staff adhered to a conventional wisdom that the divulging of a prognosis would cause irreparable mental distress, and (3) medical staff assumed that patients did not wish to be told the true extent of their illnesses when they possessed terminal conditions like cancer. Each of these beliefs or reasons for not telling patients about their condition blinded medical staff to the ethical dilemmas that (in fact) they encountered by making it appear that only one legitimate course of action existed, namely, to not disclose information. We have already noted that a serious case can be made to disclose important, even troubling, information to patients to further the principles of honesty and self-determination and to promote positive consequences such as preparations for death in the case of terminally ill individuals.

We have used a clinical, or service-oriented, example to this point to discuss the rationale for ethical reasoning, but the same rationale exists with respect to the development of policies. We noted in Chapter Four that policy-makers often develop policies by comparing policy alternatives with respect to specific criteria such as their cost, their effectiveness, and their administrative feasibility. Policy analysis becomes an ethical undertaking when these consequences are supplemented by value-laden criteria such as self-determination, honesty, social justice, and fairness. Consider the example of many agencies that have waiting lists. A policy of first-come, first-served has the ethical merit of fairness because applicants are treated alike. However, most agencies have to develop policies for breaching the doctrine of fairness by giving certain people, such as ones with particularly serious problems, immediate access to services. (This breaching of the normal policy advances the ethical principle of beneficence, i.e., the redressing of suffering.) If many exceptions are made, however, the principle of fairness is breached. Moreover, as the number and kind of exceptions increase, intake staff are provided with more discretion that might be used in turn to provide special treatment for those individuals who appeal to them or who are clever at "playing the system," that is, avoiding the waiting list. The first-come, first-served policy raises another, more subtle value issue—namely, its effects on different kinds of consumers. Assume for the moment that an analysis of an agency's waiting list divulged that relatively affluent persons were less likely than low-income persons to drop off the waiting list—and hence receive most of the services from the agency. The first-come, first-served policy might in this instance have the unintended effect of decreasing services to low-income clientele— a result that could impede the agency's efforts to provide services to a broad spectrum of the population. Should the agency in this example make exceptions to the waiting list on the basis of social class?

This example of the waiting list suggests that ethical issues lurk even behind relatively mundane policy issues. As in the case of divulging information to terminally ill patients, this example also illustrates how people often do not recognize the ethical components of policies. Policy analysts often do not make values explicit in their analysis because they concentrate on cost, effectiveness, and other quantifiable criteria. When people are accustomed to certain kinds of policies, as in the case of waiting lists, they may be impervious to their ethical implications. Or one value might be identified and examined, such as fairness, while other issues, such as egalitarian ones, are ignored.

TOWARD ETHICAL REASONING: AN ECLECTIC APPROACH

Once we have decided that an issue *is* an ethical one and when we have decided that we should take pause, we confront the brambled thicket of ethical reasoning where proponents of various styles of ethical reasoning contend with each other. We noted in prior discussions, for example, that utilitarians, deontologists, and intuitionists believe that their respective approaches should be used to analyze ethical issues.

Our approach, admittedly one that would not be accepted by the adherents of some schools, is to develop a set of orienting or sensitizing questions that are derived from *each* of the philosophical schools. We suggest that people should ask a *variety* of questions that reflect various philosophical schools when addressing ethical issues because ethical choices are not simple.[41] Indeed, using a variety of questions is supported by the preceding discussion of both the strengths and the weaknesses of each of the schools; if utilitarians, deontologists, and intuitionists each provide useful insights, their approaches contain limitations that suggest that other considerations are also needed.

Intuitionists make the useful observation that many of our ethical choices are fashioned by recourse to our personal moral impulses, which in turn derive from our upbringing, religious orientation, peer influences, culture, and interests. Indeed, we often recognize an ethical dilemma by a "gut feeling" that important values are at stake or conflict in a specific situation. When we consider lying to someone else, for example, we typically feel uncomfortable (unless we are psychopaths) because we realize that lying conflicts with ethical rules like honesty. But intuitionists risk denying the reality that binding and common ethical rules often exist and are necessary to the functioning of society and its subunits, and they fail sufficiently to recognize that our ethical conclusions are often shaped by our calculations of the consequences of specific actions or choices.

Deontologists usefully define various first-order principles that have obtained a wide following in Western societies, such as honesty, not-killing, self-determination (or freedom), confidence-keeping (or contact-keeping), beneficence, and social justice. Whether they derive these principles from a reasoning process, as in the case of Rawls, or take them from religions or other sources, they correctly note that the functioning of society could be jeopardized if these kinds of first-order principles were summarily dismissed. But deontologists fail to sufficiently recognize that first-order principles are often vague in nature and that personal or intuitive understandings often shape their meanings to specific persons. Like intuitionists, deontologists are often impervious to the consequences of specific choices or actions.

Utilitarians correctly note that it is inadvisable to completely ignore some of the practical effects, or consequences, of ethical choices. Even when we subscribe to first-order principles, we often cannot rigidly follow their dictates without examining some possible consequences of a specific course of action. If onlookers are completely honest with a deranged and armed person who threatens to kill a hostage and tell him that a police officer is about to grab him from behind, they ignore (to say the least) consequences that could have made them reconsider their ethical adherence to be honest in this situation. Like intuitionists, however, utilitarians often ignore the need for first-order principles to provide some (relatively) binding rules, and they falsely suggest that ethical reasoning can be reduced to a science that recommends only those actions that will advance the public good.

A number of considerations often shape ethical choices that cannot easily be classified under the headings of intuitionism, deontologism, and utilitarianism. For example, *practical considerations* shape our choices, such as the availability of resources and political considerations. We might want to use agency resources to redistribute resources to disadvantaged populations, but resources might not exist for this purpose in an agency. We might decide a specific course of action is ethically sensible, but political realities might render it unfeasible. Assume, for example, that we decide that active euthanasia *is* ethically advisable; if the staff of a hospital are adamantly opposed to it, it might be counterproductive to propose the policy in this hospital. We have noted that *legal realities* also intrude because existing laws sometimes preclude specific policies or actions; if active euthanasia has been ruled to be a homicide by existing legislation or by court rulings, persons who use it risk criminal penalties if they perform it. *Occupational and professional roles* shape our ethical choices; as employees, for example, we have the duty to promote the effective functioning of our organizations, so we would not normally promote conflict for its own sake or propose policies for the purpose of promoting internal discord. (We might promote conflict if we believed it to be necessary to obtain ethically correct policies, however.) In similar fashion, members of specific professions have a duty to take actions and to promote policies that are consonant with the profession and that do not undermine its credibility; one would not seek to undermine or discredit a professional colleague, for example, unless that colleague was taking actions that were ethically flawed.

Table 8.3 provides a list of sensitizing actions and questions that draws on each of the philosophical schools.

A list of sensitizing questions and actions is not, of course, a panacea because it requires us to use an array of information when addressing ethical issues. The list does not tell us what relative importance, or weight, to give to the various kinds of information; should we give more or less importance to information about consequences, to first-order principles, or to intuition?[42]

TABLE 8.3   Some Sensitizing Actions and Questions for Addressing Ethical Issues

Some Actions Drawn from Intuitionists

■ Carefully examine one's conscience and motives to select the action or choice that intuitively satisfies my values and my estimation of important consequences.

■ Select the action or choice that seems congruent with prevailing ethical mores.

Some Actions Drawn from Deontologists

■ Identify first-order principles that are relevant to an ethical dilemma and decide, on balance, which choices or actions best satisfy them.

■ When first-order principles conflict—i.e., point, respectively, to different choices—seek a compromise solution that satisfies each of them to some degree.

Some Actions Drawn from Utilitarians

■ Conduct research to identify important consequences that are likely to be associated with the selection of specific options or actions.

■ Select the option or choice that maximizes positive consequences for society or for one (or more) of its subunits.

Some Questions That Probe Additional Considerations

■ Should various situational factors influence choices such as available resources and political realities?

■ Should existing laws and policies constrain the kinds of choices that are available?

■ Should specific roles—e.g., as an employee or a member of a specific profession—shape choices?

■ Should specific persons be able to "opt out" of those ethical positions that conflict with their personal moral codes?

When should we allow situational factors, such as our loyalties to our employers or to fellow professionals, to shape our decisions to abandon choices or actions that appear ethically sensible?

An orienting and eclectic list has some virtues, however. It forces us to consider many kinds of information when making ethical choices. It requires us to integrate or synthesize the information during a **process of reasoning.** It makes us realize that ethical reasoning is more art than science because no mechanical means exist to integrate and use a range of information to reach ethically correct decisions. Indeed, a list of a range of considerations suggests that reasonable people can often reach different kinds of conclusions when examining specific ethical dilemmas, as our discussion of active euthanasia suggests.

When using the list of questions and actions, we look for points of convergence and divergence. If intuitive, deontologic, *and* utilitarian perspectives *converge* to suggest that a specific course of action or a specific policy choice is more meritorious than others, we can be fairly certain about our resulting decision. If these different perspectives lead us in *diverging* paths—that is, respectively suggest that we should make different or various actions or choices—we have to devote time and thought to seeking some resolution.[43] Perhaps we will decide to give priority to one of the perspectives and to ignore or give less weight to another. Someone might decide when using a utilitarian perspective that active euthanasia is advisable because (among other consequences) it saves many persons the indignity of medical bankruptcy when they have terminal illnesses—but she overrides this utilitarian decision with a first-order principle drawn from deontology that says "thou shalt not kill." Or we might decide to find a new solution that appears to satisfy the various perspectives more satisfactorily than do the solutions that we had previously examined; someone might decide, for example, to limit active euthanasia to brain-dead persons when the surviving relatives unanimously support it—a decision that would be less objectionable from a deontologic perspective than would "on-call" euthanasia and that would nonetheless have the positive consequence of saving the medical resources that are required to maintain comatose persons indefinitely. (Of course, some deontologists would object to this policy, which illustrates that divergence can occur even when we use a single perspective like deontology.)

We suggest that ethical evidence be sought that uses the various perspectives that are presented in Table 8.3, that is, intuitive, deontologic, and utilitarian perspectives. Of course, these perspectives need not be used in this order, although a case can be made that this order has some merit. We often start with our intuitive feelings about moral actions and choices, then consider first-order principles, and then examine consequences and situational factors that might alter our positions. (Were we to examine consequences first, we might fall victim to the utilitarian error of using a policy or action with mostly good consequences, even when it infringes on the rights and needs of some persons who do *not* benefit from it.)

AN EXAMPLE OF MORAL REASONING:
THE CASE OF EUTHANASIA REVISITED

To illustrate the use of questions and perspectives in Table 8.3, let's consider in more detail how someone might approach the tasks of developing an ethical position on euthanasia. In most situations, our intuitive feelings alert us to the existence of an ethical dilemma and provide us with some tentative resolutions. After all, unless we are psychopaths, we have internalized those moral principles that our society, or subparts thereof, have developed to provide social tranquility and predictability in social relations, such as not killing other people, blatantly lying, or imposing our will on others in a way that frustrates their self-determination or freedom. But our intuitive feelings, while providing a starting point, can lead to ethical errors.[44] We may have internalized "conventional wisdom" of persons in a specific setting that is ethically flawed, such as routinely failing to divulge information to patients about the true extent of their illness. Or we may override our internalized ethical codes with rationalizations, such as a physician's assumption that "patients do not really want to know when they are terminally ill." Our vested interests, such as our desire to be promoted or our desire not to have to deal with the tumultuous feelings of persons who know they are terminally ill, may blind us to certain positions.

We should often test our initial ethical positions against first-order principles such as honesty, not-killing, confidence-keeping, self-determination, fairness, and social justice, particularly when our intuitive choices violate one of these commonly recognized principles. (Our intuition often "red flags" those choices that infringe first-order ethical principles, although we might have blind spots in our ethical codes or we might falsely rationalize our choices as not infringing first-order principles.)

Using first-order principles has the salutary effect of requiring us to reconsider our intuitive responses to a situation. Someone might intuitively decide to help a terminally ill patient, who has made a particularly compelling and urgent plea to take him out of his misery, to commit suicide. Indeed, the health-care provider is following the dictates of the first-order ethical principle of advancing the self-determination of the patient in this instance, since he wants to end his life. On further reflection, the health-care provider realizes that the first-order principle of "not-killing" is *also* implicated because active euthanasia *is* killing, even when the health-care provider does it at the request of the patient. Indeed, two first-order principles conflict here. Different ethicists might resolve this tension in different fashion, but awareness of the conflict between first-order principles forces our health-care provider to reconsider the merits of restriction of euthanasia to passive euthanasia for a terminally ill person.[45]

Whenever people examine ethical actions in light of first-order principles, they are forced to grapple with difficult definitions—in this case, with words like *terminally ill* and *killing*.[46] If we wish to restrict the use of passive euthanasia to terminally ill patients, we need to define terminal illness. How terminal does someone have to be to qualify, and who makes this judgment? Should we declare—as some states do—that persons are terminally ill when two physicians independently declare they will not live for more than six months, or is this too stringent or too loose a standard?

When considering the definition of killing, the health-care provider soon realizes that many gradations exist. Indeed, we can even construct a gruesome continuum that extends from using procedures or medications that actively and quickly cause death, such as administering a lethal substance, to the actions (or nonactions) that eventually and passively cause death, such as withholding extraordinary and life-saving measures like surgery.[47] Many options exist between these two extremes, including withholding life-sustaining food or water and using pain-killing substances like morphine that speed the termination of life when they exceed a certain dosage. If we define killing to be *any* course of treatment that leads to an earlier cessation of life than would occur if all available medical technology were used, we adopt a broad definition that even includes the nonuse of surgery on terminally ill patients. Alternatively, we might adopt a narrow definition that declares that killing occurs only when substances or drugs are used that immediately terminate someone's life. Or we could adopt an intermediate position that includes withholding food and water in our definition of killing but that excludes using pain-killing substances like morphine. Nitpicking as these fine distinctions might appear, they are important to this ethical issue just as similar kinds of distinctions are important to many other ethical debates.[48]

The health-care provider decides to embrace a relatively restrictive definition of killing and to exclude from it the withholding of food and water, the administering of morphine in the case of pain, and the withholding of heroic measures from terminally ill patients. When used with consenting and terminally ill patients, she decides that these measures do not conflict with the first-order rule of not-killing and moreover advance the principle of self-determination. She decides that the *motives* of persons also have to be considered when deciding whether a specific action violates a first-order principle; someone who administers morphine to a consenting person to relieve pain does not commit murder even if the morphine has the side effect of hastening death.[49] (By contrast, someone who places arsenic in someone's tea to collect his insurance benefits has decidedly sinister motives.)

Let's assume for the moment that our health-care provider emerges from the intuitive and deontologic stages of her ethical reasoning with the following ethical statement: "euthanasia, which includes avoiding extraordinary measures, using morphine in the case of pain, and witholding food and water, is appropriate with terminally ill patients who inform health-care providers in writing of their desire to have one (or more) of these measures used." When the health-care provider moves to the utilitarian (or consequentialist) phase, however, she becomes less certain (again) that she has made the correct choice when someone asks her, "would not active euthanasia have adverse consequences on the morale of health-care providers, who would find it abhorrent to withdraw food and water from terminal (and often conscious) patients?"[50] Moreover, this critic continues, "could not patients be subjected to subtle pressure, particularly in money-strapped clinics that serve poor people, to agree to active euthanasia even when they do not want it?"[51] While the health-care provider retorts that positive consequences would also accompany her ethical position, such as shortening the suffering of some terminally ill patients and increasing their participation in medical decisions, she realizes that the critic has identified some possible adverse consequences of her ethical position.

Indeed, the doubts of the health-care provider increase when she considers various personal and situational factors. From discussions with some physicians in her hospital, she learns that they will not withhold food or water from any patient in any circumstances because of their personal moral codes. One of them maintained that the Hippocratic Oath, which requires physicians to "follow that method of treatment which . . . [they] consider for the benefit of [their] patients . . . and [to] abstain from whatever is deleterious," forbids them from withholding food and water. To make matters more complex, the health-care provider learns that recent court rulings have not convinced many physicians that they will not be sued if they openly subscribe to withholding food and water from patients, even when the patients consent to these procedures.[52]

When consequences, the personal positions of some physicians, and legal realities are entered into the equation, the health-care provider decides to amend her ethical statement to exclude the withdrawing of food and water from terminally ill patients but to retain the remaining provisions with the additional statement: "Health-care providers who feel they cannot comply with patients' wishes with respect to these measures because of their personal moral codes should refer them to another health-care provider."[53]

This extended example of ethical reasoning, which draws on the questions and perspectives in Table 8.3, illustrates the difficulty of resolving some issues to our satisfaction. It also suggests that each of the perspectives provides a check on the others; in this case, the health-care provider changed her position as she progressed through intuitive, deontologic, and utilitarian phases and when she considered various situational and personal factors. Even after she finished her work, she felt some doubts about her position—

a normal occurrence when dealing with complex ethical issues like this one. Of course, many ethical issues are not this complicated, and people might develop positions on them with a considerable sense of certitude.

ASCENDING LEVELS OF GENERALITY: FROM SPECIFIC CASES TO BROAD RULES

The preceding discussion of the ethics of euthanasia suggests that ethical decisions are sometimes developed in specific situations, such as when a health-care provider wrestles with the ethics of passive euthanasia in a specific case. If we *only* had case-specific and situation-specific moral rules, however, we would encounter an endless string of moral choices because we would have no general rules to guide our decisions. Every time we encountered a moral choice, we would have to decide de novo the merits of alternative choices or actions. When developing general moral rules, we still use words like *ought, should, duty,* or *responsibility,* but we identify actions or choices that are ethically desirable *whenever* specific conditions exist. For example, many states have enacted laws that require that health-care providers *not* perform heroic measures when patients have signed specific legal documents and have met certain conditions, such as being declared to be terminally ill by a specified number of physicians. Or a specific hospital might develop certain procedures or rules of its own to inform its medical staff of suggested actions or choices in certain kinds of situations.

Indeed, legislation and court rulings often provide general ethical rules. When the Supreme Court ruled in *Roe v. Wade* (1973) that states cannot prohibit abortions in the first trimester of pregnancy, for example, it struck an ethical balance between two competing first-order principles, that is, between not-killing and the woman's right to self-determination. Its decision to not allow states to declare abortion to be illegal in the first trimester upheld the rights of privacy of the woman, whereas its decision that states could declare abortion to be illegal after the first trimester upheld the rights of the fetus. (As the controversy about *Roe v. Wade* suggests, general rules often draw opposition from people who do not want to be bound or constrained by them.)

Most professions have codes of ethics, which are rules for their members. The code of the National Association of Social Workers prohibits sexual relations between social workers and their clients, for example. Like most professional codes, NASW's code possesses both negative statements (no sexual contact with clients) and positive statements (social workers have the duty to "prevent and eliminate discrimination against any person . . . [to] promote conditions that encourage respect for the diversity of cultures that constitute American society . . . [and to] advocate changes of policy and legislation to improve social conditions and to promote social justice").

SELECTED ETHICAL ISSUES IN SOCIAL WELFARE POLICY

We have focused thus far on ethical reasoning rather than on specific ethical issues that confront policymakers. If we do not know how to reason ethically, we will likely find it difficult to develop positions on myriad policy issues. Many kinds of ethical issues frequently recur in social welfare policy, including ones regarding the political process, the substantive content of policy proposals, the implementing and assessing of enacted policies, and decisions about participating in policy-making in the first instance. We briefly discuss some of these ethical issues not to develop detailed positions on them but to introduce some preliminary considerations that will spur readers to begin their own process of ethical reasoning.

Some Ethical Issues in Political Interactions

As we noted in Chapters Five and Six, policy practitioners often use power to obtain their policy preferences. It is wrong to assert that using power is intrinsically unethical or ethical because it only *becomes* ethical or unethical in specific situations as its wielders honor or violate first-order ethical principles and as they use it in a manner that creates positive or negative consequences.[54] Let's consider an example of the unethical use of power and contrast it with an ethical use. Assume that a group wants the enactment of a policy and decides that "hard-ball" tactics are needed. They decide to use a variety of negative tactics such as impugning the reputations of their opponents by spreading rumors about their personal lives, falsifying data to make their policy appear more attractive than a competing policy, and using coercive power to obtain the support of some of their subordinates. Our intuitive sense of morality would likely make us question these tactics or at least wonder if a negative campaign is necessary. Various of these tactics conflict with first-order principles such as honesty, self-determination, and beneficence. When persons seek to discredit the reputations of opponents and not merely their ideas, they violate the principle of beneficence by harming them.[55] When they falsify data to make their proposal appear more attractive than it is or to make opponents' proposals appear less attractive, they violate the principle of honesty.[56] Moreover, they risk violating the principle of self-determination when they use power in a manner that excludes persons from the decision-making process.[57] People who routinely exclude others from deliberations, such as authoritarian executives, can correctly be accused of depriving them of a chance to express their opinions on important matters. Some people are also adept at making it *appear* that they value the advice of others when in fact they accord them symbolic roles in decision making; in such cases, participants in meetings eventually realize that their contributions are not valued.[58]

Other people are adept at manipulating others; they may obtain their support for a policy by playing on their fears, by impugning the motives or reputations of individuals who favor an opposing policy, or by "staging an event" to make it falsely appear that a groundswell of support exists for a policy. They may seek the support of some individuals by using coercive power, that is, by using actual or implied threats to rally them behind a policy. In each case, the power wielder avoids direct and honest communication and manipulates the decision-making procedures or the beliefs of individuals to obtain his or her policy preferences.[59]

To be candid, it is often difficult to clearly distinguish ethical from unethical uses of power, and we usually need to explore various situational realities to render a judgment. When we seek to change the actions or beliefs of others, we often resort to tactics that are somewhat dishonest or manipulative. When using the power of expertise, for example, we might somewhat overstate the case for a policy—or perhaps omit some negative evidence or fail to make some cautionary statements.[60] It is common to try to arrange the agendas of meetings to favor certain proposals, to orchestrate some favorable comments for a proposal before a meeting, or to use parliamentary or procedural tactics that give proponents an advantage over opponents.[61] Partly because opponents of proposals often resort to similar tactics, it is often true in some settings that *completely* honest and nonmanipulative persons place their side in a dispute at a decided disadvantage.[62] Moreover, when someone encounters a forbidding political situation where opponents possess superior power, it is common to use strategies that include some deception and some use of coercive or reward power.

We often have to take into account situational factors such as the motives of persons and the distribution of power to gauge the ethics of specific tactics. If an individual uses power solely to advance personal interests, we are often more likely to negatively evaluate his use of specific tactics because we know that his motivation is entirely self-interested.[63] Someone who oversells a proposal that will redistribute resources to poor people would probably be viewed more favorably than someone who used the same tactic to obtain personal gain. Carried to an extreme, however, this argument could lead to the assertion that "good ends justify *any* tactics"—an assertion that none of us would accept.[64] When individuals encounter opponents who use manipulative tactics or who resort to lying, they may be somewhat more justified in resorting to these tactics in self-defense, although this argument can easily lead to a rationalizing of unethical actions.

Our inability to place actions neatly in all-good or all-bad categories should not deter us from grappling with ethical issues in the political interaction. Some political strategies are unethical because they *blatantly* violate first-order ethical principles. Other actions are clearly ethical. Still other actions fall between these extremes, such as not fully disclosing information, telling "relatively innocuous" untruths, or somewhat overstating the case for a policy. These actions are judged ethical or nonethical, based on the extent they violate first-order principles, the kinds of consequences that they cause, the motives of the power wielder, and the tactics of opponents.[65]

Lest we dwell excessively on ethical problems that can be associated with the use of power, we should also note that a *failure* to use power can also be unethical.[66] When we retreat from important issues and fail to voice our objections to an ill-advised policy, we might help sustain dysfunctional policies. Put differently, if existing rules are morally flawed, our disinclination to try to change them exposes us to the charge that we are accomplices of the unethical policy.

Some Ethical Issues When Devising Policy Proposals

As we discussed in Chapters Three and Four, policy practitioners often compare and contrast the merits of specific policy options when they construct policy proposals. Values intrude at numerous points in the analytic process; people have to decide how to define certain social problems, which policy options are worth considering in the first instance, and the weights or importance of criteria—and they have to meld options into an embracing proposal.[67]

Many paradigms are used to examine social problems, such as intrapsychic, ecological, and radical ones, as we discussed in Chapter Two. The definitions of problems shape the kinds of solutions that persons propose. People who define AIDS as *only* a physiological problem, for example, are likely to concentrate exclusively on the provision of medical services, whereas those who use an ecological framework are more likely to attend, as well, to efforts to help its victims cope with discrimination, economic destitution, and mental trauma.[68] The selection of paradigms has ethical implications. People who define AIDS in narrowly medical terms risk violating the principle of beneficence since their paradigm impedes the development of a range of ameliorative programs and laws, such as ones that prevent discrimination against people with AIDS in medical clinics, housing, and employment.[69]

Some policy practitioners deliberately omit certain policy options from policy deliberations to ensure that they will not be included in the final proposals. Perhaps they fear policy options that suggest the need for fundamental reforms of existing policies. Or they may fear options that could lead to proposals that would harm their personal interests or that will force them to alter traditional modes of providing services.[70] Disliked policy options can be omitted from deliberations in several ways. Individuals who are known to espouse them can be excluded from deliberations, or these individuals can be scapegoated by calling them "troublemakers" or other pejorative names. (Scapegoating is an effective means of silencing critics by exposing them to peer pressure that impugns their ideas and their reputations.) The selection of program or reform options has ethical implications. If ones that challenge existing (and defective) institutions are omitted from consideration, policy analysts risk violating the principles of beneficence and social justice. At the same time, inattention to practical political realities, which may suggest that far-reaching reforms will be difficult to enact, can be attacked on ethical grounds, as well. The enactment of modest reforms, even if they fail to achieve the full objectives of reformers, provides resources and services to people with AIDS, for example, that might otherwise not exist if no reforms were passed.

Criteria can be selected that skew the evaluations of policy options in a manner so that (for all intents) certain of them are selected or rejected. If cost is made the only criterion, for example, policy options that are somewhat more costly than other options will be rejected. When numerous criteria are selected, certain ones can be weighted more heavily than others to skew the selection process toward certain options and away from other options. A policy analyst might include criteria other than cost, such as "effectiveness in addressing the needs of clients," but weight the criterion of cost so heavily that it dominates the selection process.

Many critics of contemporary policy analysis have criticized the tendency to select only those criteria that lend themselves to quantitative measurements—a tendency that excludes important and value-based criteria such as effects in reducing specific kinds of inequalities, fairness, and effects in restoring public trust in public services.[71] To be certain, some value-based criteria are difficult to define and are likely to prompt controversy. Equality is, for example, a diffuse concept because we have to define what kind of equality we wish to emphasize; do we want, for example, to redress inequalities in access to specific services, or do we want to modify the life conditions (such as housing) of certain people to make them more equal to others?[72] *Whose* inequalities do we wish to decrease, that is, women, racial minorities, members of groups with stigmatized problems such as mental health, relatively poor people, people who reside in specific jurisdictions such as rural areas, or people who possess some combination of these (or other) characteristics? *How much* equality is feasible or desirable? Individuals who state that they wish to reduce certain kinds of inequalities for certain kinds of people are likely to stimulate spirited opposition from others who contend that the rights or needs of *other* people are jeopardized; critics of affirmative action maintain, for example, that preferential treatment of racial minorities and women in training or educational programs brings "reverse discrimination" against white males.

The difficulties of defining certain criteria, such as equality, ought not deter us from using them, however. If no one uses them, important first-order values like equality and social justice will be absent from policy deliberations.[73] Indeed, social workers, whose founders often sought to advance the interests of disadvantaged people, ought to envision their policy practice to include advocacy for unpopular causes *and* unpopular criteria.[74]

We have suggested that policy practitioners need to include a range of criteria in their analysis of policy options, but we should note that such inclusiveness often makes the selection of options more difficult. As we add criteria, we increase the chances that the criteria will conflict, as illustrated by the example of involuntary commitment procedures for mental patients. If a department of mental health uses only the criteria of "minimizing short-run costs" and "maximizing the self-determination of people with severe mental conditions," for example, it might decide to emphasize strict limits on the intake ability of psychiatric evaluation teams (PET teams) to commit persons to mental institutions. (By limiting commitments to hospitals, this policy would limit the costs of the mental health department.) If the department *also* adds the criteria of "enhancing the safety of the general public" and "decreasing the likelihood that persons with severe mental conditions will harm themselves," its process of policy selection becomes more difficult not only because it must consider more options but also because the criteria of enhancing self-determination, enhancing the safety of the general public, and enhancing the safety of people with severe mental conditions conflict with one another. The department staff are likely to feel pulled in different ways; if they do not restrict the intake staff's ability to use involuntary commitments, they decrease the self-determination of those patients who resist commitment; but if they severely restrict the intake staff's ability to use involuntary commitments, they risk jeopardizing the safety of some clients who possess life-threatening conditions, as well as members of the general public in the case of patients with violent tendencies.

It is tempting when confronting complex issues like commitment procedures to seek to simplify them to expedite solutions, but this strategy risks ignoring important issues. When different first-order principles are involved and when they suggest conflicting policy options, policy practitioners ought not avoid policy dilemmas. In the case of commitment procedures, we should value self-determination, the well-being of the patients, *and* the well-being of the general public. As we have already noted, we often should feel "pulled in different directions" when we develop policy proposals—a conflict that we can only partially resolve by seeking compromise solutions.

When resources are scarce, policy practitioners often encounter the difficult question: Which issues or problems should be given priority? For example, a mental health agency decides to focus its efforts upon programs to attract relatively affluent and fee-paying clients and fails to devote time to securing funds to help homeless or other impoverished clients. The principles of beneficence and social justice suggest that social agencies have an ethical duty to direct their scarce resources, as well as their fund-raising and political energies, to projects to help populations that are particularly needy.[75]

When people construct policy proposals, they encounter many value dilemmas. Should they seek major or minor funding for a proposal? Should they leave certain details undefined in hopes of expediting its passage, or should they insist that certain provisions be made explicit? It is not possible to develop ethical resolutions of these issues without considering situational realities. If the proponents of a proposal encounter formidable political opposition, for example, they may have to be content with a relatively modest proposal if they want it to be enacted. As with many decisions in policy practice, trade-offs usually exist; someone may facilitate the enactment of a proposal by leaving some provisions from a proposal but find subsequently that it is ineffectively implemented because these provisions were omitted.

Some Ethical Issues When Implementing and Assessing Enacted Policies

Many ethical issues arise during the implementation of policies. Let's begin with the issues of compliance and discretion. When policies are enacted, people are usually required to implement them, whether they are established by executives in agencies, the governing boards of agencies, funders, courts, government agencies, or legislatures. As we noted in Chapter One, policies are *collective and binding* rules, regulations, and objectives. If someone disagrees with a policy, however, can she ethically oppose it or even, in some cases, refuse to implement it?

The routine flaunting of official policy is unethical because it violates the first-order principles of contract-keeping and honesty.[76] When we assume specific positions in agencies, we usually agree, implicitly or explicitly, to implement existing rules and regulations, as well as ones that are developed during our tenure. Moreover, the routine flaunting of official policy carries with it negative consequences; if staff cannot be counted on to implement official policies, funders, government officials, and the general public would become cynical about agencies and their staff and would probably impose even more rules on them.

But staff can and should ameliorate deficient policies. Efforts to change policy should typically occur within "normal channels."[77] But what if individuals find specific policies—or the manner in which they are implemented—ethically flawed, such as policies or actions of implementors that are discriminatory against certain kinds of people? And what if it is impossible to change current policies or actions of implementors through normal channels because of the noninterest of superiors in changing policies or because they are inclined to use coercive power to quell dissent? An emerging literature on whistle-blowing suggests that staff can ethically publicize ethically flawed policies and actions to people outside their agencies when all else fails. They can publicly divulge information to funders, legislators, or the mass media, or they can anonymously release information to outsiders.

Certain ethical limitations provide some boundaries to whistle-blowing. Persons ought to have tried to change policies through normal channels. Moreover, the ethical dilemmas of existing problems have to be sufficiently serious to warrant whistle-blowing; some people engage in it because of personal vendettas or minor issues. The whistle-blower also has an obligation to provide accurate information to outsiders such as the press or the funders of an agency. In most cases, persons should discuss the issue with trusted colleagues to be certain that no other recourse exists.[78]

Despite recent legislation in some states that protects some whistle-blowers, people who engage in it often encounter reprisals such as loss of employment. Even with these provisos and warnings, however, it is important to reiterate that whistle-blowing is ethically meritorious when used in those rare circumstances when obedience is ethically indefensible and when traditional methods of changing policies are ineffective.

Other ethical issues arise during the implementation of policies. Implementors often advance their own interests during implementation as terms like *empire building, turf rivalry, padding statistics,* and *goal displacement* suggest. In goal displacement, staff forget their primary goal—to assist people who possess specific problems—in order to meet those criteria that funders use to calculate their grants to specific agencies, such as the volume of services provided rather than their quality or content. The realities of limited funding in the human services sometimes promote competition between agencies for clients and resources. *Some* competition between agencies is inevitable and, at least in some cases, beneficial. When competition and goal displacement lead to a hoarding of clients or a disinclination to refer them to other agencies that can address their needs effectively, however, staff risk violating the first-order principles of beneficence and honesty.[79]

Staff have to grapple with difficult issues of resource deployment during the implementation of policies. Given the reality of limited resources, they should not squander resources in ways that detract from the provision of services to consumers, such as through frivolous expenditures and the personal use of agency funds. Even when these improper uses of resources do not exist, staff encounter some dilemmas, particularly when they possess some discretion over the use of resources. How many resources should be devoted to the needs of specific clients when resources are inadequate to address the needs of all applicants? What kinds of limits, or ceilings, should be placed on the number of services or resources that particular persons receive? What kinds of clients and what kinds of problems should receive priority?

In addressing these issues, staff must resolve difficult dilemmas. On the one hand, they wish to advance the principle of beneficence by helping all people who need assistance and by providing them with as much assistance as the staff believe that they need to resolve their problems. On the other hand, generosity to specific clients can deplete resources that are available to others.[80] Moreover, staff must sometimes make difficult distinctions between *degrees* of need or suffering; if scarce resources are expended on clients with trivial or unimportant needs, others with truly serious needs may receive no or insufficient services. Staff must also decide whether to give priority to members of specific groups who are chronically underserved, such as racial minorities and poverty-stricken people who are underrepresented in the clientele of a specific program or agency. These choices about the deployment of resources are ethical because they involve first-order ethical principles of beneficence and social justice; staff must "play god" as they decide what configuration of services will best address the needs of consumers and rectify inequalities in the existing distribution of services.[81]

Administrators and staff of agencies must also wrestle with ethical issues that are associated with the amounts of discretion that are granted to front-line staff in providing services. On the one hand, many people contend that the first-order principle of fairness requires the development of explicit rules that guide the provision of services to consumers. Because rules are numerous and explicit, they deter front-line staff from displaying favoritism to specific clients, whether in their intake, service-delivery, or fee-assessing functions.[82] However, the development of numerous rules carries problems of its own. Front-line staff have to adapt their services to the idiosyncratic needs of specific clients; yet numerous rules may require them to limit this discretion. Indeed, they need some ability to make exceptions to rules as well as some latitude in interpreting rules to address the needs of specific people.[83] In the case of hospitals that develop rules to govern how long patients can remain in hospitals—rules that are shaped by the disinclination of government and private funders to reimburse them for patients who remain in the hospital for more than several days—front-line staff need to use their professional knowledge to determine when someone is truly ready to be discharged. (Premature discharges can threaten the physical and mental well-being of some patients, particularly when staff have been unable to locate community-based facilities that can meet their needs.) When discussing discretion, we also should note that staff possess certain rights, such as some degree of autonomy.[84] Judgments lie at the heart of professional practice—if the employers attempt to regulate every detail of work, they imperil the effectiveness of professional practitioners. When shaping policies about discretion then, staff have to balance the conflicting first-order principles of fairness, which supports limits on discretion, and beneficence, which suggests that staff need considerable discretion. As with many moral issues, then, the ethics of discretion suggest the need for compromises among competing principles. Some limits on discretion are needed to provide fair, equitable, and efficient services, but these limits should not exceed a threshold that threatens the effectiveness of services or the rights of staff.

Agency and program staff encounter another set of ethical dilemmas when they assess programs. They must first decide whether to obtain evaluative data if they are not required to do so by their funders. It is tempting not to evaluate programs because evaluations require the expenditure of resources and time that could be used to provide services. Moreover, evaluations that suggest programs are not effective may imperil their continued funding if the findings reach funders and decision makers. However, if professionals do not try to assess their work, they risk continuing ineffective services, which imperils the principle of beneficence. An ethical case can be made, therefore, that evaluations of programs should be required by professionals.[85] As we discuss in more detail in Chapter Thirteen, evaluations need to be conducted with sufficient rigor and professional integrity that they provide useful and valid data.[86]

SUMMARY

Policy practitioners frequently confront ethical issues, but there is surprisingly little discussion of them in existing policy literature. Perhaps this reluctance of many theorists to grapple with ethical issues stems from the lack of agreement among ethicists about how to conduct ethical reasoning in the first instance. We have contrasted intuitive, deontologic, and utilitarian approaches to ethical reasoning; although adherents of these various approaches often reach similar conclusions on specific issues, they reach their positions in strikingly different fashion and are often highly critical of alternative styles of ethical reasoning.

Rather than side with one or another school or any specific theorist, we have chosen to discuss the advantages and deficiencies of each approach and to suggest that we need to couple, or combine, the different approaches when examining ethical issues. We can begin with our intuitive responses to ethical problems, decide whether our preliminary conclusions do or do not conflict with first-order ethical principles, examine whether specific consequences of various choices or actions ought to influence our ethical choices, and (finally) include personal and situational factors in our ethical calculations. This eclectic approach has utility but, it must be noted, is not likely to be popular with those people who are determined to develop a single approach to ethical reasoning or to apply to all ethical issues the prescriptions, or style of reasoning, of a specific ethicist.

We have also contended that ethics is not a science because values shape our choices as well as our style of reasoning. Despite its intrinsic difficulties, ethical reasoning has the virtue of making us take pause before taking actions or making choices that violate commonly held principles or that threaten adverse consequences.

QUESTIONS FOR DISCUSSION

1. Review Policy-Practice Case 8. Discuss why the issue of client access to records in this case is a moral issue rather than only a technical matter.

2. Assume that you are a participant in Policy-Practice Case 8 and need to decide whether clients have access to their records and in what circumstance. Develop a position (pro or con) by using:
   a) a utilitarian mode of argument
   b) a deontological mode of argument
   c) an intuitive or subjectivist mode of argument.

3. Would persons with different philosophical perspectives in the preceding question necessarily reach different or similar conclusions? Could two people using the *same* mode of argument reach different conclusions? What do your answers to these questions tell us about the nature of ethical reasoning?

4. Identify one of the major schools of ethical reasoning that seems particularly sensible to you. Discuss some of its strengths and limitations when compared to an alternative school of ethical reasoning.

5. A dilemma in ethical reasoning is that people often encounter two (or more) "partly-good options" so that choices are often not clear cut. Discuss this reality with respect to the merits of active euthanasia or any other controversial policy issue.

6. Discuss the assertion of deontologists that utilitarianism can sometimes lead its proponents down strange and unethical paths, such as slashing funding of programs for older people in order to increase the funding of programs for children.

7. Discuss the assertion of utilitarians that deontologists resort to ill-proven "first-order principles."

8. With reference to Policy-Practice Case 8 or with reference to the traditional practice of physicians *not* to tell terminally ill persons their diagnosis, discuss the assertion that many people fail to recognize the ethical components of specific issues. Why might this be the case?

9. Discuss the assertion that "hard-ball tactics" are sometimes needed if individuals wish to be effective in the political process.

10. Discuss some ethical considerations that "whistle-blowers" confront when they attack ill-considered policies or practices of specific agencies.

11. Discuss the assertion that "some limits on the discretion or autonomy of professional staff are needed, but they should not exceed a threshold that threatens the effectiveness of services or the rights of staff."

12. In many legislative and bureaucratic settings issues like social justice and equality often receive scant attention when policies are devised. Discuss why this might be the case and whether social workers can assume an advocacy posture with respect to them.

SUGGESTED READINGS

Understanding Moral Reasoning: Utilitarian Approaches

Jeremy Bentham, *An Introduction to the Principles of Morals and Legislation* (London: Athlone Press, 1970).

Understanding Moral Reasoning: Deontological Approaches

Robert Veatch, *A Theory of Medical Ethics* (New York: Basic Books, 1981).

Understanding Moral Reasoning: Intuitionist Approaches

J. L. Mackie, *Ethics: Inventing Right and Wrong* (London: Penguin Books, 1977).

Exploring Ethical Issues in Politics

Chauncey Alexander, "Professional Social Workers and Political Responsibility," in Maryann Mahaffey and John Hanks, eds., *Practical Politics: Social Workers and Political Response* (Washington, D.C.: National Association of Social Workers, 1982), pp. 22–25.

George Brager, Harry Specht, and James Torczyner, *Community Organizing*, 2nd ed. (New York: Columbia University Press), pp. 316–339.

Joel Fleishman, "Self-Interest and Political Integrity," in Joel Fleishman, Lance Liebman, and Mark Moore, eds., *Public Duties: The Moral Obligations of Government Officials* (Cambridge, Mass.: Harvard University Press, 1981), pp. 52–92.

Exploring Ethical Issues in the Implementation of Policy

Sissela Bok, "Blowing the Whistle," in Fleishman, Liebman, and Moore, eds., *Public Duties*, pp. 204–220.

Robert Goodin, *Reasons for Welfare: The Political Theory of the Welfare State* (Princeton, N.J.: Princeton University Press, 1988), pp. 184–223.

Charles Levy, *Guide to Ethical Decisions and Actions for Social Service Administrators: A Handbook for Managerial Personnel* (New York: Haworth Press, 1982).

Donald Warwick, "The Ethics of Administrative Discretion," in Fleishman, Liebman, and Moore, eds., *Public Duties*, pp. 93–127.

Exploring Ethical Issues in Policy Analysis and Assessment

Peter Brown, "Assessing Officials," in Fleishman, Liebman, and Moore, eds., *Public Duties*, pp. 289–303.

Ruth Hanft, "Use of Social Science Data for Policy Analysis and Policymaking," in Daniel Callahan and Bruce Jennings, eds., *Ethics, the Social Sciences, and Policy* (New York: Plenum Press, 1983), pp. 213–248.

Martin Rein, "Value-Critical Policy Analysis" in Callahan and Jennings, eds., *Ethics, the Social Sciences, and Policy Analysis*, pp. 96–100.

Charles Wolf, "Ethics and Policy Analysis," in Fleishman, Liebman, and Moore, eds., *Public Duties*, pp. 131–141.

Exploring Ethical Issues That Confront Social Workers

Frank Loewenberg and Ralph Dolgoff, *Ethical Decisions for Social Work Practice*, 3rd ed. (Itasca, Ill.: F.E. Peacock, 1988).

Frederic Reamer, *Ethical Dilemmas in Social Service* (New York: Columbia University Press, 1982).

Margaret Rhodes, *Ethical Dilemmas in Social Work Practice* (Boston: Routledge and Kegan Paul, 1986).

Exploring Ethical Issues about the Nature of "The Good Society"

John Baker, *Arguing for Equality* (London: Verso, 1987).

Goodin, *Reasons for Welfare*, pp. 227–359.

John Rawls, *A Theory of Justice* (Cambridge, Mass.: Harvard University Press, 1971).

NOTES

1. Benjamin Freedman, *A Moral Theory of Consent* (Hastings-on-Hudson, N.Y.: Hastings Center Report, 1975).

2. Frederic Reamer, *Ethical Dilemmas in Social Service* (New York: Columbia University Press, 1982), p. 3.

3. Margaret Rhodes, *Ethical Dilemmas in Social Work Practice* (Boston: Routledge and Kegan Paul, 1986), p. xii.

4. Reamer, *Ethical Dilemmas in Social Service*, p. 3.

5. Robert Veatch, *A Theory of Medical Ethics* (New York: Basic Books, 1981), pp. 79–107.

6. See J. L. Mackie, *Ethics: Inventing Right and Wrong* (London: Penguin Books, 1977), pp. 107–115.

7. See Douglas Yates, "Hard Choices: Justifying Bureaucratic Decisions," in Joel Fleishman, Lance Liebman, and Mark Moore, eds., *Public Duties: The Moral Obligations of Government Officials* (Cambridge, Mass.: Harvard University Press, 1981), p. 38.

8. David Price, "Assessing Policy: Conceptual Points of Departure," in Fleishman, Liebman, and Moore, eds., *Public Duties*, pp. 151–155.

9. John Rawls, *A Theory of Justice* (Cambridge, Mass.: Harvard University Press, 1971).

10. See Charles Wolf, "Ethics and Policy Analysis," in Fleishman, Liebman, and Moore, eds., *Public Duties*, pp. 133–137.

11. Jeremy Bentham, *An Introduction to the Principles of Morals and Legislation* (London: Athlone Press, 1970).

12. Mackie, *Ethics*, pp. 125–148.

13. For a utilitarian approach to medical ethics, see Howard Brody, *Ethical Decisions in Medicine* (Boston: Little, Brown, 1976). For a critique of the use of utilitarian reasoning in medical ethics, see Veatch, *A Theory of Medical Ethics*, pp. 170–176.

14. For an overview of controversy about euthanasia, see U.S. President's Commission for the Study of Ethical Problems in Medicine and Biomedical and Behavioral Research, *Deciding to Forego Life-Sustaining Treatment* (Washington, D.C.: Government Printing Office, 1983), pp. 65–89.

15. Mark Moore, "Realms of Obligation and Virtue," in Fleishman, Liebman, and Moore, eds., *Public Duties*, pp. 14–17.

16. Ibid., pp. 14–17.

17. Ibid., pp. 16–17. Also see Mackie, *Ethics*, pp. 126–129.

18. Mackie, *Ethics*, pp. 129–134.

19. Veatch, *Theory of Medical Ethics*, p. 174.

20. Robert Binstock, "The Aged as Scapegoat," *Gerontologist*, 23 (April 1983): 136–143.

21. Veatch, *Theory of Medical Ethics*, pp. 27–78.

22. Rawls, *Theory of Justice*.

23. Ibid., pp. 12, 19, 136–142.

24. Ibid., pp. 60–65.

25. Veatch, *Theory of Medical Ethics*, pp. 234–237.

26. Freedman, "A Moral Theory of Consent."

27. Mackie, *Ethics*, pp. 151–168.

28. Ibid., pp. 182–184.

29. Ibid., pp. 36–38.

30. Carol Weiss, "Ideology, Interests, and Information: The Basis of Policy Positions," in Daniel Callahan and Bruce Jennings, eds., *Ethics, the Social Sciences, and Policy Analysis* (New York: Plenum Press, 1983), pp. 213–248.

31. Robert Heilbroner, *The Worldly Philosophers* (New York: Simon and Schuster, 1968), pp. 38–67.

32. Joel Fleishman, "Self-Interest and Political Integrity," in Fleishman, Liebman, and Moore, eds., *Public Duties*, pp. 56–61.

33. Mackie, *Ethics*, pp. 107–114.

34. Fleishman, "Self-Interest and Political Integrity," pp. 56–66.

35. Bruce Jansson, *The Reluctant Welfare State: A History of American Social Welfare Policies* (Belmont, Ca.: Wadsworth Publishing Co., 1988), pp. 52–53.

36. See Charles Levy, *Guide to Ethical Decisions and Actions for Social Service Administrators: A Handbook for Managerial Personnel* (New York: Haworth Press, 1982), pp. 17–24.

37. Ibid., pp. 47–48.

38. Ronald Munson, *Intervention and Reflection: Basic Issues in Medical Ethics* (Belmont, Ca.: Wadsworth Publishing Co., 1988), pp. 165–193.

39. Yates, "Hard Choices," pp. 32–37.

40. Ibid., pp. 32–37. Also see Reamer, *Ethical Dilemmas*, pp. 23–26, 254–257.

41. Peter Brown, "Assessing Officials," in Fleishman, Liebman, and Moore, eds., *Public Duties*, pp. 289–303. Also see Rhodes, *Ethical Dilemmas*, p. 19; and Moore, "Realms of Obligation and Virtue," pp. 289–303.

42. Moore, "Realms of Obligation and Virtue," p. 19.

43. Brown, "Assessing Officials," pp. 289–303.

44. See Moore, "Realms of Obligation and Virtue," p. 29, and Veatch, *Theory of Medical Ethics*, pp. 79–107.

45. Veatch, *Theory of Medical Ethics*, pp. 291–305.

46. Ibid., pp. 243–249. Also see Price, "Assessing Policy," pp. 142–172.

47. See U.S., Presidents Commission, *Deciding to Forego*, pp. 65–89.

48. Price, "Assessing Policy," pp. 142–172.

49. Fleishman, "Self-Interest and Political Integrity," pp. 52–92.

50. Veatch, *Theory of Medical Ethics*, p. 198.

51. See J. Gay Williams, "The Wrongfulness of Euthanasia," in Munson, *Reflections and Interventions*, pp. 168–171.

52. U.S., President's Commission, *Deciding to Forego*, pp. 32–41.

53. Veatch, *Theory of Medical Ethics*, pp. 198, 329.

54. Chauncey Alexander, "Professional Social Workers and Political Responsibility," in Maryann Mahaffey and John Hanks, eds., *Practical Politics: Social Workers and Political Response* (Washington, D.C.: National Association of Social Workers, 1982), pp. 22–25. Also see Jack Rothman, John Erlich, and Joseph Teresa, *Promoting Change in Organizations and Communities* (New York: John Wiley and Sons, 1976), pp. 17–19.

55. See the Code of Ethics of the National Association of Social Workers in Levy, *Guide to Ethical Decisions*, p. 153.

56. Ruth Hanft, "Use of Social Science Data for Policy Analysis and Policymaking," in Callahan and Jennings, eds., *Ethics, the Social Sciences, and Policy Analysis*, pp. 249–291.

57. Moore, "Realms of Obligation and Virtue," pp. 21–26.

58. Yates, "Hard Choices," pp. 40–46.

59. See George Brager, Harry Specht, and James Torczyner, *Community Organizing* (New York: Columbia University Press, 1987), p. 318.

60. Ibid., p. 318. Also see Eugene Bardach, *The Skill Factor in Politics* (Berkeley, Ca.: University of California Press, 1972), pp. 237–238.

61. Bardach, *Skill Factor in Politics*, pp. 235–237.

62. Ibid., pp. 237–238.

63. Fleishman, "Self-Interest and Political Integrity," pp. 52–92.

64. Ibid.

65. See Brager, Specht, and Torczyner, *Community Organizing,* pp. 316–336.

66. See Rothman, Erlich, and Teresa, *Promoting Innovation and Change,* pp. 17–19.

67. Wolf, "Ethics and Policy Analysis," pp. 131–141. Also see Bruce Jansson, "Combining Advocacy and Technical Skills: The Interaction of Politics and Numbers, *Administration in Social Work* (forthcoming Summer 1990).

68. Martin Rein, "Value-Critical Policy Analysis," in Callahan and Jennings, eds., *Ethics, the Social Sciences, and Policy Analysis,* pp. 96–100.

69. Katherine Briar and Scott Briar, "Clinical Social Work and Public Policies," in Mahaffey and Hanks, eds., *Practical Politics,* pp. 45–54.

70. Wolf, "Ethics and Policy Analysis," pp. 131–141.

71. Ibid., pp. 133–137.

72. John Baker, *Arguing for Equality* (London: Verso Press, 1987), pp. 3–13.

73. Ibid. Also see Wolf, "Ethics and Policy Analysis," pp. 133–137.

74. Jansson, *Reluctant Welfare State,* pp. 108–109.

75. Levy, *Guide to Ethical Decisions,* pp. 36–41.

76. Ibid., pp. 48–51.

77. Sissela Bok, "Blowing the Whistle," in Fleishman, Liebman, and Moore, eds., *Public Duties,* p. 211.

78. Ibid., pp. 210–215.

79. Levy, *Guide to Ethical Decisions,* pp. 138–139.

80. Frank Loewenberg and Ralph Dolgoff, *Ethical Decisions for Social Work Practice,* 3rd ed. (Itasca, Ill.: F.E. Peacock, 1988), pp. 84–87.

81. Levy, *Guide to Ethical Decisions,* pp. 36–41.

82. Robert Goodin, *Reasons for Welfare* (Princeton, N.J.: Princeton University Press, 1988), pp. 184–228.

83. Ibid.

84. David Mechanic, "The Sociology of Organizations," in Saul Feldman, ed., *Administration in Mental Health* (Springfield, Ill.: Charles C Thomas, 1980), pp. 174–181, 187–190.

85. Ibid., p. 192. Also see Rhodes, *Ethical Dilemmas,* pp. 142–144.

86. David Warwich, "The Ethics of Administrative Discretion," in Fleishman, Liebman, and Moore, eds., *Public Duties,* pp. 108–111.

PART IV

∎

Social Welfare Policy
in Action:
A Framework and Six
Policy-Practice Tasks

In Chapters Nine and Ten, we move from discussion of the four policy skills to discussion of social welfare policy in action. We provide a framework of social welfare policy in action in Chapter Nine that builds on the framework of policy deliberations that was presented at the end of Chapter One. This framework depicts six policy-practice tasks, namely, agenda building, problem defining, proposal writing, policy enacting, policy implementing, and policy assessing. This framework makes clear what our discussion in Chapters Two through Eight implied; policies are ultimately fashioned not by abstract forces but by the actions and behaviors of specific persons in specific settings.

Before we can turn to the way policy practitioners undertake or engage in these tasks, however, we have to examine the characteristics and orientations of specific policy practitioners, which is the subject of Chapter Nine. We examine their values and how various situational factors influence them, as well as the tactics of other participants. We ask whether the concept *style*, which is used extensively to discuss alternative approaches to direct-service and administrative practice, can be used to describe alternative approaches to policy practice.

In Chapter Ten, we analyze how policy practitioners actually engage in the practice of policy. We examine how they develop overarching strategy, which we call a *game plan*. We ask how they change or adapt their game plan to the changing realities that they encounter and how they implement their game plans. We explore methods of evaluating the policy practice of specific persons in specific situations. A policy-practice case, which is drawn from Edward Banfield's book, *Political Influence*, is used to illustrate the policy-practice framework.

To illustrate concepts in Chapters Nine and Ten, as well as to review concepts from Chapters Two through Eight, we provide an extended policy-practice case in Chapter Eleven. The case, which was developed by interviews with many of its participants and by extensive use of Congressional documents and secondary sources, examines the evolution of child development and daycare legislation in the Congress from 1967 to 1989. The case illustrates how policy practitioners use analytic, political, interactional, and value-clarification skills; how they engage in agenda-building, problem-defining, proposal-making, policy-enacting, policy-implementing, and policy-assessing tasks; and how they use various skills in tandem to accomplish the policy tasks.

CHAPTER 9

■

The Policy Practitioner in Action

Analytic, political, interactional, and value-clarification skills constitute the four building blocks of policy practice. Were we to end our discussion of policy-making with the four skills, however, we might fail to ask some broader and important questions. How do policy practitioners combine the four skills? How do policy practitioners develop an overarching strategy or game plan and modify it as events and circumstances change? How do we evaluate the work of policy practitioners?

Before we can address these questions in the next chapter, however, we need to examine some factors that shape the policy practice of specific persons. We examine various personal and situational factors in this chapter, as well as the effects of the actions and strategies of other participants. In this and the next chapter, we draw heavily on concepts that were discussed in preceding chapters; indeed, these two chapters can be viewed as ones that integrate concepts from preceding chapters and that link them to the policy practice of specific persons.

REVIEWING "THE BIG PICTURE"

Recall that a framework, which was discussed in the concluding section of Chapter One, provides an overview of the policy-making process (Figure 1.1). Policy-making, we argue, occurs in a context that includes political, economic, technical, interactional, and value components. These realities profoundly shape the actions and deliberations of persons who participate in the policy-making process.

Policy Tasks

The framework in Chapter One describes policy deliberations, which include contextual factors, a presenting policy issue, the processing of the issue, enactments, and the implementation and assessment of policies. Because we wish to examine the work of specific policy practitioners in this and the next chapter, we revise that framework to include specific and recurring tasks that correspond to various facets of policy deliberations (Figure 9.1) The term *policy task* describes the actions of policy practitioners during the various phases of policy deliberations.[1]

The **agenda-building task** describes the work of policy practitioners as they try to shape or influence the selection and placement of policy problems or issues on the agendas of decision makers. Agenda building is an important kind of power of policy practitioners; as they succeed in placing specific issues, problems, and solutions on the agendas of decision makers, they enhance their effectiveness by shaping the content and outcomes of policy deliberations. Powerful presidents, whether liberal or conservative, shape the agendas of Congress, for example, whereas weaker ones lack this critical ability. Policy practitioners in social agencies are sometimes able to project specific issues or problems to the forefront of policy deliberations by making timely presentations, discussing them with other staff, or sensitizing highly placed officials.

The **problem-defining task** describes the work of policy practitioners as

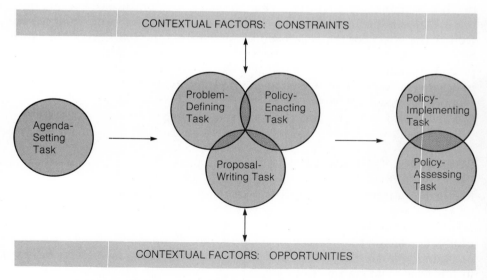

Figure 9.1   Policy Tasks During the Course of Policy Deliberations

they contribute to the analysis of the definitions, causes, nature, and prevalence of specific policy problems. We noted in Chapter Two, for example, that policymakers sometimes use theory and research that are drawn from the social sciences, economics, and medicine to inform their policy choices. Policy practitioners engage in the problem-defining task whenever they contribute to formulations of the causes, prevalence, and definitions of specific social problems.

The **proposal-writing task** describes the work of policy practitioners as they develop policy solutions to specific problems. As we noted in Chapters Three and Four, this work often requires them to examine an array of policy options, to identify and to weight criteria, and to select those policies that obtain relatively high scores or evaluations. Proposals can be srelatively ambitious ones, such as a proposed piece of legislation, or can involve relatively modest and incremental changes in existing policies.

The **policy-enacting task** describes the work of policy practitioners as they try to secure the enactment of specific policies. We noted in Chapters Five and Six that policy practitioners possess various kinds of power resources and that they fashion strategy by identifying and using their power resources to increase the likelihood of obtaining their policy preferences.

As we note in Chapters Twelve and Thirteen, policy practitioners go "beyond policy" in the wake of policy enactment when they undertake **policy-implementing** and **policy-assessing tasks**. If policy practitioners wish enacted policies to be realized in the real world, they have to identify and address barriers, or obstacles, to their implementation. Because this work requires knowledge about and use of concepts from administration and organizational theory, the implementation role requires policy practitioners to develop competencies that extend beyond the traditional boundaries of social welfare policy. In similar fashion, they have to couple their knowledge of policy with the disciplines of research and program evaluation when they assume the policy-assessing task. We noted in Chapter Four that policy practitioners often try to select meritorious policies during the proposal-writing stage, based on available information and their best guesses. But these predictions of the likely effectiveness of policies are always hazardous because the policies have not yet been implemented. Indeed, as we discuss in Chapter Twelve, many things can go wrong "twixt the lip and the cup." When assessing the effectiveness of realized or implemented policies, policy practitioners often obtain data to examine the performance of specific policies. Assessing policies can present daunting methodological and interpretative problems, but it nonetheless can provide information to revise those policies—or various details of their implementation—to enhance their effectiveness.

When we separately discuss these various policy tasks, we risk suggesting that they are separate and easily distinguishable. In fact, persons often assume several of the roles at the same time as several examples suggest.

Legislators undertake the policy-enacting task *as* they engage in the proposal-writing task when they often insert provisions in their proposals that will enhance their prospects of enactment. They couple the problem-defining task with the proposal-writing task when they modify a proposal to make it address the basic causes of a social problem or to make its services relevant to the needs of a specific segment of the population.

Moreover, policy practitioners rarely progress between the various tasks in a sequential and predictable fashion. Legislators may draft a proposal before devoting much time to defining the presenting social problem—but then revise the proposal at a subsequent point in response to comments from a social scientist who injects new perspectives at a legislative committee hearing. In this case, they start their policy practice with the proposal-writing task and then revert to the problem-defining task and then return to the proposal-writing task. In similar fashion, a legislator may attempt to rally support for a vague and ill-defined proposal (the policy-enacting task) only to return to problem-defining and proposal-writing tasks at a later time. Of course, this seemingly chaotic approach to policy-making runs counter to the maxims of some policy analysts who favor a sequential process that progresses from problem-defining to proposal-writing to policy-enacting tasks, but events in the real world often do not correspond to any orderly approach.

To underscore the fluid nature of policy-making and to underscore relationships between the different phases or stages of the policy-making process, we use interlocking circles in the center of Figure 9.1 to characterize relationships between the various roles.

The Context

A framework that describes the context and the phases of policy-making, such as the one in Figure 9.1, is useful because it provides an overview of contextual factors and policy deliberations. Indeed, it encourages us to ask difficult questions about the nature of policy-making in specific situations and in general terms. We can ask, for example, whether and when contextual political and economic forces determine the course and outcomes of policy deliberations. In some cases, for example, powerful interests possess such resources and clout that they can singlehandedly shape the outcomes of deliberations about specific issues. The National Rifle Association, for example, has such resources that it has repeatedly stymied efforts to develop controls on the possession of guns, including handguns and rapid-fire "assault weapons." Interest groups with large constituencies and major economic resources have developed extraordinary power by using mass mailing, marketing, campaign underwriting, and vote-counting technology—whether corporate ones like the American Association of Automobile Dealers or mass-membership ones like the American Association of Retired Persons.[2] With respect to other issues, however, powerful external interests do not exist or are locked in opposition to one another. In the case of strategies to cut costs of the Medicare Program by placing ceilings on physicians' fees, for example, the American Medical Association, which opposes this policy, contends with pressures from conservatives, some employers, and some unions that favor the policy to cut costs of the Medicare Program.[3] Even these few examples suggest then that a variable political and economic context exists in policy-making arenas. It provides policymakers with considerable latitude in some situations and imposes remarkable and constraining pressure on them in others.

Moreover, the context is an *evolving* one that shifts and changes during the course of time, both in response to external events and in response to policy deliberations themselves. As we shall discuss in Chapter Eleven, for example, proposals to enact major federal day-care programs would have faced certain defeat in the 1960s because few interest groups or citizens believed that women should work. By 1988, however, a determined group of children's advocates almost secured the enactment of a major daycare program. These long-term changes in the nature of the political and economic context were promoted by fundamental changes in economic and social patterns in the broader society, such as (in the case of daycare) the remarkable growth in the numbers of employed women. But short-term changes in contextual factors can also occur. As persons and interests debate issues and develop policy proposals, they change the context by altering the opinions of specific groups, drawing new groups who had been on the sidelines into the debate, or outmaneuvering potential opponents of a measure. In the extended case example of child development legislation in Chapter Eleven, for example, its advocates were able to exclude conservative politicians and interest groups from the deliberations during much of the policy delibera-tions—a tactic that led to a far more favorable context for the legislation than exists for many social reforms. But this favorable context became much bleaker when conservative politicians finally began to exert massive pressure on the incumbent president to oppose the child development legislation. Such volatility in the political context of policy deliberations is not uncommon because participants in policy-making can sometimes shape the context to make it more favorable to their proposals.

Our policy framework also poses interesting questions about relation-ships between phases, or tasks, within the policy deliberations. The way an issue is defined at the outset of deliberations (see the agenda-building and problem-defining tasks) often shapes the perceptions and choices of persons during the ensuing deliberations. Many politicians were concerned in 1987, for example, with the large enrollment in the AFDC program. To them, "welfare reform" *meant* reductions in the size of the rolls. This method of framing the issue led them to emphasize those kinds of policy solutions during the remaining phases of the policy deliberations that would reduce the size of the rolls, such as the use of work requirements and the provision of training programs. Had the welfare-reform issue been defined differently at the outset, however, policymakers might have emphasized different issues. Assume, for example, that legislators had focused on the "relative poverty of unskilled and single women with one or more children in their households." Had the issue been defined in these economic terms, legislators might have focused on methods of raising the income of women by increasing the minimum wage, increasing tax incentives to employers who hire them, decreasing Social Security payroll deductions of low-paid workers, and increasing the level of AFDC benefits for those women who remained on the rolls.[4] (None of these solutions were emphasized in the final welfare-reform package that was signed into law by President Reagan in 1988.)

In similar fashion, activities in other phases in the policy-making framework influence activities, events, and outcomes in other phases. The proposal-writing and policy-implementing phases are closely related, for example. When policymakers establish lofty goals but allocate relatively few resources in the proposal-writing phase, for example, they decrease the likelihood that their proposals will be effectively implemented during the implementation phase.[5]

POLICY TASKS AND POLICY SKILLS: CHALLENGES AND DILEMMAS

We discussed analytic, political, interactional, and value-clarification skills in Chapters Two through Eight—and we have discussed agenda-building, problem-defining, proposal-writing, policy-enacting, policy-implementing, and policy-assessing tasks in this chapter. Were we to stop our discussion at this point, some readers might wonder whether the four policy skills and the six policy tasks are related.

Policy skills and policy tasks are entwined and meshed during policy practice. Policy practitioners encounter specific analytic, political, interactional, and value-clarification challenges when they undertake the various policy tasks as succeeding discussion suggests. (We reserve discussion of policy-implementing and policy-assessing tasks until Chapters Twelve and Thirteen.)

The Agenda-Building Task

People in both agency and legislative settings can choose to address an infinite number of issues or problems, as the thousands of bills that are drafted each year in each of numerous legislatures across the nation suggest. Since most problems and issues are consigned to outbaskets, only a relatively few number of issues receive serious attention by being placed upon the agendas of legislative committees—or before the boards or committees of agencies.

Policy practitioners encounter analytic, political, interactional, and value-based challenges when they try to secure an advantaged position for specific issues or problems in agency and legislative settings.[6] Their analytic challenge is to provide technical information that convinces decision makers that their problem or issue is sufficiently important to deserve serious attention. They can conduct research—or cite research—to provide evidence that a specific problem or issue is a serious one, as our discussion in Chapter Two suggests. They can try to demonstrate that a specific problem, such as alcoholism, has sufficiently serious effects or impacts upon society that it demands attention. Policy practitioners often use trend data that suggest that a specific problem is becoming more serious with the passage of time—a tactic that suggests that inaction will result in even greater costs in the future.

Indeed, policy practitioners often use their analytic skills to create the impression that a crisis or emergency exists. When current data suggest that a problem is currently a serious one and when trend data suggest that it has become markedly more serious, decision makers are particularly likely to believe that it demands immediate attention.[7]

Policy practitioners use their political skills to try to convince decision makers that specific problems or issues are associated with a combination of political threats and opportunities. People believe a political threat exists when they fear that specific positions or actions will lead to political losses. For example, in 1989 when seeking to convince politicians of both political parties that they should *not* enact legislation within states to restrict the rights of women to obtain abortions, the National Organization for Women threatened to develop a new political party devoted to the needs of women. By using this tactic, feminists hoped to convince establishment politicians that they risked massive defections of female voters from their parties if they supported policies to restrict access to abortions. Decision makers perceive opportunities exist to attract *new* supporters by taking certain positions or actions. In the case of the Republican Party, for example, black leaders have sometimes contended that it could wrest some blacks from the Democratic Party if its leaders would take certain positions on civil rights and economic matters. Indeed, policy practitioners often attempt to create the impression that specific issues are associated with a combination of threats and opportunities to magnify the political stakes that decision makers attach to them.

Policy practitioners can convey the political importance of specific issues or problems to decision makers in many ways. They can ask the leaders of important groups and factions to attest to the significance of specific issues or problems. They can point to analogous situations to demonstrate potential political threats or opportunities; a policy practitioner might tell a decision maker, for example, that someone else obtained considerable political advantage by championing a similar issue on a prior occasion—or experienced important political losses by avoiding it. Once they have convinced a specific decision maker to commit to an issue or problem, they can try to convince others that they will "miss the boat if they fail to jump on board in the early stages."

Effective policy practitioners are skilled in selecting propitious moments for injecting specific issues into political deliberations. John Kingdon suggests that "windows of opportunity" exist when background factors are particularly favorable.[8] Perhaps a particularly scandalous condition has just been publicized, such as the neglect or abuse of a victim of Alzheimer's disease. Perhaps a newly elected city mayor, whose mother is a victim of Alzheimer's disease, is sympathetic to funding a new initiative. Perhaps a research report has just been released that documents the dearth of services to families of victims with Alzheimer's disease.

Policy practitioners use various interactional skills to promote specific issues. They often hope to propel specific issues into the consciousness of decision makers by obtaining a privileged position for them in policy deliberation. Perhaps the leader of a committee can be persuaded to place a specific issue or problem onto the agenda of his or her committee at a forthcoming meeting. Perhaps the executive of an agency can be persuaded to form a task force to examine a specific issue or problem. Perhaps the aide to an influential legislator will agree to discuss a specific issue with a highly placed member of a legislative committee so that a specific bill will be given preferential treatment in the committee's deliberations.

To secure a privileged position for specific issues, then, policy practitioners need to use a range of persuasive, group process, and credibility-enhancing strategies. In personal discussions, they need to convince others that an issue is relevant to their beliefs, values, and ideology, or that important political threats or opportunities exist, or that credible people are interested in their issue.

Policy practitioners confront value or normative issues when they seek a preferred position for specific issues or problems in policy deliberations. We discussed the question of priorities in Chapter Eight; when policy practitioners inject a specific issue into deliberations, they need to reconsider their priorities since they risk preempting other, more important issues. To increase the prominence of an issue, policy practitioners sometimes inflate figures, exaggerate the costs or negative impacts of a problem on the broader society, or magnify the political threats or opportunities. As we discussed in Chapter Eight, these tactics pose ethical issues that need to be considered. In other cases, policy practitioners may display undue caution by avoiding important issues that are relatively unpopular. In such cases, they need to decide whether their political caution leads them to ignore important policy issues that have significant consequences for oppressed or unpopular groups.

The Problem-Defining Task

In Chapter Two, we discussed how people often construct typologies or classifications of social problems. With reference to the problem of substance abuse, we also discussed alternative paradigms, such as ecological ones, that are used to examine the causes of problems. These analytic tools, when coupled with empirical research, are used to develop definitions of specific problems during the problem-defining task.

Policy practitioners also encounter the political challenge during the problem-defining task of "framing" specific issues so that they attract the attention of decision makers.[9] While technical or analytic people are accustomed to relatively complex discussions of issues and proposals, many decision makers want relatively understandable—even short-hand—presentations of problems and proposals. Policy practitioners need to develop words, titles, and explanations that are both comprehensible to decision makers and palatable or attractive to them. We have noted, for example, that advocates of reforms of the AFDC program in 1987 and 1988 emphasized "family support" rather than "welfare reform" to make their measure more acceptable to conservative politicians, who traditionally oppose those welfare reforms that are not relatively punitive in nature. (They argued that the measure would strengthen welfare families by helping the mothers to become more competitive in labor markets.) Because welfare programs are often viewed as enticing people to avoid work, the supporters of the legislation contended that it would prevent welfare by providing training and education for mothers, as well as day care for their children. To undermine the notion that social reforms necessarily increase the power of Washington bureaucrats, the supporters of the legislation emphasized its role in funding innovative programs of states and local units of government. In framing the problem and their legislation, then, the advocates of this legislation selected symbols or themes of children, families, prevention, and local innovation—and they chose these words because they would be attractive to a broad spectrum of politicians, including many legislators who would usually oppose projects to help AFDC women.[10]

Policy practitioners also need interactional skills to perform the problem-defining task. They often need to link their problem-defining work to the culture or mission of specific organizations or settings. When we discussed techniques for enhancing personal credibility in Chapter Seven, for example, we noted how people often select problems or issues that are likely to be perceived as relevant to the mission or objectives of organizations. For example, a hospital social worker who works in a hospital that wants to dramatically expand its services to older persons might identify some service needs of this population as the basis for a proposal. In similar fashion, policy practitioners often select paradigms or conceptions of social problems that are consonant with the mission and culture of specific settings. For example, someone who works in a medical setting could not ignore the prevailing focus on physiological or biological issues while seeking to expand or supplement this focus with ecological, public health, or other paradigms.[11]

Interactional skills are needed to develop and to tap into specific networks when undertaking the agenda-building and the problem-defining tasks. Policy practitioners often want to develop support for problems and issues even before they develop the proposals or programs, so they need to be conversant with the decision makers and staff who form the leader corps in specific settings. A division of labor exists in many settings with respect to the defining of issues; certain people are widely perceived to possess expertise and credibility with certain issues but possess negligible roles with respect to others. This division of labor is most obvious in legislative settings where the chairs and members of committees become known for their expertise in specific issues. While less formalized, a similar division of labor exists in some agencies. Policy practitioners need to use their interactional skills to convince officials, whose expertise and reputation are germane to a specific issue, to assume leadership roles in specific reforms.

To the extent a coalition is formed to promote action on an issue, policy practitioners need to develop some agreements about terms, definitions, and paradigms that members will use when discussing the issue with decision makers. When testifying on child welfare and welfare reform issues in 1980 and 1988, the leaders of various advocacy and professional groups developed common themes that they emphasized in their testimony to Congressional committees. We have noted, for example, that proponents of welfare reform legislation rarely referred to it as "welfare reform" but used terms, instead, like "family support," "prevention," "employment and training," and "children." These common themes in their testimony did not appear accidentally but emerged in the course of numerous meetings of the members of the coalition that was developed to promote the legislation.[12]

Value-clarification skills are needed by policy practitioners to address a number of issues. To what extent should they define and frame problems or issues to accommodate the preferences of decision makers, the culture, or the mission of specific organizations—even when those preferences pose certain risks? Indeed, some critics of the welfare reform legislation that was enacted in 1988 concluded that reformers had "sold out" to conservatives and had neglected important economic needs of welfare recipients in favor of relatively paltry training programs.[13]

The Proposal-Writing Task

In Chapter Four we discussed the analytic skills people need when they construct proposals. There we surveyed conceptual or theoretical, policy-selection, and logistical zones of proposals (see Figure 4.2). We noted, as well, how policy practitioners calculate trade-offs in order to select a preferred policy from an array of competing ones; they identify and weigh criteria, score or rank competing options, and select the option that receives the highest score.

Were proposal writing entirely an analytic or technical matter, decision makers would hire experts, give them specific instructions, and use the finished product in policy deliberations. Since political realities usually intrude, however, policy practitioners need political skills to develop proposals. Many policies are shaped during an extended process of deliberations when various amendments are made. As Ron Dear and Rino Patti note, the fate of legislation often hinges upon the willingness of its advocates to accept amendments to it; they may alter the kinds of policies that were discussed in Chapter Three, such as the title of a program, administrative details, the kinds of services it offers, its eligibility standards, the kinds of agencies that can deliver its services, and the standards that govern the kinds of staff that provide its services.[14] Moreover, amendments may be advanced to modify the magnitude of a program, such as decreasing its size.

Policy practitioners use political and value-clarification skills to decide when to accept and oppose specific amendments. Friendly amendments are offered by people who basically favor a proposal but wish to suggest relatively technical changes to improve or enhance its political prospects. Their task is more difficult when hostile amendments are advanced to scuttle or to fundamentally alter their proposal. Someone may wish to slash the size of their proposal so profoundly that it no longer remains viable. Or opponents may try to delete or modify certain standards, such as ones that govern the qualifications of staff. When faced with hostile amendments, the proponents of a proposal must decide whether the political advantages of specific amendments compensate for the substantive costs that they impose. Of course, these kinds of calculations are often complex; opposition to a hostile amendment may appear meritorious on value grounds, but someone may regret opposing an amendment if this action eventually contributes to the defeat of their proposal.

As we discussed in Chapter Four, policy practitioners often use political and value-clarification skills to decide whether to leave certain issues relatively unresolved or vague in a proposal. Political considerations, such as believing that vagueness reduces controversy and conflict, sometimes impel them *not* to define with precision the content of a proposal. Vagueness poses threats of its own, however. When proposals are vague, their implementors have considerable latitude in filling in the gaps after the policies have been enacted. If policy practitioners believe implementors are likely to possess different perspectives than their own, they are likely to want "all the i's dotted and t's crossed" in their proposals in hopes of limiting the discretion of the implementors.

Interactional skills are needed at many points during the process of developing proposals. Committees sometimes assume a central position in fashioning proposals, whether in legislative or agency settings. Personal discussions are often needed with friends and foes of a proposal to orchestrate a succession of friendly amendments and to soften or avert hostile amendments. Coalitions often assume a prominent role in the proposal-making process. For example, they may mobilize opposition to hostile amendments, or they may oppose efforts to make a proposal excessively vague, at least with respect to those matters that they deem to be particularly important.

Value-clarification skills are needed to preserve the integrity of proposals in the face of efforts to amend them. People have to decide at what point amendments or concessions violate their policy preferences so extensively that they cannot accede to them.

The Policy-Enacting Task

Policy practitioners employ analytic skills when developing political strategy. They develop force-field analyses at periodic intervals, identify specific power resources that they (or their allies) possess, and evolve a coherent political strategy. As we discussed in Chapter Five, policy practitioners often compare the relative merits of competing political strategies before they select one.

Policy practitioners use their political skills during the policy-enacting task to implement their political strategy. As we discussed in Chapter Four, power resources are exercised in transactional relationships; the wielders of power must use those person-to-person, parliamentary, process, substantive, and other power resources sufficiently skillfully that other people modify their positions and actions to accede to their wishes. To the extent they exercise their power through intermediaries, they have to convince other people to intercede for them in specific situations.

Policy practitioners use a range of interactional skills during the political process. They use various tactics to develop and maintain their credibility with decision makers, such as including in their coalition respected leaders and opinion-setters. They need access to people who possess inside information such as possible parliamentary strategy and the positions of opponents. They use their persuasive skills to win converts and to keep opponents on the defensive. Group skills are needed to determine what strategies to use to build momentum behind a policy and to avoid excessive discord within a coalition.

In Chapter Eight, we discussed some ethical issues that policy practitioners confront during the political process. They have to decide when tactics, such as dishonesty, are ill-advised or when are they necessary to defeat a well-organized opposition that resorts to its own "hard-ball" politics. It is difficult to establish inflexible rules to make these ethical choices because situational realities, such as the tactics of opponents, often influence our ethical judgments. Moreover, tactics often involve not "all-bad" options, such as blatant lying, but "partly-bad" options, such as not divulging sensitive information to the opponents of a proposal.

FACTORS THAT INFLUENCE HOW POLICY PRACTITIONERS ENGAGE IN POLICY PRACTICE

We have discussed a policy-making framework as well as some challenges that policy practitioners encounter when they use their policy skills to accomplish the six policy tasks. Our discussion of these challenges suggests, however, that no single or right method of policy practice exists. Difficult choices must sometimes be made as policy practitioners use their analytic, political, interactional, and value-clarification skills in the give-and-take of policy deliberations and in a sometimes volatile policy context.

To understand the way policy practitioners engage in their work, we need to examine some personal and stylistic factors that shape their work as well as orientations toward the issue that is contested. We also need to examine some factors, such as organizational and peer-group realities, as well as the policy deliberations themselves, that shape their work. When taken together, these kinds of factors help us understand how specific policy practitioners resolve difficult issues and make specific choices during the course of policy deliberations. An understanding of the policy practice of other people allows us to predict how others will respond to specific events and to understand our own policy practice.

PERSONAL CHARACTERISTICS OF POLICY PRACTITIONERS

When undertaking each of the policy tasks in Figure 9.1, various personal characteristics shape or influence the work of specific policy practitioners; these include attitudes, beliefs, values, ideology, and stylistic preferences. Some theorists speculate that these terms are obsolete in the modern era, but even casual perusal of the writings of speeches of leaders like Ronald Reagan, Edward Kennedy, Michael Dukakis, and Jesse Jackson suggest that they remain an important force in policy affairs. Moreover, as we discussed in Chapter Eight, values influence the shaping of policy choices and actions, even when persons lack an articulated ideology or address issues where ideology appears not to be germane.

Attitudes, Values, Beliefs, and Ideology

Social scientists encounter a daunting task when they try to define subjective factors that, singly and in tandem, influence the policy choices of people. As the predictive skills of political pollsters suggest, however, considerable conceptual and empirical work has enhanced our understanding of subjective factors. It is useful to distinguish among attitudes, values, ideologies, beliefs, and prejudice, as well as specific kinds of prejudice like sexism, racism, and homophobia.

Attitudes   **Attitudes** are evaluations of specific objects or conditions, i.e., a judgment that an object or condition is "good or bad, desirable or undesirable, something to be approached or avoided . . . the object may be literally anything: a person, an event, an idea, a proposal for action, an action itself."[15] People exhibit specific attitudes when they contend that "this welfare program is bad," "this specific tax increase is evil," or "this social program is meritorious."

Values   If the attitudes of people are judgments about the merits of particular and specific entities or conditions, their **values** represent higher order and generalized judgments. Herbert Simons defines values as "generalized attitudes that are adhered to rather consistently in judging particular attitude objects."[16] People display values when they contend that "all welfare programs should be avoided," "we should generally restrict the size of the federal government," or "programs that reduce economic inequality are good."

Beliefs   **Beliefs** are "judgments held with varying degrees of certainty that an object possesses a particular attribute."[17] Someone who says "social programs are bedeviled with red tape" believes that social programs always possess this characteristic. If they do not value red tape, they are unlikely to favor specific programs (an attitude) or social programs in general (a value).

The preceding comments suggest that attitudes, values, and beliefs are often related to one another. In the case of people who are consistent and logical, we can predict their values from their attitudes and beliefs. If I have the attitude that red tape is evil and if I have the belief that all governmental social programs possess red tape, I may dislike most or all governmental social programs (a value). Or we can work backward from values and beliefs to attitudes; if someone dislikes social programs in general, they are likely to dislike a specific social program or harbor the belief that it has negative characteristics, such as red tape.

Ideology   We define **ideology** as a cluster of values that form a distinctive and recurring pattern.[18] Conservatives tend to possess values that favor a limited role for the federal government in social welfare, use of voucher or market systems, and retention of existing economic inequalities. Moreover, they often oppose regulations of private enterprise, affirmative action, and an expansive welfare state. Socialists or radicals tend to favor expansive roles for government, governmental or public systems of provision of services, regulations for private enterprise, reduction of economic inequalities (through radical revisions of the tax code and policies like affirmative action), and an expansive welfare state. Liberals (or moderates) tend to fall midway between these polar extremes on an ideological continuum that extends between conservatism and radicalism. Many subgroups or factions like neo-conservatism and neoliberalism exist within these broad ideological camps. Some liberals, such as Democrats Michael Dukakis and Gary Hart, approach conservative positions on some social welfare issues, while other Democrats, such as the late Hubert Humphrey and Paul Simon, approach radical positions on some issues. (Democrats like former President Jimmy Carter are conservative on a range of social issues.) In similar fashion, some Republican conservatives, such as the late Nelson Rockefeller, approached liberal or even radical positions on some issues. As James Reichley suggests when discussing the ideology of various Republican leaders and placing them into groups,[19] terms like stalwarts, fundamentalists, moderates, and progressives are useful.

Is ideology no longer relevant to social welfare policy as some theorists suggest? Value-based (ideological) conflict still exists, as the debates on major pieces of social reform in the Congress suggest. We cannot understand the positions of major figures like Ronald Reagan, Jesse Jackson, and Michael Dukakis if we do not understand their ideologies. Nor can we understand general trends in political culture, such as the movement toward conservative and moderate positions in the 1980s from the relatively liberal tenor of the 1960s, without using terms like values and ideology. Indeed, people sometimes falsely declare the demise of ideology when broad shifts in public opinion toward a specific ideology make it appear that the general ideology is no longer present. (Ideology becomes more obvious when considerable ideological polarization exists, but it can shape the positions of people even when a consensus exists.[20])

Ideology is not, of course, relevant to some issues, such as relatively minor or technical ones. Its role is often less obvious in agency settings than in legislatures, since policy disputes in agencies often focus upon the details of implementation rather than dramatic issues of social obligation like the size of the welfare state or economic inequality. Ideological considerations sometimes intrude in organizational settings, however. An executive who wishes to serve affluent and fee-paying services and who envisions no role for an agency in changing or reforming policies in the external world possesses a philosophy that is akin to conservatism and that can be contrasted with the ideology of another executive who seeks redistributive and social-reform functions for his or her agency.

Prejudice   *Prejudice* can be viewed as negative values and beliefs. People who possess prejudice possess negative orientations toward members of specific groups. Racism is prejudice that is directed toward groups whose members are considered physiologically homogeneous, such as blacks and Native Americans. Someone who despises blacks, for example, may not wish to extend social welfare benefits to them on grounds that they will become "yet more lazy." Sexism and homophobia are directed toward specific genders or people who engage in sexual practices with members of the same gender. Prejudice also shapes the orientations of people toward many other groups, such as persons with mental or physical disabilities, criminal offenders, poor people, members of specific ethnic groups (such as Hispanics), and foreigners.

Prejudice often prompts people to favor relatively punitive or restrictive policies toward the members of specific groups. Widespread and pervasive prejudice, is often called *institutional prejudice*, which refers to those overt or covert policies that systematically restrict or discriminate against the members of a specific group. Assume, for example, that staff in an agency do not wish to serve Spanish-speaking people; they can discourage them from using services in the location of the facilities, not hiring bilingual staff, restricting the hours of service to times that are inconvenient, and providing insensitive services.

Our discussion of these various subjective factors suggests that it is not simple to separate them. People are not necessarily consistent; someone may believe that welfare causes freeloading, for example, but nonetheless value governmental assistance for other programs or people. As political pollsters have discovered, a person's position on specific issues or candidates can change abruptly. Beliefs sometimes change as people receive new evidence or as they are persuaded that a policy is associated with a value that they prize. As we noted earlier, welfare reformers in 1988 skillfully depicted their reforms as "saving the family," an objective that most politicians value.

It is important not to magnify the importance of attitudes, values, beliefs, and ideology excessively. These subjective orientations do not always predict positions on specific issues, since the positions of people on specific issues are shaped by many factors, such as perceptions of their self-interest.[21] While many conservatives oppose many social reforms, for example, they often support them once they have been enacted because some of their constituents benefit from them and insist upon their continuation. Some conservative politicians initiated federal daycare legislation in the 1980s because (among other motivations) they feared that female voters, who had abandoned the Republican party in large numbers in national elections of 1980 and 1984, might continue to defect to the Democratic party. People sometimes do not heed their values when taking positions because of inertia that stems from traditions or habits, because of peer pressure, or because they emulate or internalize the positions of people whom they respect, such as leaders or high-level officials.

As we discussed in Chapter Seven, effective persuaders are aware of the complex and numerous factors that contribute to the development of positions. Indeed, effective persuaders sometimes minimize value-based or ideological arguments when they believe these arguments create conflict or polarization that jeopardizes their ability to secure a consensus. On other occasions, however, they may appeal to values or ideology when they want to activate a constituency or incite conflict—or when they wish to bring an important value to the fore that has been ignored by other people.

While subjective orientations do not fully predict actions, they cannot be ignored in many situations. One often cannot conduct force-field analysis, make effective presentations, or develop proposals that are politically feasible without considering attitudes, values, beliefs, ideology, and prejudices.

Policy Styles

Various policy-practice styles exist, as can quickly be detected by even a cursory examination of existing literature. It is useful to make a distinction between analytic, value-based, political (or entrepreneurial), and consensus-building approaches to policy-making.[22]

Analytic models, such as ones that have been delineated by many economists but also by some social workers like Alfred Kahn, prescribe a step-by-step process of information collecting, identification of options, and selection of policies based on the use of research.[23] Rationalists are impatient with selection of options in the push-and-pull of the political process because such policies, they argue, do not effectively address or solve social problems. Rationalists often favor placing economists and social scientists who possess considerable technical skills in important positions in the policy-making process. Although many technical or analytic models exist, they differ primarily in the kinds of criteria that are used to assess the merits of policy options. Thus, cost–benefit models examine the extent various options deliver net benefits to society when program costs are subtracted from the value of benefits to society; cost–effectiveness models examine the extent specific expenditures on various options allow them to redress or solve social problems.[24] In each case, the "best" option is selected on the basis of its merits as determined by quantitative data and empirical research.

Some criticisms can be made of the frameworks of rationalists. Because policies often must be assessed *before* they are enacted, it is often difficult to obtain reliable data about their future costs, effectiveness, or benefits. We noted in Chapters Four and Eight that the selection of criteria, which are used to assess the merits of alternative policies, is strongly influenced by values. A rationalist who emphasizes the costs of policies may be contested by another one who places more emphasis on the effectiveness of specific policies in solving or redressing social problems.[25]

Political realities often doom the hopes of rationalists. After devoting years to locating the best solution to a problem by using sophisticated data-collection and data-analysis techniques, experts sometimes find that their recommendations receive little attention from politicians or decision makers, who proceed to enact a policy option that received low marks from the experts.

Some theorists, such as Davil Gil, espouse **value-based models** of policy-making.[26] They contend that specific value premises should be identified at the outset of policy deliberations, such as a desire to enhance equality by adopting policies that promote redistribution of resources, services, or power from affluent or well-positioned persons to less advantaged persons. Assume that two alternative models of national health insurance were proposed in a legislative setting; persons advocating a value-based model would select the model that maximized those dominant values that they prioritized at the outset of their work, such as "enhancing the redistribution of medical services and resources to poor persons."

Value-based models have advantages and disadvantages. Unlike many rationalists, who often pretend neutrality and objectivity, value-based theorists are "out front" with their values. Indeed, value-based theorists continually remind us that policy-making is influenced at many points by values and indeed can rarely be conducted without making value-based choices at numerous points. Value-based models encounter two problems, however. First, as conflict between radicals, liberals, and conservatives suggests, people often differ about which values to prioritize. The recommendations of any value-based study can be attacked by questioning those value-premises that were selected at the outset of the study.

Second, value-based theorists are vulnerable to the charge that their work neglects empirical and political components. Value-based theorists often use data in their work, but critics contend that they select only those data that confirm their policy predilections. Some conservatives contend, for example, that advocates of a socialized health-care system highlight only those data that portray the faults of the existing health-care system, such as its unresponsiveness to poor people, while ignoring data that suggest that the health-care system has led to remarkable decreases in certain kinds of diseases. Value-based theorists sometimes feel uncomfortable with political realities because they do not want to "compromise away" their policy preferences. Indeed, value-based theorists sometimes are contemptuous of allies who make concessions to opponents.

A **political,** or **entrepreneurial, model** is advocated by some theorists who argue that effective policymakers need to fashion proposals that are politically feasible.[27] Many of them contend that policy practitioners are, in effect, entrepreneurs; if the latter locate in trial-and-error fashion those products and those prices that the existing marketplace will accept, the former identify those policies that can obtain sufficient political support to be enacted. Policymakers select feasible policies by floating "trial balloons," where they gauge initial reactions to tentative proposals, by identifying and negotiating with those persons and groups that possess power, and by modifying policies to make them politically acceptable.

Interest-group or pluralist models have the merit of sensitizing policy-makers to the harsh reality that many policies cannot be enacted unless they are politically feasible and that policy practitioners have to be willing to make concessions. Many political theorists, however, become so accommodating to political realities that they ignore the importance of values; some politicians, for example, become so concerned with enhancing their reelections that they support *any* policy that has the support of well-heeled or powerful constituents or interest groups. Moreover, as many value-based theorists note, those persons who accommodate to existing political realities forget that many people and groups lack the resources, expertise, or organization to be serious players in policy deliberations; effectively excluded, their interests are often ignored by political realists who cater to powerful interests.[28] Political entrepreneurs are also criticized by policy analysts who contend that they are so preoccupied with shaping their proposals to accommodate political realities that they neglect to heed existing research and knowledge.

We noted in Chapter Six, as well, that it is often difficult to calculate the political feasibility of a specific policy. Even a seasoned veteran may underestimate or overestimate opposition to a policy. Moreover, the balance of political forces often shifts during policy deliberations so that the calculations made at the outset of deliberations are confounded by the shifting currents of the political process.

Some theorists favor using **consensus-building models** to fashion policies.[29] Consensus can be achieved, they suggest, if participants identify common objectives at the outset, engage in a process of creative and nonconflictual brainstorming to identify policy solutions, and discuss the merits of alternative policies until a consensus emerges. These theorists sometimes suggest that an outside facilitator should be used to promote consensus building. Policies that emerge from consensus building are often superior to ones that are derived from the political process, these theorists suggest, because they draw upon the combined insights of many people. Moreover, they contend, people are more likely to facilitate the implementation of those policies that have emerged from collaborative deliberations.

Although the quest for consensus is a noble one, political realities often intrude. Many issues are so encumbered with cleavages between contending factions that consensus building is difficult or impossible. Consensus builders sometimes fail to recognize that consensus decisions can sometimes be reached only by excessively diluting or compromising the policy preferences of the various participants.

To this point, we have discussed analytic, value-based, entrepreneurial, and consensus-building models. These models can be contrasted with one another on a number of dimensions (see Table 9.1).

Favored Skills   We have discussed analytic, political, interactional, and value-clarification skills in Chapters Two through Eight. Proponents of the

TABLE 9.1   Styles of Policy-Making

	Technical or Analytic	Value-Based	Political or Entrepreneurial	Consensus-Building
Favored skills	Analytic	Value-clarification and political mobilizing	Political	Process
The extent values are explicit	Implicit	Explicit	Implicit	Implicit
Orientation to the status quo	Unclear	Change-oriented	Bias to status quo	Bias to status quo
Favored policy criteria	Cost, effectiveness	Value-based criteria	Political feasibility	Those criteria that obtain a consensus
The extent data and research are emphasized	Emphasized	Deemphasized	Deemphasized	Deemphasized
Level of conflict that is favored	Little	High	Moderate	Little

various styles emphasize one or several of them. Technical models emphasize analytic skills, value-based models emphasize value-clarification skills, political (entrepreneurial) models emphasize political skills, and consensus-building models emphasize process skills.

Considerable evidence suggests that these models or styles actually exist in the real world. Arnold Meltsner notes, for example, that some federal bureaucrats equate policy practice with computer terminals, data files, and economic analysis; they have almost no interest in the political process or in processes of consensus building.[30] When they finish their technical studies and hand them to their superiors, they consider their policy work to be completed. Other policy practitioners, Meltsner found, deemphasize the use of research but are well schooled in the art of estimating patterns of support and opposition to various measures, from both their colleagues and their constituents.

The Extent Values Are Explicit   Technicians tend to deemphasize the role of values in their analysis of policies because they claim to be relatively scientific in their approach. Nor do political entrepreneurs and consensus builders emphasize their value-premises because they favor whatever policies emerge from the political or deliberative process. By contrast, value-based practitioners emphasize those basic values that undergird their analysis.

Orientation to the Status Quo   Some objectives, which are related to our policy identities and beliefs, describe our orientation to the status quo. People who want fundamental changes in existing policies—whether conservatives who want to "turn back the clock" by eliminating existing social programs or radicals who want to augment the welfare state—may be less likely to accept compromises than are people who are relatively content with existing policies. Liberal Democrats, such as Hubert Humphrey, and conservative Republicans, such as Strom Thurmond, frequently "fought to the end" against compromise legislation that they believed violated their fundamental principles. If value-based practitioners are often unhappy with the status quo, the stance of rationalists and political entrepreneurs toward the status quo is dictated by their analysis or by their political calculations. If their technical analysis indicates the need for major policy reforms, for example, policy analysts can recommend major departures from the status quo, but they may recommend minor reforms if their technical analysis leads them in that direction. Some political entrepreneurs can recommend major reforms if they believe they will benefit their interests, such as Nixon did during his first presidential term when he supported a range of social reforms to expand the base of the Republican party, but political entrepreneurs often recommend no or minor changes if their calculations suggest that they satisfy their political needs.

Favored Policy Criteria   We discussed various criteria that are used to assess the merits of specific policy options in Chapter Four, such as efficiency, equality, effectiveness, and feasibility. Policy practitioners often favor one or several of these criteria in their analysis of options, whether because of their policy beliefs, their roles within the human services, or other factors. Administrators and political entrepreneurs, who are, respectively, preoccupied with "keeping the ship afloat" and with political survival, often emphasize feasibility considerations by asking, Is this policy option administratively feasible in terms of its cost and its "doability"? Value-based practitioners seek to maximize values like redistribution (in the case of liberals) or freedom (in the case of conservatives). Practitioners who prefer technical styles often emphasize cost or effectiveness criteria—or some combination of them. Consensus builders emphasize those criteria that emerge from collaborative policy deliberations. Direct-service staff and some consumers tend to be more concerned with the effectiveness of policies in redressing specific social problems. Civil rights and advocacy groups are often concerned with the extent a policy corrects inequalities in society; they may criticize, for example, the size or scope of a policy or program. Of course, legislators, particularly ones in positions such as the chairs of committees, want to know if a policy is politically feasible or whether their support of it will increase or decrease their constituency support.

The Extent Data and Research Are Emphasized   People who use technical models emphasize the use of data and research in their work, but other policy practitioners often place less emphasis on it, or they use those pieces of data and research that confirm or support their positions. Thus, some advocates of a specific policy—whether because it conforms with their values or their political interests—will opportunistically seek data that support their positions.

Orientation Toward Conflict   Because technical practitioners hope that decisions will be made on the merits of the issue, they do not emphasize political confrontation or advocacy. By contrast many value-based practitioners expect to use conflict to overcome opposition from people with alternative values. Consensus builders hope to avoid conflict by collaborating with various participants in policy deliberations.

Hybrid Styles   Of course, policy styles that policy practitioners *actually* use often do not conform to these ideal or pure models.[31] People sometimes incorporate elements of different models in their policy practice, as when incumbent politicians merge entrepreneurial and technical models or when radicals merge value-based and technical ones. Ralph Nader exemplifies the mixture of styles when he couples relatively sophisticated technical work of experts with the traditional mobilizing and constituency-building skills of advocates.

Policy practitioners sometimes use different styles at different times, even when seeking support for a specific measure. Eric Redman notes in *The Dance of Legislation*, for example, that he began his work on a policy proposal in Congress with a style that deemphasized conflict; he sought to obtain a specific public health measure by merely attaching it to an existing program in behind-the-scenes and relatively secretive deliberations.[32] When that tactic failed, he still tried to avert conflict by developing bipartisan support for a legislative proposal, but he had to resort to a high-conflict strategy when he sought to solicit and promote the mobilizing of external pressure on key congressional representatives and on the president at strategic points when the momentum of the bill was slowed. The existence of hybrid styles suggests the difficulty of describing the policy practice of a specific practitioner in precise terms. We can nonetheless identify some major elements of the style of a policy practitioner during an episode of policy practice, ask why he used this style, and inquire about its effectiveness in achieving specific policy objectives.

It is tempting to ally ourselves with one of the models and to criticize others; indeed, considerable literature exists that debunks one or another of the styles. Theorists who like value-based models sometimes criticize people who favor political models because they are not sufficiently attentive to the needs of disadvantaged and powerless populations; in turn, theorists who favor the political and technical models sometimes contend that people who favor value-based models are fuzzy-minded or impervious to quantitative or analytic considerations.

Why not, however, acknowledge that each model provides useful tools and insights? Policy practitioners should shape their practice to their objectives and to the circumstances that they confront. Value-based models are needed when existing policies conflict with the fundamental values of a practitioner, but political calculations, quantitative data, and the need to develop a consensus sometimes must be given priority.

Policy Objectives

The objectives of policy practitioners guide their actions during policy-making. Let's make a distinction between outcome objectives and process objectives.

Some objectives can be called **outcome objectives**. Although most people ultimately want resolution of policy problems by enacting policy proposals, they often develop short-term objectives such as sensitizing persons to the existence of a serious policy problem, developing a policy proposal that meets specific criteria, enacting a specific policy proposal, or implementing a policy. Outcome objectives also define the size and ambitiousness of ultimate policy goals that specific practitioners possess. Do they want incremental changes in existing policy, major reforms, or midrange reforms? How willing are they to make concessions to opponents, even if that requires a substantial modification of their proposal?

The preceding objectives suggest an affirmative and problem-solving orientation, but some practitioners develop opposing or blocking objectives, ones that merely restate the preceding objectives in negative terms, such as to convince others that a policy problem is not sufficiently serious to merit attention, to convince others that a new policy proposal is not needed, to defeat a proposal, or to prevent the implementation of a specific policy.

Objectives are sometimes established in terms of specific criteria that describe ultimate outcomes, such as "let's find a policy that will make our operations more efficient" or "let's revise our eligibility policies to make them fairer."

Other objectives can be called **process objectives** that describe the kind of deliberations that policy practitioners want and are partly shaped by the styles of policy practice that specific policy practitioners favor. A consensus builder, for example, often wants to develop a policy solution through a participatory process; a person who favors a technical style wants a deliberative process that emphasizes the use of research and analytic reason; a political entrepreneur wants a deliberative process that emphasizes negotiating and bargaining; and advocates often favor a confrontive or conflictual process.

CHARACTERISTICS OF POLICY PRACTITIONERS: ORIENTATIONS ABOUT THE POLITICS OF SPECIFIC ISSUES

The actions and strategies of policy practitioners are partly shaped by their perceptions of the politics of a specific issue, such as the expected gains and losses that they associate with it and the importance, or salience, they attach to it.

Expected Gains and Losses

Policy practitioners are influenced by their perceptions of the expected gains and losses that are associated with an issue. They often ponder the effects of a policy on their reputations, their credibility, the security of their jobs, or their friendships. In the case of politicians, of course, issues are scrutinized with respect to their implications for support from their constituents and from those interest groups that provide them with campaign and other resources. Imagine a continuum extending from "all losses or risks" to "all gains or benefits." In the case of risk-heavy issues, practitioners fear that involvement in the issue will excessively jeopardize their interests. Moreover, risks rise to the extent that people believe that "their side" lacks the power to prevail because others often do not want to be associated with a losing cause. They will likely become bystanders in such cases, adopt extremely cautious and defensive positions, or assume the role of blockers. By contrast policy practitioners have an incentive to aggressively and publicly participate in issues associated with all benefits.

Of course, the estimation of gains and losses is seldom this clear-cut because many issues and proposals are perceived to be associated with a mixture of losses and gains. Moreover, the perceptions of policy practitioners of the likely losses and gains of an issue can change in the course of time, with resulting changes in their behaviors. People may actively pursue an issue or proposal at one time because they believe its gains (to them) exceed its losses, but they may later assume a more cautious role when they believe the ratio of gains to losses appears to be less beneficial. We should remember, of course, that the estimation by policy practitioners of the likely losses and gains of an issue or position may be inaccurate. When discussing assertiveness in Chapter Six, for example, we noted that people often wrongly believe they encounter risks by championing an issue.

The calculations of the likely gains or losses of a position or action are often influenced by perceptions of the intentions of traditional opponents.[33] Legislators who believe, for example, that members of an opposing party hope to use an issue to increase their constituencies or popularity at their expense are particularly likely to invest time and resources in contesting the issue. In such win-lose conflict, people believe that the gains of contenders necessarily require them to suffer losses. When policy practitioners do not believe that their opponents possess such sinister motives, they are less likely to believe that they have to commit time and resources to an issue.

When calculating the gains and losses that are associated with an issue, people often compare it with other competing issues. Someone may believe, for example, that she can obtain considerable gains from a specific issue but decide that other issues offer even greater gains. In such cases, she may decide to invest her time in these other issues.

It should be recognized, as well, that tensions sometimes exist between people's values and their calculations of the gains and losses that are associated with an issue. For example, a politician may believe strongly that an issue such as welfare reform is important, but decides that the issue presents political risks or that another issue, such as a proposal to increase Social Security benefits, offers more opportunities for expanding his support from constituents. Or a line worker in a social services agency may believe certain service-delivery policies violate her professional ethics but fears that "speaking out" could expose her to certain risks. It would be nice, as some economists presume, to reduce human choice to mathematical equations, but real-world choices are often made in bewildering fashion as people juggle competing impulses.

Salience

Salience describes the perceived importance of a specific issue to a person. Does he place it in an important place on his personal agenda or give it a secondary position? Does she wish to devote considerable time and resources to the issue or not emphasize it? When he encounters frustrations or risks, is he inclined to back away from an issue or to persist?

Salience is influenced by many factors. Although perceived gains and risks that are associated with an issue are a determinant of salience, they do not tell us why some people persist in battling an issue even when they encounter major risks, setbacks, opposition, or delays. We can hypothesize that salience increases as people possess multiple reasons or motivations for supporting (or opposing) an issue, such as values, ideology, vested interests, peer pressure, and loyalty to traditions. People who *also* believe that they do not face insurmountable odds and who believe that strong allies can be found are probably even more likely to possess high salience.

CHARACTERISTICS OF POLICY PRACTITIONERS: SITUATIONAL FACTORS

We have discussed to this point various personal factors that shape the decisions and actions of policy practitioners, but many situational factors intrude, as well. The influence of **role** and **role expectations** has been widely discussed by social scientists. For example, one's style of policy practice can be powerfully influenced by roles and role expectations.[34] Politicians tend to be political entrepreneurs, that is, they initiate, support, and propose those policies that will advance their political interests. Bureaucratic officials (who specialize in reporting to higher-level officials about the workings of their programs), many academicians, staff of "think tanks," and staff to legislative committees are often technicians who excel in obtaining and analyzing data. Staff and members of external pressure groups, particularly ones associated with relatively liberal or conservative causes, are advocates for specific programs and populations and seek to build constituency and lobbyist pressure on politicians to expand specific programs. Individuals who occupy strategic positions—such as party leaders, chairs of legislative and other committees, majority and minority leaders of legislative bodies, and executives of agencies—often use consensus-building strategies, particularly when they must lead relatively divided parties, agencies, or committees.

Examples abound of individuals who have changed their policy styles when they assumed new positions. David Brody notes, for example, that many Socialists, who were elected to mayoral posts in the Progressive Era, became indistinguishable from other mayors as they supplanted their advocacy and value-based styles with the entrepreneurial and consensus-building approaches of many chief executives.[35] (They needed these styles both to build political support to allow them to retain their positions and to quell excessive dissension that could imperil their reputations as effective administrators of city governments.) Radical organizers of trade unions often become more accommodationist and incrementalist when they succeed to positions as union leaders. Many consumer advocates become more concerned with cost and feasibility considerations when placed on the boards of agencies.

A variety of **organizational factors** shape policy styles. The policy practice of those salaried professionals who work within organizations is shaped by myriad factors that stem from the culture, the tasks, and the environment of the organization. As anyone knows who has worked in different organizations, certain norms and taboos shape decision-making styles. In some organizations, decisions are made by top administrators with little consultation with other staff, whereas others, such as free clinics, pride themselves on participatory management and encourage contributions from staff. Conflict rarely occurs in some organizations but is rampant in others. At points of crisis, such as just after the succession of a new leader, considerable turmoil may exist in some organizations only to be followed by periods of relative tranquility.

These styles of decision making and interaction within organizations shape in turn people's styles of policy practice. Individuals often modify their actions to conform to institutional norms or find, to their dismay, that they suffer policy losses if they do not. An abrasive and high-conflict style, which may be functional in certain organizations or at certain points in their development, is counterproductive in other organizations or at other times. People who are nonassertive in seeking their policy objectives may imperil their programs and units in organizations where cut-throat competition exists for internal resources.

Organizational norms and traditions shape not only the style and frequency of policy discourse but also the kinds of subjects that can be considered within them. The missions of organizations—that is, the set of objectives and programs to which influential people are committed—engender strong loyalties and preferences; some programs and policies cannot easily be changed, or even critically discussed, because of these institutional traditions. Of course, organizational missions, as well as the policies and programs that are supported by them, can be modified in the course of time, but a frontal attack on them can often promote divisive conflict.

Many **group factors** influence policy practitioners. Terms like *contagion, groupthink, momentum, peer pressure,* and *scapegoating* describe group phenomena that shape actions and beliefs of policy practitioners.

Policy practitioners usually are not lemmings, but they can be influenced by peer pressures of many kinds. Initially uninterested in a policy issue or wanting to use a specific style such as a low-conflict one, a policy practitioner can change directions in response to peer pressure. Groups often develop fixed ways of analyzing problems, mobilize behind specific policy options, and rigidly emphasize certain policy criteria to the exclusion of others. As we discussed in Chapter Seven, Irving Janis contends that this kind of groupthink is most pronounced under specific conditions such as when the group lacks heterogeneous membership, when its members perceive themselves to be under external attack, and when its leaders lack the ability to inject alternative perspectives.[36] Under these conditions, it can take a particularly virulent form and can lead to scapegoating of persons who introduce dissenting perspectives. But milder forms of groupthink exist in many groups at one time or another.

The **personal status** and **formal power** of individuals profoundly influence how they participate in policy practice. Consider the example of a simple simulation game. In groups of seven or eight persons, participants are given a slip of paper that connotes the number of votes that each of them possesses and that range from one to eight votes.[37] Each group is asked to select one of the members to be its leader, but each member has to prominently display the number of votes she possesses during the note-writing and discussion periods that precede the final vote. Members negotiate, build coalitions, and make nominations during these periods. As might be expected, persons with the least number of votes participate the least in the discourse of the group, feel like outcasts, and usually have little impact on the group's decision. Unexpectedly, however, persons with the most votes often do not dominate the proceedings and are often content to allow persons with midrange power to dominate discourse and to be selected as the leader. They often feel sufficiently self-conscious about their power that they do not use it. In other cases, they become so confident that their enormous power will allow them to prevail that they fail to build coalitions with others. In still other cases, their power leads to arrogance and condescension, which sufficiently angers other members of the group that they disregard their suggestions.

Like all simulations, this one only imperfectly replicates the real world, but it contains some interesting lessons. People with little formal power, such as some direct-service staff, can be effectively "written out of" policy discourse, both by others and by themselves when they create a self-fulfilling prophecy that leads them to believe that they can have little impact. But the response of a participant to ascribed or formal power is as important—and sometimes more so—than the formal power itself. Some people with relatively little power have extraordinary success by initiating or joining coalitions. Some people with great power squander it or attempt to use it in a manner that is counterproductive. But the psychology of power is also illustrated by the domination of many of the games by people with midrange power—people who are neither disillusioned by their near absence of power nor lulled into complacency by their extraordinary power. Unimpeded by hangups of people with extremes of power, these individuals often shape the outcomes of policy and are often the selected leaders.

This simulation game contains both descriptive and prescriptive lessons. Although it describes how people often respond to their power, it suggests that policy practitioners need not fall victim to mind games that make them prematurely disengage from policy practice. People who lack the power to directly shape decisions can sometimes assume a modest but significant role by joining with others, by making timely suggestions, and by indirection, that is, by working through other people. People with midrange power can often assume important roles even when their formal power is substantially eclipsed by others.

FACTORS THAT INFLUENCE THE WORK OF POLICY PRACTITIONERS: THE FLOW OF DELIBERATIONS

We have discussed various factors that influence whether and how policy practitioners participate in policy deliberations. We have neglected to discuss, however, how "the nature of the game" influences the work of policy practitioners because we have focused upon factors that influence the work of people *before* they enter policy deliberations.

Assume for the moment that the values and perceptions of self interest prompt someone to be a bystander with respect to a specific issue. When she perceives the intense interest of other people in the issue, as reflected by their emotional speeches and frantic actions, however, she might decide to become involved, whether because she emulates persons she respects, fears that traditional opponents wish to seize the issue at her expense, or comes to believe that the issue has import for her values or self interest.

We have noted that game theorists discuss how people often become involved in specific issues when they develop moves, much as in a game of chess, to counter the actions of opponents. To some extent, the practice of policy involves looking over one's shoulder at the actions of other persons to develop counterstrategies, particularly when we believe that win-lose conflict exists. In these cases, then, the strategies of other people profoundly influence our actions.

No tidy method exists for discussing the effects of the nature of the game on the actions of specific policy practitioners. Concepts drawn from small group theory (such as contagion), from social psychology (such as peer pressure), and from game theory (such as countering moves) are useful for probing the effects of policy deliberations themselves upon the actions of policy practitioners.

This dynamic perspective on policy practice suggests the futility of seeking to reduce it to a set of simple rules or maxims, such as exist in a considerable portion of traditional policy literature. It underscores, as well, the difficulties of predicting the outcomes of specific deliberations because we do not know, until play has commenced, what the moves and countermoves of specific people will be, much as a quarterback on a football team has to improvise strategy.

A dynamic perspective is needed in other practice disciplines, as well. The actions of an administrator, a community organizer, or a direct-service practitioner are often contingent upon the actions of other persons as well as clients. Rather than perceiving these dynamic realities as an inconvenience, we can, instead, view them as challenges that require us to improvise and to adapt our work to changing realities.

SUMMARY

Policy practitioners engage in agenda-building, problem-defining, proposal-writing, policy-enacting, policy-implementing, and policy-assessing tasks. Each of these tasks describes an important part of the policy-making process. The agenda-building task allows policy practitioners to place specific issues on the agendas of decision makers. In the problem-defining task, policy practitioners frame issues to stimulate interest in them and to conceptualize them so that solutions can be found. When they write proposals, policy practitioners develop preferred remedies to specific social or institutional problems, even though they must frequently amend their proposals during policy deliberations. They try to secure sufficient support for their proposals to obtain their approval when they engage in the policy-enacting task. Policy-implementing and policy-assessing tasks are undertaken in the wake of the enactment of specific proposals.

Policy practitioners use analytic, political, interactional, and value-clarification skills to accomplish these policy tasks. While their stylistic preferences may lead them to emphasize one or several of these skills, they usually use them in tandem to accomplish the various policy tasks.

We cannot understand whether and how people participate in policy deliberations if we fail to examine their subjective orientations—attitudes, beliefs, values, ideologies, as well as prejudices—that often shape their choices and actions. Stylistic preferences also influence what policy skills they emphasize, the extent values are explicit in their work, their orientation to the status quo, the policy criteria that they favor, whether they emphasize data or research, and the extent to which they use political conflict in their work. Analytic, value-based, political or entrepreneurial, and consensus-building styles often describe the policy practice of specific people, although hybrid styles are often used.

The perceptions of the politics of specific issues often influence whether and how specific people participate in policy deliberations, such as the kinds of gains and losses that they might incur. Situational factors that influence the work of policy practitioners include role expectations, organizational factors such as styles of decision making, and group factors like contagion and peer pressure. Nor can we neglect the role of personal status and formal power in shaping decisions about whether and how to contest specific issues. Once policy deliberations have begun, the actions of other people shape the choices and actions of policy practitioners, as well.

QUESTIONS FOR DISCUSSION

1. Critically discuss the assertion that "powerful interests always preclude significant policy reforms."

2. Use concepts that are germane to agenda building to discuss why issues or policies that are not feasible at one point in time become feasible at a subsequent point in time. Can you identify an example in an agency or community setting with which you are familiar? Identify another example at the national level of American politics.

3. Discuss the assertion that "the way problems are defined or framed at the outset often determines the kinds of solutions that people propose." Can you think of examples either in an agency or community setting or at the national level with which you are familiar?

4. Take any one of the six policy tasks that are defined in this chapter and discuss how policy practitioners often need to use a variety of policy skills to accomplish it.

5. Take any policy issue with which you are familiar and discuss how attitudes, beliefs, values, and ideology shape the positions of policy practitioners.

6. Speculate about the kinds of circumstances when each of the four policy styles would be appropriate and when each of them would be inappropriate. (You may wish to discuss what kinds of issues, what kinds of political realities, and what kinds of settings lend themselves to or suggest various policy styles.)

7. Compare win-lose with win-win politics. If you wanted to convert a situation that was perceived to be win-lose to a win-win situation, what kinds of tactics might you use?

8. Discuss how the personal status and formal power of individuals influence how they participate in policy practice. Apply your discussion, if possible, to a specific situation you have encountered.

SUGGESTED READINGS

An Overview of Alternative Styles

Ron Haskins and James Gallagher, eds., *Models for Analysis of Social Policy* (Norwood, N.J.: ABLEX Publishing Corp., 1981).

Barclay Hudson, "Comparison of Current Planning Theories: Counterparts and Contradictions," *Journal of the American Institute of Planners*, 45 (October 1979): 387–398.

Value-Based Styles

David Gil, *Unravelling Social Policy* (Cambridge, Mass.: Schenkman, 1976).

Robert Moroney, "Policy Analysis Within a Value Theoretical Framework," in Haskins and Gallagher, eds., *Models for Analysis of Social Policy*, pp. 78–102.

Martin Rein, "Value-Critical Policy Analysis," in Daniel Callahan and Bruce Jennings, eds., *Ethics, the Social Sciences, and Policy Analysis* (New York: Plenum, 1983), pp. 83–111.

Analytic Styles

Brian Hogwood and Lewis Gunn, *Policy Analysis for the Real World* (London: Oxford University Press, 1984).

Robert Mayer and Ernest Greenwood, *The Design of Social Policy Research* (Englewood Cliffs, N.J.: Prentice-Hall, 1980).

Carl Patton and David Sawicki, *Basic Methods of Policy Analysis and Planning* (Englewood Cliffs, N.J.: Prentice-Hall, 1986).

Political Styles

Eugene Bardach, *The Skill Factor in Politics* (Berkeley, Ca.: University of California Press, 1972).

Charles Lindblom, *The Policy Making Process* (Englewood Cliffs, N.J.: Prentice-Hall, 1968).

Consensus-Building Styles

John Friedman, *Retracking America: A Theory of Transactive Planning* (New York: Anchor Press, 1973).

Personal Factors That Shape Policy Practice

Morton Deutsch, *The Resolution of Conflict* (New Haven, Conn.: Yale University Press, 1973), pp. 143–176, 351–400.

Irving Janis, *Victims of Group-Think: A Psychological Study of Foreign Policy Decision Making* (Boston: Houghton Mifflin, 1972).

Arnold Meltsner, *Policy Analysis in the Bureaucracy* (Berkeley, Ca.: University of California Press, 1976).

Gerald Zaltman and Robert Duncan, *Strategies of Planned Change* (New York: John Wiley, 1977), pp. 185–224.

The Agenda-Building Task

John Kingdon, *Agendas, Alternatives, and Public Policies* (Boston: Little, Brown, 1984).

Hedrick Smith, *The Power Game: How Washington Works* (New York: Ballantine Books, 1988), pp. 331–444.

The Problem-Defining Task

Allison Graham, *Essence of Decision* (Boston: Little, Brown, 1971).

Arnold Green, *Social Problems: Arena of Conflict* (New York: McGraw-Hill, 1975).

Hogwood and Gunn, *Policy Analysis for the Real World*, pp. 67–87, 108–127.

Patton and Sawicki, *Basic Methods of Policy Analysis and Planning*, pp. 103–138.

The Policy-Enacting Task

Charles Jones, *The United States Congress: People, Place, and Policy* (Homewood, Ill.: Dorsey Press, 1982).

Eric Redman, *The Dance of Legislation* (New York: Simon and Schuster, 1973).

Randall Ripley, *Congress: Process and Policy*, 3rd ed. (New York: W. W. Norton, 1983).

NOTES

1. The term *task* emphasizes the work of policy practitioners rather than the more general term *phase*, so we use it in this framework. For a discussion of phases, see Bruce S. Jansson, *The Theory and Practice of Social Welfare Policy* (Belmont, Ca.: Wadsworth Publishing Co., 1984), pp. 49–53.

2. See Hedrick Smith, *The Power Game: How Washington Works* (New York: Ballantine Books, 1988), pp. 215–269.

3. Joseph Califano, *America's Health Care Revolution: Who Lives? Who Dies?* (New York: Random House, 1986).

4. For criticism of the 1988 welfare-reform legislation, see Ann Nichols-Casebolt and Jesse McClure, "Social Work Support for Welfare Reform: The Latest Surrender in the War on Poverty," *Social Work*, 34 (January 1989): 77–80.

5. Robert Montjoy and Laurence O'Toole, "The Implementation of Change in Human Service Organizations," *Public Administration Review*, 39 (September-October 1979): 465–477.

6. For a discussion of agenda building, see Robert Eyestone, *From Social Issues to Public Policy* (New York: John Wiley, 1976), and John Kingdon, *Agendas, Alternatives, and Public Policies* (Boston: Little, Brown, 1984).

7. Kingdon, *Agendas, Alternatives, and Public Policies*, pp. 95–105.

8. Ibid., pp. 182–184.

9. Smith, *The Power Game*, pp. 331–387.

10. The use of these symbols is obvious when reading testimony on the 1988 welfare reform legislation. See U.S., Congress, Senate, Committee on Finance, Subcommittee on Social Security and Family Policy, *Hearings on Welfare: Reform or Replacement?* 100th Cong., 1st Sess., January 23, February 2 and 20, March 2, 1987.

11. Bruce Jansson and June Simmons, "The Ecology of Social Work Units in Host Organizations: Empirical Findings and Strategy Implications," *Social Work in Health Care*, 11 (Winter 1985): 1–16.

12. Groups that participated in the coalition testified before Congress. See, for example, U.S., Congress, Senate, *Hearings on Welfare: Reform or Replacement?* 100th Cong., 1st Sess., January 23, February 2 and 20, March 2, 1987.

13. Nichols-Casebolt and McClure, "Social Work Support for Welfare Reform."

14. Ron Dear and Rino Patti, "Legislation Advocacy," *Encyclopedia of Social Work*, 18th ed., vol. 2 (Washington, D.C.: National Association of Social Workers), p. 371.

15. Herbert Simons, *Persuasion: Understanding, Practice, and Analysis*, 2nd ed. (New York: Random House, 1986), p. 22.

16. Ibid., pp. 22–23.

17. Ibid.

18. Milton Rokeach, *The Nature of Human Values* (New York: Free Press, 1973), pp. 3–12.

19. See James Reichley, *Conservatives in an Age of Change: The Nixon and Ford Administrations* (Washington, D.C.: Brookings Institution, 1981), pp. 22–41.

20. Louis Hartz argues that Americans are particularly likely to discount ideology because the nation has lacked ideological polarization. See Hartz, *The Liberal Tradition in America* (New York: Harcourt, Brace, and World, 1955).

21. Simons, *Persuasion*, pp. 62–67.

22. For discussion of styles, see Barclay Hudson, "Comparison of Current Planning Theories: Counterparts and Contradictions," *Journal of the American Institute of Planners*, 45 (October 1979): 387–398. Also see Ron Haskins and James Gallagher, eds., *Models for Analysis of Social Planning* (Norwood, N.J.: ABLEX Publishing, Corp., 1981).

23. Alfred Kahn, *Theory and Practice of Social Planning* (New York: Russell Sage, 1969).

24. A number of analytic techniques are discussed in Murray Gruber, ed., *Management Systems in the Human Services* (Philadelphia: Temple University Press, 1981).

25. Martin Rein, "Value-Critical Policy Analysis," in Daniel Callahan and Bruce Jennings, eds. *Ethics, the Social Sciences, and Policy Analysis* (New York: Plenum, 1983), pp. 83–111.

26. David Gil, *Unravelling Social Policy* (Cambridge, Mass.: Schenkman, 1976).

27. Charles Lindblom, *The Policy Making Process* (Englewood Cliffs, N.J.: Prentice-Hall, 1968). Also see Eugene Bardach, *The Skill Factor in Politics* (Berkeley, Ca.: University of California, 1972).

28. Paul Davidoff, "Advocacy and Pluralism in Planning," *Journal of the American Institute of Planners*, 31 (November 1965): 331–338.

29. John Friedman, *Retracking America: A Theory of Transactional Planning* (New York: Anchor Press, 1973).

30. Arnold Meltsner, *Policy Analysts in the Bureaucracy* (Berkeley, Ca.: University of California Press, 1976).

31. Jack Rothman discusses the use of hybrid styles when discussing alternative styles of community work. See Rothman, "Three Models of Community Organization Practice," in Fred Cox et al., eds., *Strategies of Community Organization* (Itasca, Ill.: Peacock, 1979).

32. Eric Redman, *The Dance of Legislation* (New York: Simon and Schuster, 1973).

33. Morton Deutsch, *The Resolution of Conflict* (New Haven, Conn.: Yale University Press, 1973), p. 369.

34. Carl Van Horn, Donald Baumer, and William Gormley, *Politics and Public Policy* (Washington, D.C.: Congressional Quarterly, Inc., 1989), pp. 59–262.

35. David Brody, *Workers in Industrial America: Essays on the Twentieth-Century Struggle* (New York: Oxford University Press, 1980), pp. 32–39.

36. Irving Janis, *Victims of Group-Think: A Psychological Study of Foreign-Policy Decisions* (Boston: Houghton Mifflin, 1972).

37. See "Power and Influence in Organizations" in Harry Knudsen, Robert Woodworth, and Cecil Bell, *Management: An Experimental Approach* (New York: McGraw-Hill, 1973), pp. 315–328.

CHAPTER 10

■

Social Welfare Policy in Action

We discussed policy-making in a general way in Chapter Nine, as well as various factors that influence the policy practice of specific persons. In this chapter, we move toward methods of describing and evaluating the actual policy practice of specific persons in specific settings.

The framework of policy-making that was discussed in Chapter Nine (Figure 9.1) provides a starting point because it "decomposes" policy-making into a series of six tasks, that is, agenda building, problem defining, proposal writing, policy enacting, policy implementing, and policy assessing. This framework suggests that we can describe the work of specific policy practitioners during specific *episodes* of policy practice, that is, during relatively brief periods of time when they engage in one of the tasks. *Or* we can examine the work of specific practitioners over a *sequence* of tasks when they engage in an extended and protracted set of actions, behaviors, verbal exchanges, and strategies and have undertaken several or more of the tasks. Indeed, we can envision a continuum extending from very brief episodes of policy practice, such as making a specific presentation, to an extended sequence that involves writing a policy proposal, seeking its enactment, and shaping its implementation.

Why do we want to focus on specific episodes or extended sequences of the policy practice of specific persons? If social welfare policy includes a policy-practice component, we have to examine actual instances of policy practice—both to describe and to evaluate them. In similar fashion, direct-service and administrative practitioners and theorists describe and evaluate the work of their respective practices by disaggregating it into specific episodes or sequences. One can examine, for example, how a direct-service practitioner "established a contract" with a specific client (a specific episode of his work) or how he managed an extended sequence of actions, verbal exchanges, and strategies from intake through the termination of the case.

Were we to evaluate his work, we could focus on the specific episode by asking whether he effectively established the contract. Or we could evaluate his extended sequence of work with this client by asking whether his work at various phases of the case, such as contract making, treatment, and termination, was effective.

DISAGGREGATING THE WORK OF POLICY PRACTITIONERS

Our discussion of the six policy tasks and four policy skills gives us an approach to describing the work of specific policy practitioners. We must first **disaggregate** their work, that is, decide what portion of it we wish to describe and evaluate. As the following list shows, we can describe and evaluate someone's policy practice in an ascending level of generality:

1. The use of specific skills when working on specific tasks
2. The use of various skills when working on specific tasks
3. The accomplishment of sequences of related tasks

At the simplest level, we examine someone's use of a specific skill when he is engaged in a single policy task. We can describe and evaluate his use of analytic skills (a single skill) when he is developing a policy proposal (a single task) by asking whether he was familiar with important research and theory from the social sciences, whether he consulted someone with technical expertise, and whether he researched possible funding sources. Or we could describe and evaluate his use of political skills by asking whether he examined the political feasibility of the proposal and whether he consulted with people who might be instrumental in securing support for it.

At a more ambitious level, we could inquire about his work in accomplishing a specific policy task, such as writing a policy proposal, at a broader level of generality. We could describe the *mix*, or *combination*, of skills that he used to develop the proposal, whether he possessed at specific times some overall strategy and whether he altered his strategy and actions as events unfolded. If this policy practitioner failed to supplement analytic skills with political ones in a situation that was politically "charged," we might decide that he failed to incorporate a needed skill in the policy practice.

At an even more general level, we can examine the work of a policy practitioner who engages in a number of related tasks. We can ask how a policy practitioner not only constructed a specific proposal (one task) but sought its enactment and its implementation (two additional tasks). We might conclude, for example, that he was technically expert at writing a proposal but lacked the political skills to obtain its approval from decision makers in a specific setting.

DISAGGREGATING AND DESCRIBING POLICY PRACTICE: A CASE EXAMPLE

When we examine the work of a policy practitioner, we often look for specific kinds of activities and strategies. We examine what task or tasks she undertook, what kinds of strategy she developed, and how she interacted with the context. As we note in the succeeding discussion, we must first *describe* these activities and strategies before we can *evaluate* them.

Some Elements of the Context

We can use a case example drawn from Edward Banfield's classic book, *Political Influence*, to illustrate the policy-practice framework presented in Figure 9.1.[1] The staff of the Welfare Council of Chicago, which was directed by a social worker, was convinced that a new branch of the Cook County Hospital was needed on the southside of Chicago where a large, low-income, black community resided. The massive Cook County Hospital was located on the westside of Chicago and could be reached by many residents only by a long ride on public transportation. Some southside blacks obtained medical assistance from local nonprofit hospitals, such as Michael Reese Hospital or the Billings Hospital of the University of Chicago, but most had to travel a considerable distance to Cook County Hospital. Moreover, some black leaders were angry that some nonprofit hospitals on the southside engaged in the "dumping" of black patients that occurred when low-income black residents were told by these hospitals to obtain medical assistance at the county hospital.

The politics of Chicago at the time this case occurred were dominated by the Democratic political machine and its "boss," Mayor Richard J. Daley. The city of Chicago, which was overwhelmingly Democratic, was tightly organized by Daley, who provided tens of thousands of Chicagoans with positions in the city services in return for their support for the machine. Chicago was circled by a ring of white and largely Republican suburbs that provided a constituency for some Republicans on the Cook County Board of Supervisors. (The county included both the city of Chicago and these white suburban communities.) Democrats nonetheless firmly controlled the county board of supervisors under the leadership of Dan Ryan, himself a close political ally of Daley's.

The construction of a branch hospital on the southside, which the Welfare Council strongly favored, would not be easy. County funds would be needed because public hospitals fell under the jurisdiction of the county. Moreover, medical staff would need to be found who were willing to work at the branch hospital, and difficult decisions would need to be made about the kinds of services it would provide. Should it, for example, only provide outpatient services, or should it provide a range of surgical and diagnostic services as well?

But these logistic, financing, and planning challenges dimmed when compared to the political problem of securing support for the branch hospital. Karl Meyer, the long-time director of Cook County Hospital, was adamantly opposed to building a branch hospital; would it not be cost-effective, he asked, to expand the existing county hospital rather than to invest funds in a new facility? He also contended that it would be difficult to obtain interns, residents, and top-notch physicians at a hospital that was not a teaching hospital (the county hospital was a teaching hospital). Some people believed that Meyer also feared that a branch hospital would dilute the fiefdom that he controlled at the county hospital, which also provided many patronage jobs for supporters of the machine.

Meyer was moreover a close friend of the powerful Dan Ryan; thus, he had an important possible ally in the forthcoming battle over the branch hospital. (It was not certain, however, where Ryan stood on the issue.) The Welfare Council by contrast was poorly connected to the power structure of city or county politics. Its large board consisted of businesspeople and professionals who in turn were often members of the governing boards of the network of hundreds of social agencies in Chicago that were funded by the federated appeal of the Welfare Council. They tended to be highly educated and affluent persons who did not participate in the politics of the machine.

Despite the seeming importance of the issue to the black communities of the southside of Chicago, no widespread support of the issue had developed to support it. Traditional spokespersons and interests on the southside included a powerful newspaper, a black congressman who was affiliated with the Democratic machine, and some civil rights groups such as the Urban League.

The Policy Tasks

Were we to disaggregate the policy practice of the leaders of the Welfare Council, we would describe how they addressed each of the specific policy tasks. (Because this is a complex and extended case, they addressed a range of tasks rather than merely one or several of them.) In their *agenda-building task*, the Welfare Council had to decide how to elevate interest in the issue because the county board of supervisors was preoccupied with countless other issues. (The county hospital system was under the jurisdiction of the board.) Their primary strategy was a technical one; they asked their research and planning department, headed by Alexander Ropchan, to examine the feasibility of constructing a branch hospital.

In their *problem-defining task*, the Welfare Council sought to establish a rationale for the construction of the branch hospital. Because there seemed to be widespread recognition of the need for an additional facility, they focused on collecting information to demonstrate that it would be feasible to build and staff the facility. Thus, they obtained information that suggested that interns, residents, and physicians could be found to staff it. Moreover, they developed data that suggested it would be less expensive to build and staff the facility than some critics suggested.

The Welfare Council undertook a *proposal-writing task* when it developed specific cost and staffing estimates and proposals for the new facility, as well as a description of the kinds of services it would provide. They hoped, for example, that it would not be merely an outpatient hospital but would provide a range of outpatient, family-practice, surgical, and specialty services. (By contrast some people seemed to suggest that it be merely a "feeder hospital" to the county facility that limited its services to relatively few outpatient services.)

They assumed a *policy-enacting task* when they sought to persuade the county board of supervisors to provide funds to build this full-service facility. When the county board eventually decided to approve a bond issue to fund a major expansion of Cook County Hospital, the Welfare Council threatened to defeat the bond issue—a tactic that enabled them to convince the board to make some concessions to them; they agreed to drop the bond issue and the expansion of Cook County Hospital and to earmark some funds for the eventual purchase of a site for a southside hospital.

Had the branch hospital been constructed, the Welfare Council might have assumed the *policy-implementing* and *policy-assessing tasks*. They would have sought to participate in some issues regarding the implementation of the policy—such as securing adequate annual funding for it from the county board, enhancing its outreach services to the surrounding community, and increasing its role in preventive programs such as fighting lead poisoning among children who ate lead-based paint in tenement houses. Or they could have participated in assessment of the policy by examining whether the branch hospital was successful in preventing or treating specific kinds of illnesses, in meeting certain cost or efficiency objectives, or in obtaining any other objective or criterion that they had established.

To understand the actions (or inactions) of the Welfare Council, we need to place the policy practice of their staff in the perspective of contextual political, technical, value-clarification, and interactional factors that were discussed in the policy-practice framework that was depicted in Figure 9.1. Indeed, we could not evaluate their work without taking into account contextual realities, such as the machine, the power of Dan Ryan, the strong preferences of Karl Meyer, and the lack of strong support on the southside for a branch hospital.

Using a Range of Skills to Accomplish Specific Policy Tasks

To describe the work of the Welfare Council in this case, we not only need to enumerate the various policy tasks that they undertook, but need to describe if and how they used analytic, political, interactional, and value-clarification skills to accomplish them.

To illustrate the use of various skills, let's examine the Welfare Council's work on problem-defining, proposal-writing, and policy-enacting tasks. When defining the problem of medical service on Chicago's southside, the Council focused on the inaccessibility of medical services to black citizens, who had to travel long distances to the westside Cook County Hospital if they could not obtain access to southside nonprofit hospitals. Moreover, the Council emphasized traditional outpatient and surgical services. Because they framed the issue in this manner, it was almost a foregone conclusion that they would advocate the construction of a full-service public hospital on the southside. Indeed, much of their analytic work was devoted to proving that it was feasible to build and operate a large public hospital on the southside. In their analytic work during the problem-defining task, then, they defined the problem as "inadequate access" by blacks to hospital services. They used their political and interactional skills to try to convince other people, such as Dan Ryan and Karl Meyer, that they had framed the issue correctly. They issued a technical report and sent people to inform Ryan and Meyer of their conclusions.

Were we to characterize their use of skills in the problem-defining task, then, we would conclude that they used analytic skills to document the dearth of hospital facilities for blacks on the southside, as well as political and interactional skills to disseminate their position to highly placed decision makers.

They used their analytic skills when they assumed the proposal-writing task to develop a proposal for the southside hospital. Essentially, their proposal sought funds for a smaller version of the existing county hospital to be built on the southside of Chicago. Interactional and political skills were used, as in the case of the definition of the problem, to inform high-level officials of their recommendations and to demand that they obtain the funds for the hospital so that construction could begin as soon as possible.

Convinced of the rectitude of their position, and assuming that other people would soon concur, they saw no need to compromise or change their proposal to make it more acceptable. Indeed, the leaders of the Council maintained a relatively intransigent posture during most of the policy deliberations. When Ryan sought Council participation in a task force that he had established to study the issue, they maintained a relatively righteous posture. At one point they read their position to the members of the task force with the clear implication that they did not want to accede to amendments. Their interactional and political skills during the policy-enacting task were devoted to enunciating their proposal in relatively strident terms.

When it became clear that other officials did not concur and, indeed, sought to enlarge the existing county hospital rather than to build a southside hospital, the Welfare Council quickly shifted strategy. It sought to mobilize widespread opposition to Ryan's plan to seek voter approval for a bond issue that would fund a major expansion of the Cook County westside hospital. Throughout the process of policy deliberations, the Council made clear that it did not want to amend or change its proposal.

When undertaking the policy-enacting task, the Welfare Council used its analytic skills to decipher the existing balance of political forces on the issue. They apparently concluded that highly placed officials, such as Ryan and Meyer, were unlikely to favor a southside hospital. But they seem to have assumed that public opinion, as well as most people on the southside, would rally to their position and would ultimately pressure the county to construct the facility. Indeed, this optimism increased their intransigence with Ryan and the task force he established to examine the issue. Their interactional skills during the policy-enacting task were used to give Ryan and others the message that they would not negotiate on the issue.

When Ryan's task force recommended that the county place a bond issue before the voters to fund an expansion of the county hospital at the westside facility instead of a new branch on the southside, the Council's analysis of political realities made it clear to them that public opinion would determine the fate of the bond issue. They assumed a negative or blocking role at this juncture as they sought to convince the county to withdraw its bond issue. They organized a coalition of social agencies in Chicago that were affiliated with the Welfare Council and with officials of Michael Reese Hospital, a nonprofit, southside hospital that wanted a public southside hospital to ease the crush of indigent black patients on their facilities. They succeeded in obtaining some coverage in a major local paper that was critical of the plan to expand the county hospital. Members of the coalition packed a public meeting on the issue and voiced their displeasure at the county's plans.

The Council was chagrined to discover that their campaign to defeat the bond issue did not attract broad support among black citizens in south Chicago. They had assumed that the major black newspaper, black politicians, and black community groups would rally to their side, since, after all, they sought to secure a major new medical facility in their district. They were so optimistic that they would receive widespread support that they had not extensively consulted black leaders or citizens. In fact, some black leaders, who were primarily concerned about discrimination against black patients by some southside nonprofit hospitals, feared that construction of the public hospital might encourage even more "dumping" of black, indigent patients. Other black politicians were beholden to the Democratic machine—and Ryan was a powerful member of that machine.

The Welfare Council eventually succeeded in forcing Ryan to change his position, since he doubted that the bond issue would be approved if public opinion was divided on the issue. He agreed to a much smaller bond issue to fund a relatively small, outpatient clinic on the southside as well as modest expansion of Cook County Hospital. It appeared in retrospect that neither side had prevailed: Ryan and Meyer failed to secure massive expansion of

Cook County Hospital and the Council failed to secure a large southside public hospital.

Were we to characterize their use of skills during the proposal-enacting task, we might conclude that the Welfare Council oscillated between a relatively optimistic posture early in the case (when they assumed most people would ultimately accept their position that a southside facility was needed) and a relatively negative posture in the latter portion of the case (where they assumed that Ryan would prevail unless a determined, high-conflict, and publicized campaign were initiated to block the bond issue).

We have not yet attempted to evaluate the Welfare Council's policy practice during the problem-defining, proposal-writing, and policy-enacting tasks. Were they too inclined to rely on their analytic skills during the problem-defining and proposal-writing tasks rather than to use political and analytic skills, as well? Did they make erroneous judgments about the political realities in the case? Could they have made skillful advances to Ryan earlier in the case and acceded to some compromises that would have led to the construction of a southside facility *and* an expansion of Cook County Hospital?

As our discussion in the last chapter suggests, the way officials from the Welfare Council chose to engage in policy deliberations was influenced by various personal, organizational, and situational factors. As officials in a charitable organization that stood outside of the political system of Chicago, the leaders of the Welfare Council did not know how to play the rough-and-tumble political game of Cook County. Since the members of the board of the Welfare Council came from the relatively affluent and well-educated corps of business and professional leaders of Chicago, they were disinclined to "play ball" with the leaders of machine politics of Chicago and Cook County. Accustomed to providing technical reports on a variety of social problems in Chicago from their detached position, it was not surprising that the Welfare Council resorted to a similar tactic in this situation. Nor is it surprising that the Welfare Council failed to communicate with the southside black leadership; in an era that preceded the Civil Rights Movement of the 1960s, its leaders, most of whom were white, were out of touch with the leaders and citizens of minority communities.

While we can explain why the Welfare Council was not more inventive in its strategy, we can nonetheless criticize it. We will discuss various kinds of policy-practice errors, some of which the Welfare Council may have committed.

POLICY PRACTICE IN ACTION: THE PLANNING AND IMPLEMENTATION OF GAME PLANS

We have discussed policy skills and policy tasks and used them to describe various policy-practice cases of preceding chapters, as well as to discuss

Banfield's case study of the Welfare Council. We have also discussed various personal and situational factors that influence the choices of policy practitioners, such as their stylistic preferences and the amounts of power they possess.

To evaluate the work of specific policy practitioners, however, we need to understand not only the kinds of choices they make during policy deliberations, but their overarching plan or strategy that allows them to decide what actions, skills, and tasks to take or perform during a specific period of time. Officials of the Welfare Council, for example, decided in the early part of the policy deliberations not to compromise with Meyer or Ryan and not to consult southside black leaders. They decided to concentrate their energies on developing a proposal for a large southside hospital and to develop technical studies to prove it feasible to build, staff, and maintain. Their strategy in the latter stages of the policy deliberations shifted toward developing a plan to block Ryan's proposal to expand the county hospital.

We use the term **game plan** to describe the overarching strategy of policy practitioners during specific time frames.[2] And we use the term **implementation of game plan** to describe the actions that policy practitioners take to implement their game plan. In discussing game plans and their implementation, we do not wish to imply that policy practitioners always develop game plans or that they take (or necessarily should take) a specific form. Rather, we use these terms to allow us to describe and analyze whether and how policy practitioners develop an overarching strategy and to facilitate critical evaluation of this strategy as well as their efforts to implement it.

When developing game plans, policy practitioners often consider nine issues (see Table 10.1). People usually establish some boundaries or parameters for their game plan, whether a specific time frame (e.g., the next three months) or a specific task (e.g., defining a problem, writing a proposal, or enacting a proposal). Parameters are needed to partialize policy practice into manageable components. The Welfare Council, for example, emphasized the development of a policy proposal in the early and middle portions of policy deliberations, while they developed and implemented a blocking strategy in the latter portion.

When developing a game plan, policy practitioners can act in tandem with others, whether through informal consultations or by developing a strategy group. (A coalition, for example, can develop an executive or strategy committee that develops its game plan.) Or a policy practitioner can develop a game plan without consulting other persons. Banfield implies that the Welfare Council developed its strategy in the early and middle part of the policy deliberations in isolation from other people and institutions, but that it developed and staffed a coalition that shared in the development of strategy in the latter portion of the case.

Game plans can be relatively simple or complex in nature. Some theorists, such as Jack Rothman, establish rather specific questions or steps that prac-

TABLE 10.1   Possible Components of Game Plans

What Is the Role or Vantagepoint of the Policy Practitioner?

What Are Some Parameters for the Game Plan?

- Time Frame
- Task or phase within the policy-making process that provides the focus of this game plan (e.g., trying to define a policy problem, selecting a policy option, trying to get a policy enacted, working to get a policy implemented, or some combination of these)

How Is a Game Plan Established?

- Through consultation with others
- By the policy practitioner

What Are Characteristics of the Game Plan?

- Formal, detailed, and written
- Informal and relatively vague
- Somewhere between these two extremes

What Objectives Exist for This Time Frame and Task?

- Outcome objectives
- Process objectives

Does the Game Plan Define How the Policy Practitioner Interacts with and Uses Contextual Factors?

- Does it define how supportive or helpful elements of the context will be used?
- Does it define how negative elements of the context will be bypassed, offset, or neutralized?

What Stylistic Choices (if any) Are Perceived as Relevant to This Issue in This Time Frame and in This Setting?

What Specific Actions Are Planned in This Time Frame?

- Ones involving political skills: ones the policy practitioner undertakes or ones other persons undertake
- Ones involving analytic skills: ones the policy practitioner undertakes or ones other persons undertake
- Ones involving interactional skills: ones the policy practitioner undertakes or ones other persons undertake

What Value-Dilemmas or Issues Are Identified?

titioners should follow, but our analysis suggests that game plans need not take any specific form; indeed, they should vary with the tasks and objectives of policy practitioners, as well as the situational realities that they confront.[3] Game plans are sometimes formal, detailed, and written. Others are relatively vague and rest upon verbal understandings between collaborating policy practitioners. Other game plans fall between these polar extremes. Banfield implies that the Welfare Council lacked a detailed game plan in the early and middle sections of policy deliberations, but that it developed a relatively detailed strategy to defeat Ryan's proposal in the latter portion of the policy deliberations.

As we discussed in Chapter Nine, policy practitioners establish objectives for their work. In the case of affirmative outcome objectives, they decide what kinds of policies they wish to enact and their willingness to compromise or amend their policies. In the case of opposing or blocking outcome objectives, they decide to what extent and in what details they wish to defeat or modify a proposal of an opposing person or faction. The Welfare Council's objectives in the early and middle portions of the policy deliberations were clear: to obtain the funding of a large, full-service public hospital facility on the southside. Their objective in the latter stages was equally unambiguous: to defeat Ryan's proposal to expand the county hospital.

Policy practitioners often develop process objectives. People may decide, for example, that they want to secure the enactment of a specific policy (an outcome objective) but not at the expense of cordial relations with people who oppose it (a process objective). The Welfare Council appeared not to care if it antagonized Ryan or Meyer, since its spokespersons were relatively hostile and abrasive. (Had they needed to collaborate with them on other matters, they might have been more concerned to maintain friendly relations.)

Game plans define how policy practitioners plan to use contextual factors to facilitate their objectives. When supportive factors exist, such as potential allies, how will they be brought into their system of action? The Welfare Council did not consult black leaders on the southside, for example, but this action might have been useful to their game plan. In similar fashion, game plans can determine how policy practitioners aim to exclude, offset, or neutralize obstructing or negative factors. Had a close friend of Mayor Daley's been on the Welfare Council for example, the Council might have tried to use this friend to impel Daley to support a southside hospital in hopes of inducing Ryan to follow the lead of his political leader.

A game plan may define a style or approach to policy practice. It will be recalled that we discussed analytic, political or entrepreneurial, consensus-building, and value-based styles in Chapter Nine. Of course, people often do not name a specific style in a game plan since their stylistic preferences are implicit in their choices and strategy. The Welfare Council used an analytic style, for example, in the early and midde portions of the policy deliberations, since they emphasized the development and defense of a policy proposal, made extensive use of technical experts, and deemphasized the use of political or interactional skills. Their style in the latter portion of the case is best described by a combination of the political or entrepreneurial style and the value-based style, since they sought to mobilize political allies to defeat Ryan's proposal by appealing to righteous indignation against the political establishment.

Game plans sometimes describe analytic, political, or interactional activities that specific people will undertake. Someone in the Welfare Council probably defined a series of analytic tasks that needed to be performed in the early and middle stages of the case, such as developing a feasibility study for the proposed southside hospital. In similar fashion, their game plan probably defined the letter-writing, coalition-building, and other activities that were required to oppose Ryan's plan in the latter portion of the policy deliberations.

Finally, game plans may identify value dilemmas or issues, as well as projected solutions to them. The Welfare Council encountered a dilemma at the start of the case: In light of the likely opposition of Meyer to a southside hospital, should they be willing to compromise their desire to obtain a large hospital on the southside? They resolved this dilemma by deciding not to seek or accept compromises or amendments to their plan.

Whatever their form and content, game plans are eventually implemented during policy deliberations. Practitioners engage in a range of actions, verbal exchanges, speeches, research, and intelligence-gathering. These activities may conform to the dictates of their game plan as in the case of a disciplined and consistent policy practitioner. Or they may improvise extensively during the course of deliberations, perhaps even contradicting their initial game plan in important respects.

EVALUATING THE POLICY PRACTICE OF SPECIFIC PEOPLE: SOME COMMON ERRORS

We have discussed thus far how we describe the work of specific policy practitioners. When we evaluate their work, we can examine specific actions, verbal exchanges, or behaviors in specific situations, such as when we say a policy practitioner made an effective or ineffective presentation at a specific meeting. Or we can ask about their strategy, or game plan; did they have one, and was it flawed or meritorious with respect to its content? We can ask whether persons used multiple policy skills or whether they neglected some of them. In short the evaluation of policy practice, like the evaluation of direct-service and administrative practice, can explore a number of factors. Indeed, several kinds of errors are possible in policy practice, including the lack of a game plan, unbalanced policy practice, poorly executed policy practice, nonadaptive policy practice, strategy that works at cross purposes, misdirected policy practice, poor selection of issues, lack of parsimony, and failure of nerve.[4]

Risks of No Game Plan

While the form and content of game plans differ, people who have *no* game plan risk undermining their effectiveness. We can speculate that the proponents of specific measures are more likely to succeed if they have an articulated game plan, particularly when dealing with a relatively turbulent environment, controversial issues, or an effective opposition. As suggested by ensuing discussion, we can also evaluate the content of a game plan: Does the strategy of a policy practitioner make sense in the context of political and economic realities, the nature of the issue, and the nature of likely opposition?

Unbalanced Policy Practice

Like jugglers, policy practitioners have to balance many kinds of skills including political, analytic, interactional, and value-clarification ones. We have noted that certain kinds of styles of policy practice exist that emphasize one or another of these skills. When policy practitioners neglect one or more of these skills in specific situations, however, they risk the error of unbalanced practice.

Examples abound. Consider the case of the Welfare Council in the aforementioned case study by Banfield where well-intentioned and data-oriented social workers developed a proposal for a branch hospital in a black community on the southside of Chicago.[5] We noted that they were opposed by the administrator (Karl Meyer) of the massive public hospital (Cook County Hospital) on the westside of Chicago, who wanted to expand his facility rather than construct a new hospital in south Chicago.

Whatever his rationale or his motives, Meyer was well connected to powerful Democratic politicians. The Welfare Council's staff chose nonetheless to emphasize the development of analytic studies to refute the various objections to building the branch hospital. Because the Welfare Council's staff became so absorbed with technical studies, they failed to accurately diagnose the strength of opposition to the branch hospital and did not develop allies within the Democratic machine. Moreover, because they envisioned themselves to be the benevolent friends of southside blacks, they also failed to realize that significant opposition to the branch hospital existed *within* the southside community; thus, some staff of the Urban League feared that the branch hospital would further intensify the inclination of many nonprofit southside hospitals to "dump" black and low-income patients to county facilities. (They wanted to integrate the staffs of existing hospitals and obtain public subsidies for the medical care of those blacks who used them in an era that preceded the federal Medicaid Program.)

In this unbalanced strategy then, the Welfare Council was badly out-maneuvered by proponents of the expansion of Cook County Hospital. They mistakenly emphasized analytic skills to the detriment of political and inter-actional ones and failed moreover to examine some value-premises within their proposal, which did not address the issue of racial discrimination within existing health facilities.

Poorly Executed Policy Practice

Assume that policy practitioners have adeptly fashioned strategy by defining their objectives, using a variety of skills, and developing game plans. Of course, persons must not only develop a sensible strategy but also must implement it skillfully. In the case of the Welfare Council, they bungled the implementation of their strategy at numerous points. When they made a presentation of their case at an important meeting, for example, they deliv-ered it in a condescending tone that infuriated many members of the audi-ence. When Dan Ryan, the president of the county board of supervisors, invited them to submit a roster of names to participate on an influential task force to consider the issue, they submitted the names of many persons who were so uninterested in the issue that they failed to attend its meetings after they were appointed. Some persons even wondered if their technical studies, on which they hinged much of their strategy, were skillfully conducted.

Nonadaptive Policy Practice

We have noted often that policy practice occurs in a changing environment. Persons who were not involved in an issue become involved, and others withdraw from the issue. Background factors emerge that modify perceptions of the issue, such as changes in the budget situation or the emergence of new leaders. New issues arise that distract the attention of persons from an older issue or that intensify their interest in it. In the give-and-take of the political process, strategies of opponents of a measure can intensify resistance to a proposal or, if counterproductive, can decrease resistance. The assump-tions that policy practitioners made at one time about the positions or moti-vations of certain persons may prove to be unfounded at later times.

Effective policy practitioners often have to modify their strategy—and sometimes their objectives—during the course of policy deliberations.[6] That strategy needs to be adaptive and flexible is most obvious in political cam-paigns; presidential candidate Michael Dukakis failed in his 1988 campaign, for example, to respond quickly and effectively to George Bush's allegation that he was "soft on crime"—an omission that led to widespread disaffection among "Reagan Democrats" whose support he desperately needed. In the aforementioned case of the branch hospital, the Welfare Council realized too late that their analytic style would not effectively counter the political and interactional strategies of their opponents. They sought belatedly to mobilize a coalition of southside proponents of a branch hospital, but their opponents had obtained the upper hand by then.

Strategy That Works at Cross Purposes

Assume that a policy practitioner wishes to use a low-conflict strategy that relies on securing support for a policy from a few highly placed officials who will expedite its enactment in behind-the-scenes negotiations. Were the practitioner simultaneously to agree to be interviewed by a member of the mass media, he could sabotage the low-conflict strategy by exposing the issue to a broad audience that could contain potential opponents. Or a policy practitioner might decide to form a supportive coalition for a policy, only to fail to sufficiently consult some important persons and interests. In the case of the Welfare Council, they failed to consult the Urban League, editors of a southside black newspaper, and some important black politicians when they tried to form a coalition. Sufficient internal consistency is needed in game plans of policy practitioners to protect them from these kinds of contradictory strategies.

Misdirected Policy Practice

As we discuss in more detail in the concluding chapter, our evaluations of the policy practice of a practitioner often hinge on our assessments of her substantive objectives. As is often illustrated by political campaigns, a policy practitioner may develop brilliant strategy that results in victory only to disillusion many supporters who assumed that she shared their ideology or their political views.[7] To put the matter succinctly, policy practice is only as good as its purposes.

When we evaluate the merits of the purposes of policy practice, we often begin with the substantive policy beliefs of practitioners. Do they seek policies that are consonant with certain moral or ethical beliefs? Are they too modest in their policy objectives, or are they too ambitious? Of course, these evaluations of the beliefs or objectives of policy practitioners are shaped by our personal perspectives.

When we assess the beliefs or objectives of policy practitioners, we often examine how they resolved competing objectives and competing values because policy practitioners often have to make trade-offs. Someone may want to develop a major social reform, for example, but decide to dilute it in light of pragmatic political considerations. Even radicals concede that relatively modest measures are often needed in light of political, administrative, or fiscal considerations. We can ask in such cases, Did they *excessively* dilute their policy objectives to secure the enactment of specific policies? Reasonable people can, of course, disagree about the merits of concessions and compromises; indeed, splits often develop within campaign staffs, within administrations, among members of a specific coalition, and among the advisors of politicians and decision makers about their resolution of competing objectives. We noted in Chapter Four moreover that policy analysts often have to make policy choices in light of different and often competing criteria such as cost, effectiveness, and equity considerations.

Poor Selection of Issues

We have noted at several points that considerable skill is needed to establish priorities in policy practice. President Jimmy Carter was relatively unsuccessful in obtaining legislation because (among other problems) he bombarded Congress with legislative proposals rather than focusing on several of them at a time.[8] Or someone may select an issue that is clearly not feasible at a specific time when he might have better selected another issue or deferred action on the first issue.

Lack of Parsimony

Policy practitioners usually want to conserve their scarce time and resources by not devoting unnecessary amounts of them to an issue or a policy. They sometimes miscalculate, however. Someone may develop an ambitious campaign to obtain the enactment of a policy when a more modest one would have sufficed. Or someone may heatedly attack someone else's policy when a more conciliatory approach would have been as or more effective. When persons use more political resources than are needed, they waste time and political resources and, at least in some cases, create animosities that may later haunt them when they need assistance from other persons on another issue at a later time. Policy practitioners should sometimes conceptualize a series of strategies; when less ambitious ones fail, they can try more complex and resource-intensive strategies.[9]

Failure of Nerve

Recall our discussion of assertiveness in Chapter Five when we noted that some policy practitioners refrain from seeking policy changes because they excessively discount their own power (or that of their allies) or exaggerate the power of their opponents.[10] Such failure of nerve—a failing that all of us experience at multiple points in our careers—underscores the fact that in policy practice failures of omission are as important as errors of commission. In some cases, we are even kinder in our assessments of persons who commit errors than persons who avoid participating because the former at least tried to take actions to correct policies that they believed were flawed.

PRACTICE "ERRORS" IN PERSPECTIVE

Mistakes in policy practice can be placed on a continuum extending from certain errors at one extreme to possible errors at the other extreme. Some of them are blatant and that can clearly be assigned to specific policy practitioners, much like the egregious miscues of an infielder on a baseball team. Those members of the Welfare Council who failed even to attend important meetings of the task force unnecessarily jeopardized support for the branch hospital.

Some actions of policy practitioners fall between the two extremes of the continuum. We may determine that some actions or strategies of policy practitioners were judgment calls that on balance were inadvisable. By saying *on balance*, however, we suggest that a case can be made that they might not have been errors. Banfield implies in his case study that the Welfare Council erred in assuming that important officials, such as Ryan, were intransigent in their opposition to a branch hospital. This paranoia prompted them, he suggests, not even to try to convince them of the merits of their position or to participate in the task force that Ryan established to consider the issue. They probably erred in not obtaining more information or in trying to test the waters, but some evidence existed—such as the fact that Ryan's close friend, Meyer, opposed the branch hospital—that influential decision makers would not have supported the branch hospital. Moreover, Mayor Richard J. Daley, the powerful head of the Chicago political machine who was also a close ally of Ryan, took no position on the issue—a silence that could easily have been interpreted as noninterest in or opposition to the branch hospital.

In truth it is often difficult to identify errors in policy practice with certainty. Because policy outcomes, such as the passage or defeat of policies, hinge on many persons and many factors, it is unwise to assume that a specific choice, encounter, or presentation was responsible for the defeat of a specific measure. When we decide retrospectively that an error was made, we risk ignoring the state of knowledge of practitioners when they made their choices or took specific actions. For example, hindsight gives us insights and knowledge that were not known to policy practitioners at the time they engaged in their work. When we are too zealous in criticizing the policy practice of persons, including ourselves, we can risk excessively personalizing and simplifying policy practice. The actions and words of many people can contribute to the defeat of a measure, as well as many background forces and factors. Indeed, persons who wrongly attribute failures to themselves may refrain from participating in policy practice on future occasions.

If we do not try to evaluate the policy practice of other people or ourselves, however, we fail to develop our own skills or our understanding of policy practice. To improve their work, many practitioners in direct-service and administrative practice often try to evaluate their practice to identify chronic as well as specific errors in their development and implementation of strategy.

When evaluating the policy practice of specific people, we should take into account the degree of difficulty that they encountered. People who undertake difficult tasks or who encounter a formidable opposition will "lose" relatively frequently—no matter how skilled they may be. Conversely, people who only contest simple issues will probably emerge victorious on numerous occasions. If we were to evaluate policy practitioners only on the basis of their success in securing policy victories, we would risk giving high marks to excessively cautious people who only become involved in relatively simple or uncontested issues.

Indeed, we should note that "defeats" do not necessarily suggest that policy practitioners have been unsuccessful. When people take the initiative to propose policies, for example, they sensitize or educate other people, who may not have been aware of specific issues or problems. While no immediate successes are recorded, the defeated policy practitioner can try to reintroduce another proposal at a subsequent and more propitious moment and hope that some other people, now aware of the issue, will change their positions. As we will note in Chapter Eleven, many versions of child development and day-care proposals were defeated in the 1960s, 1970s, and 1980s, but each of them kept the issue alive, forced decision makers to grapple with it, and activated reform-minded supporters.

We also have to take into account the context of specific policy practitioners when we assess their policy practice. We argued in Chapter Nine that many factors impinge upon people who engage in policy deliberations such as their values and beliefs, their stylistic preferences, their objectives, their perceptions of gains and losses, organizational factors, and group or peer pressures. All of us possess certain biases, preferences, and habits that derive from these kinds of factors. While we may still conclude that someone, such as an official in the Welfare Council, made a strategic blunder, we may temper our criticism with some understanding of various pressures that impinged upon that person. For example, some officials in the Welfare Council, who were used to a relatively analytic style of policy practice, were ill-equipped to participate in the rough-and-tumble politics of Chicago and Cook County, where connections with highly placed members of the Democratic machine were needed. We might be even more critical of a Chicago politician who failed to attend to political tasks than of a participant like the Welfare Council that was not as accustomed to machine politics.

STATING THINGS POSITIVELY

In emphasizing possible errors in discussing policy practice, we have risked an excessively negative cast. To balance this, we discuss some of the strengths and positive attributes of policy practitioners. (As in the case of "errors," we offer these comments in a tentative fashion because relatively little empirical research exists that probes those tactics and attributes that make someone an effective policy practitioner.)

Policy practitioners probably need a vision (or a set of visions) that provides them with some notion of a preferred state of affairs, whether in specific agencies, communities, regions or states, or in the nation. If we lack some notion of a preferred state of affairs we are unlikely, in many cases, to be discontented with existing policies and programs. This vision derives from our values, beliefs, and ideology, as well as from a desire to help vulnerable or oppressed people, who receive inferior or negligible assistance. We do not attempt to define the vision in narrowly ideological terms because policy practice benefits from a variety of perspectives. It is nonetheless promoted and fueled by a sense of discontent that derives from comparisons of existing policies and institutions with a vision that describes preferred arrangements.

Indeed, a vision not only is a driving force, but can serve the political and credibility-building interests of a policy practitioner, as reflected by sayings like, someone "has principles," "really cares," or "is committed to changing things." We tend to be somewhat mistrustful, by contrast, of people who we believe are "only in it for themselves" or "bend with the wind." Of course, inflexibility and dogmatism can be deficits in policy practice, so people have to make an accommodation between pragmatism and those beliefs or values that constitute their vision.

In the case of the profession of social work, a vision can be created by developing an overview of the evolution of policies within specific agencies and communities, as well as by understanding the policy implications of broad theoretical frameworks such as an ecological or systems approach. Assuming that we have some empathy for the downtrodden, historical perspectives sensitize us to patterns of discrimination, racism, inequalities, and suffering that have prompted the development of various policy reforms. We become, in effect, descendants of an array of social reformers, including some of the founders of the profession like Jane Addams, who devoted remarkable energy to policy practice in a society that lacked the policies that we now take for granted. In a compelling argument, Jerome Wakefield contends that "distributional justice" provides a central mission for the social work profession that distinguishes it from other professions and from traditional psychotherapy.[11]

An ecological or systems perspective, which provides an orienting perspective for social work practice, contributes to a vision by sensitizing us to an array of factors that exacerbate or cause some problems such as homelessness, drug addiction, and illness.[12] An ecological framework also sensitizes us to the way outmoded or dysfunctional forms of the human services system exacerbate clients' problems.

Policy practitioners have to be sensible risk takers. Each of us possesses a finite amount of time, energy, and political resources. It is unwise to squander them on trivial or hopeless issues, even though ethical considerations sometimes prompt us to participate in difficult, even relatively hopeless, battles. But we also need to be willing to take risks. When we try to change policies we often encounter opposition from people who benefit from those policies, who possess divergent values, or who are wedded to tradition. It is not comfortable to be attacked; nor is it easy to add policy practice onto the existing direct-service, administrative, or community-work functions that most social workers carry. As we discussed in Chapter Five, however, these risks can sometimes be exaggerated by people who find assertive and proactive behaviors to be difficult or unnatural.

Policy practitioners need to be sufficiently flexible that they can alter their style or approach situationally; like administrative, community-work, and direct-service practice, policy practitioners encounter a variable environment, different kinds of issues, and different levels of conflict. Moreover, they engage in policy practice from an array of vantagepoints from within and external to the human services delivery system. People who believe they can reduce policy practice to a simple set of recommended rules or a single style are likely to be disappointed when they discover that those rules or that style is not useful in all (or even most) situations. Policy practitioners must also be willing to compromise to secure additional support for specific proposals and to diminish opposition to them.

Policy practitioners need an array of competencies. Analytic, political, interactional, and value-clarification skills need to be used in tandem in specific situations and during extended policy deliberations. A unidimensional policy practitioner is likely to be frustrated because external realities require a combination of skills. As we discussed in Chapter One, policy practitioners need to perceive that their work is linked to, but conceptually different from, other forms of social work practice. Policy practice is not simply an extension of direct-service practice because it requires different competencies. Nor is it adequately described by concepts drawn from administrative or community-work practice, whose theorists and practitioners attend to an array of tasks that have little connection to the agenda-building, problem-defining, proposal-writing, policy-enacting, policy-implementing, and policy-assessing tasks that form the core of policy practice.

Perspective is needed by policy practitioners to avoid pessimism and self-recrimination in the wake of defeats or partial successes. As we have noted, no single person or group is likely to prevail in the complex playing field of policy deliberations. Perspective is needed to realize that defeats are more likely when people champion the needs of stigmatized and relatively powerless groups, which lack the clout of more powerful interests.

Creativity is needed during policy practice to seize opportunities, to develop innovative strategies, to develop proposals, and to identify and define issues in a manner that makes other people want to invest time and resources in them. Some policy practitioners benefit from the use of *unexpected* strategies or behaviors that catch potential opponents off guard or that serve to reduce apathy.

Policy practitioners often have to be persistent, as the inspirational lives of social reformers like Jane Addams and Martin Luther King suggest. These people had an ability to persevere even in the wake of repeated defeats and when they encountered formidable obstacles. Unlike some of their colleagues, who left reform causes once the dust had settled from the tumult of early battles, Addams and King maintained their devotion to social reform. Indeed, Jane Addams, who founded the pioneer social settlement Hull House in 1889, persevered not only during the Progressive Era, but during the 1920s to support innumerable social reforms. One can guess that had Martin Luther King not been tragically assassinated, he would have been active in social reforms for decades after the 1960s because he had demonstrated that he was not inclined to rest on his laurels after securing many victories in the South.

Of course, few of us possess the persistence or the energy of these heroic figures. But every community possesses particularly dedicated social workers who manage to participate in many policy frays within their agencies and communities, as well as in broader arenas—even while they perform heavy direct-service, administrative, or community-work functions. We do not know why some people are dedicated while others lack the ability to sustain policy practice over extended periods, but we can learn from people who possess this ability and seek, in smaller measure, to emulate them. Perhaps their persistence stems, in part, from a combination of their vision or moral purpose and an ability to not be deterred by personal attacks or policy defeats. A vision provides a rationale for policy practice that is independent of the vagaries of particular moments or the defeats and recriminations that any policy practitioner experiences.

Policy practitioners need to be able to tolerate uncertainty since policy practice often lacks structure and boundaries. If relatively few people participate in the transactions of a direct-service practitioner, an "open field" often exists in policy practice that draws new people into specific issues. Policy practitioners often do not know what to expect when they initiate a proposal: Will it be associated with conflict, consensus, or apathy? When they initiate a proposal, they often cannot predict how much time and energy will be required, as the case of child development and day-care legislation in Chapter Eleven, which spans several decades, suggests.

Our discussion of game plans in this chapter suggests that policy practitioners have to develop plans to guide their work and yet be able to improvise during changing or unexpected events. Planning allows them to organize their work into a coherent pattern that provides direction and prescribes tasks that need to be accomplished. Improvisation allows them to seize unexpected opportunities, to counter arguments and tactics of opponents, and to adopt new strategies that were not anticipated in an earlier game plan.

In one sense, game plans are comprised of a set of policy-practice hypotheses where a policy practitioner asks, "In light of the time and risk that I wish to incur, what actions and arguments will increase the likelihood that I will obtain my objectives?" Various options are considered, such as relatively simple or more complex parsimonious strategies. The resultant game plan represents, then, a judgment that specific actions and arguments, rather than alternative ones, will yield an acceptable result or outcome. In light of the uncertainties of many situations, however, these hypotheses must often be guarded in nature and subject to modification when circumstances dictate. Policy-practice hypotheses or game plans are made to be broken since they reflect best guesses at a particular point in time.

SUMMARY

We are interested in some cases in *describing* the intentions, actions, and strategies of policy practitioners as they assume agenda-building, problem-defining, proposal-writing, policy-enacting, policy-implementing, and policy-assessing tasks. In other cases, we wish to *understand* the nature of the policy practice of specific people in the context of their values and situational factors. In still other cases, we wish to *evaluate* the policy practice; were their strategies meritorious, did they implement them skillfully, were they sufficiently flexible to adapt their actions to the exigencies of contextual factors, and were they sufficiently persistent or sufficiently willing to take risks?

By defining various policy-practice tasks, the policy-making framework that we used in this and the last chapter alerts us to the sheer number of ways that persons can participate in the shaping of policies. Most ambitiously, persons sometimes undertake a range of tasks with respect to a specific issue or problem, such as placing it on the agendas of decision makers, defining the problem, writing a proposal, and securing its enactment. In other cases, persons participate in only a segment or portion of the policy-making process. Perhaps someone makes a signal contribution in a specific meeting that lends support to a proposal or suggests refinements in it. Or perhaps someone's role is restricted to sensitizing a key official to an important problem in the services of an agency.

A policy-practice framework renders social welfare policy less abstract than conventional frameworks and more attuned to the way policies are made in the real world through a mixture of analytic, political, interactional, and value-clarification skills—within a multifaceted and evolving context. Our framework makes clear that policies are developed, enacted, implemented, and assessed by specific individuals but within a policy context. By so doing, it invites bystanders to participate, at least in those circumstances where they believe existing policies are inadequate and reforms are feasible.

When evaluating the policy practice of specific persons, many factors can be considered. We noted a number of errors that the Welfare Council may have made when seeking a branch hospital on the southside of Chicago. When assessing our own policy practice or that of others, we need to retain a sense of perspective, however. Many factors often contribute to the failure of policy practitioners to obtain their policy preferences. Moreover, they can become so preoccupied with the possibility of failure that they lose the will even to participate—a failure of nerve that is itself a recurring error in policy practice.

QUESTIONS FOR DISCUSSION

1. Take a policy change or reform with which you are familiar and describe the sequence of tasks that were undertaken by those people who sought it.
2. Take an attempted policy change or reform with which you are familiar that failed to be enacted. Analyze the strategies of its proponents and discuss possible errors that they may have made.
3. Discuss some problems in "laying fault" when assessing the policy practice of specific people.
4. What personal attributes do you think are most needed by policy practitioners?

SUGGESTED READINGS

Some Extended Case Studies of Policy Practice in the Human Services

Edward Banfield, *Political Influence* (New York: Free Press, 1961), pp. 15–56, 57–90.

Eric Redman, *The Dance of Legislation* (New York: Simon and Schuster, 1973).

NOTES

1. Edward Banfield, *Political Influence* (New York: Free Press, 1961), pp. 15–56.
2. I used the term *game plan* to describe the political strategy of policy practitioners in a preceding book, but use the term in this book to describe the broader policy-making strategy of policy practitioners. See Bruce Jansson, *The Theory and Practice*

of Social Welfare Policy (Belmont, Ca.: Wadsworth Publishing Co., 1984), pp. 185–186.

3. Jack Rothman, John Erlich, and Joseph Teresa, *Promoting Change in Organizations and Communities* (New York: John Wiley and Sons, 1976).

4. Gerald Zaltman and Robert Duncan discuss "errors" in the strategy of change agents in *Strategies for Planned Change* (New York: Wiley-Interscience, 1977), pp. 204–206. Various of these kinds of errors are implied by Eugene Bardach in his discussion of the strategies of policymakers in *The Skill Factor in Politics* (Berkeley, Ca.: University of California Press, 1972).

5. Banfield, *Political Influence*, pp. 15–56.

6. Various critical analyses of the strategy of former President Jimmy Carter suggest he was not adaptive to external realities. See Joseph Califano, *Governing America* (New York: Simon and Schuster, 1981); Haynes Johnson, *In the Absence of Power* (New York: Viking Press, 1980); and Robert Shogan, *Promises to Keep: Carter's First Hundred Days* (New York: Thomas Crowell, 1977).

7. Lyndon Johnson's increasing preoccupation with the Vietnam War is a good example of misdirected policy practice at the national level. See Doris Kearns, *Lyndon Johnson and the American Dream* (New York: Harper and Row, 1976).

8. For a critical discussion of Carter's strategy, see Johnson, *In the Absence of Power*, and Shogan, *Promises to Keep*.

9. For a discussion of parsimony, see Michael Sosin and Sharon Caulum, "Advocacy: A Reconceptualization for Social Work Practice," *Social Work*, 28 (January–February 1983): 12–17.

10. See John Wax, "Power Theory and Institutional Change," *Social Service Review*, 45 (September 1971): 274–288.

11. Jerome Wakefield, "Psychotherapy, Distributive Justice, and Social Work, Parts 1 and 2," *Social Service Review*, 62 (June and September 1988): 187–210, 353–384.

12. See Carel Germain and Alex Gitterman, *The Life Model of Social Work Practice* (New York: Columbia University Press, 1980).

CHAPTER 11

■

An Extended Policy-Practice Case: Child Development and Daycare

We have discussed analytic, political, interactional, and value-clarification skills in preceding chapters. This case, an extended one that discusses the development and progression of two major pieces of legislation in the U.S. Congress (the Child Development Act of 1971 and the Act for Better Child Care in 1988 and 1989), illustrates many of the concepts and skills that were discussed previously.[1] Analytic skills are illustrated by the way legislators— often in conflict with one another—fashion the substantive content of their legislation in the course of their deliberations. Political skills are evident at innumerable points in the case; for example, legislators variously use substantive power when they fashion compromises in the legislation, procedural power when they expedite the passage of the legislation by attaching the child development legislation to other pieces of legislation, and coercive power when a presidential veto will threaten the bill if it is not changed in important respects. Interactional realities sometimes assist the progress of the legislation through the Congress, such as a friendly rivalry between legislators in the House and the Senate, and sometimes deter its progress, such as the hostility between certain staff in the Department of Health, Education and Welfare (renamed the Department of Health and Human Services in 1978) and some officials in the White House. Policy practitioners use interactional skills to persuade other people to accept their amendments to the legislation and to build and maintain coalitions. Values often intrude as reflected in the different criteria that are used by legislators to assess policy options, the magnitude of the programs they favor, and the kinds of political tactics that specific people use.

The case of the child development and daycare legislation also illustrates the six policy tasks. Legislators and reformers engage in agenda-building, problem-defining, proposal-writing, policy-enacting, policy-implementing, and policy-assessing roles at the numerous points in the case. Moreover, the case illustrates how policy practitioners use a combination of policy skills to accomplish specific tasks.

The evolution of the legislation can usefully be divided into five periods. Background legislation and developments in the period extending from 1967–1969 stimulated interest in the issue. A period of "friendly partisan rivalry" occurred during 1970 and much of 1971 when members of both parties developed different versions of the child development legislation, but by 1971 they agreed on a similar version. A conflictual period occurred in the House–Senate conference committee and its aftermath that culminated in a presidential veto. But this saga does not end with this presidential veto because the child development legislation, although defeated, became part of the historical context for succeeding efforts to enact children's legislation. Indeed we discuss many changes in the political and social contexts of the 1970s and 1980s that set the stage for renewed efforts of children's reformers to secure national daycare legislation in 1987 and 1988.

BACKGROUND LEGISLATION AND DEVELOPMENTS BETWEEN 1967 AND 1969

In the waning years of his administration, President Lyndon Johnson seriously considered proposing massive increases in funding for children's programs. He was proud of the increases that had occurred in funding for children's programs during his administration, but he wanted a dramatic initiative to revive the reform impetus of his administration that had been lost in the wake of the Vietnam debacle.[2] He considered sponsoring "a child development program" that included health and other programs. His aide, Joseph Califano, scribbled in the margin of a December 1967 letter that "LBJ wants *big* children's programs this year."[3] By November 1968, the program, renamed Kiddy Care, was to include comprehensive health insurance for all children. He also considered a fivefold increase in the popular Head Start Program.

The president almost announced the multibillion initiatives at a national Head Start Conference in Houston, Texas, in late 1968.[4] Jule Sugarman, then associate director of the Children's Bureau, wrote a presidential aide that "if the President were prepared to take some action on Head Start [the conference] would offer an excellent opportunity."[5] Other aides and friends of the president urged action; consultant Harry McPherson wrote to four presidential aides:

> I heard an extraordinary thing last night . . . . 75 percent of mental retardation is "environmentally" caused. . . . My God, what a revelation! The slums are producing ineradicably damaged children. . . . Maybe there is a mother–child program that could be put together. . . .[6]

Various task forces had suggested even earlier in the Johnson administration that new programs were needed for children, and some had suggested the development of new administrative mechanisms to coordinate the existing and fragmented programs. A task force on early child development recommended in 1966, for example, that an Office of Children be created to contain and coordinate an enlarged Head Start Program, child welfare programs of the Children's Bureau, new medical and nutritional programs, and parent–child centers for children under age three. Furthermore, the office was to oversee and fund "community commissions" to administer and monitor the children's programs at the local level. The report emphasized the urgency of the situation when it drew heavily on the research of Urie Bronfenbrenner (also a member and a leading authority in child development) who warned that a dangerous decline in the family imperiled the well-being of children in U.S. society.[7]

The Head Start Program had whetted the appetite of many officials. Begun in 1964, its enrollments increased dramatically each year so that it enrolled almost 700,000 children in full-year and summer-only preschool programs during 1968. Many people believed, however, that Head Start was "too little and too late" to constitute an effective remedy to the problems of children and families. Moreover, some advocates of the Head Start Program were nervous that it might lose its autonomy by becoming merged into some larger program.[8]

The desire for massive increases in the funding of children's programs was not universally shared. A 1968 task force on education was established to provide ideas for Vice President Hubert Humphrey's presidential campaign; although it urged "coordination, improvement and funding of (current) programs," it warned against the development of relatively expensive daycare programs because "group daycare was tried and rejected by the U.S.S.R. as too expensive."[9] Moreover, even though the number of women in the labor force had increased rapidly between 1946–1968, many people still believed that women should refrain from extended employment in order to raise their children. To these people, large, subsidized daycare programs would wrongly entice many women to abandon their parenting functions.

Other policy developments from 1967–1969 made many officials desirous of establishing an enhanced federal role with respect to children's programs. Congress enacted a work requirement for recipients of AFDC in 1967. Some officials in the Johnson administration, as well as experts like Bronfenbrenner, were petrified that local officials would place hundreds of thousands of children of working welfare recipients in "custodial" daycare programs. Indeed, Bronfenbrenner warned just before its passage that "this will be the most serious blow to the children of low income families that our nation has suffered since the Depression."[10] To cope with this threat, the president decided a "czar" was needed in the Department of Health, Education, and Welfare (HEW) to retain and improve federal daycare standards that mandated minimum ratios of children to staff in centers.[11]

When presidential aides considered who should be the "czar," there was no serious competitor to Jule Sugarman. He had been the director of the Head Start Program and was a strong ally of Wilbur Cohen, the politically powerful Secretary of HEW who wanted to strengthen the Children's Bureau by vesting in it the function of coordinating federal children's programs and who wanted to transfer the Head Start Program to it.[12] Sugarman moved from the Office of Economic Opportunity (OEO), where Head Start was lodged, to become the associate director of the Children's Bureau in April 1968. Immediately after his transfer, the Federal Interagency Panel on Early Childhood was established—with Sugarman as its chair—to coordinate the various children's programs and to establish common interagency standards to govern federal daycare programs. Soon thereafter, Sugarman and close associates devised an ambitious scheme to develop state and local agencies to coordinate children's programs at the local level. Sugarman wanted the Federal Interagency Panel to fund local agencies, known as 4–C or Community-Coordinated Child-Care Organizations, which would plan, monitor, and administer all day-care and child development programs for children in specific geographic regions. Sugarman engaged in his work with considerable urgency, for he and others feared their work could be undone by a new administration in the wake of the November elections.[13]

To the chagrin of Sugarman and others, however, the 4–C Program proved disappointing. Representatives of various children's programs were threatened by a coordination program because they feared it would "take over" their programs. In the waning days of the Johnson administration, the Federal Interagency Panel managed, however, to develop a set of standards in 1968 to govern the administration of daycare programs that were funded by the federal government. A working group of OEO, HEW, and Department of Labor officials drafted the new regulations, which were formally issued in the summer of 1968. Because they applied *only* to center-based facilities, however, they had little relevance to the day care of welfare recipients, whose daycare was overwhelmingly provided in the homes of friends or neighbors. Moreover, it soon became obvious that the standards were often not enforced at the local level, in part because of lack of interest in them by staff of federal and state welfare agencies. (Wilbur Cohen, who did not support stringent federal standards, thought even the 1968 standards were unrealistic and costly because they required a staff–child ratio of at least one to five, a far more intense ratio than currently prevailed in many daycare centers, which often had ratios of one to ten or less.)

Richard Nixon was elected president in November 1968, in a closely fought contest with Vice President Hubert Humphrey. Some children's reformers feared that the new president, who scorned many of Johnson's Great Society programs, would oppose new reforms for children and might even scuttle the popular Head Start Program. Nor were their fears altogether misplaced. Nixon favored social reforms that emphasized the distribution of resources to poor people and to local governments, such as his plan to streamline and reform the welfare system and proposals to give federal funds directly to local jurisdictions—for example, his revenue-sharing legislation. He was less enamored with service-oriented programs like daycare and was disinclined to expand the role of the federal government in service programs. The Nixon administration, which assumed office in January 1969, chose not to emphasize the 4–C enterprise, which had virtually ended by 1970. The new Republican administration did not even recognize the 1968 standards as legitimate and made no effort to enforce them. Indeed, an audit of welfare daycare in four states and Washington, D.C., in 1971 found in many instances even the basic requirements pertaining to the health and safety of the children were not being met.[14]

There were nonetheless some hopeful signs. Some Republicans wanted to expand the base of the Republican party, which had traditionally been dominated by middle- and upper-class white voters. Some of these officials began to ask, "Why not develop some federal day-care subsidies that will appeal to the growing numbers of female workers?" Moreover, some liberal Republican senators, principally Jacob Javits of New York, wanted the new administration to continue some of the coordinating programs of the Johnson administration and to support expansive new reforms including large increases in the funding of the Head Start Program. Indeed, Javits was able to persuade Nixon to establish the Office of Child Development (OCD) in HEW to coordinate children's programs—and to make Jule Sugarman, a friend of his, its director.[15]

Savvy observers of the politics of children's programs nonetheless realized that many obstacles existed to the development of major legislative proposals to help children. Many top officials in the Nixon administration, particularly in the powerful Office of Management and Budget (OMB), were uninterested in children's programs like daycare because of its high costs, particularly expensive center-based programs; they preferred use of unlicensed family daycare and the use of relatives.[16] Some officials believed that children would best be served by giving low-income families more funds through enactment of welfare reform, which quickly became the central domestic priority of the new administration. Jurisdictional and turf rivalries between various government agencies, as well as existing children's programs, made it difficult to develop comprehensive programs or legislation. Many congressional conservatives believed that children's programs should be largely funded and administered by local jurisdictions; indeed, some of them argued that "intrusion" by the federal government in family issues was akin to the practices of totalitarian societies that, they believed, used state-run daycare programs to indoctrinate children. Considerable controversy also existed between the two political parties; if many Democrats favored a Head Start model of administration, where federal authorities directly funded local programs, many Republicans wanted to enhance the administrative and policy roles of states.

Daycare was a potentially divisive issue in the late 1960s. On the one hand, in the wake of the birth of the feminist movement of the 1960s, increasing numbers of women were aware that they could not obtain parity in employment if they were not given subsidized daycare services. On the other hand, many people had misgivings about the remarkable rise in employment by women with children; would subsidized daycare, they asked, encourage many women to abdicate their "family responsibilities?" Many politicians and officials resisted the establishment of federal standards for day care. If minimum staff-to-child ratios were established, the cost of federally subsidized daycare would rise. Some politicians feared that children's advocates might require welfare departments to use center-based or institutional daycare—a policy that would vastly increase federal expenditures for daycare—as opposed to daycare that is provided in private homes. Some politicians believed that *any* involvement in daycare programs by the federal government—aside from daycare for welfare recipients—was inappropriate.

FRIENDLY PARTISAN COMPETITION AND THE GROWTH OF CHILD DEVELOPMENT LEGISLATION

Various factors promoted the growth of child development legislation in the waning days of the Johnson administration and the early years of the Nixon administration. We have already discussed the emerging interest in child development, daycare, and preschool programs in the Johnson administration, as well as the resolve of some officials to enhance the coordination of children's programs. Some Democrats, who had chafed under the budget-cutting and antireform tendencies of Johnson in the waning days of his administration, wanted to develop new domestic initiatives. Indeed, some members of each party feared that legislators from the opposing party would preempt the issue by developing major initiatives. As we see in the succeeding discussion, this "friendly rivalry" also extended to relations between the two chambers of Congress.

Representative John Brademas (D., Indiana) quickly emerged in 1969 as the major spokesman for child development legislation. A former Rhodes scholar, Brademas had been growing increasingly restive in the Committee on Education and Labor, which was chaired by Representative Carl Perkins (D., Kentucky), a veteran legislator who did not encourage members of the committee to develop their own legislative initiatives. Moreover, Perkins was a staunch defender of the Head Start Program, did not want to see it merged with other children's programs, and was wedded to its style of administration, which gave federal authorities the power to select and fund local projects rather than using the states as conduits for federal funds.[17]

When Brademas was elevated to the chair of the Select Subcommittee on

Education, a subcommittee of the Committee on Education and Labor, he obtained the power to initiate legislation even if it still had to be approved by Perkins and his committee. He chose child development as his first major initiative in part because of the influence of an aide, Jack Duncan, who had previously worked with Jule Sugarman in HEW. Indeed, the child development legislation introduced by Brademas in 1969 closely resembled the administrative structure of the 4–C Program and had been largely drafted in HEW in 1967 and 1968 by Sugarman and Duncan.[18]

Like many legislators who seize the initiative, Brademas had many motives. He was troubled by the fragmented nature of children's programs and their poor funding, believed child development legislation would be popular with his conservative and rural northern Indiana constituency, and wanted to develop his own legislative authority, which had been stifled by Perkins.[19] He also wanted to develop an initiative that would place Congress on the legislative offensive so that it did not merely react to the legislative initiatives of the Nixon administration. And he wanted to assert the legislative role of the House committee rather than letting the counterpart Senate committee exert uncontested leadership with respect to children.

The bill that Brademas sponsored was the Comprehensive Preschool Education and Child Development Act of 1969, which proposed merging the Head Start Program and a variety of children's programs into a consolidated program to be placed in the OCD. He wanted the OCD to rely on state commissions to allocate funds to specific projects within their states and to oversee their operations. The legislation made substantial numbers of blue-collar families eligible for its programs because Brademas wanted to appeal to those blue-collar voters who needed day care and who believed they had been unfairly excluded from many programs of the Great Society.[20]

As an astute politician, however, Brademas realized that he risked opposition from those legislators who favored the Head Start model of administration. (They adamantly opposed reliance on state commissions because they wanted HEW to select and fund local programs.) Accordingly, his bill allowed local agencies to appeal directly to HEW for funds if they believed that they had not received fair treatment from the state commissions. Many allies of Head Start also feared that public schools would establish custodial and poor-quality programs if they could receive funds for day care and other programs; thus the bill specified that public schools could participate in the program only with the approval of local community-action agencies that had been established by the War on Poverty. To appease Head Start advocates who favored parent participation on boards of local agencies that received funds, Brademas's legislation required one-third of the members of state commissions to be parents of enrolled children and required parent participation of unspecified amounts on the governing boards of local agencies.

Brademas decided to leave many details of local child development programs vague to avoid political conflict with some Republican and conservative politicians, as well as with the Nixon administration. The legislation was silent with respect to staff-to-child ratio and other daycare standards, did not specify the precise amount of authorization for the legislation (it allowed "such amounts as may be necessary"), did not determine how parent participation was to be implemented in local projects funded by the legislation, and did not establish precise fee or eligibility criteria.[21] Many Republicans, he realized, would oppose an "overly costly" program that provided benefits to an excessively broad segment of the population and would oppose parent-participation requirements. Moreover, he knew that some conservatives, as well as liberals who wished to target services to low-income families, would oppose the inclusion of blue-collar families.

Like many legislators, Brademas was able to perform a skillful balancing act. Many House Republicans liked the proposal's use of state commissions, its proposal that merged Head Start into its programs, and its vagueness on parent-participation requirements and authorizations.[22] Some House Democrats liked that Brademas had seized the legislative initiative rather than allowing the administration or the Senate to take credit for children's legislation. Like all high-wire balancers, however, Brademas's feat also carried dangers. Perkins and defenders of the Head Start Program were furious that he used state commissions and that he folded Head Start into the child development legislation. They wanted even greater emphasis on parent participation and wanted explicit and high authorization. Moreover, Perkins deeply resented Brademas's encroachment on his legislative prerogatives.

But the Brademas bill was not associated with extensive partisan or ideological opposition in committee hearings, in part because of its vagueness and omissions, its provisions that were conciliatory both to defenders of Head Start and to conservatives, and the fact that no one believed that the legislation would pass the House—much less make it through the Senate. Brademas benefited, as well, from the argument that the bill asserted congressional powers against the executive branch by initiating major domestic legislation, a prerogative that usually fell to the president.[23]

House Republicans became fearful, however, that Democrats would preempt an issue that could have considerable political appeal to the general public. Accordingly, some of them began to contemplate a rival Republican measure. In the spring of 1969, a task force was established under the direction of Representative John Dellenbach (R., Oregon) to study educational issues and was staffed by Martha Phillips, the wife of conservative theorist Kevin Phillips. She was convinced that the issue could be used constructively by Republicans to broaden their base of support to include blue-collar voters, because her research suggested that the largest, unfilled demand for day care existed in these families.[24]

A number of Republican leaders met with the Secretary of HEW, Robert Finch, in late October 1969, and secured his support for a legislative initiative. But he cautioned them to consult with the White House to ensure that high-level support existed. A series of subsequent meetings proved disappointing.[25] Daniel Moynihan, Nixon's presidential advisor on urban affairs, suggested in a meeting in early November 1969 that more research and development were needed and implied that the legislation would be a potential rival to the administration's Family Assistance Plan, which included a large daycare component for those welfare recipients who would be placed in training programs and jobs.[26] The staff of the OMB, the powerful agency that prepares the president's budget, were highly critical of center-based children's services because of its cost when compared to family-based day care. Indeed, Sugarman, as director of OCD, was "directed" by top officials in the White House to testify *against* Brademas's legislation despite his personal support of it.[27]

House Republicans nonetheless persevered in their quest for a Republican alternative to Brademas's legislation because of their commitment to the issue, their hostility to key White House officials, and their fear that Democrats would receive credit for child development initiatives. They felt that they had not received a "fair hearing," distrusted Moynihan who was perceived to be unable to communicate with rank-and-file Republicans, and felt they lacked access to a president who seemed uninterested in programs for children despite some symbolic promises.[28]

Dellenback asked Phillips to draft legislation during the 1969 Christmas holiday legislative recess; her draft proposal was titled the Comprehensive Head Start and Child Development Act of 1970. The bill was similar to Brademas's legislation because Phillips borrowed its framework, but she made some important changes to meet the preferences of Republicans. Because many Republicans liked "the free-market system," it allowed profit-oriented agencies to receive grants. It gave even greater power to state commissions than did Brademas's legislation by not allowing local agencies to appeal directly to HEW for funds. It merely "authorized" rather than required local agencies to include parents on their governing boards. Moreover, it *relaxed* the Federal Interagency Panel's daycare requirements by decreasing the allowable staff-to-child ratio for five-year-olds in center-based care from one to five to one to fourteen. If Brademas's legislation merely implied that Head Start would be merged into a comprehensive program, the Republican legislation specifically folded it into the overall child development budget. To be certain that the cost of the overall bill would not be exorbitant, the Republican version authorized only $500 million for fiscal year 1972 and somewhat higher amounts in the succeeding three years. Forty-three House Republicans indicated their support of the bill when it was introduced on February 2, 1970.[29]

Although Democrats and Republicans had developed different child development bills in 1969, neither bill made it to the floor of the House. Considerable sentiment arose to develop bipartisan and compromise versions of the child development legislation because some top officials in the White House and OMB suggested that high-level opposition existed to *any* child development legislation.[30] If congressional legislators hoped to avoid a presidential veto, they would have to build a bipartisan measure so popular in Congress that the White House would be afraid to oppose or veto it. Rumors filtered down that Sugarman was having scant success in obtaining White House approval for children's legislation; some high-level officials in the White House feared that child development was a *Democratic* initiative that would compete with the administration's Family Assistance Plan. Indeed, Sugarman left HEW in the spring of 1970 to take a position in New York City. Moreover, Brademas needed Republican support in the Committee on Education and Labor because its chair, Representative Perkins, might oppose Brademas's legislation; Perkins still saw no reason to supplant the Head Start Program, which he had helped enact and had often supported, with child development legislation. Brademas even suspected that Perkins would urge some Democrats not to support it.[31]

Aided by a close working relationship between Phillips and Duncan, a bipartisan version was fashioned in the House during the spring and summer of 1970 and was approved by the Select Subcommittee on Education in August 1970. This version made concessions to Democrats and Republicans.[32] Democrats were able to delete the provision that relaxed current federal day-care standards and to require that at least one-third of the members of state commissions be parents of enrolled children. Republicans were able to eliminate the right of local jurisdictions to bypass the state commissions by appealing directly to HEW and to require coordination between child development and educational programs. Many specific compromises were fashioned. If Democrats were able to delete the term *profit-oriented agencies* from the bill, Republicans made certain that the door was left open for the use of profit-oriented agencies and public schools by terminology that allowed "any qualified public agency or organization" to administer programs. If Republicans enhanced the power of state commissions in overseeing and funding local programs, Democrats obtained a provision that cities of more than 400,000 population could establish planning mechanisms of their own, that is, bypass the state commissions. Members of both parties wanted to include children from blue-collar families, but Republicans were able to restrict this permissive eligibility policy by requiring that at least 50 percent of a state's allotment be allocated to disadvantaged children.

This summary of the compromises that were fashioned should not suggest that they came easily. Many drafts of the legislation were required, with complex patterns of negotiation that often split on partisan lines, and discussion was often heated. Some Republicans were convinced that some Democrats wished to develop a version of the legislation that the president would have to veto in hopes of embarrassing the Republican administration. Some Democrats feared that some Republicans would pull out of the negotiations and attack any child development legislation.

Despite conflict, most Republicans and Democrats who participated in the negotiations displayed remarkable restraint. They assiduously kept their disputes out of the mass media to avoid further politicizing of the issue. They shielded their partisan disputes from high-level officials in OMB and the White House to induce them to believe that bipartisan agreement existed. They refrained from drawing into their disputes those ultraliberal or ultra-conservative legislators who might attack their work. They also agreed to use terms that would make their legislation more politically acceptable to a range of legislators; they emphasized the term *child development*, which connoted popular programs like Head Start, rather than the controversial term *daycare*.

But what was happening in the Senate? Republican Senator Jacob Javits and John Scales, the minority counsel of the Senate Committee on Labor and Public Welfare, had observed with growing interest in 1969 and early 1970 the emergence of child development legislation in the House. Unlike many House Republicans, however, Javits and Scales *strongly* favored a Head Start model of service, which deemphasized the role of the states, allowed federal authorities to directly fund local projects, and required parental participation in decision making. Scales had extensive discussions with Bronfenbrenner, who strongly favored involving parents in programs.[33] Nor were Javits and Scales pleased by the paltry authorizations of the House legislation.

Javits and Scales drafted a piece of legislation that emphasized local community child-care councils to administer programs that would be *directly* funded by federal authorities and that allowed authorizations to rise from $900 million in fiscal year 1973 to $2.8 billion in fiscal year 1975. But Javits could not hope to secure approval of his legislation by the Senate Committee on Labor and Public Welfare because Democrats possessed a majority on it.

Senator Walter Mondale (D., Minnesota), like Brademas in the House, quickly assumed leadership on the issue. He had championed the Head Start Program in the face of possible cutbacks in 1969 and had even introduced a short bill in May 1969 that was entitled the Head Start Child Development Act.[34] Mondale was thrust to the forefront of developments in the Senate when he was chosen to chair a newly formed Subcommittee on Children and Youth in February 1971. When Javits reintroduced his legislation in February, he quickly agreed to develop and cosponsor a bipartisan version with Mondale. Both Mondale and Javits had many reasons to cooperate. They shared similar values. Moreover, if Javits knew his legislation could not be enacted without support from the majority (Democratic) party, Mondale realized that the support of Republicans was needed to decrease the chances of a presidential veto if the Democratic Congress enacted child development legislation. He also feared that Senator Russell Long (D., Louisiana) would introduce legislation to provide massive amounts of custodial daycare to welfare recipients to advance his prime interest in forcing hundreds of thousands of women off welfare rolls. A coalition of bipartisan legislators would allow him, Mondale thought, to wrest the initiative from Long.

Knowledgeable observers realized that the Senate version of child development legislation would take a markedly different form than would the House version. Many Democrats and Republicans on the Senate Committee on Labor and Public Welfare had developed a strong affinity for the citizen-action programs of the War on Poverty during the middle and late 1960s, which emphasized grass-roots advocacy by citizen-dominated councils that received their funds directly from Washington rather than from the states.[35] They feared that states and educational institutions would seek to control child development programs and were convinced that some representatives on the House Committee on Education and Labor, and even Sugarman himself, had conspired to transfer Head Start from the War on Poverty to the Office of Education soon after the Nixon administration assumed office.[36]

Unlike Brademas who *had* to engage in complex and protracted negotiations with House Republicans because he lacked the support of the chair (Perkins) of the House Committee on Education and Labor, Mondale could fashion legislation that closely conformed to his own policy preferences because Gaylord Nelson (D., Wisconsin), the ultraliberal chair of the Senate Committee on Labor and Public Welfare, strongly favored child development legislation. Moreover, Javits, the ranking Republican, was nearly as liberal as Mondale.

The Senate version would be different from the House version, as well, because of strong pressure that was exerted on the senators by a group that came to be known as The Coalition, an ad hoc interest group that included the Child Welfare League of America, the Day Care and Child Development Council of America, the National Organization for Women, and the National League of Mayors. Its most important members, however, were the Washington Research Project and the AFL–CIO, whose staff quickly assumed leadership roles in The Coalition.

The Washington Research Project was a southern-based organization that had supported civil rights activities in the South during the 1960s. Its articulate and assertive black director, Marian Edelman, was vehemently opposed to the House version of child development legislation because she wanted strong, grass-roots, and advocacy organizations to administer child development programs.[37] Moreover, she wanted child development legislation to strongly emphasize services to disadvantaged children. She had a close working relationship with Kenneth Young of the legislative department of the AFL–CIO, which favored expanded daycare in part because of the growing numbers of women in unions like the International Ladies Garment Workers Union.[38]

Edelman and The Coalition had been unsuccessful in its bid to shape the House legislation that evolved in 1970, despite support from Carl Perkins. Having failed in the House, The Coalition turned its lobbying efforts on the Senate, which was, they feared, their last hope.

This discussion of the policy perspectives of many senators illustrates how difficult it is to understand patterns of conflict in Congress. On some issues, conflict can be described in simple partisan terms or in ideological terms where, respectively, Democrats oppose Republicans or conservatives oppose liberals. The child development legislation was more complex. Partisan disagreements existed, as we noted previously, between Democrats and Republicans in the House. But conflict also existed between the different chambers; in this case, many Republicans in the Senate, like Javits, possessed policy preferences that were similar to some of the beliefs of House Democrats such as Perkins. Moreover, the ultraliberal Edelman, who disagreed in most respects with House Republicans, wanted, like them, to focus much of the child development funds on disadvantaged children. The term *cross-cutting alliances* is often used to describe these complex patterns of agreement and disagreement on some issues.[39]

The Mondale–Javits legislation proposed local sponsorship of community-controlled child development programs that would receive their funds directly from HEW. At least 65 percent of child development funds were earmarked for disadvantaged children—a concession to Edelman—but the legislation also stipulated that free services could be given to many blue-collar families by establishing an eligibility level of $6960 for a family of four—a concession to those Democrats and Republicans who wanted to serve blue-collar families. (The figure $6960, which is not adjusted for the inflation that has occurred since 1971, would have included many blue-collar families.) The legislation required the secretary of HEW to establish national daycare standards within six months of the legislation by convening a committee to be largely composed of parents of eligible children. To emphasize a social-action component comparable to the War on Poverty and Head Start, the legislation proposed funding many child-advocacy programs and a "national child-advocacy system."

Aside from The Coalition, surprisingly little external pressure was placed on the senators. Most interest groups assumed the legislation would not pass; some hardly knew about it because, as in the House, senators kept their deliberations remarkably quiet and hidden from the press.[40] Edward Zigler, the noted child development researcher who had assumed the leadership of the OCD in the spring of 1970 when Sugarman left the post, began to pressure his superiors to develop some position on the House legislation during late 1970, but he was personally aloof from Congress.[41] In December 1970, at the insistence of the secretary of HEW, Elliot Richardson (he had replaced Robert Finch), many meetings were held among various staff in HEW to develop a position on child development, but these staff engaged in endless arguments about the details of a service-delivery system, eligibility policies, and levels of authorizations that would be acceptable to the administration. The general disinterest in child development legislation created a political vacuum that The Coalition filled.[42]

The Javits–Mondale legislation aroused little opposition in the Senate.

Testimony on it during the spring of 1971 consisted largely of enthusiastic support from child development groups and experts and included a ringing endorsement from Bronfenbrenner, who strongly defended parent-participation provisions, which he believed would enhance parents' roles.

Several ominous signs existed, however. The prepared testimony of spokespersons for the administration questioned the cost of the legislation and the administrative feasibility of HEW funding and monitoring thousands of projects around the country. (The administration wished to give states and a small number of "prime sponsors" the major task of administering the legislation.[43]) Sugarman, who had become the commissioner of the Department of Human Resources in New York City and was closely allied with House politicians who favored Brademas's legislation, also wished to enhance the policy roles of states and favored far lower authorizations on grounds that the existing supply of staff and facilities made dramatic growth of child development programs unrealistic.[44]

Mondale realized that the opposition by the administration to the legislation could imperil its passage if it inflamed opposition by Republicans. He also knew that Senator Long was vigorously promoting his own daycare program in the Senate Finance Committee to provide (he feared) custodial daycare to welfare recipients; Mondale also feared that some conservatives might inflame opposition to the legislation.[45] To enhance its speedy passage, to continue low-profile discussions of it, and to outmaneuver Long, Mondale attached the bill to pending War-on-Poverty legislation that had been relatively noncontroversial. In effect, he "hid" the child development legislation in another more popular bill.

Caught napping, the administration finally realized that Mondale's tactic could lead to the enactment of child development legislation if the House followed suit with its version of child development legislation. Only twenty-four hours before the vote on the War-on-Poverty legislation in the Senate, the administration, working through Senator Robert Taft (R., Ohio), tried to amend it on the floor of the Senate to eliminate the child-advocacy councils, to disallow cities of less than 100,000 in population from directly administering programs, and to concentrate even more of its funds on disadvantaged children. As a last resort, Taft tried to delete the child development legislation from the War-on-Poverty legislation.[46] These last-minute tactics of the administration angered many legislators in both parties, who overwhelmingly defeated the proposed amendments. Moreover, the Senate passed by voice vote an amendment of a liberal senator to ensure that the Federal Interagency Panel's day-care requirements would not be significantly relaxed.

In yet another ominous sign, however, prominent, conservative Senator James Buckley (R., New York) developed a conservative rationale for opposing the legislation that went far beyond a discussion of various administrative and program details. He "framed the issue" in highly moral terms by saying the legislation "puts the federal government fully and finally into the business of caring for each and every aspect of each and every life that happens to be born in America."[47] By raising the specter of Big Brother, Buckley implied that the legislation was un-American, that it infringed on the privacy of the home, and that it (somehow) would force parents to ascribe to parenting notions of left-wing planners. No one joined Buckley in this argument, however, and defenders of the legislation, hoping to assuage conservatives, supported an amendment by Buckley to add language to ensure some provisions would not be interpreted as infringing on the moral-legal rights of parenting.

The full Senate passed the War-on-Poverty legislation with its attached child development component, on September 9, 1971, by a one-sided vote of forty-nine to twelve.

What happened in the House in 1971? Because Brademas's legislation in 1970 had not come to a vote in the Committee on Education and Labor, he had to fashion a new proposal in his subcommittee in early 1971. Once again, Brademas encountered a formidable political dilemma that required a balancing act. He *had* to make some concessions to the Senate and The Coalition by moving his legislation somewhat toward their version if he hoped to avoid a stalemate in the conference committee that would meet after the House passed its version of child development legislation. Yet he could not make too many concessions for fear of alienating House Republicans, who disliked many facets of the Senate's version. The Coalition placed "unbelievable pressure" on him to allow even small towns to obtain funds directly from HEW for their programs, to favor disadvantaged children, to include relatively high authorizations, and to emphasize parent participation in the governance of local programs. Because he wanted a unanimous vote of the subcommittee that included some Republicans, Brademas refused to budge on some issues; he refused, for example, to allow cities with less than 100,000 in population to bypass states by receiving funds directly from HEW.[48]

Brademas announced the compromise House version on March 24, 1971. Concessions to The Coalition included lowering the population cutoff for cities that could develop their own planning councils from 500,000 to 100,000 people, increasing the share of funding to go to disadvantaged children from 50 percent to 65 percent, and stating that the secretary of HEW be required to establish federal minimum program standards with a committee whose membership would comprise at least 50 percent parents of enrolled children. But he refused to explicitly remove profit-oriented centers from the bill or to allow towns with less than 100,000 people to receive funds directly from Washington. He did not accede to The Coalition's demand that the legislation contain a provision that declared that existing federal day-care standards would not be relaxed. Nor did he include language that emphasized parent participation in local programs. Moreover, in defiance of The Coalition, he placed in the bill the relatively high eligibility standard of $6960 (for a family of four) to appease those who wanted blue-collar families to be eligible for services.[49]

Surface appearances suggested that his tightrope act had worked; a bipartisan group of liberal and conservative representatives cosponsored the legislation and it easily passed the subcommittee and the full committee. Moreover, the House version of the legislation received strong endorsement from Wilbur Mills (D., Oklahoma), the powerful chair of the House Committee on Ways and Means, who said that the legislation did not duplicate day-care provisions of the administration's welfare-reform legislation that was also under consideration in the House.[50]

FROM CONSENSUS BUILDING TO CONFLICTUAL POLITICS: HOUSE PASSAGE AND THE CONFERENCE COMMITTEE

When Brademas, like Mondale in the Senate, sought to attach the legislation to War-on-Poverty legislation on the floor of the House, however, he encountered a polarized and conflictual politics that indicated that the bipartisan coalition in support of child development legislation was fraying. Although his amendment to attach it narrowly passed by a vote of 186 to 183, most Republicans and a majority of southern Democrats opposed it. Conservatives prevailed in an amendment on the floor of the House to reduce the eligibility level to $4320, as well as an amendment *not* to allow "local policy councils" to veto plans developed by state and city planning commissions for their areas. (An unusual coalition of liberal northerners and conservative southerners was able, however, to obtain passage of an amendment introduced by Perkins, whose district contained many rural areas, to allow small towns to receive funds directly from Washington.)

The House version passed on September 30, 1971, and, with its passage, the stage was set for the conference committee. Many House Republicans came to the conference committee convinced that Democrats sought to "take over" the child development legislation to embarrass the Republican president, who would appear to be antichildren if he vetoed it. Some of them were infuriated by Perkins's amendment to allow small towns to receive funds directly from Washington.[51] Those House Republicans who were close friends of Brademas were angered by Perkins's decision not to allow Brademas even to participate on the conference committee because Perkins believed Brademas had usurped his legislative role. (Perkins could exclude Brademas because committee chairs appoint members to the conference committees from their chambers.[52]) One source close to the negotiations of the conference committee believed that Representative Albert Quie (R., Minnesota) was so angry at these various decisions that he had decided to recommend to the president that he veto the legislation if it came across his desk.

The anger of some Republicans on the conference committee was raised, as well, by clear signs that the administration disliked the House version.[53] It had supported the last-minute reduction of the eligibility level to $4320 to reduce the cost of the legislation and to make it conform to the eligibility levels for day care in its pending welfare-reform legislation. It wanted to return to the emphasis on state administration in the earlier Brademas legislation. The anger of some Democrats on the conference committee was elevated by charges of The Coalition that Brademas had "caved in" to the Republicans in the final deliberations in the House; some of them wanted to rescind many of his concessions on various points. Meanwhile, some conservatives in Congress, who had been silent about the legislation because of ignorance of it or because they believed it would not be enacted, became restive about the prospect of the passage of the kind of major social reform that they had usually opposed.

Marked hostility also existed between House and Senate conferees.[54] Many House conferees believed that some Senate conferees insisted on "unrealistic provisions" to force the president to veto the measure to embarrass him. Institutional rivalry between the House and Senate had become ideologically polarized; if senators generally supported policies that were amenable to The Coalition, most House conferees wanted a version more like what Brademas had drafted in 1969.

As the president and his top aides remained silent, fear of a presidential veto hung over the conference committee as its members wondered what concessions or compromises might be required to avert it.[55] The local-control administrative structure that senators favored was retained in the conference committee, as well as Perkins's provision that small towns could directly receive funds from Washington. The Senate's high authorizations were retained, but the senators acceded to the House provision to reduce eligibility levels from $6960 to $4320 and to delete portions of the legislation that emphasized child-advocacy programs, which were strongly opposed by many Republicans and by the administration.

The compromises did not allay partisan conflict, however. Five of the six House Republicans and three of five Senate Republicans refused to sign the report of the conference committee. If the conference report easily passed the Senate on December 2, 1971, it passed the House on December 7 in a tense atmosphere and with a close vote of 211 to 187, where almost all Republicans and a majority of southern, conservative Democrats opposed it.[56] Extensive support by Republicans in the Senate for the legislation stemmed from their anger at officials in the White House, who had refused to communicate openly with them about the legislation; indeed, it was widely rumored that even Secretary Richardson lacked access to top White House officials on this issue. As we have noted, widespread support also existed in the Senate for the local-control administrative structure of the legislation.

Opinions were divided about the actions President Nixon would take. Representative Quie, who had assumed leadership of the House Republicans, openly predicted a presidential veto, but some conferees were encouraged by a telephone call from Richardson to Javits that suggested the administration would support the legislation.[57] In fact, the administration was divided into three camps. Some officials in the White House, the OMB, and HEW were opposed to *any* child development legislation. Some officials favored legislation that enhanced coordination and consolidation of existing children's programs but without large authorizations. Finally, some favored child development legislation that was similar to the House version, that is, that authorized modest spending increases and the granting of major powers to the states to administer and coordinate children's programs.

Edward Zigler, director of the OCD, and HEW Secretary Richardson were members of the third camp. Zigler sent many memos to Richardson in late 1970 and early 1971 that supported child development programs. Like Mondale, he feared extensive use of custodial day care for welfare recipients that might accompany welfare-reform measures and that were currently used by many working welfare recipients. Zigler warned Richardson in January 1971 that the administration needed to increase its credibility with Congress with respect to children's legislation and received by April 1971 a strong commitment from Richardson to work for the House version of child development legislation. (Neither Zigler nor Richardson favored the community-control aspects of the Senate version.[58])

But many officials in OMB, such as Richard Nathan, were skeptical about child development legislation, which they regarded as expensive, unproductive, and untested. They believed partisans of child development in HEW did not use "hard analysis," such as data about the demand, supply, and standards of services, to analyze program options. They believed children's programs should be largely funded and regulated by local governments.[59] And, despite extensive participation by Republicans in Congress, many of them perceived the legislation to be a Democratic initiative.

A stalemate ensued between members of these three camps within the administration that became politically embarrassing to the administration as internal divisions began to be publicized. In an article in May 1971, for example, Kevin Phillips charged that "a little known functionary (Richard Nathan) in the OMB is blocking the Nixon Administration's endorsement of enlarged daycare. . . ."[60] Not willing to precipitate an open rift within the administration, Nathan decided not to bring the issue to the personal attention of the president but to negotiate with HEW officials to obtain a set of acceptable specifications or guidelines for possible child development legislation. These specifications emphasized the role of states in delivering and planning services, made $4320 per family of four the upper limit for free services, emphasized only an advisory role for parents in the administration of local programs, and stated that the Federal Interagency Panel's requirements needed to be revised. But the specifications merely compounded the problem because Richardson assumed that they gave permission to him to negotiate with legislators about the details of the child development legislation, whereas White House and OMB officials felt they had made clear they did not want the legislation or increased expenditures.[61] (To them, the specifications were merely minimum requirements for legislation if and when the administration decided to support some version of child development legislation.)

Zigler and Richardson were truly "caught in the middle" in the summer of 1971. They could not openly campaign for child development legislation for fear that they would precipitate open conflict against it by OMB and White House officials, yet they risked antagonizing legislators—including many Republicans—if they failed to communicate with them. Neither Richardson nor Zigler knew how the president would respond. Both of them then maintained episodic contact with legislators and gave ambiguous messages to them that led to contradictory rumors about their support of or opposition to the legislation in the summer and fall of 1971.[62]

The suspense was lifted when President Nixon resoundingly vetoed the legislation on December 9, 1971. Like Senator Buckley months before, his veto message framed the issue as a moral one. The legislation, he said, would destroy the institution of a family by usurping daycare and parenting roles. He equated the legislation with daycare when he said it "would commit the vast moral authority of the federal government on the side of communal approaches to child rearing as against the family-centered approach." If debates in the House, Senate, and conference committee had centered on administrative, program, and funding details and if most legislators had emphasized child development rather than daycare, the president emphasized moral arguments about the policy roles of federal and state government, daycare, and parental choice.[63]

By making his attack on the legislation, the president cleverly appealed to several kinds of sentiment in the nation. Conservatives had traditionally opposed the expansion of policy roles of the federal government, but Nixon suggested that a federal program would somehow undermine both states *and* families. Many Americans were amenable to the argument that the provision of subsidized daycare would encourage women to abdicate family roles. Many Americans had come to accept a variety of social programs, but some believed the family to be a "castle" that epitomized American values of freedom. The term *comprehensive services*, which was widely used by reformers to describe the child development legislation, seemed to suggest a barrage of federal programs that would in some sinister fashion violate this bastion. By cleverly emphasizing the *daycare* elements of the bill rather than the term *child development*, the president chose the most divisive portion of the reform that would appeal to people who did not want women to move beyond their traditional role of rearing children.

Why did the president take a right-wing and moralistic posture? Many sources implicate his immediate political concerns. The conservative wing of the Republican party was angry at the president for his sponsorship of major social reforms such as welfare reform during his first term. Indeed, Representative John Ashbrook (R., Ohio) had announced that he would oppose the president in the 1972 primaries but had implied that a veto of the child development legislation might change his mind.[64] Even before the veto and after the conference report had been approved by both houses of Congress, conservative grass-roots groups had begun to marshal opposition to the legislation; of the 1000 letters that were sent to the White House in late 1971, 960 opposed the legislation, mostly in hysterical terms.[65] The veto speech was written by Pat Buchanan, the most conservative of the president's speech writers.

Defenders of child development legislation, including some Republicans who had supported various versions of it, were horrified by the tenor of the veto message. By politicizing the issue in such emotional terms, the president not only defeated the legislation but also placed child-care reformers on the defensive for more than a decade. It was not until 1988 that major daycare legislation almost passed Congress when, once again, a bipartisan coalition sought the enactment of major children's legislation.

FROM CHILD DEVELOPMENT TO DAYCARE: A CHANGING CONTEXT

The child development legislation of 1971 was enacted by the Congress only because of the consummate skill and dedication of a variety of children's advocates, who battled the administration and institutional rivalries between the parties and the two houses of Congress. But contextual realities were not favorable. Daycare was widely perceived to encourage women to abdicate their parenting responsibilities and the measure competed with the Family Assistance Plan of an administration that was suspicious of federal involvement in children's programs. Moreover, relatively little pressure was exerted on federal politicians for children's measures. Feminists were so preoccupied with establishing the rights of women to obtain employment and training that they did not emphasize children's programs in their lobbying. Corporate officials were employing increasing numbers of women, but they were insensitive to their daycare needs. They also feared that their competitiveness in world markets would decrease if they had to fund the high costs of daycare (they already were alarmed about the cost of the health care benefits of their workers).

The contextual situation gradually became more favorable to children's legislation, though it was not until 1988 that the Congress almost enacted a major piece of daycare legislation. Congressional representatives began to receive pressure from a variety of quarters.[66] A tremendous acceleration of employment by women with children occurred during the 1970s and 1980s, particularly among women with preschool children. Increases in employment were most dramatic among women with children less than three years of age; if only 33 percent of these women had worked in 1975, about 54 percent of them were employed in 1987. These women not only needed daycare in extraordinary numbers, but they needed affordable daycare because many of them worked at or near the minimum wage. (A large proportion of women were under or near the official poverty standard because of the low wages of many female-dominated jobs in clerical and service sectors.)

While the supply of daycare had increased markedly during the 1970s and 1980s, it failed to keep up with the exploding needs of women and their children. There were only 2.5 million licensed daycare slots for the more than 10.4 million children who were less than six years of age and had working mothers.[67] As a labor-intensive service, it is often difficult for daycare facilities to obtain qualified workers. Their low wages, often near the minimum wage, meant that many centers had high rates of staff turnover. The bulk of daycare continued to be family daycare that was provided in the homes of neighbors and friends, but this source of daycare was imperiled by the growing numbers of women who sought employment elsewhere. Many people hoped that more employers might develop daycare facilities by following the example of some corporations, schools, and hospitals. These institutions provided only a trickle of daycare slots because of high cost and logistical problems in developing and maintaining daycare facilities, which have to meet various standards of local government.

Corporate executives had maintained a low profile on the daycare issue in the 1970s, but they became increasingly vocal in the 1980s. With the maturing of the war-baby generation, corporations were increasingly dependent upon women of child bearing age for their labor force. The careers of women, corporate executives learned, are disrupted if they lack daycare for their children. Moreover, women and men are more likely to have high rates of absenteeism if they lack dependable child care arrangements.[68]

State and local officials also began to increase pressure on federal authorities to expand their funding of daycare. In the wake of tax revolts in their jurisdictions as well as deep cuts in federal funding of many social programs in the Reagan administration, state and local officials, themselves subject to increasing pressure from citizens and corporations, told federal officials that they would need to provide a substantial share of resources for daycare.

Grassroots pressure on legislators was increased by emphasizing that expenditures on children now pay dividends later in reduced rates of truancy, poor health, and dependency. Indeed, the Reagan administration budget cuts had spurred interest in protecting and expanding programs for children. The Reagan policies also promoted cooperation among various advocacy groups for children, which had been unable to develop and maintain powerful coalitions in the 1970s. People from educational, health, juvenile justice, and child-care programs, who had often been rivals for scarce federal funds, began to communicate with one another and to form a common cause. Sparked by numerous reports of the Children's Defense Fund, which was founded by Marian Wright Edelman in 1973, as well as many academicians, a bipartisan consensus had emerged that the nation should increase the share of domestic funding that went to children. Why not, some persons asked, include in daycare a variety of educational, nutritional, and health services so that daycare, like the Head Start Program, could serve a variety of the children's needs?[69]

The increased interest in children's programs was spurred, as well, by growing concern that the nation was not competitive with Japan and some European nations in the economic sector. The expansion of federal funding for daycare would meet two needs simultaneously: (1) It would allow more women to obtain training, education, and employment and (2) It would facilitate the healthy development of children who would eventually become the future workers for the nation's imperiled industries.[70]

Conservatives from both political parties had traditionally been skeptical about increasing the role of the federal government with respect to "family matters," as Nixon's veto of the child development legislation had suggested. But a softening of opposition by many conservatives to daycare legislation occurred during the 1980s as they became aware of the critical importance of female workers to the economy and the long-term benefits of expenditures on children. Women pressured some conservatives (not to mention pressure from their wives who possessed daycare needs of their own) to abandon their traditional opposition.[71]

Changes in the Congress also promoted interest in daycare legislation. The House Select Committee on Children, Youth, and Families was established in 1982 to develop a forum for children's issues. It served as a catalyst for advocacy and research, as well as a growing number of legislative proposals.[72]

FROM A WINDOW OF OPPORTUNITY TO LEGISLATIVE PROPOSALS

In a manner reminiscent of the late 1960s, when a flurry of child development legislation was initiated, many legislators recognized that a window of opportunity existed for daycare legislation. By 1988, under pressure from various advocacy groups, Senators Edward Kennedy (D., Massachusetts) and Orrin Hatch (R., Utah) had developed competing daycare bills in the Senate. A coalition of 130 national organizations, led by the Children's Defense Fund, pressured the House Committee on Education and Labor to develop its own version known as the Act for Better Child Care (ABC). These bills differed strikingly in their overall cost, focus, and administrative structure.[73] ABC proposed $2.5 billion in federal funds to be given in categorical grants to the states, whose officials, in turn, would match these funds and distribute them to a range of providers that would meet standards to be established by state and national authorities. Hatch's legislation proposed only $250 million in its first year to be given to states as a block grant with few strings attached.

The differences between Hatch's legislation and ABC reflected marked ideological differences between many Republicans and more liberal legislators and advocates. If Hatch wanted to keep the federal role restricted to providing funds, advocates of ABC wanted to insist that federal standards needed to be developed within five years, that a considerable share of the daycare subsidies be targeted to low-income children, and that some of the funds be used to train child-care staff and to raise their salaries. Ferocious debates were waged on ideological as well as pragmatic grounds; if advocates of ABC believed the Republican legislation would do little to enhance the supply of daycare or to ensure adequate standards, some Republicans retorted that ABC would usurp parental rights by imposing specific standards and give federal authorities too significant a role in overseeing local programs. Battles were waged on other fronts as well. Advocates of ABC insisted that their legislation did not favor center-based facilities, but many Republicans, who favored family daycare, believed it deemphasized family daycare. Some Republicans wanted to target the funds to poor children, while other Republicans and many Democrats insisted that children from middle-income families needed subsidized daycare, as well.[74]

The Senate Labor and Human Resources Committee approved ABC during the summer of 1988, but the House Committee on Education and Labor became divided on another issue: If some groups wanted none of the federal funds to go to sectarian daycare centers, many sectarian groups wanted their centers to receive federal subsidies (a large share of center-based daycare is located in church-owned property).[75]

Daycare entered presidential politics in the summer of 1988 when both presidential candidates sought the votes of women. Michael Dukakis, the Democratic contender who was not liberal on many social service matters, agreed with ABC "in principle," though he refused to endorse it outright— a middle ground that would, he thought, satisfy female voters while not allowing Republicans to depict him as a "big spending liberal."[76] Not to be outdone, George Bush, the Republican contender, supported a $2.2 billion program to provide tax credits to low-income, working families.[77] (Those working families that paid no taxes would receive the credit in cash, while poor but tax-paying families could subtract the credit from their taxes.) Bush's plan, like Hatch's proposal, sought to reduce the role of the federal government by giving it no involvement in establishing standards and by allowing families to use whatever daycare programs they wished—including unlicensed ones. Like many Republicans, Bush favored targeting daycare subsidies to low-income families.

The child-care legislation died with the end of the legislative session in 1988 since it was not approved by the Senate, but immediately ABC was reintroduced in the Senate in January 1989. (Since it was a new Congress, the legislation had to work its way through the various committees, once again, in the House and in the Senate.) With the unanticipated support of Hatch, the Senate Committee on Labor and Human Resources approved ABC in March. This revised version of ABC was developed only after intensive negotiations between Democratic senators and Hatch; he finally approved it because it softened language on federal standards, which could be no stricter than the strictest existing state standard.[78] The action of the Senate committee prompted Bush to submit his tax-credit scheme, which continued not to mention federal standards and to target the tax credit to low-income families. (ABC, by contrast, allowed subsidies to families who earned up to 100 percent of the state's median income or about $33,000 on average for a family of four.) Meanwhile, yet another bill was introduced by several other powerful senators that contained a tax-credit scheme like Bush's but that also proposed to add child-care funds to the existing Social Services Block Grant, which provided federal funds for a variety of service programs.[79]

By early July 1989, intense negotiations had occurred among the proponents of the various bills. To the consternation of many advocacy groups, Senate backers of ABC made many concessions to conservatives to try to obtain a consensus on a revised bill: They agreed to abandon daycare standards, to give wide latitude to families to choose family daycare, and to target much of the subsidies to working and poor parents. The Democratic party was badly split: Many of its moderates and conservatives wanted, like many Republicans, to restrict the role of the federal government, but some of its liberals favored the approach in the original ABC legislation.[80]

It was not clear what would emerge from the legislative confusion of midsummer 1989. Unlike 1971, however, when background factors were not propitious, a constellation of factors suggested that the Congress would soon enact national daycare legislation of some sort. If so, it would come after more than twenty years of political maneuvering, seemingly endless disputes about the substantive provisions of many pieces of legislation, and sustained lobbying by a host of children's reformers.

What lessons can we draw from the tortured history of child development and daycare legislation in the United States? When dealing with complex issues in a partisan environment, the race clearly belongs to the persistent. Compromise is often needed even when it sometimes seems ethically objectionable. Our saga suggests that many people, such as Marian Edelman, are willing to invest extraordinary amounts of time in advocating the needs of powerless groups like children even when no certain or easy gains are likely and even after people with less fortitude have lost heart.

QUESTIONS FOR DISCUSSION

1. Place yourself in Brademas's position in early 1970: If you had attempted a force-field analysis to determine the feasibility of enacting child development legislation, which people or groups would you have placed in it,

and how would you have characterized their likely positions on the legislation? (Be certain to note people or institutions with uncertain or unknown positions.) Then, with the advantage of hindsight, reassess the actual positions that these people and institutions held as the case developed.

2. Discuss some elements of the political strategy of advocates of child development legislation, officials in the White House who opposed it, and Zigler in OCD and Richardson in HEW.

3. What were some of the key policy-analysis issues (refer to Table 3.1) that recurred during the evolution of the child development legislation? What policy options were considered with respect to these issues? What arguments and counterarguments were used by various persons to justify their positions with respect to specific options?

4. Discuss some interactional factors that expedited the progress and enactment of the legislation *and* that delayed its progress and contributed to its ultimate demise.

5. Place yourself in the position of Zigler and Richardson; what value-tensions do persons who are "caught in the middle" experience, and how did they appear to resolve them? What other courses of action might they have considered?

6. Does this case support the contention that it is relatively easy for determined foes of legislation to defeat it? Or was this legislation particularly easy to oppose? (If so, discuss why it was particularly vulnerable to a concerted attack by its opponents.)

7. Refer to Figure 1.1 and discuss the policy context of this case. What contextual factors supported the enactment of the legislation, and which of them deterred it?

8. How had the policy context changed in the nearly two decades after 1971, and what implications did these changes have for the politics of day care in 1988?

9. Discuss how John Brademas used the various policy-practice skills, singly and in tandem, to fashion the House version of child development legislation in 1971.

NOTES

1. This is a revised and expanded version of a case that first appeared in Bruce Jansson, "The History and Politics of Selected Children's Programs and Related Legislation in the Context of Four Models of Political Behavior," Doctoral Dissertation, School of Social Service Administration, University of Chicago, 1975.

2. Interview with Wilbur Cohen.

3. Letter from James Gaither to Joseph Califano, dated December 12, 1967.

4. Memorandum from Charles Maguire in the "White House Sitution Room" to the President, dated November 29, 1968.

5. Letter from Jules Sugarman to James Gaither, dated November 14, 1968.

6. Memorandum from Harry C. McPherson to James Gaither, Joseph Califano, and Douglas Cater, dated October 26, 1967.

7. Joseph Califano in an interview noted that the *Report* of the Task Force on Child Development made a particularly significant impact upon the president.

8. *Report* of the 1966 Task Force on Child Development, p. 122.

9. Letter of transmittal from Harold Howe to Wilbur Cohen, dated November 29, 1968.

10. The 1968 Task Force on Education noted that welfare daycare "could become a huge babysitting enterprise."

11. Undated memorandum marked "eyes only" from James Gaither to Wilbur Cohen regarding "leadership of early childhood programs."

12. Jule Sugarman, *Oral History* (Tape II), p. 15 and interview with Margaret Wirtz.

13. Interview with Wilbur Cohen.

14. U.S., H.E.W., Social Rehabilitation Service, Community Services Agency, *Audit of Children's Services*, June 1973, p. 12.

15. Interview with Martha Phillips.

16. Ibid. Documentation of bipartisan hostility toward the administration can be found in the *National Journal*, 2 (July 27, 1970): 1353-1366.

17. Interviews with many people familiar with the committee.

18. Interview with Jack Duncan.

19. Interview with Wilbur Cohen.

20. H.R. 13520.

21. Child development advocates hoped that this would not encourage battling among various parts of the child development community to control the legislation. See testimony by Milton Akers of the National Association for the Education of Young Persons in U.S., Congress, House, Committee on Education and Labor, Select Subcommittee on Education, *Hearings on the Comprehensive Preschool Education and Child Care Act of 1969*, 91st Cong., 2nd Sess., 1969, pp. 16-17.

22. Interview with Dr. Marty LaVor.

23. U.S., Congress, House, *Hearings on the Comprehensive Preschool Education and Child Care Act of 1969*, p. 825.

24. Interview with Martha Phillips.

25. Interviews with Judy Miller and Martha Phillips.

26. Ibid.

27. U.S., Congress, House, *Hearings on the Comprehensive Preschool Education and Child Care Act of 1969*, p. 102, and interview with Jules Sugarman.

28. Interview with Martha Phillips.

29. H.R. 15776. Interview with Martha Phillips.

30. Events are taken from a mimeographed *Chronology* from the files of Martha Phillips.

31. Interviews with Wilbur Cohen and Richard Orton.

32. It was H.R. 19362.

33. Interviews with John Scales, Urie Bronfenbrenner, and Jack Duncan. Richard Orton, Director of the Head Start Program, played a considerable role in urging senators to counter the House legislation with a version more similar to the Head Start Program.

34. *Congressional Record*, Senate, May 5, 1969, pp. 11294-11302.

35. Interview with Jules Sugarman.

36. Martha Phillips, "The Head Start Program."

37. Interviews with Erika Streuer, William Pierce, and Judy Asmuss.

38. Ibid.

39. Eric Schattschneider, *The Semi-Sovereign People* (Hinesdale, Ill.: Dryden Press, 1960), pp. 64-67.

40. The precise role of the administration with respect to the legislation is discussed subsequently in this chapter.

41. Interviews with many administration and congressional officials.

42. Interview with Wilbur Cohen.

43. U.S., Congress, Senate, Committee on Labor and Public Welfare, Subcommittee on Children and Youth. *Hearings on Comprehensive Child Development Act of 1971*, 92nd Cong., 1st Sess., 1971, pp. 762-789.

44. Ibid., pp. 169-175.

45. *National Journal*, 3 (October 23, 1971): 2128, and interviews with Sid Johnson and Michael Stern.

46. See a letter from Elliot Richardson to Senator Taft dated September 8, 1971.

47. *Congressional Record*, Senate, September 9, 1971, p. 31226.

48. Interview with Jack Duncan.

49. The bill was H.R. 6748.

50. Interviews with Jack Duncan and Judy Asmuss.

51. *National Journal*, 3 (October 23, 1971): 2129.

52. Ibid.

53. Ibid.

54. Ibid.

55. Interview with John Scales.

56. *Report on Preschool Education*, 3 (December 1, 1971): 2-3.

57. *Report on Preschool Education*, 3 (November 17, 1971): 2.

58. See memoranda from Zigler to James Farmer (September 21, 1970) and to Elliot Richardson (February 25, 1971 and January 15, 1970).

59. James Welch, "Child Care Plan Considered for Higher Income Families," *Washington Star* (May 24, 1971).

60. Kevin Phillips, *Washington Post* (May 20, 1971): A19.

61. Interviews with Richard Emery and James Edwards.

62. Interview with Mrs. Richard Lansburgh.

63. Interview with Martha Phillips.

64. *Chicago Daily News* (December 10, 1971): 4.

65. Interview with Marge Elsten.

66. A discussion of the changing political context in the 1980s is found in Julie Kosterlitz, "Not Just Kid Stuff," *National Journal*, 20 (November 19, 1988): 2934-2939.

67. Patrick Knudsen, "Committees Starting to Focus on Child Care," *Congressional Quarterly Weekly Report*, 46 (February 27, 1988): 514-515.

68. Kosterlitz, "Not Just Kid Stuff."

69. Ibid.

70. Ibid.

71. Ibid.

72. Ibid.

73. Knudsen, "Committees Starting to Focus on Child Care."

74. Julie Rovner, "Day-Care Package Clears First Hurdle in House," *Congressional Quarterly Weekly Report*, 46 (July 2, 1988), pp. 1833-1836.

75. Julie Rovner, "Senate Labor Committee Approves ABC Bill," *Congressional Quarterly Weekly Report*, 46 (July 30, 1988): 2077. Also see Macon Moorhouse, "Markup of Child-Care Bill Slows as Dispute Develops," *Congressional Quarterly Weekly Report*, 46 (August 6, 1988): 2200-2202.

76. Ibid.

77. Julie Rovner, "$2.2 Billion Child Care Report of Bush's Unveiled," *Congressional Quarterly Weekly Report*, 46 (December 10, 1988): 3463.

78. Julie Rovner, "Child-Care Debate Intensifies as ABC Bill Is Approved," *Congressional Quarterly Weekly Report*, 47 (March 18, 1989): 585-587.

79. Ibid.

80. Thomas Edsall, "Disputes Over Social Issues Mark Partisan Upheaval in Congress," *Washington Post* (July 6, 1989): A14.

PART V

■

Social Welfare Policy in the Postenactment Phases of Implementation and Assessment

After the enactment of specific policies, some policy practitioners, relieved that their long ordeal has ended, hope to enjoy the fruits of victory. But they sometimes discover that the battle has hardly begun because many meritorious policies meet their demise in the realities of turf rivalries, poor funding, incompetent administrators, ill-equipped staff, and special interests who seek to sabotage facets of the enacted policies. Policy-implementing and policy-assessing tasks describe the work of policy practitioners in the postenactment phases.

We explore these postenactment realities in Chapter Twelve by examining reasons why one widely heralded policy enactment, the Adoption Assistance and Child Welfare Act of 1980, did not meet some of the lofty expectations of some of its founders. As is often the case, many factors undermined its implementation. We argue in the concluding section of the chapter that social workers have an important policy-practice role during implementation; as the people who are often charged with implementing specific policies, they are often acutely aware of some of the barriers to their realization in specific agencies and communities.

In Chapter Thirteen, we discuss methods of assessing operative policies. The assessments, or evaluations, are vitally important because they tell us whether specific aims of the framers of policies are (or are not) achieved during their implementation. As with other aspects of policy, however, nontechnical factors such as politics often intrude; people often disagree about how to evaluate specific policies, how to interpret specific evaluative findings, and what policy reforms are suggested by the findings of a specific study.

CHAPTER 12

■

Implementing Policies

We have discussed various tasks that policy practitioners assume before and during the enactment of policies, but the work of policy practitioners does not stop when policies are enacted. Once policies are enacted, attention shifts to the question, To what extent and how effectively will they be implemented? Nor is this question trivial because many promising policies are severely compromised during their implementation by a host of factors. We will ask successively how we know if policies have or have not been implemented, whether nonimplementation is necessarily "bad," how we identify factors that cause the nonimplementation of policy, and how we devise corrective interventions.

We use as our lead example in this chapter the implementation of the Adoption Assistance and Child Welfare Act of 1980. Prior to its enactment, many people were alarmed by the dramatic increase in the numbers of children who were in foster-care placements because they had been removed from their natural families due to alleged abusive behavior of their parents or neglect of basic needs. (The number of children in foster care had risen to more than 500,000 children in 1979 from 177,000 children in 1961.[1])

THE NATURE OF ENACTED POLICIES

Enacted policies are merely paper directives, that is, abstract guidelines and objectives that reflect the preferences of the framers of policies, who have often balanced value, political, and analytic considerations when constructing them. To determine whether policies have been implemented, we need first to establish the content of the enacted policies, which includes formal content (i.e., policy objectives and instrumental policies that are written in legislative or policy directives) and policy intentions, or objectives, of the framers.

Written policies are relatively easy to identify, although their precise meaning may be difficult to determine because of the vagueness of certain terms. Terms like *increasing economic opportunity, full employment*, and *quality daycare* are ambiguous, but often appear in written policy.[2]

If we confined ourselves only to written policy, however, we would omit the **policy intentions** of policy framers, who devise new or modified policies because they want certain kinds of changes to occur in the external world.[3] These policy intentions are often not written in the legislation because they reflect the expectations, or hopes, of policy framers about the effects or outcomes of policies. The framers of Medicaid legislation in 1965, for example, wanted the federal program to increase the access poor people had to physicians and hospitals that were used by middle-class people, that is, to allow them to escape class-based segregation in the county and municipal hospitals that were traditionally reserved to them. The program fulfilled many of the written, or formal, policies in the legislation, but most of its recipients continued to use public hospitals so it failed to mainstream poor people into the larger medical-care system. Were we not to examine the persistence of such medical segregation, we would neglect a critically important fact when analyzing the implementation of Medicaid.[4]

When we examine implementation then, we ask, Do the actions of those officials and staff who are charged with implementing policies correspond to various of the formal or written policies, and are the enacted policies achieving the kinds of hopes or expectations that the framers had in mind when they constructed the formal policies? The importance of both official, written policy and policy expectations to implementation can be illustrated by examining the Adoption Assistance and Child Welfare Act of 1980.

To understand the policy expectations of its framers, we need to examine the child welfare system as it existed in 1980. Senators like Alan Cranston and professional associations like the Child Welfare League of America sought the passage of the legislation because they were worried that so many children, mostly minorities or teenagers, remained in foster homes or children's institutions for years after they had been removed from their natural homes.[5] The children had been taken from their natural homes by juvenile courts because the parents had neglected their children (by not providing them with sustenance or care) or subjected them to physical abuse—or because the children were "incorrigible," that is, could not be controlled or disciplined by parents. (Although some children were voluntarily relinquished, many were taken from their parents by the courts.)

Framers of the legislation wanted permanent arrangements to replace the "state of limbo" that many children experienced as they moved between a succession of placements, whether in foster homes or in institutions. They realized that two sets of officials and staff were the pillars of the child welfare system: first, the child welfare staff, who conducted most of the counseling, screening, and placement services for the children, as well as for the foster-home parents, the natural parents, and the adoptive parents; second, the juvenile court judges who made decisions about the dispositions of most children.

The framers believed that permanency was not obtained for most children who were taken from their natural families for several reasons. Many child welfare staff and juvenile court judges had become so accustomed to non-permanent arrangements for children that they did not assertively seek permanent arrangements. Despite innovative legislation in some states that provided subsidies to adoptive parents to ease the financial burdens of assuming legal responsibility for a child, relatively few persons volunteered to adopt children, particularly adolescents, minorities, or children with serious physical or mental problems. In some cases, local staff did not even try to rehabilitate the natural families of children to allow them to return to them, perhaps partly because the federal government reimbursed local authorities for the ongoing costs of foster care for AFDC children who were placed in foster care by court order.[6]

The framers hoped then to fundamentally change the kinds of decisions that were made in the child welfare system so that tens of thousands of children would be given permanent arrangements either by returning to those natural families that could be rehabilitated or by finding adoptive parents. The framers combined in an ingenious fashion the use of incentives and requirements to accomplish these sweeping objectives. Because they knew that the existing child welfare system was grievously underfunded (many social workers had caseloads exceeding eighty families), they wanted to provide additional funds to the child welfare system. Moreover, they wanted to fund adoption subsidies to help adoptive parents defray the cost of raising adopted children because they knew that many parents, particularly poor ones, were deterred from adopting children for financial reasons. Because they feared that pumping more money into the system could be counterproductive if they did not require states to promote permanent arrangements for children, they made receipt of the funds by particular states contingent on states setting in motion certain policies such as improved record-keeping systems and the establishment of periodic reviews of cases by the courts.

As they wrestled with writing these requirements, they established certain national standards. They required each state to establish a tracking system so that the progress of each child could be monitored and so that no children became "lost" in the foster-care or institutional system. Moreover, they required each state to establish reviews of the progress of each child by external reviewing bodies, whether the courts or administrative bodies. The courts had to make an initial determination that a child should be removed from its natural parents to protect the rights of natural parents. A case review was required, as well, after the child had been in foster care for six months and again at twelve months to ensure that caseworkers had established a plan for permanent arrangements. A formal review was also required at eighteen months to ensure that the permanency plan had been implemented, that is, that the child had either been returned to the natural parents or adopted. To promote the provision of preventive counseling and other services to natural parents, both before and after abusive and neglectful behavior, the legislation greatly increased the amount of federal money to be given to states to fund child welfare services in hopes it would increase efforts to reunify families, to find adoptive parents, and to develop permanent arrangements.

The federal framers of the legislation used a three-pronged strategy, then, to reform the child welfare system.[7] They provided more funds for child welfare services to encourage states to reunify families and to make permanent arrangements. They provided adoption subsidies for children who were eligible for AFDC. They established various regulations to require states and courts to track the progress of children in foster care and to review cases at point of intake as well as at six-, twelve-, and eighteen-month intervals.

HOW DO WE KNOW IF POLICIES HAVE BEEN IMPLEMENTED?

To examine the correspondence of official policy, and the policy expectations of the framers of the legislation, with implemented policy, we would need to collect data in the various states to discover whether states that used federal funds under this act established tracking systems as well as deadlines for devising and implementing a permanent plan for each child, implemented tracking systems for each child, met the six- and twelve-month requirements for reviews of the progress of each child, implemented permanency plans by the eighteen-month deadline, and markedly increased the amount and quality of services to reunify natural families. Finally, we would want ultimately to know if the well-being of children had actually been enhanced by the legislation. When any major policy is enacted, its implementors may comply with its formal requirements in a manner that subverts the intentions of some of its framers. Many advocates for children hoped that the establishment of permanent arrangements would enhance the developmental needs of children by diminishing the trauma of uncertainty and multiple placements in foster care.[8] What if some jurisdictions, anxious to comply with the formal requirements, ill advisedly returned many children to natural families that were ill suited to help them? What if many jurisdictions returned children to natural families without providing them with intensive and long-term services?

The preceding discussion suggests that it is not easy to determine whether a policy has been implemented. To obtain accurate information of the implementation of this legislation, we would need case-based data from the tens of thousands of cases of children who have been removed from their homes in the decade ensuing the 1980 legislation to discover if permanency plans had been made and implemented in accordance with deadlines established by federal legislation. Moreover, we would need to obtain data about the children themselves, such as ones that measured their developmental well-being.

Obtaining this information would be difficult. Local child welfare departments keep statistics that they forward to the state agencies that oversee foster-care and adoptive services, but their statistics would need to be viewed with some skepticism.[9] After all, they have an incentive to report data that make them appear to comply with state law even when they do not. Few officials would falsify data, but some would likely ignore nuances or subtleties in the data that would be important to researchers who were probing the implementation of the Adoption Assistance and Child Welfare Act.

These nuances and subtleties involve not just formal compliance with the requirement of the law but with the "spirit" or "direction" of implementation. A local child welfare unit could, for example, require child welfare workers to reunite children with their natural parents in order to produce permanent arrangements, but some of these reunions might be ill advised in terms of the well-being of the children. Indeed, the term *goal displacement*, which is drawn from organizational theory, captures the tendency of some policy implementors to comply with formal edicts even when sacrificing the intent of policy.[10]

Let's examine a number of ways that program statistics of local and state authorities could be misleading. First, as just suggested, a local child welfare unit might return many children to their natural families even when they had not done sufficient investigations or provided sufficient ameliorative services to be relatively certain that they would receive a minimum level of nurturance and safety. These children would be in permanent arrangements, would appear *on paper* to comply with the law, and would widely be recorded as "successes" in official statistics, but they would have fundamentally failed to meet the *intent* of the law.[11]

Second, some child welfare units might place children with adoptive parents when in fact the natural parents could have been rehabilitated with the provision of services. Concerned about the rights of natural parents, framers of the legislation wanted children to be returned to their natural homes when parents could be helped to improve their parenting skills through the provision of services or, in some cases, job training or employment. (Some children are neglected by parents because they lack the resources to provide them with basic essentials or because poverty induces stress that promotes abusive behavior.) Those jurisdictions that unnecessarily placed children in adoptions appear as successes in official statistics but violate the intent of the legislation.[12]

Third, some states developed definitions of permanency that varied from the intent of the national framers. If the national framers assumed that children would be placed with parents, whether natural or adoptive ones, some states defined permanency to include long-term residency in a single foster home or a single institution—or even the provision of a public guardian who would assume ongoing and legal responsibility for a child.[13] When defined more loosely to include these possibilities, permanency ceases to connote a fundamental change in the status of children who had been removed from their natural homes.

Fourth, some of the federal framers assumed that their legislation would lead to increased numbers of families providing assistance to children, that is, a marked increase in the aggregate number of foster families and adoptive families. Some local child welfare units, in a desperate search for adoptive parents, placed considerable pressure on foster parents to adopt one or more of the children who were placed with them. This sounds like a sensible policy—and sometimes it is—but it probably had the unfortunate effect of reducing the number of available foster parents, who, like adoptive parents, were in short supply.[14]

Fifth, the framers of the legislation wanted states to provide preventive services to natural parents to allow many of them to improve their parenting skills. Some localities might indicate that a certain percentage of the time of their direct-service staff went to various preventive activities when in fact most of it was devoted to their ongoing and regular work in responding to emergencies, completing paperwork, and testifying at juvenile courts.[15] (These errors in statistics could stem from the instrinsic difficulty of computing how staff allocate their time or from a desire by child welfare staff to impress state authorities with their compliance with the edict to provide preventive services.)

Because local units and states used any of these five devices, data about the implementation of the Adoption Assistance and Child Welfare Act would be misleading. Moreover, it would be difficult to reach sweeping conclusions in light of variations between states and between local jurisdictions within specific states. One can imagine, for example, a particular county whose chief of child welfare services and whose juvenile court judges aggressively promoted permanency planning in contrast to an adjoining county whose officials did not promote the policy. Moreover, one can imagine considerable variation between states with respect to the implementation of the various policies in the legislation.[16]

Of course, considerable data can be found that nonetheless allow certain conclusions about implementation. Many jurisdictions dramatically decreased the number of children in the foster-care system in the years following the enactment of the legislation; the number of children in foster care in the nation halved between 1977 and 1988.[17] Moreover, many states complied with the tracking and case-review requirements of the legislation.

THE ANALYTIC CHALLENGE:
IDENTIFYING FACTORS THAT IMPEDE IMPLEMENTATION

Assume in the case of the Adoption Assistance and Child Welfare Act that we discovered considerable noncompliance with the legislation in a number of counties of a state and that we were charged with locating its causes. Much like any complex problem, we would need to identify an array of possible causes as a prelude to discovering the most important ones.

The extensive literature on implementation contains many theories about possible barriers to implementation. Theorists who use a top-down approach analyze high-level factors at federal and state levels, whereas theorists who use a bottom-up approach identify factors within local agencies and communities.[18] Neither of these two alternative approaches captures the interaction of various federal, state, local, and direct-service participants who jointly participate in the implementation process. Moreover, some "sideways" and "subterranean" analysis is needed because policies require the participation of persons and agencies who are not in the formal chain of command, such as (in the case of the Adoption Assistance and Child Welfare Act) subterranean participants like adoptive parents, foster families, the children, and natural parents and sideways participants like the juvenile courts.[19] In the case of the Adoption Assistance and Child Welfare Act, these various participants are depicted in Figure 12.1.

EXAMINING THE CONTEXT OF A POLICY INNOVATION

To understand why certain policies are implemented and others are not, we need to examine implementation realities that *preceded* a policy innovation because every policy innovation that exists is inserted into a context that can help or hinder its implementation. Moreover, we need to identify societal factors that impinged on the human delivery system prior to the enactment of a specific innovation. For example, relatively little pressure was exerted on politicians by professional, community, or client groups to increase the funding of child welfare services in many jurisdictions in the decades preceding 1980.[20] Declassification of child welfare services—that is, the filling of child welfare positions by people who lacked master's degrees in social work or even bachelor's degrees in social work or the social sciences—had already

RELEVANT SOCIETAL, ECONOMIC, SOCIAL, AND POLITICAL DEVELOPMENTS

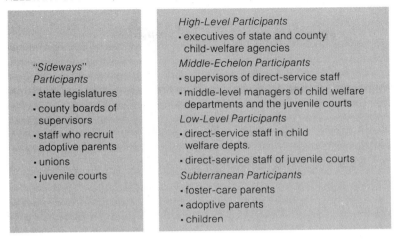

Figure 12.1   Implementation Diagram

occurred in many jurisdictions.[21] Local and state tax revolts, which began with Proposition 13 in California in 1978, represented an important contextual event with ominous implications for local funding of child welfare services.[22] Moreover, although many federal legislators did not predict it prior to the election of Ronald Reagan in November 1980, considerable public sentiment had developed to cut the size of federal social spending.[23] (We note later how these political developments had severe repercussions for the implementation of the Adoption Assistance and Child Welfare Act.) Another societal development, which also had important implications, was the rapid increase in reports of child abuse and neglect that were flooding child welfare offices in the late 1970s. These calls, which may have stemmed more from public awareness of maltreatment of children than from actual increases in its incidence, severely limited the ability of workers to devote much time to the processing of children who were already inside the foster-care system.[24] Finally, the rapidly rising number of women in labor markets, which had begun in the 1950s, continued in the 1970s and 1980s; this trend exacerbated the problem of finding women or families who were willing to be foster parents or to adopt children in the wake of the enactment of the Adoption Assistance and Child Welfare Act.[25]

We can couple our analysis of contextual factors that existed in the early 1980s with the list of various participants in child welfare programs (see Figure 12.1). Because we want to know whether various participants were favorably disposed to the underlying objectives as well as the policies of the innovation or whether they were opposed to them, we include both positive and negative orientations and realities.

High-Level Participants

Negative Factors

- Top administrators of child welfare in state and county positions are so preoccupied with responding to child-abuse and child-neglect cases that they have resigned themselves to mounting foster care and institutional care.

- A top-down mode of organizing public social services precludes communication of top officials with low-level staff.

- In light of allegations that many children have been harmed when prematurely returned to their natural parents, many high-level administrators emphasize child removal rather than efforts to improve the parenting skills of natural parents.

- Unions, which represent direct-service and clerical staff, have emphasized pay, fringe benefits, and work loads rather than service-related issues.

- Many legislators do not believe powerful constituencies support major improvements in child welfare programs.

Positive Factors

- Because rapid increases in foster care have become extraordinarily costly to local and state governments, they want to reform the system to make it more efficient.

- Many states had developed their own adoption-subsidy programs and had obtained some increases in adoptions because of them.

Middle-Echelon Participants

Negative Factors

- Supervisors devoted most of their time to hurried case consultation in the case of emergencies, threatened lawsuits from parents, and compiling program statistics.

- Declassification meant that even many supervisors no longer possessed advanced training in the social services.

Positive Factors

- Like higher officials, many supervisors feared substantial harm to children from the uncertainty and multiple placements that bedeviled children in the foster-care system.
- Despite declassification, many supervisors were holdovers from an era when child welfare services were dominated by trained social workers.

Low-Level Participants

Negative Factors

- Direct-service staff, who counsel parents and families and make critical recommendations to juvenile courts about specific children, are mainly preoccupied with investigating immediate emergencies and separating children who are in immediate danger from their natural parents. They spend relatively little time in case planning, in discussions with natural parents, or in case consultation with foster parents. Because of declassification, relatively few line workers possess M.S.W.s or even training in the social sciences at the undergraduate level.

Positive Factors

- If their caseloads were reduced, many direct-service staff wanted to develop more intensive, helping relationships with children and their families. Those who lacked training could receive in-service training.

Sideways Participants

Negative Factors

- State legislatures and county boards of supervisors do not fund child welfare services sufficiently to allow caseloads to be reduced, due to local tax revolts and the absence of political or community constituencies that are concerned about child welfare.
- Institutions, which receive funds for children who stay with them, have economic incentives not to return children to their natural families or to place them with adoptive families because state and federal authorities fund ongoing maintenance costs of the children.
- Almost no external political pressure is placed on the child welfare system by politicians or political parties because child welfare is widely perceived to be a specialized set of services that can bring little positive payoff to political candidates or members of legislatures.

Positive Factors

- Many juvenile court justices want to assume a more active role in reviewing cases and in promoting permanent arrangements.
- The rights of natural families to due process in court proceedings have been increasingly publicized and defended by attorneys—a development that has made juvenile courts and child welfare staff less inclined to quickly remove children from their natural families.

Subterranean Participants

Negative Factors

- Many parents who have troubled relations with their children need respite, homemaker, and day-care services to reduce stress and to provide children with additional caregivers. These kinds of specialized services are often not available.
- Many potential adopters of foster-care children are deterred by economic factors and fears of the burdens associated with caring for children with physical or mental problems. Many persons who would have adopted children in the past prioritize their own careers and employment, such as single and married women.
- Foster-care parents have an economic disincentive to promote permanency planning because they receive more funds if children stay with them for extended periods.
- Many natural parents view the child welfare staff and the juvenile court as adversaries who want primarily to take their children from them. Because direct-service staff are so burdened with child-removal and investigation functions, they have scant interaction with natural parents. (Increasing numbers of natural parents obtain attorneys.)

Positive Factors

- A remarkable upsurge in interest in adopting foster-care children has emerged.
- Disillusionment with transracial adoptive practice has led many leaders in minority communities to support adoption subsidies to allow indigent and minority children to be adopted by members of their own communities.
- Widespread assertion of their legal rights by natural parents suggests many of them want to pursue reunification.

Systemic Factors

Negative Factors

■ Considerable tension exists between the juvenile courts, whose judges make the ultimate decisions about the disposition of children, and child welfare workers who testify in court proceedings and who forward case material to direct-service staff who are directly hired by the juvenile courts. Many child welfare workers are demoralized when their recommendations are not accepted by the courts or when children are returned to natural parents without provision for extended services.

■ The staff who specialize in finding adoptive parents occupy a separate department from the child welfare workers, who sometimes fear that a particular child is matched with adoptive parents who lack the ability or knowledge to cope with the specific emotional or physical problems of that child.

■ Many parents neglect their children because they lack sufficient financial resources; thus, children are insufficiently fed and clothed. Moreover, poverty contributes to some abusive behavior by exacerbating intrafamilial tension. Yet no system exists within child welfare agencies for providing job-training or employment-referral services or for monitoring their provision by other agencies.

■ Innovative services, such as residential centers where troubled families can reside while receiving counseling and while testing to see if they can continue to function as an intact unit, do not exist in most localities.

Positive Factors

■ The widespread passage and implementation of adoption-subsidy programs by many states suggest a positive climate for major innovations in the child welfare system.

It can be seen in the preceding list that many orientations, practices, and capabilities describe the context of a major innovation such as the Adoption Assistance and Child Welfare Act. In this welter of positive and negative factors, it is often difficult to predict how on balance a particular innovation will fare once it has been enacted. Even a cursory examination of this list suggests an ambiguous context in the early 1980s; if considerable evidence suggests that many persons and institutions would welcome sweeping reforms, other evidence indicates that the reform could be sabotaged by numerous funding, institutional, and political factors.

The overriding question to be asked with respect to any policy innovation is, Will its provisions and resources be sufficient to overcome resistances to reforms? Because the existing child welfare system was swamped by excessive work loads and crises, many persons wondered whether the level of funding would be truly sufficient to allow the development of permanent arrangements for hundreds of thousands of children, whose ranks included many hard-to-adopt adolescent, minority, and disabled youth.[26]

CHARACTERISTICS OF THE POLICY INNOVATION AND ASSUMPTIONS ABOUT ITS IMPLEMENTATION

When a policy innovation is enacted, its implementation, of course, has not yet occurred. But the form (or substance) of the innovation and the assumptions of the framers about its impending implementation are critical to understanding its likely prospects.

Innovations take many forms. Some are relatively ambitious, such as legislation that seeks sweeping changes in existing practices and institutions. Others are relatively modest, such as pilot or demonstration projects or modifications of highly specific procedures in existing programs. If some innovations are relatively complex and involve a series of changes that must occur in tandem, other innovations are relatively simple and require only a single change in existing programs. Some innovations are relatively self-contained and can be accomplished by a specific agency or a specific set of agencies, whereas others require the collaboration of a number of organizations.[27]

Even without examining other factors, the nature of innovations provides clues about their likely implementation. Ambitious, complex, interdependent innovations are usually more difficult to implement than modest, simple, self-contained ones.[28] Moreover, they are particularly likely to be difficult to implement when they are injected into a context where many negative factors exist.

The Adoption Assistance and Child Welfare Act *was* an ambitious and complex innovation that required the collaboration of many institutions. It established a national mandate for fundamentally changing the shape of the child welfare system by proposing that hundreds of thousands of children be placed in adoptive homes or reunified with their natural families. It required the simultaneous accomplishment of a number of changes extending to actions of child welfare workers, judges, families that might become adopters, child welfare institutions, and the natural parents. Moreover, the framers assumed that state legislatures would increase their funding of child welfare services and that Congress would appropriate substantial sums for the innovation in the years following its enactment.

Ambitious and complex innovations can be successfully implemented, of course, but their prognosis is particularly guarded when they are cast into problematic and unpredictable environments, where considerable funding problems, opposition, and institutional rivalries exist. (See our prior discussion of the child welfare system in 1980, as well as tax revolts, declassification, and the shortage of foster-care and adoptive families.)

THE ANALYTIC CHALLENGE:
IMPLEMENTATION AS A MOVING TARGET

Our discussion of the implementation of the Adoption Assistance and Child Welfare Act suggests that challenges confront policy practitioners before and during implementation. First, they have to anticipate specific obstacles to the implementation of their proposals prior to their enactment. Second, they need to incorporate within their reforms policies and resources that will offset and minimize these obstacles. Third, they have to develop corrective interventions *during* the process of implementation to address emerging obstacles because it is rarely possible to foresee many of them prior to the enactment of specific reforms.

Anticipating and Minimizing Obstacles

When people shape and secure the enactment of proposals, they are often absorbed with short-term exigencies such as how to secure support from opponents of the proposal, how to move the proposal through the decision-making process, and how to keep intact the coalition or group that supports it.[29] Even if the framers and enacters of a proposal were able to concentrate on future developments, they would encounter formidable problems in shaping their proposals to increase the likelihood of their complete implementation. Indeed, the analogy of a moving target captures the intrinsic problem of predicting future developments and trying to offset them when the proposal is framed. As we have noted, for example, the framers cannot control or even predict whether legislators or funders will continue to contribute resources to their proposal in the years after its enactment.

If they are forward-looking when they construct their proposals, policy practitioners can and should develop *alternative* scenarios in which they deliberately frame worst-case situations.[30] By using charts, such as the one in Table 12.1, policy practitioners can predict patterns of response and conceptualize policies to offset or diminish patterns of resistance and rejection or possible goal displacement.

Of course, it is possible to identify only with hindsight some miscalculations of the framers of legislation. The framers of the Adoption Assistance and Child Welfare Act could not have known that Ronald Reagan would assume the presidency in November 1980. As advocates of deregulation and decentralization, his appointees in the Department of Health and Human Services did not assertively monitor the new policies and cut some of the proposed increases in federal funding of child welfare services. They even

TABLE 12.1   Scenario Building in Implementation

Predicted Patterns of Response	Possible Preventive Policies
Acceptance of ■ funding (specify who) ■ specific policy objectives (specify who) ■ certain required procedures (specify who) Resistance to ■ funding (specify who) ■ specific policy objectives (specify who) ■ certain required procedures (specify who) Rejection of ■ funding (specify who) ■ specific policy objectives (specify who) ■ certain required procedures (specify who) Goal displacement ■ What forms may it take? ■ How pervasive will it be?	

tried unsuccessfully in 1982 to rescind the legislation by including federal funds for child welfare in a general social services block grant, which (more or less) gave states complete autonomy in deciding how to use these funds.[31] This high-level disinterest in the new policy was a negative development that the framers of the legislation could not easily have predicted.

It was soon obvious, however, that neither the federal government nor the states would fund the new programs generously. Soon after its enactment, the retrenchment of federal social spending of the Reagan administration began so that considerably lesser funds were allocated to the legislation than were authorized when it was enacted.[32] Tax revolts in the various states, as well as their budgetary difficulties that stemmed from their attempt to fund programs that had been cut by federal authorities, meant that many states hardly increased their funding of child welfare programs.[33]

Other practical problems frustrated permanency planning. It had been widely assumed that many adoptive families, particularly from minority groups whose children were least likely to be adopted, would be lured by the incentive of adoption subsidies to become adoptive parents. (Some subsidy programs in various states had been successful in attracting adoptive parents.) But the framers of the 1980 legislation miscalculated on several fronts. The incentives were probably insufficient to attract many parents to adopt children with difficult mental and physical problems, particularly when free and long-term medical and counseling services were covered only for those specific conditions that existed at the point of adoption and only when adoption subsidies were available to those children who qualified for AFDC at the point when they were adopted.[34] Further, as many members of minority groups became more affluent, many of them wanted to *leave* low-income areas and were probably less likely to want to adopt foster children, who tended to be drawn from the ranks of the poor.

Other practical problems frustrated implementation. It is difficult in the best of circumstances to determine whether a specific child should return home or be adopted: the six-, twelve-, and eighteen-month reviews, which work well in clear-cut situations, can be dysfunctional when social workers encounter families that require extended counseling to be able to provide adequate parenting.[35] Moreover, despite marginal increases in the federal funding of child welfare services, the sustained and intensive provision of services to these marginal families was often not feasible because of the preoccupation of social workers with investigations of new cases.[36]

Other societal realities frustrated implementation of the legislation. Increases in substance abuse led to sharp increases in the numbers of mothers who passed their addictions to their fetuses; by 1988 about 300,000 infants were born each year who were addicted, and many of these infants were placed in the overloaded foster-care system. Reports of child abuse continued to escalate in many jurisdictions. The increase in homeless families led to escalating reports of neglect. Inundated by these kinds of problems, child welfare staff were often not able to provide sustained and intensive services to marginal families. Indeed, some critics feared that local staff often reunited children with their families without adequate investigations and with no follow-up services to see if abusive or neglectful behaviors still existed.[37]

Other logistic problems also existed in the thousands of local child welfare offices and juvenile courts across the nation. Permanency planning requires a team approach in which child welfare workers, workers who locate adoptive families, judges, social work staff from juvenile courts, natural parents, foster parents, and supervisors work together to develop and implement permanency plans. In some local offices, however, bureaucratic modes of operation, which emphasized top-down and specialized functions, precluded the formation of teams. Bureaucratic rivalries between juvenile courts and child welfare departments sometimes precluded collaboration.[38]

The top-down mode of bureaucratic organization interfered moreover with identification with and understanding of the new permanency-planning policy by direct-service staff, who often did not understand the new policy or receive in-service or technical training to allow them to implement it. High rates of turnover, which were linked to excessive work loads, poor pay, and declassification, frustrated implementation.[39] Moreover, because staff in many child welfare offices realized that most of their time had to be devoted to "fire-fighting" rather than developing well-conceived plans for specific children, little pressure was placed on line staff to complete permanency plans by specific dates. In one study, for example, the child welfare staff did not believe their promotions or pay increases were linked to their performance in implementing the new policy.[40]

Because of their optimistic assumptions, it is unlikely that most framers of the legislation realized that states and localities would resort extensively to questionable practices such as returning many children to natural parents without adequate investigations or follow-up services, pressuring foster-care parents to adopt children who had been placed with them, or placing severely disabled children with adoptive parents who were not fully informed of the extent of their physical or mental needs. (Few adoptive families received follow-up services.[41]) Each of these dubious practices was more likely to occur when the ambitious policy mandate to reform the child welfare system was not coupled with massive increases in federal funding for child welfare services.

It is interesting to speculate, for example, what the framers of the Adoption Assistance and Child Welfare Act could have included in their proposal— or how they might have altered it—had they guessed that federal and state authorities would not generously fund it or that the Reagan administration would not zealously monitor it.[42] They might have increased the federal funding of services even more substantially. Had they realized how difficult it would be to find adoptive parents, they might have provided even greater financial incentives to them or included broader health and counseling benefits. They might have questioned the feasibility of securing the rapid movement of hundreds of thousands of children from foster care—a decision that could have led them to try to upgrade the foster-care system rather than trying to eradicate it. In this scenario, they could have sought to increase the training and the reimbursement of foster-care parents, as well as to increase their status by defining their work to be a career that deserved a salary. Could community group homes have been established instead of focusing so heavily on permanency planning? Radical critiques of the Adoption Assistance and Child Welfare Act can also be made. While the legislation enhanced recordkeeping and adoptions of some children, it failed to address the poverty, unemployment, poor housing, substance abuse, and other contributors to child neglect and child abuse.[43] Of course, these policy options would have had drawbacks of their own, but the framers might have considered them more carefully had they anticipated some funding and program realities that their innovation might subsequently encounter.

Revising Policies During Implementation

Political scientist Theodore Lowi suggests that policy framers can avoid many perils during implementation by writing airtight proposals that specify with precision what implementors must do.[44] Our discussion suggests, however, that framers of proposals have some but limited power over the ensuing process of implementation. They can only imperfectly guess what forces and factors will emerge to threaten their policies—and, even when they anticipate them, they often cannot prevent them from emerging. Corrective strategies are needed *during* the implementation process.

Determining precisely why certain specific policies are not implemented constitutes the analytic challenge of policy practitioners. Nor is such determination simple; indeed, a variety of policy, administrative, attitudinal, resource, outreach, and accountability factors may obstruct implementation, whether singly or in tandem.

The policies that provide the mandate to professionals can themselves contribute to flaws in implementation. We can distinguish between *primary policies*—that is, the original policies that were enacted—and *administrative regulations*, or *guidelines*, which are issued in the wake of the enactment of primary policies.

As our discussion has already suggested, primary policies may be excessively vague, ambitious, or complex. A program may be placed in an organizational unit or a department of government that provides an inhospitable or harmful environment for it; thus, the primary policy may need to be revised to place the program in another setting.

In the case of complex government policies, numerous regulations and guidelines are issued to define those eligibility, staffing, accounting, and other details not defined in the primary legislation.[45] Less numerous but important issues are defined in the administrative regulations of agency programs. These regulations and guidelines may themselves be excessively vague, may pose onerous burdens on implementors, or may contradict some of the objectives of the primary policies.

Changing Nonpolicy Factors

Policy practitioners need familiarity with concepts drawn from administration, organizational theory, planning, and budgeting because the fate of many policies hinges on a host of nonpolicy factors. If policy focuses on the substance of proposals, these nonpolicy factors emphasize practical factors that shape the course of implementation in organizations and communities where policy is ultimately shaped.[46]

The implementation of most policies occurs within the context of organizations; thus, their success is often indirectly determined by administrative factors. Consider the example of a demoralized staff who are asked to perform complex tasks, such as permanency planning, within specific deadlines. Part of their demoralization may stem from heavy work loads, but the negative orientations of staff may also derive from dissatisfaction with working conditions, punitive patterns of supervision, high turnover rates, and lack of technical assistance from their superiors. Or staff may believe that their jobs are incorrectly structured; they may believe that they are so specialized that they require boring repetition of the same tasks. Or they may lack specific skills or perspectives to implement specific policies; some social workers contend, for example, that declassification of child welfare staff rendered many of them unable to implement permanency planning. Theorists who emphasize **personnel factors** would implicate these kinds of factors when examining the nonimplementation of policy.[47]

If the problem resides in deficiencies in the organizations that deliver the policies, policy practitioners have to identify and select policy and administrative remedies to redress implementation deficiencies in the context of a welter of theories about the implementation process and about organizations. Some theorists stress **organizational structure,** as the plethora of reorganizations of government bureaucracies suggests.[48] They may want to merge functions into single units of organizations, to decentralize operations, or to use a team approach in which persons from different professions or with different skills work together. Other theorists emphasize **process factors** such as the extent supervisors and superiors are excessively authoritarian in their relations with subordinates and the extent lower-echelon staff are allowed to participate in decisions of the broader organizations.[49] Still other theorists emphasize **leadership**; do top administrators possess the ability to develop organizational goals and to obtain the allegiance of staff to them?[50] Other theorists examine **planning and technical details** such as the extent specific objectives and goals exist that provide discipline and focus to the work of staff and the extent data are systematically obtained about the work of staff to determine its efficiency and effectiveness.[51] **Behavioral theorists** examine the orientations of staff toward specific innovations and how they are influenced by patterns of communication and organizational culture; they discuss methods of creating a milieu that is supportive of specific innovations.[52] **Innovation or dissemination theorists** examine factors that lead staff and officials to accept, resist, or reject innovations such as permanency planning; innovations that markedly depart from prior traditions are, for example, less likely to be implemented than other innovations.[53] **Exchange theorists** examine the relations of organizations with other organizations to determine patterns of referral, dominance, and subordination; they examine, for example, relationships between juvenile courts and child welfare agencies.[54] Still other theorists, whose perspectives can be broadly characterized as **political and economic** in nature, implicate environmental pressures and forces that impede, block, or divert resources from the implementation of specific policies, such as the levels of funding that they obtain from state and county officials or the kinds of pressures that public officials receive from interest groups.[55]

All these theoretical approaches yield useful perspectives when examining specific implementation problems. Of course, considerable debates occur between theorists about *which* approach or solution is most effective in addressing a specific problem. A crude analogy can be made to the plethora of theories in human behavior; although clinicians may agree that a client possesses a specific problem such as depression, they may support an array of interventions that include gestalt, transactional, task-focused, psychoanalytic, and pharmaceutical approaches. Because organizational problems are even more complex than personal ones, it is hardly surprising that schisms have developed among organizational theorists, who emphasize interventions based on various of the preceding theories and perspectives.

Our discussion suggests that policy practitioners should use a simple framework when examining problems in the human services:

1. Preinnovation system
2. Characteristics of the innovation: objectives, resources, incentives, and requirements
3. Shaping the innovation to offset likely obstacles to its implementation
4. Postenactment developments that influence the implementation of the innovation: unanticipated events, unexpected obstacles, and expected obstacles that were not addressed by preimplementation planning
5. Corrective midcourse revisions

The *context* that precedes an innovation needs to be examined because it provides clues that suggest that a specific innovation will encounter obstacles. Policy proposals should be successively revised in the course of scenario building where likely obstacles and constraints are identified. The framers of the Adoption Assistance and Child Welfare Act probably should have included even greater resources in their legislation for services and probably should not have established such sweeping goals *unless* they had been willing to increase significantly the resources devoted to the legislation.

Once policies are enacted, policy practitioners need to develop corrective interventions that include revisions in the innovation itself and proposals to address those defects in the human services delivery system that contribute to the nonimplementation of specific policies. Our discussion also suggests that policy practitioners need to develop knowledge of bureaucracies, organizational theory, and administration as they develop interventions to enhance the implementation of specific policies.

A POLICY-PRACTICE CASE FROM THE HUMAN SERVICES

We have emphasized a broader implementation perspective than would be obtained if we had begun with a single agency. In the case of the Adoption Assistance and Child Welfare Act of 1980, we examined a variety of societal, legislative, economic, and political factors that, singly and in tandem, frustrated its implementation. Had we selected only a single child welfare agency and asked why it failed to sufficiently help abused or neglected children, we would have risked "blaming the agency and its staff," that is, ignoring those extraagency factors that contributed to its failure.

Still, most social workers are employed within specific agencies and often encounter various internal problems that frustrate the implementation of specific policies.[56] Although Policy-Practice Case 12 does not focus on the implementation of a specific policy, it analyzes various factors that, from the perspective of its author, frustrated the provision of the kinds of informal and creative services that the self-help center (SHC) had provided in its early years.

Combining Skills to Overcome Implementation Barriers

Indeed, this case illustrates how policy practitioners need to couple analytic, political, interactional, and value-clarification skills when seeking to address barriers to implementation within their specific agencies. Let's discuss the author's perspectives in Policy-Practice Case 12 and how he would need to use these various skills to address problems in the SHC.

Value-Clarification Skills   Values shaped the preferences of the staff and executives in the SHC regarding the kinds of services it should provide, as well as its management style. The social worker in the case wants it to emphasize nontraditional services that stress advocacy, free services, team services, and extensive use of volunteers—services given in an informal atmosphere that contrast moreover with traditional social agencies. He believes that movement to a more bureaucratic model jeopardizes the "distinctive mission" of the SHC, a contention disputed by other agency participants who believe that SHC must move toward more traditional models of service delivery to be able to obtain grants from traditional funding sources. The social worker likes the "family atmosphere" of the original SHC, in which heavy reliance was placed on the use of unpaid volunteers. Other participants favor more traditional models of organization, including more extensive use of professional and salaried staff, an option made possible when the SHC received a large grant.

Values shape budgetary and program choices, as well. Should the SHC, when faced with a funding crisis, institute a sliding-fee schedule with its attendant means test—a policy at odds with the provision of free services to all clients in the original SHC? If fees are used, at what level should free services begin? Should the agency develop a profit-oriented subsidiary as a means of developing revenue for the SHC, or would this policy lead to increasing absorption by the executive and staff in this new "revenue center"? When are the writing and procuring of grants consonant with the mission of the SHC, or when do grants become "the tail that wags the dog"?

Value-dilemmas discussed in Chapter Eight are evident in the SHC. Some social workers in the agency confront agency administrators in a strategy that leads in some cases to demotions or dismissal. Should they try to change disliked policies even when they experience personal risks? Some social workers in the SHC leave the agency to avoid its politics; when is flight an acceptable resolution and when is it an abdication of responsibility?

Analytic Skills The social worker in the SHC tries to identify a range of factors that led to reduced staff investment in their work as well as decreasing emphasis on nontraditional services. These factors include funding instability, inadequate and volatile leadership, lack of internal communication, excessive regulations, and lack of adequate grievance procedures. In complex situations like the SHC, it is difficult to know where to begin because so many interacting factors often contribute to implementation problems. For example, funding instability is partly responsible for the growing use of regulations within the SHC because administrators hope to impress more traditional funders who are accustomed to more bureaucratic modes of organization.

People have to establish priorities when seeking to change patterns of implementation. The social worker in the SHC lists many factors that need to be changed; which of them should be addressed first? In one sense, policy practitioners in implementation face a task similar to direct-service practitioners, who identify various familial, personal, and environmental factors in specific cases and develop an initial strategy during a specific time frame. Social workers often begin with relatively simple strategies to obtain some immediate successes, even when they know that more basic factors need to be addressed subsequently.

Political Skills Many factors that the social worker identifies in the SHC cannot be addressed without the leadership of an executive who can obtain the confidence of both the staff and the board in an agency where these two groups had become polarized. An incompetent or vindictive executive poses a difficult political problem for those persons who seek administrative changes in an agency like the SHC.

Even when an enlightened and skillful executive exists, political barriers often frustrate changes in the administration of specific agencies. Major changes in agencies often encounter the opposition of specific persons, whether because they are wedded to tradition or benefit from existing arrangements. A sort of inertia develops in which standard operating procedures are perceived to be ends in themselves rather than as instrumentalities to be retained only as they contribute to quality services. Within and between organizations, turf rivalries occur in which persons and agencies jealously guard their programs and their administrative roles.

Considerable political skill is required then to develop and secure changes in agency policies. In some cases, social workers need to persuade other

POLICY-PRACTICE CASE 12

A SOCIAL WORKER DIAGNOSES A
SELF-HELP CENTER

Political conflict and difficulties generated by the uncertainty of funding sources have long been facts of life at the self-help center (SHC). Recent and unprecedented situational influences and staff and leadership changes have resulted in radical organizational changes (and, to an extent, organizational chaos). This time period can be divided into two segments. First, the SHC experienced significant changes between January and November 1978 due to receipt of a major grant. Second, from November 1978 to the present, the SHC has had three executive directors, each representing, at least in part, different leadership styles and abilities.

January 1978, when the SHC was awarded a general revenue-sharing grant (matched county and federal funds administered by Mammoth county), marked a dramatic turning point in the nature of the SHC. Prior to that time, the SHC was funded by a number of smaller grants allowing for a paid staff of only five at a low salary scale. Most of the staff and professional workers were volunteers attracted to the SHC philosophy of providing an alternative (some would say, "counterculture") model for quality community medical care. The atmosphere was described as "free," "open," and "informal." Bureaucratic structure, rules, and regulations were kept to a minimum. Staff members had considerable input into the decision-making process. Meetings tended to be informal affairs, with attention paid to ideological issues, political concerns, and innovative ideas. Conflict tended to be resolved by face-to-face confrontation and discussion within a context of mutual respect and trust. It is reported that the staff felt very much like a family, with the SHC administrator and the board organically involved in the SHC as a whole.

The SHC administrator (who was to become executive director #1) had been a part of the clinic almost since its inception, rising through the ranks from patient to volunteer to psychological counseling administrator to clinic administrator. He was highly committed to a sense of organizational mission that saw the patient as the number-one priority of the clinic operation. Although it was indicated that, to a degree, he was afraid of power, it seems fair to say that, during his tenure as leader, his stature in the clinic was almost mythical.

The sudden influx of grant monies in January 1978 had a profound impact on the various indices of organizational functioning, an impact that could have been predicted along Weberian lines: increased bureaucratic structure, that is, more formalized staff-administration relations; the development of a more hierarchical administrative structure; rules regulating staff conduct; and written formulation of administrative rules and decisions. In fact, the grant allowed for a tripling of the number of paid SHC staff members. The number of administrative positions also increased, creating a greater sense of bureaucratic structure. The SHC administrator assumed the newly created position of executive director, whose functions would include public relations, grant writing, and the role of liaison between the board and the staff. The position of SHC administrator, involving direct contact with and supervision of the staff and the day-to-day activities of the SHC, was given to a long-time SHC volunteer. The size, nature, and experience of the staff changed. Many without any previous association with the SHC were hired. More complex staffing patterns developed in what had been an agency with a relatively simple structure. And, because of the grant's extensive demands for accountability, much effort had to be directed toward retaining it.

The change in the SHC was dramatic: staff meetings became more formal and tended to involve matters of money, time, and so on, rather than innovative programming suggestions and philosophy. Regulations related to accountability were handed down, and statistics and time-sheets were required. Decisions were increasingly made on an executive level by the executive director, board president, and executive committee of the board. Even department administrators were sometimes bypassed in decisions affecting their departments. And communication within the center became less direct and effective, with conflicts no longer resolved by face-to-face discussion. Further, conflict and disagreement no longer seemed to occur within a context of mutual trust and respect.

On an administrative level, increasing polarization developed between board and staff. The board now tended to view staff members as their paid employees and themselves as having license to make demands on staff energy and time. Gone was the feeling of the center as a family. Additionally, the board evidenced significant concern for making the center acceptable to the "establishment," a source of conflict with original staff members, many of whom tended to see themselves as counterculture. Also, the executive director, although still considering himself a staff member, increasingly supported board positions against the staff.

Imposition of accountability regulations, decreased staff input and involvement in decision making, formalization of administrative structure, and a marked tendency in the direction of authoritarian leadership by both the executive director and the board resulted in conflict, job dissatisfaction, and a lowering of morale.

As might be expected, the staff resisted implementing accountability measures. In particular, some of the "old guard" were opposed to statistical requirements on the grounds that they were contrary to the spirit of the SHC. Even at this point, however, the board seemed unable to understand why they were encountering staff resistance to their decisions. They tended to label it as "childish" and as evidence that the staff did not care about the SHC as much as they did. Understandably, staff morale suffered, as did job efficiency: the amount of nonproductive small talk increased and program innovation declined.

Executive director #1 had to retire because he suffered a serious illness. His successor, an interim appointee who had briefly held a part-time administrative position at the SHC, was selected by the board the following day. No staff input was solicited. As might be expected, this interim director was

Continued

POLICY-PRACTICE CASE 12
(continued)

in a precarious position, subject to dismissal at any time by the board. It became clear at this point that the power of the organization was in the hands of the board president.

Under this executive director (#2), bureaucratic structures and procedures developed even further, although resistance was by this time largely centered in a few of the original staff. The sense of formality in the SHC was further increased when the center moved to new, larger, and in some ways more sterile quarters a few days after #2 took office.

Intraagency communication suffered under #2, who reportedly had difficulty dealing with groups of people and was weak in the areas of human relations and administration. On the positive side, however, this executive was able to tolerate criticism from staff and from other administrators; possessed good administrative, public relations, and grant-writing skills; and allowed for some autonomy on the part of department administrators.

He was removed from his position after about six months. The exact reasons for this seem unclear, although personality factors and the inevitable comparisons with his predecessor seem to have played a role. His difficulty in the areas of communication and sensitivity to human problems were stressed by the staff through their one representative on the personnel committee. With executive director #3, SHC organization and functioning approached the level of organizational chaos. In choosing this leader, the board looked for a non-SHC person. Unlike previous directors, he had no SHC experience, nor did he seem to be committed to SHC philosophy; rather, he had a managerial orientation (most recently as administrator of a private hospital). From the board's perspective, he was a director they thought they could control.

Initially, the staff had high hopes that this executive would stand up for staff positions against the board. Such hopes seemed justified when he proclaimed his intentions to revise the personnel code and solicit staff input into decision making. In fact, these hopes proved to be unfounded because there ensued a complete breakdown of communication, at least as far as the staff and most administrators were concerned. Access to the director was limited to two friends on the staff. Even his executive secretary had to make an appointment to meet with him. Criticism and disagreement were neither encouraged nor well received. Much decision making was unilateral; departmental administrators were often not even consulted on decisions affecting their departments. The quality of these decisions suffered noticeably from lack of necessary information and input.

At this point, the board still seemed blind to staff unrest and maintained their paternalistic attitude toward those who complained. Further, the executive, together with the board, brought about the precipitous firing of five staff members. The reasons for these terminations ranged from anticipated financial shortages to trivial administrative complaints. It seemed abundantly clear, however, that personal dislikes were major issues; those fired seemed to be staff members who were particularly bright, experienced, knowledgeable, and effective in their areas. Some of them were strong personalities and quite outspoken, and it is easy to see how a leader with a low sense of self-esteem could feel threatened by their presence. Indeed, he promoted some staff members who many regarded as less competent than those who had been fired.

Five months after assuming the position of executive director, the executive was fired by the board (or at least pushed to the point of offering his resignation). The board feared that they lacked sufficient control over the director and his decisions. Issues of his effectiveness and the chaotic condition of the clinic seem not to have been crucial determinants of their action. Indeed, one of the director's qualities that the board found attractive when he was hired was his public relations skill, which no doubt they felt would stand the SHC in good stead with community and funding sources. Part of their disillusionment may well have been due to his failure to achieve the desired results with the funding agencies.

The costs paid by the SHC in this chaos included low staff morale, with its effects on job efficiency and effectiveness, nondevelopment of innovative changes in SHC programs, and the departure of good workers from the organization. Further, the policy objectives, or mission, of the original center seem to have been replaced by a new ethos more akin to that of establishment agencies.

A number of steps seem to be necessary if this organization is to function on a more satisfactory and productive level. First, change is required in the style of leadership exercised by the executive director. Improvement in communication with both staff and board and an openness to innovative suggestions and constructive criticism are crucial. The director ought to have and project a significant degree of autonomy from board pressure in order that he might truly serve as a liaison rather than as an apologist for board dicta. This would allow support of staff positions on particular issues and serve, to a degree, as a check on the board's involvement in regular SHC activities. Additionally, if the present staffing structure is maintained, the executive director should properly be concerned with the acquisition of funding, public relations, and community activities, leaving the day-to-day management of the SHC in the hands of a qualified and capable administrator.

Second, the person occupying the position of SHC administrator must necessarily be a competent, confident, and trustworthy individual able to make decisions and deal in a fair and sensitive manner with staff members both as a group and as individuals. This presumes, however, that the executive director would not feel threatened by dissenting points of view.

Third, staff rights should be strictly guaranteed, with particular emphasis on due process in hiring and firing procedures. Greater autonomy should be provided for department administrators, and a mechanism should be set up to allow for and encourage input by administrators and line staff into the making of decisions that affect their departments. Staff meetings should be

Continued

POLICY-PRACTICE CASE 12
(continued)

conducted on a regular basis for administrative purposes, input into decision making, or resolution of conflict. Additionally, a grievance mechanism (a committee, ombudsman, etc.) should be set up to address problems that mutual problem-solving techniques seem unable to handle.

Reduction of emphasis on rules and regulations would also be a step in the direction of a better-functioning organization and the attainment of stated SHC goals. Also, the cost of maintaining some of the relatively trivial staff requirements should be reevaluated.

Perhaps such a realignment of SHC priorities would help to shift the focus of staff discussions and meetings back to more ideological and philosophical concerns, with exploration of the program changes and innovative methods needed to realize the organizational mission. Hopefully, this would involve a resurgence of concern with community health-care issues and increase social activism.

Fourth, board members should involve themselves in areas in which they are uniquely qualified, particularly areas involving organization of community support for SHC funding and activities. The attempt by influential board members to involve themselves in the running of the SHC itself might be a diversion of their energies from more necessary and productive tasks.

Fifth, a structure ought to be established for the organization of the many volunteer workers and professionals who are crucial to SHC functioning. A director of volunteer services is needed, someone who could identify the needs of volunteers, coordinate their training and scheduling, and represent their interests to the SHC administration. This position would hopefully allow for the development of a power base for volunteers.

Finally, because the staff is so demoralized by all the changes, an outside consultant should be hired who can facilitate the development of problem-solving groups. This would allow identification of the areas of conflict experienced by individuals, exploration of organizational assumptions and values, and frank discussion of changes that have occurred in the organization in the context of the funding turbulence of the 1980s. And people would be compelled to discuss current political realities of the SHC, its present values, and its administrative personnel, perhaps even to assume a troubleshooting role to devise methods of coupling self-help and bureaucratic models.

It is impossible and undesirable to turn the clock back to the early days of the SHC "family," as appealing as that notion might be to some. It does appear possible, even necessary, to subject the present SHC structure and operation to critical analysis and diagnosis in order to identify strategies for change.

SOURCE: This case has been contributed anonymously. Names and locations have been altered.

strategically located persons to initiate specific changes. In many cases, changes must be defended on their intrinsic merits to decrease the likelihood that others will perceive them as disguised efforts to increase the power of specific units or individuals. Indirection is often needed as direct-service staff involve the supervisors and superiors in changing specific procedures.

Conflictual strategies are sometimes needed when no recourse exists and when staff are willing to accept possible personal and organizational repercussions. The social worker in the SHC seems to believe that confrontation between staff and board might eventually become necessary if some improvements cannot be obtained by less conflictual means.

Interactional Skills   Social workers often use interpersonal and group skills to troubleshoot agency services. In some cases, staffs in service organizations believe that candid discussion of agency policies is taboo; social workers need to encourage examination of dysfunctional policies in these cases and the appraisal of actual risks that persons encounter if they call attention to implementation problems.

Group skills are needed for participating in agency committees and task forces that examine specific policies. In some cases, social workers help these groups to brainstorm alternative policies and to forestall the premature dismissal of promising ideas. When these groups do not exist, social workers can urge their formation and the placement on them of persons who possess a range of perspectives. In some cases, they can suggest including persons from the community or service populations of an agency in some of its deliberations.

Persuasive skills are needed at numerous points when seeking changes in the internal workings of an agency. When sound professional reasons exist for questioning policies, agency executives and board members are often receptive.

SUMMARY

We have discussed two cases of implementation in this chapter. Our discussion of the implementation of the Adoption Assistance and Child Welfare Act of 1980 provided a broad perspective that examined a range of societal, legislative, and economic factors that, singly and in tandem, frustrated its implementation. This political and economic perspective makes clear that barriers to the implementation of some policies sometimes exist outside specific agencies, whose staff find their work to be frustrated by deficiencies in high-level policies and shortages of resources.

Yet policies are ultimately realized or frustrated in the daily and internal workings of myriad social agencies. We provided the case example of the Self-Help Center to discuss this micro-dimension to implementation. Social workers need to be involved in efforts to secure changes in the administration of agencies so that specific policies can be more effectively implemented, but this kind of policy practice, which overlaps with administrative practice, requires a combination of analytic, political, interactional, and value-clarification skills. As we have argued throughout this book, however, this combination of skills is also needed when undertaking agenda-building, problem-defining, proposal-writing, and policy-enacting tasks.

QUESTIONS FOR DISCUSSION

1. Discuss the following dilemmas, tasks, and realities encountered by social workers in Policy-Practice Case 12.
   a) Trade-offs often have to be considered during implementation, as reflected in decisions regarding the use of fees.
   b) When they try to confront or oppose executives who they believe frustrate the implementation of specific policies, social workers may assume considerable personal risk.
   c) Since many factors often contribute to the nonimplementation of a policy, social workers have to choose their priorities and targets carefully.
   d) Unlike members of legislatures, where conflict is common, people in organizations perceive controversy to be unusual, a fact that should be considered when devising strategy to change organizational policies.
2. The case of the Adoption Assistance and Child Welfare Act of 1980 suggests some recurring problems or issues in implementation. Critically discuss:
   a) Why policymakers often establish goals or objectives that exceed the resources that they propose in their policies.
   b) Why implementing agencies often resort to goal displacement.
   c) Why it is difficult to obtain accurate data on the implementation of specific policies.
   d) How multiple factors contribute to the failure of people to implement specific policies.
   e) Why line staff are often scapegoated as the people who cause specific policies to not be implemented when, in fact, more fundamental causes exist.

SUGGESTED READINGS

An Overview of Theoretical Perspectives on Implementation

Erwin Hargrove, *The Missing Link: The Study of the Implementation of Social Policy* (Washington, D.C.: Urban Institute Press, 1975).

Robert Montjoy and Laurence O'Toole, "The Implementation of Change in Human Service Organizations," *Public Administration Review*, 39 (September–October 1979): 465–477.

Carl Van Horn and Donald Van Meter, "The Implementation of Intergovernmental Policy," in Charles Jones and Robert Thomas, eds., *Public Policy Making in the Federal System* (Beverly Hills, Ca.: Sage Publishing, 1976).

Structural-Political Perspectives on Implementation

Jeffrey Pressman and Aaron Wildavsky, *Implementation* (Berkeley, Ca.: University of California Press, 1974).

Political-Economy Perspectives on Implementation

Eugene Bardach, *The Implementation Game* (Cambridge, Mass.: MIT Press, 1977).

Mayer Zald, *Organizational Change: The Political Economy of the YMCA* (Chicago: University of Chicago Press, 1970).

Micro or Agency Perspectives on Implementation

Yeheskel Hasenfeld, "The Implementation of Change in Human Service Organizations," *Social Service Review*, 54 (December 1980): 508–520.

Mary Ann Scheirer, *Program Implementation: The Organizational Context* (Beverly Hills, Ca.: Sage Publishing, 1981).

Staff Perspectives on Implementation

Michael Lipsky, "Standing Implementation on Its Head," in Walter Burnham and Martha Wagner, eds., *American Politics and Public Policy* (Cambridge, Mass.: MIT Press, 1978).

Lyman Porter, et al., *Behavior in Organizations* (New York: McGraw-Hill, 1975), pp. 274–367.

The Effects of the Substance of Public Policy on Implementation

Theodore Lowi, *End of Liberalism* (New York: Norton, 1969).

Logistical or Procedural Perspectives on Implementation

Allen Spiegel and Herbert Hyman, *Basic Health Planning Methods* (Germantown, Md.: Aspen Systems, 1978), pp. 239–287.

Case Studies of Implementation

Franklin Chu and Sharland Trotter, *The Madness Establishment* (New York: Grossman, 1974).

NOTES

1. U.S., Congress, Senate, Committee on Finance, Subcommittee on Public Assistance, *Hearings on Proposals Related to Social and Child Welfare Services*, 96th Cong., 1st Sess., 1979, testimony of Arabella Martinez.

2. Theodore Lowi comments on the vagueness of the terms in many pieces of legislation in *The End of Liberalism* (New York: Norton, 1969).

3. Brian Hogwood and Lewis Gunn note that the stated and the real goals or objectives of people are sometimes quite different. See *Policy Analysis for the Real World* (London: Oxford University Press, 1984), p. 156.

4. The dual system is discussed by Dorothy Kupcha, "Medicaid: In or Out of the Mainstream," *California Journal*, 10 (May 1979): 181–183.

5. See U.S., Congress, Senate, Subcommittee on Public Assistance, *Hearings on Proposals*, pp. 68–69.

6. Ibid., pp. 68–126.

7. For an overview of the strategy, see U.S., Congress, House, Ways and Means Committee, Subcommittee on Public Assistance, *Hearings on Amendments to Social Services, Foster Care, and Child Welfare*, 96th Cong., 1st Sess., 1979, pp. 22–157.

8. For a discussion of the prevailing assumption that reunification was in the best interest of the child, see Michael Wald, "Family Preservation: Are We Moving Too Fast?" *Public Welfare*, 46 (Summer 1988): 33–38.

9. The absence of good data from local jurisdictions regarding children served by the Adoption Assistance and Child Welfare Act is discussed in testimony of Marylee Allen in U.S., Congress, Senate, Committee on Finance, Subcommittee on Social Security and Income Maintenance Programs, *Hearings*, 99th Cong., 1st Sess., June 24, 1985.

10. See Amitai Etzioni, *Modern Organizations* (Englewood Cliffs, N.J.: Prentice-Hall, 1964), pp. 10, 84–85.

11. This possibility is discussed by Wald, "Family Preservation."

12. This possibility is discussed by Mark Hardin in U.S. Congress, Subcommittee on Social Security and Income Maintenance Programs, June 24, 1985.

13. See Nora Gustavsson, "Implementation of Permanency Planning Legislation," Doctoral Dissertation, School of Social Work, University of Southern California, 1986, pp. 31–32, 86.

14. Ibid., pp. 31–32, 86–88.

15. In similar fashion, considerable overreporting occurred in the aftermath of the 1962 welfare amendments to the Social Security Act, which required local departments to report how much time their staff devoted to providing services; see Martha Derthick, *The Influence of Federal Grants: Public Assistance in Massachusetts* (Cambridge, Mass.: Harvard University Press, 1970), pp. 138–157.

16. See Krishna Samantrai, "Prevention in Child Welfare: States' Response to Federal Mandate," Doctoral Dissertation, School of Social Work, University of Southern California, 1988. Also see Jeffrey Koshel and Madeleine Kimmich, *Summary Report*

on the Implementation of PL 96–272 (Washington, D.C.: Urban Institute Press, 1983) and Madeleine Kimmich, *State Child Welfare Program Plans: Service Budgets Report* (Washington, D.C.: Urban Institute Press, 1983).

17. Wald, "Family Preservation."

18. It is useful to distinguish macro, mezzo, and micro factors that contribute to the nonimplementation of policies; see Mary Ann Scheirer, *Program Implementation: The Organizational Context* (Beverly Hills, Ca.: Sage Publishing, 1981).

19. Gustavsson, "Implementation of Permanency Planning," pp. 51–56.

20. We argued that child welfare and day-care issues conformed to the "politics of indifference" in the 1960s and 1970s. See Bruce Jansson, "History and Politics of Selected Children's Programs and Related Legislation," Doctoral Dissertation, University of Chicago, 1975, p. 312.

21. For a discussion of declassification, see Burton Gummer, "Is the Social Worker in Public Welfare an Endangered Species?" *Public Welfare*, 37 (Fall 1979).

22. Robert Kuttner, *Revolt of the Haves: Tax Rebellion and Hard Times* (New York: Simon and Schuster, 1980).

23. Bruce Jansson, *Reluctant Welfare State* (Belmont, Ca.: Wadsworth Publishing Co., 1988), p. 208.

24. Wald, "Family Preservation."

25. Julie Kosterlitz, "Not Just Kid Stuff," *National Journal*, 20 (November 19, 1988): 2934–2939.

26. See, for example, the testimony of Ann Klein, the Commission of Human Services of New Jersey, in U.S., Congress, House, Ways and Means Committee, Subcommittee on Public Assistance and Unemployment Compensation, *Hearings on Amendments to Social Services, Foster Care, and Child Welfare*, 96th Cong., 1st Sess., March 1979, pp. 149–154.

27. Robert Montjoy and Laurence O'Toole, "Toward a Theory of Policy Implementation," *Public Administration Review*, 39 (September–October 1979): 465–477.

28. Ibid.

29. See Jeffrey Pressman and Aaron Wildavsky, *Implementation* (Berkeley, Ca.: University of California Press, 1974).

30. Hogwood and Gunn, *Policy Analysis for the Real World*, pp. 129–149.

31. See U.S., Congress, House, Ways and Means Committee, *Joint Hearings on the Impact of the Administration's Proposed Budget Cuts on Children*, 97th Cong., 2nd Sess., March 3, 1982, pp. 90–92.

32. See testimony of Marylee Allen in U.S., Congress, Senate, *Hearings of the Subcommittee on Social Security and Income Maintenance Programs*, June 24, 1985.

33. Cuts in the child welfare staff of local jurisdictions in the early and mid-1980s are discussed by Joanne Selinske, *Public Welfare*, 41 (Summer 1983): 30–35.

34. White children are still far more likely to be adopted than minority children; see Richard Barth, "Disruption in Older Child Adoptions," *Public Welfare*, 46 (Winter 1988): 23–39.

35. Wald, "Preserving Families."

36. Ibid.

37. Ibid.

38. Gustavsson, "Implementation of Permanency Planning," pp. 106–110.

39. Ibid., pp. 106–110, 119–121.

40. Ibid., pp. 109–110.

41. Lack of follow-up services is discussed by Wald, "Preserving Families" and by Barth, "Disruption in Older Child Adoptions."

42. This need to rethink some of the assumptions of the Adoption Assistance and Child Welfare Act is suggested by different perspectives of Besharov, Brown, and Wald. See Douglas Besharov, "Rights versus Rights: The Dilemma of Child Protection," *Public Welfare*, 43 (Spring 1985): 19–27; Besharov, "The Future of Child Protective Agencies," *Public Welfare*, 45 (Spring 1987): 7–11; Larry Brown, "The Future of Child Protective Services: Seeking a National Consensus," *Public Welfare*, 45 (Spring 1987): 12–17; and Wald, "Preserving Families."

43. See, for example, Leila Whiting, "A Different Perspective," *Public Welfare*, 46 (Fall 1978): 22–25; Candace Beavers, "A Cross-Cultural Look at Child Abuse," *Public Welfare*, 44 (Fall 1986): 18–22; and Paula Dail, "Unemployment and Family Stress," *Public Welfare*, 46 (Winter 1988): 30–34.

44. Lowi, *End of Liberalism.*

45. For a discussion of administration regulations, see A. Lee Fritschler, *Smoking and Policy*, 4th ed. (Englewood Cliffs, N.J.: Prentice-Hall, 1988).

46. For a discussion of linkages between policy and other macro disciplines, such as administration, see Bruce Jansson, "From Sibling Rivalry to Pooled Knowledge and Shared Curriculum: Relations Between Community Organization, Administration, Planning, and Policy," *Administration in Social Work*, 11 (Summer 1987): 5–18.

47. See Lyman Porter, et al., *Behavior in Organizations* (New York: McGraw-Hill, 1975).

48. See, for example, the classic work by Tom Burns and George Stalker, *The Management of Innovation* (London: Tavistock, 1966).

49. A vast literature on organizational development exists; see, for example, Renesis Likert and Jane Likert, *New Ways of Managing Conflict* (New York: McGraw-Hill, 1976).

50. See, for example, the classic work by Phillip Selznick, *Leadership in Administration: A Sociological Interpretation* (New York: Harper and Row, 1957).

51. Hogwood and Gunn, *Policy Analysis for the Real World*, pp. 210–212.

52. See the discussion of persuasion in Chapter Seven.

53. For example, Gerald Zaltman and Robert Duncan, *Strategies for Planned Change* (New York: Wiley-Interscience, 1977).

54. See, for example, Eugene Litwak and Lydia Holton, "Interorganizational Interdependence, Intraorganizational Structure," *Administrative Science Quarterly*, 6 (March 1962): 395–420.

55. A classic study of relationships between bureaucracies and their political and economic environment was done by Donald Warwick, *A Theory of Public Bureaucracy: Politics, Personality, and Organization* (Cambridge, Mass.: Harvard University Press, 1975). Also see Mayer Zald, *The Political Economy of the YMCA* (Chicago: University of Chicago, 1970). Eugene Bardach places implementation squarely within the political process; see *The Implementation Game* (Cambridge, Mass.: MIT Press, 1977) as does Walter Williams, *The Implementation Perspective: A Guide for Managing Social Service Delivery Programs* (Berkeley, Ca.: University of California Press, 1980).

56. A good analysis of implementation of policies in agency settings is provided by Scheirer, *Program Implementation: The Organizational Context.*

CHAPTER 13

■

Assessing Policies

In a sense, the policy-assessing task represents both the ending and beginning of the practice of social welfare policy. Persons often regard the assessment of implemented policy as the final step in the policy-making process; having secured the enactment of a policy proposal, they wish to determine whether it has in fact been a success. But assessment is also the beginning of policy practice; when our assessments of existing policies suggest that they are flawed, we often become motivated to develop, enact, and implement policies to change them.

The policy-assessing task occupies, then, a pivotal position in the policy-making process. By triggering discontent, it stimulates people to become active in policy practice. By requiring people to ask whether a specific policy is meritorious, it stimulates critical analysis of existing policies.

To many people, however, the assessment of policies and programs seems to be a forbidding exercise because it often requires using research and technical expertise. Indeed, terms like *program evaluation, validity, statistical findings,* and *research design* are often used to describe technical issues in assessment.

Like many other facets of policymaking, however, assessment can be discussed in relatively nontechnical terms. Moreover, its technical attributes often mask the fact that assessment bears critical similarities to other topics that we have discussed in preceding chapters, such as argumentation and policy analysis. To demystify assessment, we will not focus on a highly technical discussion of it—although we will identify some technical issues—but will analyze the fundamental logic of assessment and its similarities to argumentation and policy analysis. Moreover, we will argue that assessment, like argumentation, is an enterprise that all of us can join, even if we lack the technical skills to conduct a formal and quantitative assessment of a specific policy. Indeed, we will argue that social workers can use policy assessment to develop a leadership component to their professional work.

To illustrate our discussion of assessment, we consider the example of a jurisdiction that devised and implemented policies to try to help natural parents whose children had been taken from them by the courts in the wake of allegations of abuse or neglect. (The jurisdiction vastly increased resources for this preventive work in hopes that the project would enhance the well-being of the children—and, not incidentally, save public resources by obviating the need to place some of the children in extended foster care.)

THE FUNDAMENTAL LOGIC OF ASSESSMENT

Policy practitioners often want to know whether an existing policy is flawed or meritorious, not just as a matter of idle curiosity but because the answers have important implications for a number of persons and institutions. A policy that harms (or at least fails to help) its intended beneficiaries, such as the consumers of a program, would widely be regarded as a dispensable one. A policy that helps consumers but absorbs "unacceptable" amounts of resources will likely be attacked by people who wish to use resources more efficiently. A policy that helps some people but that discriminates against others, such as a program that helps the male victims of a social problem while providing little help to its female victims, would be widely regarded as an unfair or inequitable policy that needed revising.

Policy assessment then requires examining *relationships* between specific policies that have been enacted and implemented, on the one hand, and their specific effects or consequences, on the other hand. Put differently, the process of assessment forces us to ask, How (if at all) is the external world different because a specific policy exists, and what (if any) difference would it make if we removed, deleted, or modified the policy?

When examined in this fashion, of course, policy assessment is not that different from *any* kind of assessment. Direct-service practitioners who examine their work in a critical fashion often wonder, Will such-and-such an intervention improve the well-being of specific clients—or will it be counter-productive—or has the sum total of our interventions over a specific time period led to improvements in their well-being?

SOME SIMILARITIES BETWEEN POLICY ASSESSMENT AND POLICY ANALYSIS

Those readers who remember the discussion of Chapter Four, where we examined the fundamental logic of analytic reasoning, have a head start in understanding the nature of policy assessment because assessment and analysis are strikingly similar. The decision-making matrix that we discussed in Chapter Four (see Table 4.1) is similar to a policy-assessment matrix (Table 13.1). To illustrate this matrix, let's consider the example of a jurisdiction that provides special services to the natural parents of children who have been removed by the courts because of abuse or neglect. And, to take this from the abstract, let's imagine a particular person, who works for the jurisdiction's bureau of child welfare, "thinking through" the approach she will take when trying to develop an assessment of the new program. (Assume that she has been hired to make this assessment.)[1]

The policy-assessment matrix (Table 13.1) contains one or more policy alternatives that describe (1) the policy innovation (in this case, the provision of special services to the natural parents) and (2) one or more policy alternatives (in this case, the usual or typical kinds of services that are provided to natural parents under these circumstances). Persons who assess policies usually want to *compare* an enacted policy with something else because it gives them some standard of comparison. If our policy evaluator could not make comparisons, she might wonder on balance whether the provision of special services to the natural parents "made a difference" over existing arrangements where they received relatively few services.

As she wrestles with the problem of evaluating the new policy, the policy practitioner asks, With respect to what criteria (i.e., outcomes) do I wish to compare the two policy alternatives? At first glance, this would seem to be a relatively simple decision, but she soon realizes that she must choose between an extraordinary array of possible measures of outcomes. She could look at the costs of the new policy, the effects on the parents and families, the effects on the children, the implications for staff and juvenile courts, and the effects on the foster parents. Of course, as she adds more and more

TABLE 13.1 Policy-Assessment Matrix

Policy Alternatives	Evaluative Criteria		
	Rates of Reunification	Costs per Case During the First 18 Months	Developmental Well-Being of Children
1. Special services to natural parents			
2. The existing situation, i.e., the provision of relatively few services			

criteria or outcomes, she makes her work more difficult because the addition of each successive criterion or outcome requires her to obtain more data or information. After discussing this problem with many people, she finally selects three criteria: the effects of increased services to natural parents on (1) the rates of reunification of children with their natural parents, (2) the average cost of each case during the first eighteen months—to include the costs to taxpayers for providing services, paying foster parents, and paying for litigation in juvenile courts—and (3) the "developmental status" of the children at the end of eighteen months.

Why did the policy practitioner select three measures of outcomes rather than settling for only one? She knew, of course, that many legislators and government officials were particularly concerned about the relative costs of the new policy experiment; would the additional *costs* of providing special services, they wondered, be partially or completely offset by the *savings* that could accrue to government by reducing the numbers of children in foster-care placements or (eventually) in subsidized adoptions? Indeed, some of these legislators had only grudgingly approved the policy in the first instance because they doubted that it would on balance save funds. (One conservative legislator called it "another scheme by do-gooder social workers to get more money to fund their pet projects.")

She also wanted to check the rates of reunification of children who received and who did not receive the special services. Many people wanted families to be reunified to the extent possible because of speculation that the long-term or permanent removal of children from their natural families is detrimental to their well-being. Surely, she reasoned, we should obtain information about whether special services do or do not increase the likelihood of family reunification.

But she realized that analysis of costs, as well as rates of reunification, could yield an incomplete, and even misleading, evaluation of the new policy. Recall our discussion of goal displacement in the preceding chapter—a phenomenon whereby implementors mistake certain secondary goals or objectives for the *basic* or most important ones. Unlike some legislators, social workers (let us hope) are concerned about the ultimate effects of policies on the well-being of their clients; were public authorities to use the services as a means to return most children to their natural parents to save the costs of providing foster care, they could easily forget that some parents do not provide a healthy environment *even after* (or while) they receive intensive services. In other words, a potential exists for harming some children in order to save money. Moreover, praiseworthy as reunification may often be, she discovered when searching existing literature that no research had definitively shown that reunification necessarily is in the child's best interest.[2] Some children may thrive in foster care if it provides emotional supports that are lacking in the natural home.

The researcher chooses three measures of outcomes then to obtain a clearer picture of the workings of the new policy. She realizes, of course, that she may discover mixed outcomes; the new policy might save the tax-payers monies, for example, but not yield advantages over the existing policies in promoting the developmental needs of the children.

SOME SIMILARITIES BETWEEN POLICY ASSESSMENT AND ARGUMENTATION

Let's leap ahead three years after the policy practitioner has obtained her data. Assume for the moment that her evaluations suggest that the provision of special services to some, but not to other, children has indeed reduced the costs of child welfare by a small but nonetheless significant amount; if the jurisdiction spent an average of $7,000 on each child in the special services program, it spent an average of $9,500 on each child in the regular program when the costs of foster care and services were aggregated.[3] Moreover, some increases in reunification had in fact occurred; if 27 percent of children were reunified with their parents in the special services program, only 19 percent of children were reunified with parents in the regular program.[4] To the surprise of the practitioner, however, the children in the special services program did not on average achieve higher scores on several measures of child development than did children in the regular program.

We have invented these findings, but they nicely illustrate some dilemmas or problems that evaluators of programs and policies often encounter. When subjected to rigorous and quantitative evaluations, many policies and programs are associated with relatively modest gains—they either appear not significantly different from existing or alternative programs and policies or show relatively modest changes.[5] Of course, the relatively modest changes can sometimes occur in a negative direction—in this case, for example, the children in the special services program *could* have obtained somewhat lower scores than did other children on measures of their development. In some cases, new policies and programs may be associated with striking findings, but, alas, evaluative research often provides less dramatic findings.

We can conjecture why many policies and programs do not lead to a marked transformation of the external world in the direction that their framers intended. Because *many* factors shape the behaviors and development of individuals—such as their prior experiences, their economic condition, and the persons with whom they associate on a daily basis—the programs or assistance of specific staff in the human services system cannot be expected to dramatically and quickly transform the lives of clients, patients, and consumers.[6] Perhaps the instruments that researchers use often fail to capture some important dimensions of human behavior, as well.

Whatever the reasons, the findings of the assessments of policies and programs often fail to provide definitive evidence about their merits. Indeed, assessments sometimes are greeted by considerable controversy wherein the persons who evaluated specific policies or programs are placed in the position of debating or arguing "the meaning" of their findings with others. Indeed, a noted researcher, Donald Campbell, provocatively suggests that program evaluation should be regarded as a form of "argument"—a position that suggests that the evaluator of programs and policies seeks to make a good case that can be (and sometimes is) contested by others.[7] In other words, policy evaluators are often like debaters whose arguments are sometimes contested or countered by other persons.

We can illustrate the similarities between assessment and argumentation by returning to our discussion of the policy practitioner who obtained "mixed findings" when evaluating the child welfare programs. Let's assume that she concluded her work by saying that, "on balance, my findings suggest that the special services program should be enlarged so that it covers all children (and their families) who are removed by the courts from their natural homes because of abusive or neglectful behavior by their parents." Let us also assume that this proposal is strongly contested by some conservative legislators, who continue to wonder if "hiring a lot more social workers to provide intensive services to the natural parents will really cut our costs."

The debate, or argument, between the policy evaluator and conservative politicians could easily involve five dimensions, or axes.[8] First, the evaluator and conservative politicians could debate whether "the glass is half-full or half-empty." Were the reductions in cost and the increased rates of reunification, for example, *sufficiently large* to support the contention that the special services program should be continued and enlarged? No scientific method exists for resolving this dispute because the positions of persons are strongly influenced by their values. Conservatives who opposed the development of the special services program at the outset—and who have a considerable suspicion of social workers—are likely to insist on a higher standard or threshold of evidence than are persons who favored the program at the outset. Indeed, we have already noted that many policies and programs make, at best, marginal improvements over existing ones; thus, evaluators often encounter this kind of threshold or magnitude-of-change argument.

Conservatives might also question the time frame of the research by asking whether the eighteen-month period is sufficiently long to truly discover whether the special services program is effective. "How do we know," one of them asks, "whether some of the children who have been reunified with their parents will not have to be placed in foster homes at some point in the near future?" (Recall that the researcher followed the cases of the children only during an eighteen-month interval.) The evaluator responded that "eighteen months constitutes a sufficiently long interval to make reasonable inferences." However, like the threshold argument, this one cannot be easily resolved because values often shape one's position; someone who is skeptical about a policy or program is likely to want a stricter standard of proof such as a study that follows the consumers or beneficiaries of a policy or program for an extended period of time.

People who wish to question the special services program would have other options, as well. They could question the relative weighting, or importance, of the objectives or criteria that the policy practitioner used to evaluate the program. Someone might say, for example, "It is all well and good that the special services program saves some funds and that it (somewhat) increases the rate of reunification, but *I* think that the well-being of the children ought to be the *prime* consideration—and, on this objective, the data do not seem to demonstrate an improvement over the regular program!" Such a person develops a fundamental criticism of the special services program *not* by questioning its superiority over the regular program in some respects but by suggesting that it is not superior with respect to a specific objective. Here, too, the values and perspectives of individuals influence their responses to evaluative information—someone who favors the program from the outset, for example, might be willing to deemphasize a specific and negative finding and to emphasize more positive ones. Or a cost-conscious conservative, who had opposed the special services program in the first instance, might now support it because it appeared to reduce costs—just as a child development expert, who had initially supported the innovation, might now oppose its continuation because it failed to improve the scores of children on child development tests.

As the policy practitioner presented her findings, she could easily encounter some questions about the accuracy of her data. "How do we know," someone could ask, "whether your findings are truly accurate? Maybe, for example, the children and families you chose for the special services program were ones who did not have as severe problems as other children and families." Or someone else might ask, "How do we know that you did not select particularly talented and motivated social workers to staff the special services program? Maybe the success of the program stemmed from their skills rather than from the special services program itself." Someone else might ask whether the instruments that were used to measure the well-being of the children—that is, the child development instruments— provided accurate information about the children's self-esteem.

SOME TECHNICAL STRATEGIES FOR DECREASING UNCERTAINTY?

To counter some of these latter kinds of questions about the accuracy of the data, evaluators have developed many technical tools. It is beyond the scope of this discussion to analyze these tools in detail, but we can describe some of them briefly. Every evaluation possesses a design, a sampling strategy, and instruments or measures.[9]

Before discussing these technical tools, let's quickly review what criticisms evaluators wish (if possible) to minimize or avoid in the wake of the completion of their studies. They fear that critics will contend that any successes of the policy or program are caused by extraneous or external factors that have nothing to do with the policy or program itself. This kind of criticism is, to say the least, damaging to the credibility of evaluators because it undermines the veracity of their claims, as a simple illustration suggests. Suppose that a direct-service counselor claims remarkable rates of success in treating depression but lacks systematic evidence and indeed develops a for-profit clinic known as the "Sure-Cure for Depression Clinic." Critics could easily question the claims of this entrepreneur by asking how the counselor knows (1) if his clients had not obtained their "miraculous recoveries" because of the normal course of life events rather than because of his intervention (many persons "mature out of" their problems); (2) if background events, such as an improving economy or improved marital situations, had not caused their improvement; (3) if he had selected only certain types of clients whose prognosis was particularly promising so that his rates of improvement seemed extraordinary; and (4) if his measures of the well-being of clients were not flawed ones that made it falsely appear that his clients had suffered from depression in the first instance—or had recovered from it.

Design, sampling, instruments, and statistics allow the evaluator to minimize these various threats to her findings. The *design* of an evaluation describes the strategy that is employed by the researcher to obtain comparisons between the so-called experimental group (the beneficiaries of a specific policy or program) and the control group (persons not receiving benefits from the policy or program). Let's contrast three designs to illustrate options that the evaluator encounters that can be placed on a continuum extended from relatively simple (or nonrigorous) to relatively complex (and rigorous).

In a **correlational design**, the evaluator does not try to establish a new project or program but seeks to analyze the outcomes of projects or programs that have already been implemented. Assume, for example, that the program evaluator in the case of the special services program had encountered a situation where local officials had been unwilling to approve the program so that she could not develop a study of a new program to test the effects of special services on rates of reunification of families. Also assume that the regular program of the child welfare services agency maintained excellent records of all cases during the past ten years, including detailed records of the numbers of visits that child welfare staff had made to the natural parents of children who had been removed by the courts from their homes. It might occur to the evaluator that she could examine the effects of provision of services on rates of reunification by studying *past* cases. Why not, she might ask, compare cases where extensive services had been provided to the natural parents with cases where minimal services had been provided to see if higher rates of reunification were associated with cases that received relatively intensive services?

At first glance, this evaluative strategy seems to be brilliant because the case materials already exist on which to construct the project. As she ponders the issue, however, the evaluator soon realizes that the criticisms that greeted the aforementioned claims of the Sure-Cure for Depression Clinic could also be leveled at her findings, even if they showed a dramatic and positive relationship between the intensiveness of services and the rates of reunification. Might these higher rates of reunification be caused *not* by the intensive services but because astute social workers gave intensive services primarily to those families that *already* were relatively stable and well functioning? (Because the cases had already transpired, the evaluator would be unable to eliminate this possibility.) Nor would she be able to eliminate the possibility that certain events, such as an improving economy, had influenced rates of reunification *independently* of the kinds of services that specific families received. The evaluator would encounter even more formidable research problems if she sought to examine the effects of services upon the social and psychological functioning of the children. Because the cases had already transpired, she could not administer special tests to the children, nor would the case records be likely to yield accurate rankings of the children on social and psychological functioning.

Indeed, evaluators realize that **forward-looking research**—that is, research that analyzes current phenomena—is less subject to external criticism than is retrospective or correlational research precisely because they can (in considerable measure) control or limit factors that might provide alternative explanations for their findings. By controlling who is and who is not given special or intensive services, for example, the evaluator could (largely) eliminate the effects of family characteristics, such as stability and level of functioning, as explanations of rates of reunification. She could decrease the likelihood that external events, such as economic events, influence rates of reunification by making certain that all families in the project are exposed to the same background events—a task that is more achievable when events have not occurred in the past so that the evaluator can be more certain that participants have been exposed to similar events. When the evaluator controls the terms of the experiment, she can directly administer tests or instruments to participants—in this case, tests that examine the social and psychological functioning of the children.

Using **statistical techniques** allows investigators to examine the likelihood that successful results could have occurred by chance rather than because of the special services themselves. In studies with small numbers of subjects, it is highly possible that the investigator may have drawn successful cases merely by chance. Statistical tests allow evaluators to make definitive statements such as "there is only one chance in one hundred that special services could have improved rates of reunification this much if chance were the explanation." **Sampling techniques** allow evaluators to reduce the likelihood that the findings of evaluations are shaped by the characteristics of persons who were selected to participate in a special program. Were families randomly assigned to the special services program, for example, the researcher could more confidently contend that its successes were not due to the fact that its families were *already* functioning at a relatively high level. To decrease the likelihood that positive findings are a function of the instrument—such as the way questions are asked—evaluators can develop or use **instruments** that have been subjected to rigorous scrutiny to ferret from them questions that are likely to achieve erroneous answers.

Evaluators want then to eliminate or reduce the likelihood of **rival explanations** of their findings that critics can use to question their findings. In the case of the special services program, the evaluator hopes that she can reduce the currency of arguments by opponents of the special services program who might seize on the possibility of rival explanations to discredit her findings. One can hear a conservative asking, for example, "How do we know that the special services themselves were responsible for higher rates of reunification and not some other factor, such as 'creaming' by social workers who gave services to families who were relatively stable or well functioning?" The evaluator is likely to feel more confident if she can respond that she has used specific design, sampling, instrumentation, and statistical procedures to decrease the likelihood that rival explanations could account for whatever positive outcomes were achieved by the special services program.

We have noted that it is beyond the scope of this discussion to examine the many design, instrumentation, and sampling options that the evaluator possesses in forward-looking studies. Research literature explores alternative designs such as experimental and quasi-experimental ones, various sampling techniques such as random sampling and stratified sampling, and a host of instrumentation or testing options that include questionnaires and observational techniques.[10] Suffice it to say that studies can be placed on a continuum according to their relative degree of "rigor." In highly rigorous studies, techniques such as random selection of persons to "control" (persons not receiving the special services) and to "experimental" groups (persons receiving the special services) are used.

If highly rigorous studies eliminate rival explanations, why are they not routinely used to assess the effectiveness of specific policies and programs? As the rigor of evaluations increases, so also do their costs and the amount of time that it takes to conduct them. Experts must be hired who are versed in the details of research and who are given the time—often many years— to devise and implement relatively complex studies. Moreover, some of the techniques of evaluators require officials and staff in agencies to subscribe to practices that can raise ethical problems. In the case of the special services program, for example, the evaluator might need to ask whether she could ethically *deny* special services to those families that were randomly placed in the control group.

Nor should we discount the role of politics when explaining the failure of many officials to commission sophisticated assessments of specific policies and programs, to not heed certain findings, or to bias their design or interpretations to protect their interests.[11] The advocates of new policies and programs often have to laud their likely benefits and successes in order to secure their enactment because few politicians or officials will support policies and programs that they believe are likely to fail! But evaluations pose potential risks to the advocates of a specific policy or program, as well as to the staff who work in them and the persons who use them, because they *may* suggest that the innovations do *not* lead to any, some, or most of the benefits that their advocates predicted. In the case of the special services program, only modest reductions in cost and modest increases in rates of reunification were achieved, and no improvements in the social and psychological functioning of children were obtained. Such mixed or modest findings, which are typical in evaluative research, do not seem to provide a ringing endorsement of the innovation and make the interpretations of the findings problematic. (As we noted earlier, it is difficult to determine what threshold or magnitude of success is required to support the continuation of a policy or program.) Moreover, evaluators are often trained to condition or hedge even their positive findings, such as noting those limitations in their design or methodology that *might* render even their modest findings somewhat suspect.

The interpretations of technical data are often shaped by political considerations. When a program or proposal receives unfavorable scores, people can question the validity of the data and demand a new study. Or they can contend that the unfavorable score suggests the program or option should be terminated. Or they may contend that, while the program or policy receives low scores on those criteria that were used in the study, it would or might receive higher scores on other criteria that were not used in the evaluation. Or they can maintain that the unfavorable score is not sufficiently strong to merit the termination of the policy or program. To make matters still more complicated, someone can argue that an unfavorable score for a program or policy emanates not from its intrinsic defects, but because it has not received the funds to allow it to function properly.

The production of data, then, sometimes inaugurates a period of controversy where conflicting parties vie with one another in their interpretations of the findings. If people who favor a program or policy are disposed to provide interpretations that are relatively supportive of it, people who dislike it may seize upon negative findings to urge its termination.

Before we dismiss officials and staff who do not routinely promote or support rigorous evaluations of specific policies and programs then, we should note that evaluations often occur in a politicized context, that they require significant investments of resources and time, and that they sometimes pose ethical dilemmas. We should also note that it is not yet certain that the technical advances in evaluation methodology suffice to render many findings above criticism. Indeed, as can be seen in Figure 13.1, which sum-

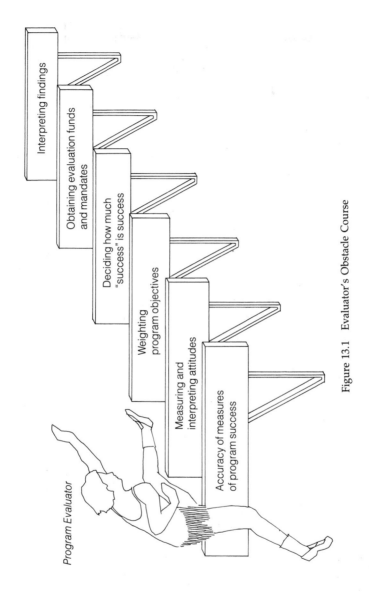

Figure 13.1   Evaluator's Obstacle Course

marizes points made in the preceding discussion, evaluators encounter many obstacles during their work—each one of which can lead to controversy and disputed findings, even among experts who are highly trained in technical procedures.

WHY EVERYONE CAN (AND SHOULD) PARTICIPATE IN THE ASSESSMENT OF POLICIES

We have discussed the technical challenges of policy evaluation at considerable length, as well as the important role of technically trained evaluators. This discussion may convey the misleading impression, however, that only experts can contribute to the assessment of policies and programs. In fact, all social workers can engage in the policy-assessing task even when they lack extended training in research, by actively participating in argumentation about research findings, by citing research, by using theory that is based on practice wisdom, and by using moral standards.

Even when they do not themselves produce research findings, social workers can participate in critical discussions of specific evaluation projects. Rather than being intimidated by research, social workers should instead be eager to participate in discussions about the merits of specific research projects by critically examining their choice of criteria, their interpretations of findings, their methodological choices, and their instruments. Indeed, in some cases, social workers should vigorously challenge evaluations that appear ill advised, such as ones that prematurely suggest that specific policies or programs should be abolished or terminated. Our discussion of evaluation-as-argumentation strongly suggests that many persons can and should address important issues in evaluations because they often contain biases that predispose them to cast aside policies and programs that possess considerable merit.

Even when they have not conducted their own studies, social workers can cite and draw on the research of others as they evaluate specific programs. For example, when evaluating a social program that lacks a bilingual staff, they can cite available research that examines whether and when persons who speak only a foreign language are deterred from seeking or using services when no translators exist. These *suggestive findings* can be used to evaluate specific programs even when they have been obtained in other settings and with different kinds of programs; we can infer, for example, that findings about the impact of a bilingual staff on services to refugees in health services could also apply to other kinds of services given to refugees.

Nor should social workers be reluctant to use professional wisdom as well as theory drawn from the social and human sciences when evaluating specific programs and policies. Empirical research is not available with respect to the vast majority of decisions and policies that exist within the human services; were we to insist on limiting our inputs to ones derived from empirical research, we would consign ourselves to silence on most issues! When they confront policies and programs that appear to conflict with professional wisdom or specific theories that are widely respected, social workers should draw on them to criticize or support specific policies.

In the 1960s, many people supported decision-making control by consumers or citizens in many social agencies. Of course, consumers or citizens can make mistakes, like any of us, but their perceptions can often be used to provide support of or opposition to specific policies. Even when their opinions are not systematically surveyed, social workers can inject their perspectives into debates about the merits of specific policies and programs. When AIDS victims in a major city suggested that they wanted special wards to be established that were devoted to their problems, their preferences importantly influenced hospital officials to develop them.

Persons can also support or oppose specific kinds of policies and programs on purely moral grounds. We discussed in Chapter Eight, for example, some moral reasons why social programs can be defended even *without* specific empirical evidence about the success in rehabilitating or changing people. As one example, we can support hospice programs for terminally ill people because they provide caring and humanistic services to those who are suffering from devastating trauma; this support does not need to be hinged on empirical findings that hospice programs save the government money by reducing the number of days people spend in hospitals. (This empirical finding provides an *additional* justification, but the hospice program could be defended exclusively on moral grounds.) As Glenn Tinder notes:

> Consequences do not count, at least not decisively (when defending social programs). If someone restores a lost wallet to the owner we do not ask how the money it contained will be spent in order to determine whether this was an appropriate act. If someone helps save a friend from unemployment and poverty and the friend later dies of drink, we do not conclude that the original assistance was unwise. Indeed, a strict sense of justice is apt to be severely indifferent to consequences. . . .[12]

The preceding discussion suggests then that the evaluation of policies and programs ought not be reserved to technical experts. All of us can make important contributions and we can use many kinds of evidence and arguments to support or oppose specific policies and programs. Indeed, as we note later, the assessment of policies is the starting point for the assumption of leadership roles in the human services system.

SUMMARY

When policy practitioners undertake the policy-assessing task, they encounter conceptual challenges that are similar to ones that they encounter when they engage in policy analysis. They have to identify and weight those criteria, such as cost and effectiveness, that will be used to assess specific policies and programs. They have to gather data that allow them to isolate the effects, outcomes, or impacts of a policy or program on those people it targets. Moreover, they have to obtain the data in a manner that reduces or eliminates the effects of external factors. When they use sophisticated design and sampling strategies, they try to reduce the effects of rival explanations, such as background economic factors.

The evaluation of policies, like other policy tasks, is often associated with politics. People may differ about the choice and weighting of criteria, the accuracy of data, and the interpretation of findings. Some officials resist systematic evaluations of those policies that they favor or select those design and sampling strategies that cast their favored programs in a positive light.

While evaluations are often difficult to undertake, policy practitioners need to use evaluative techniques to test the effectiveness of specific programs and policies. They can participate in assessing programs even without evaluative data, however, as normative or value-based evaluations of social programs suggest.

QUESTIONS FOR DISCUSSION

1. Why is the evaluation of policies, seemingly an essentially technical undertaking, often embroiled in controversy and politics?

2. The selection of the criteria to be used in evaluating specific policies is strongly influenced by values. Discuss this assertion with respect to the case of the evaluation of special services that is described in this chapter.

3. Discuss some similarities and differences between policy analysis and policy evaluation.

4. Discuss the following assertion: "Negative findings may sometimes mean that a program should be expanded."

5. Take a policy or program with which you are familiar. Discuss some design options that you could consider and some of their strengths and weaknesses.

6. Do you agree with Tinder's assertion that "consequences do not count, at least not decisively (when defending social programs)" since moral considerations, such as the extending of help to vulnerable or suffering people, are the most important considerations?

7. Discuss how people can participate in policy-assessing tasks even when they are not themselves charged with developing research studies.

SUGGESTED READINGS

General Discussions of Policy Evaluation

Scarvia Anderson and Samuel Ball, *The Profession and Practice of Program Evaluation* (San Francisco: Jossey-Bass, 1978).

Richard Berk, et al., "Social Policy Experimentation: A Position Paper," *Evaluation Review*, 9 (August 1985): 387–431.

Carl Patton and David Sawicki, *Methods of Policy Analysis and Planning* (Englewood Cliffs, N.J.: Prentice-Hall, 1986), pp. 300–328.

Tony Tripodi, et al., *Differential Social Program Evaluation* (Itasca, Ill.: Peacock, 1978).

Discussions of Policy Evaluation in Its Political and Economic Context

Carol Weiss, "Where Politics and Evaluation Meet," *Evaluation*, 1 (1973): 37–46.

Carol Weiss, "Ideology, Interests, and Information: The Basis of Policy Positions," in Daniel Callahan and Bruce Jennings, eds., *Ethics, the Social Sciences, and Policy Analysis* (New York: Plenum Press, 1983), pp. 213–248.

Richard Nathan, *Social Science in Government: Uses and Misuses* (New York: Basic Books, 1988).

Discussions of Ethical or Value Issues in Policy Evaluation

Bruce Jansson, "Combining Advocacy and Technical Skills: The Intersection of Politics and Numbers," *Administration in Social Work* (forthcoming, Summer 1990).

Martin Rein, "Value-Critical Policy Analysis," in Callahan and Jennings, eds., *Ethics, the Social Sciences, and Policy Analysis*, pp. 83–111.

Case Studies of Policy Evaluation

Emil Posavic and Raymond Carey, *Program Evaluation: Methods and Case Studies* (Englewood Cliffs, N.J.: Prentice-Hall, 1980).

Carol Weiss, ed., *Evaluation Action Programs* (Boston: Allyn and Bacon, 1972).

NOTES

1. This example was suggested by Michael Wald's discussion in his article, "Family Preservation: Are We Moving Too Fast?" *Public Welfare*, 46 (Summer 1988): 33–38.
2. Ibid.
3. These are hypothetical numbers.
4. These are hypothetical numbers.
5. This point is made by Richard Berk, et al., "Social Policy Experimentation: A Position Paper," *Evaluation Review*, 9 (August 1985): 387–431.
6. See Scarvia Anderson and Samuel Ball, *The Profession and Practice of Progam Evaluation* (San Francisco: Jossey-Bass, 1978), pp. 6, 110–125.
7. Donald Campbell, "Experiments as Arguments," *Knowledge*, 3 (1982): 327–337.
8. For a discussion of the kinds of value-laden choices in program evaluations, see Bruce Jansson, "Combining Advocacy and Technical Skills: The Intersection of

Politics and Numbers," *Administration in Social Work* (forthcoming, Summer 1990). Also see Martin Rein, "Value-Critical Policy Analysis," in Daniel Callahan and Bruce Jennings, eds., *Ethics, the Social Sciences, and Policy Analysis* (New York: Plenum Press, 1983), pp. 83–111.

9. An extended overview of program evaluation is found in Anderson and Ball, *The Profession and Practice of Program Evaluation*; and Tony Tripodi, et al., *Differential Social Program Evaluation* (Itasca, Ill.: Peacock, 1978). For a brief overview, see Carl Patton and David Sawicki, *Methods of Policy Analysis and Planning* (Englewood Cliffs, N.J.: Prentice-Hall, 1986), pp. 300–328.

10. Ibid.

11. See Carol Weiss, "Where Politics and Evaluation Meet," *Evaluation*, 1 (1973): 37–46; Carol Weiss, "The Politicization of Evaluation Research, *Journal of Evaluation Research*, 26 (1970): 57–68; and Carol Weiss, "Ideology, Interests, and Information: The Basis of Policy Positions," in Callahan and Jennings, eds., *Ethics, the Social Sciences, and Policy Analysis*, pp. 213–248. For a discussion of the uses of social science by decision makers, see Henry Aaron, *Politics and the Professors* (Washington, D.C.: Brookings Institution, 1981) and Richard Nathan, *Social Science in Government: Uses and Misuses* (New York: Basic Books, 1988).

12. Glenn Tinder, "Defending the Welfare State," *New Republic* (March 10, 1979), pp. 21–23.

PART VI

■

Mainstreaming Policy Practice into Professional Practice

We have discussed various policy skills and tasks in preceding chapters. With our conceptual work completed, we can ask some questions about the place of social welfare policy and its practice component within professional work. We argue in Chapter Fourteen that policy practice should become integral to the professional role of direct-service, administrative, and community-organizing social workers. Various obstacles exist, however, such as a lack of comfort with power by many social workers, a failure of theorists to make policy practice a central component of ecological or systems frameworks, and a failure of policy theorists to articulate frameworks and interventions to guide the policy practice of social workers.

We argue that social workers are likely to practice policy in somewhat different fashion than the members of other professions because they possess values that place emphasis upon social justice and beneficence. If this hypothesis is correct, social workers can make a distinctive and needed contribution to policy-making in agency, community, and legislative settings. Policy practice may also serve, we argue, as a unifying theme in a profession that is splintered into many specializations.

CHAPTER 14

■

Integrating the Practice of Policy
with the Professional Role

Social welfare policy ought to be integral to the professional role because the needs of clients and oppressed people require assistance that extends to the policies that shape the human services delivery system, as well as to the institutions of the wider society. In this chapter we enumerate the number of ways that direct-service, administrative, and community-organization social workers can participate in the practice of policy. We also argue, however, that policy practice is not integral to the professional role of many social workers because they lack comfort with the development and use of power, and also because theorists have failed to fully define a role for policy practice within the systems or ecological frameworks that have gained prominence. Nor have social welfare theorists devoted sufficient attention to developing a practice component of policy.

THE UBIQUITOUSNESS OF POLICY IN
PROFESSIONAL WORK

Social workers confront policy issues at virtually every turn in the road. The nature of services that they provide is dictated by a host of policies that emanate from different sources; these include policies of legislatures, government agencies, courts, funders such as United Way, contracts and grants that governmental authorities use to purchase services from agencies, professional associations such as the Code of Ethics of the National Association of Social Workers, licensing and accrediting bodies, boards of directors of agencies, and administrative staff. We argued in Chapter One, as well, that some policies emanate from the informal culture and agreements of the staff who implement policies.

We do not suggest that these various kinds of policies provide a straitjacket because they often provide implementing staff with considerable discretion. But these policies in many ways, singly and in tandem, shape the lives and work of citizens, clients, and implementing staff.

These policies vary in their effects and their importance. Trivial policies have little importance such as some of the detailed policies that exist in agencies and programs. Other policies, however, have considerable impact on citizens and professionals; reformers should give these policies attention when they believe them to be dysfunctional.

Policies also vary in their malleability. Some policies are relatively simple to change because of their source, nature, and context. Policy practitioners find it easy to modify an administrative policy in an agency that is relatively simple in nature and that is enveloped in a nonconflictual context when compared to modifying a legislative policy that requires the concurrence of hundreds of legislators and that is highly controversial in nature.

Policy practitioners need not focus on a single kind of policy in their work; they can variously seek to change simple policies, complex policies, policies in their agencies, legislative policies, controversial policies, and policies that are not enveloped in conflict. Our focus in this book, indeed, is relatively generic since we try to provide concepts, such as the various policy skills and tasks, that apply to *any* effort to change existing policies.

It would be possible, of course, to study policy practice in a more specialized way, such as focusing upon policy practice in specific settings (such as agencies or legislatures). Or we could have focused upon a specific style of policy-making, such as the analytic style. Or we could have geared our discussion of policy in a specific sector, such as child welfare policy, rather than using a range of policy examples.

But a generic or broad-based treatment of policy practice has many advantages. Were we to concentrate upon a single kind of policy, such as agency-based or legislative, we would imply that it should take preeminence in policy practice to the detriment of other kinds of policies. Were we to concentrate upon those policies that are relatively easy to change, such as some agency-based ones, we would imply that social workers ought not try to change more complex and controversial policies, such as legislative policies. If we concentrated exclusively upon agency and legislative policies, we would imply that social workers should have no connections with social movements or broad community coalitions. Were we to concentrate upon a single style of policy-making, such as an analytic style, we would imply that this style is effective in all or most situations.

A generic or broad-based approach to policy practice underscores the need for policy practitioners to be flexible and adaptable. Policy practice occurs in many kinds of settings and takes many forms. It varies with the nature of the issue and the context. Better, we argue, to understand concepts, skills, tasks, and frameworks that apply to a range of policy-practice situations than limit ourselves to a single style or situation.

The need for versatility in policy practice is underscored by a brief enumeration of the kinds of policy practice that social workers can undertake. We have noted that policy practice can occur in agency and extraagency sites; these variously include the work of line staff, supervisors, executives, community organizers who work with community groups and social movements, and lobbyists. Policy practice can occur in formally sanctioned or official projects, such as task forces that are established by executives to examine policy issues, or it can be informal in nature, as when a direct-service worker decides to pursue an issue without the approval of higher officials. Policy practice occurs in structured and planned fashion when someone develops a game plan or it can occur in improvisational fashion; someone may attend a meeting, for example, and decide on the spot to make a specific statement. Policy practitioners can variously assume affirming, blocking, and bystander roles. Policy practice can involve an extended sequence of actions, as when someone successively undertakes agenda-building, problem-defining, proposal-writing, policy-enacting, policy-implementing, and policy-assessing tasks, or it can be confined to one or several episodes, as when someone confines his work on an issue to several meetings. Policy practitioners can emphasize specific policy skills in specific situations, such as analytic skills, or they can use a variety of skills in tandem. Policy practitioners can be leaders or initiators with respect to a specific issue or they can be followers.

A generic approach to policy practice, then, sensitizes us to the variety of policy-practice situations and actions that exist in the real world. It does not limit policy practice to specific styles, settings, or issues. It invites us to become participants in many ways and at different points in our professional work.

This generic approach offers no quick-fixes or panaceas, however. Some issues are difficult to address and some policies are relatively intractable in nature. Policy-making does not occur on a level playing field; some people bring to the game more power resources, can invest more time, and have more skill than other people. Policy practitioners experience some risks when they engage in the practice of policy.

These cautionary notes should not, however, obscure the challenges and the rewards that are associated with the practice of policy. It allows professionals to expand their boundaries and to obtain the satisfaction that accompanies successful projects by modifying dysfunctional policies.

LACK OF COMFORT WITH POWER

Many social workers do not participate in policy practice because of a disinclination to develop and use power.[1] We noted in Chapter Five that relatively powerless people sometimes enter a vicious circle; they are aware that they are relatively powerless and avoid participating in policy practice, which makes them even more powerless. Social workers often work in programs that receive relatively little support from the broader society or even from within bureaucracies where their units often have to battle to maintain their existence.

Moreover, most social workers are women, and Rosabeth Kanter suggests that women are particularly subject to exclusion from the inner circles of power within bureaucracies, which may erode their confidence to participate in the practice of policy.[2] Women are also subject to the values of a male-dominated society, which has accorded them relatively background and supportive roles.

While the development and use of power is only one of the four policy skills that we have discussed in preceding chapters, it is essential to the various policy tasks. To elevate an issue or problem to prominence during the agenda-building task, for example, people have to convince decision makers that it merits attention by using power resources such as expertise and authority, by using procedural power to place it in favorable positions on the agendas of committees, by encouraging intermediaries (such as highly placed officials) to assume leadership, and by using substantive power to define the issue or problem in a manner that makes it seem important to decision makers. When engaging in the problem-defining task, social workers have to use symbols and paradigms that make a problem appear important to those decision makers whose support is needed when proposals are subsequently developed. When constructing proposals, policy practitioners have to select criteria and options with an eye to political realities, since a proposal that is wholly unacceptable to decision makers will not be successful. And they must be willing to use substantive power during the proposal-making process to initiate and accept those amendments that are needed to secure support for their proposal. Policy practitioners have to use process power when engaging in the agenda-building, problem-defining, and proposal-writing tasks; they have to decide whom to try to include in (or to exclude from) policy deliberations and when to escalate or to decrease conflict.

In addition to using power in skillful and assertive fashion, effective policy practitioners have to devote considerable time to developing power resources in the first instance. They need to enhance their credibility by making useful contributions to policy discourse. They need access to networks of people who possess information and power within specific settings.

If the use of power is endemic to the agenda-building, problem-defining, and proposal-writing tasks, it is most obvious in the policy-enacting task when policy practitioners must use a full armory of power resources to obtain the enactment of specific proposals—or to block those proposals that they dislike. But power is also integral to the policy-implementing and policy-assessing tasks. It is often as difficult to secure reforms during implementation as to secure the enactment of policies. Matters of turf, prestige, organizational hierarchies, and tradition induce many people to resist basic changes in implementation. Our brief discussion of assessment in Chapter Thirteen suggests that it, too, is associated with politics. The selection of criteria and the interpretation of findings—indeed, the decision whether even to undertake an evaluation in the first instance—are strongly influenced by the values and the interests of the various people who implement or are associated with an operating program.

Since the development and use of power resources are integral to policy-making, social workers severely jeopardize their ability to be policy practitioners if they are uncomfortable with power. Moreover, social workers need to develop skills in leadership—assuming "out front" and initiating roles in the policy-making process.[3]

LEGITIMIZING POWER, ASSERTIVENESS, AND POLICY LEADERSHIP

Power needs to be legitimized in social work so that it is seen as a resource in professional work, much like empathy, timing, and contracting in direct-service work. Social workers need to realize that the development and use of power are already endemic to ther work. Yeheskel Hasenfeld suggests, for example:

1. Clinical social workers often use power.
2. They variously cast interpretations on the problems of their clients that conform to the mission or services of their agencies; they establish certain expectations about the actions and roles that clients should take during the helping process.
3. They use subtle (and not-so-subtle) sanctions and penalties for those clients whose responses to services fall outside specific norms or expectations.
4. They enforce (or choose not to enforce) agency procedures that govern eligibility, referrals, and termination.
5. They proffer "guiding comments and suggestions" that steer clients toward certain actions or decisions.
6. They "take sides" with one or another person in family or other conflicts, sometimes in subtle (and not-so-subtle) ways.[4]

Indeed, were power *not* used in clinical transactions, clients would probably be disappointed because they expect their helpers, who presumably have considerable expertise, to guide them, to offer their informed suggestions, and to establish realistic expectations. As the employees of agencies, moreover, most social workers enforce and follow a host of policies, procedures, and protocols that derive from their agencies, not to mention those paradigms and expectations that staff share in particular agencies. While certain ethical limits should be placed on the use of power, as we discussed in Chapter Eight, power is integral to the clinical roles of social workers and not, as some imply, an unprofessional, unethical, or unnatural adjunct to professional work. In similar fashion, administrators and community organizers use power resources at innumerable places in their work, though the literature of these disciplines is less likely to deny the use of power by their practitioners.

We need to demystify power, then, and declare it a professional resource that is necessary not only in clinical work, but in policy practice, as well. While power can usefully be discussed as an abstract concept, it needs to be practiced, observed, and modeled like other professional skills. Simulations, role plays, video tapes, and films, not to mention incorporation of the concept in field work, should be used to make the subject relevant to social workers.

Assertiveness also needs to receive greater attention in the profession because it provides concepts and skills that are particularly germane to people who occupy low-status or low-power positions—or who are subject to repeated reminders of their lack of power. As the helpers of populations that are relatively stigmatized and as employees in programs that are chronically underfunded, social workers need to grapple with the psychology of power. They need to address difficult issues: When is it futile to change specific policies or conditions? When can the limited power of specific individuals be augmented by coalitions? How does one overcome a vicious circle of helplessness that sometimes exists among people with relatively little power?

We define "policy leadership" to mean "taking the initiative in a specific situation to facilitate the examination and the development of remedies to important problems."[5] (Leadership is often used to discuss different styles of management and the role of the leaders of specific groups.) People who initiate policy deliberations expose themselves to some risk, but they also can experience many gains such as recognition from others and psychological rewards that stem from assuming constructive and problem-solving roles.

Leadership needs to be perceived not as an onerous burden, but, like the use of power, as an integral part of the professional role. If social workers fail to exert policy leadership, they allow other people, who often possess less commitment to the well-being of clients and the needs of oppressed minorities, to shape the human services delivery system.

Power, assertiveness, and leadership are related and mutually-reinforcing concepts. Each of them underlies a propensity to engage in the practice of policy, as well (probably) as an ability to be an effective policy practitioner. They should be viewed as both means and ends. If the development and use of power allow people to be assertive and to assume leadership roles, for example, their assertiveness and leadership contribute, in turn, to their stock of power and their ability to convince others to heed their suggestions.

MAKING POLICY A CENTRAL FEATURE OF ECOLOGICAL FRAMEWORKS

Policy practice has always been implied in systems and ecological frameworks, which continue to receive prominence in the social work literature that discusses direct service and human behavior. Perhaps because the writers of this literature tend not to come from the macro or indirect-service segments of the profession, they usually fail to devote sufficient attention to professional practice that seeks to change agency, community, and legislative policies that exacerbate or create the problems of clients. The logic of systems and ecological frameworks is clear: Social workers, who wish to help their clients, possess a professional duty to try to reform and modify those environmental factors that contribute to the problems of people whom social workers serve.

In similar fashion, social welfare policy theorists have been remiss in not linking their discipline more explicitly to systems and ecological frameworks. Indeed, the terms are rarely present in policy (or other macro) literature, perhaps because its theorists tend to view direct-service practice as essentially different from and unrelated to policy issues.[6] The ecological framework ought not be avoided by policy theorists, however, because it provides a mechanism for linking policy to the activities of most social workers.

BUILDING POLICY-PRACTICE TECHNIQUES THAT ACTUALLY CHANGE POLICIES

It doesn't help to link social work practice to ecological frameworks, however, if theorists don't describe in considerable detail *how* social workers should implement the framework, which is relatively abstract in nature. On the direct-service side, some theorists have described a range of tasks and skills of how people can use the framework.[7] Policy theorists need to follow suit within their own discipline so that social workers possess a range of skills and strategies that will be effective in specific situations.

The development of a policy-practice discipline has been hindered, however, by the preoccupation of theorists with defining specific rules, norms, or techniques that social workers should use to develop "correct" positions. The analytic literature, in social work and in other disciplines, provides rational recommendations that reflect the use of data and research. The normative literature seeks to identify those values, such as redistribution, that should guide the development of recommendations. Both of these streams of policy literature assume that decision makers will be influenced to accept those recommendations that are technically correct (analytic theorists) or normatively correct (value-based theorists). Moreover, both the analytic and normative literature imply that policymakers are relatively cloistered experts who devise their recommendations in isolation.[8]

Policy-making is a more complex and challenging process than many rationalists and value-oriented theorists have recognized. While analytic and value considerations often assume a major role in policy deliberations, they are often superseded by political and interactional factors. It is not enough merely to take positions; social workers have to enter the fray, develop game plans, and implement strategy. They have to use a range of competencies that extend beyond the framing of positions. And, pragmatically, social workers have to adapt their practice to the realities they confront. If decision makers are not amenable to technical presentations, for example, they need to use political or advocacy styles of policy practice.

Analytic and normative literature also underplays the competitive aspects of policy-making. Many people participate in policy-making, present a variety of viewpoints, and sometimes engage in win-lose conflict where they seek to defeat their opponents. People often have to be willing to compromise their positions in the give-and-take of policy deliberations.

Policy practice will flourish only as we identify those actions, behaviors, and strategies that allow us to change policies in specific settings. Terms like skills, tasks, context, and style, which are given considerable attention in the existing direct-service, administrative, and community-work practice literature, need to appear in policy literature if the discipline is to become relevant to the everyday activities of a wide range of professional social workers.

WILL SOCIAL WORKERS PRACTICE POLICY IN DIFFERENT FASHION FROM OTHER PEOPLE?

It is worth asking in the concluding section of this book whether social workers are likely to engage in policy practice in a different fashion than the members of other disciplines or than people in general. This is, of course, a question that eventually needs to be resolved empirically, although it will be difficult to obtain solid evidence because of problems in observing and comparing the actions, behaviors, and arguments of different people in identical or similar situations. Such comparisons are needed to ascertain whether the members of different professions practice policy in different or similar fashion. While it is useful to compare the attitudes or preferences of social workers with those of members of other professions or of other people in general, these comparisons do not necessarily predict their behaviors. Three possibilities exist: (1) Social workers may practice policy in virtually identical fashion as other people. (2) They may use entirely different approaches. (3) They may practice policy somewhat differently than other people (an intermediary position). Let's discuss these three possibilities.

We reject the possibility that social workers will practice policy in an entirely different fashion than other people because people who try to change policies confront certain realities and contingencies no matter their discipline. If social workers want to change policies, they will encounter power realities, for example, no matter what their world view may be—and they will have to use power resources in their work or suffer a string of defeats. Since none of us like to experience repeated failures in any endeavor, we try to adapt our actions, behaviors, and arguments to decrease their likelihood. Over time, then, we can guess that social work practitioners, even those people who are not well equipped to engage in policy practice at the outset, will likely modify their work so that it resembles the policy practice of other people.

We surmise, however, that social workers are likely to practice policies in different fashion than the members of other professions because they possess somewhat different values. Values provide a lens that shapes the goals and tactics of policy practice as our discussion in many of the preceding chapters suggests. People who favor the criterion of social justice, for example, are likely to develop a different kind of policy proposal than someone who focuses on cost-cutting, as comparisons of liberal and conservative legislators in the Congress suggest. They are more likely to try to place issues and problems on the agendas of decision makers that pertain to the social needs of oppressed minorities. They are more likely during the implementation of policies to try to correct those administrative processes that promote inequitable treatment of stigmatized people.

If social workers possess somewhat different values than other people, it is plausible to contend that their practice of policy may share some commonalities with the policy practice of other people, but that it will be somewhat different. The possibility that social workers do possess different values than other people is suggested by the comments of Maurice Bischeff, who runs simulations games in different professional schools of the University of Southern California. He compared the tactics of students in the business school with tactics of social work students when they played a simulation game known as End of the Line. This simulation game asks participants to assume the role of elderly people who have limited resources, such as money and food, symbolized by paper clips. While various services are created to augment the supply of paper clips, a process of competition and attrition occurs that leads some people to symbolically die when they lose their stock of paper clips. Students in the business school usually created a win-lose situation that led to a few winners and many losers. Social workers, by contrast, often invited destitute players to join supportive groups that shared their dwindling supplies of paper clips. The social workers defined the game in win-win terms that emphasized cooperative rather than competitive strategies.

While this anecdote does not provide definitive evidence, it suggests that social workers are somewhat more likely to identify with underdogs, the downtrodden, and the oppressed. These groups include racial minorities, poor people, stigmatized groups such as gay and lesbian persons, or people who are viewed as deviants such as mental patients.

We do not argue that social workers possess radical or socialist ideology because they are somewhat more likely to empathize with the downtrodden than are members of other professions, although a radical faction exists within the profession. As critics of the profession often suggest, its leaders have often been willing to accommodate the interests of relatively conservative funders and boards of their agencies rather than engaging in vigorous advocacy for their clients.[9] Nor do we wish to contend that an interest in the downtrodden is always altruistic; the jobs of social workers in the many agencies that serve members of oppressed groups depend, after all, upon their continued funding.

But these cautionary comments ought not draw attention from the likelihood that social workers place *relatively* more emphasis upon social justice than do the members of business, legal, public administration, and medical professions. They choose, after all, a profession that is widely known to emphasize work with stigmatized and oppressed groups and that possesses less status than alternative professions.

Nor does the preoccupation with clinical work by most social workers imply that the profession does not value social justice, as some critics of the profession have implied. Jerome Wakefield suggests that those persons who aspire to clinical work often possess a distributive-justice ethic; they want to help persons obtain self-respect and self-esteem who often come from families and environments that have made it difficult for them to cope with crises and dilemmas in life.[10] People with mental difficulties are like a disadvantaged group in a familial and sociological sense, if not in an economic sense, since they often reach adulthood with profound relationship and problem-solving deficits. Or they develop mental problems because they experience stress from environmental causes, such as unemployment and lack of support systems. People with severe or chronic mental problems are often subject to the kinds of job, housing, and social discrimination that we commonly associate with racial minorities and with other stigmatized groups. Their mental disabilities sometimes entrap them in poverty when they are sufficiently severe to impede their ability to obtain and keep employment. By devoting much of their time to helping people with these kinds of familial and environmental deficits, clinical social workers *are* practitioners of distributive justice even though they emphasize clinical rather than policy interventions. They invest their professional energy in helping people who are members of a disadvantaged group and seek to provide them with skills to help them to improve their lot, not to mention advocacy, brokering, and liaison assistance. While their work does not appear as obviously redistributive as that of civil rights activists, it is focused upon the needs of disadvantaged people who are subject to discrimination and poverty.

We should not overstate the extent clinical social workers emphasize distributive justice in their work. Many of them practice psychotherapy that does not emphasize the imparting of social-survival and coping skills to clients, the provision of services to impoverished people, or assistance to people whose families were particularly insensitive to their material or developmental needs.[11] Even casual perusal of a range of texts and writings in social work, in both direct and indirect service, suggests, however, that social justice continues to receive considerable attention.

Even when they do not favor redistributing goods and services to impoverished or disadvantaged populations, social workers often adhere to the principle of beneficence—helping people with their problems regardless of their affiliation. Increases in the funding of mental health programs, for example, do not need to be justified by recourse to social justice, but merely on grounds that mentally distressed people benefit from counseling.

To the extent social workers place relatively more emphasis than other people on social justice and beneficence, then, we would expect their policy practice to reflect these values. When using analytic skills, they should weight social-justice and equity criteria more heavily than those people who emphasize cost or feasibility criteria. They should be more inclined to join or endorse coalitions that support reforms for disadvantaged populations than those people who are more inclined to cast their lot with other projects. They should be more inclined to define problems in redistributive terms—in the context of the relative deprivation of certain people when compared to other people.

Social workers should realize, of course, that they cannot rely exclusively upon their values in their practice of policy, since they need to use political, interactional, and analytic skills, as well. And they will often have to reach compromise positions when different criteria, such as cost considerations, are valued by other people.

POLICY PRACTICE AS A UNIFYING THEME

As Phillip Popple suggests, it is romantic to aspire to a profession that is wholly unified when its members work in such different settings and undertake such different tasks. Indeed, he calls social work a "federated profession" that is comprised of various groups that possess different specializations and perspectives.[12]

At the same time, however, some unifying themes serve psychological and political functions. If the profession lacks *any* cohesion, it will fail to develop united positions and political clout on issues that affect our profession, such as licensing, declassification, and funding. Moreover, to the extent social workers wish to help oppressed minorities, they will lack the kind of strong professional organizations that can exert effective pressure on decision makers.[13]

Perhaps policy practice can serve as one unifying theme—something that all social workers do, no matter their specialization. It will allow social workers, singly and in tandem, to shape the external world so that it is more congruent with their values. It will allow social workers to extend the boundaries of their work to influence those policies that profoundly affect the well-being of oppressed populations. And it will allow social workers to infuse their professional work with the broader vision that the founders of the profession, such as Jane Addams, possessed when they tried to persuade decision makers of their time to enact humane policies.

NOTES

1. See Eleanor Brilliant, "Social Work Leadership: A Missing Ingredient," *Social Work*, 31 (September–October 1986): 327–328.
2. Rosabeth Kanter, *Men and Women of the Corporation* (New York: Basic Books, 1977).
3. Brilliant, "Social Work Leadership."
4. Yeheskel Hasenfeld, "Power in Social Work Practice," *Social Service Review*, 61 (September 1987): 475–476.
5. See Aileen Hart's discussion of leadership in "Training Social Administrators for Leadership in Coming Decades," *Administration in Social Work*, 12 (1988): 1–11. Also see Brilliant, "Social Work Leadership," p. 326.
6. For an exception, see Carel Germaine's contribution to Samuel Taylor and Robert Roberts, *Theory and Practice of Community Work* (New York: Columbia University Press, 1985), pp. 30–58.
7. See, for example, Aaron Brower, "Can the Ecological Model Guide Social Work Practice?" *Social Service Review*, 62 (September 1988): 411–429.
8. See our discussion of this literature in Chapter Nine.
9. See Michael Reisch and Stanley Wenocur, "The Future of Community Organization in Social Work: Social Activism and the Politics of Profession Building," *Social Service Review*, 60 (March 1986): 70–93.
10. Jerome Wakefield, "Psychotherapy, Distributive Justice, and Social Work: Part 1, Distributive Justice as a Conceptual Framework for Social Work," *Social Service Review*, 62 (June 1988): 187–210. Also see "Part 2, Psychotherapy and the Pursuit of Justice," *Social Service Review*, 62 (September 1988): 353–384.
11. Ibid., pp. 377–378.
12. Phillip Popple, "The Social Work Profession: A Reconceptualization," *Social Service Review*, 59 (December 1985): 560–577.
13. See Nancy Humphreys, "Saving Social Services: Leading the Fight Against Cutbacks," *NASW News*, 26 (February 1981): 2.

APPENDIX A

■

Three Simulation Games

If policy is (at least in part) a practice discipline, we need to develop methods of providing social workers with analytic, political, interactional, and value-clarification skills. To facilitate the use of this book in educational settings, we include three simulation games in this appendix. We have chosen ones that are relatively easy to implement during a single class and with classes of different sizes. We note at the start of each simulation which chapters are particularly relevant to it.

SIMULATION 1

The Case of Dr. Breeze and the San Marcos
Community Mental Health Center

This simulation can be used in conjunction with Chapters Four and Five to illustrate the uses of power and coalitions. It can also be used as an introduction to policy, to the controversial nature of policy, to policy practice in agency settings, and to the nature of policy proposals—topics that are discussed in Chapter One.

Have the students read the case "Agency in Policy Turmoil." Then divide the class into four groups by having people sign up for one of them on the board. (If some of the groups are undersubscribed, the instructor needs to reassign people to them.)

The groups are (1) "Traditionalists" led by Dr. Jones, (2) "Insurgents" led by Dr. Storm, (3) Group for "Responsible Change" led by Dr. Virtue, (4) "Board of Directors" led by Dr. Cautious. (Other groups can be added, such as a community group of activists and a conservative community group.)

AGENCY IN POLICY TURMOIL

Exactly one year ago, Dr. George Breeze came to San Marcos, a metropolitan suburb of Los Angeles with a population of 60,000 people, to direct the recently established San Marcos Community Mental Health Center. Dr. Breeze had previously worked in Philadelphia, where he had acquired a reputation as the innovative, inspiring, and flexible director of Manford University's Outreach Mental Health Services Department.

When Dr. Breeze initially interviewed for his position, several board members expressed some reservations about how he would fit in, since he did not wear a tie and seemed almost overconfident. Dr. Sedgwick, the retiring director, calmed the board by saying that, as a young psychoanalyst, he too had been fairly unconventional. The board had to keep in mind that this was no longer the San Marcos Clinic, it was a new mental health center, and it needed new ideas and the dedication of youth. "He will work out," Dr. Sedgwick reassured them.

Shortly after George Breeze arrived at the San Marcos Community Mental Health Center, he made it clear to the staff that waiting lists, long-term therapy, and supervision were outdated. In the following months, he:

1. urged short-term, crisis-oriented management of cases
2. requested and received permission to establish an advisory board of citizens from the catchment area and another board composed of consumers
3. abolished the supervision system and established a flexible peer-consultation system
4. asked staff members to work evenings in order to see families
5. got into an argument with the Chief of Police about how officers were handling youngsters and emotionally ill persons
6. hired paraprofessionals from a human services program of a community college to serve as community aides
7. told the staff that he wanted to know personally about the service and disposition of each case that involved a racial or ethnic minority client because he suspected that staff members were allowing biases to influence case management

Within six months, the staff in the agency had become deeply divided. Three major groups had formed and developed leadership. First, some of the original clinic staff members (who had helped Dr. Sedgwick prepare the mental health center application) resented Dr. Breeze's nontraditional ways and felt that they had had no chance to introduce their ideas. They rallied behind Dr. Jones, met privately, and decided that they must take their case to other agencies in San Marcos and to local civic leaders and then must present their complaints to the agency board with the support of these other groups and leaders.

The staff hired by Dr. Breeze (young activist professionals and community aides) learned of the strategy and immediately alerted Asian, black, and Chicano groups in San Marcos and rallied behind Dr. Smith, who contacted both the National Institute of Mental Health (the prime federal funder of the center) and the Citizen and Consumer Advisory Boards. They were ready to ask for termination of federal and state funds if Dr. Breeze was fired.

Finally, a number of agency supervisors formed a group behind Dr. Virtue that advocated "responsible change." They were not opposed to all the changes instituted by Dr. Breeze but particularly opposed to those that deprived "professionals" of their rightful positions of authority and prestige within the agency. They wanted restoration of the supervisory system and curtailment of hiring of new careerists.

The issue reached crisis proportions when a patient being cared for by a community aide committed suicide in a most sensational manner. A reporter from the newspaper interviewed a member of the original staff and was told that "this would never have happened if Dr. Sedgwick had been there; Dr. Breeze's ideas just don't work."

The board decided to hold a meeting to settle the issue, and they agreed to allow representatives of all sides to present their evidence. They felt that Dr. Breeze had introduced some good programs but also felt that he was unconventional. At this meeting, they hoped to reach a final decision as to whether Dr. Breeze should be fired, retained (but only after placing limits on the reforms he had issued), or given a vote of complete confidence.

"Traditionalists," then, rallied behind Dr. Jones and wanted to restore the traditional mission of the agency—long-term therapy with white and middle-class clients. "Insurgents" supported Dr. Breeze and his various reforms with no qualifications. "Advocates of responsible change" wanted some innovations but not at the expense of the traditional prerogatives of professionals. The board wished to bring unity to the agency as soon as possible to avoid further adverse publicity as well as possible loss of funds.

SOURCE: This case was developed by Professor Samuel H. Taylor, Graduate School of Social Work, University of Southern California. Names and locations have been altered.

The exercise is divided into a series of periods. The times and numbers of periods can be altered. The schedule should be placed on the blackboard at the outset of the exercise to orient the players to the game. The class should be told that a period of extended deliberations will ensue and will culminate in a decision by the board (1) to fire Dr. Breeze, (2) to retain him with a vote of complete confidence, (3) to retain him but with specific restrictions, or (4) to retain him along with specific policies the board wishes to enact.

Period #1 (15 minutes): Each group meets by itself in a specific part of the room. They select a leader and talk in general terms about the kinds of policies or steps they would favor in this situation. The board decides which of its members will preside at the meeting and who will keep time.

Period #2   (*15 minutes*): The board convenes a public meeting of the groups and asks a spokesperson from each group to discuss in general terms its perspectives on the situation and its initial recommendations. (Each group is given a time allotment.)

Period #3   (*20 minutes*): This is a period of discussions and negotiations among members of the various groups. A member of a group can approach members of other groups to seek common agreements on specific points.

Period #4   (*10-15 minutes*): This is a final meeting of the board, which has asked each group very specifically to indicate what policies or actions it wishes the board to take.

Period #5   (*10 minutes*): The board votes its recommendations in front of other participants (only board members can speak during this session). The board announces its recommendations.

Points to Be Discussed During the Debriefing

1. What does the exercise tell us about the way social policies (in this case agency policies) are fashioned? Why are policy issues often controversial?
2. Why are some policy issues resolved amicably while others are associated with relatively conflictual deliberations?
3. What factors impeded or facilitated the success of each of the groups in obtaining its policy preferences?
4. Which group was "most successful" and which "least successful" in obtaining its policy preferences and why?
5. Does this exercise confirm or reject the statement that "vantagepoint profoundly shapes how people perceive specific policy issues and what kinds of solutions or recommendations they support"?
6. What kinds of power resources did the various groups use in the game to obtain support for their positions?

SIMULATION 2*

This simulation is relevant to the discussion of power in Chapter Five. Assume that you are a member of a social agency. A certain problem has been festering in the agency for several years. For some reason, the executive

*This simulation is a modified version of "Power and Influence in Organizations," which appeared in Harry Knudson, Robert Woodworth, and Cecil Bell, *Management: An Experiential Approach* (New York: McGraw-Hill, 1973), pp. 315–328.

director decides that "the only way to resolve this problem is to convene a group of people—and let them select a chairperson for their group as a prelude to devising a solution to the problem."

The choice of the chairperson is, everyone realizes, very important because the problem has caused considerable conflict within the agency. Indeed, some members of the group aspire to the position so that it will be more likely that *their* preferences will receive consideration.

Divide the class into groups of roughly six to eight people. The instructor gives a slip of paper to each member of a group. The various slips read:

- client, 50 units
- community resident, 75 units
- direct-service worker, 100 units
- supervisor, 200 units
- assistant administrator, 350 units
- board member, 500 units
- agency funder, 750 units

(Subtract a slip in the case of groups of six in size, and add slips with similar designations for groups of more than seven.) Each person has to fold his or her slip and place it on the table or chair so that it can be viewed by the other members of the group.

Group members are told the situation and asked to elect a chairperson. But they must follow a specific procedure. They can only write messages to each other for the first period of five minutes—no verbal communication is allowed. After allowing five minutes for people to read the messages that they received, they must engage in another message-writing period of fifteen minutes, followed by a second five-minute reading period. Finally, they engage in discussion for fifteen minutes, which may include negotiations and one-on-one discussions. At the conclusion of this discussion, they vote their units of power in an open fashion, which leads to the selection of a chairperson.

Questions for Discussion

1. What did it feel like to have relatively little power? How did it affect or influence the kinds of actions or behaviors that you took?

2. What did it feel like to have extraordinary power? How did it affect or influence the kinds of actions or behaviors that you took?

3. How did your amount of power influence the *reactions* of other people to you? And how, in turn, did these reactions shape your behaviors or actions?

4. How does this simulation game confirm (or not confirm) the assertion that power-wielding is a transactional phenomenon?

5. What kinds of people wrote the most notes and the least notes?

6. What kinds of person-to-person, coalitional, or other power resources did people use in the game to obtain support for their preferred leader?

7. What kinds of power seemed most effective or least effective?

SIMULATION 3*

This simulation can be used in conjunction with Chapter Twelve, which discusses the implementation of social policies.

The top administration of a mental hospital with many units has decided to adopt the policy that a "token economy approach" will be used to decrease "acting out" and other deviant behaviors in the hospital. It is based on the notion that rewards and penalties are useful in shaping the behaviors of mental patients in constructive ways.

They select a specific unit in the hospital as a place to initiate the policy. The unit has 22 women with chronic schizophrenia living in it who have been in the institution for an average of 17 years. There are four social workers, four nurses, and five therapy aides. (The nurses supervise the therapy aides, who do most of the daily work on the unit.) The social workers are responsible for the daily treatment plans for each patient, which are ultimately approved by a consulting psychiatrist.

A top management team comes to the unit to explain the token economy program to the staff and patients.

1. A list of "desirable behaviors" will be established for the patients that includes personal hygiene, independent behaviors such as attending recreation programs, and constructive interpersonal behaviors such as helping other people.

2. Case conferences will be held where the staff decide which patients should be rewarded because of their desirable behaviors.

3. Residents will be given "tokens" as a reward for desirable behavior; they can be used to purchase goods.

4. There will be an on-unit store, with candy, sodas, and other goods. (No cash can be used.)

Divide the class into seven groups by having people sign up for groups on the board. The groups should include: (1) a top management team from the

*We have drawn on the fifth chapter of a book by Mary Ann Scheirer to develop this simulation. See Scheirer, *Program Implementation: The Organizational Context* (Beverly Hills, Ca.: Sage Publications, 1981), pp. 145–181.

wider hospital, (2) a management team within the unit, (3) a consulting psychiatrist, (4) social workers, (5) nurses, (6) therapy aides, and (7) patients.

A series of meetings are held:

1. A meeting of each of the groups separately to discuss their general orientations or positions toward the innovation (about fifteen minutes).
2. A public meeting where spokespersons for each group present their position to the top management of the hospital (ten minutes).
3. Several planning groups are established that are each comprised of at least one member from each of the seven groups to discuss "what it will take to make this innovation work" so that it will serve constructive purposes and not be sabotaged (fifteen minutes).
4. A final public meeting where each planning group presents its recommendations (ten minutes).

Questions for Discussion

1. What barriers to the implementation of this policy appear most serious?
2. How does this simulation confirm the assertion "most policies are relatively vague, so many gaps and omissions need to be filled in during the process of implementation"?
3. Could one or more of the groups sabotage this policy? How?
4. How did it feel to be told by the hospital administration that this policy would have to be implemented with no prior consultation? Does this often happen in the real world?
5. What are problems and advantages of inviting patients or clients into the decision-making process with respect to a new policy like this one?
6. What ethical issues arose with respect to this policy and its implementation?

APPENDIX B

■

Researching Policy Issues

Whether social workers prepare memoranda, extended papers, or oral presentations, they need skills in obtaining information that can be used to build and defend positions. The amount of evidence required varies from project to project. More materials are available for some topics than for others. In some cases, time considerations preclude an exhaustive inventory of available sources of information.

Specifically, they need to be able to build bibliographies, i.e., lists of sources of information that include books, government publications, and journal articles. They need to be able to obtain important policy documents such as government reports. In some cases, written evidence is supplemented with interviews.

The precise sequence followed in obtaining information varies from project to project. In some cases, position takers interview knowledgeable persons prior to conducting library research. More commonly, however, they use the kind of sequence outlined in the following discussion, in which they begin with general library materials, locate more specialized documents, and then obtain information from persons in the field who can provide firsthand perspectives.

CLASSIFYING PROBLEMS AND ISSUES

As a prelude to building bibliographies, social workers need to be able to classify problems, i.e., identify key words that enable them to find available reading material. In many cases, relevant information is listed under a number of headings. In the case of policies pertaining to the issue of rape, for example, a policy researcher might want to examine literature pertaining to women's issues, family violence, crime, and sexual harassment. Literature might also be discovered under other headings that describe specific kinds of rape (e.g., "incest") or special kinds of institutions or staff members that encounter or address the problem (e.g., "hospital emergency rooms" or "free clinics"). In some cases, information can be discovered in literature that explores more general subjects, such as feminism, women's rights, or crimes of violence. Finally, relevant information can be found by examining literature that explores related topics, such as deviance, crime, criminology, and sexism.

Policy researchers need to be creative, then, in brainstorming a variety of concepts and words that subsequently lead to important streams of research and writing. In some cases, their work is facilitated when a specific problem or issue is relatively narrow or focused, since literature is likely to be concentrated under a relatively small number of headings. In the case of policies to assist children with reading disorders, for example, a policy researcher might discover most information under headings like "education," "dyslexia," "handicapped children," or "reading disorder." Other broad problems, such as poverty, are classified under a seemingly endless list of headings and subjects. Even a seemingly specific problem like alcoholism may be discussed in the literature on a number of topics, including substance abuse, addiction, mental health, crime, accidents, mortality, health, and occupational disease, not to mention specific populations such as adolescents and women.

PRELIMINARY SEARCH

With key concepts and words identified, policy researchers can quickly identify an array of information sources by conducting library research, i.e., using indexes and abstracts, finding relevant bibliographies, searching card catalogs, and scanning footnotes in seminal articles and books. In initial library research, a useful strategy is to identify relevant titles under various key concepts and words by using (1) the card catalog that identifies holdings under subject headings, and (2) the *Library of Congress Subject Headings* (two volumes) to see if additional key concepts or words are listed that appear important to the policy (these volumes are catalogs of subject headings used in card catalogs). Further, book-length bibliographies are often found in the card catalog under specific subjects, as illustrated by a card with the heading "Child Abuse—Bibliography." A reference librarian should be consulted during the process of preliminary search for assistance in locating bibliographies and other reference aids that are useful to beginning research on a topic.

Policy researchers are often surprised to find that they can readily find a series of important books merely by browsing shelf holdings near a relevant volume, because library books are shelved according to their subject matter. A book on women's issues, for example, is shelved next to other books covering similar material, though books relevant to this topic are also found in other locations in the library. When books are not on the shelf because they are missing, have been checked out, are on reserve, or are in a pre-shelving area, researchers should inquire at the circulation desk.

After identifying books on a topic by using the card catalog and browsing the shelves, researchers can use indexes and abstracts to identify journal articles. Indexes are publications, usually published at regular intervals, that list citations under subject and author headings. In the *Social Science Citation Index*, for example, articles from over 2000 journals in the social sciences published during specific time periods are arranged by subject matter and author. Specialized indexes exist as well, as illustrated by the index *Child Abuse and Neglect Research*. Abstracts list books and articles and provide a brief description of their content, as illustrated by *Social Work Research and Abstracts*, a compilation of material from social work and related literature. (See Table 1 for a selective list of abstracts and indexes that often prove useful in social welfare policy research projects.)

As policy researchers soon discover, indexes and abstracts can be a curse as well as a blessing. They provide quick access to many titles but use different subject headings and often inundate the researcher with excessive material. The problem of inundation is particularly acute if the researcher opts for a computer search of literature, a technology now available in most libraries at relatively modest cost. As an example, titles and abstracts of articles listed in 780 educational journals can be obtained through the computer-based Educational Resources Information Center (ERIC) or through 120 different but similar files in the Lockheed Dialogue system, which covers, among others, the Social Science Citation Index and the Public Affairs Informational Service. These computer searches can sometimes lead to identification of large numbers of articles, so care is needed to choose relatively narrow terms that allow the researcher to restrict titles to those specifically germane to the policy topic.

Another approach for generating titles is to use the indexes of journals that specialize in issues or topics relevant to the researcher's inquiry. A policy researcher, for example, might wish to examine annual indexes of journals like *Public Interest*, *Social Policy*, and *Public Welfare*. In the case of popular literature on current events, the annual and monthly update volumes of the *Reader's Guide to Periodical Literature* can be consulted.

FINDING SEMINAL WORKS

Although titles of relevant books and articles are helpful, the researcher often needs to locate pivotal or seminal works that provide an overview of the policy topic, including historical and other information about the policy context, and information about specific facets of the topic. In some cases, the

TABLE 1   User's Guide: Abstracts and Indexes Frequently Used in Social Welfare Policy Research

Abstracts on Criminology and Penology
American Statistical Index (ASI)
Congressional Information Service (CIS)
Crime and Delinquency Abstracts
Crime and Delinquency Literature
Cumulated Index Medicus
Cumulative Index to Nursing and Allied Health
Current Index to Journals in Education (ERIC)
Current Literature on Aging
Developmental Disabilities Abstracts (formerly Mental Retardation Abstracts)
Dissertation Abstracts International (used with Comprehensive Dissertation Index)
ERIC (Educational Resources Information Center)
Excerpta Medica
Government Reports Index
Human Resources Abstracts (formerly Poverty and Human Resources Abstracts)
Index of Economic Articles
Journal of Human Service Abstracts
Medical Socioeconomic Research Sources
Monthly Catalog of U.S. Government Publications
New York Times Index
Poverty and Human Resources Abstracts
Psychological Abstracts
Public Affairs Information Service
Reader's Guide to Periodical Literature
Rehabilitation Literature
Research in Education (ERIC)
Research Relating to Children
Selective Index to Health Literature
Social Science Citation Index
Social Sciences Index (formerly Social Sciences and Humanities Index)
Social Work Research and Abstracts (formerly Abstracts for Social Workers)
Sociological Abstracts
United Way of America: Digest of Selected Reports
Women's Studies Abstracts

Ruth Britton assisted in developing this list.

researcher can obtain listings of important works from someone—a reference librarian, a researcher, or a participant in policy development—who is deeply versed in the literature associated with a specific policy topic.

Examination of footnotes and bibliographies of recent books and articles can lead to identification of basic works that are referenced more frequently than others. Journals publish critical book reviews that often allow identification of the perspectives of authors, reviews that can be located by referring to the *Book Review Digest*, *Book Review Index*, or the *Social Sciences Index*.

The collected writings of important authors can be identified by using the card catalog in the library or referring to author listings in specific indexes or abstracts. In some cases, researchers may wish to begin their research by reading a few well-chosen seminal works and then proceed to development of more extensive bibliographies. They can also consult basic reference books, such as the *Encyclopedia of Social Work*, to obtain initial information about a policy topic. Other useful reference books include the *International Encyclopedia of the Social Sciences*, *Dictionary of the Social Sciences*, *Dictionary of Sociology*, *Encyclopedia of Psychology*, and the *Encyclopedia of Bioethics*.

POLICY COMMENTARY

In many cases, policy researchers supplement bibliographies with readings from newspapers and journals that discuss current issues. Annual indexes and periodic updates are available in most libraries for major newspapers such as the *New York Times*, the *Christian Science Monitor*, the *Washington Post*, the *Los Angeles Times*, and the *Wall Street Journal*. Timely articles on current policy issues in these publications are often available on microfilm and provide a wealth of material drawn from interviews with strategically placed participants in policy or program arenas. The *National Journal* provides excellent coverage of current policy issues and includes frequent update indexes to facilitate location of a range of articles on health and welfare issues. At the state level, researchers should consult indexes of major newspapers in their particular state as well as policy journals such as the *California Journal*. Information about public opinion on public issues can be found in various publications listed under the *Gallup Report* and the *Harris Survey*.

CURRENT LEGISLATIVE DEVELOPMENTS

The *Congressional Quarterly Almanac* is an indispensable and easy-to-use resource for current policy papers, since it provides a yearly summary of legislative developments in the Congress. At the end of each volume, a subject index allows location of discussion of (1) legislative developments associated with particular pieces of legislation and (2) an overview of developments in health, public welfare, and related sectors. (The *Almanac* is particularly useful because it allows ready identification of congressional publications that present public hearings held by congressional committees on specific pieces of legislation.) The researcher who is interested in legislative developments that occurred after publication of the most recent edition of the *Almanac* can consult weekly editions of the *Congressional Quarterly Weekly Reports*. The *Congressional Quarterly's Guide to the Congress* is a reference book that discusses congressional procedures. Another useful book is the *Almanac of American Politics* that includes profiles of important elected officials as well as their voting records.

GOVERNMENT DELIBERATIONS

While secondary accounts are useful, policy researchers often want to read transcripts of legislative deliberations, such as committee hearings or debates on the floor of Congress. (Important policy documents are often inserted into these transcripts as well.) Committee hearings are printed and distributed to many libraries; they can be easily found by locating the name of the relevant committee and dates of the hearings in the aforementioned *Congressional Quarterly Almanac* or in the *Congressional Information Service* (CIS) that indexes hearings, committee publications, and legislation. The call numbers of congressional hearings that are used to shelve and retrieve government hearings in libraries can be found in the CIS, which indexes hearings by subject matter and by the name of the committee that holds the hearings. Government and congressional publications are sometimes cataloged under a section of the author card catalog beginning with "U.S." As an example, perusal of the 1971 volume of the *Congressional Quarterly Almanac* indicates that child-care provisions of welfare reform legislation introduced by President Richard Nixon were discussed before the Finance Committee of the Senate on September 22, 23, and 24, 1971. This particular committee hearing had been bound by the library; its call number was located by looking in the author card catalog under the heading "U.S., Congress, Senate, Finance Committee, Hearings on S. 2003, Child Care Provisions of H.R. 1." In some libraries, government documents do not appear in the card catalog, but appear in a separate catalog or in listings maintained in the "hearings section" of the government documents room. (A reference librarian should be consulted to ascertain how government documents are cataloged in a specific library.) For titles of very recent committee hearings, the researcher should consult issues of the *Congressional Quarterly Weekly Report*.

Annual volumes of the *Congressional Record* contain transcripts of deliberations in the House and Senate. A researcher who wanted to examine testimony in the Senate on specific legislation could find the dates it was discussed in the *Congressional Quarterly Almanac* and then proceed to the appropriate dates in the bound volume of the *Congressional Record*. A *Congressional Index* is published each year and is indexed by subject matter, enabling a researcher to quickly find floor testimony on specific issues that arose during the year (periodic updates allow location of recent hearings).

LEGISLATION AND REGULATIONS

Many policy papers require examination of legislation, whether proposed bills or enacted public laws. Proposed legislation is usually included in the text of hearings of committees in the House or Senate as well as transcripts of floor debates in the *Congressional Record*. In Case Example 1, a bill that proposes amending the Public Health Service Act to establish a National Health Service Corps—legislation that was eventually enacted—is included in this section because some readers may want to examine Eric Redman's excellent case study of its development and passage. In this particular example, the bill proposes adding a section to existing public law (i.e., "Part J—National Health Service Corps"). Note how the legislation discusses a number of the core policy issues discussed in this book, including those pertaining to staffing of the National Health Service Corps, its financing, and establishment of decision-making procedures through formation of a National Health Corps Advisory Council. Many policy details are also not defined in the legislation, details that had to be addressed subsequently in administrative regulations. Redman and his allies chose not to include detailed policies concerning eligibility, for example, to avert controversy.

Proposed bills become public laws when they are formally approved by the legislature and the president. Major provisions of public legislation laws are summarized in the *Congressional Quarterly Almanac* as well as the *Congressional Quarterly Weekly Reports*.

Within a year of enactment, public laws are printed in a series of books published by West Publishing Company known as the *U.S. Code Annotated*, as well as in the *U.S. Code* published by the U.S. Government Printing Office. Enacted legislation is classified under one of fifty titles that correspond to specific subjects. Thus, for example, additions to and amendments of the Social Security Act are placed under Title 42 of the *U.S. Code*.

The policy researcher often wants to examine regulations pertinent to implementation that are issued by government authorities in the wake of passage of legislation. The *Code of Federal Regulations* contains rules that are in force at the time it is published each quarter and has fifty titles, like the *U.S. Code*, to assist the reader in locating regulations that correspond to specific pieces of enacted legislation. An excerpt from the *Code of Federal Regulations* presented in Case Example 2 discusses the use of social workers in skilled nursing facilities. Often technical and uninteresting in appearance, these administrative regulations can have profound implications for consum-

CASE EXAMPLE 1

S. 4106; 91st CONGRESS, 2d SESSION

In the Senate of the United States, July 21, 1970
Mr. Magnuson (for himself, Mr. Jackson, Mr. Cranston, Mr. Hughes, Mr. Kennedy, Mr. Nelson, Mr. Randolph, and Mr. Williams of New Jersey) introduced the following bill; which was read twice and referred to the Committee on Labor and Public Welfare.

A Bill
To amend the Public Health Service Act in order to provide for the establishment of a National Health Service Corps. *Be it enacted by the Senate and House of Representatives of the United States of America in Congress assembled,* That this Act may be cited as the "National Health Service Corps Act of 1970."

Sec. 2. Title III of the Public Health Service Act is amended by adding at the end thereof a new part as follows:

"Part J—National Health Service Corps, Establishment of National Health Service Corps; Functions
"Sec. 399h. (a) There is established in the Service a National Health Service Corps (hereinafter in this part referred to as the 'Corps') which shall be under the direction and supervision of the Surgeon General.

"(b) It shall be the function of the Corps to improve the delivery of health services to persons living in communities and areas of the United States where health personnel, facilities, and services are inadequate to meet the health needs of the residents of such communities and areas. Priority under this part shall be given to those urban and rural areas of the United States where poverty conditions exist and the health facilities are inadequate to meet the needs of the persons living in such areas.

"Staffing; Term of Service
"Sec. 399i. (a) The Surgeon General shall assign selected commissioned officers of the Service and such other personnel as may be necessary to staff the Corps and to carry out the functions of the Corps under this part.

"(b) Commissioned officers of the Service in the Corps and other Corps personnel shall be detailed for service in the Corps for a period of twenty-five months. An individual detailed to the Corps may voluntarily extend his service in the Corps for a period not to exceed an additional twenty-five months. An individual shall have the right to petition the Director (appointed pursuant to section 399j of this part) for early release from service in the Corps at the end of twenty-four months of service therein.

"Director of the National Health Service Corps
"Sec. 399j. The Corps shall be headed by a Director who shall be appointed

by the President, by and with the advice and consent of the Senate. It shall be the responsibility of the Director to direct the operations of the Corps, subject to the supervision and control of the Surgeon General.

"Authority of Secretary to Utilize Corps Personnel

"Sec. 399k. The Secretary is authorized, whenever he deems such action appropriate, to utilize commissioned officers of the Service and other personnel detailed to duty with the Corps to—

"(1) perform services in connection with direct health care programs carried out by the Service;

"(2) perform services in connection with any direct health care program carried out in whole or in part with the Department of Health, Education, and Welfare funds or the funds of any other department or agency of the Federal Government; or

"(3) perform services in connection with any other health care activity in furtherance of the purposes of this Act. Should services provided under this subsection require the establishment of health care programs not otherwise authorized by law, the Secretary is authorized and directed to establish mechanisms whereby recipients of such services shall pay, to the extent practicable, for services received. Any funds collected in this manner shall be used to defray in part the operating expenses of the Corps.

"National Health Corps Advisory Council

"Sec. 399l. (a) There is established a council to be known as the National Health Corps Advisory Council (hereinafter in this section referred to as the 'Council'). The Council shall be composed of twelve members appointed as follows:

"(1) three members from the Department of Health, Education, and Welfare, serving outside the Corps, to be appointed by the Secretary;

"(2) three members appointed by the Secretary from private life;

"(3) three members detailed to duty with the Corps, at least two of whom shall be commissioned officers of the Service, to be appointed by the Secretary; and

"(4) three persons who have received more than minimal health care services from the Corps, to be appointed by the Secretary after the Corps has been in operation for a period of at least one hundred and twenty days and to be appointed from geographically dispersed areas to the extent practicable.

"(b) Members of the Council shall be appointed for a term of three years and shall not be removed, except for cause. Members may be reappointed to the Council.

"(c) It shall be the function of the Council—

"(1) to establish guidelines with respect to how the Corps shall be utilized and to consult with and advise the Director generally regarding the operation of the Corps;

"(2) to assist the Surgeon General, at his request, in the selection of

Continued

CASE EXAMPLE 1
(continued)

commissioned officers of the Service and other personnel for assignment to the Corps, and to approve all assignments of Corps members;

"(3) to establish criteria for determining which communities or areas will receive assistance from the Corps, taking into consideration—

"(A) the need of any community or area for health services provided under this part;

"(B) the willingness of the community or area and the appropriate governmental agencies therein to assist and cooperate with the Corps in providing effective health services to residents of the community or area;

"(C) the prospects of the community or area for utilizing Corps personnel after their tour of duty with the Corps;

"(D) the recommendations of any agency or organization which may be responsible for the development, under section 314(b), of a comprehensive plan covering all or any part of the area or community involved; and

"(E) recommendations from the medical, dental, and other medical personnel of any community or area considered for assistance under this part.

ers, providers, and professionals. Policy researchers who want to examine recent or proposed regulations can examine daily issues of the *Federal Register* and its quarterly index. (All proposed regulations have to be printed in this publication prior to their adoption to allow interested persons to comment on them.)

STATISTICAL INFORMATION

The *Statistical Abstract of the United States* annually summarizes crime, health, and other selected statistics published by government agencies. Thus, the researcher need only search the index of this publication for relevant trend data. At periodic points in this book, charts are used that are drawn from *Social Indicators III*, the third in a series of publications of the U.S. Bureau of the Census. Census data are summarized in the *U.S. Census of Population*. The Bureau of the Census also publishes many *Current Population Reports* that draw on census and other studies. The beginning researcher can often consult a reference librarian and ask about the availability of trend data relevant to such policy topics as child abuse, malnutrition, infant mortality, and poor housing. The *American Statistical Index* lists titles of all government publications that provide statistical information as well as the agencies that issue them (from which copies can be obtained). Other books that provide statistics include the *Handbook of Labor Statistical Yearbook*, the *Historical Statistics of the*

CASE EXAMPLE 2

**CODE OF FEDERAL REGULATIONS; TITLE 42,
PUBLIC HEALTH; CHAPTER IV, HEALTH CARE
FINANCING ADMINISTRATION; HS OF
OCTOBER 1, 1980**

405.1130 Condition of participation—social services The skilled nursing facility has satisfactory arrangements for identifying the medically related social and emotional needs of the patient. It is not mandatory that the skilled nursing facility itself provide social services in order to participate in the program. If the facility does not provide social services, it has written procedures for referring patients in need of social services to appropriate social agencies. If social services are offered by the facility, they are provided under a clearly defined plan, by qualified persons, to assist each patient to adjust to the social and emotional aspects of his illness, treatment, and stay in the facility.

(a) Standard: Social service-functions The medically related social and emotional needs of the patient are identified and services provided to meet them, either by qualified staff of the facility, or by referral, based on established procedures, to appropriate social agencies. If financial assistance is indicated, arrangements are made promptly for referral to an appropriate agency. The patient and his family or responsible person are fully informed of the patient's personal and property rights.

(b) Standard: Staffing If the facility offers social services, a member of the staff of the facility is designated as responsible for social services. If the designated person is not a qualified social worker, the facility has a written agreement with a qualified social worker or recognized social agency for consultation and assistance on a regularly scheduled basis. (See § 405.1121(i).) The social service also has sufficient supportive personnel to meet patient needs. Facilities are adequate for social service personnel, easily accessible to patients and medical and other staff, and ensure privacy for interviews.

U.S., *Business Statistics,* the *Statistical Yearbook,* and the *Demographic Yearbook* (the latter two publications are issued by the United Nations).

ADDITIONAL RESOURCES

As policy researchers obtain familiarity with the resources discussed thus far, they can use other resources as well. For example, titles, abstracts, and the names of sponsors of proposed legislation can be obtained by using the

Digest of the Public General Bills and Resolutions published by the Congressional Research Service of the Library of Congress or the *Congressional Index* published by the Commerce Clearing House. Persons who want information on recently enacted legislation that has not yet been published in the *U.S.Code* can consult the *United States Code Congressional and Administrative News*. Government publications can also be accessed by referring to the *Monthly Catalog of U.S. Government Publications*, a rich repository of titles of publications that are relevant to many policy topics. (Libraries designated as "depository libraries" are required to have many of these government publications in their holdings.)

Whether using these or other resources discussed in this section, policy researchers should not be intimidated by the plethora of resources or their seeming complexity. Researchers who begin with the easy-to-use and indispensable *Congressional Quarterly Almanac* can easily obtain additional information about other sources from reference libraries, and librarians in law libraries can assist them in locating copies of legislation or relevant administrative regulations.

Many researchers need to obtain legislation and administrative guidelines enacted at the state level. Each state has a series of volumes that present state laws as well as administrative regulations. (Consult a reference or law librarian to obtain references applicable to a specific state as well as transcripts of committee and legislative deliberations.)

INTERVIEWING

No substitute exists for interviewing people who, because of their strategic location, know about important facets of policy. Line staff, supervisors, and administrators can discuss issues associated with implementation of existing policies. Aides to legislators and staff in government agencies can provide invaluable information, whether in local, state, or federal arenas.

Preparation for interviews is essential. In many cases, the policy researcher should already have invested considerable time in library research to enable more productive use of the interview, including a focusing of questions on topics not discussed in written materials. Although relatively open-ended or unstructured questions are often used, the researcher should carefully develop a set of questions to be used during a portion of the interview that direct attention to important facets of the policy topic. Similarly, time should be given to developing an initial list of interviewees who (1) represent several or more perspectives on the policy topic and (2) are positioned to provide specific kinds of information about it.

People who conduct interviews on sensitive policy topics soon realize that good fortune is required to find key informants willing to discuss controversial issues. Some interviewees are extremely guarded in divulging information and personal perspectives; others not only assist the researcher but provide names of additional interviewees.

In order to increase the likelihood that interviewees will share information, researchers should maintain a posture that is relatively neutral yet supportive, even with informants whose personal perspectives diverge markedly from their own. Interviewers from academic settings should not cut off exchange of information with moderate or conservative interviewees by appearing to fit liberal academic stereotypes.

Exercises and Research Projects to Enhance the Use of Policy Practice in Educational Settings

In this section, we discuss exercises and research projects to enhance the teaching of social welfare policy and policy practice. We divided these exercises and research projects into five groups according to their focus:

1. Exploring policies of specific settings
2. Analyzing the evolution of policy in specific settings
3. Linking social welfare policy to other social work disciplines
4. Linking policy practice to policy sectors
5. Projects to link social welfare policy to social reform

This listing of exercises and research projects is meant not to be all-inclusive, but to serve as a catalyst to develop innovative ways to teach the practice of policy.

EXPLORING POLICIES OF SPECIFIC SETTINGS

A Point-of-Origin Exercise

Take any social agency and construct a "map" of some of its important social welfare policies. At the periphery of the map, identify those policies that influence the work of agency staff that emanate from external sources such as funders, government agencies, and courts. (You will need to interview executive-level staff to obtain a relatively complete picture of these policies.) Also identify some policies that emanate from high-level sources of the agency itself, such as from its mission statement and from its bylaws. (You may wish to interview executive-level staff and some middle-management staff to obtain a view of the important objectives or goals that emanate from within the agency.) Finally, try to find a policy that has its origins in specific units of the agency or that derives from direct-service staff. (These may be informal policies that reflect common practice of staff and rest on common and informal agreements about how to treat clients.)

Discuss whether you find any contradictions between specific policies, whether you see any omissions, whether certain policies seem unclear, and whether any policies appear detrimental to specific needs of clients.

Exploring Policy-Practice Tasks in Specific Settings

With the policy map completed (see above), try to identify one or more policies that could be targets of a policy-practice endeavor—whether to change it (the proposal-writing and policy-enacting task), to improve its implementation (the policy-implementing task), or to assess it (the policy-assessing task).

Try to identify some social problem or need in the community that is not adequately met by the agency. Speculate about the process someone might follow to place it on the agendas of decision makers in this setting (the agenda-building and problem-defining tasks).

ANALYZING THE EVOLUTION OF POLICY IN SPECIFIC SETTINGS

Analyzing the Emergence and Enactment of Specific Policies

Take a specific legislature (such as the Congress, a state legislature, or a city governing body) or a specific agency. Select an example of a major change in policy that occurred during the last ten years. Research the evolution of the policy by using terms and concepts that are relevant to: the agenda-building task, the problem-defining task, the proposal-writing task, and the policy-enacting task. To conduct this kind of research project, you need information from secondary sources or from key informants. (Secondary sources pertaining to congressional policy are suggested in Appendix B.) Present an account of the evolution of the policy by describing how people undertook the various policy tasks and how they used analytic, political, interactional, or value-clarification skills.

When examining the agenda-building task, for example, you should ask why a particular measure received a high position on the agendas of decision makers by noting background factors and the actions of specific people who enabled it to be placed on the agendas. When examining the policy-defining task, examine how people defined the issue or problem. What paradigms or social-science research did they use? When examining the proposal-writing task, you might discuss how a proposal emerged in the course of policy deliberations, who assumed the lead, what substantive topics or issues were controversial, and what the provisions of the proposal were. When researching the policy-enacting task, examine the politics of the measure, the political strategies of one or more of the central figures, and the kinds of changes or amendments that were made in the proposal.

This kind of research can also be used to examine the evolution of policies that were seriously considered by decision makers but not enacted by them. For example, the evolution of the child development legislation of the late 1960s and early 1970s, which was not enacted by the Congress, is examined in Chapter Eleven.

Analyzing the Implementation and Assessment of Specific Policies

You can examine, as well, the postenactment fate of specific policies. What information exists about the nature of the implementation of a specific policy like the Adoption Assistance and Child Welfare Act of 1980 (see the discussion in Chapter Twelve)? Were the framers of the policy realistic when they shaped the policy about "what it would take" to obtain its adequate implementation? What barriers or obstacles have frustrated its implementation? What corrective measures might enhance its implementation?

You can also obtain information about whether a policy seems to be achieving specific objectives or meeting specific criteria. Does information exist about its effects? If you assess a policy, what criteria should be selected and given importance? How might you design an assessment strategy?

LINKING SOCIAL WELFARE POLICY TO OTHER SOCIAL WORK DISCIPLINES

We argue in Chapter Fourteen that social welfare policy and policy practice can be a unifying force within the profession of social work, but they are unlikely to assume this role if their connections to other disciplines are not examined.

Linking Social Welfare Policy to Human Behavior and Direct-Service Practice

Take a specific case of a client who possesses a specific problem and construct a "policy map" that identifies an array of policies that are germane to the client. First, identify some policies that shape or determine the kinds and nature of assistance that the client receives for this problem. (Identify policies that dictate the approaches or paradigms of staff who help the client in a specific setting and the duration or intensity of assistance the client receives in this setting.) Second, identify some policies in the external society that exacerbate the ability of the client to cope with the problem. For example, discuss patterns of discrimination that the client may encounter. Third, what policies in the community or society might have contributed to the development of the client's problem? For example, do patterns of segregation, poor wages, and poor housing contribute to this client's problem?

This policy map, which begins with policies that immediately influence the kinds of assistance that the client receives, moves toward broader, societal policies that shape the response of people and institutions to the client, and toward policies that contribute to the development of the problem.

Use this exercise to identify how a social worker might use case-based and class-based advocacy to help the client.

Linking Social Welfare Policy to Community Organization

Take a major social problem and examine the extent and nature of pressure that is placed upon specific decision makers, such as state legislators, by (1) people who possess the problem, (2) people who sympathize with people who have the problem, and (3) people who possess relatively restrictive or punitive perceptions of those people who possess the problem. You may want to ask whether a social movement exists that is relevant to the problem. By interviewing someone from a social movement or an advocate, discuss whether and how more community pressure might be generated to induce a sympathetic response from decision makers.

Linking Social Welfare Policy to Administration

Linkages between social welfare policy and administration are most obvious when examining the implementation of specific policies. Examine the implementation of a policy in a specific agency. Identify some barriers or obstacles that exist and discuss how top executives might overcome or address them.

Linking Social Welfare Policy to Research

In examining the assessment of a specific policy, the linkages between social welfare policy and research are most obvious. Develop an assessment strategy for a specific policy by developing a policy-assessment matrix such as the one that was discussed in Chapter Thirteen. Identify an array of methodological options, such as alternative designs, sampling strategies, and data-gathering strategies. Select some of these options to shape an assessment strategy.

Research is linked to social welfare policy when people use data or social-science research while undertaking the agenda-building, problem-defining, or proposal-writing tasks. Examine the kinds of research and data that people use when they seek to frame a specific measure, such as the welfare reform in 1988. Or, identify a data-collection strategy that could be used to document the need to develop a specific policy.

LINKING POLICY PRACTICE TO POLICY SECTORS

An extensive literature exists on policies of health, mental health, child and family, and income maintenance in the field of social welfare policy. This literature can be linked to the concepts of policy practice by focusing upon specific themes when reading this broader literature. Instead of reading the broader literature in a descriptive way, concepts from policy practice help to illuminate how policies evolved and some substantive issues. When reading literature on health policy, for example, ask the following kinds of questions:

1. When designing a major reform, such as national health insurance, what analytic challenges confront policymakers when wrestling with competing criteria of cost, effectiveness, and social justice?

2. What political forces and factors assume a dominant role in shaping the nation's health-care strategy?

3. What value-based objections can be made of the way the nation allocates its health-care resources?

4. What forces and factors in the nation in the 1990s might place national health insurance high on the agendas of national policymakers?

PROJECTS TO LINK SOCIAL WELFARE POLICY TO SOCIAL REFORM

A Conceptual Approach: Brainstorming a Reform

Identify an issue or problem in an agency, community, or state and develop a strategy or proposal to address it by interviewing various people who are familiar with the issue or problem.

When developing the proposal or strategy, you need to use a combination of analytic, political, interactional, and value-clarification skills. Analytic skills are needed to develop a proposal that possesses technical merit (see Chapters Two, Three, and Four). Political skills are needed to be certain that the proposal and strategy possess or can obtain sufficient political support to make them feasible. Interactional skills are needed to develop a persuading strategy, coalitions, networks, and credibility to facilitate support for the proposal. Value-clarification skills are needed to decide what tactics to use and whether to dilute or compromise a proposal to make it politically accept-able to decision makers.

In effect, you are engaged in a sort of conceptual policy practice because you are defining a proposal, discussing methods of securing support for it, and wrestling with analytic, political, interactional, and value-clarification considerations.

Seeking an Actual Reform

It may be feasible in some cases to go the next step, i.e., to try to convince a decision maker, such as a legislator, an aide, or an administrator, to support the proposal or to use it as a catalyst for developing her own proposal. Or, you might seek to convince leaders of a community group or interest group to adopt the proposal or use it to stimulate one of their own.

Name Index

Subject Index